THE HISTORY OF SALT LAKE CITY

and its Founders

VOLUME 1

EDWARD WILLIAM TULLIDGE

JUERGEN BECK

The History of Salt Lake City 1, Tulidge/Beck
Jazzybee Verlag Jürgen Beck
86450 Altenmünster, Loschberg 9
Deutschland

ISBN: 9783849671624

www.jazzybee-verlag.de
admin@jazzybee-verlag.de

Printed by Createspace, North Charleston, SC, USA

CONTENTS:

CHAPTER I. 1

CHAPTER II. 6

CHAPTER III. 21

CHAPTER IV. 28

CHAPTER V. 39

CHAPTER VI. 46

CHAPTER VII. 51

CHAPTER VIII. 58

CHAPTER IX. 66

CHAPTER X. 78

CHAPTER XI. 90

CHAPTER XII. 95

CHAPTER XIV. 105

CHAPTER XV. 112

CHAPTER XVI. 134

CHAPTER XVII. 147

CHAPTER XVIII. 155

CHAPTER XIX. 164

CHAPTER XX. 177

CHAPTER XXI. 185

CHAPTER XXII. 189

CHAPTER XXIII. 195

CHAPTER XXIV. 201

CHAPTER XXV. 207

CHAPTER XXV. 212

CHAPTER XXVI. 225

CHAPTER XXVII.	231
CHAPTER XXVIII.	238
CHAPTER XXIX.	245
CHAPTER XXX.	253
CHAPTER XXXI.	259
CHAPTER XXXII.	269
CHAPTER XXXIII.	276
CHAPTER XXXIV.	296
CHAPTER XXXV.	302
CHAPTER XXXVI.	308
CHAPTER XXXVII.	314
CHAPTER XXXVIII.	320
CHAPTER XXXIX.	333
CHAPTER XL.	341
CHAPTER XLI.	346
CHAPTER XLII.	356
CHAPTER XLIII.	361
CHAPTER XLIV.	373
CHAPTER XLV.	380
CHAPTER. XLVI.	384
CHAPTER XLVII.	408
CHAPTER XLVIII.	413
CHAPTER XLIX.	419

CHAPTER I.

PREFATORY REVIEW OF THE PEOPLE WHO FOUNDED SALT LAKE CITY. GRAND COLONIZING DESIGN OF THE MORMON PROPHET.

It will be well affirmed in history that the Pioneers who founded Salt Lake City, were as the crest of that tidal wave of colonization which peopled these Pacific States and Territories. And the colonies which this wonderful state-founding community has sent to the West, since that tidal wave rose in the exodus from Nauvoo, will stand as the most marked example of organic colonization which has occurred in the growth and spread of the American nation. Other States and cities, which have been founded since the first colonization of America by the Pilgrims of New England, have grown up and increased in their population upon the ordinary laws of national growth, to which has been superadded the promiscuous emigration of Europeans to this country; but not even in the extraordinary case of the growth of the Western States and Territories, excepting that shown by the Mormon people, has there been a spectacle of colonization proper, to mark the history of America in the present century. Thus considered, it is a most unique fact of the age that Salt Lake City was founded by a colony of the strictest type. In most of its leading features, the founding and growth of Utah resembles the founding of the American nation by the Pilgrim colonies, which sailed from England and Holland to establish religious liberty on a virgin continent, driven by the cruel force of persecution, yet whose every exile from the dear mother land became big with the genius of colonization, until the little companies of emigrants who left their native shores, very much in the character of religious outlaws, grew into a galaxy of States. Persecution undoubtedly at the onset drove the Mormons hitherward, as it drove the Puritans to this continent—drove them in fact into the very path of their destiny—but as they came westward from Ohio, where their Zion first rose, they so fast imbibed the genius of colonization, that extermination brought forth in the mind of the Mormon Prophet the grand scheme to colonize the Pacific Slope with his people, and with them form in the West the nucleus of a new galaxy of American States.

The first recorded note of the grand design of the Mormon Prophet to colonize the Pacific Slope with his people, will be seen in the following entry from his diary: "Saturday, 6th [August, 1842]. Passed over the river to Montrose, Iowa, in company with General Adams, Colonel Brewer, and others, and witnessed the installation of the officers of the Rising Sun Lodge of Ancient York Masons, at Montrose, by Gen. James Adams, Deputy Grand Master of Illinois. While the Deputy Grand Master was engaged in giving the requisite instructions to the Master elect, I had a conversation with a number of brethren, in the shade of the building, on the subject of our persecutions in Missouri, and the constant annoyance which has followed us since we were driven from that State. I prophesied that the Saints would continue to suffer much affliction and would be driven to the Rocky Mountains. Many would apostatize, others would be put to death by our persecutors, or lose their lives in consequence of exposure or disease, and some would live to go and assist in making settlements and building cities, and see the Saints become a mighty people in the midst of the Rocky Mountains."

A year and a half later his design was matured, and his people ready to execute it. Here is a diary note of that date: "Tuesday, Feb. 20th [1844]. I instructed the Twelve

Apostles to send out a delegation and investigate the locations of California and Oregon and hunt out a good location where we can remove to after the Temple is completed, and where we can build a city in a day and have a government of our own." * * * On the evening of the following day the Twelve met at the Mayor's office, and, according to the above instructions, appointed the following committee: Jonathan Dunham, Phineas H. Young, David D. Yearsley, David Fullmer, Alphonso Young, James Emmett, George D. Watt, Daniel Spencer. Subsequent action was also taken on the same subject, and volunteers were added to the committee.

It was at this date that the Elders undertook a political campaign through the States to nominate Joseph Smith for the Presidential chair of the nation, but it is very evident that the removal of the Saints to the Rocky Mountains, or to California, was the real action contemplated by the Prophet, and not a successful campaign for the presidency of the United States. The event, however, did afford a rare opportunity for sending out the Apostles and a company of the ablest Elders, to make another missionary effort in the States before the contemplated exodus.

A few days later we find Joseph Smith alluding to himself in connection with the presidential chair, but he at once branches off to a subject which more particularly attracted his thoughts, namely, the annexation of Texas and the possession of the Pacific Coast by the United States. Said he: "As to politics, I care but little about the Presidential chair. I would not give half as much for the office of President of the United States as I would for the one I now hold as Lieutenant-General of the Nauvoo Legion. * * * "What I have said in my views in relation to the annexation of Texas is, with some, unpopular. The people are opposed to it. Some of the Anti-Mormons are good fellows. I say it, however, in anticipation that they will repent.* * * We should grasp all the territory we can. * * The government will not receive any advice or counsel from me: they are self-sufficient. * * "The South holds the balance of power. By annexing Texas I can do away with this evil. As soon as Texas was annexed I would liberate the slaves in two or three States, indemnifying their owners, and send the negroes to Texas, and from Texas to Mexico, where all colors are alike. And if that was not sufficient, I would call upon Canada and annex it."

Mark next his bold empire-founding move, in petitioning Congress to raise a volunteer force of a hundred thousand in the service of the United States, to possess the Pacific Coast. Says he, under date of March 30th: "I had prepared a memorial to his Excellency, John Tyler, the President of the United States, embodying in it the same sentiments as are in my petition to the Senate and House of Representatives of the United States, dated March 26th, 1844, asking the privilege of raising 100,000 men to extend protection to persons wishing to settle Oregon and other portions of the Territory of the United States, and extend protection to the people in Texas. * * * "Also signed an introductory letter for Elder Orson Hyde, who is going to carry the memorials to Washington."

To found empire for America was just in the line of his character. Destiny was pushing the Saints westward and had Joseph Smith reached California at the head of an army of 20,000 pioneers, backed by the remainder of the 100,000 as emigrants, he would have given quite a Napoleonic account of himself, and opened the war with Mexico. This was clearly his intention, and it may be observed that he did not overrate his forces.

And what makes the Prophet's bold national design so deserving of attention is the fact that the United States Government and the British Government were at that moment in an attitude of rivalry for the possession of the Pacific Coast, and that the United States barely escaped being worsted. , Thus prefaced, let us listen to the report of Elder Hyde to the Prophet from the capital: "* * Judge Douglas has been quite ill, but is just recovered. He will help all he can; Mr. Hardin likewise. But Major Semple says that he does not believe anything will be done about Texas or Oregon this session, for it might have a very important effect upon the Presidential election; and politicians are slow to move when such doubtful and important matters are likely to be affected by it. * * * "I will now give you my opinion in relation to this matter. It is made up from the spirit of the times in a hasty manner, nevertheless I think time will prove it to be correct:—That Congress will pass no act in relation to Texas or Oregon at present. She is afraid of England, afraid of Mexico, afraid the Presidential election will be twisted by it. The members all appear like unskillful players at checkers—afraid to move, for they see not which way to move advantageously. * *"

"The most of the settlers in Oregon and Texas are our old enemies, the mobocrats of Missouri. If, however, the settlement of Oregon and Texas be determined upon, the sooner the move is made the better; and I would not advise any delay for the action of our Government, for there is such a jealousy of our rising power that Government will do nothing to favor us.

* * Your superior wisdom must determine whether to go to Oregon, to Texas, or to remain within these United States and send forth the most efficient men to build up churches, and let them remain for the time being; and in the meantime send some wise men among the Indians and teach them civilization and religion, to cultivate the soil, to live in peace with one another and with all men." * * In a subsequent letter Elder Hyde said: "We have this day [April 26th] had a long conversation with Judge Douglas. He is ripe for Oregon and California. He said he would resign his seat in Congress if he could command the force that Mr. Smith could, and would be on the march to that country in a month. 'In five years,' said he, 'a noble State might be formed, and then if they would not receive us into the Union, we would have a government of our own.'"

So we see that the American nation was not at that time prepared for the Prophet's bold design of occupying the Pacific Coast by an irresistible American emigration; yet several years afterward Fremont, with his volunteers in California, and Houston and Taylor by their action in forcing the war with Mexico, proved that a manifest destiny was in some such plan as that proposed; and an American emigration swept on like a tidal wave. And as it was, the Saints, per ship Brooklyn, were the first company of American emigrants to arrive in California; while simultaneous was the exodus of the entire community to the Rocky Mountains.

Perhaps it were well also to note here that this petition of Joseph Smith, in 1844, was probably the original basis of the action of President Polk in calling the "Mormon Battalion," and designing to use the Saints for the national convenience of possessing California. The whole of Polk's action in the case, and the instructions of the Secretary of War to General Kearney to "make a dash into California, conquer the country, and set up a government there" in the name of the United States, show that the Cabinet were not only familiar with the Prophet's scheme, but that certain statesmen, at this date, endorsed it.

A passing review of our national affairs of that period, will connect here most suggestively with the Mormon Prophet's bold proposition to the United States Government to possess the Pacific Coast by a hundred thousand Mormon colonists.

From the period of Mr. Jefferson's administration the United States had been striving to checkmate the European Powers, especially Great Britain, France Russia and Spain, in their schemes to occupy the Pacific coast and firmly establish thereon the dominion of Europe. At length the contest for the Pacific Coast laid between the United States and Great Britain, Mexico herself resigning to our ambitious mother country to prevent the march of American empire upon herself. The ships of both nations were riding in the Bay of San Francisco, the admirals were watching for their respective opportunities.

In 1845 Great Britain had matured a masterly scheme to forestall our government in the possession of California, with the co-operation of Mexico. Mr. Forbes the British Vice-Consul, was the principal agent of his government in carrying out this finely conceived design. A declaration of the independence of California from Mexico was to be made, to be followed by a petition from a convention of Californians, to be taken under the protection of Great Britain. 1 But the most diplomatic part of the scheme of the British government was to emigrate ten thousand of its subjects to the valley of San Joaquin, to own and occupy the country. An Irish priest by the name of MacNamara was chosen to fill this part of the scheme, and he went to Mexico in 1845, on n's mission to arouse the holy zeal of that republic against the "usurpation of the anti-Catholic and irreligious nation." He urged that no time should be lost or "within a year, California would become a part of the American nation, be inundated by cruel invaders, and their Catholic institutions the prey of Methodist wolves." Thus the Irish priest worded his petition to the Mexican government, urging an Irish emigration to that country for colonization in the interest of Great Britain. The Mexican government listened to this petition, and everything moved on favorably to the completion of the diplomatic scheme, which would have given California into the hands of Great Britain. Indeed, a treaty to this effect was actually signed between the British and the authorities of Mexico and her province of California, and then came events of another shaping, culminating in the war between Mexico and the United States.

Thus may be seen from the counterpart records of those times, that the Mormon Prophet was before-hand with Great Britain in the design of possessing the Pacific Coast by colonization, as the record shows that early in 1844 he petitioned the United States for the privilege of raising 100,000 men "to extend protection to persons wishing to settle Oregon and other portions of the territory of the United States, and extend protection to the people in Texas," while at the same time he was planning the removal of his entire people on to the Pacific slope, as seen in his diary note of February 20th, 1844, already presented. And it is a singular fact in American history that two years later, and nearly simultaneously with the signing of the contract between the British Consul Forbes, Governor Pice of California, and General Castro, President Polk and his cabinet were entertaining the policy of sending a battalion of one thousand Mormon soldiers (this being the original number) overland into California fully equipped and armed, to take possession of and defend that country, while another thousand were designed to be sent from the Eastern States by way of Cape Horn for the same service.

President Polk, at this later date, designed to checkmate the British Government, with its ten thousand Irish emigrants, with from twenty to forty thousand Mormon Protestants under the American flag. Thus the true history of those times compared, shows the extraordinary fact that, two years after the assassination of the Mormon Prophet, the United States Government was actually prepared to accept his grand colonizing plan to take possession of the Pacific territory, which he offered in his memorial to President Tyler and the Congress of the United States, bearing date March 26th, 1844. Nothing seems more certain in the record than the fact that had not the assassination of the Mormon Prophet so soon followed his colonizing offer to the United States, he had moved with his people to the Pacific Coast two or three years earlier than the occupation of Utah. And had he gone on to California he would have raised the American flag there, and struck the first blow with his Legion, instead of Fremont doing it in 1846 with his volunteers.

Had the Prophet moved with his people, either to the Rocky Mountains or California proper, it had been at the head of his Legion. Force of circumstances, it seems, would have made him thenceforth a Prophet-General, while the very strength of his Napoleonic character would have shot him, like Jove's thunderbolt, into the action between the United States and Mexico.

CHAPTER II.

GOVERNOR FORD URGES THE MIGRATION OF THE MORMONS TO CALIFORNIA. COMPACT OF THE REMOVAL. ADDRESS TO THE PRESIDENT OF THE UNITED STATES. THE EXODUS MORMON LIFE ON THE JOURNEY. A SENSATION FROM THE UNITED STATES GOVERNMENT.

Soon after the assassination of the Prophet and his brother Hyrum, Governor Ford, in a letter to President Young, under date of April 8th, 1845, urging the migration of the Mormons to California, said: "If you can get off by yourselves you may enjoy peace; but, surrounded by such neighbors, I confess that I do not see the time when you will be permitted to enjoy quiet. I was informed by General Joseph Smith last summer that he contemplated a removal west: and from what I learned from him and others at that time, I think, if he had lived, he would have begun to move in the matter before this time. I would be willing to exert all my feeble abilities and influence to further your views in this respect if it was the wish of your people.

"I would suggest a matter in confidence. California now offers a field for the prettiest enterprise that has been undertaken in modern times. It is but sparsely inhabited, and by none but the Indian or imbecile Mexican Spaniards. I have not enquired enough to know how strong it is in men and means. But this we know, that if conquered from Mexico, that country is so physically weak, and morally distracted, that she could never send a force there to reconquer it. Why should it not be a pretty operation for your people to go out there, take possession of and conquer a portion of the vacant country, and establish an independent government of your own, subject only to the law of nations? You would remain there a long time before you would be disturbed by the proximity of other settlements. If you conclude to do this, your design ought not to be known, or otherwise it would become the duty of the United States to prevent your emigration. If once you cross the line of the United States Territories, you would be in no danger of being interfered with."

Knowing the intentions of Joseph Smith to remove the Mormon people, Senator Douglas and others had given similar advice to him; and the very fact that such men looked upon the Mormons as quite equal to the establishment of an independent nationality, is most convincing proof that not their wrongdoing, but their empire-founding genius has been, and still is, the cause of the "irrepressible conflict" between them and their opponents. The advice of Governor Ford, however, was neither sought nor required.

Brigham Young, carrying out Joseph Smith's plan, had nearly matured every part of the movement, shaping also the emigration from the British Mission; but the Rocky Mountains, not California proper, was the place chosen for his people's retreat.

It was then that the Mormon leaders addressed the famous petition to President Polk and the Governors of all the States, excepting Missouri and Illinois, changing simply the address to each person. Here it is: "Nauvoo, April 24th, 1845.

"His Excellency James K. Polk, President of the United States.

"Hon. Sir: Suffer us, in behalf of a disfranchised and long afflicted people, to prefer a few suggestions for "your serious consideration, in hope of a friendly and unequivocal response, at as early a period as may suit your convenience, and the extreme urgency of the case seems to demand.

"It is not our present design to detail the multiplied and aggravated wrongs that we have received in the midst of a nation that gave us birth. Most of us have long been loyal citizens of some one of these United States, over which you have the honor to preside, while a few only claim the privilege of peaceable and lawful emigrants, designing to make the Union our permanent residence.

"We say we are a disfranchised people. We are privately told by the highest authorities of the State that it is neither prudent nor safe for us to vote at the polls; still we have continued to maintain our right to vote, until the blood of our best men has been shed, both in Missouri and Illinois, with impunity.

"You are doubtless somewhat familiar with the history of our expulsion from the State of Missouri, wherein scores of our brethren were massacred. Hundreds died through want and sickness, occasioned by their unparalleled sufferings.

Some millions worth of our property was destroyed, and some fifteen thousand souls fled for their lives to the then hospitable and peaceful shores of Illinois: and that the State of Illinois granted to us a liberal charter, for the term of perpetual succession, under whose provision private rights have become invested, and the largest city in the State has grown up, numbering about twenty thousand inhabitants.

"But, sir, the startling attitude recently assumed by the State of Illinois, forbids us to think that her designs are any less vindictive than those of Missouri.

She has already used the military of the State, with the executive at their head, to coerce and surrender up our best men to unparalleled murder, and that too under the most sacred pledges of protection and safety. As a salve for such unearthly perfidy and guilt, she told us, through her highest executive officers, that the laws should be magnified and the murderers brought to justice; but the blood of her innocent victims had not been wholly wiped from the floor of the awful arena, ere the Senate of that State rescued one of the indicted actors in that mournful tragedy from the sheriff of Hancock County, and gave him a seat in her hall of legislation; and all who were indicted by the grand jury of Hancock County for the murder of Joseph and Hyrum Smith, are suffered to roam at large, watching for further prey.

"To crown the climax of those bloody deeds, the State has repealed those chartered rights, by which wo might have lawfully defended ourselves against aggressors. If we defend ourselves hereafter against violence, whether it comes under the shadow of law or otherwise (for we have reason to expect it in both ways), we shall then be charged with treason and suffer the penalty; and if we continue passive and non-resistant, we must certainly expect to perish, for our enemies have sworn it.

"And here, sir, permit us to state that General Joseph Smith, during his short life, was arraigned at the bar of his country about fifty times, charged with criminal offences, but was acquitted every time by his country; his enemies, or rather his religious opponents, almost invariably being his judges. And we further testify that, as a people, we are law-abiding, peaceable and without crime; and we challenge the world to prove to the contrary; and while other less cities in Illinois have had special courts instituted to try their criminals, we have been stript of every source of arraigning marauders and murderers who are prowling around to destroy us, except the common magistracy.

"With these facts before you, sir, will you write to us without delay as a father and friend, and advise us what to do. We are members of the same great confederacy. Our fathers, yea, some of us, have fought and bled for our country, and we love her Constitution dearly.

"In the name of Israel's God, and by virtue of multiplied ties of country and kindred, we ask your friendly interposition in our favor. Will it be too much for us to ask you to convene a special session of Congress, and furnish us an asylum, where we can enjoy our rights of conscience and religion unmolested? Or, will you, in a special message to that body, when convened, recommend a remonstrance against such unhallowed acts of oppression and expatriation as this people have continued to receive from the States of Missouri and Illinois? Or will you favor us by your personal influence and by your official rank? Or will you express your views concerning what is called the "Great Western Measure" of colonizing the Latter-day Saints in Oregon, the north-western Territory, or some location remote from the States, where the hand of oppression shall not crush every noble principle and extinguish every patriotic feeling?

"And now, honored sir, having reached out our imploring hands to you, with deep solemnity, we would importune you as a father, a friend, a patriot and the head of a mighty nation, by the Constitution of American liberty, by the blood of our fathers who have fought for the independence of this republic, by the blood of the martyrs which has been shed in our midst, by the waitings of the widows and orphans, by our murdered fathers and mothers, brothers and sisters, wives and children, by the dread of immediate destruction from secret combinations now forming for our overthrow, and by every endearing tie that binds man to man and renders life bearable, and that too, for aught we know, for the last time,—that you will lend your immediate aid to quell the violence of mobocracy, and exert your influence to establish us as a people in our civil and religious rights, where we now are, or in some part of the United States, or in some place remote therefrom, where we may colonize in peace and safety as soon as circumstances will permit.

"We sincerely hope that your future prompt measures towards us will be dictated by the best feelings that dwell in the bosom of humanity, and the blessings of a grateful people, and many ready to perish, shall come upon you.

"We are, sir, with great respect, your obedient servants, Brigham Young, Willard Richards, Orson Spencer, Orson Pratt, y Committee, W. W. Phelps, A. W. Babbitt, J. M. Bernhisel, In behalf of the Church of Jesus Christ of Latter-day Saints, at Nauvoo, Illinois.

"P.S.—As many of our communications, post-marked at Nauvoo, have failed of their destination, and the mails around us have been intercepted by our enemies, we shall send this to some distant office by the hand of a special messenger."

The appeal itself is not a mere attempt at rhetoric. The very inelegance of multiplied ties and sacred objects invoked and crowded upon each other, to touch the hearts of men in power, is truly affecting. There is a tragic burden in the circumstances and urgency of the case. But the prayer was unanswered.

Towards the close of the year 1845, the leaders, in council, resolved to remove their people at once and seek a second Zion in the valleys of the Rocky Mountains. It was too clear that they could no longer dwell among so-called civilized men. They knew that they must soon seek refuge with the children of the forest; and as for humanity, they must seek it in the breasts of savages, for there was scarcely a smoldering spark of it left for them, either in Missouri or Illinois, nor indeed anywhere within the borders of the United States.

They had now no destiny but in the West. If they tarried longer their blood would fertilize the lands which they had tilled, and their wives and daughters would be ravished within the sanctuary of the homes which their industrious hands had built. Their people were by a thousand ancestral links joined to the Pilgrim Fathers who founded this nation, and with the heroes who won for it independence, and it was as the breaking of their heartstrings to rend them from their fatherland, and send them as exiles into the territory of a foreign power. But there was no alternative between a Mormon exodus or a Mormon massacre.

Sorrowfully, but resolutely, the Saints prepared to leave; trusting in the Providence which had thus far taken them through their darkest days and multiplied upon their heads compensation for their sorrows. But the anti-Mormons seemed eager for the questionable honor of exterminating them. In September of the year 1845, delegates from nine counties met in convention, at Carthage, over the Mormon troubles, and sent four commissioners: General Hardin, Commander of the State Militia; Senator Douglass; W. B. Warren; and J. A. McDougal, to demand the removal of the Mormons to the Rocky Mountains. The commissioners held a council with the Twelve Apostles at Nauvoo, and the Mormon leaders promptly agreed to remove their people at once, a movement, as we have seen, which they had been considering for several years. Now were they brought face to face with the issue. The Mormon leaders sought not to evade it; but, with their characteristic Israelitish methods, resolved to grapple with the tremendous undertaking of the exodus of a people.

On that exodus, hung, not only the very destiny of the people, but the peace of the State of Illinois. Probably it was a sensible comprehension of this fact that prompted General Hardin to ask of the Twelve Apostles, at the council in question, what guarantee they would give that the Mormons would fulfill their part of the covenant. To this Brigham Young replied, with a strong touch of common-sense severity: "You have our all as the guarantee; what more can we give beyond the guarantee of our names?" Senator Douglass observed, "Mr. Young is right." But General Hardin knew that the people of Illinois, and especially the anti-Mormons, would look to him more than to Douglass, who had been styled the Mormon-made senator; so the commissioners asked for a written covenant, of a nature to relieve themselves of much of the responsibility, and addressed the following: "Nauvoo, Oct. 1st, 1845.

"To the President and Council of the Church at Nauvoo: "Having had a free and full conversation with you this day, in reference to your proposed removal from this country, together with the members of your church, we have to request you to submit the facts and intentions stated to us in the said conversations to writing, in order that we may lay them before the Governor and people of the State. We hope that by so doing it will have a tendency to allay the excitement at present existing in the public mind.

"We have the honor to subscribe ourselves,
Respectfully yours,
John J. Hardin,
W. B. Warren,

S. A. Douglass,
J. A. McDougal."

The covenant itself is too precious to be lost to history; here it is: "Nauvoo, Ill., Oct. 1st, 1845.

"To Gen. J. Hardin, W. B. Warren, S. A. Douglass, and J. A. McDougal: "Messrs:—In reply to your letter of this date, requesting us ' to submit the facts and intentions stated by us in writing, in order that you may lay them before the Governor and people of the State,' we would refer you to our communication of the 24th ult. to the 'Quincy Committee,'etc., a copy of which is herewith enclosed.

"In addition to this we would say that we had commenced making arrangements to remove from the country previous to the recent disturbances; that we have four companies, of one hundred families each, and six more companies now organizing, of the same number each, preparatory to a removal.

"That one thousand families, including the Twelve, the High Council, the trustees and general authorities of the Church, are fully determined to remove in the Spring, independent of the contingencies of selling our property; and that this company will comprise from five to six thousand souls.

"That the Church, as a body, desire to remove with us, and will, if sales can be effected, so as to raise the necessary means.

"That the organization of the Church we represent is such that there never can exist but one head or presidency at any one time. And all good members wish to be with the organization: and all are determined to remove to some distant point where we shall neither infringe nor be infringed upon, so soon as time and means will permit.

"That we have some hundreds of farms and some two thousand houses for sale in this city and county, and we request all good citizens to assist in the disposal of our property.

"That we do not expect to find purchasers for our Temple and other public buildings; but we are willing to rent them to a respectable community who may inhabit the city.

"That we wish it distinctly understood that although we may not find purchasers for our property, we will not sacrifice it, nor give it away, or suffer it illegally to be wrested from us.

"That we do not intend to sow any wheat this Fall, and should we all sell, we shall not put in any more crops of any description.

"That as soon as practicable, we will appoint committees for this city, La Harpe, Macedonia, Bear Creek, and all necessary places in the county, to give information to purchasers.

"That if these testimonies are not sufficient to satisfy any people that we are in earnest, we will soon give them a sign that cannot be mistaken—we will LEAVE THEM.

"In behalf of the council, respectfully yours, etc.,
Brigham Young, President.
Willard Richards, Clerk.'"

The covenant satisfied the commissioners, and for a time also satisfied the anti-Mormons.

But their enemies were impatient for the Mormons to be gone. They would not keep even their own conditions of the covenant, much less were they disposed to lend a helping hand to lighten the burden of this thrice-afflicted people in their exodus, that their mutual bond might be fulfilled—a bond already sealed with the blood of their Prophet, and of his brother the Patriarch. So the High Council issued a circular to the Church, January 20, 1846, in which they stated the intention of their community to locate "in some good valley in the neighborhood of the Rocky Mountains, where they will infringe on no one, and not be likely to be infringed upon." "Here we will make a resting place," they said, '.' until we can determine a place for a permanent location. * * * We also further declare, for the satisfaction of some who have concluded that our grievances have alienated us from our country, that our patriotism has not been overcome by fire, by sword, by daylight nor by midnight assassination which we have endured, neither have they alienated us from the institutions of our country."

Then came the subject of service on the side of their country, should warbreak out between it and a foreign country, as was indicated at that time by our growing difficulties with Mexico. The anti-Mormons took advantage of this war prospect, and not satisfied with their act of expulsion, they raised the cry, "The Mormons intend to join the enemy!" This was as cruel as the seething of the kid in its mother's milk, but the High Council answered it with the homely anecdote of the Quaker's characteristic action against the pirates in defense of the ship on which he was a passenger, when he cut away the rope in the hands of the boarder, observing: "If thee wants that piece of rope I will help thee to it."

"The pirate fell," said the circular, "and a watery grave was his resting place."

Their country had been anything but a kind protecting parent to the Saints, but at least, in its hour of need, they would do as much as the conscientious Quaker did in the defense of the ship. There was, too, a grim humor and quiet pathos in the telling, that was more touchingly reproachful than would have been a storm of denunciations. In the same spirit the High Council climaxed their circular thus: "We agreed to leave the country for the sake of peace, upon the condition that no more persecutions be instituted against us. In good faith we have labored to fulfill this agreement. Governor Ford has also done his duty to further our wishes in this respect, but there are some who are unwilling that we should have an existence anywhere; but our destinies are in the hands of God, and so are also theirs."

Early in February, 1846, the Mormons began to cross the Mississippi in flat boats, old lighters, and a number of skiffs, forming, says the President's Journal, "quite a fleet," which was at work night and day under the direction of the police, commanded by their captain, Hosea Stout. Several days later the Mississippi froze over, and the companies continued the crossing on the ice.

On the 15th of the same month, Brigham Young, with his family, accompanied by Willard Richards and family, and George A. Smith, also crossed the Mississippi from Nauvoo, and proceeded to the " Camps of Israel," as they were styled by the Saints, which waited on the west side of the river, a few miles on the way, for the coming of their leaders. These were to form the vanguard of the migrating Saints, who were to follow from the various States where they were located or had organized themselves into flourishing branches and conferences; and soon after this period also began to pour across the Atlantic that tide of emigration from Europe which has since swelled to the number of over one hundred thousand souls.

As yet the "Camps of Israel" were unorganized, awaiting the coming of the President, on Sugar Creek, which he and his companions reached at dusk.

The next day he was busy organizing the company, and on the following, which was February 17th, at 9:50 a. m., the brethren of the camp had assembled near the bridge, to receive their initiatory instructions, and take the word of command from their leader, who ended his first day's orders to the congregation with a real touch of the law-giver's method. He said, " We will have no laws we cannot keep, but we will have order in the camp. If any want to live in peace when we have left this place, they must toe the mark." He then called upon all who wanted to go with the camp to raise their right hands. "All hands flew up at the bidding," says the record.

After the dismissal of the congregation, the President took several of the Twelve with him half a mile up a valley east of the camp and held a council. A letter was read from Mr. Samuel Brannan, of New York, with a copy of a curious agreement between him and a Mr. A. G. Benson, which had been sent west, under cover, for the authorities to sign.

To make clear to the reader a story, which now belongs to our national history, in connection with the first settling of California, it must be observed that Brannan, once known as one of the millionaires of the Golden State, had been the editor of The Prophet, published at New York. He seems to have been one of those sagacious men who saw in Mormonism the means to their own ends.

At the date of the exodus he was in the charge of a company of Saints, bound for the Pacific Coast, in the ship Brooklyn. They took all necessary outfit for the first settlers of a new country, including a printing press, upon which was afterwards struck off the first regular newspaper of California. This company was, also, the earliest company of American emigrants that arrived in the bay of San Francisco, and really the pioneer emigration of American citizens to the Golden State, for Fremont's volunteers cannot be considered in that character. Indeed, it is not a little singular that the Mormons were not only the pioneers of Utah, but also the pioneers of California, the builders of the first houses, the starters of the first papers, and, what has contributed so much to the growth of the Pacific Slope, the men who discovered the gold, under Mr. Marshal, the foreman of Sutter's mills. These facts, however, the people of California seem somewhat to hide in the histories of their State.

Relative to the sailing of this company, Samuel Brannan had written to the Mormon authorities. Ex-Postmaster Amos Kendall, and the said Benson, who seems to have been Kendall's agent, with others of political influence, represented to Brannan that, unless the leaders of the Church signed an agreement with them, to which the President of the United States, he said, was a "silent party," the government would not permit the Mormons to proceed on their journey westward.

This agreement required the pioneers " to transfer to A. G. Benson & Co., and to their heirs and assigns, the odd numbers of all the lands and town lots they may acquire in the country where they may settle." In case they refused to sign the agreement the President, it was said, would issue a proclamation, setting forth that it was the intention of the Mormons to take sides with either Mexico or Great Britain against the United States, and order them to be disarmed and dispersed. Both the letter and contract are very characteristic, and the worldly-minded man's poor imitation of the earnest religionist has probably often since amused Mr. Brannan himself. In his letter he said: "I declare to all that you are not going to California, but Oregon, and that my information is official. Kendall has also learned that we have chartered the ship Brooklyn, and that Mormons are going out in her; and, it is thought, she will be searched for arms, and, if found, they will be taken from us; and if not, an order will be sent to Commodore Stockton on the Pacific to search our vessel before we land. Kendall will be in the city next Thursday again, and then an effort will be made to bring about a reconciliation. I will make you acquainted with the result before I leave."

The "reconciliation" between the Government and the Mormons, as the reader will duly appreciate, was to be effected by a division of the spoils among the political chiefs, including, if Brannan and Kendall are to be relied on, the President of the United States. The following letter of fourteen days later date is too rich and graphic to be lost to the public: "New York, January 26, 1846.

"Dear Brother Young: "I haste to lay before your honorable body the result of ray movements since I wrote you last, which was from this city, stating some of my discoveries, in relation to the contemplated movements of the General Government in opposition to our removal.

"I had an interview with Amos Kendall, in company with Mr. Benson, which resulted in a compromise, the conditions of which you will learn by reading the contract between them and us, which I shall forward by this mail. I shall also leave a copy of the same with Elder Appleby, who was present when it was signed. Kendall is now our friend, and will use his influence in our behalf, in connection with twenty-five of the most prominent demagogues in the country.

You will be permitted to pass out of the States unmolested. Their counsel is to go well armed but keep them well secreted from the rabble.

"I shall select the most suitable spot on the Bay of San Francisco for the location of a commercial city. When I sail, which will be next Saturday, at one o'clock, I shall hoist a flag with ' Oregon' on it.

"Immediately on the reception of this letter, you must write to Mr. A. G. Benson, and let him know whether you are willing to coincide with the contract I have made for our deliverance. I am aware it is a covenant with death, but we know that God is able to break it and will do it. The Children of Israel, in their escape from Egypt, had to make covenants for their safety, and leave it for God to break them; and the Prophet has said, 'As it was then, so shall it be in the last days.' And I have been led by a remarkable train of circumstances to say, amen; and I feel and hope you will do the same.

"Mr. Benson thinks the Twelve should leave and get out of the country first, and avoid being arrested, if it is a possible thing; but if you are arrested, you will find a staunch friend in him; and you will find friends, and that a host, to deliver you from their hands. If any of you are arrested, don't be tried west of the Alleghany Mountains; in the East you will find friends that you little think of.

"It is the prayer of the Saints in the East night and day for your safety, and it is mine first in the morning and the last in the evening.

"I must now bring my letter to a close. Mr. Benson's address is No. 39 South Street; and the sooner you can give him answer the better it will be for us.

He will spend one month in Washington to sustain you, and he will do it, no mistake. But everything must be kept silent as death on our part, names of parties in particular.

"I now commit this sheet to the post, praying that Israel's God may prevent it from falling into the hands of wicked men. You will hear from me again on the day of sailing, if it is the Lord's will, amen.

"Your's truly, a friend and brother in God's kingdom.

S. Brannan."

The contract in question was signed by Samuel Brannan and A. G. Benson and witnessed by W. I. Appleby. To it is this postscript: "This is only a copy of the original, which I have filled out. It is no gammon, but will be carried through, if you say, amen. It was drawn up by Kendall's own hand; but no person must be known but Mr. Benson."

The following simple minute, in Brigham Young's private journal, is a fine set-off to these documents: "Samuel Brannan urged upon the council the signing of the document.

The council considered the subject, and concluded that as our trust was in God, and that, as we looked to him for protection, we would not sign any such unjust and oppressive agreement. This was a plan of political demagogues to rob the Latter-day Saints of millions and compel them to submit to it by threats of Federal bayonets."

No matter what view the reader may take of the Mormons and their leaders relative to the intrinsic value to the world of their social and theological problems, no intelligent mind can help being struck with the towering superiority of men trusting in their God, in the supremest hour of trial, compared with the foremost politicians in the country, including a President of the United States, as illustrated in the above example. It is charitably to be hoped, however, that President Polk was a very "silent party" to this scheme, and that his name was merely used to give potency to the promise of protection-, and to the threat that the General Government would intercept the Mormons in their exodus.

Little did the political demagogues of the time, and these land speculators, understand the Mormon people, and still less the character of the men who were leading them; nor did "Elder Brannan" know them much better. From the beginning the Mormons never gave up an inch of their chosen ground, never, as a people, consented to a compromise, nor allowed themselves to be turned aside from their purposes, nor wavered in their fidelity to their faith. They would suffer expulsion, or make an exodus if need be, yet ever, as in this case, have they answered, "Our trust is in God. We look to Him for protection." So far "Elder Brannan" understood them; hence his profession of faith that the Lord would overrule and break the "covenant with death." But these men did wiser and better. They never made the covenant, but calmly defied the consequences, which they knew too well might soon follow. Not even as much as to reply to Messrs. Benson, Kendall & Co. did they descend from the pinnacle of their integrity.

But, be it not for a moment thought that the Mormon leaders did not fully comprehend their critical position in all its aspects. A homely anecdote of the apostle George A. Smith will illustrate those times. At a council in Nauvoo, of the men who were to act as the captains of the people in that famous exodus, one after the other brought up difficulties in their path until the prospect was without one poor speck of daylight. The good nature of "George A." was provoked at last, when he sprang up and observed with his quaint humor that had now a touch of the grand in it, " If there is no God in Israel we are a 'sucked in' set of fellows. But I am going to take my family and cross the river, and the Lord will open the way." He was one of the first to set out on that miraculous journey to the Rocky Mountains.

Having resolved to trust in their God and themselves, quietly setting aside the politicians, Brigham Young and several of the Twelve left the Camp of Israel for a few days, and returned to bid farewell to their beloved Nauvoo, and hold a parting service in the Temple. This was the last time Brigham Young ever saw that sacred monument of the Mormons' devotion.

The Pioneers had now been a month on Sugar Creek, and during the time had, of course, consumed a vast amount of the provisions; indeed, nearly all, which had been gathered up for their journey. Their condition, however, was not without its compensation; for it checked the movements of the mob, among whom the opinion prevailed that the outfit of the Pioneers was so utterly insufficient that, in a short time, they would break in pieces and scatter. Moreover, it was mid-winter. Up to the date of their starting from this first camping ground, detachments continued to join them, crossing the Mississippi, from Nauvoo, on the ice; but before starting they addressed the following memorial: "To His Excellency Governor of the Territory of Iowa: Honored Sir: The time is at hand in which several thousand free citizens of this great Republic are to be driven from their peaceful homes and firesides, their property and farms, and their dearest constitutional rights, to wander in the barren plains and sterile mountains of western wilds, and linger out their lives in wretched exile, far beyond the pale of professed civilization, or else be exterminated upon their own lands by the people and authorities of the State of Illinois.

"As life is sweet, we have chosen banishment rather than death, but, sir, the terms of our banishment are so rigid, that we have not sufficient time allotted us to make the necessary preparations to encounter the hardships and difficulties of these dreary and uninhabited regions. We have not time allowed us to dispose of our property, dwellings and farms, consequently many of us will have to leave them unsold, without the means of procuring the necessary provisions, clothing, teams, etc., to sustain us but a short distance beyond the settlements; hence our persecutors have placed us in very unpleasant circumstances.

"To stay is death by ' fire and sword;' to go into banishment unprepared is death by starvation. But yet, under these heartrending circumstances, several hundred of us have started upon our dreary journey, and are now encamped in Lee County, Iowa, suffering much from the intensity of the cold. Some of us are already without food, and others have barely sufficient to last a few weeks: hundreds of others must shortly follow us in the same unhappy condition, therefore: "We, the presiding authorities of the Church of Jesus Christ of Latter-day Saints, as a committee in behalf of several thousand suffering exiles, humbly ask Your Excellency to shield and protect us in our constitutional rights, while we are passing through the Territory over which you have jurisdiction. And, should any of the exiles be under the necessity of stopping in this Territory for a time, either in settled or unsettled parts, for the purpose of raising crops, by renting farms or upon public lands, or to make the necessary preparations for their exile in any lawful way, we humbly petition Your Excellency to use an influence and power in our behalf, and thus preserve thousands of American citizens, together with their wives and children, from intense sufferings, starvation and death. And your petitioners will ever pray."

In the diary of the President is a sort of valedictory, written before starting on their journey from Sugar Creek, which concludes thus: "Our homes, gardens, orchards, farms, streets, bridges, mills, public halls, magnificent temple, and other public improvements we leave as a monument of our patriotism, industry, economy, uprightness of purpose, and integrity of heart, and as a living testimony of the falsehood and wickedness of those who charge us with disloyalty to the Constitution of our country, idleness and dishonesty."

The Mormons were setting out under their leaders, from the borders of civilization, with their wives and their children, in broad daylight, before the very eyes of ten thousand of their enemies, who would have preferred their utter destruction to their " flight," notwithstanding they had enforced it by treaties outrageous beyond description, inasmuch as the exiles were nearly all American born, many of them tracing their ancestors to the very founders of the nation. They had to make a journey of fifteen hundred miles over trackless prairies, sandy deserts and rocky mountains, through bands of warlike Indians, who had been driven, exasperated, towards the West; and at last, to seek out and build up their Zion in valleys then unfruitful, in a solitary region where the foot of the white man had scarcely trod. These, too, were to be followed by the aged, the halt, the sick and the blind, the poor, who were to be helped by their little less destitute brethren, and the delicate young mother with her new-born babe at her breast, and still worse, for they were not only threatened with the extermination of the poor remnant at Nauvoo, but news had arrived that the parent-government designed to pursue their pioneers with troops, take from them their arms, and scatter them, that they might perish by the way, and leave their bones bleaching in the wilderness.

Yet did Brigham Young deal with the exodus of the Mormon people as simply in its opening as he did in his daily record of it. So, indeed, did the entire Mormon community. They all seemed as oblivious of the stupendous meaning of an exodus, as did the first workers on railroads of the vast meaning to civilization of that wonder of the age. A people trusting in their God, the Mormons were, in their mission, superior to the greatest human trials, and in their childlike faith equal to almost superhuman undertakings. To-day, however, with the astonishing change which has come over the spirit of the scene, on the whole Pacific Slope, since the Mormons pioneered our nation towards the setting sun, the picture of a modern Israel in their exodus has almost faded from the popular mind; but, in the centuries hence, when the passing events of this age shall have each taken their proper place, the historian will point back to that exodus in the New World of the West, as one quite worthy to rank with the immortal exodus of the children of Israel.

At about noon, on the 1st of March, 1846, the " Camp of Israel" began to move, and at four o'clock nearly four hundred wagons were on the way, traveling in a north-westerly direction. At night, they camped again on Sugar Creek, having advanced five miles. Scraping away the snow, they pitched their tents upon the hard-frozen ground; and after building large fires in front, they made themselves as comfortable as possible under the circumstances. Indeed, it is questionable whether any other people in the world could have cozened themselves into a happy state of mind amid such surroundings, with such a past, fresh and bleeding in their memories, and with such a prospect as was before both themselves and the remnant of their brethren left in Nauvoo to the tender mercies of the mob. In his diary Apostle Orson Pratt wrote that night, "Notwithstanding our sufferings, hardships and privations, we are cheerful, and rejoice that we have the privilege of passing through tribulation for the truth's sake."

These Mormon pilgrims, who took much consolation on their journey in likening themselves to the pilgrim fathers and mothers of this nation, whose descendants many of them actually were, that night made their beds upon the frozen earth. "After bowing before our great Creator," wrote Apostle Pratt, "and offering up praise and thanksgiving to him, and imploring his protection, we resigned ourselves to the slumbers of the night."

But the weather was more moderate that night than it had been for several weeks previous. At their first encampment the thermometer, at one time, fell twenty degrees below zero, freezing over the great Mississippi. The survivors of that journey will tell you they never Suffered so much from the cold in their lives as they did on Sugar Creek. And what of the Mormon women? Around them circles an almost tragic romance. Fancy may find abundant subject for graphic story of the devotion, the suffering, the matchless heroism of the "Sisters," in the telling incident that nine children were born to them the first night they camped out on Sugar Creek, February 5th, 1846. That day they wept their farewells over their beloved city, or in the sanctuary of the Temple, in which they had hoped to worship till the end of life, but which they left, never to see again; that night suffering nature administered to them the mixed cup of woman's supremest joy and pain.

But it was not prayer alone that sustained these pilgrims. The practical philosophy of their great leader, daily and hourly applied to the exigencies of their case, did almost as much as their own matchless faith to sustain them from the commencement to the end of their journey. With that leader had very properly come to the "Camp of Israel" several of the Twelve and the chief bishops of the Church, but he also brought with him a quorum humble in pretensions, yet useful as high priests to the Saints in those spirit saddening days.

It was Captain Pitt's brass band. That night the President had the "brethren and sisters" out in the dance, and the music was as glad as at a merry-making. Several gentlemen from Iowa gathered to witness the strange interesting scene. They could scarcely believe their own senses when they were told that these were the Mormons in their "flight from civilization," bound they knew not whither, except where God should lead them by the "hand of his servant."

Thus in the song and the dance the Saints praised the Lord. When the night was fine, and supper, which consisted of the most primitive fare, was over, some of the men would clear away the snow, while others bore large logs to the camp fires in anticipation of the jubilee of the evening. Soon, in a sheltered place, the blazing fires would roar, and fifty couples, old and young, would join, in the merriest spirit, to the music of the band or the rival revelry of the solitary fiddle. As they journeyed along, too, strangers constantly visited their camps, and great was their wonderment to see the order, unity and good feeling that prevailed in the midst of the people. By the camp fires they would linger, listening to the music and song; and they fain had taken part in the merriment had not those scenes been as sacred worship in the exodus of a God-fearing people. To fully understand the incidents here narrated, the reader must couple in his mind the idea of an exodus with the idea of an Israelitish jubilee; for it was a jubilee to the Mormons to be delivered from their enemies at any price.

The sagacious reader will readily appreciate the wise method pursued by Brigham Young. Prayers availed much. The hymn and the prayer were never forgotten at the close of the dance, before they dispersed, to make their bed within the shelter of the wagon, or under it, exposed to the cold of those bitter nights. But the dance and the song kept the Mormon pilgrims cheerful and healthy in mind, whereas, had a spirit of gloomy fanaticism been encouraged, such as one might have expected, most likely there would soon have been murmuring in the congregation against their Moses, and the people would have been sighing for the flesh-pots of Egypt. The patriarchal care of Brigham Young over the migrating thousands was also something uncommon. It was extended to every family, every soul; even the very animals had the master friend near to ease and succor them. A thousand anecdotes could be told of that journey to illustrate this. When traveling, or in camp, he was ever looking after the welfare of all. No poor horse or ox even had a tight collar or a bow too small but his eye would see it. Many times did he get out of his vehicle and see that some suffering animal was relieved.

There can be no doubt that the industrious habits of the Mormons, and the semi-communistic character of their camps, enabled them to accomplish on their journey what otherwise would have been impossible. They were almost destitute at the start, but they created resources on the way. Their pioneers and able-bodied men generally took work on farms, split rails, cleared the timber for the new settlers, fenced their lands, built barns and husked their corn. Each night brought them some employment; and, if they laid over for a day or two at their encampment, the country around was busy with their industry. They also scattered for work, some of them going even into Missouri among their ancient enemies to turn to the smiter the "other cheek," while they were earning support for their families.

At one of their first camping grounds, on a ten-acre lot which the pioneer had cleared of timber, they made the acquaintance of its owner, a Dr. Jewett.

The worthy doctor was an enthusiast over mesmerism and animal magnetism, so he sought to convert the Mormon leaders to his views. Brigham Young replied, "I perfectly understand it, Doctor. We believe in the Lord's magnetizing.

He magnetized Belshazzar so that he saw the hand-writing on the wall." The Mormons, too, had seen the hand-writing on the wall, and were hastening to the mountains.

The citizens of Farmington came over to invite the Nauvoo Band, under Captain Pitt, to come to their village for a concert. There was some music left in the " brethren." They had not forgotten how to sing the " Songs of Zion," so they made the good folks of Farmington merry, and for a time forgot their own sorrows.

As soon as the "Camp of Israel" was fairly on the march, the leader, with the Twelve and the captains, divided it into companies of hundreds, fifties, and tens; and then the companies took up their line in order, Brigham Young directing the whole, and bringing up the main body, with the chief care of the families.

The weather was still intensely cold. The Pioneers moved in the face of keen-edged northwest winds; they broke the ice to give their cattle drink; they made their beds on the soaked prairie lands; heavy rains and snow by day, and frost at night, rendered their situation anything but pleasant. The bark and limbs of trees were the principal food of their animals, and after doubling their teams all day, wading through the deep mud, they would find themselves at night only a few miles on their journey. They grew sick of this at last, and for three weeks rested on the head waters of the Chariton, waiting for the freshets to subside.

These incidents of travel were varied by an occasional birth in camp. There was also the death of a lamented lady early on the journey. She was a gentle, intelligent wife of a famous Mormon missionary, Orson Spencer, once a Baptist minister of excellent standing. She had requested the brethren to take her with them. She would not be left behind. Life was too far exhausted by the persecutions to survive the exodus, but she could yet have the honor of dying in that immortal circumstance of her people. Several others of the sisters also died at the very starting. Ah, who shall fitly picture the lofty heroism of the Mormon women!

It was near the Chariton that the organization of the " Camp of Israel" was perfected, on the 27th of March, when Brigham Young was formally chosen as the President; and captains of hundreds, fifties, and tens were appointed.

Thus the Twelve became relieved of their mere secular commands, and were placed at the heads of divisions, in their more apostolic character, as presidents.

The provisioning of the camp was also equally brought under organic management. Henry G. Sherwood was appointed contracting commissary for the first fifty; David D. Yearsley for the second; W. H. Edwards for the third; Peter Haws for the fourth; Samuel Gulley for the fifth: Joseph Warburton for the sixth. Henry G. Sherwood ranked as acting commissary-general. There were also distributing commissaries appointed. Their duties, says the President's diary, "are to make a righteous distribution of grain and provisions, and such articles as shall be furnished for the use of the camp, among their respective fifties."

Thus it will be seen that the "Camp of Israel" now partook very much of a military character, with all of an army's organic efficiency.

Towards the end of April the camp came to a place the leaders named Garden Grove. Here they determined to form a small settlement, open farms, and make a temporary gathering place for "the poor," while the better prepared were to push on the way and make other settlements.

On the morning of the 27th of April the bugle sounded at Garden Grove, and all the men assembled to organize for labor. Immediately hundreds of men were at work cutting trees, splitting rails, making fences, cutting logs for houses, building bridges, digging wells, making plows, and herding cattle. Quite a number were sent into the Missouri settlements to exchange horses for oxen, valuable feather beds and the like for provisions and articles most needed in the camp, and the remainder engaged in plowing and planting. Messengers were also dispatched to call in the bands of pioneers scattered over the country seeking work, with instructions to hasten them up to help form the new settlements before the season had passed; so that, in a scarcely conceivable time, at Garden Grove and Mount Pisgah, industrious settlements sprang up almost as if by magic. The main body also hurried on towards old Council Bluffs, under the President and his chief men, to locate winter quarters, and to send on a picked company of pioneers that year to the Rocky Mountains. Reaching the Missouri River, they were welcomed by the Pottowatomie and Omaha Indians.

By this time Apostle Orson Hyde had arrived at headquarters from Nauvoo, and Apostle Woodruff, home from his mission to England, was at Mount Pisgah.

To this place an express from the President at Council Bluffs came to raise one hundred men for the expedition to the mountains. Apostle Woodruff called for the mounted volunteers, and sixty at once followed him out into the line; but the next day an event occurred which caused the postponement of the journey to the mountains till the following year.

It was on the 26th of June when the camp at Mount Pisgah was thrown into consternation by the cry, "The United States troops are upon us!" But soon afterwards, Captain James Allen arriving with only three dragoons, the excitement subsided. The High Council was called, and Captain Allen laid before it his business, which is set forth in the following " Circular to the Mormons: I have come among you, instructed by Col. S. F. Kearney, of the U. S. Army, now commanding the Army of the West, to visit the Mormon camp, and to accept the service for twelve months of four or five companies of Mormon men who may be willing to serve their country for that period in our present war with Mexico; this force to unite with the Army of the West at Santa Fe, and be marched thence to California, where they will be discharged.

"They will receive pay and rations, and other allowances, such as other volunteers or regular soldiers receive, from the day they shall be mustered into the service, and will be entitled to all comforts and benefits of regular soldiers of the army, and when discharged, as contemplated, at California, they will be given gratis their arms and accoutrements, with which they will be fully equipped at Fort Leavenworth. This is offered to the Mormon people now. This year an opportunity of sending a portion of their young and intelligent men to the ultimate destination of their whole people, and entirely at the expense of the United States, and this advanced party can thus pave the way and look out the land for their brethren to come after them.

"Those of the Mormons who are desirous of serving their country on the conditions here enumerated, are requested to meet me without delay at their principal camp at the Council Bluffs, whither I am now going to consult with their principal men, and to receive and organize the force contemplated to be raised.

"I will receive all healthy, able-bodied men of from eighteen to forty-five years of age.

J. Allen, Capt., 1st Dragoons.

"Camp of the Mormons at Mount Pisgah, 138 miles east of Council Bluff, June 26th, 1846.

"Note.—I hope to complete the organization of this battalion in six days after my reaching Council Bluffs, or within nine days from this time."

The High Council of Mount Pisgah treated the military envoy with studied courtesy, but the matter was of too great importance for even an opinion to be hazarded in the absence of the master mind; so Captain Allen was furnished with a letter of introduction to Brigham Young and the authorities at headquarters, and a special messenger was dispatched by Apostle Woodruff to prepare the President for the business of the government agent.

CHAPTER III.

THE CALL FOR THE MORMON BATTALION. INTERVIEWS WITH PRESIDENT POLK. THE APOSTLES ENLISTING SOLDIERS FROM THEIR PEOPLE FOR THE SERVICE OF THE NATION. THE BATTALION ON THE MARCH.

We now come to a subject in Mormon history of which two opposite views have been taken, neither of which, perhaps, are unqualifiedly correct. It is that of the calling of a Mormon battalion to serve the nation in its war with Mexico, as set forth in the circular already given. One view is that the Government, prompted by such men as Senator Benton of Missouri, sought to destroy, or at least to cripple the Mormons, by taking from them five hundred of their best men, in an Indian country, and in their exodus; while the other view is that the Government designed their good and honor. The truth is that a few honorable gentlemen like Colonel Thomas L. Kane did so design; but it is equally true that the great majority heartily wished for their utter extinction; while Senator Douglass and many other politicians, seeing in this vast migration of the Mormons towards the Pacific the ready and most efficient means to wrest California from Mexico, favored the calling of the battalion for national conquest, without caring what afterwards became of those heroic men who left their families and people in the " wilderness," or whether those families perished by the way or not. Moreover, the Mormon leaders are in possession of what appears to be very positive evidence that, after President Polk issued the " call," Senator Thomas Benton obtained from him the pledge that, should the Mormons refuse to respond, United States troops should pursue, cut off their route, and disperse them.

Such a covenant was villainous beyond expression; for, to have dispersed the Mormon pilgrims at that moment would have been to have devoted a whole people to the crudest martyrdom.

In any view of the case, it shows that the Mormons were an essentially loyal and patriotic people; and, if we take the darkest view, which be it emphatically affirmed was the one of that hour, then does the masterly policy of Brigham Young, and the conduct of the Mormons, stand out sublime and farseeing beyond most of the examples of history. The reader has noted Mr. Brannan's letter, received by the leaders before starting on their journey; they looked upon this "call" for, from five hundred to a thousand, of the flower of their camps as the fulfillment of the "threat." The excuse to annihilate them they believed was sought; even the General Government dared not disperse and disarm them without an excuse. At the best an extraordinary test of their loyalty was asked of them, under circumstances that would have required the thrice hardening of a Pharaoh's heart to have exacted.

Here it will only be just to both sides to give Colonel Kane's statement, in his historical discourse on the Mormons, delivered before the Historical Society of Pennsylvania, as that gentleman sustained in the case very much the character of a special agent of the Administration to the Mormons. He said: "At the commencement of the Mexican war, the President considered it desirable to march a body of reliable infantry to California, at as early a period as practicable, and the known hardihood and habits of discipline of the Mormons were supposed peculiarly to fit them for this service. As California was supposed also to be their ultimate destination, the long march might cost them less than other citizens. They were accordingly invited to furnish a battalion of volunteers early in the month of July.

"The call could hardly have been more inconveniently timed. The young and those who could best have been spared, were then away from the main body, either with pioneer companies in the van, or, their faith unannounced, seeking work and food about the north-western settlements, to support them till the return of the season for commencing emigration. The force was, therefore, to be recruited from among the fathers of families, and others, whose presence it was most desirable to retain.

"There were some, too, who could not view the invitation without distrust; they had twice been persuaded by Government authorities in Illinois and Missouri, to give up their arms on some special appeals to their patriotic confidence and had then been left to the malice of their enemies. And now they were asked, in the midst of the Indian country, to surrender over five hundred of their best men for a war march of thousands of miles to California, without the hope of return till after the conquest of that country. Could they view such a proposition with favor?

"But the feeling of country triumphed; the Union had never wronged them. 'You shall have your battalion at once, if it has to be a class of elders,' said one, himself a ruling elder. A central mass-meeting for council, some harangues at the more remotely scattered camps, an American flag brought out from the storehouse of things rescued and hoisted to the top of a tree-mast, and, in three days, the force was reported, mustered, organized and ready to march."

The foregoing is a graphic summary, but the reader will ask for something more of detail of this one of the chief episodes of the Pioneer history.

On the first of July Captain Allen was in council at the Bluffs with Brigham Young, Heber C. Kimball, Orson Hyde, Orson Pratt, Willard Richards, George A. Smith, John Taylor, John Smith and Levi Richards. At head-quarters they had not nearly sufficient force to raise the battalion. Yet they lost not a moment.

In the character of recruiting sergeants Brigham, Heber and Willard at once set out for Mount Pisgah, a distance of 130 miles, on the back track. Here they met Elder Jesse C. Little, home from Washington, having had interviews with President Polk and other members of the Government. A condensation of Elder Little's report will, at least, give to the public the original plan of the Government in the call of the battalion: "To President Brigham Young and the Council of the Twelve Apostles: "Brethren: In your letter of appointment to me dated Temple of God, Nauvoo, January 26th, 1846, you suggested, 'If our Government should offer facilities for emigrating to the western coast, Embrace those facilities if possible.

As a wise and faithful man, take every honorable advantage of the times you can.

Be thou a savior and deliverer of the people, and let virtue, integrity and truth be your motto—salvation and glory the prize for which you contend.' In accordance with my instructions, I felt an anxious desire for the deliverance of the Saints, and resolved upon visiting James K. Polk, President of the United States, to lay the situation of my persecuted brethren before him, and ask him, as the representative of our country, to stretch forth the Federal arm in their behalf. Accordingly, I called upon Governor Steele, of New Hampshire, with whom I had been acquainted from my youth, and other philanthropic gentlemen to obtain letters of recommendation to the heads of the departments."

Governor Steele gave to Elder Little a letter of introduction to Mr. Bancroft, Secretary of the Navy, in which the Governor said: "Mr. Little visits Washington, if I understand it correctly, for the purpose of procuring, or endeavoring to procure, the freight of any provisions or naval stores which the Government may be desirous of sending to Oregon, or to any portion of the Pacific. He is thus desirous of obtaining freight for the purpose of lessening the expense of chartering vessels to convey him and his followers to California, where they intend going and making a permanent settlement the present summer.

Yours truly, John Steele."

From Colonel Thomas L. Kane, Elder Little received a letter of introduction to the Hon. George M. Dallas, Vice-President of the United States, in which the writer said: "This gentleman visits Washington, with no other object than the laudable one of desiring aid of Government for his people, who, forced by persecution to found a new commonwealth in the Sacramento Valley, still retain American hearts, and would not willingly sell themselves to the foreigner, or forget the old commonwealth they leave behind."

Armed with these and other letters, Mr. Little started to Washington from Philadelphia, where he had enlisted, for his afflicted people, the zealous friendship of the patriotic brother of the great Arctic explorer; and, soon after his arrival at the capital, he obtained an introduction to President Polk, through Ex-Postmaster-General Amos Kendall. The Elder was favorably received by Mr. Polk, which emboldened him to address a formal petition to the President, which he closed as follows: "From twelve to fifteen thousand Mormons have already left Nauvoo for California, and many others are making ready to go; some have gone around Cape Horn, and I trust, before this time, have landed at the Bay of San Francisco. We have about forty thousand in the British Isles, all determined to gather to this land, and thousands will sail this fall. There are also many thousands scattered through the States, besides the great number in and around Nauvoo, who will go to California as soon as possible, but many of them are destitute of money to pay their passage either by sea or land.

"We are true-hearted Americans, true to our native country, true to its laws, true to its glorious institutions; and we have a desire to go under the outstretched wings of the American Eagle; we would disdain to receive assistance from a foreign power, although it should be proffered, unless our Government should turn us off in this great crisis, and compel us to be foreigners.

"If you will assist us in this crisis, I hereby pledge my honor, as the representative of this people, that the whole body will stand ready at your call, and act as one man in the land to which we are going; and should our Territory be invaded, we will hold ourselves ready to enter the field of battle, and then, like our patriotic fathers, make the battle-field our grave, or gain our liberty."

There were present at the first interview between the Mormon Elder and the President of the United States, Gen. Sam. Houston, just from Texas, upon Mexican affairs, and other distinguished men. A singular circumstance in American history is here connected; for at that important juncture in the history of our nation, as well as the Mormons, Washington was thrown into great excitement by the news that General Taylor had fought two battles with the Mexicans. This important event was directly bearing on the affairs of the Mormons, as much as upon those of the nation at large. The news of the actual commencement of the war between the two rival republics came in the very nick of time. Had Elder Little arrived in Washington six months before, or six months later, there would have been a marked variation from that which came to pass. We know not what the exact difference would have been, but it is most certain that President Polk would not then have designed to possess California by the help of these State-founding Saints, nor would their shovels have turned up the gold at Sutter's Mill, nor would General Stephen F. Kearney have had at his back the Mormon Battalion as his chief force, when he made himself master of the land of precious metals, and put his rival, Fremont, under arrest.

The day alter his first interview with President Polk, Elder Little called again upon ex-Postmaster-General Kendall, who informed him that the President had determined to take possession of California; that he designed to use the Mormons for this purpose, and that they would receive orders to push through to fortify the country. This induced the Elder to address the petition already quoted.

The President now laid the matter before the Cabinet. The plan offered to his colleagues was for the Elder to go direct to the Mormon camp, to raise from among them "one thousand picked men, to make a dash into California and take possession of it in the name of the United States." The Battalion was to be officered by their own men, excepting the commanding officer, who was to be appointed by President Polk, and to take cannon and everything necessary for the defense of the country. One thousand more of the Mormons from the Eastern States were proposed to be sent by way of Cape Horn, in a U. S. transport, for the same service. This was the original plan which President Polk laid before his Cabinet.

After this Elder Little had his second interview with President Polk, who told the Elder that he "had no prejudices against the Saints, but that he believed them to be good citizens;" that he "was willing to do them all the good in his power consistently ;" that " they should be protected ;'" and that he had "read the petition with interest." He further emphatically observed that he had "confidence in the Mormons as true American citizens, or he would not make such propositions as those he designed." This interview lasted three hours, so filled was the President with his plan of possessing California by the aid of the Mormons. But this generous design was afterwards changed through the influence of Senator Benton.

Before his departure west, Elder Little had another special interview with the President, who further said that he had "received the Mormon suffrages," that " they should be remembered;" and that he had "instructed the Secretary of War to make out dispatches to Colonel Kearney, commander of the Army of the West, relative to the Mormon Battalion."

On the 12th of June, Elder Little, in company with Colonel Thomas L. Kane, started for the West, the Colonel bearing special dispatches from the Government to General Kearney, who was at Fort Leavenworth. Judge Kane journeyed with his son as far as St. Louis.

The following is the order under which the Battalion was mustered into service:

"Headquarters, Army of the West, Fort Leavenworth, June 19, 1846.

"Sir: It is understood that there is a large body of Mormons who are desirous of emigrating to California, for the purpose of settling in that country, and I have therefore to direct that you will proceed to their camps and endeavor to raise from amongst them four or five companies of volunteers, to join me in my expedition to that country, each company to consist of any number between 73 and 109, the officers of each company will be a captain, first lieutenant, and second lieutenant, who will be elected by the privates, and subject to your approval, and the captains then to appoint the non-commissioned officers, also subject to your approval. The companies, upon being thus organized, will be mustered by you into the service of the United States, and from that day will commence to receive the pay, rations, and other allowances given to the other infantry volunteers, each according to his rank. You will, upon mustering into service the fourth company, be considered as having the rank, pay, and emoluments of a lieutenant-colonel of infantry, and are authorized to appoint an adjutant, sergeant-major, and quartermaster-sergeant for the battalion.

"The companies, after being organized, will be marched to this post, where they will be armed and prepared for the field, after which they will, under your command, follow on my trail in the direction of Santa Fe, and where you will receive further orders from me.

"You will, upon organizing the companies, require provisions, wagons, horses, mules, etc. You must purchase everything that is necessary and give the necessary drafts upon the quartermaster and commissary departments at this post, which drafts will be paid upon presentation.

"You will have the Mormons distinctly to understand that I wish to have them as volunteers for twelve months; that they will be marched to California, receiving pay and allowances during the above time, and at its expiration they will be discharged, and allowed to retain, as their private property, the guns and accoutrements furnished to them at this post.

"Each company will be allowed four women as laundresses, who will travel with the company, receiving rations and other allowances given to the laundresses of our army.

"With the foregoing conditions, which are hereby pledged to the Mormons, and which will be faithfully kept by me and other officers in behalf of the Government of the United States, I cannot doubt but that you will in a few days be able to raise five hundred young and efficient men for this expedition.

"Very respectfully your obedient servant, (Signed) S. F. Kearney, Col. of First Dragoons.

Per Capt. James Allen, First. Reg. Dragoons, Fort Leavenworth."

The following from important documents sent from the War Office a quarter of a century later, to aid this author in his investigation of the call of the Mormon Battalion is presented here to perfect the view: "Adjutant General's Office.

"Sir. I send herewith such papers as I have been able to find relating to the way the Mormon Battalion was received into service during the Mexican war.

Your obedient servant, E. D. Townsend, Adjutant-General."

"Hon. W. L. Marcy, Secretary of War, in a letter to General Kearney, dated June 3, 1846, states that it is known that a large body of Mormon emigrants are en route to California, for the purpose of settling in that country, desires the General to use all proper means to have a good understanding with them, to the end that the United States may have their co-operation in taking possession of and holding the country; authorizes the General to muster into service such as can be induced to volunteer, not, however, to a number exceeding one third of his entire force. Should they enter the service they were to be paid as other volunteers; to be allowed to designate, as far as it could be properly done, the persons to act as officers.

"This appears to be the authority under which General Kearney mustered the Mormon Battalion into service.

"The command was mustered out of service in California, in 1847, and one company was again mustered in immediately after to serve for twelve months.

This company was mustered out in 1848 at San Diego."

The other document of this Battalion history, furnished by the Adjutant General, is General Kearney's order under which the Battalion was mustered into service.

It will be seen from the above abstract of Secretary Marcy's letter to General Kearney, that there exists in the War Office to-day positive proof that the United States did design to colonize California by the aid of the Mormons.

Extraordinary was the wording, that the United States Government " desires the General to use all proper means to have a good understanding with them, to the end that the United States may have their co-operation in taking possession of and holding the country.'" We return to the Pioneer narrative: It will be remembered that Brigham Young, while believing the Battalion call to be a test of loyalty, hastened with Heber C. Kimball and Willard Richards to Mount Pisgah, 130 miles, to execute the "demand," as they deemed it, for a battalion of their picked men to serve their country. They immediately sent messengers, with official dispatches from their High Council to Nauvoo, Garden, Grove, and the regions around, calling to headquarters their old men and able-bodied boys to supply the place of their picked men going for the service of their country.

Returning to Council Bluffs, the Twelve gathered the " Camp of Israel" to enroll the companies of volunteers. While Major Hunt, of the volunteers, was calling out the first company, Brigham Young conversed with Colonel Kane in Woodruff's carriage about the affairs of the nation and told him the time would come when the Mormons would "have to save the Government of the United States, or it would crumble to atoms."

Forty minutes after twelve of the same day, July 15, the Elders and the people assembled in the Bowery. President Young then delivered to the congregation a simple but earnest speech, in which he told the brethren, with a touch of subdued pathos, "not to mention families to-day;" that they had "not time to reason now." "We want," he said, "to conform to the requisition made upon us, and we will do nothing else until we accomplish this thing. If we want the privilege of going where we can worship God according to the dictates of our consciences, we must raise the Battalion. I say, it is right; and who cares for sacrificing our comfort for a few years?"

Nobly did the Mormons respond to this call of their country. The Apostles acted as recruiting sergeants; nor did they wait for their reinforcements, but moved as though they intended to apply their leader's closing sentence literally; he said: "After we get through talking, we will call out the companies; and if there are not young men enough we will take the old men, and if they are not enough we will take the women. I want to say to every man, the Constitution of the United States, as framed by our fathers, was dictated, was revealed, was put into their hearts by the Almighty, who sits enthroned in the midst of the heavens; although unknown to them it was dictated by the revelations of Jesus Christ, and I tell you, in the name of Jesus Christ, it is as good as ever I could ask for. I say unto you, magnify the laws. There is no law in the United States, or in the Constitution, but I am ready to make honorable."

"There was no sentimental affectation at their leave-taking," said Thomas L. Kane, in relating the story to the Historical Society of Pennsylvania. "The afternoon before their march was devoted to a farewell ball; and a more merry rout I have never seen, though the company went without refreshments, and their ball was of the most primitive. It was the custom, whenever the larger camps rested for a few days together, to make great arbors, or boweries, as they called them, of poles, and brush, and wattling, as places of shelter for their meetings of devotion or conference. In one of these, where the ground had been trodden firm and hard by the worshippers, of the popular Father Taylor's precinct, was gathered now the mirth and beauty of the Mormon Israel.

"If anything told that the Mormons had been bred to other lives, it was the appearance of the women as they assembled here. Before their flight they had sold their watches and trinkets as the most available recourse for raising ready money; and hence like their partners, who wore waistcoats cut with useless watch pockets, they, although their ears were pierced and bore the marks of rejected pendants, were without earrings, chains or broaches. Except such ornaments, however, they lacked nothing most becoming the attire of decorous maidens. The neatly-darned white stockings, and clean white petticoat, the clear-starched collar and chemisette, the something faded, only because too-well washed lawn or gingham gown, that fitted modishly to the waist of its pretty wearer—these, if any of them spoke of poverty, spoke of a poverty that had known better days.

"With the rest attended the elders of the Church within call, including nearly all the chiefs of the High Council, with their wives and children. They, the bravest and most trouble-worn, seemed the most anxious of any to throw off the burden of heavy thoughts. Their leading off the dance in a double cotillion was the signal which bade the festivity to commence. To the canto of debonair violins, the cheer of horns, the jingle of sleigh bells and the jovial snoring of the tambourines, they did dance! None of your minuets or other mortuary possessions of gentles in etiquette, tight shoes and pinching gloves, but the spirited and scientific displays of our venerated and merry grandparents, who were not above following the fiddle to the lively fox-chase, French fours, Copenhagen jigs, Virginia reels, and the like forgotten figures, executed with the spirit of people too happy to be slow, or bashful, or constrained. Light hearts, lithe figures, and light feet had it their own way from an early hour till after the sun had dipped behind the sharp sky-line of the Omaha hills. Silence was then called, and a well-cultivated mezzo-soprano voice, belonging to a young lady with fair face and dark eyes, gave with quartette accompaniment, a little song, the notes of which I have been unsuccessful in repeated efforts to obtain since—a version of the text touching to all earthly wanderers: "By the rivers of Babylon we sat down and wept; We wept when we remembered Zion.

"There was danger of some expression of feeling when the song was over, for it had begun to draw tears, but, breaking the quiet with his hard voice, an elder asked the blessing of heaven on all who, with purity of heart and brotherhood of spirit, had mingled in that society, and then all dispersed, hastening to cover from the falling dews."

CHAPTER IV.

THE MORMONS SETTLE ON INDIAN LANDS. A GRAND COUNCIL HELD BETWEEN THE ELDERS AND INDIAN CHIEFS. A COVENANT IS MADE BETWEEN THEM, AND LAND GRANTED BY THE INDIANS TO THEIR MORMON BROTHERS. CHARACTERISTIC SPEECHES OF FAMOUS INDIAN CHIEFS. WINTER QUARTERS ORGANIZED. THE JOURNEY OF THE PIONEERS TO THE ROCKY MOUNTAINS.

With the departure of the Battalion, the flower of their strength, vanished all expectation of going to the Rocky Mountains that year, and the elders immediately set to work to locate and build their winter quarters. Ever exact to the organic genius of their community, their first business was to organize the High Council of a "Traveling Stake of Zion." This was done at Council Bluffs, July 21st, with Father Morley at the head of an incorporated council of twelve high priests.

The Indians welcomed their " Mormon brothers" with a touch of dramatic pathos. "They would have been pleased," said Colonel Kane, "with any whites who would not cheat them, nor sell them whiskey, nor whip them for their poor gipsy habits, nor bear themselves indecently toward their women, many of whom among the Pottawatomies, especially those of nearly unmixed French descent, are singularly comely, and some of them educated. But all Indians have something like a sentiment of reverence for the insane, and admire those who sacrifice, without apparent motive, their worldly welfare to the triumph of an idea. They understand the meaning of what they call a great vow, and think it is the duty of the right-minded to lighten the votary's penance under it.

To this feeling they united the sympathy of fellow sufferers for those who could talk to them of their own Illinois and tell the story how from it they also had been ruthlessly expelled.

"Their hospitality was sincere, almost delicate. Fanny Le Clerc, the spoiled child of the great brave, Pied Riche, interpreter of the nation, would have the pale face, Miss Divine, learn duets with her to the guitar; and the daughter of substantial Joseph La Framboise, the interpreter of the United States (she died of the fever that summer) welcomed all the nicest young Mormon Kitties and Lizzies and Jennies and Susans, to a coffee feast at her father's house, which was probably the best cabin in the river village. They made the Mormons at home there and elsewhere. Upon all they formally gave them leave to tarry just so long as it suited their own good pleasure.

"The affair, of course, furnished material for a solemn council. Under the auspices of an officer of the United States, their chiefs were summoned, in the form befitting great occasions, to meet in the dirty yard of one Mr. P. A. Sarpy's log trading house, at their village; they came in grand toilet, moving in their fantastic attire with so much aplomb and genteel measure, that the stranger found it difficult not to believe them high-born gentlemen attending a costumed ball.

When the red men had indulged to satiety in tobacco smoke from their peace pipes, and in what they love still better, their peculiar metaphoric rodomontade, which, beginning with celestial bodies, and coursing downwards over the grandest sublunary objects, always managed to alight at last on their great Father Polk, and the tenderness of him for his affectionate colored children; all the solemn funny fellows present, who played the part of chiefs, signed formal articles of convention with their unpronounceable names.

"The renowned chief, Pied Riche (he was surnamed Le Clerc on account of his remarkable scholarship) then rose and said: "' My Mormon Brethren: The Pottawatomie came sad and tired into this unhealthy Missouri bottom, not many years back, when he was taken from his beautiful country beyond the Mississippi, which had abundant game and timber, and clear water everywhere. Now you are driven away the same from your lodges and your lands there, and the graves of your people. So we have both suffered. We must keep one another and the Great Spirit will keep us both.

You are now free to cut and use all the wood you may wish. You can make your improvements and live on any part of our actual land not occupied by us. Because one suffers and does not deserve it, it is no reason he should suffer always.

I say, we may live to see all right yet. However, if we do not, our children will. Bonjour!'"

And thus ended the pageant. But the Mormons had most to do with the Omaha Indians, for they located their camps on both the east and west sides of the Missouri River. Winter Quarters proper was on the west side, five miles above the Omaha of to-day. There, on a pretty plateau, overlooking the river, they built, in a few months, over seven hundred houses, neatly laid out with highways and by-ways, and fortified with breastwork, stockade, and block-houses. It had, too, its place of worship, "tabernacle of the congregation;" for in everything they did they kept up the character of the modern Israel. The industrial character of the people also typed itself on their city in the wilderness, which sprang up as by magic, for it could boast of large workshops, and mills and factories provided with water power. They styled it a "Stake of Zion." It was the principal stake, too; several others, such as Garden Grove and Mount Pisgah having already been established on the route.

The settlement of headquarters brought the Mormons into peculiar relationship with the Omahas. A grand council was also held between their chiefs and the Elders. Big Elk made a characteristic speech for the occasion, yet not so distinguished in its Indian eloquence as that of Le Clerc. Big Elk said, in response to President Young: "My son, thou hast spoken well. I have all thou hast said in my heart. I have much I want to say. We are poor. When we go to hunt game in one place, we meet an enemy, and so in another place our enemies kill us. We do not kill them. I hope we will be friends. You may stay on these lands two years or more. Our young men may watch your cattle. We would be glad to have you trade with us. We will warn you of danger from other Indians."

The council closed with an excellent feeling; the pauper Omahas were treated to a feast, very gracious even to the princely appetite of Big Elk; and then they returned to their wigwams, satisfied for the time with the dispensation of the Great Spirit, who had sent their " Mormon brethren" into their country to care for and protect them from their enemies—the warlike Sioux.

The Omahas were ready to solicit as a favor the residence of white protectors among them. The Mormons harvested and stored away for them their crops of maize; with all their own poverty they spared them food enough besides, from time to time, to save them from absolutely starving; and their entrenched camp to the north of the Omaha villages, served as a sort of a breakwater between them and the destroying rush of the Sioux.

But the Mormons were as careful in their settlement on the Indian lands as they had been in the Battalion case, to make their conduct irreproachable in the eyes of the General Government, and to do nothing, even in their direst necessities, that would not force the sanction of the nation. They were, therefore, particular in obtaining covenants from the Indians and forwarding them to the President of the United States. Here is the covenant of the Omahas: "West Side of the Missouri River, Near Council Bluffs, August 31, 1846.

"We, the undersigned chiefs and braves, representatives of the Omaha nation of Indians, do hereby grant to the Mormon people the privilege of tarrying upon our lands for two years or more, or as long as may suit their convenience for the purpose of making the necessary preparations to prosecute their journey west of the Rocky Mountains, provided that our great father, the President of the United States, shall not counsel us to the contrary.

And we also do grant unto them the privilege of using all the wood and timber they shall require.

And furthermore agree that we will not molest or take from them their cattle, horses, sheep, or any other property.

Big Elk, his x mark,
Standing Elk, his x mark,
Little Chief, his x mark."

On this matter Brigham Young wrote to the President in behalf of his people: Near Council Bluffs, Butler's Park, Omaha Nation, Sept. 7, 1846.

"Sir: Since our communication of the 9th ult. to Your Excellency, the Omaha Indians have returned from their Summer hunt, and we have had an interview in general council with their chiefs and braves, who expressed a willingness that we should tarry on their lands, and use what wood and timber would be necessary for our convenience, while we were preparing to prosecute our journey, as may be seen by a duplicate of theirs to us of the 21st of August, which will be presented by Col. Kane.

"In council they were much more specific than in their writings, and Big Elk, in behalf of his nation requested us to lend them teams to draw their corn at harvest, and help keep it after it was deposited, to assist them in building houses, making fields, doing some blacksmithing, etc., and to teach some of their young men to do the same, and also keep some goods, and trade with them while we tarried among them.

We responded to all their wishes in the same spirit of kindness manifested by them and told them we would do them all the good we could, with the same proviso they made—if the President is willing; and this is why we write.

Hitherto we have kept aloof from all intercourse except in councils, as referred to, and giving them a few beeves when hungry, but we have the means of doing them a favor by instructing them in agricultural and mechanical arts, if it is desirable.

It might subject us to some inconvenience in our impoverished situation, to procure goods for their accommodation, and yet, if we can do it, we might receive in return as many skins and furs as would prove a valuable temporary substitute for worn-out clothing and tents in our camp, which would be no small blessing.

"A small division of our camp is some two or three hundred miles west of this, on the rush bottoms, among the Puncaws, where similar feelings are manifested towards our people.

"Should Your Excellency consider the requests of the Indians for instruction, etc., reasonable, and signifying the same to us, we will give them all the information in mechanism and farming the nature of the case will admit, which will give us the opportunity of getting the assistance of their men to help ns herd and labor, which we have much needed since the organization of the Battalion.

"A license, giving us permission to trade with the Indians while we are tarrying on or passing through their lands, made out in the name of Newel K. Whitney, our agent in camp, would be a favor to our people and our red neighbors. All of which is submitted to Your Excellency's considerations and the confidence of Colonel Kane.

"Done in behalf of the council of the Church of Jesus Christ of Latterday Saints, at the time and place before mentioned, and Camp of Israel.

'Most respectfully,
Brigham Young, President,
Willard Richards, Clerk."
"To James K. Polk, President U. S."

Out of an absolute destitution, and in spite of their expulsion, the Mormons had flourished and increased in the wilderness, so that at the end of the year 1846, Winter Quarters had grown into twenty-two wards, with a bishop over each.

As the spring opened, they began to prepare for their journey to the mountains, which at that day was almost appalling to the imagination. They had still over a thousand miles to the valley of the Salt Like, and so little was known of the country any more than its name implied—the Great American Desert— that the Mormons could not look forward to much of a land of promise to repay them for all the past. Yet sang their poet, Eliza R. Snow, who has ever on their great occasions fired them with her Hebraic inspiration:

"The time of winter now is o'er.
There's verdure on the plain;
We leave our shelt'ring roofs once more,
And to our tents again.
Chorus :—O Camp of Israel, onward move,
O, Jacob, rise and sing;
Ye Saints the world's salvation prove,
All hail to Zion's King!"

The pioneer song (as it was called) was, like their journey, quite lengthy.

But the pioneers sang it with a will. It told them of their past; told them in exultation, that they were leaving the "mobbing Gentile race, who thirsted for their blood, to rest in Jacob's hiding place," and it told of the future, in prophetic strains.

The word and will of the Lord concerning the Camp of Israel in its journeyings to the West, was published from head-quarters, on the 14th of January, 1847. As it is the first written revelation ever sent out to the Church by President Young, the following passages from it will be read with interest: "Let all the people of the Church of Jesus Christ of Latter-day Saints and those who journey with them, be organized into companies, with a covenant and promise to keep all the commandments and statutes of the Lord our God. Let the companies be organized with captains of hundreds, and captains of fifties, and captains of tens, with a president and councilor at their head, under the direction of the Twelve Apostles; and this shall be our covenant, that we will walk in all the ordinances of the Lord.

"Let each company provide itself with all the teams, wagons, provisions and all other necessaries for the journey that they can. When the companies are organized, let them go to with all their might, to prepare for those who are to tarry. Let each company, with their captains and presidents, decide how many can go next spring; then choose out a sufficient number of able-bodied and expert men to take teams, seed, and farming utensils to go as pioneers to prepare for putting in the spring crops. Let each company bear an equal proportion, according to the dividend of their property, in taking the poor, the widows, and the fatherless, and the families of those who have gone with the army, that the cries of the widow and the fatherless come not up into the ears of the Lord against his people.

"Let each company prepare houses, and fields for raising corn for those who are to remain behind this season; and this is the will of the Lord concerning this people."

"Let every man use all his influence and property to remove this people to the place where the Lord shall locate a Stake of Zion; and if ye do this with a pure heart, with all faithfulness, ye shall be blessed in your flocks, and in your herds, and in your fields, and in your houses, and in your families." * * On the 7th of April, 1847, the day after the general conference, the pioneers started from Winter Quarters.

As soon as they got fairly on the journey, they were organized as a military body, into companies of hundreds, fifties and tens. The following order of the officers will illustrate:

Brigham Young, Lieutenant-General; Stephen Markham, Colonel; John Pack, 1st Major; Shadrach Roundy, 2nd Major; Captains of hundreds, Stephen Markham and A. P. Rockwood.

Captain of Company 1, Wilford Woodruff; Company 2, Ezra T. Benson; Company 3, Phineas H. Young; Company 4, Luke Johnson; Company 5, Stephen H. Goddard; Company 6, Charles Shumway; Company 7, James Case: Company 8, Seth Taft; Company 9, Howard Egan; Company 10, Appleton M. Harmon; Company 11, John Higbie; Company 12, Norton Jacobs; Company 13, John Brown; Company 14, Joseph Mathews.

The camp consisted of 73 wagons; 143 men, 3 women and 2 children— 148 souls. Nothing could better illustrate the perfection of Mormon organization than this example of the pioneers, for they were apostles and picked elders of minute companies, and under strict discipline.

Lieutenant-General Young issued general orders to the regiment. The men were ordered to travel in a compact body, being in an Indian country; every man to carry his gun loaded, the locks to be shut on a piece of buckskin, with caps ready in case of attack; flint locks, with cotton and powder flask handy, and every man to walk by the side of his wagon, under orders not to leave it, unless sent by the officer in command, and the wagons to be formed two abreast, where practicable, on the march. At the call of the bugle in the morning, at five o'clock, the pioneers were to arise, assemble for prayers, get breakfast, and be ready to start at the second call of the bugle at seven. At night, at half-past eight, at the command from the bugle, each was to retire for prayer in his own wagon, and to bed at nine o'clock. Tents were to be pitched on Saturday nights and the Sabbath kept.

The course of the pioneers was up the north bank of the Platte, along which they traveled slowly. They crossed Elk Horn on a raft, forded the Loup Fork with considerable danger in consequence of the quicksands, and reached Grand Island about the 1st of May.

This was the day on which the pioneers had their first buffalo hunt. There was much exciting interest in the scene, for scarcely one of the hunters had chased a buffalo before. They killed four cows, three bulls, and five calves.

While on a hunt, several days after, the hunters were called in, a party of four hundred Indian warriors nearby having shown signs of an attack. The Indians had previously been threatening and were setting fire to the prairie on the north side of the Platte. The pioneers fired their cannon twice to warn the Indians that they were on the watch.

A council was now held to consider whether or not it were wise to cross the river and strike the old road to Laramie, there being good grass on that side, while the Indians were burning it on the north. In view, however, of the thousands who would follow in their track, it was concluded to continue as before, braving the Indians and the burning prairies; for, said the pioneers: "A new road will thus be made, which shall stand as a permanent route for the Saints."

Thus the pioneers broke a new road across the plains, over which tens of thousands of their people have since traveled, and which was famous as the "old Mormon road," till the railway came to blot almost from memory the toils and dangers of a journey of more than a thousand miles, by ox teams, to the valleys of Utah. (It is a curious fact that for several hundred miles the grade of the great transcontinental railway is made exactly upon the old Mormon road).

The pioneers were wary. Colonel Markham drilled his men in good military style, and the cannon was put on wheels. William Clayton, formerly the scribe of the Prophet, and, in the pioneer journey, scribe to President Young, and Willard Richards, the Church historian, invented a machine to measure the distance. General Young himself marked the entire route, going in advance daily with his staff. This service was deemed most important, as their emigrations would follow almost in the very footprints of the pioneers.

Those were days for the buffalo hunt, scarcely to be imagined, when crossing the plains a quarter of a century later. Some days they saw as many as fifty thousand buffalo.

They came to the hunting ground of the Sioux, where, a few days before, five hundred lodges had stood. Nearly a thousand warriors had encamped there.

They had been on a hunting expedition. Acres of ground were covered with buffalo wool and other remains of the slaughter. No wonder the Indian of the plains bemoans his hunting grounds, now lost to him forever. Several days later there were again fears of an Indian attack, and the cannon was got ready.

The pioneers were within view of Chimney rock on Sunday, the 23rd of May. Here they held their usual Sabbath service.

On the first of June they were opposite Laramie. Here they were joined by a small company of Mormons from Mississippi, who had been at Pueblo during the winter. They reported news of a detachment of the battalion at Pueblo that expected to start for Laramie about the first of June and follow the pioneer track. This addition to the camp consisted of a brother Crow and his family (fourteen souls, with seven wagons).

The next day President Young and others visited Fort Laramie, then occupied by thirty-eight persons, mostly French, who had married the Sioux.

Mr. Burdow, the principal man at the Fort, was a Frenchman. He cordially received General Young and his staff, invited them into his sitting-room, gave them information of the route, and furnished them with a flat-bottom boat on reasonable terms, to assist them in ferrying the Platte. Ex-Governor Boggs, who had recently passed with his company, had said much against the Mormons, cautioning Mr. Burdow to take care of his horses and cattle. Boggs and his company were quarreling, many having deserted him; so Burdow told the ex-Governor that, let the Mormons be what they might, they could not be worse than himself and his men.

It is not a little singular that this exterminating Governor of Missouri should have been crossing the Plains at the same time with the Pioneers. They were going to carve out for their people a greater destiny than they could have reached either in Missouri or Illinois—he to pass away, leaving nothing but a transitory name.

It was decided to send Amasa Lyman, with several other brethren, to Pueblo, to meet the detachment of the Battalion, and hurry them on to Laramie to follow the track.

At the old Fort they set up blacksmith shops and did some necessary work for the camp. Then commenced the ascent of the Black Hills, on the 4th of June.

Fifteen miles from Laramie, at the Springs, a company of Missouri emigrants came up. The pioneers kept the Sabbath the next day; the Missourians journeyed. Another company of Missourians appeared and passed on. A party of traders, direct from Santa Fe, overtook the Pioneers, and gave information of the detachment of the battalion, at Santa Fe, under Captain Brown.

The two Missouri companies kept up a warfare between themselves on the route. They were a suggestive example to the Mormons. After they had traveled near each other for a week, on the Sunday following, President Young made this the subject of his discourse. He said of the two Missourian companies: "They curse, swear, rip and tear, and are trying to swallow up the earth; but though they do not wish us to have a place on it, the earth might as well open and swallow them up; for they will go to the land of forgetfulness, while the Saints; though they suffer some privations here, if faithful, will ultimately inherit the earth, and increase in power, dominion and glory."

General Young called together the officers, to consult on a plan for crossing the river. He directed them to go immediately to the mountains with teams, to get poles. They were then to lash from two to four wagons abreast, to keep them from turning over, and float them across the river with boats and ropes; so a company of horsemen started to the mountains with teams.

The "brethren" had previously ferried over the Missourians, who paid them $1.50 for each wagon and load, and paid it in flour at $2.50; yet flour was worth ten dollars per cwt., at least, at that point. They divided their earnings among the camp equally. It amounted to five and a half pounds of flour each, two pounds of meal, and a small piece of bacon.

"It looked," says Wilford Woodruff, "as much of a miracle to me to see our flour and meal bags replenished in the Black Hills as it did to have the Children of Israel fed with manna in the wilderness. But the Lord had been truly with us on our journey and had wonderfully preserved and blessed us."

These little stores of flour were supposed to have saved the lives of some of the pioneers, for they were by this time entirely destitute of the " staff of life."

The pioneers were seven days crossing the river at this point. While here they established a ferry and selected nine men to leave in charge of it, with instructions to divide the means accumulated equally, to be careful of the lives and property of those they ferried, to "forget not their prayers," and "to come on with the next company of Saints." They reached Independence Rock on the 21st of June, and the South Pass on the 26th.

Several days later they met Major Harris, who had traveled through Oregon and California for twenty-five years. He spoke unfavorably of the Salt Lake country for a settlement. Next day Col. Bridger came up. He desired to go into council with the Mormon leaders. The apostles held the council with the colonel. He spoke more favorably of the great basin; but thought it not prudent to continue emigration there until they ascertained whether grain would grow there or not. He said he would give a thousand dollars for the first bushel of wheat raised in the valley of the Salt Lake.

At Green River they were met by Elder Samuel Brannan from the Bay of San Francisco. He came to give an account of the Mormon company that sailed with him in the ship Brooklyn. They had established themselves two hundred miles up the river, were building up a city, and he had already started a newspaper. They were several days fording Green River. Here the pioneers kept the 4th of July.

The Mormon battalion now began to reinforce the pioneers. Thirteen of these soldiers, returning from the service of their country, joined them at Green River, and reported that a whole detachment of 140 were within seven days' drive.

As the pioneers approached the valley of the Great Salt Lake, the interest became intense. The gold-finders of California, and the founders of the Pacific States and Territories generally, had but a fever for precious metals, or were impelled westward by the migrating spirit of the American people; but these Mormon pioneers were seeking the "Pearl of Great Price," and their thoughts and emotions, as they drew near the Salt Lake Valley were akin to those of the Pilgrim Fathers as they came in sight of Plymouth Rock.

During the last days of the journey, President Young was laid up with the "mountain fever," from which he did not fully recover till on the return trip to Winter Quarters.

After passing Bear River, a council of the whole was called, and it was resolved that Apostle Orson Pratt should take a company of about twenty wagons, with forty men, to go forward and make a road. Twenty-three wagons started the next morning. For a while we will follow the journal of Orson Pratt: "July 21st —We resumed our journey, traveled two and a half miles, and ascended a mountain for one and a half miles; descended upon the west side one mile; came upon a swift running creek, where we halted for noon: we called this Last Creek. Brother Erastus Snow (having overtaken our camp from the other camp, which he said was but a few miles in the rear,) and myself proceeded in advance of the camp down Last Creek four and a half miles, to where it passes through a canyon and issues into a broad open valley below. To avoid the canyon the wagons last season had passed over an exceedingly steep and dangerous hill. Mr. Snow and myself ascended this hill, from the top of which a broad open valley, about twenty miles wide and thirty long, lay stretched out before us, at the north end of which the broad waters of the Great Salt Lake glistened in the sunbeams, containing high mountainous islands from twenty-five to thirty miles in extent. After issuing from the mountains among which we had been shut up for many days and beholding in a moment such an extensive scenery open before us, we could not refrain from a shout of joy which almost involuntarily escaped from our lips the moment this grand and lovely scenery was within our view. We immediately descended very gradually into the lower parts of the valley, and although we had but one horse between us, yet we traversed a circuit of about twelve miles before we left the valley to return to our camp, which we found encamped one and a half miles up the ravine from the valley, and three miles in advance of their noon halt. It was about nine o'clock in the evening when we got into camp. The main body of the pioneers who were in the rear were encamped only one and a half miles up the creek from us, with the exception of some wagons containing some who were sick, who were still behind.

"July 22nd.—This morning George A. Smith and myself, accompanied by seven others, rode into the valley to explore, leaving the camp to follow on and work the road, which here required considerable labor, for we found that the canyon at the entrance of the valley, by cutting out the thick timber and underbrush, connected with some spading and digging, could be made far more preferable than the route over the steep hill mentioned above. We accordingly left a written note to that effect and passed on. After going down into the valley about five miles, we turned our course to the north, down towards the Salt Lake. For three or four miles north we found the soil of a most excellent quality.

Streams from the mountains and springs were very abundant, the water excellent, and generally with gravel bottoms. A great variety of green grass, and very luxuriant, covered the bottoms for miles where the soil was sufficiently damp, but in other places, although the soil was good, yet the grass had nearly dried up for want of moisture. We found the drier places swarming with very large crickets, about the size of a man's thumb. This valley is surrounded with mountains, except on the north, the tops of some of the highest being covered with snow. Every one or two miles streams were emptying into it from the mountains on the east, many of which were sufficiently large to carry mills and other machinery.

As we proceeded towards the Salt Lake the soil began to assume a more sterile appearance, being probably at some seasons of the year overflowed with water. We found as we proceeded on, great numbers of hot springs issuing from near the base of the mountains. These springs were highly impregnated with salt and sulphur: the temperature of some was nearly raised to the boiling point. We traveled for about fifteen miles down after coming into the valley, the latter parts of the distance the soil being unfit for agricultural purposes. We returned and found our wagons encamped in the valley, about five and one-fourth miles from where they left the canyon.

"July 21st.—This morning we dispatched two persons to President Young, and the wagons which were still behind, informing them of our discoveries and explorations. The camp removed its position two miles to the north, where we encamped near the bank of a beautiful creek of pure cold water. This stream is sufficiently large for mill sites and other machinery. Here we called the camp together, and it fell to my lot to offer up prayer and thanksgiving in behalf of our company, all of whom had been preserved from the Missouri, river to this point; and, after dedicating ourselves and the land unto the Lord, and imploring His blessings upon our labors, we appointed various committees to attend to different branches of business, preparatory to putting in crops, and in about two hours after our arrival we began to plow, and the same afternoon built a dam to irrigate the soil, which at the spot where we were plowing was exceedingly dry.

Towards evening we were visited by a thunder shower from the west; not quite enough rain to lay the dust. Our two messengers returned, bringing us word that the remainder of the wagons belonging to the pioneer company were only a few miles distant, and would arrive the next day. At 3 p. M. the thermometer stood at 960."

Returning to the main body of the Pioneers, a few simple but graphic passages from the diary of Apostle Wilford Woodruff will illustrate their entrance into the valleys of Utah better than an author's imagination.

"July 20th.—We started early this morning, and stopped for breakfast after a five miles' drive. I carried Brother Brigham in my carriage. The fever was still on him, but he stood the journey well. After breakfast we travelled over ten miles of the worst road of the whole journey.

"July 21st.—We are compelled to lay over in consequence of the sick.

"July 22nd.—Continued our journey.

"July 23rd.—We left East Canyon; reached the summit of the mountain and descended six miles through a thick-timbered grove. We nooned at a beautiful spring in a small birch grove. Here we were met by Brothers Pack and Mathews from the advance camps. They brought us a dispatch. They had explored the Great Salt Lake Valley as far as possible and made choice of a spot to put in crops.

"July 24th.—This is one of the most important days of my life, and in the history of the Church of Jesus Christ of Latter-day Saints.

"After traveling six miles through a deep ravine ending with the canyon, we came in full view of the valley of the Great Salt Lake; the land of promise, held in reserve by God, as a resting place for his Saints.

"We gazed in wonder and admiration upon the vast valley before us, with the waters of the Great Salt Lake glistening in the sun, mountains towering to the skies, and streams of pure water running through the beautiful valley. It was the grandest view we had ever seen till this moment. Pleasant thoughts ran through our minds at the prospect that, not many years hence, the house of God would be established in the mountains and exalted above the hills; while the valleys would be converted into orchards, vineyards, and fruitful fields, cities erected to the name of the Lord, and the standard of Zion unfurled for the gathering of the nations.

"President Young expressed his entire satisfaction at the appearance of the valley as a resting place for the Saints and felt amply repaid for his journey. While lying upon his bed, in my carriage, gazing upon the scene before us, many things of the future, concerning the valley, were shown to him in vision.

"After gazing awhile upon this scenery, we moved four miles across the table land into the valley, to the encampment of our brethren who had arrived two days before us. They had pitched upon the banks of two small streams of pure water and had commenced plowing. On our arrival they had already broken five acres of land and had begun planting potatoes in the valley of the Great Salt Lake.

"As soon as our encampment was formed, before taking my dinner, having half a bushel of potatoes, I went to the plowed field and planted them, hoping, with the blessing of God, to save at least the seed for another year.

"The brethren had damned up one of the creeks and dug a trench, and by night nearly the whole ground, which was found very dry, was irrigated.

"Towards evening, Brothers Kimball, Smith, Benson and myself rode several miles up the creek (City Creek) into the mountain, to look for timber and see the country.

"There was a thunder shower, and it rained over nearly the whole valley; it also rained a little in the forepart of the night. We felt thankful for this, as it was the generally conceived opinion that it did not rain in the valley during the summer season."

How well this arrival of the Pioneers into their "Land of Promise" illustrates the character of the Mormon people. Empire founding on the first day; planting their fields before rest or dinner. Rain on the day of Brigham Young's arrival—to them a miracle of promise! Already had his vision begun to be fulfilled!

CHAPTER V.

THE FIRST SABBATH IN THE VALLEY. THE PIONEERS APPLY THE PROPHECIES TO THEMSELVES AND THEIR LOCATION. ZION HAS GONE UP INTO THE MOUNTAINS. THEY LOCATE THE TEMPLE AND LAY OFF THE "CITY OF THE GREAT SALT LAKE." THE LEADERS RETURN TO WINTER QUARTERS TO GATHER THE BODY OF THE CHURCH.

The arrival of the main body of the Pioneers in the valley of the Great Salt Lake was on a Saturday. The next day to them was a Sabbath indeed.

"We shaved and cleaned up," says Apostle Woodruff, in his graphic story of the Pioneers, "and met in the circle of the encampment."

In the afternoon the whole "Congregation of Israel" partook of the Sacrament of the Lord's Supper.

Then the valleys rang with the exultant themes of the Hebrew Prophets, and the "everlasting hills" reverberated to the hosannas of the Saints.

Orson Pratt was the preacher of the great subject, which, to the ardent faith of those Pioneers, never lived in fulfillment till that moment. The sublime flights of the matchless Isaiah gave the principal theme.

"O Zion, that bringest good tidings, get thee up into the high mountains!"

But Isaiah is not alone in the culminating inspiration. There is such a grand unity among the Hebrew prophets, when touching this subject of a Latter-day Zion, that undoubtedly, it was the burden of the divine epic to which the Hebraic genius soared. Notwithstanding the mental diversity of these poet-prophets, in this crowning theme they gave us, not poetic fragments, but a glorious continued composition, as from a manifold genius.

"Thy watchmen shall lift up their voice; with the voice together shall they sing; and they shall see eye to eye when they Lord shall bring again Zion."

This was fulfilled to those Anglo-American Pioneers on that day. They felt they were the watchmen! With the voice together they sang the theme and did literally shout their hosannas. They saw eye to eye. "The Lord hath brought again Zion."

Nor were these Mormon Apostles figurative in their applications; they rendered most literally to themselves every point. Orson Pratt declared, with an Apostle's assurance, that their location, in the valleys of the Rocky Mountains, was in the view of the ancient seers. That which was before seemingly contradictory in the extreme, relative to the Latter-day Zion, especially its location and the rapid transformation of its founding, was now made plain and most literal.

Apostle Pratt reconciled it all. The Pioneers saw the vision of Zion harmonized on that first Sabbath in the valley, as they might have seen their own faces in a mirror.

God would "hide his people in the chambers of the mountains!" Yet, in these "last days" he would "establish his house on the tops of the mountains and exalt it above the hills!"

And here were these Pioneers of Mormon Israel in a valley nearly thirty miles in diameter, encircled by a chain of mountains; here, in a valley nearly five thousand feet above the level of the sea—"exalted above the hills"—yet belted by mountains with everlasting caps of snow. It was indeed as the "chambers of the Lord," and the name which it popularly bore—the "Great Basin "—was nearly as striking to the imagination as its prophetic name.

Latter-day Zion, too, was to be a place "sought out"—a place "not forsaken." They had sought it out by an exodus, and an unparalleled journey of a people, nearly fifteen hundred miles, over unbroken prairies, sandy deserts, and rocky mountains; and they were about to found their Zion in a primeval valley, where no city, since the creation, had ever stood—a place "not forsaken" by civilized people of the ages long since dead. The " solitary places" were to be "made glad," the " wilderness" was to "blossom as the rose," and the " desert" suddenly to be converted into the " fruitful field." Such was the sermon of the first Sabbath in the Great Salt Lake Valley. The Pioneers had chosen for the location of their Zion and her temples, the "Great American Desert," and they were about to make real the strange and highly colored picture. So much like the change in an enchanted scene has been the transformation which has since come over those desert valleys and canyons of the Rocky Mountains, that for the last quarter of a century the Mormons have been popularly described in nearly every nation of the earth as that peculiar people who have made the "desert to blossom as the rose." Look upon the valley of the Salt Lake today as the Spring opens, when the gardens and orchards are in one universal rose blossom, and there never was a prophetic picture more literally realized.

Though feeble with that most languishing of diseases, the mountain fever, and scarcely able to stand upon his feet, Brigham Young was still the law-giver on that first Sabbath. If he had not the strength to preach a great sermon on the Latter-day Zion, like that of the Mormon Paul—Orson Pratt—he was "every inch" the Moses of the Mormon Exodus.

"He told the brethren," says the historian Woodruff, "that they must not work on Sunday; that they would lose five times as much as they would gain by it. None were to hunt or fish on that day; and there should not any man dwell among us who would not observe these rules. They might go and dwell where they pleased but should not dwell with us. He also said, no man should buy any land who came here; that he had none to sell; but every man should have his land measured out to him for city and farming purposes. He might till it as he pleased, but he must be industrious, and take care of it.

"On Monday ten men were chosen for an exploring expedition. I took President Young into my carriage, and, traveling two miles towards the mountain, made choice of a spot for our garden.

"We then returned to camp, and went north about five miles, and we all went on to the top of a high peak, on the edge of the mountain, which we considered a good place to raise an ensign. So we named it 'Ensign Peak.'

"I was the first person to ascend this hill, which we had thus named. Brother Young was very weary, in climbing to the peak, from his recent fever.

"We descended to the valley, and started north to the Hot Sulphur Springs, but we returned two miles to get a drink of cold water, and then went back four miles to the Springs. We returned to the camp quite weary with our day's explorations. Brothers Mathews and Brown had crossed the valley in the narrowest part, opposite the camp, to the west mountain, and found it about fifteen miles.

"Next day Amasa Lyman came into camp and informed us that Captain Brown's detachment of the Mormon Battalion would be with us in about two days.

"We again started on our exploring expedition. All the members of the quorum of the Twelve belonging to the pioneers, eight in number, were of the company. Six others of the brethren, including Brannan of San Francisco, were with us.

"We started for the purpose of visiting the Great Salt Lake, and mountains on the west of the valley. We traveled two miles west from Temple Block and came to the outlet of the Utah Lake; thence fourteen miles to the west mountain and found that the land was not so fertile as on the east side.

"We took our dinner at the fresh water pool, and then rode six miles to a large rock, on the shore of the Salt Lake, which we named Black Rock, where we all halted and bathed in the salt water. No person could sink in it but would roll and float on the surface like a dry log. We concluded that the Salt Lake was one of the wonders of the world.

"After spending an hour here, we went west along the lake shore, and then returned ten miles to our place of nooning, making forty miles that day.

"In the morning we arose refreshed by sleep in the open air. Having lost my carriage whip the night before, I started on horseback to go after it. As I approached the spot where it was dropped, I saw about twenty Indians. At first they looked to me in the distance like a lot of bears coming towards me. As I was unarmed I wheeled my horse and started back on a slow trot.

"But they called to me, and one, mounting his horse, came after me with all speed. When he got within twenty rods I stopped and met him. The rest followed. They were Utes and wanted to trade. I told them by signs that our camp was near, so he went on with me to the camp. From what we had yet seen of the Utes they appeared friendly, though they had a bad name from the mountaineers. The Indian wanted to smoke the pipe of peace with us, but we soon started on and he waited for his company.

"We traveled ten miles south under the mountain. The land laid beautifully, but there was no water, and the soil was not so good as on the east. We saw about a hundred goats, sheep and antelope playing about the hills and valleys. We returned, weary, to the pioneer encampment, making thirty miles for the day.

"After our return to the camp, President Young called a council of the quorum of the Twelve. There were present: Brigham Young, Heber C. Kimball, Willard Richards, Orson Pratt, Wilford Woodruff, George A. Smith, Amasa Lyman and Ezra T. Benson.

"We walked from the north camp to about the center between the two creeks, when President Young waved his hand and said: 'Here is the forty acres for the Temple. The city can be laid out perfectly square, north and south, east and west.' It was then moved and carried that the Temple lot contain forty acres on the ground where we stood. It was also moved and carried that the city be laid out into lots of ten rods by twenty each, exclusive of the streets, and into blocks of eight lots, being ten acres in each block, and one and a quarter in each lot.

"It was further moved and carried that each street be laid out eight rods wide, and that there be a side-walk on each side, twenty feet wide, and that each house be built in the center of the lot twenty feet from the front, that there might be uniformity throughout the city.

"It was also moved that there be four public squares of ten acres each, to be laid out in various parts of the city for public grounds.

"At eight o'clock the whole camp came together on the Temple ground and passed the votes unanimously, and, when the business part of the meeting was closed, President Young arose and addressed the assembly upon a variety of subjects.

"In his remarks the President said that he was determined to have all things in order, and righteousness should be practiced in the land. We had come here according to the direction and counsel of Brother Joseph, before his death; and, said the President, Joseph would still have been alive if the Twelve had been in Nauvoo when he re-crossed the river from Montrose.

" During his remarks, President Young observed that he intended to have every hole and corner from the Bay of San Francisco to Hudson Bay known to us.

"On the 29th, President Young, with a number of brethren, mounted and started to meet the Battalion detachment, under the command of Captain Brown.

"We met some of them about four miles from camp, and soon afterwards met Captains Brown and Higgins, Lieutenant Willis, and the company. There were 140 of the Battalion, and a company of about 100 of the Mississippi Saints, who came with them from Pueblo. They had with them 60 wagons, 100 horses and mules, and 300 head of cattle, which greatly added to our strength.

"While we were in the canyon, a water cloud burst, which sent the water into the creeks from the mountains, with a rush and roar like thunder, resembling the opening of a flood gate. The shower spread over a good share of the valley where we settled.

"We returned at the head of the companies and marched into camp with music. The Battalion took up their quarters between our two camps on the bank of the creek.

"While we had been exploring, the rest of the pioneers had been farming.

"By the 1st of August (Sunday) the brethren constructed the Bowery on Temple block, in which Heber C. Kimball was the first to preach. Orson Pratt followed in a discourse upon the prophecies of Isaiah, proving that the location of Zion in the mountains by our people was the fulfillment.

"On Monday we commenced laying out the city, beginning with the Temple block. In forming this block, forty acres appeared so large, that a council was held to determine whether or not it would be wisdom to reduce it one-half. Not being decided in our views, we held council again, two days later, when we gave as our matured opinions that we could not do justice to forty acres; that ten acres would be sufficient.

"As we were under the necessity of returning soon to Winter Quarters for the Saints, it was thought best to go at once to the mountains for logs to build ourselves cabins, as the adobe houses might not be ready for our use.

"On the 6th of August, the Twelve were re-baptized. This we considered a privilege and a duty. As we had come in a glorious valley to locate and build up Zion, we felt like renewing our covenants before the Lord and each other.

We soon repaired to the water, and President Young went down into the water and baptized all his brethren of the Twelve present. He then confirmed us, and sealed upon us our apostleship, and all the keys, powers and blessings belonging to that office. Brother Heber C. Kimball baptized and confirmed President Brigham Young. The following were the names and order of those present: Brigham Young, Heber C. Kimball, Orson Pratt, Willard Richards, Wilford Woodruff, George A. Smith, and

Amasa Lyman. Ezra T. Benson had been dispatched several days before to meet the companies on the road.

"In the afternoon of the next day, the Twelve went to the Temple Block to select their inheritances.

"President Young took a block east of the Temple, and running southeast, to settle his friends around him; Heber C. Kimball a block north of the Temple; Orson Pratt, south and running south; Wilford Woodruff, a block cornering the Temple Block, the southwest corner joining Orson Pratt's; Amasa Lyman took a block forty rods below Wilford Woodruff's; George A. Smith one joining the Temple on the west, and running, due west. It was supposed that Willard Richards would take his on the east, near President Young's. None others of the Twelve were present in the camp.

"During the same evening the Twelve went to City Creek, and Heber C. Kimball baptized fifty-five members of the camp, for the remission of their sins; and they were confirmed under the hands of President Young, Orson Pratt, Wilford Woodruff, George A. Smith, and Amasa Lyman; President Young being mouth.

"On the next day (Sunday, August 8th), the whole Camp of Israel renewed their covenants before the Lord by baptism. There were two hundred and twenty-four baptized this morning, making two hundred and eighty-four re-baptized in the last three days.

"In the afternoon we partook of the Sacrament. At the close of the meeting one hundred and ten men were called for, to go into the adobe yard, and seventy-six volunteered.

"Brother Crow had a child drowned on the 11th.

"On the 13th the Twelve held council. Each one was to make choice of the blocks that they were to settle their friends upon. President Young took the tiers of blocks south through the city; Brother Kimball's runs north and northwest; Orson Pratt, four blocks; Wilford Woodruff eight blocks; George A. Smith, eight; and Amasa Lyman, twelve blocks, according to the companies organized with each.

"Next day four of the messengers returned from Bear River and Cache Valley.

"They brought a cheering report of Cache Valley. The brethren also returned who went to Utah Lake for fish. They found a mountain of granite.

"The quorum of the Twelve decided in council that the name of the city should be the ' City of the Great Salt Lake.'

"Sunday, August 15th, President Young preached on the death of Brother Crow's child; a most interesting discourse, full of principle.

"Sunday, the 22nd, we held a general conference, when the public assembly resolved to call the city the 'City of the Great Salt Lake.'

"It was also voted to fence the city for farming purposes the coming year and to appoint a President and High Council, and all other officers necessary in this Stake of Zion, and that the Twelve write an epistle to leave with the Saints in the valley. The conference then adjourned until the 6th of October, 1848.

"On the morning of the 26th of August, 1847, the Pioneers, with most of the returning members of the Mormon Battalion, harnessed their horses and bade farewell to the brethren who were to tarry. The soldiers were very anxious to meet their wives again, whom they had left by the wayside, without a moment's notice, for their service in the war with Mexico. These being, too, the 'Young Men of Israel,' had left many newly wedded brides; and not a few of those gallant fellows were fathers of first-born babes whom they had not yet seen.

"The brethren in the valley were placed under the presidency of the Chief Patriarch of the Church—Father John Smith, uncle of the Prophet. The members of the quorum of the Twelve Apostles Brigham took with him; but he left reliable men, among whom was Albert Carrington.

"There were a number of companies also on the road, under principal men and chief 'Captains of Israel,' such as Apostles Parley P. Pratt and John Taylor, Bishop Hunter, Daniel Spencer, and Jedediah M. Grant, who was afterwards one of the first presidents of the Church.

"On the fourth day of their return journey, the Pioneers were met by their messengers, under Ezra T. Benson, whom President Young had sent forward with instructions to the outcoming companies. These messengers gladdened the hearts of the Pioneers, with letters from their wives and brethren, and reported the coming ' Camp of Israel' as divided into nine companies, numbering 600 wagons.

On the 3rd of September, they met the first division of fifty, under President Daniel Spencer, upon the Big Sandy; and, on the following day, on the Little Sandy, two more fifties, one under the command of Captain Sessions and the other under Apostle Parley P. Pratt.

"They continued daily to meet the companies, Apostle Taylor bringing up his hundred on the Sweetwater. In this company was Edward Hunter, afterwards presiding Bishop of the whole Church. These brethren prepared a great feast in the wilderness. They made it a sort of a surprise party, the Pioneers being unexpectedly introduced to the richly-laden table. The feast consisted of roast and boiled beef, pies, cakes, biscuit, butter, peach sauce, coffee, tea, sugar, and a great variety of good things. In the evening the camp had a dance, but the Twelve met in council to adjust important business.

"Next day they met Jedediah M. Grant, with his hundred. He was direct from Philadelphia. He informed them that Senator Thomas Benton, the inveterate enemy of the Mormons, was doing all he could against them.

"At Fort Laramie Presidents Young, Kimball, and others of the Apostles dined with Commodore Stockton, from the Bay of San Francisco, with forty of his men, eastward bound.

"On the 19th of October, the Pioneers were met by a troop of mounted police from Winter Quarters, under their captain, Hosea Stout, who had come to meet them, thinking they might need help."

As they drew near Winter Quarters, the sisters, mothers and wives came out to meet the brave men who had found for them a second Zion. They also sent teams laden with the richest produce of Winter Quarters and the delicacies of the household table, which loving hands had prepared.

When within about a mile of Winter Quarters a halt was called; the company was drawn up in order and addressed by President Young, who then dismissed the Pioneer camp with his blessing.

They drove into the city in order. The streets were lined with people to shake hands with them as they passed. Each of the Pioneers drove to his own home. This was October 31st.

The Pioneers on their return found the Saints at Winter Quarters well and prosperous. They, like the leaders, had been greatly blessed. The earth, under their thorough habits of cultivation and industry, had brought forth abundantly.

During the first three months of the year 1848, the Saints at Winter Quarters were busy preparing for the general migration of the Church to the Valley of the Great Salt Lake; but they also petitioned the Legislature of Iowa for the organization of a county in the Pottawattamie tract of land, and for a post office.

On the 3rd of February those who were in the "Battle of Nauvoo" commemorated it with a feast.

On the 6th of April the regular general conference was held, celebrating the organization of the Church; and on the 11th messengers arrived from Great Salt Lake City. They were of the Battalion.

A feast was made by President Young on the 29th for his immediate associates, some of whom were going on missions, others were designed to stay on the frontiers to conduct and bring up the emigration; while President Young himself was about to lead the vanguard of the people to the mountains.

About the middle of May, all was bustle at Winter Quarters. President Young addressed the people Sunday, 14th, blessed those who were going with him to the valley, and those who were to tarry. He also blessed the Pottawatomie land and prophesied that the Saints would never be driven from the Rocky Mountains.

On the 24th of May, President Young started for Elk Horn to organize his company. There were 600 wagons in the encampment. They formed the largest pioneer force which had yet set out to build up the States and Territories destined to spring up on the Pacific Slope.

We need not follow the Pioneers on their second journey to the Rocky Mountains. Suffice it to say that Brigham led the body of the Church in safety to these mountain retreats, arriving in the City of the Great Salt Lake in September, 1848.

CHAPTER VI.

PROGRESS OF THE COLONY. DESTRUCTION OF THE CROPS BY CRICKETS. DESCRIPTION OF GREAT SALT LAKE CITY.

Of the colony in its first year's growth and doings, Parley P. Pratt says: "After many toils, vexations and trials, such as breaking wagons, losing cattle, upsetting, etc., we arrived in the Valley of Great Salt Lake late in September, 1847. Here we found a fort commenced and partly built by the Pioneers, consisting of an enclosure of a block of ten acres with a wall, or in part of buildings of adobes or logs. We also found a city laid out and a public square dedicated for a temple of God. We found also much ground planted in late crops, which, however, did not mature, being planted late in July; although there were obtained for seed a few small potatoes, from the size of a pea upward to that of half an inch in diameter. These being sound and planted another year produced some very fine potatoes, and, finally, contributed mainly in seeding the Territory with that almost indispensable article of food.

"After we had arrived on the ground of Great Salt Lake City we pitched our tents by the side of a spring of water; and, after resting a little, I devoted my time chiefly to building temporary houses, putting in crops, and obtaining fuel from the mountains.

Having repented of our sins and renewed our covenants, President John Taylor and myself administered the ordinances of baptism, etc., to each other and to our families, according to the example set by the President and Pioneers who had done the same on entering the valley.

"These solemnities took place with us and most of our families, November 28, 1847.

"Sometime in December, having finished sowing wheat and rye, I started, in company with a Brother Higby and others, for Utah Lake with a boat and fish net. We travelled some thirty miles with our boat, etc., on an ox wagon, while some of us rode on horseback. This distance brought us to the foot of Utah Lake, a beautiful sheet of fresh water, some thirty-six miles long by fifteen broad.

Here we launched our boat and tried our net, being probably the first boat and net ever used on this sheet of water in modern times.

"We sailed up and down the lake shore on its western side for many miles but had only poor success in fishing. We, however, caught a few samples of mountain trout and other fish.

"After exploring the lake and valley for a day or two, the company returned home, and a Brother Summers and myself struck westward from the foot of the lake on horseback, on an exploring tour. On this tour we discovered and partly explored Cedar Valley, and there crossed over the west mountain range and discovered a valley beyond; passing through which, we crossed a range of hills northward, and entered Tooele Valley. Passing still northward, we camped one night on a bold mountain stream, and the next day we came to the southern extreme of Great Salt Lake and passing round between it and the West Mountain we journeyed in an eastern course, and, crossing the Jordan, arrived in Great Salt Lake City—having devoted nearly one week to our fishing, hunting, and exploring expedition. During all this time we had fine weather and warm days; but the night we arrived home was a cold one, with a severe snow storm. And thus closed the year 1847.

"January 1st, 1848.—The opening of the year found us and the community generally in good, comfortable, temporary log or adobe cabins, which were built in a way to enclose the square commenced by the Pioneers, and a portion of two other blocks of the city plot. * * * "We had to struggle against great difficulties in trying to mature a first crop. We had not only the difficulties and inexperience incidental to an unknown and untried climate, but also swarms of insects equal to the locusts of Egypt, and also a terrible drought, while we were entirely inexperienced in the art of irrigation; still we struggled on, trusting in God."

Thus was the fair promise of the first harvest in the Valley destroyed by the - desolating crickets. Their ravages were frightful. They came down from the mountains in myriads. Countless hosts attacked the fields of grain. The crops were threatened with utter destruction. The valleys appeared as though scorched by fire. Famine stared the settlers in the face. All were in danger of perishing.

Every effort was made by the settlers to drive the crickets off by bushes, long rods, and other like means—whole families and neighborhoods turning out en masse until the people were almost exhausted. At this frightful moment, when the utter destruction of their crops stared the little colony in the face,—while also on their journey were the companies under President Young, who would need supplies until the second harvest, the manifestation of a special Providence was sent to save the people—so these reverent colonists believed. Immense flocks of gulls came up from the islands of the Lake to make war upon the destroying hosts. Like good angels, they came at the dawn; all day they feasted upon the crickets. The gulls covered every field where the crickets had taken possession, driving them into the streams and even into the door-yards, devouring them until gorged, then vomiting them and devouring more.

Even as it was, there was a season of famine in Utah; but none perished from starvation. The patriarchal character of the community saved it. As one great family they shared the substance of the country. An inventory of provisions was taken in the Spring of 1849, and the people were put upon rations.

Still their breadstuffs were insufficient, and many went out with the Indians and dug small native roots, while some, in their destitution, took the hides of animals, which covered the roofs of their houses, and cut them up and cooked them. But the harvest of 1849 was abundant and the people were saved.

A passage of Indian history should not be lost here, as given by Parley P. Pratt in a letter to his brother Orson, in England, bearing date, Great Salt Lake City, September 5th, 1848. He wrote: "A few weeks since, Mr. Joseph Walker, the celebrated Utah Chief, mentioned in the journey of Colonel Fremont, paid a visit to this place, accompanied by Soweite, the king of the whole Utah nations, and with them some hundreds of men, women and children; they had several hundred head of horses for sale.

"They were good looking, brave, and intelligent beyond any we had seen on this side of the mountains. They were much pleased and excited with everything they saw, and finally expressed a wish to become one people with us, and to live among us and we among them, and to learn to cultivate the earth and live as we do. They would like for some of us to go and commence farming with them in their valleys, which are situated about three hundred miles south.

"We enjoined it on them to be at peace with one another, and with all people, and to cease to war."

The following from the First General Epistle sent out from the Mormon Presidency, in the spring of 1849, is valuable as a page of the early history.

"On our arrival in this valley, we found the brethren had erected four forts, composed mostly of houses, including an area of about forty-seven acres, and numbering about 5,000 souls, including our camp. The brethren had succeeded in sowing and planting an extensive variety of seeds, at all seasons, from January to July, on a farm about twelve "miles in length, and from one to six in width, including the city plot. Most of their early crops were destroyed, in the month of May, by crickets and frost, which continued occasionally until June; while the latter harvest was injured by drought and frost, which commenced its injuries about the 10th of October, and by the out-breaking of herds of cattle. The brethren were not sufficiently numerous to fight the crickets, irrigate the crops, and fence the farm of their extensive planting, consequently they suffered heavy losses; though the experiment of last year is sufficient to prove that valuable crops may be raised in this valley by an attentive and judicious management.

"The winter of 1847-8 was very mild, grass abundant, flocks and herds thriving thereon, and the earth tillable most of the time during each month; but the winter of 1848-9 has been very different, more like a severe New England winter. Excessive cold commenced on the 1st of December and continued till the latter part of February. Snow storms were frequent, and though there were several thaws, the earth was not without snow during that period, varying from one to three feet in depth, both in time and places. The coldest day of the past winter was the 5th of February, the mercury falling 330 below freezing point, and the warmest day was Sunday, the 25th of February, mercury rising to 21° above freezing point, Fahrenheit. Violent and contrary winds have been frequent.

The snow on the surrounding mountains has been much deeper, which has made the wood very difficult of access; while the cattle have become so poor, through fasting and scanty fare, that it has been difficult to draw the necessary fuel, and many have had to suffer more or less from the want thereof. The winter commenced at an unusual and unexpected moment and found many of the brethren without houses or fuel, and although there has been considerable suffering, there has been no death by the frost. Three attempts have been made by the brethren with pack animals or snow shoes to visit Fort Bridger, since the snow fell, but have failed; yet it is expected that Compton will be able to take the mail east soon after April conference.

"In the former part of February, the bishops took an inventory of the breadstuff in the valley, when it was reported that there was little more than three-fourths of a pound per day for each soul, until the 5th of July; and considerable was known to exist which was not reported. As a natural consequence some were nearly destitute while others had abundance. The common price of corn since harvest has been two dollars; some have sold for three; at present there is none in the market at any price. Wheat has ranged from four to five dollars, and potatoes from six to twenty dollars per bushel, and though not to be bought at present, it is expected that there will be a good supply for seed by another year.

"Our public works are prosperous, consisting of a Council House, 45 feet square, two stories, building by tithing; also a bridge across the Western Jordan, at an expense of seven hundred dollars, and six or seven bridges across minor streams, to be paid by a one per cent, property tax; also, a bath-house at the warm spring.

"A field of about 8000 acres has been surveyed south of and bordering on the city, and plotted in five and ten acre lots, and a church farm of about 800 acres. The five and ten acre lots were distributed to the brethren, by casting lots, and every man is to help build a pole, ditch, or a stone fence.as shall be most convenient around the whole field, in proportion to the land he draws; also, a canal on the east side, for the purpose of irrigation. There are three grist mills, and five or six saw mills in operation, and several more in contemplation.

"The location of a tannery and foundry are contemplated as soon as the snows leave the mountains.

"The forts are rapidly breaking up, by the removal of the houses on to the city lots; and the city is already assuming the appearance of years, for any ordinary country; such is the industry and perseverance of the Saints.

"A winter's hunt, by rival parties of one hundred men each, has destroyed about 700 wolves and foxes, 2 wolverines, 20 minx and pole cats, 500 hawks, owls, and magpies, and 1,000 ravens, in this valley and vicinity.

"On the return of a portion of the Mormon Battalion through the northern part of Western California, they discovered an extensive gold mine, which enabled them by a few days delay to bring a sufficient of the dust to make money plentiful in this place for all ordinary purposes of public convenience; in the exchange the brethren deposited the gold dust with the presidency, who issued bills or a paper currency."

Captain Stansbury describing Salt Lake City and its environs, as viewed about the year 1850, wrote: "A city has been laid out upon a magnificent scale, being nearly four miles in length and three in breadth; the streets at right angles with each other, eight rods or one hundred and thirty-two feet wide, with sidewalks of twenty feet; the blocks forty rods square, divided into eight lots, each of which contains an acre and a quarter of ground. By an ordinance of the city, each house is to be placed twenty feet back from the front line of the lot, the intervening space being designed for shrubbery and trees. The site for the city is most beautiful: it lies at the western base of the Wasatch Mountains, in a curve formed by the projection westward from the main range of a lofty spur which forms its southern boundary. On the west it is washed by the waters of the Jordan, while to the southward for twenty-five miles extends a broad, level plain, watered by several little streams, which flowing down from the eastern hills, form the great element of fertility and wealth to the community. Through the city itself flows an unfailing stream of pure, sweet water, which, by an ingenious mode of irrigation, is made to traverse each side of every street, whence it is led into every garden spot, spreading life, verdure and beauty over what was heretofore a barren waste.

On the east and north the mountain descends to the plain by steps, which form broad and elevated terraces, commanding an extensive view of the whole valley of the Jordan, which is bounded on the west by a range of rugged mountains, stretching far to the southward, and enclosing within their embrace the lovely little Lake of Utah.

"On the northern confines of the city, a warm spring issues from the base of the mountain, the water of which has been conducted by pipes into a commodious bathing house; while, at the western point of the same spur, about three miles distant, another spring flows in a bold stream from beneath a perpendicular rock, with a temperature too high to admit the insertion of the hand, (128 Fahrenheit.) At the base of the hill it forms a little lake, which in the autumn and winter is covered with large flocks of waterfowl, attracted by the genial temperature of the water.

Beyond the Jordan, on the west, the dry and otherwise barren plains support a hardy grass, (called bunch grass,) which is peculiar to these regions, requiring but little moisture, very nutritious and in sufficient quantities to afford excellent pasturage to numerous herds of cattle. To the northward, in the low grounds bordering the river, hay in abundance can be procured, although it is rather coarse and of an inferior quality.

"The facilities for beautifying this admirable site are manifold. The irrigating canals, which flow before every door, furnish abundance of water for the nourishment of shade trees, and the open space between each building, and the pavement [sidewalk] before it, when planted with shrubbery and adorned with flowers, will make this one of the most lovely spots between the Mississippi and the Pacific.

"The city was estimated to contain about eight thousand inhabitants, and was divided into numerous wards, each, at the time of our visit, enclosed by a substantial fence, for the protection of the young crops: as time and leisure will permit, these will be removed, and each lot enclosed by itself, as with us. The houses are built, principally of adobe or sun-dried brick, which, when well covered, with a tight projecting roof, make warm, comfortable dwellings, presenting a very neat appearance. Buildings of a better description are being introduced, although slowly, owing to the difficulty of procuring the necessary lumber, which must always be dear in a country so destitute of timber.

"Upon a square appropriated to the public buildings, an immense shed had been erected upon posts, which was capable of containing three thousand persons. It was called 'The Bowery,' and served as a temporary place of worship until the construction of the great Temple. * * * A mint was already in operation, from which were issued gold coins of the Federal denominations, stamped without assay, from the dust brought from California."

CHAPTER VII.

THE PRIMITIVE GOVERNMENT OF THE COLONY, PROVISIONAL STATE OF DESERET ORGANIZED. PASSAGE OF THE GOLD-SEEKERS THROUGH THE VALLEY.

During the first four years the colony grew up under the peculiar rule of the Mormon community. There was the "City of the Great Salt Lake" in name, but no regular incorporation until after the setting up of the Territory of Utah, under the United States administration. At first the city was simply a "Stake of Zion," with no secular functions in the common sense, nor a secular administration in any form, until the election for officers of the Provisional Government of the State of Deseret, when the bishops became magistrates of their several wards.

Previous to their return to Winter Quarters, the Twelve Apostles organized a Stake of Zion, and appointed John Smith President, Charles C. Rich and John Young his counselors; Tarleton Lewis, Bishop, and a High Council. This organization went into effect on the arrival of the emigrant companies, in the fall of 1847, when about 700 wagons, laden with families, located on the site of Great Salt Lake City. This, however, may be considered rather as a temporary Stake than the organization proper, for Great Salt Lake City was destined to be the permanent headquarters of the Church. With the Twelve and First Presidency at Winter Quarters, the Church herself was still in that place, and it was there that the First Presidency was re-established, with Brigham Young and his counselors, Heber C. Kimball and Willard Richards. This done, the Church evacuated Winter Quarters to establish herself in the valley of the Great Salt Lake, designing to send out therefrom her colonies, to found cities in every valley of these Rocky Mountains.

Immediately on the arrival of the body of the Church, under the presidency of Brigham Young in September, 1848, the regular social and ecclesiastical organizations of the community were effected, and the chief Stake of Zion organized in Great Salt Lake City. Commencing the re-organization at the general October Conference of that year, Brigham Young was acknowledged President of the Church in all the world, with Heber C. Kimball and Willard Richards as his counselors. On the 1st of January, 1849, John Smith, uncle to the Prophet Joseph Smith, was ordained Patriarch of the Church, and on the 12th of February the Presidency and Twelve proceeded, to fill up the vacant places in the quorum of the Twelve Apostles. They next, in the words of their General Epistle, "proceeded to organize a Stake of Zion at the Great Salt Lake City, with Daniel Spencer, president, and David Fullmer and Willard Snow, counselors. They also ordained and set apart a High Council of the Stake, consisting of Isaac Morley, Phinehas Richards, Shadrach Roundy, Henry G. Sherwood, Titus Billings, Eleazer Miller, John Vance, Levi Jackman, Ira Eldredge, Elisha H. Groves, William W. Major, and Edwin D. Wooley. The other quorums of the Church were also re-organized. The Presidency of the Seventies was composed of Joseph Young, Zera Pulsipher, Levi W. Hancock, Jedediah M. Grant, Henry Herriman, Benjamin L. Clapp, and Albert P. Rockwood. John Young was ordained president of the High Priests' quorum, with counselors Reynolds Cahoon and George B. Wallace; John Nebeker, president of the Elders' quorum, with counselors James H. Smith and Aaron Savery. This re-organization took place at the house of George B. Wallace, in the Old Fort.

After these branches of the "spiritual" organization were perfected, the city was divided into nineteen wards, over which bishops were appointed with their counselors.

Under the direction of Brigham Young, who, throughout his lifetime, was the "all in all" in the colonization of Utah, the Apostles and Bishops commenced to lay off the city, from the southeast corner, running west five wards, then returning, running east five wards, then west again, and so on.

Bishop Newel K. Whitney was the presiding Bishop over the whole. The original Bishops of the nineteen wards were as follows: First Ward, Peter McCue; Second Ward, John Lowrey; Third Ward, Christopher Williams; Fourth Ward, Benjamin Brown; Fifth Ward (which for quite a while was without a Bishop), Thomas Winters; Sixth Ward, William Hickenlooper; Seventh Ward, William G. Perkins; Eighth Ward, Addison Everett; Ninth Ward, Seth Taft; Tenth Ward, David Pettegrew; Eleventh Ward, John Lytle; Twelfth Ward, Benjamin Covey; Thirteenth Ward, Edward Hunter; Fourteenth Ward, John Murdock, Sen.; Fifteenth Ward, Nathaniel V. Jones; Sixteenth Ward, Shadrach Roundy; Seventeenth Ward, J. L. Heywood; Eighteenth Ward, Presiding Bishop Whitney; Nineteenth Ward, James Hendricks.

Under the government of the Bishops, Utah grew up, and, until the regular incorporation of Great Salt Lake City in 1851, they held what is usually considered the secular administration over the people; Brigham Young was their director, for he formulated and constructed everything in those early days.

Each of these nineteen wards developed, during the first period, before the regular incorporation of the city, like so many municipal corporations, over which the Bishops were as chief magistrates or mayors. Under their temporal administration all over Utah, as well as in Salt Lake, cities were built, lands divided off to the people, roads and bridges made, water-ditches cut, the land irrigated, and society governed. In fact, under them all the revenue was produced and the work done of founding Great Salt Lake City.

Perhaps the most unique ecclesiastical order of government belonging to the Christian era is that which has sprung up in the Mormon Church in the organizations and government of its Bishops. It is altogether out of the common ecclesiastical order and church regime; and the duties and calling of those belonging to the Mormon Bishopric have originated a form of government peculiarly its own. Indeed, this branch of the Mormon development has not only shaped considerable of the history of this peculiar people but given to the world something of a new social problem. We may not be able to determine how much the influence and life-work of these Bishops will in the future affect the growth of the Pacific States and Territories; but, so far as the past is concerned, we know that under the Bishops the hundreds of cities and settlements of Utah and some of the adjacent Territories have been founded.

Almost from the first organization of the Church and long before the organization of the quorum of the Twelve Apostles, it was shown in the peculiar history of the people that the Bishops were as the organic basis of the Mormon society, and the proper business managers of the Church; but it was not until the Mormons came to the Rocky Mountains that the society-work of the Bishops grew rapidly into the vast proportions of their present social and church government. In Utah, they soon became the veritable founders of our settlements and cities; and, having founded them, they have also governed them and directed the people in their social organization and material growth, while the Apostles and Presidents of Stakes have directed spiritual affairs.

It may be further explained, that a Stake of Zion, the initial of which we have seen organized in that of the Salt Lake Stake, is analogous to a county; and the High Council is a quorum of judges, in equity for the people, at the head of which is the President of the Stake, with his counselors.

The community grew so rapidly that before the close of the second year it was deemed wise to establish a constitutional secular government, and accordingly representatives of the people met in convention in the month of March, 1849 and formed the Provisional Government of the State of Deseret. A constitution was adopted, and delegates sent to Washington asking admission into the Union. Here is what they said: "We, the people, grateful to the Supreme Being for the blessings hitherto enjoyed, and feeling our dependence on Him for a continuation of those blessings, do ordain and establish a free and independent government by the name of the State of Deseret, including all the Territory of the United States within the following boundaries, to-wit: Commencing at the 33rd degree of north latitude, where it crosses the 108th degree of longitude west from Greenwich; thence running south and west to the boundary of Mexico; thence west to and down the main channel of the Gila River (or the northern part of Mexico), and on the northern boundary of Lower California to the Pacific Ocean; thence along the coast northwesterly to the 118th degree, 30th minute of west longitude; thence north to where said line intersects the dividing ridge of the Sierra Nevada Mountains to the dividing range of mountains that separates the waters flowing into the Columbia River from the waters running into the Great Basin on the south, to the summit of the Wind River chain of mountains; thence southeast and south by the dividing range of mountains that separates the waters flowing into the Gulf of Mexico from the waters flowing into the Gulf of California, to the place of beginning, as set forth in a map drawn by Charles Preuss, and published by order of the Senate of the United States, in 1848."

The Twelve, in their general epistle, under date, "Great Salt Lake City, March 9, 1849, thus explains this organic movement: "We have petitioned the Congress of the United States for the organization of a Territorial government here, embracing a territory of about seven hundred miles square, bounded north by Oregon, latitude 42 degrees, east by the Rio Grande Del Norte, south by the late lines between the United States and Mexico, near the latitude 32 degrees, and west by the sea coast and California Mountains. Until this petition is granted, we are under the necessity of organizing a local government for the time being, to consist of a governor, chief-justice, secretary, marshal, magistrates, etc. elected by the people: the election to take place next Monday."

Accordingly, on Monday, March 12th, 1849, the State election was held in Great Salt Lake City, resulting in the unanimous choice of Brigham Young as Governor; Willard Richards, Secretary; N. K. Whitney, Treasurer; Heber C. Kimball, Chief Justice; John Taylor and N. K. Whitney, Associate Justices; Daniel H. Wells, Attorney-General; Horace S. Eldredge, Marshal; Albert Carrington, Assessor and Collector of taxes; Joseph L. Heywood, Surveyor of Highways; and the Bishops of the several wards as Magistrates.

The first celebration in the mountains was held on the 24th of July, 1849— the second anniversary of the entrance of the Pioneers.

The following description of the celebration, by the " Chief Scribe," may be of interest to many: "The inhabitants were awakened by the firing of cannon, accompanied by music. The brass band, playing martial airs, was then carried through the city, returning to the Bowery by seven o'clock. The Bowery is a building 100 feet long by 60 feet wide, built on 104 posts, and covered with boards; but for the services of this day a canopy or awning was extended about 100 feet from each side of the Bowery, to accommodate the vast multitude at dinner.

"At half-past seven the large national flag, measuring sixty-five feet in length, was unfurled at the top of the liberty pole, which is 104 feet high, and was saluted by the firing of six guns, the ringing of the Nauvoo bell, and spirit-stirring airs from the band.

"At eight o'clock the multitude were called together by music and the firing of guns, the Bishops of the several wards arranging themselves on the sides of the aisles, with the banners of their wards unfurled, each bearing some appropriate inscription.

"At a quarter past eight, the Presidency of the Stake, the Twelve, and the bands, went to prepare the escort in the following order, at the house of President Brigham Young, under the direction of Lorenzo Snow, J. M. Grant, and F. D. Richards: "(1) Horace S. Eldredge, marshal, on horseback, in military uniform; (2) brass band; (3) twelve bishops bearing the banners of their wards; (4) seventy-four young men dressed in white, with white scarfs on their right shoulders, and coronets on their heads, each carrying in his right hand a copy of the Declaration of Independence and the Constitution of the United States, and each carrying a sheathed sword in his left hand; one of them carrying a beautiful banner, inscribed on it, ' The Zion of the Lord ;' (5) twenty-four young ladies, dressed in white, with white scarfs on their right shoulders, and wreaths of white roses on their heads, each carrying a copy of the Bible and Book of Mormon, and one carrying a very neat banner, inscribed with 'Hail to our Captain;' (6) Brigham Young, Heber C. Kimball, Willard Richards, Parley P. Pratt, Charles C. Rich, John Taylor, Daniel Spencer, D. Fullmer, Willard Snow, Erastus Snow; (7) twelve Bishops, carrying flags of their wards; (8) twenty-four Silver Greys, led by Isaac Morley, Patriarch, each having a staff, painted red at the upper part, and a bunch of white ribbon fastened at the top, one of them carrying the Stars and Stripes, bearing the inscription, 'Liberty and Truth.' "The procession started from the house at nine o'clock. The young men and young ladies sang a hymn through the streets, the cannon roared, the musketry rolled, the Nauvoo bell pealed forth its silvery notes, and the air was filled by the sweet strains of the brass band. On arriving at the Bowery the escort was received with shouts of 'Hosanna! to God and the Lamb!' While the Presidency, Patriarch, and presiding Bishops were passing down the aisle, the people cheered and shouted, 'Hail to the Governor of Deseret.' These being seated by the committee on the stand, the escort passed round the assembly, singing a hymn of praise, marched down the aisle, and were seated in double rows on either side. The assembly was called to order by Mr. J. M. Grant. On being seated, Mr. Erastus Snow offered up a prayer.

"Richard Ballantyne, one of the twenty-four young men, came to the stand, and, in a neat speech, presented the Declaration of Independence and the Constitution of the United States to President Young, which was received with three shouts, 'May it live forever,' led by the President.

"The Declaration of Independence was then read by Mr. Erastus Snow, the band following with a lively air.

"The clerk then read 'The Mountain Standard,' composed by Parley P. Pratt:—

"Lo, the Gentile chain is broken,

Freedom's banner waves on high.' "

After the above had been sung by the twenty-four young men and young ladies, Mr. Phinehas Richards came forward in behalf of the twenty-four aged sires in Israel and read their congratulatory address on the anniversary of the day. At the conclusion of the reading, the assembly rose and shouted three times, 'Hosanna! hosanna! hosanna! to God and the Lamb, forever and ever, Amen,' while the banners were waved by the Bishops. The band next played a lively air, and the clerk then rose and read an 'Ode on Liberty.' "The ode was then sung by the twenty-four Silver Greys, to the tune of 'Bruce's Address to his Army,' "The hour of intermission having arrived, the escort was reformed, the Bishops of each ward collected the inhabitants of their respective wards together, and marched with them to the dinner tables, where several thousand of the Saints dined sumptuously on the fruits of the earth. Several hundred emigrants also partook of the repast, as did also three score Indians."

Orson Hyde, President of the Twelve Apostles, in the Frontier Guardian, published at Kanesville, Iowa, thus explains this first celebration, at which, it will have been noticed, the Declaration of American Independence was read: "Our people celebrated the 24th of July instead of the 4th, for two reasons—one was because that was the day on which Brother Young and the Pioneers first entered the valley; and the other was, they had little or no bread, or flour to make cakes, etc., that early, and not wishing to celebrate on empty stomachs, they postponed it until their harvest came in."

The explanation of Apostle Hyde has historical pertinence, when it is remembered that in the Spring of this year the community were put on rations; it was this very harvest of 1849, that saved the people from a continuance of the famine, caused by the destruction of the crops by the grasshoppers in 1848.

Here a passage of history seems due to the soldiers of the Mormon Battalion, relative to their connection with the early times of California, and the finding of gold, which largely tended to the rapid growth of Great Salt Lake City and started its currency.

On being discharged from the United States service, four of the Mormon Battalion found employ with Mr. Thomas Marshall, in digging Captain Sutter's mill race, on the Sacramento River. One day these brethren were attracted by the mysterious movements of their foreman, Mr. Marshall, whom they partly surprised in the act of washing something which his shovel had just turned up.

That something was gold! The discovery was at once shared by Mr. Marshall and his men. Of course, at first there was some secrecy preserved, but such a discovery could not be long hid, and soon the Mormons of California, both those of the Battalion and those who sailed to the Bay of San Francisco with Mr. Samuel Brannan in the ship Brooklyn, were working in the gold diggings.

So that notwithstanding Mr. Marshall's shovel brought the initial glitter of California gold to light, it was the shovels of Mormon Elders that spread the golden tidings to the world.

No sooner was the discovery bruited than the whole civilized world seemed flocking to the new El Dorado. Scarcely a nation but sent its adventurous spirits to the paradise of gold. From the American States themselves came colony after colony pouring daily towards the west. Gold was the incentive at first, but as that wondrous emigrational tide swelled, it became more like the migration of a dominant race for the purpose of founding a new empire. This did finally become the proper character of the movement.

The best blood of America was in those emigrant companies, and they took with them enough resources to found a new State; but there was no "royal road" to the land of gold; fifteen hundred miles then intervened between the western frontier of the States and Great Salt Lake City. The Mormon Zion became the "half-way house" of the nation.

But the ambitious and spirited emigrants to California could not endure the tedious journey as the Saints had done. Before they reached the mountains they began to leave fragments of their richly-laden trains by the wayside. All along the route was strewn valuable freight, with the ruins of wagons and the carcasses of oxen and mules.

By the time the gold-seekers reached the valley of the Great Salt Lake, they were utterly impatient and demoralized. Many had loaded their trains with clothing, dry goods, general merchandise, mechanics' tools and machinery, expecting to find a market where gold was dug and a new country to be settled.

But the merchant, alike with the adventurer, was at last subdued by the contagion of the gold fever and provoked into a mania of impatience by the tedious journey. News also reached the overland emigrants that steamers, laden with merchandise had sailed from New York to California. The speculations of the merchants lost their last charm. That which was destined for California was left in Utah. In absolute disgust for their trains of merchandise and splendid emigrant outfits, they gave the bulk to the Mormons at their own price, and for the most ordinary means of barter. A horse or a mule outfit to carry the gold hunter quickly to his destination, was taken as an equivalent for wagons, cattle, and merchandise.

Parley P. Pratt, writing to his brother Orson under date July 8th, 1849, says: "The present travel through this place, or near it, will, it is thought, amount to some thirty or forty thousand persons. All will center here another year, as much of it does this year. This employs blacksmiths, pack-saddlers, washing, board, etc., and opens a large trade in provisions, cattle, mules, horses, etc. Scores or hundreds of people now arrive here daily, and all stop to rest and re-fit."

The Frontier Guardian, giving the news of the arrival of the gold-seekers in Great Salt Lake City related the story thus: "The valley has been a place of general deposit for property, goods, etc., by Californians. When they saw a few bags and kegs of gold dust brought in by our boys, it made them completely enthusiastic. Pack mules and horses that were worth twenty-five dollars in ordinary times, would readily bring two hundred dollars in the most valuable property at the lowest price. Goods and other property were daily offered at auction in all parts of the city. For a light Yankee wagon, sometimes three or four great heavy ones would be offered in exchange, and a yoke of oxen thrown in at that.

Common domestic sheeting sold from five to ten cents per yard by the bolt. The best of spades and shovels for fifty cents each. Vests that cost in St. Louis one dollar and fifty cents each, were sold at Salt Lake for thirty-seven and one half cents. Full chests of joiner's tools that would cost one hundred and fifty dollars in the East, were sold in Salt Lake City for twenty-five dollars. Indeed, almost every article, except sugar and coffee, were selling on an average fifty per cent, below wholesale prices in the eastern States."

In the fall, a company of Mormon Elders started from Salt Lake City, designing to work for a while in the gold mines, after which some were to proceed on missions to the Sandwich Islands. The company consisted of General Charles C. Rich, Major Hunt of the Mormon Battalion, Captain Flake, captain of the company, George Q. Cannon, Joseph Cain, Thomas Whittle, Henry E. Gibson and other prominent Mormons. This was the first company that undertook to go to California by the southern route. The expedition started with only about thirty days' provisions; yet sixty days on the road were passed before the first settlement was reached. The men went with pack animals. In crossing the desert they had often to turn back and retake up their march in some other direction, which made the journey very long and severe, killing nearly all of their animals, so that the last three hundred and fifty miles were mostly performed on foot. But it was a fine company of men, and they were enabled to survive one of the hardest journeys ever made to the State of California.

CHAPTER VIII.

ARRIVAL OF CAPTAIN STANSBURY. HIS INTERVIEW WITH GOVERNOR YOUNG GOVERNMENT SURVEY OF THE LAKES. COMMENCEMENT OF INDIAN DIFFICULTIES.

In August of that year (1849) Captain Howard Stansbury, of the United States Army Topographical Engineers, with his assistants, arrived in the valley for the purpose of making a government survey of the lakes. He was accompanied by Lieutenant Gunnison who was, like Captain Stansbury, one of the earliest and most intelligent writers upon the Utah community. Of his arrival, Captain Stansbury thus reports to the chief of his department: "Before reaching Great Salt Lake City, I had heard from various sources that much uneasiness was felt by the Mormon community at my anticipated coming among them. I was told that they would never permit any survey of their country to be made; while it was darkly hinted that if I persevered in attempting to carry it on, my life would scarce be safe. Utterly disregarding, indeed, giving not the least credence to these insinuations, I at once called upon Brigham Young, the President of the Mormon Church and the Governor of the Commonwealth, stated to him what I had heard, explained to him the views of the Government in directing an exploration and survey of the lake, assuring him that these were the sole objects of the expedition. He replied, that he did not hesitate to say that both he and the people whom he presided over had been very much disturbed and surprised that the Government should send out a party into their country so soon after they had made their settlement; that he had heard of the expedition from time to time, since its onset from Fort Leavenworth; and that the whole community were extremely anxious as to what could be the design of the Government in such a movement. It appeared, too, that their alarm had been increased by. the indiscreet and totally unauthorized boasting of an attaché of General Wilson, the newly appointed Indian agent for California, whose train on its way thither had reached the city a few days before I myself arrived. This person, as I understood, had declared openly that General Wilson had come clothed with authority from the President of the United States to expel the Mormons from the lands which they occupied, and that he would do so if he thought proper. The Mormons very naturally supposed from such a declaration that there must be some understanding or connection between General Wilson and myself; and that the arrival of the two parties so nearly together was the result of a concerted and combined movement for the ulterior purpose of breaking up and destroying their colony. The impression was that a survey was to be made of their country in the same manner that other public lands are surveyed, for the purpose of dividing into townships and sections, and of thus establishing and recording the claims of the Government to it, and thereby anticipating any claim the Mormons might set up from their previous occupation. However unreasonable such a suspicion may be considered, yet it must be remembered that these people are exasperated and rendered almost desperate by the wrongs and persecutions they had previously suffered in Illinois and Missouri; that they had left the confines of civilization and fled to these far distant wilds, that they might enjoy undisturbed the religious liberty which had been practically denied them: and that now they supposed themselves to be followed up by the General Government with the view of driving them out from even this solitary spot, where they had hoped they should at length be permitted to set up their habitation in peace.

"Upon all these points I undeceived Governor Young to his entire satisfaction. I was induced to pursue this conciliatory course, not only in justice to the Government, but also because I knew, from the peculiar organization of this singular community, that, unless the 'President' was fully satisfied that no evil was intended to his people, it would be useless for me to attempt to carry out my instructions. He was not only civil Governor, but the President of the whole Church of Latter-day Saints upon the earth, their prophet and their priest, receiving, as they all firmly believed, direct revelations of the Divine will, which, according to their creed, form the law of the Church. He is, consequently, profoundly revered by all, and possesses unbounded influence and almost unlimited power. I did not anticipate open resistance; but I was fully aware that if the President continued to view the expedition with distrust, nothing could be more natural than that every possible obstruction should be thrown in our way by a 'masterly inactivity.' Provisions would not be furnished; information would not be afforded; labor could not be procured; and no means would be left untried, short of open opposition, to prevent the success of a measure by them deemed fatal to their interests and safety. So soon, however, as the true object of the expedition was fully understood, the President laid the subject matter before the council called for that purpose, and I was informed, as the result of their deliberations, that the authorities were much pleased that the exploration was to be made; that they had themselves contemplated something of the kind, but did not yet feel able to incur the expense; but that any assistance they could render to facilitate our operations would be most cheerfully furnished to the extent of their ability. This pledge, thus heartily given, was as faithfully redeemed; and it gives me pleasure here to acknowledge the warm interest manifested and efficient aid rendered, as well by the President as by all the leading men of the community, both in our personal welfare and in the successful prosecution of the work.

"Matters being thus satisfactorily adjusted, as the provisions which had been laid in at the beginning of the journey were nearly exhausted, I left the city on the 12th of September, with teams and pack-mules, for Fort Hall, to procure the supplies for the party which had been forwarded to that post by the supply train attached to Colonel Loring's command; and at the same time to carry out that portion of my instructions which directed me to explore a route for a road from the head of Salt Lake to Fort Hall. The main party was left under the command of Lieutenant Gunnison, with instructions to commence the survey upon the basis already laid down."

Returning from his exploration of a route from Great Salt Lake City to Fort Hall, and reconnaissance of Cache Valley, Captain Stansbury continues a narrative intimately connected with the early history of this city. He says: "Upon my arrival at Salt Lake City, I found that the camp, under Lieutenant Gunnison, was then about sixty miles to the southward, upon Utah Lake. I accordingly joined him as soon as possible. The work, during my absence, had been carried forward by that officer with energy, industry and judgment.

"I had hoped, from the representations which had been made to me of the mildness of the two previous winters, that we should be able to keep the field the greater part, if not the whole of the season; but, in the latter part of November, the winter set in with great and unusual severity, accompanied by deep snows, which rendered any farther prosecution of the work impracticable. I was therefore compelled to break up my camp, and to seek for winter quarters in the city.

These were not obtained without some difficulty, as the tide of emigration had been so great that houses were very scarce, and not a small portion of the inhabitants, among whom was the president himself, were forced to lodge portions of their families in wagons.

"Upon terminating the field-work for the season, I dispatched three men, one of whom was my guide and interpreter, with a small invoice of goods, to trade for horses among the Uintah Utahs, with directions to await my orders at Fort Bridger. Reports afterward reached us that a bloody fight had taken place between the Sioux and the Yampah Utahs, which latter tribe reside in the vicinity of the Uintahs, and great fears were entertained that the little party had been cut off by one or the other of the contending tribes. Such a calamity, aside from the loss of life, would have been of serious consequence to the expedition, as the horses I expected to obtain were almost indispensable to the return of the party to the States, the number of our animals having been much diminished by death and robbery.

"It may as well be mentioned here, that the party thus dispatched subsequently joined me in the spring, as soon as the melting of the snows rendered communication with Fort Bridger practicable, bringing with them a drove of twenty-five horses. They had met with very rough usage from the Indians, having been robbed of a number of their horses, besides the whole of what remained of their goods and narrowly escaped with their lives.

"From the report by Lieutenant Gunnison of his operations during my absence, I make the following synopsis.

"A thorough exploration was made, with the view of ascertaining the points for such a base line as would best develop a system of triangles embracing both the Salt Lake and Utah Valleys.

"A line was selected, and carefully measured by rods constructed for the purpose, and tripod stations erected over the termini, which were marked by metal points set in wooden posts sunk flush with the surface of the ground. The length of the base is thirty-one thousand six hundred and eighty feet.

"Fourteen principal triangulation stations were erected, consisting of large pyramidal timber tripods, strongly framed, to be covered, when required for use, by cotton cloth of different colors, according to the background. The triangles extended to the south shore of Utah Lake, and embraced an area of about eighty by twenty-five miles.

"A survey and sounding had been made of the Utah Lake, and also of the river connecting it with Salt Lake: this operation requiring a line to be run of one hundred and twenty-six miles, principally by the back angle, with the theodolite.

"Although such a result, from less than two months' labor, would be entirely satisfactory under ordinary circumstances anywhere, and would reflect credit on the energy and capacity of the officer in charge of the work, yet it may be remarked that it would be very unfair to judge of it by a comparison with similar results obtained in the Eastern States. There, all the accessories to such a work, especially water and timber, are abundant, and generally at a convenient distance: here, on the contrary, both are very scarce and hard to be obtained.

All the water, for instance, used both for cooking and drinking, that was consumed on the base line, (requiring seven days of incessant labor in its measurement,) had to be transported upon mules from the river, which lay a mile east of its eastern terminus; and the force employed in the erection of most of the triangulation stations had to be supplied in a like manner. But the principal difficulty was the scarcity of timber. Wood grows nowhere on the plains; all the wood used for cooking in camp, and all the timber, both for posts on the base line and for the construction of the stations, had to be hauled from the mountains in many cases fifteen or twenty miles distant, over a rough country without roads. Almost every stick used for this purpose cost from twenty to thirty miles travel of a six-mule team. This, together with the delays of getting into the canyons, where alone the timber can be procured, cutting down the trees, and hauling them down the gorges by hand to the nearest spots accessible to the teams, involved an amount of time and labor which must be experienced before it can be appreciated. All this had to be done, however, or the prosecution of the work would have been impracticable.

"Before leaving the Salt Like City for Fort Hall, I had engaged the services of Albert Carrington, Esq., a member of the Mormon community, who was to act as an assistant on the survey. He was without experience in the use of instruments; but, being a gentleman of liberal education, he soon acquired, under instruction, the requisite skill, and, by his zeal, industry, and practical good sense, materially aided us in our subsequent operations. He continued with the party until the termination of the survey, accompanied it to this city, [Washington] and has since returned to his mountain home, carrying with him the respect and kind wishes of all with whom he was associated.

"The winter season in the valley was long and severe. The vicinity of so many high mountains rendered the weather extremely variable; snows fell constantly upon them, and frequently to the depth of ten inches in the plains. In many of the canyons it accumulated to the depth of fifty feet, filling up the passes so rapidly that, in more than one instance, emigrants who had been belated in starting from the States, were overtaken by the storms in the mountain gorges, and forced to abandon everything, and escape on loot, leaving even their animals to perish in the snows. All communication with the world beyond was thus effectually cut off; and, as the winter advanced, the gorges became more and more impassable, owing to the drifting of the snow into them from the projecting peaks.

"We remained thus shut up until the 3rd of April. Our quarters consisted of a small unfurnished house of unburnt brick or adobe, unplastered, and roofed with boards loosely nailed on, which, every time it stormed, admitted so much water as called into requisition all the pans and buckets in the establishment to receive the numerous little streams which came trickling down from every crack and knot-hole. During this season of comparative inaction, we received from the authorities and citizens of the community every kindness that the most warmhearted hospitality could dictate: and no effort was spared to render us comfortable as their own limited means would admit. Indeed, we were much better lodged than many of our neighbors; for, as has been previously observed, very many families were obliged still to lodge wholly or in part in their wagons, which, being covered, served, when taken off from the wheels and set upon the ground, to make bedrooms, of limited dimensions it is true, but yet exceedingly comfortable. Many of these were comparatively large and commodious, and, when carpeted and furnished with a little stove, formed an additional apartment or back building to the small cabin, with which they frequently communicated by a door.

It certainly argued a high tone of morals and a habitual observance of good order and decorum, to find women and children thus securely slumbering in the midst of a large city, with no protection from midnight molestation other than a wagon cover of linen and the regis of the law. In the very next enclosure to that occupied by our party, a whole family of children had no other shelter than one of these wagons, where they slept all the winter, literally out of doors, there being no communication whatever with the inside of their parents' house."

Stansbury's report to the Government also supplies the initial pages of the Indian history of Utah. He says:

"The native tribes with whom we came in contact in the valley were the most degraded and lowest in the scale of being of any I had ever seen. They consisted of the ' root-diggers,' a class of Indians which seemed to be composed of outcasts from their respective tribes, subsisting chiefly upon roots dug from the ground, and the seeds of various plants indigenous to the soil, which they grind into a kind of flour between two flat stones. Lizards and crickets also form a portion of their food. At certain seasons of the year they obtain from the tributaries of both the Salt Lake and Lake Utah, a considerable quantity of fish, which they take in weirs or traps, constructed of willow bushes. Those that we saw were branches of the Shoshones or Snakes, and from the large and warlike tribe of Utahs, which latter inhabit a large tract of country to the southward. They are known among the traders by the designation of 'snake-diggers,' and 'Utes;' those of the latter tribe, which inhabit the vicinity of the lakes and streams and live chiefly on fish, being distinguished by the name of 'Pah Utahs,' or 'Pah Utes,'—the word Pah, in their language, signifying water.

"While engaged in the survey of the Utah Valley, we were no little annoyed by numbers of the latter tribe, who hung around the camp, crowding around the cook-fires, more like hungry dogs than human beings, eagerly watching for the least scrap that might be thrown away, which they devoured with avidity and without the least preparation. The herdsmen also complained that their cattle were frequently scattered, and that notwithstanding their utmost vigilance, several of them had unaccountably disappeared and were lost. One morning, a fine fat ox came into camp with an arrow buried in his side, which perfectly accounted for the disappearance of the others.

"After the party left Lake Utah for winter quarters in Salt Lake City, the Indians became more insolent, boasting of what they had done—driving off the stock of the inhabitants of the southern settlements, resisting all attempts to recover them, and finally firing upon the people themselves as they issued from their little stockade to attend to their ordinary occupations. Under these circumstances, the settlers in the Utah Valley applied to the supreme government, at Salt Lake City, for counsel as to the proper course of action. The President was at first extremely averse to the adoption of harsh measures; but, after several conciliatory overtures had been resorted to in vain, he very properly determined to put a stop, by force, to further aggressions, which, if not resisted, could only end in the total destruction of the colony. Before coming to this decision, the authorities called upon me to consult as to the policy of the measure, and to request the expression of my opinion as to what view the Government of the United States might be expected to take of it. Knowing, as I did, most of the circumstances, and feeling convinced that some action of the kind would ultimately have to be resorted to, as the forbearance already shown had been only attributed to weakness and cowardice, and had served but to encourage further and bolder outrages, I did not hesitate to say to them that, in my judgment, the contemplated expedition against these savage marauders was a measure not only of good policy, but one of absolute necessity and self-preservation. I knew the leader of the Indians to be a crafty and bloodthirsty savage, who had been already guilty of several murders, and had openly threatened that he would kill every white man that he found alone upon the prairies. In addition to this, I was convinced that the completion of the yet unfinished survey of the Utah Valley, the coming season, must otherwise be attended with serious difficulty, if not actual hazard, and would involve the necessity of a largely increased and armed escort for its protection. Such being the circumstances, the course proposed could not but meet my entire approval.

"A force of one hundred men was accordingly organized, and, upon the application of President Young, leave was given to Lieutenant Howland, of the Mounted Rifles, then on duty with my command, to accompany the expedition as its adjutant: such assistance also was furnished as it was in my power to afford, consisting of arms, tents, camp-equipage, and ammunition.

"The expedition was completely successful. The Indians fought very bravely, but were finally routed, some forty of them killed, and as many more taken prisoners; the latter, consisting principally of women and children, were carried to the city and distributed among the inhabitants, for the purpose of weaning them from their savage pursuits, and bringing them up in the habits of civilized and Christian life. The experiment, however, did not succeed as was anticipated, most of the prisoners escaping upon the very first opportunity.

"On the 22nd of February, about three p. m., a slight shock of an earthquake was felt in the southern part of the city, the vibrations being sufficient to shake plates from the shelves and to disturb milk in the pans."

The historical importance of the first Indian expedition of this Territory, which was the beginning of the organization of the Utah militia, calls for the following supplementary pages to Captain Stansbury's report.

The organization of a militia for the protection of these colonies in an Indian country was an imperative necessity, and to Daniel H. Wells, who had already distinguished himself in military affairs, was given the task of creating it, and the rank of Lieutenant-General was conferred upon him by the Governor.

The first company organized was under the command of Captain George D. Grant, who was afterwards Brigadier-General. They were called " Minute Men," a name which soon became famous in the Indian service throughout Utah. The company originated in Great Salt Lake City, and from time to time it was called out to the relief of those colonies which were sent from the parent colony to explore and populate the country. The first engagement of any importance was on the spot where the city of Provo now stands; there had, however, occurred a slight affray at Battle Creek, at which Colonel John Scott commanded, but none were killed on either side.

On the call by Governor Young for one hundred mounted men General Wells immediately dispatched a company of fifty under the command of Captain George

D. Grant. Among the subordinate officers were William H. Kimball, James A. Little, James Ferguson and Henry Johnson, the two latter having been officers in the Mormon Battalion; and among the privates were such men as Robert T. Burton, Lot Smith, Ephraim Hanks, Jesse Martin, Orson Whitney, and others who afterwards figured prominently in the Utah militia.

The second fifty was forwarded under the command of Captain Lytle, who was an officer in the Mormon Battalion.

The company under the command of Captain George D. Grant started from Great Salt Lake City on the 7th day of February. The men marched all night in the snow for the purpose of coming upon the Indians unawares. The weather was intensely cold; from ten to twelve inches of snow covered the entire Utah Valley. They arrived early in the morning of the 8th, having suffered severely on the march from the inclement weather.

The Indians had fortified themselves on the Provo River. They were encamped in a bend of the river bottom, under a low bluff, from which the ground receded to the river. All this bottom, at that time, was covered with willow brush and cottonwood timber, some of the latter having been cut down by them to construct their fortifications.

These Indians were of a warlike tribe, under the command of Old Elk, and not of the lower class of which Stansbury speaks. There were about seventy warriors, possessing arms equal to those of the expedition sent out against them,—their arms having been obtained from the mountaineers, traders, and settlers. Their squaws and children were sent into the canyons, while the warriors thus strongly fortified awaited the attack. They also held possession of a double log house. The settlers had retired to the shelter of their fort, but some of them joined the assailants on their arrival and did effective service in the defense of their city.

Thus fortified, the Indian warriors kept the militia at bay till the evening of the second day, before the latter obtained any decided advantage. Meantime the Indians had killed one and wounded five or six. They frequently sallied out from their entrenchments, delivered their fire, then quickly retreated to the brush. At length Lieutenant Howland, of Stansbury's command, suggested a moveable battery, which was forthwith constructed of plank, laid up edgewise on the top of runners, over which were thrown camp blankets and buffalo robes.

This battery was handled by the assailants effectively and pushed towards the Indian line of defense. On the afternoon of the second day, a small company of cavalry (sixteen in number) was ordered by Captain Grant to make a charge upon the Indian quarters, and especially to get possession of the log house, previously referred to, from which the Indians had greatly annoyed the men. The little company of cavalry made a dashing charge, but were met with such a volley of fire, wounding two or three of their number, that the impetuosity of the charge was for a moment checked, but Burton and Lot Smith, dashing on, succeeded in riding their horses into the passage that divided the rooms of the double log house, of which they took possession, the Indians having deserted it at the onslaught. The Indians, recovering from the surprise of the charge, fired on the remainder of the detachment with such violence that the men had to take shelter under the end of the house, but seven or eight of their best horses were shot down in a very few minutes. Between the firing the men got into the house, upon which the Indians continued to fire for several hours. In this company of sixteen picked men were Lot Smith, Robert T. Burton, William H. Kimball, Jas. Ferguson, Ephraim Hanks, Henry Johnson, Isham Flyn, (who was wounded,) Orson Whitney, and eight others whose names we have not been able to obtain.

This charge was complimented by Lieutenant Howland as being as fine as regular cavalry would make. It gave the advantage of the engagement into the hands of the militia; for the Indians retired in the night after the charge, leaving their dead on the ground, carrying their wounded with them; but before their retreat they supplied themselves abundantly with the horse beef.

So much bravery was exhibited by the Indians, and such a desperate defense made, that dispatches had been sent to Great Salt Lake City, repeatedly requesting General Wells to come and take personal command, which he did, but arrived after the second day's engagement. There was afterwards quite an engagement on the south end of Utah Lake, at which General Wells was present and had personal command.

Captain Stansbury omitted to mention that Dr. Blake, of his command, was in this expedition, but his presence and services to the wounded have been remembered and gratefully acknowledged by the commanding officers of the old Minute Men. And it is worthy of note that it was this very expedition which brought out the men who have since figured as generals of the Utah militia. In it Lot Smith and Robert T. Burton for the first time met, and with that charge together on the log house began the lifelong friendship of these two men who, next to the Lieutenant-General, Daniel H. Wells, have figured the most conspicuously in the military history of Utah.

Having completed their surveys and explorations, the topographical engineers left the City of the Great Salt Lake for home on the 28th of August, 1850, Stansbury, closing the record of his sojourn among the founders of this Territory, with the following tribute to them: "Before taking leave of the Mormon community, whose history has been the subject of no little interest in the country, I cannot but avail myself of the opportunity again to acknowledge the constant kindness and generous hospitality which was ever extended to the party during the sojourn of rather more than a year among them. The most disinterested efforts were made to afford us, both personally and officially, all the aids and facilities within the power of the people, as well to forward our labors as to contribute to our comfort and enjoyment.

Official invitations were sent by the authorities to the officers of the party, while engaged in distant duty on the lake, to participate in the celebration of their annual jubilee, on the 24th of July, and an honorable position assigned them in the procession on that occasion. Upon our final departure, we were followed with the kindest expressions of regard, and anxious hopes for the safety and welfare of the party upon its homeward journey."

CHAPTER IX.

INCORPORATION OF GREAT SALT LAKE CITY. ITS ORIGINAL CHARTER. THE FIRST CITY COUNCIL AND MUNICIPAL OFFICERS. ORGANIZATION OF THE TERRITORY. ARRIVAL OF THE NEWS OF GOVERNOR YOUNGS APPOINTMENT. DISSOLUTION OF THE STATE OF DESERET. GOVERNORS PROCLAMATION. LEGALIZING THE LAWS PASSED BY THE PROVISIONAL GOVERNMENT. CORRESPONDENCE BETWEEN COLONEL KANE AND PRESIDENT FILLMORE. STANSBURY'S VOUCHER FOR BRIGHAM YOUNG.

The cities of Utah needing their due municipal orders and having waited so long for the action of Congress, the Governor and the General Assembly of the State of Deseret, at the opening of the year 1851, effected the incorporation of the cities of Great Salt Lake, Ogden, Provo, Manti and Parowan. The following is the original charter of Great Salt Lake City, entitled

"AN ORDINANCE TO INCORPORATE GREAT SALT LAKE CITY.

"Sec. i. Be it ordained by the General Assembly of the State of Deseret: That all that district of country embraced in the following boundaries, to wit:— beginning at the southeast corner of the Church Pasture, about half a mile north of the Hot Spring; thence west to the west bank of the Jordan River; thence south, up the west bank thereof, to a point in said bank directly west from the southwest corner of the five-acre lots, south of said city; thence east to the aforesaid southwest corner of said five-acre lots, and along the south line thereof; thence east to the base of the mountains; thence directly north to the point directly east of the southeast corner of the Church Pasture; thence west to the place of beginning:—including the present survey of said city, shall be known and designated as Great Salt Lake City; and the inhabitants thereof are hereby constituted a body corporate and politic, by the name aforesaid, and shall have perpetual succession, and may have and use a common seal, which they may change and alter at pleasure.

"Sec. 2. The inhabitants of said city, by the name and style aforesaid, shall have power to sue and be sued; to plead and be impleaded; defend and be defended in all courts of law and equity, and in all actions whatsoever; to purchase, receive and hold property, real and personal, in said city; to purchase receive and hold real property beyond the pity, for burying grounds, or other public purposes, for the use of the inhabitants of said city; to sell, lease, convey, or dispose of property, real and personal, for the benefit of said city; to improve and protect such property, and to do all other things in relation thereto, as natural persons.

Sec. 3. There shall be a City Council, to consist of a Mayor, four Aldermen, and nine Councilors, who shall have the qualifications of electors of said city, and shall be chosen by the qualified voters thereof, and shall hold their for two years, and until their successors shall be elected and qualified. The City Council shall judge of the qualifications, elections, and returns of their own members, and a majority of them shall form a quorum to do business; but a smaller number may adjourn from day to day, and compel the attendance of absent members, under such penalties as may be prescribed by ordinance.

Sec. 4. The Mayor, Aldermen, and Councilors, before entering upon the duties of their offices, shall take and subscribe an oath or affirmation, that they will support the Constitution of the United States, and of this State, and that they will well and truly perform the duties of their offices, to the best of their skill and abilities.

Sec. 5. On the first Monday of April next, and every two years thereafter, on said day, an election shall be held for the election of one Mayor, four Aldermen, and nine Councilors; and at the first election under this ordinance, three judges shall be chosen, viva voce, by the electors present. The said judges shall choose two clerks, and the judges and clerks, before entering upon their duties, shall take and subscribe an oath or affirmation, such as is now required by law to be taken by judges and clerks of other elections; and at all subsequent elections the necessary number of judges and clerks shall be appointed by the City Council. At the first election so held, the polls shall be opened at nine o'clock a. m., and closed at six o'clock p. m. At the close of the polls, the votes shall be counted, and a statement thereof proclaimed at the front door of the house at which said election shall be held; and the clerks shall leave with each person elected, or at his usual place of residence, within five days after the election, a written notice of his election; and each person so notified, shall within ten days after the election, take the oath or affirmation herein before mentioned, a certificate of which oath shall be deposited with the Recorder, whose appointment is hereinafter provided for, and be by him preserved. And all subsequent elections shall be held, conducted, and returns thereof made, as may be provided for by ordinance of the City Council.

Sec. 6. All free white male inhabitants of the age of eighteen years, who are entitled to vote for State officers, and who shall have been actual residents of said city sixty days next preceding said election, shall be entitled to vote for city officers.

Sec. 7. The City Council shall have authority to levy and collect taxes for city purposes, upon all taxable property, real and personal, within the limits of the city, not exceeding one-half per cent, per annum, upon the assessed value thereof, and may enforce the payment of the same in any manner to be provided by ordinance, not repugnant to the Constitution of the United States, or of this State.

Sec. 8. The City Council shall have power to appoint a Recorder, Treasurer, Assessor and Collector, Marshal and Supervisor of Streets. They shall also have the power to appoint all such other officers, by ordinance, as may be necessary, define the duties of all city officers, and remove them from office at pleasure.

Sec. 9. The City Council shall have power to require of all officers appointed in pursuance of this ordinance, bonds with penalty and security, for the faithful performance of their respective duties, such as may be deemed expedient, and also to require all officers appointed as aforesaid, to take an oath for the faithful performance of the duties of their respective offices.

Sec. 10. The City Council shall have power and authority to make, ordain, establish, and execute all such ordinances not repugnant to the Constitution of the United States, or of this State, as they may deem necessary for the peace, benefit, good order, regulation, convenience, and cleanliness of said city; for the protection of property therein, from destruction of property by fire or otherwise, and for the health and happiness thereof. They shall have power to fill all vacancies that may happen by death, resignation, or removal, in any of the offices herein made elective; to fix and establish all the fees of the officers of said corporation, not herein established; to impose such fines, not exceeding one hundred dollars for each offense, as they may deem just, for refusing to accept any office in or under the corporation, or (or misconduct therein; to divide the city into wards, and specify the boundaries thereof, and create additional wards; to add to the number of Aldermen and Councilors, and apportion them among the several wards, as may be just, and most conducive to the interest of the city.

Sec. 11. To establish, support and regulate common schools; to borrow money on the credit of the city,—provided that no sum or sums of money be borrowed on a greater interest than six per cent, per annum,—nor shall the interest on the aggregate of all the sums borrowed and outstanding ever exceed one half of the city revenue, arising from taxes assessed on real estate within this corporation.

Sec. 12. To make regulations to prevent the introduction of contagious diseases into the City, to make quarantine laws for that purpose, and enforce the same.

Sec. 13. To appropriate and provide for the payment of the expenses and debts of the city.

Sec. 14. To establish hospitals and make regulations for the government of the same; to make regulations to secure the general health of the inhabitants; to declare what shall be nuisances, and to prevent and remove the same.

Sec. 15. To provide the City with water, to dig wells, lay pump logs, and pipes, and erect pumps in the streets for the extinguishment of fires, and convenience of the inhabitants.

Sec. 16. To open, alter, widen, extend, establish, grade, pave, or otherwise improve and keep in repair, streets, avenues, lanes, and alleys; and to establish, erect and keep in repair aqueducts and bridges.

Sec. 17. To provide for lighting of the streets, and erecting lamp posts; and establish, support and regulate night watches; to erect market houses, establish markets and market places, and provide for the government and regulations thereof.

Sec. 18. To provide for erecting all needful buildings for the use of the City; and for enclosing, improving, and regulating all public grounds belonging to the City.

Sec. 19. To license, tax and regulate auctioneers, merchants, and retailers, grocers and taverns, ordinaries, hawkers, peddlers, brokers, pawnbrokers, and money changers.

Sec. 20. To license, tax and regulate hacking, carriages, wagons, carts and drays, and fix the rates to be charged for the carriage of persons, and for wagonage, cartage and drayage of property; as also to license and regulate porters, and fix the rates of porterage.

Sec. 21. To license, tax and regulate theatrical and other exhibitions, shows and amusements.

Sec. 22. To tax, restrain, prohibit, and suppress tippling houses, dram shops, gaming houses, bawdy, and other disorderly houses.

Sec. 23. To provide for the prevention and extinguishment of fires; to regulate the fixing of chimneys, and the flues thereof, and stove pipes, and to organize and establish fire companies.

Sec. 24. To regulate the storage of gunpowder, tar, pitch, rosin, and other combustible materials.

Sec. 25. To regulate and order parapet walls, and other partition fences.

Sec. 26. To establish standard weights and measures and regulate the weights and measures to be used in the city, in all other cases not provided for by law.

Sec. 27. To provide for the inspection and measuring of lumber and other building materials, and for the measurement of all kinds of mechanical work.

Sec. 28. To provide for the inspection and weighing of hay, lime and stone coal, and measuring of charcoal, firewood, and other fuel, to be sold or used within the City.

Sec. 29. To provide for and regulate the inspection of tobacco, and of beef, pork, flour, meal; also beer and whisky, brandy, and all other spirituous or fermented liquors.

Sec. 30. To regulate the weight, quality, and price of bread sold and used in the City.

Sec. 31. To provide for taking the enumeration of the inhabitants of the City.

Sec. 32. To fix the compensation of all city officers, and regulate the fees of jurors, witnesses, and others, for services rendered under this or any city ordinance.

Sec. 33. The City Council shall have exclusive power within the city by ordinance, to license, regulate, suppress, or restrain billiard tables, and from one to twenty pin alleys, and every other description of gaming or gambling.

Sec. 34. The City Council shall have exclusive power within the City, by ordinance, to license, regulate, or restrain the keeping of ferries, and toll bridges; to regulate the police of the city; to impose fines, forfeitures and penalties, for the breach of any ordinance, and provide for the recovery of such fines and forfeitures, and the enforcement of such penalties, and to pass such ordinances as may be necessary and proper for carrying into effect and execution, the powers specified in this ordinance, provided such ordinances are not repugnant to the Constitution of the United States, or of this State.

Sec. 35. All ordinances passed by the City Council, shall, within one month after they shall have been passed, be published in some newspaper, printed in said City, or certified copies thereof, be posted up in three of the most public places in the City.

Sec. 36. All ordinances of the City may be proven by the seal of the corporation; and when printed or published in book or pamphlet form, purporting to be printed or published by the authority of the corporation, the same shall be received in evidence in all courts, or places, without further proof.

Sec. 37. The Mayor and Aldermen shall be conservators of the peace within the limits of the city and shall have all the powers of justices of the peace therein, both in civil and criminal cases, arising under the laws of the State. They shall, as justices of the peace within said city, perform the same duties, be governed by the same laws, give the same bonds and securities, as other justices of the peace, and be commissioned as justices of the peace, in and for said city, by the Governor.

Sec. 38. The Mayor and Aldermen shall have exclusive jurisdiction in all cases arising under the ordinances of the corporation and shall issue such process as may be necessary to carry said ordinances into execution and effect. Appeals may be had from any decision or judgment of said Mayor or Aldermen, arising under the ordinances of said city, to the Municipal Court, under such regulations as may be prescribed by ordinance; which court shall be composed of the Mayor as chief justice, and the Aldermen as associate justices; and from the final judgment of the Municipal

Court to the Probate Court of Great Salt Lake County, in the same manner as appeals are taken from the justices of the peace; provided that the parties litigant shall have a right to a trial by jury of twelve men in all cases before the Municipal Court. The Municipal Court shall have power to grant writs of habeas corpus, and try the same, in all cases arising under the ordinances of the City Council.

Sec. 39. The Municipal Court may sit on the first Monday of every month, and the City Council, at such times and places as may be prescribed by city ordinance, special meetings of which may at any time be called by the Mayor or any two Aldermen.

Sec. 40. All process issued by the Mayor, Aldermen, or Municipal Court shall be directed to the Marshal, and in the execution thereof, he shall be governed by the same laws as are or may be prescribed for the direction and compensation of constables in similar cases. The Marshal shall also perform such other duties as may be required of him under the ordinances of said City and shall be the principal ministerial officer.

Sec. 41. It shall be the duty of the Recorder to make and keep accurate records of all ordinances made by the City Council, and of all their proceedings in their corporate capacity, which record shall at all times be open to the inspection of the electors of said City, and shall perform all other duties as may be required of him by the ordinances of the City Council, and shall serve as clerk of the Municipal Court.

Sec. 42. When it shall be necessary to take private property for opening, widening, or altering any public street, lane, avenue, or alley, the corporation shall make a just compensation therefor; to the person whose property is so taken; and if the amount of such compensation cannot be agreed upon, the Mayor shall cause the same to be ascertained by a jury of six disinterested men, who shall be inhabitants of the City.

Sec. 43. All jurors empaneled to enquire into the amount of benefits or damages, that shall happen to the owners of property so proposed to be taken, shall first be sworn to that effect, and shall return to the Mayor their inquest in writing, signed by each juror.

Sec. 44. In case the Mayor shall, at any time, be guilty of a palpable omission of duty, or shall willfully or corruptly be guilty of oppression, malconduct, or partiality, in the discharge of the duties of his office, he shall be liable to indictment in the Probate Court of Great Salt Lake County, and on conviction he shall be liable to fine and imprisonment; and the court shall have power on the recommend of the jury, to add to the judgment of the court, that he be removed from office.

Sec. 45. The City Council shall have power to provide for the punishment of offenders and vagrants, by imprisonment in the county or city jail, or by compelling them to labor upon the streets, or other public works, until the same shall be fully paid; in all cases where such offenders or vagrants shall fail or refuse to pay the fine and forfeitures which may be recovered against them.

Sec. 46. The inhabitants of Great Salt Lake City shall, from and after the next ensuing two years, from the first Monday of April next, be exempt from working on any road or roads, beyond the limits of said City. But all taxes devoted to road purposes, shall, from and after said term of two years, be collected and expended by, and under the direction of, the supervisor of streets, within the limits of said City.

Sec. 47. The Mayor, Aldermen, and Councilors of said City shall, in the first instance, be appointed by the Governor and Legislature of said State of Deseret; and shall hold their office until superseded by the first election.

Approved January 9th, 1851.

The first municipal Council of Great Salt Lake City was composed of Jedediah M. Grant, Mayor; Nathaniel H. Felt, William Snow, Jesse P. Harmon and Nathaniel V. Jones, Aldermen; Vincent Shurtliff, Benjamin L. Clapp, Zera Pulsipher, William G. Perkins, Harrison Burgess, Jeter Clinton, John L. Dunyon and Samuel W. Richards, Councilors.

The City Council met pursuant to notice from the clerk of Great Salt Lake County. The members having been severally sworn in by the county clerk "to observe the Constitution of the United States and of this State," organized in due form.

The ordinance incorporating Great Salt Lake City was then read by the clerk of the county, when the Mayor informed the Council that it would be necessary to appoint a Recorder, Treasurer and Marshal of the city: whereupon Robert Campbell was appointed Recorder, and Elam Luddington Marshal and Assessor and Collector of Great Salt Lake City. Afterwards Leonard W. Hardy was appointed Captain of the City police.

At the afternoon's session committees were appointed to formulate governmental methods for the City. Enquiry was made relative to the disposition of taxes, when it was stated that the State taxes would be applied as formerly for State purposes, and that a city tax of one half of one per cent, should be levied for city purposes.

The Mayor brought forward the subject of dividing the City into municipal wards.

The county clerk then submitted a city plot to the council, and the following municipal wards were laid out from the map, and their proper boundaries designated: First Ward: bounded on the north by Third South Street; west, by East Temple Street; south, by southern limits; east, by eastern limits: Alderman, Jesse P. Harmon. Second Ward: east, by East Temple Street; south, by southern limits; west, by Jordan River; north, by South Temple Street: Alderman, N. V. Jones. Third Ward: east, by East Temple Street; south, by South Temple Street; west, by Jordan River; north, by northern limits: Alderman, Nathaniel H. Felt. Fourth Ward: east, by eastern limits; south, by Third South Street; west, by East Temple Street; north, by northern limits: Alderman, William Snow.

The Mayor instructed the Marshal and Collector to proceed to assessing property and levying taxes. The Council then adjourned.

In April the first municipal election for Great Salt Lake City was held, as provided for by the charter, and the following members were returned: Mayor; Jedediah M. Grant; Aldermen: Nathaniel Felt, William Snow, J. P. Harmon, N. V. Jones; Councilors: Lewis Robinson, Robert Pierce, Zera Pulsipher, Wm. G. Perkins, Jeter Clinton, Enoch Reese, Harrison Burges, Samuel W. Richards, Vincent Shurtliff.

In the meantime Congress had passed an act, approved on the 9th of September, 1850, organizing the Territory of Utah within the following limits: "Bounded on the west by the State of California; on the north by the Territory of Oregon; on the east by the summits of the Rocky Mountains; and on the south by the 37th parallel of north latitude: with the proviso that Congress should be at liberty, when it might be deemed "convenient and proper" to cut it up into two or more Territories, or to attach any portion of it to any other State or Territory. On the 28th of the same month, President Fillmore, "with the advice and consent of the Senate," appointed Brigham Young Governor of Utah; B. D.Harris, of Vermont, Secretary; Joseph Buffington, of Pennsylvania, Chief Justice; Perry E. Brocchus, of Alabama, and Zerubbabel Snow, of Ohio, Associate Justices; Seth M. Blair, of Utah, United States Attorney; and Joseph L. Heywood of Utah, United States Marshal; but Mr. Buffington declining the office of Chief Justice, Lemuel G. Brandebury was appointed in his stead.

The postal communication between Washington and Great Salt Lake City at this period being scarcely opened, an interval of six months passed before the news officially reached Utah. It came first unofficially by way of California, brought by a portion of that same company which explored the southern route to California in the fall of 1849. The returning company consisted of Major Hunt, of the Mormon Battalion, Mr. Henry E. Gibson and five others. To bear the important news, they started on Christmas day, and travelled with pack animals from Los Angeles to Great Salt Lake City. Major Hunt stopped at his home on the way; but Mr. Gibson posted on to Great Salt Lake City, where he arrived on the 27th of January, and presented to Governor Young published reports, in Eastern papers, of the passage of the Organic Act that created Utah a Territory. The news being certain and so many months having passed since the passage of the act and his own appointment, Governor Young at once took the oath of office, on the 3rd of February, 1851; and on the 26th of March he issued the following special message to the General Assembly of the State of Deseret: Gentlemen: —Whereas the Congress of the United States passed an Act. September 9th, 1850, and received the approval of the President to "establish a Territorial Government for Utah," and made appropriations for erecting public buildings for said Territory, etc.; the appointments under said law also having been made, official announcement of which has not as yet been received, but is shortly expected; sufficient intelligence, however, has been received to justify us in preparing for the adoption and organization of the new Government under said Act.

I have therefore thought proper to suggest to you, previous to your final adjournment, the propriety of making such arrangements, as in wisdom you may consider necessary, in view of the aforesaid Act of Congress, that as little inconvenience as possible may arise in the change of governmental affairs, and in relation to the organization of the Territorial Government for erecting public buildings for said territory, etc.

And now, upon the dissolving of this Legislature, permit me to add, the industry and unanimity which have ever characterized your efforts, and contributed so much to the pre-eminent success of this government, will, in all future time, be a source of gratification to all; and whatever may be the career and destiny of this young, but growing republic, we can ever carry with us the proud satisfaction of having erected, established, and maintained a peaceful, quiet, yet energetic government, under the benign auspices of which, unparalleled prosperity has showered her blessings upon every interest.

With sentiments of the highest esteem and gratitude to the Giver of all good for His kind blessings, I remain,

Respectfully yours, Brigham Young, Governor.

Great Salt Lake City, Utah Territory,

March 26th, 1851.

The Legislature of Deseret, in joint session, March 28th, 1851, unanimously passed the following Preamble and Resolutions, pertaining to the organization of a Territorial Government for Utah: —

PREAMBLE.

Whereas, in the winter and spring of the year of our Lord, 1849, the people of this territory did form and establish a Provisional State Government, until the United States Congress should otherwise provide by law for the government of this territory; and Whereas, it was under this authority and by virtue thereof, that this body have acted and legislated, for and in behalf of the people of said State, now Utah Territory; and Whereas the United States Congress has finally legislated in behalf of this territory, by passing an act for the organization of the Territory of Utah; making appropriations for public buildings, and extending the Constitution of the United States over said territory; and Whereas, previous to the first election under said law, the census has to be taken, and apportionments made, which will necessarily consume much time; and Whereas the public buildings for said territory are very much needed, and the United States Congress having made an appropriation of twenty thousand dollars towards defraying the expense thereof;—and in order to facilitate the speedy erection of said public buildings for the use of the territory, and further promote the mutual and easy organization of said territorial government;— Therefore, be it resolved by the General Assembly of the State of Deseret:

1. That we cheerfully and cordially accept of the legislation of Congress in the Act to establish a Territorial Government for Utah.

2. That we welcome the Constitution of the United States—the legacy of our fathers—over this territory.

3. That all officers under the Provisional State Government of Deseret, are hereby requested to furnish unto their successors in office every facility in their power, by returning and delivering unto them public documents, laws, ordinances, and dockets, that may or can be of any use or benefit to their said successors in office.

4. That Union Square, in Great Salt Lake City, be devoted for the use of public buildings of said Territory.

5. That Governor B. Young be our agent to make drafts upon the treasury of the United States for the amount appropriated for said buildings, and to take such other measures as he shall deem proper for their immediate erection.

6. That we appoint an architect to draft designs, and a committee of one, to superintend the erection of said buildings.

7. That Truman O. Angel, of said city, be said architect, and Daniel H. Wells, of said city, the committee; and that they proceed immediately to the designing and erection of said buildings.

8. That, whereas, the State House in Great Salt Lake City having been originally designed for a "Council House," and erected by and at the expense of the " Church of Jesus Christ of Latter-day Saints," for the purpose, as well as to accommodate the Provisional Government; that we now do relinquish unto said Church the aforesaid building, tendering unto them our thanks for the free use thereof during the past session.

9. That we fix upon Saturday, the 5th day of April next, for the adjustment and final dissolving of the General Assembly of the State of Deseret.

H. C. Kimball, President of the Council.
J. M. Grant, Speaker of the House.
"T. Bullock, Clerk"

Governor Young issued a proclamation on July 1st, 1851, calling the election for the first Monday in the following August, when it was accordingly held, August 4th, and the Territorial Legislature of Utah duly created by the people.

The first session of the Legislative Assembly of the Territory of Utah, was convened in pursuance of the proclamation of the Governor, on the 22nd day of September, A. D. 1851; and continued by adjournments to the 18th day of February, A. D. 1852. This was succeeded by a special session, called by proclamation of the Governor, and convened the day following, continuing until the 6th day of March, A. D. 1852.

Brigham Young, Governor.

MEMBERS OF THE COUNCIL:

Great Salt Lake County.—Willard Richards (President), Heber C. Kimball, Daniel H. Wells, Orson Spencer, Ezra T. Benson (resigned September 24th, 1851), Orson Pratt (elected November 15th, 1851), Jedediah M. Grant (resigned September 23rd, 1851), Edward Hunter (elected November 15th, 1851).

Davis County.—John S. Fullmer.

Weber County.—Lorin Farr, Charles R. Dana.

Utah County.—Alexander Williams, Aaron Johnson.

San Pete County.—Isaac Morley.

Iron County.—George A. Smith.

MEMBERS OF THE HOUSE OF REPRESENTATIVES:

Great Salt Lake County.—William W. Phelps (Speaker), Daniel Spencer, Albert P. Rockwood, Nathaniel H. Felt, David Fullmer, Edwin D. Woolley, Phinehas Richards, Joseph Young, Henry G. Sherwood, Wilford Woodruff, Benjamin F. Johnson, Hosea Stout, Willard Snow (resigned September 24th, 1851), John Brown (elected November 15, 1851).

Davis County.—Andrew J. Lamereaux, John Stoker, Gideon Brownell.

Weber County.—David B. Dille, James Brown, James G. Browning.

Utah County.—David Evans, William Miller, Levi W. Hancock.

San Pete County.—Charles Shumway.

Iron County.—Elisha H. Groves, George Brimhall (elected November 15. 1851)

Tooele County,—John Rowberry.

The first printed volume of laws of Utah Territory, had the following title page:

"Acts, Resolutions, and Memorials, passed by the First Annual, and Special Sessions, of the Legislative Assembly, of the Territory of Utah, begun and held at Great Salt Lake City, on the 22nd day of September, A. D. 1851. Also the Constitution of the United States, and the Act organizing the Territory of Utah. Published by Authority of the Legislative Assembly. G. S. L. City, U. T. 1852. Brigham H. Young, Printer."

To this was appended a certificate of authenticity, signed by "Willard Richards, Secretary pro tem., appointed by the Governor."

At its opening session the members passed the following

"Joint Resolution Legalizing the Laws of the Provisional Government of the State of Deseret: "Resolved, by the Legislative Assembly of the Territory of Utah:

That the laws heretofore passed by the Provisional Government of the State of Deseret, and which do not conflict with the Organic Act of said Territory be, and the same are hereby declared to be legal, and in full force and virtue, and shall so remain until superseded by the action of the Legislative Assembly of the Territory of Utah.

"Approved October 4, 1851."

This Resolution preserved the original charter of Great Salt Lake City.

The second Resolution, passed on the same day, transferred the political capital from Great Salt Lake City to "Pauvan Valley," where the City of Fillmore was afterwards founded, and Millard County organized and named in honor of the President of the United States, who had so cordially recognized the right of the people of Utah to local self-government and the choice of their own officers.

Severe strictures, however, were passed upon President Fillmore by a portion of the American press, for appointing Brigham Young Governor of Utah, which called forth the following correspondence between the President and Colonel Thomas L. Kane:

"Washington, July 4, 1851.

"My Dear Sir:—I have just cut the enclosed slip from the Buffalo Courier. It brings serious charges against Brigham Young, Governor of Utah, and falsely charges that I knew them to be true. You will recollect that I relied much upon you for the moral character and standing of Mr. Young. You knew him and had known him in Utah. You are a democrat, but I doubt not will truly state whether these charges against the moral character of Governor Young are true.

"Please return the article with your letter.

"Not recollecting your given name, I shall address this letter to you as the son of Judge Kane.

"I am, in great haste, truly yours,

Millard Fillmore.

"Mr. Kane, Philadelphia:"

"Philadelphia, July 11th, 1851.

"My Dear Sir:—I have no wish to evade the responsibility of having vouched for the character of Mr. Brigham Young of Utah, and his fitness for the station he now occupies. I reiterate without reserve, the statement of his excellent capacity, energy and integrity, which I made you prior to his appointment.

I am willing to say I volunteered to communicate to you the facts by which I was convinced of his patriotism, and devotion to the interests of the Union. I made no qualification when I assured you of his irreproachable moral character, because I was able to speak of this from my own intimate personal knowledge.

"If any show or shadow of evidence can be adduced in support of the charges of your anonymous assailant, the next mail from Utah shall bring you their complete and circumstantial refutation. Meanwhile I am ready to offer this assurance for publication in any form you care to indicate, and challenge contradiction from any respectable authority.

"I am, Sir, with high respect and esteem, your most obedient servant,

"Thomas L. Kane.

"The President."

Captain Stansbury, in his official report to the government, giving his views and testimony relative to Brigham Young, both as the leader of the Mormon people and the Governor of Utah, said: "Upon the personal character of the leader of this singular people, it may not, perhaps, be proper for me to comment in a communication like the present.

I may, nevertheless, be pardoned for saying, that to me, President Young appeared to be a man of clear, sound sense, fully alive to the responsibilities of the station he occupies, sincerely devoted to the good name of the people over whom he presides, sensitively jealous of the least attempt to under-value or misrepresent them, and indefatigable in devising ways and means for their moral, mental, and physical elevation. He appeared to possess the unlimited personal and official confidence of his people; while both he and his councilors, forming the Presidency of the Church, seem to have but one object in view, the prosperity and peace of the society over which they preside.

"Upon the action of the Executive in the appointment of the officers within the newly-created Territory, it does not become me to offer other than a very diffident opinion. Yet the opportunities of information to which allusion has already been made, may perhaps justify me in presenting the result of my own observations upon this subject. With all due deference, then, I feel constrained to say, that in my opinion the appointment of the President of the Mormon Church, and the head of the Mormon community, in preference to any other person, to the high office of Governor of the Territory, independent of its political bearings, with which I have nothing to do, was a measure dictated alike by justice and by sound policy. Intimately connected with them from their exodus from Illinois, this man has indeed been their Moses, leading them through the wilderness to a remote and unknown land, where they have since set up their tabernacle, and where they are now building their temple. Resolute in danger, firm and sagacious in council, prompt and energetic in emergency, and enthusiastically devoted to the honor of his people, he had won their unlimited confidence, esteem and veneration, and held an unrivaled place in their hearts. Upon the establishment of the provisional government, he had been unanimously chosen as their highest civil magistrate, and even before his appointment by the President, he combined in his own person the triple character of confidential adviser, temporal ruler, and prophet of God. Intimately acquainted with their character, capacities, wants, and weaknesses; identified now with their prosperity, as he had formerly shared to the full in their adversities and sorrows; honored, trusted,—the whole wealth of the community placed in his hands, for the advancement both of the spiritual and temporal interest of the infant settlement, he was, surely, of all others, the man best fitted to preside, under the auspices of the general government, over a colony of which he may justly be said to have been the founder. No other man could have so entirely secured the confidence of the people; and the selection by the Executive of the man of their choice, besides being highly gratifying to them, is recognized as an assurance that they shall hereafter receive at the hands of the general government that justice and consideration to which they are entitled. Their confident hope now is that, no longer fugitives and outlaws, but dwelling beneath the broad shadow of the national aegis, they will be subject no more to the violence and outrage which drove them to seek a secure habitation in this far distant wilderness.

"As to the imputations that have been made against the personal character of the Governor, I feel confident they are without foundation. Whatever opinion may be entertained of his pretensions to the character of an inspired prophet, or of his views and practice of polygamy, his personal reputation I believe to be above reproach. Certain it is that the most entire confidence is felt in his integrity, personal, official, and pecuniary, on the part of those to whom along and intimate association, and in the most trying emergencies, have afforded every possible opportunity of forming a just and accurate judgment of his true character.

"From all I saw and heard, I am firmly of the opinion that the appointment of any other man to the office of governor would have been regarded by the whole people, not only as a sanction, but as in some sort a renewal, on the part of the General Government, of that series of persecutions to which they have already been subjected, and would have operated to create distrust and suspicion in minds prepared to hail with joy the admission of the new Territory to the protection of the supreme government.'"

Very pertinent to the closing paragraph of this testimony of Captain Stansbury is the following passage of an epistle of the Presidency of the Mormon Church announcing to "the Saints abroad" the event of the organization of the Territory of Utah: "We anticipate no convulsive revolutionary feeling or movement, by the citizens of Deseret in the anticipated change of governmental affairs; but an easy and quiet transition from State to Territory, like weary travelers descending a hill nearby their way side home.

"As a people, we know how to appreciate, most sensibly, the hand of friendship which has been extended towards our infant State, by the General Government. Coming to this place as did the citizens of Deseret, without the means of subsistence, except the labor of their hands, in a wilderness country, surrounded by savages, whose inroads have given occasion for many tedious and expensive expeditions; the relief afforded by our mother land, through the medium of the approaching territorial organization, will be duly estimated; and from henceforth, we would fondly hope the most friendly feelings may be warmly cherished between the various States and Territories of this great nation, whose constitutional charter is not to be excelled."

CHAPTER X.

ARRIVAL OF THE FEDERAL JUDGES. FIRST APPEARANCE OF THE UNITED STATES OFFICIALS BEFORE THE CITIZENS AT A SPECIAL CONFERENCE. JUDGE BROCCHUS ASSAULTS THE COMMUNITY. PUBLIC INDIGNATION. CORRESPONDENCE BETWEEN JUDGE BROCCHUS AND GOVERNOR YOUNG. THE "RUNAWAY" JUDGES AND SECRETARY. DANIEL WEBSTER, SECRETARY OF STATE, SUSTAINS GOVERNOR YOUNG AND REMOVES THE OFFENDING OFFICIALS. FIRST UNITED STATES COURT. THE NEW FEDERAL OFFICERS. ARRIVAL OF COLONEL STEPTOE. RE-APPOINTMENT OF BRIGHAM YOUNG. JUDGE SHAVER FOUND DEAD. JUDGES DRUMMOND AND STILES.

In July, 1851, four of the Federal officers arrived in Great Salt Lake City and waited upon his Excellency Governor Young. They were Lemuel G. Brandebury, Chief Justice, and Perry E. Brocchus and Zerubbabel Snow, Associate Justices of the Supreme Court of the Territory, and B. D. Harris, the Secretary.

Governor Brigham Young, United States Attorney Seth M. Blair, and United States Marshal Joseph L. Heywood were all residents of Great Salt Lake City.' At this time there had not been any session of the Legislative Assembly of the Territory under the Organic Law. The newly arrived Federal officers enquired the reason why the legislature had not been organized, upon which they were informed that there were no mails from the States during the winter season, and that the official news of the passage of the Act did not reach this city till March, of that year. Soon after their arrival Governor Young issued a proclamation, as provided in Section 16 of the Organic Law, defining the judicial districts of the Territory, and assigning the judges to their respective districts. His other proclamation, calling for an election in August, brought the Legislature into existence, and the two branches of the Territorial Government were thus duly established.

Early in the following September, a special conference of the Mormon Church was held in Great Salt Lake City, one of the purposes of which was to send a block of Utah marble or granite as the Territorial contribution to the Washington Monument at the Capital. It was the first time that the Federal officers had found the opportunity to appear in a body before the assembled citizens, as the representatives of the United States, since the organization of the Territory. An excellent occasion surely was this, in the design of the leaders of the community, who called that special conference, and there can be no doubt that harmony and good will were sought to be encouraged between the Federal officers and the people.

Chief Justice Brandebury, Secretary Harris and Associate Justice Brocchus were honored with an invitation to sit on the platform with the leaders of the community. This association of Mormon and Gentile on the stand was very fitting on such an occasion, considering that Governor Brigham Young, Associate Justice Zerubbabel Snow, United States Attorney Seth M. Blair, and United States Marshall Joseph L. Heywood, though Mormons, were also their Federal colleagues.

But it seems that one of their number—Associate Justice Brocchus—had chosen this as a fitting time to correct and rebuke the community relative to their peculiar religious and social institutions. The following correspondence, which subsequently took place between Governor Young and Judge Brocchus is most important and relevant to the entire history of this city and territory, as it is the commencement of that long controversy which has existed between the people of Utah and the Federal Judges, and in which, in the latter period, Congress and the Governors of the Territory have also taken an active part:

B. YOUNG TO P. E. BROCCHUS.

"Great Salt Lake City, Sept. 19, 1851.

Dear Sir.—Ever wishing to promote the peace, love and harmony of the people, and to cultivate the spirit of charity and benevolence to all, and especially towards strangers, I propose, and respectfully invite your honor, to meet our public assembly at the Bowery, on Sunday morning next, at 10 a.m., and address the same people that you addressed on the 8th inst., at our General Conference; and if your honor shall then and there explain, satisfy, or apologize to the satisfaction of the ladies who heard your address on the 8th, so that those feelings of kindness that you so dearly prized in your address can be reciprocated by them, I shall esteem it a duty and a pleasure to make every apology and satisfaction for my observations which you as a gentleman can claim or desire at my hands.

"Should your honor please to accept of this kind and benevolent invitation, please answer by the bearer, that public notice may be given, and widely extended, that the house may be full. And believe me, sir, most sincerely and respectfully, your friend and servant, Brigham Young.

"Hon. I'. E. Brocchus, Asste. Justice'

"P. S.—Be assured that no gentleman will be permitted to make any reply to your address on that occasion. B. Y."

P. E. BROCCHUS TO GOVERNOR YOUNG.

"Great Salt Lake City, Sept. 19, 1851.

Dear Sir:—Your note of this date is before me. While I fully concur in, and cordially reciprocate, the sentiments expressed in the preface of your letter, I must be excused from the acceptance of your respectful invitation, to address a public assembly at the Bowery to-morrow morning.

"If, at the proper time, the privilege of explaining had been allowed me, I should, promptly and gladly, have relieved myself from any erroneous impressions that my auditors might have derived from the substance or tone of my remarks.

But, as that privilege was denied me, at the peril of having my hair pulled, or my throat cut, I must be permitted to decline appearing again in public on the subject.

"I will take occasion here to say, that my speech, in all its parts, was the result of deliberation and care—not proceeding from a heated imagination, or a maddened impulse, as seems to have been a general impression. I intended to say what I did say; but, in so doing, I did not design to offer indignity and insult to my audience.

"My sole design, in the branch of my remarks which seems to be the source of offence, was to vindicate the Government of the United States from those feelings of prejudice and that spirit of defection which seemed to pervade the public sentiment. That duty I attempted to perform in a manner faithful to the government of which I am a citizen, and to which I owe a patriotic allegiance, without unjustly causing a chord to vibrate painfully in the bosom of my hearers.

Such a duty, I trust, I shall ever be ready to discharge with the fidelity that belongs to a true American citizen—with firmness, with boldness, with dignity— always observing a due respect towards other parties, whether assailants or neutrals.

"It was not my intention to insult or offer disrespect to my audience; and "farthest possible was it from my design, to excite a painful or unpleasant emotion in the hearts of the ladies who honored me with their presence and their respectful attention on the occasion.

"In conclusion, I will remark that, at the time of the delivery of my speech, I did not conceive that it contained anything deserving the censure of a just-minded person. My subsequent reflections have fully confirmed me in that impression.

"I am, sir, very respectfully, your obedient servant, Perry E. Brocchus.

" To His Excellency Brigham Young."

BRIGHAM YOUNG TO P. E. BROCCHUS.

"Great Salt Lake City, Sept. 20, 1851.

Dear Sir:—The perusal of your note of the 19th inst. has been the source of some sober reflections in my mind, which I beg leave to communicate in the same freedom with which my soul has been inspired in the contemplation.

With a war of words on party politics, factions, religious schisms, current controversy of creeds, policy of clans, or State clipper cliques, I have nothing to do; but when the eternal principles of truth are falsified, and light is turned into darkness by mystification of language or a false delineation of facts, so that the just indignation of the true, virtuous, upright citizens of the commonwealth is aroused into vigilance for the dear-bought liberties of themselves and fathers, and that spirit of intolerance and persecution, which has driven this people time and time again from their peaceful homes, manifests itself in the flippancy of rhetoric for female insult and desecration, it is time that I forbear to hold my peace, lest the thundering anathemas of nations born and unborn should rest upon my head when the marrow of my bones shall be illy prepared to sustain the threatened blow.

"It has been said that a wise man foreseeth evil, and hideth himself. The evil of your course I foresee, and I shall hide myself—not by attempting to screen my conduct, or the conduct of this people from the gaze of an assembled universe, but by exposing some of your movements, designs, plans, and purposes, so that the injury which you have designed for this people may fall upon your own head, unless you shall choose to accept the proffered boon—the friendship which I extended to you yesterday—by inviting you to make satisfaction to the ladies of this valley, who felt themselves insulted and abused by your address on the 8th inst., and which you have declined to do in your note, to which this is a reply.

"In your note, you remark—'If, at the proper time, the privilege of explaining had been allowed me, I should promptly and gladly have relieved myself from any erroneous impressions that my auditors might have derived from the substance and tone of my remarks; but, as that privilege was denied me, at the peril of having my hair pulled, or my throat cu I must be permitted to decline appearing again in public on the subject.' "Sir, when was the 'proper time' to which you refer? Was it when you had exhausted the patience of your audience on the 8th, after having given a personal challenge to any who would accept? Was it a proper time to challenge for single combat, before a general assembly of the people, convened especially for religious worship?

"How could you then have 'promptly and gladly relieved yourself from any erroneous impression your auditors might have derived from the substance and tone of your remarks' when you knew not from what source your auditors derived those impressions? And was it your boasted privilege, your proper time to fire and 'fight your battles o'er again,' as quick as you had given a challenge, without waiting to see if anyone accepted it? If so, who would you have been likely to hit—ladies or gentlemen?

"It was true, sir, what I said, at the close of your speech, and I repeat it here, that my expressions may not be mistaken—I said in reference to your speech, 'Judge Brocchus is either profoundly ignorant—or willfully wicked—one of the two. There are several gentlemen who would be very glad to prove the statements that have been made about Judge Brocchus, and which he has attempted to repel; but I will hear nothing more on either side at this Conference.' And why did I say it? To quell the excitement which your remarks had caused in that audience; not to give or accept a challenge, but to prevent any one (of which there were many present wishing the opportunity,) and everyone from accepting your challenge, and thereby bringing down upon your head the indignation of an outraged people, in the midst of a Conference convened for religious instruction and business, and which, had your remarks continued, must have continued the excitement, until there would have been danger "of pulling of hair and cutting of throats," perhaps, on both sides, if parties had proved equal—for there are points in human actions and events, beyond which men and women cannot be controlled. Starvation will revolutionize any people, and lead them to acts of atrocity that human power cannot control; and will not a mother's feelings, in view of her murdered offspring, her bleeding husband, and her dying sire, by hands of monocratic violence, and especially when tantalized to the highest pitch by those who stand, or ought to stand, or sit, with dignity on the judgment seat, and impart justice alike to all?

"Sir, what confidence can this persecuted, murdered, outcast people have in your decisions from the Bench, after you have tantalized their feelings from the stand, by informing them there is yet hope in their case, if they will apply to Missouri and Illinois. I ask you, sir, if you did not know, when you were thus making your plea, that this people have plead with the authorities of those States, which are doomed to irretrievable ruin by their own acts, from their lowest magistrate to their highest judge, and from their halls of legislature to their governors, times, and times, and times again, until they, with force of arms, have driven us from their midst, and utterly refused the possibility of the cries of murdered innocence from reaching their polluted ears? I ask, sir, did you know this? If not, you were profoundly ignorant; you were possessed of ignorance not to be tolerated in children of ten years, in these United States. But, on the other hand, if you were in possession of the facts, you were willfully wicked in presuming to tantalize, and rouse in anger dire, those feelings of frail humanity on one hand, and offended justice on the other, which it is our object to bury in forgetfulness, and leave the issue to the decision of a just God.

"Your motive, action, or design, you wholly concealed, or you could never have gained a hearing on such an occasion.

"As presiding officer in said Conference, did I permit any man to accept your challenge? No, sir, you know I did not; and could you, as a gentleman, ask the privilege to defend your challenge before it was accepted? Don Quixote should not be named in such a farce. No, sir, out of mercy to you I prohibited any man from accepting your challenge. And until the challenge was accepted you had nothing to reply to. When, then, was the proper time you refer to, when you would have replied, and the privilege was denied you? No such time as you supposed, existed.

"And now, sir, as it appears from the whole face of the subject, that tomorrow might have been the first 'proper time' that might have given you the 'privilege of explaining,' and as this courtesy you have utterly refused, and thereby manifest a choice to leave an incensed public incensed still, against your (as they now view it) dishonorable course, I shall take the liberty of doing my duty, by adverting still further to your reply of yesterday. Charity would have induced me hope, at least, that your speech, in part, was prompted by the impulse of the moment; but I am forbid this pleasing reflection by your note, wherein you state that 'my speech, in all its parts, was the result of deliberation and care, proceeding from a heated imagination or a maddened impulse.' 'I intended to say what I did say.' Now, if you did actually ' intend to say what you did say,' it is pretty strong presumptive testimony that you were not ignorant, for if you had been ignorant, from whence arose your intentions? And if you were not » ignorant you must have been willfully wicked; and I cannot conceive of a more charitable construction to put upon your conduct on that occasion than to believe you designedly and deliberately planned a speech to excite the indignation of your hearers to an extent that would cause them to break the bonds of propriety by pulling your hair or cutting your throat, willing, no doubt, in the utmost of your benevolence to die a martyr's death, if you could only get occasion to raise the hue and cry, and re-murder a virtuous people, as Missouri and Illinois have so often done before you. Glorious philanthropy this; and corresponds most fully with the declaration which, it is reported, on pretty good authority, that Judge Brocchus made while on his journey to the valley, substantially as follows: "If the citizens of Utah do not send me as their delegate to Washington, by God, I'll use all my influence against them, and will crush them. I have the influence and the power to do it, and I will accomplish it if they do not make me their delegate.' "Now, sir, I will not stop to argue the point whether your honor made those observations that rumor says you did; but I will leave it to an intelligent world, or so much of that world as are acquainted with the facts in the case, to decide whether your conduct has not fully proved that you harbored these malicious feelings in your heart, when you deliberately planned a speech calculated in its nature to rouse this community to violence, and that, too, on a day consecrated to religious duties, your declaration to the contrary notwithstanding, that you 'did not design to offer indignity or insult.' When a man's words are set in direct opposition to his acts, which will men believe? His acts all the time.' Where, then, is the force of your denial?

"One item more from your note reads thus: 'My sole design in the branch of my remarks which seems to be the source of offence, was to vindicate the government of the United States from those feelings of prejudice, and that spirit of defection which seemed to pervade the public sentiment, &c." Let me inquire what 'public sentiment' you referred to? Was it the sentiments of the States at large? If so, your honor missed his aim, most widely, when he left the city of Washington to become the author of such remarks. You left home when you left Washington. If such 'prejudice and defection' as you represent, there existed, there you should have thundered your anathemas, and made the people feel your 'patriotic allegiance;' but, if ever you believed for a moment—if ever an idea entered your soul that the citizens of Utah, the people generally whom you addressed on the 8th, were possessed of a spirit of defection towards the general government, or that they harbored prejudices against it unjustly, so far you proved yourself 'profoundly ignorant' of the subject in which you were engaged, and of the views and feelings of the people whom you addressed; and this ignorance alone might have been sufficient to lead you into all the errors and fooleries you were guilty of on that occasion. But had you known your hearers, you would have known, and understood, and felt that you were addressing the most enlightened and patriotic assembly, and the one furthest removed from ' prejudice and defection" to the general government that you had ever seen, that you had ever addressed, or that would be possible for you or any other being to find on the face of the whole earth. Then, sir, how would it have been possible for you to have offered your hearers on that occasion a greater insult than you did? The most refined and delicate ladies were justly incensed to wrath against you for intimating that their husbands were ever capable of being guilty of such baseness as you represented, "prejudice and defection" towards a constitution which they firmly believe emanated from the heavens, and was given by a revelation, to lay the foundation of religious and political freedom in this age—a constitution and union which this people love as they do the gospel of salvation. And when you, sir, shall attempt to fasten the false and odious appellation of treason to this community, even ignorantly, as we had supposed you did it, you will find plenty, even among the ladies, to hurl the falsehood back to its dark origin, in tones of thunder; but if, as you say, you know, (or else how could the whole have been 'the result of deliberation and care,') the plea of ignorance ceases again to shield you, and you stand before the people in all the naked deformity of willful wickedness,' who can plead your excuse? Who, under such circumstances, can make an apology? I wonder not that you should excuse yourself from the attempt, 'or decline appearing again in public on the subject.' "Permit me sir, to subscribe myself, as ever,

Most respectfully, your servant, Brigham Young.

"Hon. P. E. Brocchus, Asste. Justice.'"

The speech of Judge Brocchus is not extant, nor is there to be found any report of that exciting conference, for it was before the existence of the Deseret News; but the subject and offence appear well defined in the correspondence itself, which is strikingly illustrated in the following paragraph from Governor Young's third letter: "Another important item in the course of your remarks, on the 8th instant, in connection with the expose of your own exalted virtue—you expressed a hope that the ladies you were addressing would 'become virtuous.' Let me ask you, most seriously, my dear sir, how could you hope thus? How could you hope that those dear creatures, some of whose acts of benevolence to the stranger drew tears from your eyes while you were yet speaking—how could you hope—what possible chance was there for you to hope—they would become virtuous? Had you ever proved them unvirtuous? If so, you could have but a faint hope of their reformation. But, if you had not proved them unvirtuous, what testimony had you of their lack of virtue? And if they were unvirtuous, how could they 'become virtuous'? Sir, your hope was of the most damning dye, and your very expression tended to convey the assertion that those ladies you then and there addressed were prostitutes—unvirtuous—to that extent you could only hope, but the probability was they were so far gone in wickedness you dare not believe they ever could become virtuous. And now, sir, let your own good sense, if you have a spark left, answer—could you, had you mustered all the force that hell could lend you—could you have committed a greater indignity and outrage on the feelings of the most virtuous and sensible assemblage of ladies that your eyes ever beheld? If you could, tell me how. If you could not, you are at liberty to remain silent. Shall such insults remain unrequited, unatoned for?"

Judge Brocchus made no written reply to the review of his conduct, but in person acknowledged that it was unanswerable and authorized the Governor to apologize for him to the community.

This very singular and suggestive correspondence, which itself is quite a chapter of the history of Great Salt Lake City, was published in the New York Herald, and was the commencement of a great sensation over Utah affairs.

Having rendered themselves unpopular and being neither able to arraign a whole community for their religious institutions, nor strong enough to set aside Governor Young and his three Federal colleagues, who stood with the people, Chief Justice Brandebury, Associate Justice Brocchus, and Secretary Harris resolved to leave the Territory. But previous to their leaving, they called a Supreme Court, which was held in Great Salt Lake City, though no law had been passed fixing the time and place for holding it. At this court, as an original suit, an injunction was granted. Associate Justice Snow dissented. He said, the bill, he thought, was a good case for the injunction, yet he opposed it on two grounds:

"1st.—There was not any law fixing the time and place of holding the Supreme Court.

"2nd.—The Supreme Court had not original jurisdiction, and the District Court had, which was provided for in the Governor's proclamation."

Chief Justice Brandebury and Associate Justice Brocchus left Great Salt Lake City together. Soon afterwards Secretary Harris followed their example, carrying away with him the $24,000 which had been appropriated by Congress for the per diem and mileage of the Legislature.

It would seem that these three Federal officers expected to be applauded by the public, and sustained by the Government, their assault being against polygamy, but they indiscreetly stated, in their communication to the Government, that "polygamy monopolized all the women, which made it very inconvenient for the Federal officers to reside there."

"Loose as people might suppose frontier life to be," observes Mr. Stenhouse in his Rocky Mountain Saints, "no one anticipated that representatives of the Federal Government would thus express themselves. That one sentence annihilated them. Over the signature of Jedediah M. Grant [the Mayor of Great Salt Lake City] a series of letters was addressed to the New York Herald, under the title, 'Truth for the Mormons,' in which the Federal officers were turned into ridicule and fiercely handled. The Herald gave the public only one letter; but Grant, nothing daunted, published the whole series in pamphlet form, and scattered them broadcast. The Grant letters, from their forcible and pungent style, attracted the attention of literary men as gems of wit and vigorous English. * * * In his moments of calm reflection, Judge Brocchus may have concluded that his zeal against polygamy had outstripped his prudence. The Government took that view of it, and quietly dropped the 'runaway judges and secretary.'"

This view presented in the felicitous vein of the New York Herald's special correspondent on Utah affairs, well describes the scandalized sense of the American public over the conduct of the " runaway judges and secretary;" but it does not sufficiently express the offended judgment of the United States Government over their conduct. Congress had only just created the new Territory. In doing this both the legislative and executive departments had a very clear pre-knowledge that the United States was extending its rule over a religious community, whose institutions, though peculiar, were founded on the strict examples of the Bible. The President and his advisers, among whom was that gigantic statesman, Daniel Webster, had with an intelligent intent appointed Brigham Young Governor, with three other of his co-religionists, to represent the Federal authority to their people; while to the minority of the Federal officers was given the controlling power of the judiciary, and the secretaryship, with the custody of the appropriations; all of this had been done to bring the Mormon colony harmoniously into the Union under its supremacy; yet ere they had held a single United States District Court in the new Territory, or its Legislature had assembled, or the Territorial government itself was fully set up, the Chief Justice, his Associate, and the Secretary deserted their posts. The General Government was reasonably incensed over such a case; Congress was scarcely less offended; and Daniel Webster, who was Secretary of State, peremptorily ordered the judges and secretary back to their deserted positions or to resign.

After the departure of these Federal officers from Great Salt Lake City, Governor Young appointed Willard Richards Secretary of the Territory pro tem.

This appointment, and several other informal acts, which had become necessary in the absence of the regular officials in a newly organized Territory, was duly reported to the Department of State. Daniel Webster sustained them, and the bills of Willard Richards, which were signed "Secretary pro tem, appointed by the Governor," were allowed by the Department, and paid.

The Utah Legislature also, finding the United States Judiciary in the Territory inoperative, passed the following act authorizing Associate Justice Zerubbabel Snow to hold the Courts in all the districts:

"AN ACT CONCERNING THE JUDICIARY, AND FOR JUDICIAL PURPOSES.

Sec. 1. "Be it enacted by the Governor and Legislative Assembly of the Territory of Utah, That the first Judicial District for said Territory, shall consist of, and embrace the following counties and districts of country, to wit:—Great Salt Lake. Davis, Weber, Tooele, and Utah Counties, and all districts of country lying east, north, and west of said counties in said Territory. The Second Judicial District shall consist of Millard and San Pete Counties, and all districts of country lying south of the south line of latitude of Utah County, and north of the south line of latitude of Millard County, within said Territory. And the Third Judicial District shall consist of Iron County, and all districts of country lying south of the south line of latitude of Millard County, in said Territory.

"Sec. 2. The Honorable Zerubbabel Snow, Associate Justice of the Supreme Court of the United States for the Territory of Utah, shall reside within the First Judicial District, and hold Courts in the following order, viz: on the first Monday in January and July at Great Salt Lake City; on the first Monday of April at Ogden City, in Weber County; and on the first Monday of October at Provo City, in Utah County, in each year: Provided, the said Zerubbabel Snow, Associate Justice, shall hold his first Court on the first Monday of October in the year eighteen hundred and fifty-one, at Great Salt Lake City, and omit said Court during said year at Provo, in Utah County.

"Sec. 3. The Honorable Zerubbabel Snow is hereby authorized and required to hold two Courts in the Second Judicial District in each year, to-wit: on the first Monday of November at Manti, in San Pete County; and on the first Monday in May at Fillmore, in Millard County.

"Sec. 4. The Honorable Zerubbabel Snow is further authorized and required to hold one Court for the Third Judicial District, viz: on the first Monday in June of each year, at Parowan City, in Iron County; and each session of said Court in its several districts shall be kept open at least one week, and may adjourn to any other place in each of said districts respectively: Provided, the business of said Court shall so require!

"Sec. 5. The foregoing acts are and shall be in force until a full Bench of the Supreme Court of the United States for the Territory of Utah, shall be supplied by the President and Senate of the United States, after which the said Zerubbabel Snow shall serve only in the First Judicial District.

"Approved October 4, 1851."

This officer afterwards, in a letter upon the first United States Courts held in Utah, thus states: "The Legislative Assembly met and, as the other Judges had returned to the States, a law was passed authorizing me to hold the courts in all the districts.

At my first court I examined the proceedings of the Governor in calling the Legislative Assembly, and held them legal, though somewhat informal. This was reported to the Department of State, the Honorable Daniel Webster being Secretary, who sustained Governor Young and myself. This was the commencement of my judicial services."

That first United States District Court was held in Great Salt Lake City.

At the first term Judge Snow made use of the United States Attorney and the United States Marshal, for Territorial business, there having been at that time no Territorial fee bill passed, which led to a correspondence between the Judge and the Honorable Elisha Whittlesey, Comptroller of the Treasury, the former asking a number of questions relative to the practice of the United States in defraying the expenses of the Territorial courts, which was answered by the latter that the United States simply defrayed the expenses of its own business in the courts. The answers closed thus: "Lastly, I will observe that if the clerk, marshal, or attorney render any service in suits to which the Territory is a party the officer must obtain his pay from the Territory or from the county in which such suit may be prosecuted. It should appear affirmatively on the face of every account that every item of it is a legal and just claim against the United States; and the details and dates should be stated, as required by my circular of December 5th, otherwise the marshal should not pay it."

This led to the passage of a Territorial fee bill.

In 1852 the law was passed giving jurisdiction to the Probate courts in civil and criminal cases and creating the offices of Attorney-General and Marshal for the Territory.

An historical note may here be made that the proceedings of the first United States District Court, held in Great Salt Lake City, were published in the Deseret News, No. 1, Vol. I, November 15th, 1851, Willard Richards, editor and proprietor.

Under the censure of the great statesman, Daniel Webster, and with ex-Vice-President Dallis and Colonel Kane using their potent influence against them, and also Stephen A Douglass, (to whom Kane in his letter to Fillmore personally refers as surety for Governor Young), Brandebury, Brocchus and Harris were forced to retire. They were succeeded by Chief Justice Reed, Associate Justice Shaver, and Secretary Ferris on August 31st, 1852.

On their arrival in Great Salt Lake City the new appointees received a cordial welcome from the Governor and citizens, which was reciprocated by the Chief Justice and his Associate, but Secretary Ferris approved the course of his predecessor and condemned the Mormons and their institutions. The new judges, however, turned the tide of public feeling for a while in favor of this community, by the speeches which they delivered, and the very friendly letters which they wrote on Utah affairs. Shortly after his arrival in Great Salt Lake City, Chief Justice Reed wrote as follows: "I waited on his Excellency, Governor Young, exhibited to him my commission, and by him was duly sworn and installed as Chief Justice of Utah. I was received by Governor Young with marked courtesy and respect. He has taken pains to make my residence here agreeable. The Governor, in manners and conversation, is a polished gentleman, very neat and tasty in dress, easy and pleasant in conversation, and I think, a man of decided talent and strong intellectual qualities, * * * I have heard him address the people once on the subject of man's free agency. He is a very excellent speaker. His gesture uncommonly graceful, articulation distinct, and speech pleasant. * * * The Governor is a first-rate business man. As civil Governor of the Territory and Superintendent of Indian Affairs, we would naturally suppose he had as much to do as one man could well attend to; but in addition to those employments, he is also President of the Church—a station which is no sinecure by any means. His private business is extensive; he owns several grist and saw mills, is extensively engaged in farming operations, all of which he superintends personally. I have made up my mind that no man has been more grossly misrepresented than Governor Young, and that he is a man who will reciprocate kindness and good intentions as heartily and as freely as anyone, but if abused, or crowded hard, I think he may be found exceedingly hard to handle."

But Secretary Ferris soon after published a book expressing sentiments and views, concerning Brigham Young and the Mormon community, the very antipodes of those uttered by his Federal associates. After a short residence in Great Salt Lake City Secretary Ferris retired and went to California; Chief Justice Reed returned to New York and died; he was succeeded by Chief Justice John F. Kinney, August 24th, 1853. Associate Justice Zerubbabel Snow occupied his full term and was succeeded by Associate Justice George P. Stiles, August 1st, 1854. Almon W. Babbitt succeeded Ferris as Secretary, and District Attorney Hollman succeeded Seth M. Blair. John M. Bernhisel was Delegate to Congress.

In 1854, Lieutenant-Colonel E. J. Steptoe, with his command, arrived in Great Salt Lake City, and the term of Governor Young's appointment expiring about this time, President Pierce tendered the office to Colonel Steptoe; but he was a gentleman, and a true republican, and he had too much wisdom withal to accept the honor, for he knew that Brigham was the choice of the people. The following document, expressive of the movement which he inspired, will be of interest at this point: "To His Excellency, Franklin Pierce, President of the United States: "Your petitioners would respectfully represent that, whereas Governor Brigham Young possesses the entire confidence of the people of this Territory without distinction of party or sect; and from personal acquaintance and social intercourse we find him to be a firm supporter of the constitution and laws of the United States, and a tried pillar of Republican institutions; and having repeatedly listened to his remarks, in private as well as in public assemblies, do know he is the warm friend and able supporter of constitutional liberty, the rumors published in the States notwithstanding; and having canvassed to our satisfaction his doings as Governor and Superintendent of Indian affairs, and also the disposition of the appropriation for public buildings for the Territory; we do most cordially and cheerfully represent that the same has been expended to the best interest of the nation; and whereas his re-appointment would subserve the Territorial interest better than the appointment of any other man, and would meet with the gratitude of the entire inhabitants of the Territory, and his removal would cause the deepest feeling of sorrow and regret; and it being our unqualified opinion, based upon the personal acquaintance which we have formed with Governor Young, and from our observation of the results of his influence and administration in this Territory, that he possesses in an eminent degree every qualification necessary for the discharge of his official duties, and unquestioned integrity and ability, and he is decidedly the most suitable person that can be selected for that office.

"We therefore take pleasure in recommending him to your favorable consideration, and do earnestly request his re-appointment as Governor, and Superintendent of Indian affairs for this Territory."

This document was signed by Colonel Steptoe and every other United States Army officer in the Territory, as well as by all of the Federal civil officials, and by every merchant and prominent citizen of Great Salt Lake City on the Gentile side. The petition was headed by Chief Justice Kinney, followed by Colonel Steptoe. Associate Justice Shaver's name was also to the document.

Not long after the signing of this document, which obtained from President Pierce the re-appointment of Governor Young, Judge Shaver, on the morning of the 29th of June, 1855, was found dead in his bed, in Great Salt Lake City.

The judge the previous night was apparently in good health, but he had long suffered terribly from a wound, the pain of which he relieved by the constant administration of opiates, and occasionally by stimulants; so that, though unexpected, the cause of his death required but little explanation. The citizens sincerely mourned the loss of Judge Shaver. He was buried by them with professional honors; his funeral sermon was preached by Jedediah M. Grant, the then Mayor of Great Salt Lake City, and his memory is embalmed in the history of the Mormon Church, as an upright judge and a friend of the community. Yet notwithstanding the friendly relations which had existed between the deceased judge and the citizens, his sudden death gave an opportunity for the circulation of a malicious story of his being poisoned, on account of some supposed difficulty with Governor Young.

W. W. Drummond succeeded the lamented Judge Shaver, September 12th, 1854; and Drummond and Associate Justice George P. Stiles were principally instrumental in working up the Buchanan Expedition, or the "Utah war" as it was popularly termed; but we must leave the Federal thread for a while and review events connected with the community, the growth and peopling of Great Salt Lake City, and the colonization of Utah in general, from about the time of the setting up of the Territorial government.

CHAPTER XI.

SOCIOLOGICAL EXPOSITION. SOURCES OF OUR POPULATION. EMIGRATION. POLYGAMY

For the completeness of the history a sociological exposition of the peopling of Utah should be here presented, with its ethnological elements and methods out of which society first grew in the isolation of these Rocky Mountains; nor should the causes be ignored which have brought so many tens of thousands of souls from Europe to this country, for the very purpose of organizing a new society and creating a State of the American nation.

In the history of Great Salt Lake City, the Mormon emigrations from Europe may be considered as the most relevant to its population; for, especially at the onset, this city grew out of. those emigrations. The American pioneers did no more, in the matter of population, than plant the germs of society in these valleys, nor could they possibly do more with so small a community as that which left Nauvoo in the exodus. A decade must have passed before there could have been any perceptible increase to the population by offspring, had not the emigrations from abroad yearly poured into these valleys, vitalizing a community almost exhausted by repeated exterminations. Thus replenished, by a new fusion from the dominant parent races, from which the pioneers had themselves descended, population was increased ten-fold within the first decade. Great Britain and Scandinavia gave the bulk of this population, by their tens of thousands of emigrants, and next by their prolific increase of offspring; but the American pioneers were the originators of that emigrational movement of the Mormon people from Europe to this country.

The following general epistle from the Twelve, dated at Winter Quarters, Omaha Nation, December 23rd, 1847, will be of interest in this connection:

"To the Saints in England, Scotland, Ireland, Wales, and adjacent islands and countries, we say, emigrate as speedily as possible to this vicinity, looking to and following the counsel of the Presidency at Liverpool: shipping to New Orleans, and from thence direct to Council Bluffs, which will save much expense.

Those who have but little means, and little or no labor, will soon exhaust that means if they remain where they are, therefore it is wisdom that they remove without delay; for here is land on which, by their labor, they can speedily better their condition for their further journey. And to all Saints in any country bordering upon the Atlantic, we would say. pursue the same course, come immediately and prepare to go west,—bringing with you all kinds of choice seeds, of grain, vegetables, fruit, shrubbery, trees, and vines—everything that will please the eye, gladden the heart, or cheer the soul of man, that grows upon the face of the whole earth; also the best stock of beast, bird, and fowl of every kind; also the best tools of every description, and machinery for spinning, or weaving, and dressing cotton, wool, flax, and silk, etc., etc., or models and descriptions of the same, by which they can construct them; and the same in relation to all kinds of farming utensils and husbandry, such as corn shelters, grain threshers and cleaners, smut machines, mills, and every implement and article within their knowledge that shall tend to promote the comfort, health, happiness, or prosperity of any people. So far as it can be consistently done, bring models and drafts, and let the machinery be built where it is used, which will save great expense in transportation, particularly in heavy machinery, and tools and implements generally."

And here must be noticed the covenant of the emigration. Previous to leaving Nauvoo President Young prompted the Mormons to enter into a solemn covenant in the temple, that they would not cease their exertions until every individual of them who desired and was unable to gather to the valley by his own means was brought to that place. No sooner were they located in the Rocky Mountains, than the Church prepared to fulfill this covenant, extending its application to the Saints in all the world. The subject was introduced at the October Conference, in 1849, by President Heber C. Kimball, and a unanimous vote was there and then taken to raise a fund for the fulfillment of the promise. A committee was appointed to raise money, and Bishop Edward Hunter sent to the frontiers to purchase wagons and cattle, to bring the poor Saints from Pottawatomie lands. About $5,000 were raised that season. The fund was designated "The Perpetual Emigration Fund," and the method of its application is well set forth in the following from a letter to Apostle Orson Hyde, who was at the time presiding at Winter Quarters:

Great Salt Lake City, October 16th, 1849.

President Orson Hyde:—Beloved brother, we write to you more particularly at this time, concerning the gathering, and the mission of our general agent for the Perpetual Emigration Fund for the coming year, Bishop Hunter, who will soon be with you, bearing the funds already raised in this place.

In the first place, this fund has been raised by voluntary donations, and is to be continued by the same process, and by so managing as to preserve the same and cause it to multiply.

* * * As early in the Spring as it will possibly do, on account of feed for cattle, Brother Hunter will gather all his company, organize them in the usual order, and preside over the camp, travelling with the same to this place, having previously procured the best teamsters possible, such as are accustomed to driving, and will be kind and attentive to their teams.

When the Saints thus helped arrive here, they will give their obligations to the Church to refund to the amount of what they have received, as soon as circumstances will permit; and labor will be furnished, to such as wish, on the public works, and good pay; and as fast as they can procure the necessaries of life, and a surplus, that surplus will be applied to liquidating their debt, and thereby increase the perpetual fund.

By this it will readily be discovered that the funds are to be appropriated in the form of a loan rather than a gift; and this will make the honest in heart rejoice, for they have to labor and not live on the charity of their friends, while the lazy idlers, if any such there be, will find fault and want every luxury furnished them for the journey, and in the end pay nothing. * * * "Brother Hunter will return all the funds to this place next season, when the most judicious course will be pursued to convert all the cattle and means into cash, that the same may be sent abroad as speedily as possible on another mission, together with all that we can raise besides to add to it; and we anticipate that the Saints at Pottawatomie and in the States will increase the fund by all possible means the coming winter, so that our agent may return with a large company.

"The few thousands we send out by our agent at this time is like a grain of mustard seed in the earth; we send it forth into the world, and among the Saints — a good soil—and we expect it will grow and flourish, and spread abroad in a few weeks: that it will cover England, cast its shadow on Europe, and in process of time compass the whole earth; that is to say, these funds are destined to increase until Israel is gathered from all nations, and the poor can sit under their own vine, and inhabit their own house, and worship God in Zion.

"We remain your brethren in the gospel,
Brigham Young,
Heiser C. Kimball,
Willard Richards."

A similar epistle was written to Orson Pratt, President of the British Mission, saying at the close: "Your office in Liverpool is the place of deposit for all funds received either for this or the tithing funds for all Europe, and you will not pay out only upon our order, and to such persons as we shall direct."

These instructions and general epistles are the more important in the emigrational history, as they are substantially the basis upon which all the emigrations and business thereof have been conducted from that time to the present.

Donations in England were made straightway. The first received was 2s. 6d. from Mark and Charlotte Shelley, of Woolwich, on the 19th of April, 1850.

The next was £1, from George P. Waugh, of Edinburgh, on the 19th of June; but in time the various emigration funds of the British Mission alone became immense.

The mode of conducting the emigrations from Europe was as patriarchal as the Church itself. As the emigration season came round, from every branch and conference the Saints would be gathered and taken to Liverpool by their elders, who saw them on shipboard in vessels chartered for their use. Not a moment were they left to the mercy of "runners" and shipping agents. When on board, the companies, which in some cases have amounted to more than a thousand souls per ship, were divided into wards, each ward being under its president or bishop, and his two councilors, and each company under its president and councilors; and besides these were the doctor, steward, and cook, with their assistants. During the passage, regular service was daily observed, —morning and evening prayers, preaching meetings and councils. Besides these were numerous entertainments, concerts, dances, etc., so that the trips across the Atlantic were like merry makings, enjoyed by the captains and their officers as much as by the Saints. Reaching America a similar system was pursued up the rivers, on the railroads, and across the plains until the Saints arrived in the valleys, when they were received, in the old time, by Brigham and "the authorities in Zion," and sent by Bishop Hunter to the various settlements where they were most needed to people the fast-growing cities of Utah.

It may be here suggestively noted that, at the date of this emigrational circular, there were not in all Utah more than eight thousand souls; while, at about the same date, in the British mission there were thirty thousand members of the Mormon Church. The resources of population the community possessed abroad; at home the resources were not sufficient to people Great Salt Lake City. The colonizing genius of this "peculiar people" was now greatly in demand; and it soon began to manifest itself in gigantic efforts to populate these valleys, and to found the hundreds of cities and settlements which Utah possesses to-day, and which the Mormon leaders designed to people when they laid off the City of the Great Salt Lake in 1847. This genius of colonization the community had manifested from the beginning, as was observed in the opening chapter, but it had hitherto operated chiefly abroad, in creating a population for the "building up of a Zion" on the American continent. True there had sailed a few ship loads of Mormons from the shores of Great Britain for Nauvoo; but only a few thousand of the British people were mixed in the actual society problem of the Mormons in America, until after the settlement in the valleys of the Rocky Mountains. Indeed, it had not been possible for the Mormon leaders to have emigrated a large European population to any of the eastern States, for the formation of a community. As it was, the American Mormon population was too large for both Missouri and Illinois. But in Utah, with a Territory given them by the United States, that they might people with their fruitful resources of population from foreign missions, the Mormons for the first time found full aim and scope for their colonizing genius and religion. From that moment Mormonism meant the peopling of Utah and the building of cities and settlements, and that too, chiefly at the onset, by yearly emigrations of converts from Europe; Great Salt Lake City being the initial society work.

Accordingly at the October Conference of 1849, held in this city, after establishing the Provisional Government of the State of Deseret, and the organization of the Perpetual Emigration Fund Company, "for the gathering of Israel from the nations," as set forth in the circular, the Presidency and Twelve Apostles set apart John Taylor, for France, to open a mission in that country; Lorenzo Snow for a similar purpose to Switzerland and Italy; Franklin D. Richards for England, to start the operations of the Perpetual Emigration Fund Company in Europe; while Apostle Erastus Snow was sent to open the "new dispensation" to the Scandinavian races.

In 1849, there was not a branch of the Mormon Church in all Scandinavia; to-day (1883) nearly one-third of the Mormon population of Utah, including their offspring, is Scandinavian. In 1849, the emigrations from Great Britain, direct for Utah commenced; from that date to their suspension for a while, in consequence of the Buchanan expedition, with which we shall presently deal, the Mormon emigrations to America embraced about thirty thousand souls, the majority of whom became compounded in the population of Utah; and still on, down to the present time, the British mission, though greatly depleted by her supplies has continued emigrations to this Territory. During this time a large accession to the population also poured in from every State of the Union, sustaining the native American element.

In connection with this subject of population, it is proper that polygamy should be considered, as a social factor of this Territory. Polygamy as a system of family relations was published in 1851. With it as a religious institution the historian has nothing to do, nor is it his province either to question or approve of the special legislation passed against it; but sociologically and ethnologically history has much to do with it in the peopling of Utah. The population of this Territory, in fact, has grown largely out of Mormon polygamy; and instead of deteriorating the race it has, in this case, replenished and improved it. Emigrations from Europe pouring in yearly, bringing a surplus of females from the robust and fruitful races of Scandinavia and

Great Britain, their marriage with a dominant pioneer element of the American stock has given stamina to families and population to the country. Indeed, Mormon polygamy has done nearly as much for the population of Utah as emigration itself; and with it, further than the statement of its facts, the writer has nought to do in a sociological exposition. Thus it will be seen that, having planted the germs of society in these valleys, the American portion of the population united in marriage with the emigrants—and the whole became one people in the colonization of Utah—one people very much in race as they were already in faith. The exposition will further show that though the population a quarter of a century ago was largely foreign, today it must naturally be chiefly native American, for while the emigrant parents have by thousands passed away by death, their children born in these valleys have grown up to manhood and womanhood, and are themselves parents to day.

CHAPTER XII.

PICTURES OF MORMON SOCIETY IN THE FOUNDING OF UTAH. LIFE AMONG THE SAINTS. THEIR SOCIAL AND RELIGIOUS PECULIARITIES AND CUSTOMS. ECSTASY OF THE GOLD-HUNTERS WHEN THEY CAME UPON "ZION." VIEWS BY STANSBURY, GUNNISON, AND NOTED ENGLISH TRAVELERS, OF THE MORMONS AND THEIR INSTITUTIONS. PETITION FOR A RAILROAD. GENERAL EVENTS.

It is thought that a few pictures of the early days of Utah, and of Mormon society in its primeval forms, may have a special interest to visitors of to-day, who go up to the New Jerusalem of the West in luxurious palace cars. They shall be the pictures which struck the fancy, or the judgment, of the intelligent "Gentile" who first came upon the peculiar people, just settled in the valleys of Utah, jet they described them in wonderment, much as they would have done had they come upon the strange habitation and inhabitants of another world. There is a graphic life-touch in some of those sketches—mere letters though they were—that the imagination of the best artist could not equal. They are realistic pictures of what was; romances of social life, so to speak, that were not dreams.

Here is a graphic sketch from the artistic pen of a gold digger, a correspondent of the New York Tribune, under date of July 8th, 1849: "The company of gold diggers which I have the honor to command, arrived here on the 3rd instant, and judge our feelings when, after some twelve hundred miles travel through an uncultivated desert, and the last one hundred miles of the distance through and among lofty mountains, and narrow and difficult ravines, we found ourselves suddenly, and almost unexpectedly, in a comparative paradise. * * * At first sight of all these signs of cultivation in the wilderness, we were transported with wonder and pleasure. Some wept, some gave three cheers, some laughed, and some ran and fairly danced for joy, while all felt inexpressibly happy to find themselves once more amid scenes which mark the progress of advancing civilization. We passed on amid scenes like these, expecting every moment to come to some commercial center, some business point in this great metropolis of the mountains, but we were disappointed. No hotel, sign post, cake and beer shop, barber pole, market house, grocery, provision, dry goods, or hardware store distinguished one part of the town from another; not even a bakery or a mechanic's sign was anywhere discernible.

"Here, then, was something new: an entire people reduced to a level, and all living by their labor—all cultivating the earth or following some branch 01 physical industry. At first I thought it was an experiment, an order of things established purposely to carry out the principles of 'socialism' or ' Mormonism.' In short, I thought it very much like Owenism personified. However, on inquiry, I found that a combination of seemingly unavoidable circumstances had produced this singular state of affairs. There were no hotels because there had been no travel; no barber shops, because everyone chose to shave himself, and no one had time to shave his neighbor; no stores, because they had no goods to sell, nor time to traffic; no center of business, because all were too busy to make a center.

"There was abundance of mechanic's shops, of dressmakers, milliners and tailors, etc.; but they needed no sign, nor had they time to paint or erect one, for they were crowded with business. Beside their several trades, all must cultivate the land or die, for the country was new, and no cultivation but their own within a thousand miles. Everyone had his own lot, and built on it; everyone cultivated it, and perhaps a small farm in the distance.

"And the strangest of all was, that this great city, extending over several square miles, had been erected, and every house and fence made, within nine or ten months of the time of our arrival; while at the same time, good bridges were erected over the principal streams, and the country settlements extended nearly one hundred miles up and down the valley.

"This Territory, State, or, as some term it, 'Mormon empire,' may justly be considered one of the greatest prodigies of our time, and, in comparison with its age, the most gigantic of all Republics in existence—being only in its second year since the first seed of cultivation was planted, or the first civilized habitation commenced. If these people were such thieves and robbers as their enemies represented them to be in the States, I must think they have greatly reformed in point of industry since coming to the mountains.

"I this day attended worship with them in the open air. Some thousands of well dressed, intelligent-looking people assembled; a number of them on foot, some in carriages, and some on horses. Many were neatly and even fashionably clad. The beauty and neatness of the ladies reminded me of some of our best congregations of New York. They had a choir of both sexes, who performed exceedingly well, accompanied by a band, playing well on almost every musical instrument of modern invention. Peals of the most sweet, sacred and solemn music filled the air; after which, a solemn prayer was offered by Mr. Grant (a Latter-day Saint), of Philadelphia. Then followed various business advertisements, read by the clerk. * * * After this, came a lengthy discourse by Mr. Brigham Young, President of the Society, partaking somewhat of politics, much of religion and philosophy, and a little on the subject of gold; showing the wealth, strength and glory of England, growing out of her coal mines, iron and industry, and the weakness, corruption and degradation of Spanish America, Spain, etc., growing out of their gold and silver, and idle habits.

"He further observed that the people here would petition to be organized into a Territory under the American Government, notwithstanding its abuses, and that, if granted, they would stand by the constitution and laws of the United States; while, at the same time, he denounced their corruption and abuses.

"' But,' said the speaker, 'we ask no odds of them, whether they grant our petition or not! We will never ask any odds of a nation that has driven us from our homes. If they grant us our rights, well; if not, well; they can do no more than they have done. They, and ourselves, and all men, are in the hands of the great God, who will govern all things for good; and all will be right, and work together for good to them that serve God.' "Such, in part, was the discourse to which we listened in the strongholds of the mountains. The Mormons are not dead, nor is their spirit broken. And, if I mistake not, there is a noble, daring, stern and democratic spirit swelling in their bosoms, which will people these mountains with a race of independent men, and influence the destiny of our country and the world for a hundred generations.

In their religion they seem charitable, devoted and sincere; in their politics, bold, daring and determined; in their domestic circle, quiet, affectionate and happy, while in industry, skill and intelligence they have few equals, and no superiors on earth.

"I had many strange feelings while contemplating this new civilization, growing up so suddenly in the wilderness. I almost wished I could awake from my golden dream and find it but a dream; while I pursued my domestic duties as quietly, as happily, and contentedly as this strange people."

"These Mormons," says Gunnison, "are certainly the most earnest religionists I have ever been among. It seems to be a constant self-sacrifice with them, which makes me believe that the masses of the people are honest and sincere.

"While professing a complete divorce of Church and State, their political career and administration is made subservient to the theocratical or religious element. They delight to call their system of government a 'theo-democracy', and that, in a civil capacity, they stand as the Israelites of old under Moses. For the rule of those not fully imbued with the spirit of obedience, and sojourners not of the faith, as well as for things purely temporal, tribunals of justice and law-making assemblies are at present rendered necessary.

"The influence of their nomenclature of 'brethren and sisters' is apparent in their actions and creates the bond of affection among those who are more frequently thrown together. It is impressed on infantile minds by the constant repetition and induces the feeling of family relationship. A little boy was asked the usual question, 'whose son are you?' and he very naively replied, 'I am Brother Pack's son;' a small circumstance, truly, but one that stamps the true mark of Mormon society. The welfare of the order becomes, therefore, paramount to individual interest; and the union of hearts causes the hands to unite in all that pertains to the glory of the State; and hence we see growing up and prospering the most enterprising people of the age—combining the advantages of communism, placed on the basis of religious duty and obedience to what they call the law of the gospel—transcending the notion of socialistic philosophers, that human regulations can improve and perfect society, irrespective of the revealed word of God.

"Right or wrong, in the development of the principle, and in its application, they have seized upon the most permanent element of the human mind in its social relations—not yielding fully to the doctrines of earnestness and universal intention, and making man his own regenerator, as the fountain head of truth, and passing thence into mysticism, pantheism and atheism, neither endeavoring to cure the ills of society by political notions of trade and commerce, nor by educating in the sentiment of honor, and by political inculcation of high thoughts and noble images, independent of being ' born of the water and of the spirit.' "Nor must we look upon all as ignorant and blindfolded, guided along the ditch of enthusiasm by self-deluded leaders. Indeed, almost every man is a priest, or eligible to the office, and ready armed for the controversial warfare.

His creed is his idol. And while among the best proselytes we class many that are least versed in literary attainments, still among them we find liberally educated men, and those who have been ministers in other denominations—in fact there seems to be as fair a sample of intelligence, moral probity, and good citizenship, as can be found in any nominal Christian community.

"Sincerity and simplicity of purpose mark the masses, which virtues have been amply proved by the sacrifices and suffering endured. And among the people, so submissive to counsel, are those who watch with eagle eye that first principles are adhered to and stand ready to proclaim apostacy in chief or laymen and scrutinizing all revelations to discover whether they are from the Lord, or given, through his permission, by Satan, to test the fidelity and watchfulness of the disciples of truth. Litigation is much discouraged, and it is specially thought improper for brother to go to law with brother, and that before unbelievers; so each bishop is a sort of county court judge between man and man, with an appeal to the whole 'bench,' and a final resort to Brigham, who does good practical justice without any embarrassment from statute or common law.

"This people are jealous of their rights and feel themselves entitled to enforce order by their own laws, and severely punish contempt of them. The administration of justice is of the most simple kind and based on the equity and the merits of the question, without reference to precedents and technicalities."

Another correspondent writing to a New York paper said: "It is now three years since the Mormons arrived in Salt Lake Valley, and their energy in laying out a city, building, fencing farms, raising crops, etc., is truly wonderful to behold, and is but another striking demonstration of the indefatigable enterprise, industry, and perseverance of the Anglo-Saxon race.

"The Mormons, take them as a body, I truly believe are a most industrious people, and, I confess, as intelligent as any I have met with when in the East or West. It is true they are a little fanatical about their religious views, which is not at all strange when compared with the majority of religious denominations in the East. But let no man be deceived in his estimation of the people who have settled here. Any people who have the courage to travel over plains, rivers and mountains, for twelve hundred miles, such, probably, as cannot be traveled over in any other part of the world, to settle in a region which scarcely ever received the tread of any but the wild savages and beasts who roam the wilderness, must be possessed of an indomitable energy that is but rarely met with." W. Kelly, in his "Excursions in California in the Early Days," says: "The houses are small, principally of adobes, built up only as temporary abodes, until the more urgent and. important matter of enclosure is attended to; but I never saw anything to surpass the ingenuity of arrangement with which they are fitted up, and the scrupulous cleanliness with which they are kept. There were tradesmen and artisans of all descriptions, but no regular stores or workshops, except forges. Still, from the shoeing of an ox to the mending of a watch, there was no difficulty experienced in getting it done as cheap and as well put out of hand as in any other city in America. Notwithstanding the oppressing temperature, they were all hard at work at their trades, and abroad in the fields, weeding, molding, and irrigating; and it certainly speaks volumes for their energy and industry, to see the quantity of land they have fenced in, and the breadth under cultivation, considering the very short time since they founded the settlement in 1847.

"After bathing, we dressed in our best attire, and prepared to attend the Mormon service, held for the present in the large space adjoining the intended Temple, which is only just above the foundations, but will be a structure of stupendous proportions, and, if finished according to the plan, of surpassing elegance. I went early and found a rostrum in front of which there were rows of stools and chairs for the townsfolks; those from the country, who arrived in great numbers, in light wagons, sitting on chairs, took up their stations in their vehicles in the background, after unharnessing the horses. There was a very large and moat respectable congregation; the ladies attired in rich and becoming costumes, each with parasol; and I hope I may say, without any imputation of profanity, a more bewitching assemblage of the sex it has rarely been my lot to look upon."

A still more important authority on Mormon society, in the early days of Utah, was Captain Stansbury. He says in his official report; "The founding, within the space of three years, of a large and flourishing community upon a spot so remote from the abodes of men, so completely shut out by natural barriers from the rest of the world, so entirely unconnected by water-courses with either of the oceans that wash the shores of this continent—a country offering no advantages of inland navigation or of foreign commerce, but, on the contrary, isolated by vast uninhabited deserts, and only to be reached by long, painful, and often hazardous journeys by land—presents an anomaly so very peculiar, that it deserves more than a passing notice. In this young and prosperous country of ours, where cities grow up in a day, and States spring up in a year, the successful planting of a colony, where the natural advantages have been such as to hold out the promise of adequate reward to the projectors, would have excited no surprise; but the success of an enterprise under circumstances so much at variance with all our preconceived ideas of its probability, may well be considered one of the most remarkable incidents of the present age.

Their admirable system of combining labor, while each has his own property, in lands and tenements, and the proceeds of his industry, the skill in dividing off the lands, and conducting the irrigating canals to supply the want of rain, which rarely falls between April and October; the cheerful manner in which everyone applies himself industriously, but not laboriously; the complete reign of good neighborhood and quiet house and fields, form themes for admiration to the stranger coming from the dark and sterile recesses of the mountain gorges into this flourishing valley; and he is struck with wonder at the immense results, produced in so short a time, by a handful of individuals.

"This is the result of the guidance of all those hands by one master mind; and we see a comfortable people residing where, it is not too much to say, the ordinary mode of subduing and settling our wild lands could never have been applied.

"Nothing can exceed the appearance of prosperity, peaceful harmony, and cheerful contentment that pervaded the whole community. Ever since the first year of privation, provisions have been abundant, and want of the necessaries and even comforts of life are unknown. A design was at one time entertained (more, I believe, as a prospective measure than anything else) to set apart a fund for the purpose of erecting a poor-house; but, after strict inquiry it was found that there were in the whole population but two persons who could be considered objects of public charity, and the plan was consequently abandoned.

This happy external state of universally diffused prosperity, is commented on by themselves as an evidence of the smiles of heaven, and of the special favor of the Deity; but I think it may be most clearly accounted for in the admirable discipline and ready obedience of a large body of industrious and intelligent men, and in the wise counsels of prudent and sagacious leaders, producing a oneness and concentration of action, the result of which has astonished even those by whom it has been effected. The happy consequences of this system of united and well-directed action, under one leading and controlling mind, is most prominently apparent in the erection of public buildings, opening of roads, the construction of bridges, and the preparation of the country for the speedy occupation of a large and rapidly growing population, shortly to be still further augmented by an immigration even now on its way, from almost every country in Europe.

"In their dealings with the crowds of immigrants that passed through their city, the Mormons were ever fair and upright, taking no advantage of the necessitous condition of many, if not most of them. They sold them such provisions as they could spare, at moderate prices, and such as they themselves paid in their dealings with each other. In the whole of our intercourse with them, which lasted rather more than a year, I cannot refer to a single instance of fraud or extortion to which any of the party was subjected; and I strongly incline to the opinion that the charges that have been preferred against them in this respect, arose from interested misrepresentation or erroneous information. I certainly never experienced anything like it in my own case, nor did I witness or hear of any instance of it in the case of others, while I resided among them. Too many that passed through their settlements were disposed to disregard their claim to the land they occupied, to ridicule the municipal regulations of their city, and to trespass wantonly upon their rights. Such offenders were promptly arrested by the authorities, made to pay a severe fine, and in some instances were imprisoned or made to labor on the public works; a punishment richly merited, and which would have been inflicted upon them in any civilized community. In short, these people presented the appearance of a quiet, orderly, industrious, and well-organized society, as much so as one would meet with in any city of the Union, having the rights of personal property as perfectly defined and as religiously respected as with ourselves; nothing being farther from their faith or practice than the spirit of communism, which has been most erroneously supposed to prevail among them. The main peculiarity of the people consists in their religious tenets, the form and extent of their church government, (which is a theocracy), and in the nature especially of their domestic relations."

Another early writer says: "The masses are sincere in their belief: if they are credulous, and have been deceived by their leaders, the sin, if any, rests on them. I firmly believe the people to be honest and imbued with true religious feelings; and when we take into consideration their general character previously, we cannot but believe in their sincerity. Nine-tenths of this vast population are the peasantry of Scotland, England and Wales, originally brought up with religious teachings at Protestant parish churches. They place implicit faith in their leaders, who, in a pecuniary point of view have fulfilled their promise; each and all of them are comfortably provided with land and tenements. At first they, of course, suffer privation, until they build their houses, and reap their crops, yet all their necessities in the meantime are provided for by the Church, and in a social point of view they are much happier than they could ever hope to have been at their native homes. From being tenants at the will of an imperious and exacting landlord, they suddenly became landholders in their own right, free men, living on free soil, under a free and enlightened government.

"Considering, again, how all efforts for the improvement of these advantages must necessarily be self-dependent in such a place, one cannot say they have been tardily developed. Indeed, to me, the manufactures, few as they were, and the products and settlements sprung up so extensively in so short a time, spoke not of a sensual but of a thrifty and industrious population, who, whatever may be their delusions in matters of belief, or the corrupting influence of their customs, at least determined to put their hands to the plow, and, looking forward, to work, out of hardship and adversity, a comfortable, if not an enviable, prosperity.

Observe Salt Lake City—not a San Francisco, certainly—but remember that eight years ago not a house stood here, nor a stick, nor a stone to build one of.

"The cheerful happy face, the self-sacrificed countenances, the cordial salutation of brother or sister on all occasions of address, the lively strains of music pouring forth from merry hearts in every domicile, as women and children sing their "Songs of Zion," while plying the domestic tasks, give an expression of a happy society in the vales of Deseret.

"They have determined to keep themselves distinct from the vices of civilization. During a residence of ten weeks in Great Salt Lake City, and my observations in all their various settlements, it is worthy of record that I never heard any obscene or improper language, never saw a man drunk, never had my attention called to to the exhibition of vice of any sort. There are no gambling houses, grog shops, or houses of ill-fame in all their settlements. They preach morality in their churches and from their stands, and, what is as strange as it is true, their people practice it, and religiously believe their salvation depends upon fulfilling the behests of the religion which they have adopted.

"A liquor law, enforced pretty strictly, compels sobriety, which virtue is, therefore, no subject for praise. Swearing, at least blasphemous swearing, in the public streets, is prohibited under pain of a five-dollar fine for each offense; the fine is scarcely ever imposed, but violation of the law is uncommon, and very rarely in public or private do you hear an oath. Theft, even in petty things, such as vegetables and fuel, is prevented, not by prosecution, but by the known rule, that if a man steals two or three times he is ordered to become honest or leave the country for good. Not that Mormons ever pretend that there are no bad men among them; nay, agreeable to their principles, they will tell you that a Mormon, if bad, will be worse than other men, because he sins against greater light and knowledge, and after receiving the Spirit of God. Confirmatory of this, I have met at Salt Lake with two or three very proper scoundrels; but, taking the people all around, I consider them as moral, industrious, fair-dealing and hospitable a set as one is apt to fall in with.

"In social parties and lively meetings the Mormons are pre-eminent, and their hospitality would be more readily extended to strangers had they suitable dwellings to invite them into. In their social gatherings and evening parties, patronized by the presence of the prophets and apostles, it is not unusual to open the ball with prayer, asking the blessing of God on their amusements, as well as upon any other engagement; and then will follow the most sprightly dancing, in which all join with hearty good will, from the highest dignitary to the humblest individual; and this exercise is to become part of the temple-worship, to ' praise God in song and dances.' "These private balls and soirees are frequently extended beyond the time of cock-crowing by the younger members, and the remains of the evening repast furnish the breakfast for the jovial guests.

"Toward the end of April, in 1854, about ten days previous to the departure of Governor Brigham Young, on his annual visit to the southern settlements of Utah, tickets of invitation to a grand ball were issued in his name. I had the honor to receive one of them.

"At the appointed hour I made my appearance, chaperoned by Governor Young, who gave me a general introduction. A larger collection of fairer and more beautiful women I never saw in one room. All of them were dressed in white muslin, some with pink and others with blue sashes. Flowers were the only ornaments in the hair. The utmost order and the strictest decorum prevailed. Polkas and waltzes were not danced; country dances, cotillions, quadrilles, etc., were permitted. At the invitation of Governor Young I opened the ball with one of his wives. The Governor, with a beautiful partner, stood vis-a-vis. An old-fashioned cotillion was danced with much grace by the ladies, and the Governor acquitted himself very well on the ' light fantastic toe.' After several rounds of dancing, a march was played by the band, and a procession was formed; I conducted my first partner to the supper room, where I partook of a fine entertainment at the Governor's table. There must have been at least two hundred ladies present, and about one hundred gentlemen. I returned to my quarters at twelve o'clock, most favorably impressed with the exhibition of public society among the Mormons."

In 1852 the people had a grand celebration of the Fourth of July. This was the first notable celebration of our national birthday by the Mormons since their arrival in the valley, though it was kept by the Pioneers on the way, both at Winter Quarters and as they approached the haven of their search. They had afterwards, in a manner, blended the idea and spirit of the Fourth with the Twenty-Fourth, which they esteem as the natal day of Utah. On the first celebration of the Twenty-Fourth, the Constitution of the United States was, as we have seen, presented to the Governor of the State of Deseret, and the Declaration of Independence read, but the honor of the year in 1852, was given to the Fourth of July.

At the first session of the Territorial Legislature, held in 1851-2, in Salt Lake City, memorials to Congress were adopted, praying for the construction of a national central railroad, and also a telegraph line from the Missouri River, via Salt Lake City to the Pacific. The following memorial was signed and approved by Governor Young, March 3rd, 1852: "To the Honorable the Senate and House of Representatives of the United States, in Congress assembled: "Your memorialists, the Governor and Legislative' Assembly of the Territory of Utah, respectfully pray your honorable body to provide for the establishment of a national central railroad from some eligible point on the Mississippi or Missouri River, to San Diego, San Francisco, Sacramento, or Astoria, or such other point on or near the Pacific Coast as the wisdom of your honorable body may dictate.

"Your memorialists respectfully state that the immense emigration to and from the Pacific requires the immediate attention, guardian care, and fostering assistance of the greatest and most liberal government on the earth. Your memorialists are of the opinion that not less than five thousand American citizens have perished on the different routes within the last three years, for the want of proper means of transportation. That an eligible route can be obtained, your memorialists have no doubt, being extensively acquainted with the country. We know that no obstruction exists between this point and San Diego, and that iron, coal, timber, stone, and other materials exist in various places on the route; and that the settlements of this Territory are so situated as to amply supply the builders of said road with material and provisions for a considerable portion of the route, and to carry on an extensive trade after the road is completed.

"Your memorialists are of opinion that the mineral resources of California and these mountains can never be fully developed to the benefit of the United States, without the construction of such a road; and upon its completion, the entire trade to China and the East Indies will pass through the heart of the Union, thereby giving to our citizens the almost entire control of the Asiatic and Pacific trade; pouring into the lap of the American States the millions that are now diverted through other commercial channels; and last, though not least, the road herein proposed would be a perpetual chain or iron band, which would effectually hold together our glorious Union with an imperishable identity of mutual interest; thereby consolidating our relations with foreign powers in times of peace, and our defense from foreign invasion, by the speedy transmission of troops and supplies in times of war.

"The earnest attention of Congress to this important subject is solicited by your memorialists, who, in duty bound, will ever pray."

On the 31st of January, 1854, there was another movement of the people for a Pacific Railroad. The citizens of Salt Lake and surrounding country, men and women, gathered en masse to make a grand demonstration in its favor.

As the Salt Lake Temple, when completed, will be one of the finest and most unique architectural piles in America, it will be proper for us to give a synopsis of the laying of the corner stones. We cull the following from the Deseret News: "Wednesday, April 6th, 1853, could not have dawned a more lovely day, or have been more satisfactory to Saints or Angels. The distant valleys sent forth their inhabitants, this valley swarmed forth its thousands, and a more glorious sight has not been seen for generations than at Great Salt Lake City this day.

"The Deseret national flag was unfurled to the breeze. The Nauvoo Brass Band, Captain Ballo's Band, and the Military Band enlivened the air with their sweetest strains. The Silver Greys made a venerable appearance, and the minute men, true to their duty, were at their posts at an early hour. The police, under the efficient management of Captain Hardy, were at their posts at the time appointed; and the countenances of the Saints were as glad and cheerful as though each had been favored with the visitation of an angel. * * * The procession then formed at the vestry door in the following order: "1st, Martial music. Colors. 2nd, Nauvoo Brass Band. Colors. 3rd, Ballo's Band. Colors. 4th, Captain Pettegrew with relief guards. Colors. 5th, Singers. 6th, First President and Counselors, and aged Patriarch. 7th, The Twelve Apostles, first Presidency of the Seventies, and President and Counselors of the Elders' Quorum. 8th, President of the High Priests' Quorum, and Counselors, in connection with the President of the Stake, and the High Council. 9th, Presiding Bishop, with his Council, and the Presidents of the lesser Priesthood, and their Council. 10th, Architects and workmen selected for the day, with banner, representing 'Zion's Workmen.' 11th, Captain Merrill, with relief guard, in uniform.

"The procession then marched through the line of guards to the southeast corner of the Temple ground, the singers taking their position in the center, the Nauvoo Brass Band on the east bank, Captain Ballo's Band on the west bank, and the Marshal Band on the mound southwest. Captains Pettegrew, Hardy, and Merrill, with their commands, occupying the front of the bank (which was sixteen feet deep,) and moving from corner to corner with the laying of the several stones, prevented an undue rush of the people, which might, by an excavation, have endangered the lives of many, when Presidents Young, Kimball, and Richards, with Patriarch John Smith, proceeded to lay the southeast cornerstone, and ascended the top thereof, when the choir sang; President Young delivered the chief oration, and Heber C. Kimball offered the consecration prayer.

"The procession again formed, and proceeded to the southwest corner, when the Presiding Bishop, Edward Hunter, his counsel, and the various Presidencies of the lesser Priesthood, with their associates, laid the southwest corner stone, when, from its top, Bishop Hunter delivered the oration, and Bishop Alfred Cordon offered the consecration prayer.

The procession again formed, and moved to the northwest corner stone, accompanied with martial music, when John Young, President of the High Priests' Quorum, with his Council, and the President of the Stake, with the High Council, proceeded to lay the stone. That being done they ascended the stone, and President John Young delivered the oration, and George B. Wallace offered the consecration prayer.

The procession again formed, and proceeded to the northeast corner stone, which was laid by the Twelve Apostles, the First Presidency of the Seventies, and the Presidency of the Elders' Quorum. The Apostles then ascended the stone, and Elder P. P. Pratt delivered the oration, and Orson Hyde offered the consecration prayer.

On the 31st of October, 1853, Governor Young received an express giving an account of the massacre on the 16th of that month, by Indians, of Captain John W. Gunnison and seven of his party, near the swamps of the Sevier River.

Captain Gunnison and twelve of his party had departed from the rest, and while at breakfast, a band of Indians, intending to destroy a Mormon village near at hand, came upon them and fired with rifles, and then used bows and arrows.

Shots were returned by the Gunnison party, but they were overpowered, and only four escaped. Gunnison had twenty arrows shot into his body, and, when found, had one of his arms off. The notes of the survey, which had been nearly completed, instruments, and the animals, were taken by the Indians. Governor Young immediately sent aid to Captain Morris, to release him from his critical position in the midst of the Indians, and endeavor to obtain the lost property.

In his message to the Legislature that year, the Governor said: "In the military department of the Territory there is but little change from last year's report, except an increase of about seven hundred names to the muster rolls. In the southern settlements a great portion of the troops have been kept in almost constant service in order to preserve the inhabitants and their property from Indian aggressions. * * * "During the late troubles, twelve of our citizens have been killed at different times, and many wounded; and seven of the exploring party, including the lamented Captain Gunnison, have been killed on the Sevier."

CHAPTER XIV.

CARSON COLONY. THE GREAT FAMINE IN UTAH THE HAND-CART COMPANIES. CONSTITUTIONAL CONVENTION. DEATH OF J. M. GRANT. MAYOR OF GREAT SALT LAKE CITY. BIOGRAPHICAL SKETCH.

In 1854-5, the Mormon colonists pushed forward to the western frontier of the Territory and settled a large portion of the country now known as Nevada. This mission was given to about seventy families, who were directed, to go to Carson Valley under the supervision of Orson Hyde, President of the Apostles.

Soon afterwards the Legislature of Utah organized the whole of that district under the name of Carson County, appointing at the same time Orson Hyde as probate judge. Hon. Enoch Reese was its representative. Governor Young, in his message to the Legislature, in the winter of 1855-6, said: "In accordance with a law passed by the Assembly in 1854-5, the Hon. Orson Hyde repaired to Carson County, accompanied by the Hon. Judge Stiles and Marshal Heywood, and, in connection with authorized persons from California, approximately established the boundary line between this Territory and that State in the region of Carson Valley, and fully organized the county."

The first house in Genoa was built by Col. John Reese, of Great Salt Lake City, in 1850. It was called Reese's Station. A few persons—namely, Orson Hyde, Chester Loveland, Christopher Merkley, Seth Dustin, George Hancock, Reuben Perkins, Jesse Perkins, and William Hutchings—colonized that country in 1855, but in the spring of 1856, an organized colony of about seventy families went, among were Christopher Layton, William Jennings, William Nixon, Joseph R. Walker (in the employ of Nixon), Peregrine Sessions (the founder of Sessions' settlement), Albert Dewey, farmer Cherry from Bountiful, William Kay (founder of Kaysward), George Nebeker, and a number of others who would rank as first class men in the formation of a new colony.

In the winter of 1855-6, the Legislature was removed from Great Salt Lake to Fillmore, which had been designated as the capital in former sessions.

There was a famine in Utah in 1856. The crops of the two previous years had failed, and in some of the settlements the winters had been very severe, and the cattle ranging in the valleys died in great numbers. The best provided families throughout the winter of 1855-6 had to ration themselves to the smallest amount of breadstuffs per day in order to subsist until the following harvest. The condition of the poor was appalling; and nothing but the semi-patriarchal character of the community preserved thousands from perishing.

The following letter from Heber C. Kimball to his son in England, gives a graphic picture of the famine of 1856: "Great Salt Lake City, February 29, 1856.

To my dear son William, and to all whom it may concern.—My family, with yours, are all in good health and spirits. I have been under the necessity of rationing ray family, and also yours, to two-thirds of a pound of bread stuff per day each; as the last week is up to day, we shall commence on half-a-pound each. This I am under the necessity of doing. Brother Brigham told me to-day that he had put his family on half-a-pound each, for there is scarcely any grain in the country, and there are thousands that have none at all scarcely. We do this for the purpose of feeding hundreds that have none.

"My family, at this time, consists of about one hundred souls, and I suppose that I feed about as many as one hundred besides. My mill has not brought me in, for the last seven months, over one bushel of toll per day, in consequence of the dry weather, and the water being frozen up—which would not pay my miller. When this drouth came on, I had about seven hundred bushels of wheat, and it is now reduced to about one hundred and twenty-five bushels, and I have only about twenty-five bushels of corn, which will not provide for my own family until harvest. Heber has been to the mill to-day, and has brought down some unbolted flour, and we shall be under the necessity of eating the bran along with the flour and shall think ourselves doing well with half-a-pound a day at that.

Martin Wood stated to him that he had ground thirty bushels yesterday, but last night was a very cold night, which will check the water again, as the weather has not modified a great deal. Although the sun shines pleasantly through the day, the nights are still quite cold. You must remember that I did not raise one spoonful of wheat last year, and I have not received any from any other source than the mill. Brother James planted some late corn from which we obtained about forty bushels, and rather poor at that. We have some meat and, perhaps about seventy bushels of potatoes, also a very few beets and carrots; so you can judge whether or not we can get through until harvest without digging roots; still we are altogether better off than the most of the people in these valleys of the mountains. There are several wards in this city who have not over two weeks' provisions on hand.

"I went into the tithing office with Brother Hill, and examined it from top to bottom, and, taking all the wheat, corn, buckwheat and oats, there were not to exceed five hundred bushels, which is all the Public Works have or expect to have, and the works are pretty much abandoned, the men having been all turned off, except about fifteen who are at work on Brother Brigham's house, and making seed drills for grain, as we shall be obliged to put in our grain by drilling, on account of the scarcity, which probably will not take over one-third of the grain it would to sow broadcast.

"We shall not probably do anything on the Public Works until another harvest. The mechanics of every class have all been counseled to abandon their pursuits and go to raising grain. This we are literally compelled to do, out of necessity. Moreover, there is not a settlement in the Territory, but is in the same fix that we are. Some settlements can go two months, some three, some can, probably, at the rate of half-a-pound per day, till harvest. Hon. A. W. Babbitt, even, went to Brother Hyde's provision store the other day, and begged to get twenty or twenty-five pounds of flour, but could not. This I was told by William Price, who is the salesman of the store. Money will not buy flour or meal, only at a few places, and but very little at that. I can assure you that I am harassed constantly; I sell none for money, but let it go where people are truly destitute. Dollars and Cents do not count now, in these times, for they are the tightest that I have ever seen in the Territory of Utah. You and your brethren can judge a little by this. As one of the old 'prophets said, anciently, 'As with the people, so with the priest,' we all take it together."

This second famine was likened to the famine of Egypt. For months some families knew not the taste of bread. Settlements usually noted for good crops were so destitute that they sent teams several hundred miles to other settlements to get bran and shorts, and even that supply was considered a great luxury. The community had also to feed the thousands of emigrants who arrived that year in a starved condition in the handcart companies. The famine was the great subject of the discourses of the Tabernacle; and, much to the credit of Governor Young and other leading men of substance, it is to be observed that they urged all the community to share with each other, and faithfully set the example themselves. So much were the people appalled with the prospect of famine at some future period, by the experience of this year, that for nearly twenty years thereafter they every season stored surplus wheat to be prepared when famine should come again. It took the railroad to dissipate this terror of famine from the people's mind.

It was also the year of the handcart emigration, in which several hundred perished in the snows and for lack of food. The story of the terrible sufferings of the poor emigrants and of the victims whose graves daily marked the journey can never be fully told, and it is too harrowing to the feelings of the people, even to-day, to render the effort desirable for the historian's pen. It is a page of history in the peopling of Utah which the people would fain have forgotten; but it is due to Brigham Young and the noble conduct of the entire community to record something of the rescue of those companies. The following passages are culled from Mr. John Chislett's very graphic chapters on the handcart emigration: "We traveled on in misery and sorrow day after day. Sometimes we made a pretty good distance, but at other times we were only able to make a few miles' progress. Finally we were overtaken by a snow-storm which the shrill wind blew furiously about us. The snow fell several inches deep as we traveled along, but we dared not stop, for we had a sixteen-mile journey to make, and short of it we could not get wood and water.

"As we were resting for a short time at noon a light wagon was driven into our camp from the west. Its occupants were Joseph A. Young and Stephen Taylor. They informed us that a train of supplies was on the way, and we might expect to meet it in a day or two. More welcome messengers never came from the courts of glory than these two young men were to us. They lost no time after encouraging us all they could to press forward but sped on further east to convey their glad news to Edward Martin and the fifth hand-cart company who left Florence about two weeks after us, and who it was feared were even worse off than we were. As they went from our view, many a hearty 'God bless you' followed them."

"Joseph A.," as the Prophet's eldest son is familiarly termed, was the last of the returning missionaries to leave the emigrant camp on the banks of the Platte River. Though ignorant of the apprehension that he felt for their welfare, and the presentiments he had of the inevitable suffering that awaited them, many of the emigrants clung to him with more than ordinary affection and detained him till the warning of approaching night urged him to follow his companions.

When he bade them good-by, he could scarcely say more than "You shall see me again soon." All speed was made by him and his companions, and immediately on arrival in Salt Lake City he reported to his father how far the emigrants were yet behind.

Brigham comprehended their situation in a moment. Though his son had been absent two years from his home, he ordered him instantly to make ready to return to the assistance of the emigrants and gave him authority to take all the provisions, clothing, and vehicles that he could find on the way and press them forward to the rescue. Brigham Young on that occasion earned the good opinions of foes as well as friends. Mr. Chislett continues: "The storm which we encountered, our brethren from the Valley also met and, not knowing that we were so utterly destitute, they encamped to await fine weather. But when Captain Willie found them and explained our real condition, they at once hitched up their teams and made all speed to come to our rescue. On the evening of the third day after Captain Willie's departure, just as the sun was sinking beautifully behind the distant hills, on an eminence immediately west of our camp several covered wagons, each drawn by four horses, were seen coming towards us. The news ran through the camp like wild-fire, and all who were able to leave their beds turned out en masse to see them. A few minutes brought them sufficiently near to reveal our faithful captain slightly in advance of the train. Shouts of joy rent the air; strong men wept till tears ran freely down their furrowed and sun-burnt cheeks, and little children partook of the joy which some of them hardly understood, and fairly danced around with gladness. Restraint was set aside in the general rejoicing, and as the brethren entered our camp the sisters fell upon them and deluged them with kisses. The brethren were so overcome that they could not for some time utter a word, but in choking silence repressed all demonstration of those emotions that evidently mastered them. Soon, however, feeling was somewhat abated, and such a shaking of hands, such words of welcome, and such invocation of God's blessing have seldom been witnessed.

"I was installed as regular commissary to the camp. The brethren turned over to me flour, potatoes, onions, and a limited supply of warm clothing for both sexes, besides quilts, blankets, buffalo robes, woolen socks, etc. I first distributed the necessary provisions, and after supper divided the clothing, bedding, etc., where it was most needed. That evening, for the first time in quite a period, the songs of Zion were to be heard in the camp, and peals of laughter issued from the little knots of people as they chatted around the fires. The change seemed almost miraculous, so sudden was it from grave to gay, from sorrow to gladness, from mourning to rejoicing. With the cravings of hunger satisfied, and with hearts filled with gratitude to God and our good brethren, we all united in prayer, and then retired to rest.

"Among the brethren who came to our succor were Elders W. H. Kimball and G. D. Grant. They had remained but a few days in the Valley before starting back to meet us. May God ever bless them for their generous, unselfish kindness and their manly fortitude! They felt that they had, in a great measure, contributed to our sad position; but how nobly, how faithfully, how bravely they worked to bring us safely to the Valley—to the Zion of our hopes!

"After getting over the Pass we soon experienced the influence of a warmer climate, and for a few days we made good progress. We constantly met teams from the Valley, with all necessary provisions. Most of these went on to Martin's company, but enough remained with us for our actual wants. At Fort Bridger we found a great many teams that had come to our help. The noble fellows who came to our assistance invariably received us joyfully and did all in their power to alleviate our sufferings. May they never need similar relief!

"After arriving in the Valley, I found that President Young, on learning from the brethren who passed us on the road of the lateness of our leaving the frontier, set to work at once to send us relief. It was the October Conference when they arrived with the news. Brigham at once suspended all conference business and declared that nothing further should be done until every available team was started out to meet us. He set the example by sending several of his best mule teams, laden with provisions. Heber Kimball did the same, and hundreds of others followed their noble example.

People who had come from distant parts of the Territory to attend conference, volunteered to go out to meet us, and went at once. The people who had no teams gave freely of provisions, bedding, etc.—all doing their best to help us.

"We arrived in Salt Lake City on the 9th of November, but Martin's company did not arrive until about the 1st of December. They numbered near six hundred on starting and lost over one-fourth of their number by death. The storm which overtook us while making the sixteen-mile-drive on Sweetwater, reached them at North Platte. There they settled down to await help or die, being unable to go any farther. Their camp-ground became indeed a veritable grave-yard before they left it, and their dead lie even now scattered along from that point to Salt Lake. They were longer without food than we were, and being more exposed to the severe weather, their mortality was, of course, greater in proportion.

"Our tale is their tale partly told; the same causes operated in both cases, and the same effects followed.

"Immediately that the condition of the suffering emigrants was known in Salt Lake City, the most fervent prayers for their deliverance were offered up.

There, and throughout the Territory, the same was done as soon as the news reached the people. Prayers in the Tabernacle, in the school-house, in the family circle, and in the private prayer circles of the priesthood, were constantly offered up to the Almighty, begging Him to avert the storm from us. Such intercessions were invariably made on behalf of Martin's company, at all the meetings which I attended after my arrival.

"But it was the stout hearts and strong hands of the noble fellows who came to our relief, the good teams, the flour, beef, potatoes, the warm clothing and bedding, and not prayers nor prophecies, that saved us from death."

In March, 1856, a constitutional convention was held at Great Salt Lake City, and a constitution drafted, the preamble of which stated that the last census showed a sufficient population to justify the people to petition Congress for a State government. The State was named Deseret.

At the close of the year 1856, Great Salt Lake City met a sad bereavement in the death of its first mayor, to whose distinguished memory is dedicated the following brief biographical sketch: Jedediah Morgan Grant, first mayor of Great Salt Lake City, was the son of Joshua and Thalia Grant, and was born in Windsor, Broome County, New York, February 21, 1816. We have been unable to procure definite intelligence of his childhood and education, but the foundation for mental pursuits and the love of books and study was evidently laid at that early period of life, before he appeared as a candidate for baptism in the Church of Jesus Christ of Latter-day Saints.

He was baptized by Elder John F. Boynton, afterwards one of the Apostles, on the 21st of March, 1833. In the spring of the following year, when he was eighteen years of age, he accompanied "Zion's Camp" in the wonderful march to Missouri, "and in the fatigues, privations, trying scenes and arduous labors endured by that handful of valiant men, exhibited a goodly portion, for one so young, of that integrity, zeal, and unwavering effort and constancy in behalf of the cause of truth, that invariably characterized his life." The experience the young men of this expedition obtained, on this memorable journey, was such as few ever passed through in life.

He was among the first who left Nauvoo in the exodus of 1846, crossing the river in February, and with the body of the Saints turning his back upon the tyrannical oppression of mobs and treacherous friends to seek an asylum of peace in the fastnesses of the mountains of the great West.

He went east from Winter Quarters in the winter of 1846-7, on a short mission, during which he purchased the materials for making a flag, which tor several years floated over " the land of the free and the homes of the blest" in this city and was familiarly known as "the mammoth flag." After transacting important business in the interests of the exodus, he returned in June, 1847 to the Missouri River, and was appointed Captain of the Third Hundred of the emigrating Saints, which he successfully led to the Salt Lake Valley, arriving in the following October. A year after, with characteristic energy and promptness, he went out beyond Fort Bridger with several men and teams to relieve President Willard Richards and accompany and assist them in.

May 26, 1849, he was elected Brigadier General of the first brigade of the Nauvoo Legion, and October 23rd, 1852, was promoted to the Major Generalship of the First Division, which military office he held unto his death. He was an efficient officer, valiant, energetic and just. In the difficulties with the Indians he manifested considerable skill, and always was regarded as eminently jealous of the rights of the red men as well as of the safety of the whites.

In the fall of 1849, Elder Grant went to the States on business, together with about forty missionaries, who elected him captain of the company. Among the number were President John Taylor, Apostles Erastus Snow, Lorenzo Snow, F. D. Richards, Bishop Hunter, Colonel Reese, Curtis E. Bolton, and several other prominent elders.

Great Salt Lake City was incorporated on the 19th of January, 1851, and at the first election held under the charter, on the first Monday of the next April, Jedediah M. Grant was elected mayor, which office he magnified in an eminent degree and held uninterruptedly, by the unanimous vote of the people, until his death. During the period of his administration, the first ordinances for the government, safety and general welfare of the people were enacted, forming the basis of the municipal regulations under which the city has grown and prospered to the present time.

The following introduction to his famous series of letters, published in the New York Herald, upon the "runaway judges," will fitly represent Mayor Grant's bold, independent style, and thoroughly honest character: "Sir: I will thank you to print, as soon as you can, the substance of this letter. Considered only as news, it ought to be worth your while. There is great curiosity everywhere to hear about the Mormons, and eagerness to know all the evil that can be spoken of them. Announce you that I am a Mormon Elder, just arrived from Utah—mayor, in fact, of Salt Lake City, where my wife and family are still living—a preacher, brigadier of horse, and president of the quorum of Seventies, and the like; and not one subscriber that waded over shoe tops through the slime of details you gave of the play-actor's divorce trial lately, will not be greedy to read all I have to say about the filthier accusations that have been brought against me and my friends and brethren. This is what I have to count upon, thank falsehood. And if you publish my letter entire, I will ask for no editorial help from you. I am no writer; but, with the help of the Power of Light, I am not afraid of what you can say against us. So long as I walk by the rule of my Master, you walk by the rude working of your fancies.

" I must say I have had my doubts about writing out upon these matters; my doing so not being approved by our Delegate in Congress, Dr. Bernhisel. The Doctor is one of our gentlemen at home, a real gentleman, and would not say a rough word or do a rough thing to hurt the feelings or knock off the spectacles of any man for the world. But I am no gentleman, in his sense at least; and have had slights enough put upon me, personally, since I came eastward, to entitle me to any amount of stand-up self-defense. Dr. Bernhisel's official course in this matter, I suppose I am bound to accept; for I have understood that he had the advice of experienced men, who said to him: 'Take up the report of the three officers criminating your constituents, when it comes from the State Department into the House; ask for a special committee with power to send for persons and papers, and put the false witnesses on oath; but don't stoop to wrangle upon your religion, morals and political opinions with Mr. Webster or the Congressmen at large, whom the country considers to have enough to do to take care of their own.' "This is all very well, and very high and mighty and dignified, certainly; but while the grass grows, the cow starves; while Congress is taking its months to do the work of a day, the verdict of the public goes against us, as the law-word is, by default, and we stand substantially convicted of anything and everything that any and every kind of blackguard can make up a lie about. And now I hear that the charges are not to be pushed; two of the officers want to come back to us as friends—they are to be virtually abandoned after doing us all the harm they can. What Mr. Webster thinks, we care a little; what is the opinion of most members of Congress, you can hardly believe, in your part of the world, how very little, but Public Opinion, that power we respect as well as recognize; and, therefore, I am now determined, on my own responsibility, to write myself, and blurt out all the truth I can. I may not be discreet, but I will be honest."

J. M. Grant was chosen Speaker of the House of Representatives in the Legislative Assembly of the Territory in 1852, and at three subsequent sessions, filling that office with dignity and honor, to the fullest satisfaction of the members over whom he presided. As a legislator he was quick and talented and brought to the law-making department a high practical sense of justice and right, which qualified him to propose and render valuable aid in framing wholesome laws for the political and domestic welfare of the community.

On December 1st, 1856, Mayor Grant breathed his last, and his spirit went joyfully to mingle with those of his friends, family and brethren that had gone before. He was forty years of age when he died but had spent those years to such advantage in laboring for the welfare of his fellow-men that he was mourned by thousands and left in their memories a name that will be forever cherished as a symbol of virtue, integrity and honor. The editor of the Deseret News in closing his obituary, says: "Brother Grant needs no eulogy, and least of all such an one as our language could portray, for his whole life was one of noble and diligent action upon the side of truth, of high-toned and correct example to all who desire to be saved in the Kingdom of our God. As a citizen, as a friend, a son, a husband, a father, and above all as a Saint, and in every station and circumstance of life, whether military, civil, or religious, he everywhere, and at all times, shed forth the steady and brilliant light of lofty and correct example, and died as he lived and counseled, with his 'armor on and burnished.' Though all Saints deeply feel his departure," yet they can fully realize that it redounds to his and our 'infinite gain.'"

CHAPTER XV.

EXPOSITION OF THE CAUSES AND CIRCUMSTANCES OF THE UTAH WAR. GENERAL SCOTT S CIRCULAR AND INSTRUCTIONS TO THE ARMY. MAGRAW'S LETTER TO THE PRESIDENT. DRUMMONDS CHARGES. THE REPUBLICAN PARTY ASSOCIATES UTAH WITH THE SOUTH. THE " IRREPRESSIBLE CONFLICT." FREMONT AND DOUGLAS.

The subject of the Utah Expedition occupies nearly the entire history of Salt Lake City, and of Utah in general, from the year 1857 to 1861, when Camp Floyd was evacuated. On the part of the U. S. Government the extraordinary record commenced with the issuing of the following

CIRCULAR.

To the Adjutant General, Quartermaster General, Commissary General, Surgeon General, Paymaster General, and Chief of Ordnance.

Headquarters of the Army, May 28, 1857.

Orders having been dispatched in haste for the assemblage of a body of troops at Fort Leavenworth, to march thence to Utah as soon as assembled, the general-in-chief, in concert with the War Department, issues the following instructions, to be executed by the chiefs of the respective staff departments, in connection with his general orders of this date:

1. The force—2nd dragoons, 5th infantry, 10th infantry and Phelps' battery of the 4th artillery—to be provided with transportation and supplies, will be estimated at not less than 2,500 men.

2. The Adjutant General will, in concert with the chiefs of the respective departments, issue the necessary orders for assigning to this force a full complement of disbursing and medical officers, an officer of ordnance and an Assistant Adjutant General, if the latter be required. He will relieve Captains Phelps' 4th artillery and Hawes' 2nd dragoons from special duty and order them to join their companies. He will also give the necessary orders for the movement of any available officers, whose services may be desired by the Quartermaster General or Commissary General in making purchases. Lieutenant Col. Taylor and Brevet Major Waggaman will be ordered to exchange stations. All available recruits are to be assigned to the above-named regiments up to the time of departure.

3. About 2,000 head of beef cattle must be procured and driven to Utah. Six months' supply of bacon (for two days in a week) must be sent—desiccated vegetables in sufficient quantity to guard the health of the troops for the coming winter.

4. Arrangements will be made for the concentration and temporary halt of the 5th infantry at Jefferson Barracks. The squadron of dragoons at Fort Randall taking their horse equipments with them will leave their horses at that post, and a remount must be provided for them at Fort Leavenworth. Also, horses must be sent out to the squadron at Fort Kearney, and the whole regiment, as also Phelps' battery, brought to the highest point of efficiency.

Besides the necessary trains and supplies, the quartermaster's department will procure for the expedition 250 tents of Sibley's pattern, to provide for the case that the troops shall not be able to hut themselves the ensuing winter. Storage tents are needed for the like reason. Stoves enough to provide, at least, for the sick, must accompany the tents.

5. The Surgeon General will cause the necessary medical supplies to be provided, and requisition made for the means of transporting them with the expedition.

6. The chief of ordnance will take measures immediately to put in position for the use of this force, three travelling forges and a full supply of ammunition, and will make requisition for the necessary transportation of the same.

WINFIELD SCOTT.

The command of the Expedition was at first given to Brigadier General W. S. Harney but was afterwards transferred to Col. Albert Sidney Johnston. It is due to the Government to accompany this circular with the letter of instructions to General Harney, explanatory of its views and designs concerning Utah and her people: Headquarters of the Army, New York, June 29, 1857.

Sir: The letter which I addressed to you in the name of the general-in-chief, on the 28th ultimo, his circular to the chiefs of staff departments same date; his general order No. 8, current series, and another now in press, have indicated your assignment to the command of an expedition to Utah Territory, and the preparatory measures to be taken.

The general-in-chief desires me to add in his name the following instructions, prepared in concert with the War Department, and sanctioned by its authority, whenever required.

The community and, in part, the civil government of Utah Territory are in a state of substantial rebellion against the laws and authority of the United States A new civil governor is about to be designated, and to be charged with the establishment and maintenance of law and order. Your able and energetic aid, with that of the troops to be placed under your command, is relied upon to insure the success of his mission.

The principles by which you should be guided have been already indicated in a somewhat similar case and are here substantially repeated.

If the governor of the Territory, finding the ordinary course of judicial proceedings of the power vested in the United States' Marshals and other proper officers inadequate for the preservation of the public peace and the due execution of the laws, should make requisition upon you for a military force to aid him as *posse comilatus* in the performance of that official duty, you are hereby directed to employ for that purpose the whole or such part of your command as may be required; or should the governor, the judges, or marshals of the Territory find it necessary directly to summon a part of your troops, to aid either in the performance of his duties, you will take care that the summons be promptly obeyed.

And in no case will you, your officers or men, attack anybody of citizens whatever, except on such requisition or summons, or in sheer self-defense.

In executing this delicate function of the military power of the United States the civil responsibility will be upon the governor, the judges and marshals of the Territory. While you are not to be, and cannot be subjected to the orders, strictly speaking, of the governor, you will be responsible for a jealous; harmonious and thorough co-operation with him, or frequent and full consultation, and will conform your action to his requests and views in all cases where your military judgment and prudence do not forbid, nor compel you to modify, in execution, the movements he may suggest. No doubt is entertained that your conduct will fully meet the moral and professional responsibilities of your trust; and justify the high confidence already reposed in you by the government.

The lateness of the season, the dispersed condition of the troops and the smallness of the numbers available, have seemed to present elements of difficulty, if not hazard in this expedition. But it is believed that these may be compensated by unusual care in its outfit, and great prudence in its conduct. All disposable recruits have been reserved for it.

So well is the nature of this service appreciated, and so deeply are the honor and the interest of the United States involved in its success, that I am authorized to say that the government will hesitate at no expense requisite to complete the efficiency of your little army, and to insure health and comfort to it, as far as attainable. Hence, in addition to liberal orders for its supply heretofore given —and it is known that ample measures, with every confidence of success, have been dictated by chiefs of staff departments here—a large discretion will be made over to you in the general orders for the movement. The employment of spies, guides, interpreters or laborers may be made to any reasonable extent you may think desirable. The prudence expected of you requires that you should anticipate resistance, general, organized and formidable, at the threshold, and shape your movements as if they were certain, keeping the troops well massed and in hand when approaching expected resistance. Your army will be equipped, for a time, at least, as a self-sustaining machine. Detachments will, therefore, not be lightly hazarded, and you are warned not to be betrayed into premature security or over confidence.

A small but sufficient force must however, move separately from the main column, guarding the beef cattle and such other supplies as you may think would too much encumber the march of the main body. The cattle may require to be marched more slowly than the troops, so as to arrive in Salt Lake Valley in good condition, or they may not survive the inclemency and scanty sustenance of the winter. This detachment, though afterwards to become the rear guard, may, it is hoped, be put in route before the main body, to gain as much time as possible before the latter passes it.

The general-in-chief suggests that feeble animals, of draught and cavalry, should be left ten or twelve days behind the main column, at Fort Laramie, to recruit and follow.

It should be a primary object on arriving in the valley, if the condition of things permits, to procure not only fuel, but materials for hutting the troops.

Should it be too late for the latter purpose or should such employment of the troops be unsafe or impracticable, the tents (of Sibley's pattern) furnished will, it is hoped, afford a sufficient shelter.

It is not doubted that a surplus of provisions and forage, beyond the wants of the resident population, will be found in the valley of Utah; and that the inhabitants, if assured by energy and justice, will be ready to sell them to the troops. Hence no instructions are given you for the extreme event of the troops being in absolute need of such supplies and their being withheld by the inhabitants. The necessities of such an occasion would furnish the law for your guidance.

Besides the stated reports required by regulations, special reports will be expected from you, at the headquarters of the army, as opportunity may offer. The general-in-chief desires to express his best wishes, official and personal, for your complete success and added reputation.

"I have the honor to be, sir, very respectfully, your obedient servant,
GEORGE W. LAY,
Lieutenant Colonel
Aide-de-Camp.
Brevet Brigadier General W. S. Harney, Commanding &c.,
Fort Leavenworth, K. T.

P. S.—The general-in-chief (in my letter of the 26th instant) has already conveyed to you a suggestion—not an order, nor even a recommendation—that it might be well to send forward in advance a part of your horse to Fort Laramie, there to halt and be recruited in strength, by rest and grain, before the main body comes up.

Respectfully, G. W. L., Li. Col., Aide-de-Camp.

Though the foregoing document shows no desire on the part of the Government to destroy those colonies of Mormons which were fast spreading over this western country, yet upon its face it bears remarkable evidence that the Buchanan expedition was projected without a sufficient knowledge of the real condition of Utah at that precise period, or of the feelings of her people towards the parent Government, whether loyal or disloyal. Take for instance the passage of instructions from the general-in-chief relative to supplies: "It is not doubted that a surplus of provisions and forage, beyond the wants of the resident population will be found in the Valley of Utah," etc.

The great military capacity and experience of General Scott, to say nothing of his humane character, would be sufficient evidence in the history that, when these instructions were given, he knew absolutely nothing of the real condition of the people of Utah during the year preceding; for that was the very year of the great famine in Utah, described in the foregoing chapter, which was likened to the famine in Egypt. There were thousands of people in Utah who had been hungry an entire year when those instructions were penned, and multitudes of little children in her valleys who had so often cried themselves to sleep and forgotten the gnawings of. hunger, till, sleeping or waking, hunger became as second nature to them; nor were there sufficient supplies in all the valleys of Utah to satisfy that hunger till the harvest of 1857, three months later than the date of General Scott's circular. Yet that general was about to quarter an army in or near Salt Lake City, with the full assurance that there were, at the lime of the issuance of his orders, abundant supplies in the "Valley of Utah" " beyond the wants of the resident population" to feed his army. In view of this famine how suggestive of the ignorance of the Government concerning the condition of Utah, and the loyalty or disloyalty of her people, is the addendum of the commander-in-chief to General Harney: "Hence no instructions are given you for the extreme event of the troops being in absolute need of such supplies and their being withheld by the inhabitants. The necessities of such an occasion would furnish the law for your guidance." Had an army been ordered to Utah before the harvest of 1857, for the very purpose to literally devour the country and destroy the Mormon community root and branch by famine, rather than by the sword, the order, though inhuman, would not have been so inconsistent as General Scott's instructions with his undoubted humane intentions.

The only justification indeed of the Buchanan administration for sending the expedition, which all America soon confessed was the most humiliating blunder to be found in the whole history of the nation, was just in the fact that the Government knew scarcely anything of Utah affairs; and the simple explanation of this ignorance is that for six months preceding the inception of the expedition there had been no postal communication between Utah and the Eastern States. The mails had failed; Utah had been shut out from the rest of the world by an early and extraordinarily severe winter; the handcart companies of Mormon emigrants came nearly perishing on the plains, buried in the snows; the entire Territory had risen to the rescue; the leaders had been absorbed in saving the community from perishing in the valleys in consequence of the famine, and their companies on the plains from a disaster which, but for the rescue, would have been as frightful to those emigrants as the retreat of Napoleon's army from Moscow, and withal the devoted people, whose homes were even then threatened with invasion, and their social and religions organization with utter dissolution were oblivious of the war cloud gathering over their heads. Meantime, a few Government officials, principal among whom were Judge Drummond and the very mail contractor who had failed to carry the mails, had betrayed the Government into the commission of a series of blunders, which soon provoked a general public condemnation and the investigation of Congress. The New York Herald, at the time, stated:

"Some of our cotemporaries have been publishing long letters dated from Utah and containing heart-rending accounts of the sufferings inflicted on poor helpless women, by the brutality of the Mormon leaders. It is perhaps as well that the public should know that these letters are made up on this side of the Mississippi, and we have no doubt do more credit to the imagination than to the memory of their writers. No journal has a correspondent in Utah at the present time. It reflects some credit on the ingenuity of our cotemporaries to have bethought themselves of getting up an excitement about Utah just as Kansas died out.

"Of the facts of the case in Utah, it is very difficult to form a reliable judgment, simply because our most reliable authorities, such as Judge Drummond, now in Washington, are tainted with a suspicion of interested motives. * * "There is no authority in the Constitution to justify an interference by Congress or the Federal Government with such an institution as polygamy in a Territory. It is as clearly without the pale of Congressional or executive regulation as slavery; if Congress may not pass a law to govern the one, it may not pass a law to govern the other; if the President cannot interfere to drive slavery out of Kansas; neither can he assume to drive polygamy out of Utah. Marriage, a civil contract, is essentially subject to the control of local, municipal, or civil laws; the Federal Government has nothing to do with it, and Congress can make no laws defining its nature, altering its effect, or prescribing penalties for breaches of its obligations committed by people residing within a Territory of the United States.

"Those, therefore, who assumed that Mr. Buchanan was going to carry fire and sword among the Mormons because they were polygamists, and to put down polygamy by force of arms, gave the President very little credit for judgment or knowledge of the instrument under which he holds his powers."

The passage of the general-in-chiefs instructions relative to "a surplus of provisions and forage," in a land of famine, is not more remarkable in the history than the information given to General Harney, as the reason and justification for the invading expedition which he was to command: "The community and, in part, the civil government of Utah Territory are in a state of substantial rebellion against the laws and authority of the United States. A new civil governor is about to be designated, and to be charged with the establishment and maintenance of law and order. Your able and energetic aid, with that of the troops to be placed under your command, is relied to issue the success of his mission."

Read a century hence, isolated from the well-connected history of Utah, whose every fact and circumstance now can be verified, the circular and letter of instructions, representing the views of the Administration, would be received as an established record that the people of Utah had made public demonstrations of rebellion; that Brigham Young was in actual usurpation, and that defiant word had been sent by the citizens that they would not receive any Governor other than of their own choice; nor would even this view be sufficient coupled with the following passage indicating that Utah was in actual attitude of war at that moment against the United States: "The prudence expected of you requires that you should anticipate resistance, general, organized and formidable, at the threshold, and shape your movements as if they were certain, keeping the troops well massed and in hand when approaching expected resistance. * * * You are warned not to be betrayed into premature security or over confidence."

Nothing, however, up to this date, had occurred to warrant the conclusion that the people of Utah were "in a state of substantial rebellion." No mass meetings had been held during 1856 to utter any protest, not even of the mildest form permitted by the Constitution, much less had they made any public demonstration that could reasonably be construed either into an act or intent of rebellion against the United States government. But in the reverse of this, as noted in the preceding chapter, a constitutional convention was held that very year; a republican constitution adopted, with the declaration of rights already exhibited, and delegates were sent to Congress to ask for the admission of Utah into the Union. For historical suggestiveness, lay by the side of the documents proceeding from General Scott the following extract from the Deseret News: "The delegates of the convention, from the various counties, except Green River, met in the Council House on the 17th inst. (March). The event was announced by the firing of cannon and music from Captain Ballo's band.

Throughout the day flags floated from the cupolas of the Governor's mansion and Council House, also from the tall flag poles on the Temple Block and in front of the Deseret, and Livingston, Kinkead & Co.'s stores, from flag staffs on the roof of Gilbert & Gerrish's store, and from those on the roofs of many other public buildings.

"At an early hour a large concourse of citizens had assembled, anxiously awaiting the commencement of those deliberations and acts, which have for their object the addition of another star to the brilliant and thickly spangled constellation styled, E Pluribus Unum.

"The convention organized by unanimously electing the Hon. J. M. Grant, president; Mr. T. Bullock, secretary; Mr. J. Grimshaw, assistant secretary; Mr. R. T. Burton, sergeant-at-arms; Mr. W. C. Staines, messenger; Mr. T. Hall, doorkeeper; and Messrs. G. D. Watt and J. V. Long, reporters. At 12:30, adjourned until 2 p.m. * * * * "In the afternoon the freedom of the convention was unanimously tendered to His

Excellency the Governor, the United States officers of the Territory, President H. C. Kimball, the members of the Legislative Assembly, Hons. E. Snow, A. Lyman and E. Hunter, Hon. Elias Smith, Probate Judge of G. S. L. County, and the Aldermen of G. S. L. City.

"After a remarkably short, efficient, and harmonious session, the convention dissolved on Thursday, March 27.

' Hon. George A. Smith, and Hon. John Taylor, editor of the Mormon, were unanimously elected delegates to proceed to Washington, and lay before Congress Utah's request for admission into the Union.

"The Constitution of the State of Deseret was signed by every member of the convention, though they were from various climes and of diverse creeds, government officials, merchants, etc., etc., thus indicating, beyond controversy, the represented feelings of all classes of our Territorial population. If our memory correctly serves us, so general and fair a representation of the views and feelings of the various districts of Territory, and so frank and hearty a blending of party interests, have never been excelled, if even equaled, in the initiatory action required for the admission of a new state. * * * "Is Utah loyal? Aye, most loyal, beyond successful challenge or contradiction, as is and always had been proved by all her sayings and doings. But does she love corruption and oppression? Verily no, for her sons and daughters, with few exceptions, have been reared in the cradle of liberty, in common with the citizens of the States, and the pure mountain breezes keep that love fanned to a bright and unquenchable flame. And the few exceptions just named, those who were not born citizens of our Republic, are congenial descendants of that stock from which sprang our "Revolutionary Sires." They have left their fatherlands, as did our forefathers, to escape the oppressor's rod and find a loved asylum "in the home of the free." Then can Congress refuse to extend the broad folds of equal rights and constitutional liberty over that portion of the public domain, whose inhabitants will stand by the Union while a vestige thereof exists and blood flows in their veins? It is not to be presumed that any Congress could wish so to do, but if it might, by any possibility, be imagined that an opposite feeling could be indulged, who would like to face the mingled whirlwind of scorn and indignation that would then arise in the breast of every lover of truth and justice throughout the world?

"Utah is isolated, is full of rugged mountains, desert plains, and barren valleys, and peculiarly uncomely in the eyes of lovers of rich, well timbered soil, broad rivers, extended seaboards, and commercial marts. Let her present population leave her borders, and the few oases, now gladdened with the busy hum of civilized life, would soon revert to the occupancy of the rude savage, and crumbling desolation would mark the site of stately edifices.

"Utah, with but little aid from the parent, has grown rapidly amid all her disadvantages, and, amid the jealousy and hostility of numerous Indian tribes, to high position in wealth and numbers. And are not the intelligence and energy which have so rapidly produced such laudable results, where none others would thrust in their sickles, sufficient guarantee that Utah is most emphatically deserving of a state organization?

"She has wealth, a numerous, intelligent, and highly patriotic population, is accustomed to make her own public buildings, roads, and bridges, has successfully conducted the Indian wars waged within her boundaries, has nearly expelled litigation through a wise system of legislation and policy, furnishes few abominable and illegal acts to swell the record of earth's corruptions, not even enough to make her news spicy and interesting to the corrupt taste of a perverse generation, then is there any good, fair, valid reason why Utah should not be speedily admitted into the Union as a free, sovereign, and independent State named Deseret? Not one. Hence it is but fair to infer that Senators and Representatives in Congress will grant the prayer of Utah for admission as unanimously as she presents it, independent of sectional prejudices, strife and debate of every name and description, for only two questions are to be asked, viz: is her constitution republican? Is she willing and able to maintain a state government? Everyone knows that those questions, and every legitimate question that can be asked, admit of only affirmative answers."

The people of Utah waited hopefully for the favorable action of Congress until December, when Governor Young, in his annual message to the Legislature, thus reported upon the matter: "In accordance with Acts of the Legislative Assembly, a Constitution was formed and adopted, the census taken, and delegates chosen to present our application to Congress for admission into the Union as a sovereign and independent State. Recent advices from our delegates show that our application has not been presented, owing to the intolerance evinced by the predominant party in the House of Representatives.

"The enumeration of the inhabitants showed a population of near 77,000 in this Territory, and it is presumed that the addition to our numbers, since that was taken, would amount to about twenty thousand. This gives an aggregate equal to or exceeding the ratio of representation for Congressmen, removing every objection, if any were made, to our admission, on the score of insufficient population."

Simply a bare notice is here seen of opposition in Congress to the admission of Utah; bat no indignant protest, much less anything to indicate a condition of rebellion ; yet a few months later the United States ordered a military expedition to Utah to put down rebellion, restore its rule which had not been broken, while the President appointed a new Governor for the Territory, Hon. Alfred Cumming, of Georgia who when he did come was received by them with a loyal good will.

The Buchanan administration, however, had not acted without some information and prompting, which were considered by it sufficient at the time, but very insufficient soon afterwards; and it is with that information and prompting, or rather conspiracy, that this historical exposition has now to deal.

When in less than a year from the issuing of General Scott's circular, the House of Representatives passed a resolution requesting President Buchanan "to communicate to the House of Representatives the information which gave rise to the military expedition ordered to Utah" Lewis Cass, Secretary of State, reported that "the only document on record or on file in this department, touching the subject of the resolution, is the letter of Mr. W. F. Magraw to the President, of the 3rd of October last, a copy of which is hereto annexed :"

MR. MAGRAW TO THE PRESIDENT.

Independence, Missouri, October 3rd, 1856.

"Mr. President: I feel it incumbent upon me as a personal and political friend, to lay before you some information relative to the present political and social condition of the Territory of Utah, which may be of importance.

"There is no disguising the fact, that there is left no vestige of law and order, no protection for life or property; the civil laws of the Territory are overshadowed and neutralized by a so-styled ecclesiastical organization, as despotic, dangerous and damnable, as has ever been known to exist in any country, and which is ruining not only those who do not subscribe to their religious code, but is driving the moderate and more orderly of the Mormon community to desperation. Formerly, violence committed upon the rights of persons and property were attempted to be justified by some pretext manufactured for the occasion, under color of law as it exists in that country. The victims were usually of that class whose obscurity and want of information necessary to insure proper investigation and redress of their wrongs were sufficient to guarantee to the perpetrators freedom from punishment. Emboldened by the success which attended their first attempts at lawlessness, no pretext or apology seems now to be deemed requisite, nor is any class exempt from outrage; all alike are set upon by the self-constituted theocracy, whose laws, or rather whose conspiracies, are framed in dark corners, promulgated from the stand of tabernacle or church, and executed at midnight, or upon the highways, by an organized band of bravos and assassins, whose masters compel an outraged community to tolerate in their midst. The result is that a considerable and highly respectable portion of the community, known from the Atlantic to the Pacific, whose enterprise is stimulated by a laudable desire to improve their fortunes by honorable exertions, are left helpless victims to outrage and oppression, liable at any moment to be stripped of their property or deprived of life, without the ability to put themselves under the protection of law, since all the courts that exist there at present are converted into engines and instruments of injustice.

"For want of time I am compelled thus to generalize, but particular case?, with all the attendant circumstances, names of parties and localities are not wanting to swell the calendar of crime and outrage to limits that will, when published, startle the conservative people of the States, and create a clamor which will not be readily quelled; and I have no doubt that the time is near at hand, and the elements rapidly combining to bring about a state of affairs which will result in indiscriminate bloodshed, robbery and rapine, and which in a brief space of time will reduce that country to the condition of a howling wilderness.

"There are hundreds of good men in the country, who have for years endured every privation from the comforts and enjoyments of civilized life, to confront every description of danger for the purpose of improving their fortunes.

These men have suffered repeated wrong and injustice, which they have endeavored to repair by renewed exertions, patiently awaiting the correction of outrage by that government which it is their pride to claim citizenship under, and whose protection they have a right to expect; but they now see themselves liable, at any moment, to be stripped of their hard earned means, the lives of themselves and their colleagues threatened and taken; ignominy and abuse, heaped upon them day after day, if resented, is followed by murder.

"Many of the inhabitants of the Territory possess passions and elements of character calculated to drive them to extremes and have the ability to conceive and have the courage to carry out the boldest measures for redress, and I know that they will be at no loss for a leader. When such as these are driven by their wrongs to vindicate, not only their rights as citizens, but their pride of manhood, the question of disparity in numerical force is not considered among their difficulties, and I am satisfied that a recital of their grievances would form an apology, if not sufficient justification, for the violation on their part of the usages of civilized communities.

"In addressing you, I have endeavored to discard all feelings arising from my personal annoyances in the Mormon country but have desired to lay before you the actual condition of affairs, and to prevent, if possible, scenes of lawlessness which, I fear, will be inevitable unless speedy and powerful preventives are applied. I have felt free to thus address you, from the fact that some slight requests made of me when I last left Washington, on the subject of the affairs of Kansas, justified me in believing that you had confidence in my integrity, and that what influence I could exert would not be wanting to terminate the unfortunate difficulties in that Territory; I have the pleasure of assuring you that my efforts were not spared.

"With regard to the affairs and proceedings of the probate court, the only existing tribunal in the Territory of Utah, there being but one of the three federal judges now in the Territory, I will refer you to its records, and to the evidence of gentlemen whose assertions cannot be questioned; as to the treatment of myself, I will leave that to the representation of others; at all events, the object I have in view, the end I wish to accomplish for the general good, will preclude my wearying you with a recital of them at present.

"I have the honor to be very truly yours, etc.

W. M. F. MAGRAW."

John B. Floyd, Secretary of War, was only able to furnish to the House the correspondence of the expedition itself, commencing with the foregoing circular, and including the proclamation of Governor Young and the correspondence between him and Col. Alexander; the Department of the Interior furnished several letters from David H. Burr, Surveyor General of Utah, the office of Indian affairs made up a budget from the Indian Agents of the Territory, and the Attorney General's office supplied the following: "Attorney General's Office, February 24, 1858.

"Sir: In reply to so much of the resolution of the House of Representatives, of the 27th ult., referred by you to this office, calling for 'information which gave rise to the military expeditions to Utah Territory,' etc., I have the honor to transmit herewith: "

1. The letter of resignation of W. W. Drummond, Associate Justice of Supreme Court of Utah Territory.

"2. The letter of Curtis Bolton, deputy clerk of the Supreme Court of Utah Territory, in reply to allegations contained in W. W. Drummond's letter of resignation; the above being all the correspondence on the files of this office relating to the subject.

"I am, very respectfully, J. S. BLACK.

The President.

"New Orleans, La, April 2, 1857.

"Dear Sir: When I started for my home in Illinois, I designed reaching Washington before the executive session adjourned, but could not accomplish the long and tedious journey in time; thence I concluded to come this way, and go up the Mississippi river to Chicago.

"You will see that I have made bold charges against the Mormons, which I think I can prove without doubt. You will see by the contents of the enclosed paper, wherein is inserted my resignation, some of the reasons that induced me to resign. I now refer you to Hon. D. W. Burf, surveyor general of Utah Territory, Hon. Garland Hurt, Indian agent; also C. L. Craig, Esq., D. L. Thompson, Esq., John M. Hockaday, Esq., John Kerr, Esq., Gentiles of Great Salt Lake City, for proof of the manner in which they have been insulted and abused by the leading Mormons for two years past. I shall see you soon on the subject.

In haste, yours truly, W. W. DRUMMOND.

Hon. Jeremiah S. Black, Attorney General, etc."

RESIGNATION OF JUDGE DRUMMOND.

"March 30, 1857.

"My Dear Sir: As I have concluded to resign the office of Justice of the Supreme Court of the Territory of Utah, which position I accepted in A. D., 1854, under the administration of President Pierce, I deem it due to the public to give some of the reasons why I do so. In the first place, Brigham Young, the Governor of Utah Territory, is the acknowledged head of the 'Church of Jesus Christ of Latter-day Saints,' commonly called 'Mormons;' and, as such head, the Mormons look to him, and to him alone, for the law by which they are to be governed: therefore no law of Congress is by them considered binding in any manner.

"Secondly. I know that there is a secret oath-bound organization among all the male members of the Church to resist the laws of the country, and to acknowledge no law save the law of the 'Holy Priesthood,' which comes to the people through Brigham Young direct from God; he, Young, being the vicegerent of God and Prophet, viz: successor of Joseph Smith, who was the founder of this blind and treasonable organization.

"Thirdly. I am fully aware that there is a set of men, set apart by special order of the Church, to take both the lives and property of persons who may question the authority of the Church; the names of whom I will promptly make known at a future time.

"Fourthly. That the records, papers, etc., of the Supreme Court have been destroyed by order of the Church, with the direct knowledge and approbation of Governor B. Young, and the Federal officers grossly insulted for presuming to raise a single question about the treasonable act.

"Fifthly. That the Federal officers of the Territory are constantly insulted, harassed, and annoyed by the Mormons, and for these insults there is no redress.

"Sixthly. That the Federal officers are daily compelled to hear the form of the American government traduced, the chief executives of the nation, both living and dead, slandered and abused from the masses, as well as from all the leading members of the Church, in the most vulgar, loathsome, and wicked manner that the evil passions of men can possibly conceive.

"Again: That after Moroni Green had been convicted in the District Court before my colleague, Judge Kinney, of an assault with intent to commit murder, and afterwards, on appeal to the Supreme Court, the judgment being affirmed and the said Green being sentenced to the penitentiary, Brigham Young gave a full pardon to the said Green before he reached the penitentiary; also, that the said Governor Young pardoned a man by the name of Baker, who had been tried and sentenced to ten years' imprisonment in the penitentiary, for the murder of a dumb boy by the name of White House, the proof showing one of the most aggravated cases of murder that I ever knew being tried; and to insult the Court and Government officers, this man Young took this pardoned criminal with him, in proper person, to church on the next Sabbath after his conviction; Baker, in the meantime, having received a full pardon from Governor Brigham Young.

These two men were Mormons. On the other hand, I charge the Mormons, and Governor Young in particular, with imprisoning five or six young men from Missouri and Iowa, who are now in the penitentiary of Utah, without those men having violated any criminal law in America. But they were anti-Mormons— poor, uneducated young men en route for California; but because they emigrated from Illinois, Iowa, or Missouri, and passed by Great Salt Lake City, they were indicted by a probate court, and most brutally and inhumanly dealt with, in addition to being summarily incarcerated in the saintly prison of the Territory of Utah. I also charge Governor Young with constantly interfering with the federal courts, directing the grand jury whom to indict and whom not; and after the judges charge the grand juries as to their duties, that this man Young invariably has some member of the grand jury advised in advance as to his will in relation to their labors, and that his charge thus given is the only charge known, obeyed, or received by all the grand juries of the federal courts of Utah Territory.

"Again, sir, after a careful and mature investigation, I have been compelled to come to the conclusion, heart-rending and sickening as it may be, that Captain John W. Gunnison, and his party of eight others, were murdered by the Indians in 1853, under the orders, advice, and direction of the Mormons; that my illustrious and distinguished predecessor, Hon. Leonidas Shaver, came to his death by drinking poisoned liquors, given to him under the order of the leading men of 1 he Mormon Church in Great Salt Lake City; that the late secretary of the Territory, A. W. Babbitt, was murdered on the plains by a band of Mormon marauders, under the particular and special order of Brigham Young, Heber C.

Kimball, and J. M. Grant, and not by the Indians, as reported by the Mormons themselves, and that they were sent from Salt Lake City for that purpose, and that only; and as members of the Danite Band they were bound to do the will of Brigham Young as the head of the church or forfeit their own lives. These reasons, with many others that I might give, which would be too heart-rending to insert in this communication, have induced me to resign the office of justice of the Territory of Utah, and again return to my adopted State of Illinois.

My reason, sir, for making this communication thus public is, that the democratic party, with which I have always strictly acted, is the party now in power, and, therefore, is the party that should now be held responsible for the treasonable and disgraceful state of affairs that now exists in Utah Territory. I could, sir, if necessary, refer to a cloud of witnesses to attest the reasons I have given, and the charges, bold as they are, against those despots, who rule with an iron hand their hundred thousand souls in Utah, and their two hundred thousand souls out of that notable Territory; but I shall not do so, for the reason that the lives of such gentlemen as I should designate in Utah and in California, would not be safe for a single day.

In conclusion, sir, I have to say that, in my career as justice of the supreme court of Utah Territory, I have the consolation of knowing that I did my duty, that neither threats nor intimidations drove me from that path. Upon the other hand, I am pained to say that I accomplished little good while there, and that the judiciary is only treated as a farce. The only rule of law by which the infatuated followers of this curious people will be governed, is the law of the church, and that emanates from Governor Brigham Young, and him alone.

I do believe that, if there was a man put in office as governor of that Territory, who is not a member of the church, (Mormon), and he supported with a sufficient military aid, much good would result from such a course; but as the Territory is now governed, and as it has been since the administration of Mr. Fillmore, at which time Young received his appointment as governor, it is noonday madness and folly to attempt to administer the law in that Territory. The officers are insulted, harassed, and murdered for doing their duty, and not recognizing Brigham Young as the only law-giver and law-maker on earth. Of this every man can bear incontestable evidence who has been willing to accept an appointment in Utah; and I assure you sir, that no man would be willing to risk his life and property in that Territory after once trying the sad experiment.

With an earnest desire that the present administration will give due and timely aid to the officers that may be so unfortunate as to accept situations in that Territory, and that the withering curse which now rests upon this nation by virtue of the peculiar and heart-rending institutions of the Territory of Utah, may be speedily removed, to the honor and credit of our happy country, I now remain your obedient servant,

W. W. DRUMMOND, Justice Utah Territory.

Hon. Jeremiah S. Black, Attorney General of the United States, Washington City, D. C.

"Great Salt Lake City, Utah Territory.

"Sir: My attention having been drawn to the letter of Justice W. W. Drummond, under the date of March 30, 1857, addressed to yourself, tendering his resignation as associate justice for Utah, wherein my office is called in question, I feel it incumbent upon me to make to you the following report: "Justice W. W. Drummond, in his 'fourth' paragraph, says: 'The records, papers, &c, of the supreme court have been destroyed by order of Governor B. Young, and the federal officers grossly insulted for presuming to raise a single question about the treasonable act.' "I do solemnly declare this assertion is without the slightest foundation in truth. The records, papers, &c, of the supreme court in this Territory, together with all decisions and documents of every kind belonging thereto, from Monday, September 22, 1851, at which time said court was first organized, up to this present moment, are all safe and complete in my custody, and not one of them missing, nor have they ever been disturbed by any person.

"Again, in the decision of the supreme court in the case of Moroni Green, the which decision was written by Judge Drummond himself, I find the following words: 'That as the case, for which Green was convicted, seems to have been an aggravated one, this court does remit the costs of the prosecution, both in this court and in the court below.' Green was provoked to draw a pistol in self-defense but did not point it at any one. He was a lad of 18 years old. Much feeling was excited in his favor, and he was finally pardoned by the governor, upon a petition signed by the judges, and officers of the United States, courts, the honorable secretary of state, and many of the influential citizens of Great Salt Lake City.

"Again: in relation to the incarceration of five or six young men from Missouri and Iowa, who are now (March 30, 1857,) in the penitentiary of Utah, without those men having violated any criminal law in America, &c. This statement is also utterly false.

"I presume he alludes to the incarceration, on the 22nd January, 1856, of three men, and on the 29th of January, 1856, of one more; if so these are the circumstances:
"There were quite a number of persons came here as teamsters in Gilbert and Gerrish's train of goods, arriving here in December, 1855, after winter had set in. They arrived here very destitute; and at that season of the year there is nothing a laboring man can get to do. Some of these men entered the store of S. M. Blair & Co., at various times in the night, and stole provisions, groceries, &c. Some six or eight were indicted for burglary, and larceny. Three plead guilty, and a fourth was proven guilty; and the four were sentenced to the penitentiary for the shortest time the statute allowed for the crime; and just as soon as the spring of 1856 opened, and a company was preparing to start for California, upon a petition setting forth mitigating circumstances, the governor pardoned them, and they went on their way to California. It was a matter, well understood here at the time, that these men were incarcerated more particularly to keep them from committing further crime during the winter.

"Since that time there have been but four persons sentenced to the penitentiary, one for forgery and three for petty larceny, for terms of sixty and thirty days, to wit: One on the 19th November, 1856, for larceny, thirty days; two on the 24th November, 1856, for aggravated larceny, sixty days and one on the 26th January, 1857, for forgery, thirty days. So that on the 30th March, 1857, (the date of W. W. Drummond's letter,) there was not a white prisoner in the Utah penitentiary; nor had there been for several days previous, nor is there at this present writing.

"I could, were it my province in this affidavit, go on and refute all that Judge W. W. Drummond has stated in his aforesaid letter of resignation, by records, dates, and facts; but believing the foregoing is sufficient to show you what reliance is to be placed upon the assertions or word of W. W. Drummond, I shall leave this subject.

"In witness of the truth of the foregoing affidavit, I have hereunto subscribed my name and affixed the seal of the United States supreme court [l. s.] for Utah Territory, at Great Salt Lake City, this twenty-sixth day of June, A. D. 1857.

CURTIS E. BOLTON,

Deputy Clerk of said U. S. Supreme Court for Utah, in absence of W. J. Appleby, Clerk.

Hon. Jeremiah S. Black, Attorney General of the United States, Washington, D. C."

But these documents furnished to the House alone give no sufficient exposition of causes, though there is seen much relation between the letters quoted and the action of the Government. For a thorough exposition commensurate with the aims and purposes of a true and impartial history, we must go to a general review of Utah affairs, not only as regards the Mormon community in their own conduct, but also the conduct of the people of the United States towards them, whether friendly or hostile, which exposition will show that the Utah question has long been intensely a national question.

Strange as the assertion may appear, the real beginning of the train of causes and circumstances which led to the "Utah War," and its many complications, was the continuation of Brigham Young by President Pierce in the governorship, in 1855. That is to say, the United States gave the chief cause of offence against itself, and afterwards, by construction, made the potent and thorough administration of Governor Young, and the submission of the community to Federal rule under him, to signify a condition of actual rebellion. That which 'in the Governor and people of any other Territory or State would have been esteemed by the nation as legitimate and admirable was, in Brigham Young and the Mormons, a present treason and a direct intent to overturn and supplant the national rule with a Mormon Theocracy. The case had entirely changed since Stansbury had said in his report to the Government, "I feel constrained to say, that in my opinion the appointment of the President of the Mormon Church, and the head of the Mormon community, in preference to any other person to the high office of Governor of the Territory, independent of its political bearings, with which I have nothing to do, was a measure dictated alike by justice and sound policy. This man has been their Moses. * * * He had been unanimously chosen as their highest civil magistrate, and even before his appointment by the President, he combined in his own person the triple character of confidential adviser, temporal ruler, and prophet of God."

So far as Governor Young and the Mormons were concerned, this was also all true when he was re-appointed by President Pierce, and therein was the in harmony which developed between Utah and the nation, resulting in the expedition. That which at first so eminently fitted Brigham Young for Governor of the colony which he led to these valleys and multiplied substantially into a little State of the Union, now unfitted him in the eyes of the nation. To be the President of the Mormon Church and Governor of Utah Territory was made to signify the existence of a political Mormon Theocracy. The Mormon Moses, clothed with the mantle of Federal authority at the head of his people, appeared to the "Gentile" as an Israelitish rebeldom in the heart of the American republic. Thus the wording of a Stansbury, a Gunnison and a Thomas L. Kane was substituted by the wording a Drummond and a Magraw, without any real change of subject, or substitution of some new and reversed cause. In his masterly treatise of the Mormons and their institutions Gunnison had said: "For those who desire facts in the history of humanity, on which to indulge in reflection, is this offered. It were far easier to give a romantic sketch in lofty metaphors, of the genesis and exodus of the empire-founding Saints—the subject is its own epic of heroism, whose embellishment is left to imaginative genius, and its philosophy to be deduced by the candid philanthropist." This treatise of Gunnison is the loftiest exposition of the Israelitish theocracy of the Mormons ever written by Gentile pen. As his wording shows, he has treated his historical subject as an "Israelitish epic" wrought in modern times. In view of this epic monument of their history which the hand of Gunnison essayed to rear for the Mormons, it is both astonishing and monstrous that Judge Drummond, in his resignation, should charge Brigham Young with the instigation of his murder by the Indians. Such an act is not within our comprehension of human atrocities and ingratitude, especially when applied to a leader of Brigham Young's cast and sagacity, whose every act marked his deliberate anticipation of a sufficient compensation to himself or his people. The cruel and cowardly murder of Gunnison, by the order of Brigham Young, could not possibly have brought to him or his community such compensation; for, next to Colonel Thomas L. Kane, Captain Stansbury and Lieutenant Gunnison had done Governor Young and the Mormon community more service than any other men in America.

And it is scarcely less astonishing and monstrous that Drummond in his resignation should charge Governor Young and the Mormons with the poisoning of Associate Justice Shaver, and the tomahawking on the plains of Secretary Babbitt, seeing that Judge Shaver, was mourned by Salt Lake City, arid his funeral sermon preached by its Mayor, just as the untimely fate of Gunnison was mourned in the message of Governor Young to the Legislature, and his memory thus honorably preserved on the official tablet of Utah's early history; while Secretary Babbitt was himself a Mormon, the chief politician of the community, the man whom the citizens chose and sent to Congress as their Delegate, when they set up the Provisional State of Deseret. Monstrous, however, as these charges of the murder of Government officials at the order of Governor Young must appear in any just exposition of the times of 18567, they were sent to the House of Representatives as among the chief causes of the Utah Expedition; yet it is worthy of note that there is an air of protest to the Drummond document in the presentation of the Attorney General. It is probable that, had the Hon. Jeremiah S. Black been the Executive, as well as the Judicial head of the Administration at this juncture, he would have viewed Utah and her affairs very much as Daniel Webster had done before, when Brocchus, Brandebury, Harris, Day and Ferris deserted three departments of the newly created Territory, and sought the invasion which was accomplished in 1857. Indeed, the sequel does actually show that the Attorney General, after the Proclamation of Pardon, by his constitutional decision prevented the re-opening of difficulties, and perhaps an actual war, between General Johnson and his troops on the one side, and Governor dimming and the Utah militia on the other, which decision restored the Territory to the exact place where it stood, under Governor Brigham Young.

The true historical exposition, then, is that Utah was not in rebellion when the expedition was projected; and that the cause of all the offence on the Mormon side was simply that which the community has given from the beginning—in Ohio, in Missouri, in Illinois, in Utah. They were seeking to build up the Kingdom of God upon the earth; and Brigham Young, their Prophet and President of their Church, was also now, for the second time, Governor of Utah, in virtue of his being the great colonizer and founder of the Territory. "The strange and interesting people" were just as admirable when Drummond and Magraw wrote their communications to the Government, making the community hideous and instigating a war crusade against them, as they were when Stansbury reported them to the nation as the most wonderful colony of modern times, worthy of acceptance into the Union as a model state. But, as observed, a change had come over the vision; and the presence of the Mormon community, in 1857, had become as intolerable to the majority of the people of the United States as they had been to Missouri and Illinois. The spirit and temper which had possessed those States which had driven the Mormons from their borders, now possessed the whole of the United States. That little colony of religious exiles which had planted itself in the Valley of the Great Salt Lake in 1847, and, lifting reverently the Stars and Stripes on foreign soil, claimed it for the nation in that nation's own august name, had grown by their wonderful emigrations into a hundred colonies; but for this very reason, of their marvelous growth and organism, the people of the States east and west desired to rid themselves of the Mormons altogether; and, if needs be, to drive them with guns and bayonets from American soil. Senators and Representatives saw clearly that if the Mormons were allowed to remain within the American domains, they must inevitably become a State of the Union, and in the end play, perhaps, a controlling part in party politics and the national destiny. This had been illustrated in Illinois, where they had held the balance of power between the Democrats and the Whigs. Their colonies were now fast spreading over this western country; they would settle territory which would come within the political boundaries of half a dozen States, in which they would cast their potent united vote; they would, by continued emigrations and rapid increase of offspring by their polygamy, which had offspring for its aim, multiply into a million of United States citizens within the century, whose united political power would be really formidable. Such were the anticipations and talk about Mormon Utah in those times in the newspapers of the country, as may be seen by consulting their files of 1855-6-7. The New York Herald in one of its leaders declared seriously, and with some admiration withal, that the Mormons held "the whip handle" over the United States, Fillmore and Pierce had given it into the hands of Brigham Young. With Brigham, Governor, Utah was always right, and the United States always wrong. Such Was the inference, and the reason clearly because such men as Brocchus, Ferris and Drummond were the representatives of the United States, as versus Brigham Young the Governor of Utah and President of the Mormon Church. And the New York Herald was verily right. It was just the difference in the officials who represented the United States versus Mormondom, and the governor who represented the United States to the glory and political destiny of the Utah which he had founded. Let alone for another decade, and what would this man, Brigham Young, and his Utah amount to in our national affairs?—he as Governor, exercising almost absolute authority in the name of the United States, in consequence of the potency of his own character, in consequence of the impotency of those sent against him to overbalance him, and in consequence of the constitutional rights of the people of Utah, as citizens of the United States, who earnestly and loyally supported his lawful and potent administration of Federal authority over the Territory; and, furthermore, in consequence of the fact that nearly all the other Federal officials, except the Mormon branch, first measured arms with the great Mormon Governor, and then deserted their posts, leaving the sole government of the Territory almost entirely in his hands. Invariably it was the anti-Mormon branch of the administration that commenced hostilities. They constituted themselves as missionaries delegated to put down Mormon rule in Utah, and this they did even when not a score of Gentiles were in the Territory, thus tantalizing the entire community and opposing the legitimate administration of the Governor. The opposing Judges were the most conspicuous, as also very potent, they usually forming a majority of the judicial branch of the Territorial administration antagonistic not only to Mormon rule, but to Mormon citizenship, as subsequent issues have shown. The Indian agents, on their part, though subordinate to Governor Young as Superintendent of Indian Affairs, aimed to frustrate his Indian policy, sought to stir up the Indians under his superintendency against him and the Mormons, spied upon his actions, and like spies made insidious and hostile reports against him as their chief, not only impeaching him, but recommending to the Government not to pay his accounts for expenditure in the Indian wars of the Territory, Every time this "irrepressible conflict" between Governor Young and the anti-Mormon branch was manifested to the Government and the nation, resulting as it always did in the discomfiture and generally in the resignation of the antagonists of the Governor, the administration at Washington was both perplexed and provoked, and the country thrown into a state of excitement, and exasperated anger over Utah, and the Mormons. It was evident to the nation that this conflict and anomalous condition in the affairs of one of the Territories could not be permitted to continue another decade, and the demand for the removal of Brigham Young from the Governorship, and the appointment of a Gentile Governor in his place was very generally made by the country as the only solution to the Utah difficulty. This President Franklin Pierce had sought to accomplish in the appointment of Colonel Steptoe, at the expiration of Governor Young's first term; but the declining and the petition which Steptoe and his officers headed, recommending the reappointment of Governor Young forced the action of the President and Brigham into a second term of office. The re-appointment was probably quite in accord with President Pierce's own mind, but he soon found that the sentiment of the country was decidedly against it, and that a Gentile Governor was in popular demand, and that too for the very purpose of putting down Mormondom. Indeed the expressive epithet " Mormondom" was coined to fit the case, used first in the New York Herald and made to signify, in this connection, that the Mormon Church should be tolerated with all other Churches, but that the " Mormon theocracy'" must be invaded and overthrown. This was first proposed to be accomplished by a Gentile Governor, supported by a new corps of Federal officers in accord with him, but later on as the irrepressible conflict grew, and the rage for an anti-Mormon crusade became general, the overthrow of political Mormondom was given to a United States army, sent to depose Brigham Young as a rebel Governor and to set another in his place.

President Pierce was charged with a political mistake in the continuation of Brigham Young, from the exception taken to his act both by political friends and political enemies, but the administration of Pierce was drawing to a close and it did not choose to inaugurate any new measures, which seeming indifference on the part of the Government only stirred up the opponents of Brigham Young to greater exertions, and every measure was adopted to secure some decided action. President Pierce, in disgust over this dissatisfaction of political friends and political foes, declared that he would make no more appointments for the Governorship of Utah as long as he held office, and thus Governor Young remained a colossus on his pedestal, on which anti-Mormon rage spent itself in vain, so far as disturbing the condition of affairs in Utah, but an action was worked up in the States against Utah and the Mormons scarcely less virulent in its animus than that which prevailed in the Republican party against slavery and the South.

The rise of the Republican party into power lifted Utah into a political situation, which while it gave her no political advantages, such as her admission as a State, exposed her to danger and left her open to the assault of her enemies. In the framing of its first platform the Republican party raised her to a kindred association with the South and, in every campaign where John C. Fremont was the standard bearer of the party, there could be read "The abolishment of slavery and polygamy; the twin relics of barbarism."

Undoubtedly General Fremont had much to do with the sharpening of this political directness that associated Utah and the South in the "irrepressible conflict," which the Republican party was inspiring in the country for the overthrow of the Democratic party, and which struck Utah with a military expedition before it struck the South. And though it would fall short of Fremont's dignity and national reputation to class him with Drummond, or to charge him with malice towards Utah, yet it should not be forgotten that there had existed a relation between him and the Mormons for many years, in which there was nascent much of the "irrepressible conflict" which he sought to infuse into the political contest of the nation against Mormon Utah. He was the son-in-law of Senator Thomas H. Benton, whom the Mormons at that time looked upon as the greatest political enemy they ever had, and there had been something of a rivalry between the Mormons and Fremont, relative to the possession of California. This had dated as far back as the lifetime of Joseph Smith, who, at the very moment when Fremont was designing the conquest of California with a volunteer army, had petitioned the President of the United States and Congress to allow him to occupy that Mexican province with a colony of a hundred thousand Mormons. Senator Douglass favored "General" Smith's project versus General Fremont's; and accompanied with Fremont's report on California, which had just been printed by the Senate, but not yet made public, the Senator from Illinois dispatched his urgent advice to " General" Smith to at once start for the possession of the Pacific coast with his Mormon colony. It was undoubtedly a knowledge of the Mormon Prophet's design to possess California by his colony, as preferred by Douglass to the somewhat filibustering character of his son-in-law's proposed expedition, that so strongly set Benton against this Mormon colonization in the west, the wonderful success of which the simple relation of the historical fact is proving to be the real cause, not only of the Utah Expedition, but also of all the special legislation in Congress to this day against " Mormon Utah." This at the last effort was very strikingly illustrated by General Cullom in his affirmation to the Senate, substantially to the effect that, if the successful Mormon colonization of the west was not stopped by some radical treasure of Congress, the Mormons would control half a dozen States in the west, and thus give the balance of power in the national politics against the Republican party, which at its birth made proclamation of war against Mormondom. Now it is just in this political vein that the historian finds the real cause and animus of the Utah Expedition, and of all the action and special legislation against Mormon Utah to this day, and not in the charges of Magraw and Drummond, nor even polygamy, though the former furnished excuse for the Expedition, as the other does protest for special legislation.

In Missouri and Illinois, this political vein of the Mormon question was only locally defined. It was Senator Benton who first gave it a national significance, and now, upon the political banners of his son-in-law, it was proclaimed with mottoes classing Utah and polygamy with slavery and the South. This development of the history, gives interest and significance to a brief review of the case of Fremont and the Mormons, in the occupation of the Pacific Slope.

Destiny led the Mormon pioneers to the valleys of Utah. Destiny went with the Mormon battalion to California in the expedition of General S. W. Kearney, whose instructions from the Secretary of War were to " conquer" California and set up a provisional military government there in the name of the United States. California, however, was won by Fremont and his volunteers, and the United States flag was hoisted in the Bay of San Francisco by Commodore Stockton before the arrival of General Kearney. A battle or two, by the regular troops, under Kearney, completed the conquest. Had not the General been forestalled by Fremont, the Mormons would have been among his most reliable soldiers in the conquest of that country. As it was, Kearney found the situation claimed by several rival governors. Fremont was the hero. Fremont was his great rival. The hero was in rebellion. He refused at first to resign to the military chief the government of the conquered Province. He might have even won the position from the rightful Governor on the strength of his claims as conqueror, supported by his popularity; but at this crisis of affairs, Col. Phillip St. George Cooke arrived in California with his command—the Mormon battalion. Their coming gave to Kearney the victory over his rival. He consulted with Colonel Cooke, who assured him that he could rely on his Mormon soldiers to a man. This decided the General. He resolved to force the issue and arrest his rival. This was consummated, and Fremont was carried to Washington for trial, under a Mormon guard. The famous case of Kearney and Fremont, forms quite a chapter of American history, but it is not so well known how conspicuous a part the Mormon soldiers played in the case.

The political banners of Fremont as a candidate for the Presidential chair, with their motto, "The abolition of slavery and polygamy; the twin relics of barbarism," are scarcely more significant than the foregoing review, touching the personal case of himself and the Mormons.

After the rise of the Republican party, this political vein of the Mormon question grew so broad and rapidly in the political mind of the great parties, at this time struggling for the supremacy, that even Senator Douglass was overwhelmed with the necessity of taking up the conflict against the Mormons, whose united vote had sent him to the Senate, and towards whom, up to the present time, he had manifested not merely political gratitude, but even personal friendship.

In politics, Senator Douglas and the Mormons were in perfect accord. His "squatter-sovereignty" was their political creed, and while they sought his influence at the seat of Government, he found in them the living exponents of the sovereignty doctrine to which he devoted his life. Just here, his advice to the Mormon Prophet, as reported by Orson Hyde may be repeated with much historical pertinence:

"We have this, day [April 26] had a long conversation with Judge Douglass. He is ripe for Oregon and California. He said he would resign his seat in Congress, if he could command the force that Mr. Smith could, and would be on the march to that country in a month. 'In five years,' he said, 'a noble State might be formed, and then if they would not receive us into the Union, we would have a government of our own.'"

The Mormons had not gone to the extent of Senator Douglass' counsel. They had, indeed, built up what they considered a "noble State" of the Union and had repeatedly offered it to Congress for acceptance, which had been rejected; but they had not in consequence of this rejection "set up an independent government of their own," which fidelity to the nation doubtless Douglas approved seeing that the treaty had ceded this then Mexican Territory to the United States. There had been then no political change between Douglass and the Mormons. The case was simply that Douglass was at that time an aspirant for the Presidency of the United States, and this position he could only reach as the candidate of the State which had expelled the Mormons.

In the spring of 1856 Senator Douglass delivered a great speech at Springfield, Illinois. It was the announcement of his platform before the assembling of the conventions that were to nominate the successor of President Pierce. In that speech the senator characterized Mormonism as "the loathsome ulcer of the body politic" and recommended the free use of the scalpel as the only remedy in the hands of the nation. But there were those in the States, such as Thomas L. Kane, who had given Douglass' name to President Filmore as surety for Governor Young, and Mr. Fred. Hudson, the great manager at the time of the New York Herald, who viewed the speech of the Senator from Illinois in its true light. Hudson's confidant, an assistant, on Utah affairs, noticing this passage in American politics of himself, wrote: "My first impulse was to notice the speech, but a careful examination of it rendered the expediency of such a course very doubtful. There were so many 'ifs,' and so often 'should it be,' that it was at last concluded to leave it alone, for the senator might, after all, have said what he did from the necessity of sailing with the popular tide against the Mormons, while, at the same time, he might in the Senate demand evidence of the criminality of the Mormons before any action was taken against them."

But the Mormon leaders were so incensed at the action of Douglass that it became impossible for him to prompt the Senate to an investigation of Utah affairs by a commission. An irreconcilable breach was made. The Deseret News (undoubtedly speaking with Governor Young's voice) replied to the speech, and the Illinois statesman was reminded of the time when he was " but a county judge,"

and when the Prophet Joseph told him that he would someday be an aspirant for the chair of Washington; that, if he continued the friend of the Mormons, he should live to be President of the United States; but if he ever lifted his finger or his voice against them, his plans should be frustrated and his hopes utterly disappointed. All this, the successor of the Mormon Prophet circumstantially related to the senator in reply to his Springfield speech and closed in the name of the Lord, with the prediction that Douglass should fail, and never attain the goal of his ambition.

The prediction of the Mormon Prophet in his conversation with Douglass is singularly authentic and was published years before the Illinois Senator recommended the Government to "cut the loathsome ulcer out," which recommendation makes the story pertinent here as referring to Utah and the causes of the Buchanan expedition.

The Democratic convention meet in Cincinnati soon after the speech, and Senator Douglas was a candidate for the Presidency of the United States: Buchanan was nominated and Douglass defeated.

But neither the defeat of Douglass nor the triumph of Buchanan changed the "manifest destiny" that so singularly made Utah the political scapegoat of the times. She was declared to be the sister of the South, with a common fate, but the South had not yet chosen to recognize her. During that campaign, in the fall of 1856, Republicans carried the banner hostile to polygamy, and Democrats made speeches against the same institution. The only difference was, that the Republicans saw more clearly, or sensed more instinctively than the Democrats, that the Mormons and the Democrats had a common cause and a common fate.

In fine the political action in the country in the fall of 1856 left the Mormons no friends in any of the States and it was this very fact and not their right doings nor their wrong doings, in Utah that determined the Government to send the expedition.

On the 4th of March, 1857, Mr. Buchanan was inaugurated President of the United States, and he and his cabinet, like Douglas, was soon overwhelmed with the popular wave that rose at that time, to lash to fury in vain upon the Rocky Mountain Zion; but which, astonishingly to be told, immediately thereafter swept over the South and baptized the United States in the blood of civil war.

CHAPTER XVI.

REVIEW OF JUDGE DRUMMONDS COURSE IN UTAH. HE ASSAULTS THE PROBATE COURTS AND DENOUNCES THE UTAH LEGISLATURE AT THE CAPITOL. JUDGE SNOWS REVIEW OF THE COURTS OF THE TERRITORY. HIS LETTER TO THE COMPTROLLER OF THE TREASURY. JUDGE DRUMMOND LEAVES UTAH AND COMMENCES HIS CRUSADE. THE CONSPIRACY TO WORKUP THE "UTAH WAR." THE CONTRACTORS. CHARGES OF INDIAN AGENT TWISS. POSTAL SERVICE. CONTRACT AWARDED TO MR. HYRUM KIMBALL. GOVERNOR YOUNG ORGANIZES AN EXPRESS AND CARRYING COMPANY. NEW POSTAL SERVICE. WAR AGAINST UTAH. POST OFFICE DEPARTMENT REPUDIATES ITS CONTRACT. "TROOPS ARE ON THE WAY TO INVADE ZION!"

Thus it appears in reviewing the political history of 1856, that the complications of the nation herself, tending towards the great war conflict between the North and the South, drew Utah into the vortex, almost without any action of her own, whether good or bad; but no military expedition could be sent against her without circumstantial causes. The charges of Drummond and Magraw were considered to be sufficient, which fact makes a review of themselves and their action in Utah affairs necessary to the development of the history of a crusade that cost the nation fifty millions of money, and, for a while, threatened these valleys with desolation.

The following passage from a letter of a member of the Utah Legislature, Samuel W. Richards, to his brother in England, dated Fillmore City, December 7th, 1855, gives a very suggestive opening to Judge Drummond's administration in this Territory:

"You have, no doubt, heard of the appointment and arrival of Judge Drummond in this Territory. He has lately been holding court in this place, which has given him an opportunity to show himself. * * * He has brass to declare, in open court, that the Utah laws are founded in ignorance, and has attempted to set some of the most important ones aside. This being the highest compliment he has to pay to Utah legislators, we shall all endeavor to appreciate it, and he, no doubt from his great ability to judge the merits of law, will be able to appreciate the merits of a return compliment someday. His course and policy so far seem to be to raise a row if possible and make himself notorious.
****

"In speaking of Judge Drummond, I might have named the fact that he compliments a Mormon jury by taking his wife on to the judgment-seat with him, which she occupies almost constantly. There was-one case, however, of such a character that she did not appear."

In a letter of a later date (January 5th, 1856,) the same correspondent wrote.

"Some little excitement prevails in town to-day. An affair took place between Judge Drummond and a Jew trader here, which was rather amusing at the time, but may be something more than that for the Judge before he gets through with it. A grand jury is meeting this evening, which will bring in an indictment against the Judge and his negro, Cato, for assault and battery with intent to murder; and he will be arrested and brought before the probate court on Monday morning next, a 9 o'clock, just at the time he should answer to his name in the supreme court, which sits at that hour. * * * "He has virtually ruled our probate courts out of power in his decisions, but we will now know whether probate courts can act or not, especially in his case. * * *

"Judges Kinney and Stiles, Babbitt, Blair, and nearly all the lawyers in the Territory, United States' Marshal, etc., are expected in here to-morrow, as the supreme court opens on Monday. There is only one case that I am aware of to come up before that court, and that of not much account. * *

Evening.

"The party alluded to just above have arrived. A. W. Babbitt comes in a prisoner. He has been arrested by order of Judge Drummond, on the supposition that he was concerned in the escape of Carlos Murray, who was brought here a prisoner some time since, but is not here now. There is quite an excitement in town about matters and things. I wish this letter was to go one week later, so as to give you the result of the present commotion, which will probably decide the jurisdiction of our probate courts."

The case of the "wife" was a greater outrage both to the government and the community than this indignant member of the Legislature knew at the time.

Associate Justice Drummond had brought with him to the Territory a " lady companion," while his wife and family were left in Illinois. After the notice of his arrival had been published in the Deseret News, some of the relatives of Mrs. Drummond paid a visit to the judge's "companion," and, unfortunately for the honor of the bench, the "lady" from St. Louis did not answer to the description of the wife in Oquawkee. The discovery was noised abroad, yet so shameless was the conduct of this judge and his paramour that she traveled with him wherever he held court, and on some occasions sat beside him on the bench.

"Plurality of wives," comments Stenhouse, "was to the Mormons a part of their religion openly acknowledged to all the world. Drummond's plurality was the outrage of a respectable wife of excellent reputation for the indulgence of a common prostitute, and the whole of his conduct was a gross insult to the Government which he represented, and the people among whom he was sent to administer law. For any contempt the Mormons exhibited towards such a man, there is no need of apology."

Here is exhibited the very onset of the conflict, relative to the jurisdiction of the probate courts in this Territory, and the existence and business of a Territorial marshal, a conflict that continued to the days of Chief Justice McLean; but it is clear from the record that, whether the Utah Legislature made its laws in ignorance or not, it had shown no intent to subvert the federal rule, or to set aside United States Courts to give the jurisdiction to the probate courts; yet this is the very charge made against Governor Young and the Utah Legislature—namely, that they did both with intent and treason so set aside federal rule, substituting, an ecclesiastical rule under the guise of probate courts. "With regard to the affairs and proceeding of the probate court, (wrote Magraw to the President) the only existing tribunal in the Territory of Utah, there being but one of the three federal judges now in the Territory, I will refer you to its records, and to the evidence of gentlemen whose assertions cannot be questioned," while the associate justice wrote, "The judiciary is only treated as a farce. * * It is noonday madness and folly to attempt to administer the law in that Territory.

The officers are insulted, harassed and murdered for doing their duty, and not recognizing Brigham Young as the only lawgiver and lawmaker upon earth."

In the reverse of this the foregoing notes, from one of the legislators to his brother, show us a judge, who was sent to execute the laws of the Territory, rudely assaulting the lawmaking department and ruling out of power the probate courts, which it had endowed with a jurisdiction necessary to the commonwealth under peculiar circumstances. This conflict thus begun by Judge Drummond, in 1855-6, against the Territorial commonwealth, falsely interpreted to Buchanan's administration, is rendered in General Scott's instructions as "state of substantial rebellion against the laws and authority of the United States."

The burden of the subject resting then, at this point with the jurisdiction of our probate courts, and the Territorial business generally; it is needful that we enlarge the review of previous chapters relative to the reasons of the superior jurisdiction given to those courts, and the creation of the offices of Territorial Marshal, Attorney General and District Attorney. The reason in fine was the desertion of the Chief Justice and one of his associates, accompanied by the Secretary of the Territory and Indian Agent, carrying away all the government funds. It is not necessary to again review their conduct, or to reaffirm the justification of Governor Young and the Mormon community, but simply to repeat the connecting cause of the powers which the legislature conferred upon the probate courts and the creation of the Territorial officers. Associate Justice Snow was not set aside by the Legislature, but an enabling act was passed authorizing him to hold United States Courts in all the districts; at the same time jurisdiction was given to the probate courts in civil and criminal affairs in the interest of the commonwealth, lest it should be left altogether unable to administer in the departments of justice, which would have been the case at that moment had Associate Justice Snow died or left the Territory. Mr. Magraw himself unintentionally illustrated this point, when he told the President that the probate court was the only existing tribunal in Utah, "there being but one of the three federal judges now in the Territory." This was the exact case at the onset when the probate court was created.

Already extracts have been made from the correspondence between Judge Snow and the Hon. Elisha Whittlesey, who drew a strong line of demarcation between United States and Territorial business, making it absolutely necessary for the Territory to assume the responsibility and cost of its own business.

This, however, the legislature did against its own judgment, holding that the Territorial District Courts were really United States Courts. Judge Snow, continuing the correspondence, discussing the subject with the comptroller of the treasury in behalf of his court and the legislature, said in his letter of February 8, "853-"To enable you to fully understand the present situation of things, before proceeding further, I will inform you that the Legislative Assembly passed an act, approved October 4th, 1851, authorizing and requiring me, for a limited time, to hold all the courts in the Territory, but said nothing about jurisdiction, appellate or original. (See Utah Laws, p. 37.) "February 4, 1852, another act was approved, giving jurisdiction to the district courts in all cases, civil and criminal, also in chancery. (See ib., p. 38, sec. 2.) The same law gave jurisdiction to the probate courts, civil and criminal, also in chancery. (See ib., p. 43, sec. 36.) An act was approved March 3rd, 1852, providing for the appointment of a Territorial Marshal, Attorney General and District Attorneys, to attend to legal business in the district courts when the Territory should be interested. (See ib., pp. 56, 57.) "I do not intend to be understood as expressing any opinion in relation to the legality of these several enactments, but I only mention them to enable you to understand the present views of the Legislative Assembly, as expressed in a report to which I shall soon refer. This report was called out by reason of the non-payment of these costs. I having referred the claimants to the Legislative Assembly, they procured my certificate of their correctness and petitioned for payment. The petition was referred to a committee on claims, and, to enable that committee to understand the subject, the Council passed a resolution, requesting me to inform them of the amount of costs of holding the courts for the past year, distinguishing those which in my opinion should be paid by the general government from those payable by the Territory.

"With this request I complied, and gave the reasons of my opinion, acting on the principle that the reasons of an opinion are often of far more value than the opinion itself. In so doing I laid before them my correspondence with you and referred to such of the laws of the United States as in my opinion had a bearing on the subject, and to the enactments. I also went minutely into the usual officers of the courts and expenses attendant upon them and showed how these officers and courts are usually paid, in both civil and criminal cases, together with the payment of the incidental expenses, making my answer quite lengthy, too much so for insertion in this communication.

"This committee reported adversely to payment by the Territory, but upon what principle I have not been informed. The subject was then referred to a judiciary committee, composed of some of the best members of the council. This committee reported adversely to payment by the Territory and gave their reasons.

This report was adopted, therefore I proceed to notice the positions taken by them.

"They commence with what they call the equity of the principle involved in the question presented, saying that nearly all the costs of courts here have accrued by reason of emigration passing through here to California and Oregon, and that justice requires the United States to pay such expenses.

"My experience in the courts thus far justifies the firm belief that the facts here assumed are correctly stated. See my concluding remark in my letter of July 10. But with this equitable consideration, I am unable to see what I have to do, though I can see its bearing when addressed to the political branches of the government by whom and to whom that matter was then addressed.

"They further take the position that the United States and the Territory of Utah respectively must sustain and bear the expenses, direct and incidental, of the officers and offices of its own creation, that the supreme and district courts were created, not by a law of Utah, but by a law of the United States; and as such, by the Organic Act, they have jurisdiction, civil and criminal, in all cases not arising out of the constitution and laws of the United States, unless such jurisdiction should be limited by a law of the Territory; that congress, by extending the constitution and laws of the United States over the Territory, and creating courts and appointing officers to execute these laws, had done what was her right and duty to do, but, as she had seen fit to go further and give jurisdiction to her courts and require her officers to execute the laws of the Territory, it had become her duty to sustain these courts and officers, and bear their expenses; that the Territorial Legislature, by giving jurisdiction to these courts and dividing the Territory into districts, had done nothing but discharge a duty which Congress had required at their hands, but this did not require them to bear any part of the expenses; that these courts took jurisdiction in all cases, not by virtue of the Territorial laws, but by a law of Congress; that the Territories, by their Organic Acts, are not independent governments within the meaning of the term that all just powers emanate from the government, but are subordinate, dependent branches of government; that Congress did not intend to give any court jurisdiction in civil and criminal cases at common law and in chancery, but the supreme and district courts, and, as she had reserved the right to nullify any act of the Legislative Assembly, she could enforce obedience to her mandates; that, with such a state of things, it is contrary to every principle of justice and sound legislation to require so dependent a branch of government to bear any part of the expenses of enforcing the laws; that the officers, having charge of that branch of public service, ought not to so construe the acts of Congress as to produce such results, so long as the long as the laws will admit of a construction consistent with justice and sound legislation; that, in their opinion, the acts of Congress did not require such a construction, but on the contrary they strongly indicated, if they did not require, the construction contended for by them; and that the same principle which would require such dependencies to pay a part (of the expenses) would require them to pay the whole, and with that construction Congress might, at the expense of the Territories, impose upon them any embodiment of officers she, in her discretion, might see fit to send, which never could have been intended by the framers of the constitution.

"This report concludes by recommending that these costs be referred to me, with the opinion of the council that they are payable out or the annual appropriations made by Congress for defraying the expenses of the circuit and district courts of the United States, and by recommending that the laws of Utah be so amended as to take away the jurisdiction of the probate courts at common law, civil and criminal, and in chancery, and abolish the offices of territorial marshal, attorney-general, and district attorneys, so that the United States, by her judges, attorneys and marshals may execute the laws of the Territory. But, as this report was not made until a late day in the session, the laws were not so amended.

Should the next Legislative Assembly in these matters concur with this, the laws above referred to will either be repealed or modified."

It will be seen by this report of the committee that the Utah Legislature, as early as 1852-3, desired to do what, after twenty years of conflict, was accomplished,— namely, to limit the jurisdiction of the probate court and to abolish those Territorial officers which had been created from necessity, "so that the United States, by her judges, attorneys and marshals may execute the laws of the Territory."

It appears, then, from this review made by Associate Justice Snow, long before the date of the Utah Expedition that the conflict which arose in the courts of Judges Drummond and Stiles, furnishing the most direct cause of said expedition, was not in consequence of the Legislature desiring to limit the legitimate rule of the federal officers, much less to put the Territory in the attitude of rebellion, but rather that Drummond and others sought the conflict with the very design so soon afterwards expressed in the Utah war. Such, at least, was the opinion of the Mormon people.

In the Spring of 1857, Associate Justice Drummond went to Carson Valley ostensibly to hold court, instead of which he immediately left Carson for California to commence his crusade. As soon as he reached the Pacific Coast he made a fierce attack upon the Mormons in the papers of San Francisco. He next from New Orleans April 2, 1857, dispatched his resignation to the Government that it might reach Washington before the executive session adjourned.

His exposure—much of it false and much of it exaggerated—added to the affidavit of Judge Stiles who was then in Washington, aroused Congress to demand immediate action.

Meantime, while this war crusade was being worked up against Utah, she was making extraordinary efforts to bring herself into closer relations with the Eastern States, and a broader intercourse with the world generally. As already seen, early in the year 1856, she had made a grand demonstration for admission into the Union, and now the close of the year saw her undertaking a great enterprise to aid the Government in its postal service, enlarge her own commerce, and establish a line of settlements between Great Salt Lake City and the Eastern frontiers. One of the citizens of Utah, Mr. Hiram Kimball, had obtained the contract from the Post Office Department for the transportation of the United States mails across the plains between Independence, Missouri, and this city.

Hitherto the postal service with Utah had been very unsatisfactory, the contracts being exceedingly low, which gave the contractors, who were only commercially interested in Utah, nothing of the citizen's impulse and ambition to perfect the mail service. Feramorz Little, indeed, as a sub-contractor, had on former occasions made exceedingly short time, but up to the letting of the contract to Mr. Hiram Kimball, the enterprising men of Salt Lake City, whose commercial facilities would be greatly enhanced by the organization of a grand carrying company, had found no opportunity for such a design. The contract of Mr. Hiram Kimball amounted to only $23,600 for the mail service, but Governor Young saw in it the foundation of a gigantic express company, such as only he could possibly organize, having at his back an entire community who was so vitally concerned in the enterprise.

Locked out by deep snows on the mountains from nearly all intercourse with the Eastern States during the terrible winter of 1856, and almost as destitute of news from the Pacific, the Mormons had little idea of the stir which Utah had created everywhere throughout the Union since the former contractor, Magraw, had written his letter to the President of the United States, dated Independence, Missouri, October 3, 1856, since which time, they had received no mail; much less did they know of the inception of the "contractors' war," as in the sequel the Utah Expedition was very generally considered to be.

Taking up the mail contract of the Government in good faith, and with that executive promptness and confidence in his resources which were so characteristic of the man, Governor Young bent all his energies to organize the "B. Y. Express." He gathered around him the most intrepid men of the mountains, urged the brethren who had stock to join in the enterprise, and succeeded in controlling all that was necessary to make such a gigantic company as that which he designed successful. There were many companies organized with outfitting teams, tools, farming utensils, etc., to form settlements over the entire line, though at that date there were only a few mountaineers living between Salt Lake City and the terminal point.

The winter snows of 1856-7 had tarried long on the mountains and the plains, and this rendered the stocking of the road and the building of stations over the long distance of 1,200 miles a very severe task. But there was every incentive to more than ordinary diligence. The Government had never exhibited much favor to any Mormon citizen. The acting postmaster at that time, Judge Elias Smith, was only a deputy of the gentile postmaster, Mr. William Bell. Any delay now in commencing the new mail contract might be seized as a pretext for repudiating the new contractor, which really turned out to be the case when the expedition made it convenient for the Government to find such a pretext. With this fully impressed upon their minds, the most daring and hardy of the mountaineers were called by Governor Young to assist, and in an incredibly short space of time, and in the midst of very severe weather, stations were built and relays of horses and mules were strung all the way along the traveled route, from the mountains to the Missouri river. There was a fair prospect that the "B. Y. Express Carrying Company" would soon grow into the vast enterprise as designed, conveying all the merchandise and mails from the East and placing Utah, by means of express messengers, in daily intercourse with the rest of the world, a decade before that desired end was accomplished by the railroad.

But this very enterprise, undertaken in the service of the Government, having for its aim also the general good and commercial advancement of this western country, and for the safety of the emigrations, which were fast peopling these young States and Territories, was construed against the Mormons as one of the causes which gave rise to the Utah Expedition. This will be exemplified in document, No. 33, furnished to the House from the Indian Department.

"Indian Agency of the Upper Platte, On Raw Hide Creek, July 15, 1857.

"Sir: In a communication addressed to the Indian Office, dated April last, I called the attention of the department to the settlements being made within the boundaries of this agency by the ' Mormon Church,' clearly in violation of law, although the pretext or pretense under which these settlements are made is under the cover of a contract of the Mormon Church to carry the mail from Independence, Missouri, to Great Salt Lake City.

"On the 25th May, a large Mormon colony took possession of the valley of Deer Creek, one hundred miles west of Fort Laramie, and drove away a band of Sioux Indians whom I had settled there in April and had induced them to plant corn.

"I left that Indian band on the 23rd May, to attend to matters connected with the Cheyenne band, in the lower part of the agency.

"I have information from a reliable source that these Mormons are about three hundred in number, have plowed and planted two hundred acres of prairie, and are building houses sufficient for the accommodation of five hundred persons, and have a large herd of cattle, horses and mules.

"I am persuaded that the Mormon Church intend, by this plan thus partially developed, to monopolize all of the trade with the Indians and whites within, or passing through, the Indian country.

"I respectfully and earnestly rail the attention of the department to this invasion and enter my protest against this occupation of the Indian country, in force, and the forcible ejection of the Indians from the place where I had settled them.

"I am powerless to control this matter, for the Mormons obey no laws enacted by Congress. I would respectfully request that the President will be pleased to issue such order as, in his wisdom and judgment, may seem best in order to correct the evil complained of.

"Very respectfully, your obedient servant,

THOS. S. TWISS, Indian Agent, Upper Platte.

"Hon. J. W. Denver, Commissioner of Indian Affairs." The date of the communication referred to, (of April, 1857), is prior to the circular of General Scott, and cotemporary with the letter of Judge Drummond to the Attorney General, which was dated April 2nd, 1857, enclosing his resignation dated March 30th, 1857. These three letters quoted—from the contractor, Magraw, Associate Justice Drummond, and Indian Agent Twiss—are the very documents which, both in subject and date, bore most directly upon the "information which gave rise to the military expedition ordered to Utah Territory, * * * throwing light upon the question as to how far said Brigham Young and his followers are in a state of rebellion or resistance to the government of the United States." Moreover, in most of the documents furnished to the House, excepting those from the War Department, of date subsequent to the determination of the Expedition, there is seen not only a marked, and almost serial connection with the three documents in example, but the evidence of a decided conspiracy; that is to say, those documents were concocted both with malice and intent to bring on the "Utah War," by leading the Government astray with false information that "Brigham Young and his followers" were "in a state of rebellion or resistance to the government of the United States." It will be noticeable, that two of the six " Gentiles of Great Salt Lake City," to whom Judge Drummond refers the Attorney General " for proof of the manner in which they have been insulted and abused by leading Mormons for two years past," are Garland Hurt, Indian Agent, and John M. Hockaday, merchant and mail contractor. There was no call for proof from the Chief Justice, John F. Kinney, then in the east, nor from such Gentile merchants as Livingston and Bell, the latter of whom was also the postmaster of Great Salt Lake City, nor from William H. Hooper, who in that period must be considered as a Gentile merchant rather than as a Mormon.

Now, the pertinency of this mail business in the historical exposition of causes which led to the Utah war will appear at the very naming of the fact that Hockaday and Magraw were the former contractors to carry the mail between Independence, Missouri, and Great Salt Lake City.

Notice at this point a remarkable connection of causes suggestive of conspiracy, when laid side by side with subsequent events, and the acts of the principal factors who gave to the Government the information that led to the sending of the Expedition to put down a rebellion, which had no existence in fact or intent, so far as the citizens of Utah were concerned.

In the fall of 1856, Hockaday and Magraw lost the mail contract, which, as noticed, was awarded to Mr. Hiram Kimball, a citizen of Utah. This award was not as any favor from the department, which, there is every reason to believe, preferred the former contractors, but in compliance with the rule, requiring the lowest responsible bid. The mail service for Utah was now in the hands of the community so vitally concerned in its success, rather than in the mere emoluments of the contract; and Governor Young, in the interest of the commerce of the Territory, and of their emigrations, as well as for the quick and reliable postal intercourse with the Eastern States, had already designed the gigantic "B. Y. Express Carrying Company."

Doubtless the former contractor, one of whom, Mr. Hockaday, was a resident merchant of Salt Lake City, knew of the conception of such a design of Governor Young, sometime before the new contract was awarded, seeing the contract was sought for that very purpose. The great Mormon colonizer and city founder, had already proclaimed his intention of establishing a line of settlements from Great Salt Lake City to Carson Valley, and a line of intercourse east to the Missouri River; and it was quite certain that, on this eastern line, a chain of settlements would spring up out of the Mormon emigrations, as soon as permitted by the Government in its treaties for Indian lands. This example was given by the Mormons in their exodus, when they established "stakes of Zion " on the route to the Mountains—laid the foundations indeed of what have since become our great frontier cities. No sooner did the Indian agent, Thomas S. Twiss, see the establishment of the mail stations, by the "Y. X. Company," than he predicted to the Government, the Mormon control of the trade of the plains, and urged hostilities to prevent this colonization of the eastern line, exaggerating a mail station into a settlement of five hundred, and charging the Mormons with driving off the Indians and unlawfully settling on their lands.

The contractor, W. M. F. Magraw, on the side of his personal interest, seems to have been in full understanding and perfect accord with Indian Agent Twiss; and immediately upon the award of the contract to Mr. Hiram Kimball, upon which was to be based the operation of the " B. Y. Express and Carrying Company," he wrote to the President of the United States, addressing him "as a personal and political friend," to lay before him "some information relative to the present political and social condition of the Territory of Utah," in which "there is left no protection for life or property," but a condition of things, which, (to follow the contractor's words) "will, when published, startle the conservative people of the States, and. create a clamor which will not be readily quelled; and I have no doubt that the time is near at hand, and the elements rapidly combining to bring about a state of affairs which will result in indiscriminate bloodshed, robbery and rapine, and which, in a brief space of time will reduce that country to a condition of a howling wilderness."

Very suggestive is this prediction of the contractor Magraw, in view of the fact that it was afterwards nearly fulfilled. It was the prospect of the ensuing two years—a prospect, moreover, which was known in the States, and even in Europe, quite six months before it was known to the people of Utah—which reasonably suggests that it was an anticipation not of prescient sagacity, but of a direct conspiracy to accomplish that foreshadowed in Magraw's letter, presented by Secretary Cass as the first link of the information which gave rise to the Utah Expedition. And the prediction is the more striking the closer it is viewed, and the nearer the altar is approached upon which the sacrifice to be offered up was laid. The Mormon community is the sacrifice seen upon the altar, just as it had been in Missouri and Illinois,—a sacrifice which, when it was revealed in the actual offering to the gaze of the good wife of Governor Cummings, caused that lady to weep, and in anguish to implore her noble-hearted husband to use his influence with the Government to save the devoted people. It was the "country" which the Mormons had changed from " the desert to the fruitful field," and made it "blossom as the rose," that in "a brief space of time" was to be reduced "to a condition of a howling wilderness," which, when General Johnston and his army were brought face to face with the prospect, as they rode through the deserted city of the Great Salt Lake, appalled even those familiar with the desolations of war.

The prediction of this mail contractor, then, has a deep significance in the history, especially when coupled with his statement to the President, to the effect that there was about to be " published" charges against the Mormon community which would "startle the conservative people of the States, and create a clamor which will not be readily quelled." This was fulfilled to the letter, when a few months later Judge Drummond fulminated his monstrous charges, both in California and the Eastern States, and aroused a fury in the nation to "wipe" the Mormon community out.

But there is another part of the narrative to be yet told, relative to the mail service and the contracts in question, that ramifies itself in every branch of the history, from the date of Mr. Magraw's letter to the President, to the time of the repudiation of the Kimball contract by the General Post Office Department, and the arrival of the news in Utah that an army was on the way. The major thread of this subject shall be left to the hereafter review, in the next message of the Governor Young to the Legislature, so ponderous and important is the matter; but a few minor threads is here necessary for the completeness of the historic story.

The failure of the contractor Magraw to bring the last mails, which kept Utah and "the world" so long without news of each other, made it necessary for the postmaster of Great Salt Lake City, to make a special contract to carry the mail east to the terminal point, Independence, Missouri. Feramorz Little was entrusted with the contract, and he and Ephraim K. Hanks left Great Salt Lake City with the mail, December 11, 1856. Beyond the Devil's Gate on the way they met the former contractor's outfit—Mr. Magraw and company. They were bringing their last mail through and picking up their stock. Having tarried so long, however, this contractor and his company failed to come through, in consequence of the deep snows in the mountains, and they returned to the Platte River Bridge and wintered. The important item will by and by appear in Governor Young's message, that the official letter of the award of the new contract to Mr. Hiram Kimball wintered with them, in the pocket of one of the contractor's agents, which circumstance had a sequel not greatly to the honor of the post office department, in its repudiation of Mr. Kimball's contract, on the pretext of the service not being commenced by him in the stipulated time.

Mr. Little with the special mail arrived at Independence, Missouri on the 27th of February, 1857, after a very severe trip. He forthwith proceeded to Washington to collect his money for taking the mail down, which having accomplished, he went to New York. The charges of Judge Drummond were just at that moment published in the Eastern papers, creating a great excitement. The following letter to the public from Mr. Little was called forth in answer:

"Merchant's Hotel, N. Y., April 15, 1857.

"Editor Herald.

"Sir: As myself and Mr. E. K. Hanks are the last persons who have come to the States from Great Salt Lake City, I deem it my duty to bear testimony against the lying scribblers who seem to be doing their utmost to stir up a bad feeling against the Utonians. We left our homes on the 11th of December, brought the last mail to the States, and certainly should know of the state of things there. The charges of Judge Drummond are as false as he is corrupt. Before I left for the States, I was five days every week in Great Salt Lake City, and I witness to all the world that I never heard one word of the burning of nine hundred volumes of law, records, etc., nor anything of that character, nor do I know, or ever heard of anything of the dumb boy story he talks of.

"There is only one house between my house and the Penitentiary, said to contain "five or six young men from Missouri and Iowa," and I do know that up to the day I left, there were only in that place of confinement three Indians, who were convicted at the time of Colonel Steptoe's sojourn there, for having taken part in the massacre of Captain Gunnison and party, which Drummond now charges upon the Mormons, even though Colonel Steptoe and the United States' officers then in Utah investigated the affair thoroughly and secured the conviction of the three Indians alluded to. This is an unblushing falsehood, that none but a man like Drummond could pen.

"The treasonable acts alleged against the Mormons in Utah are false from beginning to end. At Fort Kearney we learned all about the murder of Colonel Babbitt and do know that that charge against the Mormons is but another of Drummond's creations.

"I have but a short time at my disposal for writing, but must say, that I am astonished to find in the States, rumors against Utah. We left our homes in peace, dreaming of no evil, and we come here and learn that we are the most corrupt of men, and are preparing for war.

"Yours, etc.,
FERAMORZ LITTLE."

At New York, Mr. Little learned from Mr. James Monroe Livingston, one of the firm of Livingston and Kinkead, of Great Salt Lake City, that the "Y. X." company for carrying the mails had been started, and that he, Mr. Little, was expected to take charge of the returning mails. He immediately hastened to Independence, Missouri, where he found the agents who had come down from the mountains with the Utah mails. There was at Independence a large accumulation of mail matter, amounting to several tons. The men in charge fitted up two or three wagons, and Mr. John R. Murdock, with the latest mail selected, started home on the 1st of May, while Mr. Little remained to get up the June mail, and on the 1st of June, he started himself with three wagon loads of postal matter.

While at Independence, gathering up the mails, Mr. Little had much intercourse with the numerous contractors at that point, who were waiting the contracts for the Utah Expedition, with which, though not yet announced officially from the War Department, they were well posted in the design. The Mormon mail agent at first could not believe it possible that the Government was about to send an army against Utah for being in a state of rebellion which, he assured them was not the case, while they in turn assured him that such an expedition was projected and certain. What a suggestion of "the Contractor's war"!

A short distance from Fort Laramie, Mr. Little met Abraham O. Smoot, Esq., the then Mayor of Great Salt Lake City, in charge of the June mail going east. Of his trip Mayor Smoot furnishes us the following: "On the 2nd of June, 1857, I left Salt Lake City in company with a young man from the Thirteenth Ward, by the name of Ensign, (whose father still resides in that ward), in charge of the last mail going east by the Y. Express.

"We met between Fort Laramie and Kearney, some two or three hundred United States troops, who said they were reconnoitering the country in search of hostile Indians, who at that time were very troublesome on the plains. The officer in command (whose name has gone from me) treated us very kindly, and proposed to furnish us an escort as far east as Fort Kearney, I thanked him for his kind consideration in offering the escort, but told him I feared his escort would not be able to keep up with me, as I proposed to drive about sixty miles a day, until 1 reached Fort Kearney, and at that speed I thought there would be little, if any, danger of the Indians overtaking us.

"About one hundred miles west of Independence we began to meet heavy freight teams. The captains and teamsters all seemed to be very reticent in relation to giving their destination, and all I was able to learn from them was that they had Government freight, and were bound for some western post, and the trains belonged to William H. Russell.

"In less than two days from that time I reached Kansas City, twelve miles west of Independence, where I met Nicholas Groesbeck who had charge of the Y. X. Company at that end of the route. In company with him we immediately proceeded to the office of William H. Russell, and there learned that the destination of his freight trains was Salt Lake City, with supplies for Government troops who would soon follow, I also learned from William H. Russell of the appointment of Governor Cumming and other Federal officers that came out with the United States troops that year.

"The next morning Mr. Groesbeck sent the mail into Independence and I remained in Kansas City to learn more of the movements of the Government, if possible.

"The mail we took down was received by the postmaster and he informed the carrier that he had received instructions from the Government to deliver no more mail for Salt Lake City at present.

That denial implied that we had no more use for our stock and mail stations on the route; so, in consultation with Bro. N. Groesbeck and others, we concluded to move our stock and station outfits homeward. Myself and Judson Stoddard were given the responsibility, and two or three other young men (Bro. Ensign being one) were detailed to assist us.

"We moved slowly gathering everything as we went, until we reached South Platte about 120 miles east of Fort Laramie where we met Porter Rockwell with the July mail from Salt Lake City, he proceeded no further east but returned with us to Fort Laramie, 513 miles east of Salt Lake, arriving there on the 17th of July.

"On the 18th Bro. O. P. Rockwell and myself, believing that we had passed all danger of Indian troubles, concluded to leave the stock in the care of Bro. J. Stoddard and others to bring in at their leisure and we would make our way home by the 24th of July, the tenth anniversary of the arrival of the Pioneers in Salt Lake Valley. This arrangement did not meet with the approval of Bro. Stoddard against which he strongly protested but without effect, so he finally accepted the alternative of leaving his stock (some eight or ten which were his personal property) with his trusty hired men and accompany us to the Salt Lake Valley.

"We hitched up two span of our best animals to a small spring wagon and left Fort Laramie on the evening of the 18th of July, and reached Salt Lake City on the evening of the 23rd of July, making the 513 miles in five days and three hours.

Yours respectfully, A. O. SMOOT.

Prow City, Utah, February 14th, 1884."

CHAPTER XVII.

THE PIONEER JUBILEE. CELEBRATION OF THEIR TENTH ANNIVERSARY. ARRIVAL OF MESSENGERS WITH THE NEWS OF THE COMING OF AN INVADING ARMY. THE DAY OF JUBILEE CHANGED TO A DAY OF INDEPENDENCE. CAPTAIN VAN VLIET AND THE MORMON PEOPLE.

The people were celebrating the twenty-fourth of July—the anniversary of the pioneers—in Big Cottonwood Canyon, when the news reached them of the coming of the troops to invade their homes.

They had conquered the desert. Cities were fast springing up in the solitary places, where cities had never been planted before, and in valleys that had once been the bed of the great sea; civilization was spreading.

A plentiful harvest was promised that year, and every circumstance of their situation seemed favorable, except the lack of postal communication with the East. Their isolation, in this particular, had kept them in ignorance, up to that time, of the movements of the Government concerning them.

On the 22nd of July, 1857, numerous teams were seen wending their way, by different routes, to the mouth of Big Cottonwood Canyon, where they halted for the night. Next morning Governor Young led the van of the long line of carriages and wagons, and before noon the cavalcade reached the camp ground at the Cottonwood Lake, which nestles in the bosom of the mountain, 8,000 feet above the level of the sea. Early in the afternoon, the company, numbering 2,687 persons, encamped, and soon all were busy with the arrangements for the morrow. It will be seen, at a glance, that this was intended to be a pioneer's jubilee indeed; not in a city, but in primitive surroundings, suggestive of their entrance into these valleys ten years before.

There were in attendance: Captain Ballo's band, the Nauvoo brass band, the Ogden City brass band, and the Great Salt Lake City and Ogden martial bands; also, of the military, the 1st company of light artillery, under Adjutant General James Ferguson; a detachment of four platoons of life guards and one platoon of the lancers, under Colonel Burton; and one company of light infantry cadets, under Captain John W. Young. Colonel J. C. Little was marshal of the day.

Early on the following morning the people assembled, and the choir sang: "On the mountain tops appearing." Then, after prayers the Stars and Stripes were unfurled on the two highest peaks, in sight of the camp, on two of the tallest trees. At twenty minutes past nine a. m., three rounds from the artillery saluted the First Presidency, and at a quarter past ten three rounds were given for the "Hope of Israel," Captain John W. Young, with his company of light infantry, answered to this last salute, and went through their military evolutions to the admiration of the beholders.

This company numbered fifty boys, at about the age of twelve, who had been uniformed by Governor Young.

At noon, Mayor A. O. Smoot, Elder Judson Stoddard, Judge Elias Smith, and O. P. Rockwell, rode into camp, the two former from the "States" (Missouri River), in twenty days. They brought news of the coming of the troops.

It was the first tidings of war. Any other people in the world would have been stricken with a terrible fear; but not so these Mormon Saints. The well-known Avar cry of Cromwell, when he entered into battle, "The Lord of Hosts is with us!" was the undaunted explanation of every heart, and soon it was the burden of every speech.

In a moment the festive song was changed to the theme of war; the jubilee of a people swelled into a sublime declaration of independence. Never before did such a spirit of heroism so suddenly and completely possess an entire community.

Men and women shared it alike. The purest and most graphic passage of Stenhouse's "Rocky Mountain Saints" is the description of this eventful day. It is worthy of quotation. He says: "On the 24th of July, 1857, there were probably gathered at the lake about two thousand persons—men women, and children—in the fullest enjoyment of social freedom. Some were fishing in the lake, others strolling among the trees, climbing the high peaks, pitching quoits, playing cricket, engaging in gymnastic exercises, pic-nicking, and gliding through the boweries that were prepared for the mazy dance. It was a day of feasting, joy, and amusement for the silver-haired veteran and the tottering child. The welkin rang with the triumphant songs of Zion, and these, accompanied by the sweet melody of many-toned instruments of music, thrilled every bosom with enthusiastic joy. Their exuberance was the pure outgushing of their souls' emotion, and owned no earthly inspiration, for their only beverage was the sparkling nectar of Eden, while their sympathies were united by a sacred and fraternal bond of affectionate love, which for the time rendered them oblivious of the artificial distinctions of social life. The highest and the lowest rejoiced together, rank and authority were set aside; it was a day in which the dreary past could be favorably contrasted with the joyous present, and hearts were made glad in the simple faith that the God of their fathers was their protector, and that they were his peculiar people.

"But before the sun had crimsoned the snowy peaks that surrounded the worshiping, rejoicing Saints, Brigham was in possession of the news, and the people were listening with breathless attention to the most stirring, important address that ever their leader had uttered, for upon his decision depended peace or war.

"Brigham was undaunted. With the inspiration of such surroundings—the grandeur of the Wasatch range of the Rocky Mountains everywhere encircling him, the stately trees whose foliage of a century's growth towered proudly to the heavens, the multitude of people before him who had listened to his counsels as if hearkening to the voice of the Most High—men and women who had followed him from the abodes of civilization to seek shelter in the wilderness from mobs, prattling innocents and youths who knew nothing of the world but Utah, and' who looked to him as a father for protection—what could he not say?"

To say that the Mormons were taken with astonishment would be to-misstate the case. They had long looked for this issue. They had seen mobs marshaled against them from the beginning, but they had also been told by their Prophet Joseph Smith, early in his career, that "Someday they would see the United States come against them in war, and that the Lord should deliver them and bring glory to His name," Nothing more unlikely could have been uttered by this prophet of a few hundred disciples; as likely was it that the stars of heaven should make war upon the earth in impotent wrath. They were not even in a location at that time where this was possible. The very prophecy foreshadowed their removal to the mountains, as though to invite the nation to the issue; and its fulfillment bespoke a destiny in them superior to the destiny even of the United States.

The nation was now coming against them, to verify the prophecy in the most literal manner. Hence, doubtless, the extraordinary trust and fortitude of the people, and the self-possession of their leaders. They had no doubt as to the issue, though how God would work out their deliverance they saw not fully.

Everything the Mormons did at that time was done in the most deliberate earnestness. Two messengers were immediately dispatched to England, to call home the American Elders in Europe, and ten thousand British Saints would have gathered that year, had it been possible, to share the fate of their brethren and sisters in the mountains; but all emigration was, of course now cut off.

Never was there so much enthusiasm in the foreign missions as then. One could judge of the sublime enthusiasm at home by that which animated the Saints abroad. Yet they saw a mighty nation moving against the handful in the mountains and moving with a settled resolve to annihilate the Mormon power at once and forever, leaving no seed on American territory from which that power might re-germinate. The papers of America and Europe teemed with these anticipations.

It was broadly suggested that volunteers from every State should pour into Utah, make short work of the Saints, possess their cities, fill their Territory with a gentile population, and take their wives and daughters as spoil, thus breaking up the polygamic institution. For a time there was a prospect of this. Tens of thousands were eager for this thorough work of regeneration for Utah; and, had the Government dared to encourage it, the attempt would have been made. For such a crusade, however, a civilized judgement could have found no excuse, not even on the plea of rebellion. At least, President Buchanan was made to see this much, and to appreciate that he could only use United States regular troops, and these only in the guise of a posse comitatus to the new Governor.

The sentiments that actuated the Mormon community at that time were of no doubtful tenor, as may be judged by the following extracts from Brigham's discourses to his people immediately after the receipt of the news.

"Liars have reported that this people have committed treason, and upon their misrepresentations the President has ordered out troops to aid in officering this Territory. If those officers are like many who have previously been sent here—and we have reason to believe that they are, or they would not come where they know they are not wanted—they are poor, broken down political hacks, not fit for the civilized society whence they came, and so they are dragooned upon us for officers. I feel that I won't bear such treatment (and that is enough to say,) for we are just as free as the mountain air. * * * This people are free; they are not in bondage to any Government on God's footstool. We have transgressed no law, neither do we intend so to do; but as for any nation coming to destroy this people, God Almighty being my helper, it shall not be! * * * We have borne enough of their oppression and abuse, and we will not bear any more of it, for there is no just law requiring further forbearance on our part.

And I am not going to permit troops here for the protection of the priests and the rabble in their efforts to drive us from the land we possess. The Lord does not want us to be driven, for He has said, 'If you will assert your rights, and keep my commandments, you shall never again be brought into bondage by your enemies' * * * They say that the coming of their army is legal; and I say that it is not; they who say it are morally rotten. Come on with your thousands of illegally-ordered troops, and I promise you in the name of Israel's God, that they shall melt away as the snow before a July sun. * * * You might as well tell me that you can make hell into a powder-house as to tell me that they intend to keep an army here and have peace! * * * I have told you that if this people will live their religion all will be well; and I have told you that if there is any man or woman who's not willing to destroy everything of their property that would be of use to an enemy if left, I would advise them to leave the Territory. And I again say so to-day; for when the time comes to burn and lay waste our improvements, if any man undertakes to shield his he will be treated as a traitor; for 'judgement will be laid to the line, and righteousness to the plummet.' * * * Now the faint-hearted can go in peace; but should that time come, they must not interfere. Before I will again suffer as I have in times gone by there shall not one building, nor one foot of lumber, nor a fence, nor a tree, nor a particle of grass or hay, that will burn, be left in reach of our enemies. I am sworn, if driven to extremity, to utterly lay waste this land in the name of Israel's God, and our enemies shall find it as barren as when we came here."

It was at such a moment, as the picture suggests, that Capt. Van Vliet arrived in the city of the Saints. The Governor, the Lieut. General, Daniel H. Wells, Adjt. General Furguson, and the Apostles, received him with marked cordiality, but with an open programme. They took him into their gardens. The sisters showed him the paradise that their woman hands would destroy if that invading army came. He was awed by the prospect—his ordinary judgment confounded by such extraordinary examples. To the wife of Albert Carrington, in whose garden he was walking, in conversation with the Governor and his party he exclaimed:

"What, madam! would you consent to see this beautiful home in ashes and this fruitful orchard destroyed?"

"Yes!" answered Sister Carrington, with heroic resolution, "I would not only consent to it, but I would set fire to my home with my own hands and cut down every tree and root up every plant!"

The following extracts from conversations between Governor Young and Captain Van Vliet, on the 12th and 13th of September, 1857, will be of interest, insomuch as they were had previous to the receipt, in Salt Lake City, of the news of the Mountain Meadow Massacre. Their accuracy may be relied on, as they are transcribed from Apostle Woodruff's private journal, and were originally recorded within a few hours of their occurrence, and are amply verified by many persons then present:

"President Young. We do not want to fight the United States, but if they drive us to it, we shall do the best we can; and I will tell you, as the Lord lives, we shall come off conquerors, for we trust in Him. * * * God has set up his kingdom on the earth, and it will never fall. * * * We shall do all we can to avert a collision, but if they drive us to it, God will overthrow them. If they would let us alone and say to the mobs: 'Now you may go and kill the Mormons if you can, but we will have nothing to do with it,' that would be all we would ask of them; but for the Government to array the army against us, is too despicable and damnable a thing for any honorable nation to do, and God will hold them in derision who do it. * * * The United States are sending their armies here to simply hold us still until a mob can come and butcher us, as has been done before. * * * We are the supporters of the constitution of the United States, and we love that constitution and respect the laws of the United States; but it is by the corrupt administration of those laws that we are made to suffer. If the law had been vindicated in Missouri, it would have sent Governor Boggs to the gallows, along with those who murdered Joseph and Hyrum, and those other fiends who accomplished our expulsion from the States. * * * Most of the Government officers who have been sent here have taken no interest in us, but, on the contrary, have tried many times to destroy us.

"Capt. Van Vliet This is the case with most men sent to the Territories. They receive their offices as a political reward, or as a stepping-stone to the Senatorship; but they have no interest in common with the people. * * * This people has been lied about the worst of any people I ever saw. * * The greatest hold that the Government now has upon you is in the accusation that you have burned the United States records.

"President Young. I deny that any books of the United States have been burned! All I ask of any man is, that he tell the truth about us, pay his debts and not steal, and then he will be welcome to come or go as he likes. * * If the Government has arrived at that state that it will try to kill this people because of their religion, no honorable man should be afraid of it. * * We would like to ward off this blow if we can; but the United States seem determined to drive us into a fight. They will kill us if they can. A mob killed Joseph and Hyrum in jail, notwithstanding the faith of the State was pledged to protect them. * * * I have broken no law, and under the present state of affairs I will not suffer myself to be taken by any United States officer, to be killed as they killed Joseph.

"Capt. Van Vliet: I do not think it is the intention of the Government to arrest you, but to install a new governor in the Territory.

"President Young: I believe you tell the truth—that you believe this—but you do not know their intentions as well as I do. When you get away from here you will think of a great many things that you have seen and heard: for instance, people have accused us of colleaguing with the Indians against the Government: they were much afraid that Joseph Smith would go among the Indians, and they wanted to keep him away from them; but now they have driven us into their midst. I want you to note the signs of the times; you will see that God will chastise this nation for trying to destroy both the Indians and the Mormons.

* * * If the Government persists in sending an army to destroy us, in the name of the Lord we shall conquer them. If they dare to force the issue, I shall not hold the Indians by the wrist any longer, for white men to shoot at them; they shall go ahead and do as they please. If the issue comes, you may tell the Government to stop all emigration across this continent, for the Indians will kill all who attempt it. And if an army succeeds in penetrating this valley, tell the Government to see that it has forage and provisions in store, for they will find here only a charred and barren waste.

"Capt. Van Vliet: * * * If our Government pushes this matter to the extent of making war upon you, I will withdraw from the army, for I will not have a hand in shedding the blood of American citizens.

"President Young: We shall trust in God. * * * Congress has promptly sent investigating committees to Kansas and other places, as occasion has required; but upon the merest rumor it has sent 2,000 armed soldiers to destroy the people of Utah, without investigating the subject at all.

"Capt. Van Vliet. The Government may yet send an investigating committee to Utah, and consider it good policy, before they get through.

"President Young. I believe God has sent you here, and that good will grow out of it. I was glad when I heart you were coining.

"Capt. Van Vliet. I am anxious to get back to Washington as soon as I can. I have heard officially that General Harney has been recalled to Kansas to officiate as Governor. I shall stop the train on Ham's Fork on my own responsibility.

"President Young. If we can keep the peace for this Winter I do think there will something turn up that may save the shedding of blood."

The reader cannot fail to perceive that the terrible butchery at the Mountain Meadow—was farthest from Brigham Young's policy at that time, to say nothing of humanitarian considerations.

But, though Governor Young was aiming for some such consummation as that which came, he neither allowed himself nor his people to retreat a step from their chosen position. Indeed, in their stern fidelity to their cause was their only safety and successful outcome.

Captain Van Vliet thus reported to the commanding general of the army:

Ham's Fork, September 16, 1857.

"Captain: I have the honor to report, for the information of the commanding general, the result of my trip to the Territory of Utah.

"In obedience to special instructions, dated headquarters army for Utah, Fort Leavenworth, July 28, 1857, I left Fort Leavenworth, July 30, and reached Fort Kearny in nine travelling days, Fort Laramie in ten, and Great Salt Lake City in thirty-three and a half. At Fort Kearny I was detained one day by the changes I had to make and by sickness, and at Fort Laramie three days, as all the animals were forty miles from the post, and when brought in all had to be shod before they could take the road. I traveled as rapidly as it is possible to do with six mule wagons. Several of my teams broke down, and at least half of my animals are unserviceable and will remain so until they recruit. During my progress towards Utah I met many people from that Territory, and also several mountain men at Green river, and all informed me that I would not be allowed to enter Utah, and if I did I would run great risk of losing my life. I treated all this, however, as idle talk, but it induced me to leave my wagons and escort at Ham's Fork, 143 miles this side of the city, and proceed alone. I reached Great Salt Lake City without molestation, and immediately upon my arrival I informed Governor Brigham Young that I desired an interview, which he appointed for the next day. On the evening of the day of my arrival Governor Young, with many of the leading men of the city, called upon me at my quarters. The governor received me most cordially and treated me during my stay, which continued some six days, with the greatest hospitality and kindness.

In this interview the governor made known to me his views with regard to the approach of the United States troops, in plain and unmistakable language.

"He stated that the Mormons had been persecuted, murdered, and robbed in Missouri and Illinois both by the mob and State authorities, and that now the United States were about to pursue the same course, and that, therefore, he and the people of Utah had determined to resist all persecution at the commencement, and that the troops now on the march for Utah should not enter the Great Salt Lake valley. As he uttered these words all those present concurred most heartily in what he said.

"The next day, as agreed upon, I called upon the governor and delivered in person the letter with which I had been entrusted. In that interview, and in several subsequent ones, the same determination to resist to the death the entrance of the troops into the valley was expressed by Governor Young and those about him.

"The governor informed me that there was abundance of everything I required for the troops, such as lumber, forage, etc., but that none would be sold to us. In the course of my conversations with the governor and the influential men in the Territory, I told them plainly and frankly what I conceived would be the result of their present course. I told them that they might prevent the small military force now approaching Utah from getting through the narrow defiles and rugged passes of the mountains this year, but that next season the United States government would send troops sufficient to overcome all opposition. The answer to this was invariably the same: "We are aware that such will be the case; but when those troops arrive they will find Utah a desert. Every house will be burned to the ground, every tree cut down, and every field laid waste.

We have three years' provisions on hand, which we will 'cache,' and then take to the mountains and bid defiance to all the powers of the government." I attended their service on Sunday, and, in course of a sermon delivered by Elder Taylor, he referred to the approach of the troops and declared they should not enter the Territory. He then referred to the probability of an overpowering force being sent against them, and desired all present, who would apply the torch to their own buildings, cut down their trees, and by waste their fields, to hold up their hands. Every hand, in an audience numbering over 4,000 persons, was raised at the same moment. During my stay in the city I visited several families, and all with whom I was thrown looked upon the present movement of the troops towards their Territory as the commencement of another religious persecution and expressed a fixed determination to sustain Governor Young in any measures he might adopt. From all these facts I am forced to the conclusion that Governor Young and the people of Utah will prevent, if possible, the army for Utah from entering their Territory this season. This, in my opinion, will not be a difficult task, owing to the lateness of the season, the smallness of our force, and the defenses that nature has thrown around the valley of the Great Salt Lake.

"There is but one road running into the valley on the side which our troops are approaching, and for over fifty miles it passes through narrow canyons and over rugged mountains, which a small force could hold against great odds. I am inclined however, to believe that the Mormons will not resort to actual hostilities until the last moment. Their plan of operations will be, burn the grass, cut up the roads, and stampede the animals, so as to delay the troops until the snow commences to fall, which will render the road impassable. Snow falls early in this region, in fact last night it commenced falling at Fort Bridger, and this morning the surrounding mountains are clothed in white. Were it one month earlier in the season I believe the troops could force their way in, and they may be able to do so even now; but the attempt will be fraught with considerable danger, arising from the filling up of the canyons and passes with snow. I do not wish it to be considered that I am advocating either the one course or the other. I simply wish to lay the facts before the general, leaving it to his better judgment to decide upon the proper movements. Notwithstanding my inability to make the purchases I was ordered to, and all that Governor Young said in regard to opposing the entrance of the troops into the valley I examined the country in the vicinity of the city, with the view of selecting a proper military site. I visited the military reserve, Rush Valley, but found it, in my opinion, entirely unsuitable for a military station. It contains but little grass and is very much exposed to the cold winds of winter; its only advantage being the close proximity of fine wood. It is too far from the city, being between thirty-five and forty miles, and will require teams four days to go there and return.

I examined another point on the road to Rush Valley, and only about thirty miles from the city, which I consider a much more eligible position. It is in Tuelle Valley three miles to the north of Tuelle city, and possesses wood, water, and grass; but it is occupied by the Mormons, who have some sixty acres under cultivation, with houses and barns on their land. These persons would have to be dispossessed or bought out. In fact there is no place within forty, fifty or sixty miles of the city suitable for a military position, that is not occupied by the inhabitants and under cultivation. On my return I examined the vicinity of Fort Bridger and found it a very suitable position for wintering the troops and grazing the animals, should it be necessary to stop at that point. The Mormons occupy the fort at present, and also have a settlement about ten miles further up Black's Fork, called Fort Supply. These two places contain buildings sufficient to cover nearly half the troops now en route for Utah; but I was informed that they would all be laid in ashes as the army advances. I have thus stated fully the result of my visit to Utah, and trusting that my conduct will meet the approval of the commanding general, I am, very respectfully, your obedient servant, STEWART VAN VLIET, Captain A. Q. M.

"Captain Pleasanton,

A. A. Adjt. Gen. Army for Utah, Fort Leavenworth.

"P. S.—I shall start on my return to-morrow, with an escort often men."

CHAPTER XVIII.

GOVERNOR YOUNG PLACES THE TERRITORY UNDER MARTIAL LAW. THE MILITIA ORDERED OUT. THE SEAT OF WAR. CORRESPONDENCE BETWEEN GOVERNOR YOUNG AND COLONEL ALEXANDER. BURNING THE GOVERNMENT TRAINS. LOT SMITHS STORY. CONGRESS DECLARES UTAH IN A STATE OF REBELLION.

The next day after the departure of Van Vliet, the Governor issued the following proclamation, placing the Territory under martial law: "Citizens of Utah:—We are invaded by a hostile force, who are evidently assailing us to accomplish our overthrow and destruction.

"For the last twenty-five years we have trusted officials of the Government, from constables and justices to judges, governors and presidents, only to be scorned, held in derision, insulted and betrayed. Our houses have been plundered and then burned, our fields laid waste, our principal men butchered while under the pledged faith of the Government for their safety, and our families driven from their homes to find that shelter in the barren wilderness, and that protection among hostile savages which were denied them in the boasted abodes of Christianity and civilization.

"The constitution of our common country guarantees to us all that we do now, or have ever, claimed.

"If the constitutional rights which pertain to us as American citizens were extended to Utah according to the spirit and meaning thereof, and fairly and impartially administered, it is all that we could ask—all that we ever asked.

"Our opponents have availed themselves of prejudices existing against us because of our religious faith, to send out a formidable host to accomplish our destruction. We have had no privilege, no opportunity of defending ourselves from the false, foul and unjust aspersions against us, before the nation.

"The Government has not condescended to cause an investigating committee or other persons to be sent to enquire into and ascertain the truth, as is customary in such cases.

"We know those aspersions to be false, but that avails us nothing. We are condemned unheard, and forced to an issue with an armed mercenary mob, which has been sent against us at the instigation of anonymous letter-writers, ashamed to father the base, slanderous falsehoods which they have given to the public; of corrupt officials who have brought false accusations against us to screen themselves in their own infamy; and of hireling priests and howling editors, who prostitute the truth for filthy lucre's sake.

"The issue which has been thus forced upon us compels us to resort to the great first law of self-preservation, and stand in our own defense, a right guaranteed to us by the genius and institutions of our country, and upon which the government is based. Our duty to ourselves, to our families, requires us not to tamely submit to be driven and slain, without an attempt to preserve ourselves; our duty to our country, our holy religion, our God, to freedom and liberty, requires that we should not quietly stand still, and see those fetters forging around us which are calculated to enslave, and bring us in subjection to an unlawful military despotism, such as can only emanate in a country of constitutional law, from usurpation, tyranny and oppression.

"Therefore, I, Brigham Young, governor and superintendent of Indian affairs for the Territory of Utah, in the name of the people of the United States, in the Territory of Utah, forbid:

"First. All armed forces of every description from coming into this Territory, under any pretense whatever.

"Second. That all the forces in said Territory hold themselves in readiness to march at a moment's notice to repel any and all such invasion.

"Third. Martial law is hereby declared to exist in this Territory from and after the publication of this proclamation, and no person shall be allowed to pass or repass into or through or from this Territory without a permit from the proper officer.

"Given under my hand and seal, at Great Salt City, Territory of Utah, this fifteenth day of September, A. D. eighteen hundred and fifty-seven, and of the independence of the United States of America the eighty-second.

BRIGHAM YOUNG."

While Captain Van Vliet was listening to the discourses of the Mormon leaders and witnessing the heroic demonstrations of the people of Great Salt Lake City the militia of the Territory was everywhere preparing for active service. Six weeks before the proclamation of martial law the following extraordinary dispatch was issued to the district commanding officers:

Headquarters Nauvoo Legion,

Adjt. General's Office, G. S. L. City, Aug. 1, 1857.

"Sir: Reports, tolerably well authenticated, have reached this office that an army from the Eastern States is now en route to invade this Territory.

"The people of this Territory have lived in strict obedience to the laws of the parent and home governments and are ever zealous for the supremacy of the Constitution and the rights guaranteed thereby. In such time, when anarchy takes the place of orderly government and mobocratic tyranny usurps the power of rulers, they have left the inalienable right to defend themselves against all aggression upon their constitutional privileges. It is enough that for successive years they have witnessed the desolation of their homes; the barbarous wrath of mobs poured upon their unoffending brethren and sisters; their leaders arrested, incarcerated and slain, and themselves driven to cull life from the hospitality of the desert and the savage. They are not willing to endure longer these unceasing outrages; but if an exterminating war be purposed against them and blood alone can cleanse pollution from the Nation's bulwarks, to the God of our fathers let the appeal be made.

"You are instructed to hold your commend in readiness to march at the shortest possible notice to any part of the Territory. See that the law is strictly enforced in regard to arms and ammunition, and as far as practicable that each Ten be provided with a good wagon and four horses or mules, as well as the necessary clothing, etc., for a winter campaign. Particularly let your influence be used for the preservation of the grain. Avoid all excitement but be ready.

"DANIEL H. WELLS.

Lieutenant General Commanding

"By James Ferguson, Adjutant General."

Copies of this letter were sent to the following: Colonel W. H. Dame, Parowan; Major L. W. McCullough, Fillmore; Major C. W. Bradley, Nephi; Major Warren S. Snow, Sanpete; General Aaron Johnson, Peteetneet; Colonel William B. Pace, Provo;

Major Samuel Smith, Box Elder; Colonel C. W. West, Weber; Colonel P. C. Merrill, Davis; Major David Evans, Lehi; Major Allen Weeks, Cedar; Major John Rowberry, Tooele.

Within a few days these instructions reached the various districts and were quietly acted upon. There was a universal cleaning of arms, filling up of cartridge boxes, and attention given to the equipment of horses, teams and camping outfits.

The Nauvoo Legion (the territorial militia), consisted at this time of all able bodied men between the ages of eighteen and forty-five, and was organized into military districts. The general officers of the Legion detailed for the campaign were: Daniel H. Wells, Lieut. General, commanding; Generals Geo. D. Grant, Wm. H. Kimball, James Ferguson, H. B. Clawson; Colonels R. T. Burton, N. V. Jones, James Cummings, C. W. West, Thos. Callister, John Sharp, W. B. Pace, Lot Smith, Warren Snow, Jos. A. Young, A. P. Rockwood; J. L. Dunyon, Surgeon; Majors H. W. Lawrence, J. M. Barlow, Israel Ivins, R. J. Golding, J. R. Winder, J. D. T. McAllister. Besides these officers, scouts and rangers were detailed to perform special duties. Among these were O. P. Rockwell, Ephraim Hanks and many others. The nature of the campaign was such that individuals were selected for certain service without regard to their official station thus officers of the highest rank were found performing the duties of company captains or sharing the labors of men of the line.

On the thirteenth of August orders was issued for the first movement of the forces. It was directed to Col. Robert T. Burton, instructing him to take the field with one hundred and sixty men from the first regiment. He, however, started on the fifteenth with but seventy men from the Life Guards. Among the officers accompanying this expedition were Col. James Cummings, of the general staff, Maj. J. M. Barlow, quartermaster and commissary, Maj. H. W. Lawrence, Capt. H. P. Kimball, Lieuts. J. Q. Knowlton and C. F. Decker. They were afterwards joined by a company from Provo, commanded by Capt. Joshua Clark.

The instructions given Col. Burton were to march to the east on the main traveled road, affording aid and protection to the incoming trains of immigrants, and to act as a corps of observation to learn the strength and equipments of forces reported on the way to Utah, and report to headquarters; but not to interfere with life or property of any one they might encounter on the road. Speaking of this trip, Gen. Burton says: "We arrived at Fort Bridger August 21st and met the first company of immigrants at Pacific Springs on the 26th. On the following day we met Moody's company from Texas, also several large supply trains, entirely unprotected by any escort. On the 29th I left my wagons and half of the men and animals on the Sweetwater, proceeding with pack animals. On the 30th I arrived at Devil's Gate, with Kimball, Cummings and Decker's command coming up the next day; here on the 31st we met Jones, Stringham, and others, on their way from Deer Creek to Salt Lake City, and on the day after Captain John R. Murdock from the States. The latter brought word of the intense bitterness expressed all over the Union against the Mormons, and of the expectations that many entertained that the people of Utah were about to be annihilated by the strong arm of the military power."

These companies proceeded immediately on their way to the city, while Col. Burton and command were engaged caching provisions for future use. On September 8th, he sent an express to the Platte; which returned on the 12th. From this time the expedition returned slowly towards the city, thoroughly examining the country and posting themselves upon all points likely to be of advantage later in the campaign. They also kept a good lookout on the scouting and other military movements, forwarding by express all information of interest to General Wells and Governor Young. On the 17th they received an express from Salt Lake, by J. M. Simmons and O. Spencer, and from this date men were kept in the saddle night and day between the front and headquarters. September 16th, N. V. Jones and Stephen Taylor brought an express from the city, and on the 21st Colonel Burton took three men, H. W. Lawrence, H. P. Kimball, and John Smith, and again moved east to the vicinity of Devil's Gate and camped. September 22nd. within half a mile of Colonel E. B. Alexander's command. Here they first met the advance of the Utah army, and from that time were its immediate neighbors until it arrived at Ham's Fork.

On September 29th, Lieut. Gen. D. H. Wells left Salt Lake City and proceeded to establish headquarters in the narrows of Echo Canyon. He was accompanied by Adjt. Gen. James Ferguson, Col. N. V. Jones, Maj. Lot Smith, and other staff officers Companies of militia from the several military districts, aggregating about 1,250 men were ordered to report at Echo, with provisions for thirty days.

At Echo, Gen. Wells divided his staff, leaving Col. N. V. Jones and J. D. T. McAllister in command of the force there. These engaged in digging trenches across the canyon, throwing up breast works, loosening stones on the heights, and in every way preparing to resist the progress of any body of men that might attempt to pass through the canyon. The day after reaching Echo, Gen. Wells, with a small escort, proceeded to Fort Bridger, where he met Col. Burton and Gen. Robison, and was informed of all movements that had been made by the troops, of the location of their supply trains, their strength, probability of reinforcements, etc.

From this information it was ascertained that for several days previously the army had been making very rapid forced marches, to overtake and protect their supplies on Ham's Fork, which had been forwarded several weeks before. It was apprehended, as they had been successful in securing these advance supply trains so near the mountain passes, that the troops would shoulder rations for three days an attempt to force their way on to the city.

In view of this a Mormon writer on the "Echo Canyon War" thus explains the situation: "The activity of the enemy required the utmost vigilance and some decisive action on the part or our forces to delay any such movement. It was the policy to 'fight this war without bloodshed.' How to do it successfully was the question. It was a difficult one to solve while the weather remained fair, the advancing troops well supplied with food and ammunition, and eager to try their strength with their Mormon foes. Yet it was extremely necessary that the advance should be checked and the power of the people of Utah to defend themselves felt."

Just at this point the extraordinary correspondence commences between Governor Young and the commanding officers of the U. S. Expedition, as presented to Congress by President Buchanan, opening with the following to Col. Alexander:

Fort Bridger,
September 30, 1857.

"Sir: I have the honor to forward you the accompanying letter from His Excellency Governor Young, together with two copies of his proclamation and a copy of the laws of Utah, 1856-'57, containing the organic act of the Territory.

"It may be proper to add that I am here to aid in carrying out the instructions of Governor Young.

"General Robison will deliver these papers to you and receive such communication as you may wish to make.

"Trusting that your answer and actions will be dedicated by a proper respect for the rights and liberties of American citizens.

"I remain, very respectfully, etc.,
"DANIEL H. WELLS,
"Lieutenant General Commanding, Nauvoo Legion."

Governor's Office, Utah Territory,
Great Salt Lake City, September 29, 1857.

"Sir: By reference to the act of Congress passed September 9, 1850, organizing the Territory of Utah, published in the Laws of Utah, herewith forwarded, pp. 146-7, you will find the following: "' Sec. 2. And be it further enacted, That the executive power and authority in and over said Territory of Utah shall be vested in a governor, who shall hold his office for four years, and until his successor shall be appointed and qualified, unless sooner removed by the President of the United States. The governor shall reside within said Territory, shall be commander-in-chief of the militia thereof, etc., etc.

"I am still the governor and superintendent of Indian affairs for this Territory, no successor having been appointed and qualified, as provided by law; nor have I been removed by the President of the United States.

"By virtue of the authority thus vested in me, I have issued, and forwarded you a copy of, my proclamation forbidding the entrance of armed forces into this Territory. This you have disregarded. I now further direct that you retire forthwith from the Territory, by the same route you entered. Should you deem this impracticable, and prefer to remain until spring in the vicinity of your present encampment, Black's Fork, or Green River, you can do so in peace and unmolested, on condition that you deposit your arms and ammunition with Lewis Robison, quartermaster general of the Territory, and leave in the spring, as soon as the condition of the roads will permit you to march; and should you fall short of provisions, they can be furnished you, upon making the proper applications therefor. General D. H. Wells will forward this and receive any communication you may have to make.

"Very respectfully, BRIGHAM YOUNG
"Governor and Superintendent of Indian Affairs, Utah Territory.
"The Officer Commanding the forces now invading Utah Territory'

Headquarters 10th Regiment of Infantry,
Camp Winfield, on Ham's Fork, October 2, 1857.

"Sir: I have the honor to acknowledge the receipt of your communication of September 29, 1857; with two copies of Proclamation and one of "Laws of Utah," and have given it an attentive consideration.

"I am at present the senior and commanding officer of the troops of the United States at this point, and I will submit your letter to the general commanding as soon as he arrives here.

"In the meantime I have only to say that these troops are here by the orders of the President of the United States, and their future movements will depend entirely upon the orders issued by competent military authority.

I am, sir, very respectfully, etc.,
"E. B. ALEXANDER,
"Col. 10th U. S. Infantry, commanding.

"Brigham Young, Esq.,
"Governor of Utah Territory
"Headquarters 10th Infantry, October 2, 1857.
"Official.

HENRY E. MAYNADIER, Adjutant 10th Infantry."

General Robison and Major Lot Smith were dispatched with these documents, instructed to deliver them personally or send them by a Mexican if it should be dangerous to enter Col. Alexander's camp; the latter course was adopted. On the return of Major Lot Smith with the answer of Col. Alexander to Governor Young, General Wells resolved on the immediate execution of his programme of the campaign.

The plan of the campaign had been thoroughly digested by Brigham Young, as commander-in-chief of the Utah militia, and his Lieutenant General, before the latter left Great Salt Lake City for "the seat of war;" and with General Wells, Apostles John Taylor and George A. Smith had gone out to Echo Canyon, undoubtedly to give their voice in the councils of war. Therefore, there was no need for General Wells to seek further consultation with his chief previous to the execution of the plan, which was substantially that embodied in the order, found upon the person of major Joseph Taylor when he was captured: Headquarters Eastern Expedition, Camp near Cache Cave, Oct. 4, 1857.

"You will proceed, with all possible dispatch, without injuring your animals, to the Oregon road, near the bend of Bear river, north by east of this place. Take close and correct observations of the country on your route.

When you approach the road, send scouts ahead, to ascertain if the invading troops have passed that way. Should they have passed, take a concealed route, and get ahead of them. Express to Colonel Burton, who is now on that road and in the vicinity of the troops, and effect a junction with him, so as to operate in concert. On ascertaining the locality or route of the troops, proceed at once to annoy them in every possible way. Use every exertion to stampede their animals and set fire to their trains. Burn the whole country before them, and on their flanks. Keep them from sleeping by night surprises; blockade the road by felling trees or destroying the river fords where you can. Watch for opportunities to set fire to the grass on their windward, so as if possible to envelope their trains. Leave no grass before them that can be burned. Keep your men concealed as much as possible, and guard against surprise. Keep scouts out at all times, and communications open with Colonel Burton, Major McAllister and O. P. Rockwell, who are operating in the same way. Keep me advised daily of your movements, and every step the troops take, and in which direction.

"God bless you, and give you success.

"Your brother in Christ.
DANIEL H. WELLS.

"P. S.—If the troops have not passed, or have turned in this direction, follow in their rear, and continue to annoy them, burning any trains they may leave. Take no life, but destroy their trains, and stampede or drive away their animals, at every opportunity.

D. H. WELLS.

"Major Joseph Taylor.
"Headquarters Army of Utah,
Black's Fork, 16 miles from Fort Bridger,
En route to Salt Lake City, November 7, 1857.

"A true copy of instructions in the possession of Major Joseph Taylor, when captured.

"F. J. PORTER,
Assistant Adjutant General.'"

After delivering the dispatch of Col. Alexander, Major Lot Smith was invited to take dinner with his commanding-general and his aides. Among all the warriors of the Mormon Israel there was, perhaps not one so fitted to open this very peculiar campaign as Lot Smith. His lion-like courage and absolute fearlessness of personal danger, when most in its presence, marked him out as the man of men to execute an exploit of such daring as that designed—to astonish the American nation into a realization of the Mormon earnestness, yet at the same time to do it without the shedding of a drop of "the enemy's" blood.

"During the meal," says Maj. Lot Smith, in his piquant narrative of one of the most daring guerilla exploits on record, "General Wells, looking at me as straight as possible, asked if I could take a few men and turn back the trains that were on the road or burn them? I replied that I thought that I could do just what he told me to. The answer appeared to please him, and he accepted it, telling me he could furnish only a few men, but they would be sufficient, for they would appear many more to our enemies."

At 4 o'clock in the evening of October 3rd, Major Lot Smith's troop, numbering forty-four men rank and file, started on their expedition. They rode all night and early the next morning came in sight of an ox train headed westward.

On calling for the captain, Maj. Smith ordered him to turn his train and go the other way till he reached the States. The Captain "swore pretty strongly," faced about and started to go east, but as soon as out of sight he would turn again towards the mountains. The troops met him that day and took out his lading, leaving the wagons and teams standing. Lot Smith camped near these troops on that night on the banks of the Green River. His story continues: "Losing the opportunity to make much impression on Rankin's train, I thought something must be done speedily to carry out the instructions received, so I sent Captain Haight with twenty men to see if he could get the mules of the Tenth Regiment on any terms. With the remaining twenty-three men I started for Sandy Fork to intercept trains that might be approaching in that direction.

On the road, seeing a large cloud of dust at a distance up the river, on the old Mormon road, I sent scouts to see what caused it. They returned, overtaking me at

Sandy, and reported a train of twenty-six large freight wagons. We took supper and started at dark. After traveling fourteen miles, we came up to the train, but discovered that the teamsters were drunk, and knowing that drunken men were easily excited and always ready to fight and remembering my positive orders not to hurt anyone except in self-defense, we remained in ambush until after mid-night. I then sent scouts to thoroughly examine the appearance of their camp, to note the number of wagons and men and report all they discovered. When they returned and reported twenty-six wagons in two lines a short distance apart, I concluded that counting one teamster to each wagon and throwing in eight or ten extra men would make their force about forty. I thought we would be a match for them, and so ordered an advance to their camp.

"On nearing the wagons, I found I had misunderstood the scouts, for instead of one train of twenty-six wagons there were two, doubling the number of men, and putting quite another phase on our relative strength and situation.

There was a large camp-fire burning, and a number of men were standing around it smoking. It was expected by my men that on finding out the real number of wagons and men, I would not go farther than to make some inquiries and passing our sortie upon the trains as a joke would go on until some more favorable time. But it seemed to me that it was no time for joking. I arranged my men, and we advanced until our horses' heads came into the light of the fire; then I discovered that we had the advantage, for looking back into the darkness, I could not see where my line of troops ended and could imagine my twenty followers stringing out to a hundred or more as well as not. I inquired for the captain of the train.

Mr. Dawson stepped out and said he was the man. I told him that I had a little business with him. He inquired the nature of it, and I replied by requesting him to get all of his men and their private property as quickly as possible out of the wagons for I meant to put a little fire into them. He exclaimed: 'For God's sake, don't burn the trains.' I said it was for His sake that I was going to burn them and pointed out a place for his men to stack their arms, and another where they were to stand in a group, placing a guard over both. I then sent a scout down towards Little Mountaineer Fork, failing to put one out towards Ham's Fork on the army. While I was busy with the train a messenger from the latter surprised us by coming into camp. I asked him if he had dispatches and to hand them to me. He said he had but they were verbal. I told him if he lied to me his life was not worth a straw. He became terrified, in fact I never saw a man more frightened. He said afterwards that he expected every moment to be killed. His orders to the train men were from the commander at Camp Winfield and were to the effect that the Mormons were in the field and that they must not go to sleep but keep night guard on their trains, and that four companies of cavalry and two pieces of artillery would come over in the morning to escort them to camp." After thus dealing with the first train, the other was treated in like manner.

The closing of Lot Smith's story gives a striking dramatic denouement.

"When all was ready, I made a torch, instructing my Gentile follower, known as Big James, to do the same, as I thought it was proper for the 'Gentiles to spoil the Gentiles.' At this stage of our proceedings an Indian came from the Mountaineer Fork and seeing how the thing was going asked for some presents.

He wanted two wagon covers for a lodge, some flour and soap. I filled his order and he went away much elated. Out of respect to the candor poor Dawson had showed, I released him from going with me when we fired the trains, taking Big James instead, he not being afraid of saltpeter or sulphur either.

"While riding from wagon to wagon, with torch in hand and the wind blowing, the covers seemed to me to catch very slowly. I so stated it to James. He replied, swinging his long torch over his head: 'By St. Patrick, ain't it beautiful! I never saw anything go better in all my life.' About this time I had Dawson send in his men to the wagons, not yet fired, to get us some provisions, enough to thoroughly furnish us, telling him to get plenty of sugar and coffee, for though I never used the latter myself, some of my men below, intimating that I had a force down there, were fond of it. On completing this task I told him that we were going just a little way off, and that if he or his men molested the trains or undertook to put the fire out, they would be instantly killed. We rode away leaving the wagons all ablaze."

The burning of the Government trains accomplished the very purpose designed. The nation was thrown into a fearful state of excitement over the daring deed, and at the issue of Governor Young's Proclamation. Congress passed a resolution declaring Utah in a state of rebellion and referred a motion to the committee on Territories to expel the Utah Delegate. Burning the supplies of an army of the United States, sent by the Government to put down an incipient rebellion, was declared to be an extraordinary overt act of actual war, while the proclamation of Governor Young was considered as a veritable declaration of war as from an independent power. A terrible wrath was aroused against Mormon Utah. At that moment, had the season been favorable, and the Government made the call, a hundred thousand volunteers would have quickly mustered into service to annihilate the whole Mormon community. Yet, be it repeated, the very purpose had been accomplished which Brigham Young designed. It was a most dramatic illustration of his words to Captain Van Vliet, "We are aware that such will be the case; but when those troops arrive they will find Utah a desert. Every house will be burned to the ground, every tree cut down and every field left waste. We have three years' provisions on hand, which we will 'cache,' and then take to the mountains and bid defiance to all the powers of the government." The nation could now believe that this was not mere bravado or bombast of Brigham Young, nor the insane rage of fanatics, but the extraordinary resolve of a Puritanic people, such as those who fought "in the name of the Lord" for the commonwealth of England and founded the American nation. And though Colonel C. F. Smith of the Expedition wrote to headquarters: "As the threats of their leaders to Captain Van Vliet, coupled with the burning of our supply trains—in itself an act of war—is evidence of their treason, I shall regard them as enemies, and fire upon the scoundrels if they give me the least opportunity;" yet from that moment President Buchanan saw cause for pause. Brigham Young would keep his word! Strange as it may seem his Proclamation, and the order of Lieutenant General Wells, followed so quickly by the burning of the supply trains, ultimately brought the Peace Commission, and the Proclamation of pardon to the entire Mormon people.

CHAPTER XIX.

CORRESPONDENCE BETWEEN GOVERNOR YOUNG AND COLONEL ALEXANDER. UNFLINCHING ATTITUDE OF BOTH SIDES. EXCHANGE OF COURTESIES. THE GOVERNOR INVITES A PEACEFUL VISIT OF THE OFFICERS TO THE CITY. A REMARKABLE LETTER FROM APOSTLE JOHN TAYLOR TO CAPTAIN MARCY.

"Great Salt Lake City, U. T , October 14, 1857.

"Colonel: In consideration of our relative positions—you acting in your capacity as commander of the United States forces, and in obedience, as you have stated, to orders from the President of the United States, and I as governor of this Territory, impelled by every sense of justice, honor, integrity and patriotism to resist what I consider to be a direct infringement of the rights of the citizens of Utah, and an act of usurpation and tyranny unprecedented in the history of the United States—permit me to address you frankly as a citizen of the United States, untrammeled by the usages of official dignity or military etiquette.

"As citizens of the United States, we both, it is presumable, feel strongly attached to the Constitution and institutions of our common country; and, as gentlemen, should probably agree in sustaining the dear bought liberties bequeathed by our fathers—the position in which we are individually placed being the only apparent cause of our present antagonism; you, as colonel commanding, feeling that you have a rigid duty to perform in obedience to orders, and I, a still more important duty to the people of this Territory, "I need not here reiterate what I have already mentioned in my official proclamation, and what I and the people of this Territory universally believe firmly to be the object of the administration in the present expedition against Utah, viz: the destruction, if not the entire annihilation of the Mormon community, solely upon religious grounds, and without any pretext whatever; for the administration do know, from the most reliable sources, that the base reports circulated by Drummond, and others of their mean officials, are barefaced calumnies. They do, moreover, know that the people of Utah have been more peaceable and law abiding than those of any other Territory of the United States, and have never resisted even the wish of the President of the United States, nor treated with indignity a single individual coming to the Territory under his authority although the conduct and deportment of many of them have merited, and in any other State or Territory would have met with summary punishment. But when the President of the United States so far degrades his high position, and prostitutes the highest gift of the people as to make use of the military power (only intended for the protection of the people's rights) to crush the people's liberties, and compel them to receive officials so lost to self-respect as to accept appointments against the known and expressed wish of the people, and so craven and degraded as to need an army to protect them in their position, we feel that we should be recreant to every principle of self-respect, honor, integrity, and patriotism, to bow tamely to such high-handed tyranny, a parallel for which is only found in the attempts of the British government, in its most corrupt stages, against the rights, liberties and lives of our forefathers.

"Now, Colonel, I do not charge you, nor those serving under you, with the instigation of these enormities. I consider that you are only the agent made use of by the administration, probably unwillingly so, to further their infamous designs. What high-minded gentleman can feel comfortable in being the mere catspaw of political jugglers and hucksters, penny-a-liners, hungry speculators and disgraced officials? Yet it is from the statements of such characters only that the administration has acted, attaching the official seal to your movements. Now, I feel that, when such treason is perpetrated, unblushingly, in open daylight, against the liberties and most sacred rights of the citizens of this Territory, it is my duty, and the duty of every lover of his country and her sacred institutions, to resist it, and maintain inviolate the constitution of our common country.

"Perhaps, colonel, you may feel otherwise; education and associations have their influences; but I have yet to learn that United States officers are implicitly bound to obey the dictum of a despotic President, in violating the most sacred constitutional rights of American citizens.

"We have sought diligently for peace. We have sacrificed millions of dollars worth of property to obtain it and wandered a thousand miles from the confines of civilization, severing ourselves from home, the society of friends, and everything that makes life worth enjoyment. If we have war, it is not of our seeking; we have never gone nor sought to interfere with the rights of others, but they have come and sent to interfere with us. We had hoped that, in this barren and desolate country, we could have remained unmolested; but it would seem that our implacable, blood-thirsty foes envy us even these barren deserts.

Now, if our real enemies, the mobocrats, priests, editors and politicians, at whose instigation the present storm has been gathered, had come against us, instead of you and your command, I should never have addressed them thus. They never would have been allowed to reach the South Pass. In you we recognize only the agents and instruments of the administration, and with you, personally, have no quarrel. I believe it would have been more consonant with your feelings to have made war upon the enemies of your country than upon American citizens.

But to us the end to be accomplished is the same, and while I appreciate the unpleasantness of your position, you must be aware that circumstances compel the people of Utah to look upon you, in your present belligerent attitude, as their enemies and the enemies of our common country, and notwithstanding my most sincere desires to promote amicable relations with you, I shall feel it my duty, as do the people of the Territory universally, to resist to the utmost every attempt to encroach further upon their rights.

"It, therefore, becomes a matter for your serious consideration, whether it would not be more in accordance with the spirit and institutions of our country to return with your present force rather than force an issue so unpleasant to all, and which must result in great misery and, perhaps, bloodshed and, if persisted in, the total destruction of your army. And, furthermore, does it not become a question whether it is more patriotic for officers of the United States army to ward off, by all honorable means, a collision with American citizens or to further the precipitate move of an indiscreet and rash administration, in plunging a whole Territory into a horrible, fratricidal and sanguinary war.

"Trusting that the foregoing considerations may be duly weighed by you, and that the difficulties now impending may be brought to an amicable adjustment, with sentiments of esteem, I have the honor to remain most respectfully etc.,

BRIGHAM YOUNG."

"Headquarters Army for Utah.
Camp on Ham's Fork, October 12, 1857.

"Sir: Yesterday two young men, named Hickman, were arrested by the rear guard of the army, and are now held in confinement. They brought a letter from W. A. Hickman to Mr. Perry, a sutler of one of the regiments, but came under none of the privileges of bearers, of dispatches, and are, perhaps, liable to be considered and treated as spies. But I am convinced, from conversation with them, that their conduct does not merit the serious punishment awarded to persons of that character, and I have accordingly resolved to release the younger one, especially in consideration of his having a wife and three children, dependent upon him, and to make him the bearer of this letter. The elder I shall keep until I know how this communication is received, and until I receive an answer to it, reserving, even then, the right to hold him a prisoner, if, in my judgment, circumstances require it. I need hardly assure you that his life will be protracted, and that he will receive every comfort and indulgence proper to be afforded him.

"I desire now, sir, to set before you the following facts: the forces under my command are ordered by the President of the United States, to establish a military post at or near Salt Lake City. They set out on their long and arduous march, anticipating a reception similar to that which they would receive in any other State or Territory in the Union. They were met at the boundary of the Territory of which you are the Governor, and in which capacity alone I have any business with you, by a proclamation issued by yourself, forbidding them to come upon soil belonging to the United States, and calling upon the inhabitants to resist them with arms. You have ordered them to return and have called upon them to give up their arms in default of obeying your mandate. You have resorted to open hostilities, and of a kind, permit me to say, far beneath the usages of civilized warfare, and only resorted to by those who are conscious of inability to resist by more honorable means, by authorizing persons under your control, some of the very citizens, doubtless, whom you have called to arms, to burn the grass apparently with the intention of starving a few beasts, and hoping that men would starve after them. Citizens of Utah, acting, I am bound to believe, under your authority, have destroyed trains containing public stores, with a similar humane purpose of starving the army. I infer also from your communications received day before yesterday, referring to "a dearth of news from the east and from home," that you have caused public and private letters to be diverted from their proper destination, and this, too, when carried by a public messenger on a public highway. It is unnecessary for me to adduce further instances to show that you have placed yourself, in your capacity of governor, and so many of the citizens of the Territory of Utah as have obeyed your decree, in a position of rebellion and hostility to the general government of the United States. It becomes you to look to the consequences, for you must be aware that so unequal a contest can never be successfully sustained by the people you govern.

"It is my duty to inform you that I shall use the force under my control, and all honorable means in my power, to obey literally and strictly the orders under which I am acting. If you, or any acting under your orders, oppose me, I will use force, and I warn you that the blood that is shed in this contest will be upon your head. My means I consider ample to overcome any obstacle; and I assure you that any idea you may have formed of forcing these troops back, or of preventing them from carrying out the views of the government, will result in unnecessary violence and utter failure. Should you reply to this in a spirit which our relative positions give me a right to demand, I will be prepared to propose an arrangement with you. I have also the honor to inform you that all persons found lurking around or in any of our camps, will be put under guard and held prisoners as long as circumstances may require.

"I remain sir, very respectfully, your obedient servant,
  E. B. ALEXANDER, Colonel 10th Infantry, Commanding.
"His Excellency Brigham Young,
  Governor of Utah Territory."

"Governor's Office,
Great Salt Lake City, Utah Territory, October 16, 1857.
"Sir: I have the honor to acknowledge the receipt of your letter of the 12th instant, at 8:30 this morning, and embrace the earliest opportunity to reply, out of courtesy to your position, at this late season of the year.

"As you officially allege it, I acknowledge that you and the forces have been sent to the Territory by the President of the United States, but we shall treat you as though you were open enemies, because I have so many times seen armies in our country, under color of law, drive this people, commonly styled Mormons, from their homes, while mobs have followed and plundered at their pleasure, which is now most obviously the design of the general government, as all candid, thinking men know full well. Were not such the fact, why did not the government send an army here to protect us against the savages when we first settled here, and were poor and few in number? So contrary to this was their course, that they sent an informal requisition for five hundred of our most efficient men, (while we were in an Indian country and striving to leave the borders of the United States, from which its civilization (?) had expelled us,) with a preconcerted view to cripple and destroy us. And do you fancy for a moment that we do not fully understand the tender (?) mercies and designs of our government against us? Again, if an army was ordered here for peaceful purposes, to protect and preserve the rights and lives of the innocent, why did government send here troops that were withdrawn from Minnesota, where the Indians were slaughtering men, women, and children, and were banding in large numbers, threatening to lay waste the country?

"You mention that it is alone in my gubernatorial capacity that you have any business with me, though your commanding officer, Brevet-Brigadier General Harney, addressed his letter by Captain Van Vliet to 'President Brigham Young, of the society of Mormons.' "You acknowledge the receipt of my official proclamation, forbidding your entrance into the Territory of Utah, and upon that point I have only to again inform you that the matter set forth in that document is true, and the orders therein contained will be most strictly carried out.

"If you came here for peaceful purposes, you have no use for weapons of war. We wish, and ever have wished for peace, and have ever sued for it all the day long, as our bitterest enemies know full well; and though the wicked, with the administration now at their head, have determined that we shall have no peace, except it be to lie down in death, in the name of Israel's God we will have peace, even though we be compelled by our enemies to fight for it.

"We have as yet studiously avoided the shedding of blood, though we have resorted to measures to resist our enemies, and through the operations of those mild measures, you can easily perceive that you and your troops are now at the mercy of the elements, and that we live in the mountains, and our men are all mountaineers. This the government should know, and also give us our rights and then let us alone.

"As to the style of those measures, past, present, or future, persons acting in self-defense have of right a wide scope for choice, and that, too, without being very careful as to what name their enemies may see fit to term that choice; for both we and the Kingdom of God will be free from all hellish oppressors, the Lord being our helper. Threatenings to waste and exterminate this people have been sounded in our ears for more than a score of years, and we yet live. The Zion of the Lord is here, and wicked men and devils cannot destroy it.

"If you persist in your attempt to permanently locate an army in this Territory, contrary to the wishes and constitutional rights of the people therein, and with a view to aid the administration in their unhallowed efforts to palm their corrupt officials upon us, and to protect them and blacklegs, black-hearted scoundrels, whore masters, and murderers, as was the sole intention in sending you and your troops here, you will have to meet a mode of warfare against which your tactics furnish you no information.

"As to your inference concerning 'public and private letters,' it contains an ungentlemanly and false insinuation; for, so far as I have any knowledge, the only stopping or detaining of the character you mention has alone been done by the Post Office Department in Washington; they having, as you must have known, stopped our mail from Independence, Missouri, by which it was but fair to presume that you, as well as we, were measurably curtailed in mail facilities.

"In regard to myself and certain others, having placed ourselves 'in a position of rebellion and hostility to the general government of the United States,' I am perfectly aware that we understand our true and most loyal position far better than our enemies can inform us. We, of all people, are endeavoring to preserve and perpetuate the genius of the Constitution and constitutional laws, while the administration and the troops they have ordered to Utah are, in fact, themselves the rebels, and in hostility to the general government. And if George Washington were now living, and at the helm of our government, he would hang the administration as high as he did Andre, and that, too, with a far better grace and to a much greater subserving the best interests of our country.

"You write: 'It becomes you to look to the consequences, for you must be aware that so unequal a contest can never be successfully sustained by the people you govern.' We have counted the cost it may be to us; we look for the United States to endeavor to swallow us up, and we are prepared for the contest, if they wish to forego the Constitution in their insane efforts to crush out all human rights. But the cost of so suicidal a course to our enemies we have not wasted our time considering, rightly deeming it more particularly their business to figure out and arrive at the amount of so immense a sum. It is now the kingdom of God and the kingdom of the devil. If God is for us we will prosper, but if He is for you and against us, you will prosper, and we will say amen; let the Lord be God, and Him alone we will serve.

"As to your obeying ' orders,' my official counsel to you would be for you to stop and reflect until you know wherein are the just and right, and then, David Crocket like, go ahead. But if you undertake to come in here and build forts, rest assured that you will be opposed, and that you will need all the force now under your command, and much more. And, in regard to your warning, I have to inform you that my head has been sought during many years past, not for any crime on my part, or for so much as even the wish to commit a crime, but solely for my religious belief, and that, too, in a land of professed constitutional religious liberty.

"Inasmuch as you consider your force amply sufficient to enable you to come to this city, why have you so unwisely dallied so long on Ham's Fork at this late season of the year?

"Carrying out the views of the government, as those views are now developing themselves, can but result in the utter overthrow of that Union which we, in common with all American patriots, have striven to sustain; and as to our failure in our present efforts to uphold rights justly guaranteed to all citizens of the United States, that can be better told hereafter.

"I presume that the 'spirit' and tenor of my reply to your letter will be unsatisfactory to you, for doubtless you are not aware of the nature and object of the service in which you are now engaged. For your better information, permit me to inform you that we have a number of times been compelled to receive and submit to the most fiendish proposals, made to us by armies virtually belonging to the United States, our only alternative being to comply therewith. At the last treaty forced upon us by our enemies, in which we were required to leave the United States, and with which we, as hitherto, complied, two United States Senators were present, and pledged themselves, so far as their influence might reach, that we should be no more pursued by her citizens. That pledge has been broken by our enemies, as they have ever done when this people were a party, and we have thus always proven that it is vain for us to seek or expect protection from the officials or administrators of our government. It is obvious that war upon the Saints is all the time determined, and now we, for the first time, possess the power to have a voice in the treatment that we will receive, and we intend to use that power, so far as the Constitution and justice may warrant, which is all we ask. True, in struggling to sustain the Constitution and constitutional rights belonging to every citizen of our republic, we have no arm or power to trust in but that of Jehovah and the strength and ability that He gives us.

"By virtue of my office as governor of the Territory of Utah, I command you to marshal your troops and leave this Territory, for it can be of no possible benefit to you to wickedly waste treasures and blood in prosecuting your course upon the side of a rebellion against the general government by its administrators.

You have had and still have plenty of time to retire within reach of supplies at the east, or to go to Fort Hall. Should you conclude to comply with so just a command, and need any assistance to go east, such assistance will be promptly and cheerfully extended. We do not wish to destroy the life of any human being, but, on the contrary, we ardently desire to preserve the lives and liberties of all, so far as it may be in our power. Neither do we wish for the property of the United States, notwithstanding they justly owe us millions.

"Colonel, should you, or any of the officers with you, wish to visit this city, unaccompanied by troops, as did Captain Van Vliet, with a view to personally learn the condition and feelings of this people, you are at liberty to do so, under my cheerfully proffered assurance that you will be safely escorted from our outposts to this city and back, and that during your stay in our midst you will receive all that courtesy and attention your rank demands. Doubtless you have supposed that many of the people here would flee to you for protection upon your arrival, and if there are any such persons they shall be at once conveyed to your camp in perfect safety, so soon as such fact can be known.

"Were you and your fellow-officers as well acquainted with your soldiers as I am with mine, and did they understand the work they are now engaged in as well as you may understand it, you must know that many of them would immediately revolt from all connection with so ungodly, illegal, unconstitutional and hellish a crusade against an innocent people, and if their blood is shed it shall rest upon the heads of their commanders. With us it is the kingdom of God or nothing. I have the honor to be,
Your obedient servant,
BRIGHAM YOUNG,
Governor and Superintendent of Indian Affairs, U. T."
"E. B. Alexander, Colonel 10th Infantry, U.S.A."

"Headquarters Army for Utah,
Camp on Ham's Fork, October 19, 1857.

"Sir: I have received by the hands of Lieutenant Colonel Beatie your letter of the 16th instant. It is not necessary for me to argue the points advanced by you, and I have only to repeat my assurance that no harm would have happened to any citizen of Utah through the instrumentality of the army of the United States, in the performance of its legitimate duties without molestation.

My disposition of the troops depends upon grave considerations not necessary to enumerate and considering your order to leave the Territory illegal and beyond your authority to issue, or power to enforce, I shall not obey it.

"I am, sir, with respect, your obedient servant,
E. B. ALEXANDER,
Colonel Commanding, 10th Infantry U. S. A.
"His Excellency Brigham Young,
Governor of Utah Territory."

"Governor's Office, Great Salt Lake City, October 28, 1857.

"Sir: Having learned that Mrs. Mago, with her infant child, wishes to join her husband in your camp, also that Mr. Jesse Jones, who has been in this city a few weeks, was anxious to see Mr. Roup, it has afforded me pleasure to cause the necessary arrangements to be made for their comfortable and safe conveyance to your care, under the conduct and protection of Messrs. John Harvey, Joseph Sharp, Adam Sharp, and Thomas J. Hickman, the bearers of this communication.

"Mrs. Mago and her infant are conveyed to your camp in accordance with my previously often expressed readiness to forward to you such as might wish to go and is the only resident of that description in Utah, as far as I am informed.

Her husband made his first appearance here in the capacity of a teamster for Captain W. H. Hooper. He was then in very destitute circumstances; and has since been in the employ of the late United States surveyor general of Utah, and I am not aware that he has any property or tie of any description in this Territory, except the wife and child now conveyed to him in your cmp. Should Colonel Conby and lady wish to partake of the hospitalities proffered by Mr. Heywood and family, and should Captain R. B. Marcy desire to favor me with a visit, as I infer from his letter of introduction forwarded and in my possession, or should you or any other officers in your command wish to indulge in a trip to this city, you will be kindly welcomed and hospitably entertained, and the vehicle and escort now sent to your camp are tendered for conveyance of such as may receive your permission to avail themselves of this cordial invitation.

"It is also presumed that your humane feelings will prompt you, in case there are any persons who wish to peacefully leave your camp for this city, to permit them to avail themselves of the protection and guidance of the escort now sent.

"Trusting that this communication will meet your entire approval and hearty co-operation, I have the honor, sir, to be your obedient servant,
BRIGHAM YOUNG,
Governor and Superintendent of Indian Affairs, U. T.
"Colonel E. B. Alexander,
Tenth Infantry, U. S. A., Camp Ham's Fork."

"Great Salt Lake City, October 21, 1857.

"My Dear Sir: I embrace this the earliest opportunity of answering your communication to me, embracing a letter from Mr. Fuller, of New York, to you, an introductory letter to me, and also one from W. I. Appleby to Governor Young; the latter, immediately on its receipt, I forwarded to His Excellency; and here let me state, sir, that I sincerely regret that circumstances now existing have hitherto prevented a personal interview.

"I can readily believe your statement, that it is very far from your feelings, and most of the command that are with you, to interfere with our social habits or religious views. One must naturally suppose that among gentlemen educated for the army alone, who have been occupied by the study of the art of war, whose pulses have throbbed with pleasure at the contemplation of the deeds of our venerated fathers, whose minds have been elated by the recital of the heroic deeds of other nations, and who have listened almost exclusively to the declamations of patriots and heroes, that there is not much time, and less inclination, to listen to the low party bickerings of political demagogues, the interested twaddle of sectional declaimers, or the throes and contortions of contracted religious bigots. You are supposed to stand on elevated ground, representing the power and securing the interests of the whole of a great and mighty nation. That many of you are thus honorable, I am proud, as an American citizen, to acknowledge; but you must excuse me, my dear sir, if I cannot concede with you that all your officials are so high-toned, disinterested, humane and gentlemanly, as a knowledge of some of their antecedents expressly demonstrates. However, it is not with the personal character, the amiable qualities, high-toned feelings, or gentlemanly deportment of the officers in your expedition, that we at present have to do. The question that concerns us is one that is independent of your personal, generous, friendly and humane feelings or any individual predilection of yours; it is one that involves the dearest rights of American citizens, strikes at the root of our social and political existence, if it does not threaten our entire annihilation from the earth. Excuse me, sir, when I say that you are merely the servants of a lamentably corrupt administration; that your primary law is obedience to orders, and that you came here with armed foreigners with cannon, rifles, bayonets, and broadswords, expressly, and for the openly avowed purpose of 'cutting out the loathsome ulcer from the body politic' I am aware what our friend Fuller says in relation to this matter, and I entertain no doubt of his generous and humane feelings, nor do I of yours, sir; but I do know that he is mistaken in relation to the rabid tone and false, furious attacks of a venal and corrupt press. I do know that they are merely the mouthpiece, the tools, the barking dogs of a corrupt administration. I do know that Mr. Buchanan was well apprised of the nature of the testimony adduced against us by ex-Judge Drummond and others; for he was informed of it, to my knowledge, by a member of own cabinet, and I further know, from personal intercourse with members of the Senate and House of Representatives of the United States, that there have been various plans concerted at headquarters for some time past, for the overthrow of this people. Captain, Mr. Fuller informs me that you are a politician; if so, you must know that in the last presidential campaign the republican party had opposition to slavery and polygamy as two of the principal planks in their platform. You may know, sir, that Utah was picked out, and the only Territory excluded from a participation in pre-emption rights to land. You may also be aware that bills were introduced into Congress for the persecution of the Mormons; but other business was too pressing at that time for them to receive attention. You may be aware that measures were also set on foot, and bills prepared to divide up Utah among the Territories of Nebraska, Kansas, Oregon and New Mexico (giving a slice to California), for the purpose of bringing us into collision with the people of those Territories, not to say anything about thousands of our letters detained at the post office at Independence. I might enumerate injuries by the score, and if these things are not so, why is it that Utah is so 'knotty a question?' If people were no more ready to interfere with us and our institutions than we are with them and theirs, these difficulties would vanish into thin air. Why, again I ask, could Drummond and a host of others, mean scribblers, palm their barefaced lies with such impunity, and have their infamous slanders swallowed with so much gusto? Was it not that the administration and their satellites, having planned our destruction, were eager to catch at anything to render specious their contemplated acts of blood? Or, in plain terms, the democrats advocated strongly popular sovereignty. The republicans tell them that, if they join in maintaining inviolable the domestic institutions of the South, they must also swallow polygamy. The democrats thought this would not do, as it would interfere with the religious scruples of many of their supporters, and they looked about for some means to dispose of the knotty question. Buchanan, with Douglass, Cass, Thompson and others of his advisers, after failing to devise legal measures, hit upon the expedient of an armed force against Utah; and thus thought, by the sacrifice of the Mormons, to untie the knotty question; do a thousand times worse than the republicans ever meant; fairly out-Herod Herod, and by religiously extirpating, destroying, or killing a hundred thousand innocent American citizens, satisfy a pious, humane, patriotic feeling of their constituents; take the wind out of the sails of the republicans, and gain to themselves immortal laurels. Captain, I have heard of a pious Presbyterian doctrine that would inculcate thankfulness to the all-wise Creator for the privilege of being damned. Now, as we are not Presbyterians, nor believe in this kind of self-abnegation, you will, I am sure, excuse us for finding fault at being thus summarily dealt with, no matter how agreeable the excision or expatriation might be to our political, patriotic or very pious friends. We have lived long enough in the world to know that we are a portion of the body politic, have some rights as well as other people, and that if others do not respect us, we, at least, have manhood enough to respect ourselves.

"Permit me here to refer to a remark made by our friend Mr. Fuller, to you, viz: 'That he had rendered me certain services in the city of New York, and that he had no doubt that when you had seen us and known us as he had, that you would report as favorably as he had unflinchingly done.' Now, those favors to which Mr. Fuller refers were simply telling a few plain matters of fact that had come under his own observation during a short sojourn at Salt Lake.

This, of course, I could duly appreciate, for I always admired a man who dare tell the truth. But, Captain, does it not strike you as humiliating to manhood and to the pride of all honorable American citizens, when among the thousands that have passed through and sojourned among us, and knew as well as Mr. Fuller did our true social and moral position, that perhaps one in ten thousand dare state their honest convictions; and further, that Mr. Fuller, with his knowledge of human nature, should look upon you as a rara avis, possessing the moral courage and integrity to declare the truth in opposition to the floods of falsehood that have deluged our nation. Surely, we have (alien on unlucky times, when honesty is avowed to be at so great a premium.

"In regard to our religion, it is perhaps unnecessary to say much; yet, whatever others' feelings may be about it, with us it is honestly a matter of conscience. This is a right guaranteed to us by the Constitution of our country; yet it is on this ground, and this alone, that we have suffered a continued series of persecutions, and that this present crusade is set on foot against us. In regard to this people, I have traveled extensively in the United States, and through Europe, yet have never found so moral, chaste, and virtuous a people, nor do I expect to find them. And, if let alone, they are the most patriotic, and appreciate more fully the blessings of religious, civil, and political freedom than any other portion of the United States. They have, however, discovered the difference between a blind submission to the caprices of political demagogues and obedience to the Constitution, laws, and institutions of the United States; nor can they, in the present instance, be hoodwinked by the cry of 'treason.' If it be treason to stand up for our constitutional rights; if it be treason to resist the unconstitutional acts of a vitiated and corrupt administration, who, by a mercenary armed force, would seek to rob us of the rights of franchise, cut our throats to subserve their party, and seek to force upon us its corrupt tools, and violently invade the rights of American citizens; if it be treason to maintain inviolate our homes, our firesides, our wives, and our honor from the corrupting and withering blight of a debauched soldiery; if it be treason to keep inviolate the Constitution and institutions of the United States, when nearly all the States are seeking to trample them under their feet, then, indeed, we are guilty of treason. We have carefully considered all these matters and are prepared to meet the ' terrible vengeance' we have been very politely informed will be the result of our acts. It is in vain to hide it from you that this people have suffered so much from every kind of official that they will endure it no longer. It is not with them an idle phantom, but a stern reality. It is not, as some suppose, the voice of Brigham only, but the universal, deep-settled feeling of the whole community. Their cry is, 'Give us our Constitutional rights; give us liberty or death!' A strange cry in our boasted model republic, but a truth deeply and indelibly graven on the hearts of 100,000 American citizens by a series of twenty-seven years' unmitigated and unprovoked, yet unrequited wrongs. Having told you of this, you will not be surprised that when fifty have been called to assist in repelling our aggressors, a hundred have volunteered, and, when a hundred have been called, the number has been more than doubled; the only feeling is 'don't let us be overlooked or forgotten.' And here let me inform you that I have seen thousands of hands raised simultaneously, voting to burn our property rather than let it fall into the hands of our enemies. They have been so frequently robbed and despoiled without redress, that they have solemnly decreed that, if they cannot enjoy their own property, nobody else shall. You will see by this that it would be literally madness for your small force to attempt to come into the settlements.

It would only be courting destruction. But, say you, have you counted the cost? have you considered the wealth and power of the United States and the fearful odds against you? Yes; and here let me inform you that, if necessitated, we would as soon meet 100,000 as 1,000, and, if driven to the necessity, will burn every house, tree, shrub, rail, every patch of grass and stack of straw and hay, and flee to the mountains. You will then obtain a barren, desolate wilderness, but will not have conquered the people, and the same principle in regard to other property will be carried out. If this people have to burn their property to save it from the hands of legalized mobs, they will see to it that their enemies shall be without fuel; they will haunt them by day and by night. Such is, in part, our plan. The three hundred thousand dollars' worth of our property destroyed already in Green River County is only a faint sample of what will be done throughout the Territory. We have been twice driven, by tamely submitting to the authority of corrupt officials, and left our houses and homes for others to inhabit, but are now determined that, if we are again robbed of our possessions, our enemies shall also feel how pleasant it is to be houseless at least for once, and be permitted, as they have sought to do to us, 'to dig their own dark graves, creep into them, and die.' "You see we are not backward in showing our hands. Is it not strange to what lengths the human family may be goaded by a continued series of oppressions? The administration may yet find leisure to muse over the consequences of their acts, and it may yet become a question for them to solve whether they have blood and treasure enough to crush out the sacred principles of liberty from the bosoms of 100,000 freemen and mike them bow in craven servility to the mendacious acts of a perjured, degraded tyrant. You may have learned already that it is anything but pleasant for eve 1 a small army to contend with the chilling blasts of this inhospitable climate. How a large army would fare without resources you can picture to yourself. We have weighed those matters; it is for the administration to post their own accounts. It may not be amiss, however, here to state that, it they continue to prosecute this inhuman fratricidal war, and our Nero would light the fires and, sitting in his chair of state, laugh at burning Rome, there is a day of reckoning even for Neros. There are generally two sides to a question. As I before said, we wish for peace, but that we are determined on having it if we have to fight for it. We will not have officers forced upon us who are so degraded as to submit to be sustained by the bayonet's point. We cannot be dragooned into servile obedience to any man.

"These things settled, Captain, and all the like preliminaries of etiquette are easily arranged; and permit me here to state, that no man will be more courteous and civil than Governor Young, and nowhere could you find in your capacity of an officer of the United States a more generous and hearty welcome than at the hands of his excellency. But when, instead of battling with the enemies of our country, you come (though probably reluctantly) to make war upon my family and friends, our civilities are naturally cooled, and we instinctively grasp the sword; Minie rifles, Colt's revolvers, sabers, and cannon may display very good workmanship and great artistic skill, but we very much object to having their temper and capabilities tried upon us. We may admire the capabilities, gentlemanly deportment, heroism and patriotism of United States officers; but in an official capacity of enemies, we would rather see their backs than their faces. The guillotine may be a very pretty instrument, and show great artistic skill, but I don't like to try my neck in it.

"Now, Captain, notwithstanding all this, I shall be very happy to see you if circumstances should so transpire as to make it convenient for you to come, and to extend to you the courtesies of our city, for I am sure you are not our personal enemy. I shall be happy to render you" any information in my power in regard to your contemplated explorations.

"I am heartily sorry that things are so unpleasant at the present time, and I cannot but realize the awkwardness of your position, and that of your compatriots, and let me here say that anything that lays in my power compatible with the conduct of a gentleman you can command. If you have leisure, I should be most happy to hear from you. You will, I am sure, excuse me, if I disclaim the prefix of reverend to my name; address John Taylor, Great Salt Lake City.

"I need not here assure you that personally there can be no feelings of enmity between us and your officers. We regard you as the agents of the administration in the discharge of a probably unpleasant duty, and very likely ignorant of the ultimate designs of the administration. As I left the East this summer, you will excuse me when I say I am probably better posted in some of these matters than you are, having been one of a delegation from the citizens of this Territory to apply for admission into the Union. I can only regret that it is not our real enemies that are here instead of you. We do not wish to harm you or any of the command to which you belong, and I can assure you that in any other capacity than the one you now occupy, you would be received a« civilly and treated as courteously as in any other portion of our Union.

"On my departure from the States, the fluctuating tide of popular opinion against us seemed to be on the wave. By this time there may be quite a reaction in the public mind. If so, it may probably affect materially the position of the administration, and tend to more constitutional, pacific and humane measure. In such an event our relative positions would be materially changed, and instead of meeting as enemi.es, we could meet, as all Americans should, friends to each other, and united against our legitimate enemies only. Such an issue is devoutly to be desired, and I can assure you that no one would more appreciate so happy a result to our present awkward and unpleasant position, than yours truly,

JOHN TAYLOR.

Captain Marcy.
Headquarters Army of Utah, Black's Fork,
16 miles from Fort Bridger, en route to Salt Lake City,
November 7th. 1857.
Official: F. J. PORTER,
Assistant Adjutant General.

CHAPTER XX.

REVIEW OF THE EXPEDITION, KANSAS TROUBLES. GENERAL HARNEY RELIEVED OF THE COMMAND. GENERAL PERSIFER F. SMITH APPOINTED IN HIS STEAD. HE DIES AND COLONEL ALBERT SIDNEY JOHNSTON IS APPOINTED. DISASTROUS MARCH OF THE SECOND DRAGOONS TO UTAH. SCENE OF THE ARMY IN WINTER QUARTERS.

At this point must be given a circumstantial review of the history of the Expedition from the issuing of General Scott's circular to the close of the winter of 18-;7-8, so bitter in its experience to the ill-fated troops who composed the army sent to invade the Rocky Mountain Zion.

The force consisted of two regiments of infantry — the Fifth and Tenth; one regiment of cavalry — the old Second Dragoons; and two batteries of artillery—Reno's and Phelps'. Of the equipments, it may be said there was nothing forgotten and nothing grudged, to make the Expedition a splendid and thorough success.

"So well is the nature of this service appreciated," wrote the commander-in-chief to General Harney, by the pen of his aid de camp, "and so deeply are the honor and interests of the United States involved in its success, that I am authorized to say that the government will hesitate at no expense requisite to complete the efficiency of your little army, and to insure health and comfort to it, as far as attainable. Hence, in addition to the liberal orders for its supply heretofore given—and it is known that ample measures, with every confidence of success, have been dictated by the chiefs of staff departments here—a large discretion will be made over to you in the general orders for the movement. The employment of spies, guides, interpreters or laborers may be made to any reasonable extent you may think desirable."

The chief officers were gentlemen of thorough military education. There were names connected with that army, which rank to day in the national galaxy of America's great generals. There was General Harney, who at that period held the reputation of being the greatest Indian fighter of all the commanding officers of the American army; and for that reason he was probably singled out at the onset for this campaign against the Mormons, which in a mountainous country must necessarily have partaken much of the guerilla warfare, if it came to the action. There was General Persifer F. Smith, a distinguished officer; Captain Van Vliet, afterwards a Major-General; Colonel Philip St. George Cooke, also afterwards a Major General, and of before time the honored commander of the Mormon Battalion; Captain Marcy a distinguished officer and father in-law of General McClellen; Colonel Alexander who himself was able to command an expedition; and greater than all besides Colonel Albert Sidney Johnston, the brilliant soldier who afterwards commanded the Confederate army of the battle of Shiloh, and fell as one of the laurelled heroes of Southern rebeldom, but in 1857 he was sent as the commander to put down Mormon rebeldom. What a strange fatality! and what a parallel! It was the flower of the American army that was sent to Utah, and its history is more remarkable from that very fact. When the order was given for the march of the troops, no one of that command could have divined that such terrible disasters were in store as befell them before the close of the year. The prospect appeared auspicious at the commencement of the march. Writing from Fort Kearney, August 10th, Colonel Alexander reported all well. "The men are in good health and condition and have surprised me by the endurance they exhibited from the commencement. The march from Fort Leavenworth here occupied nineteen days, giving an average of fifteen and a half miles per day."

Writing from Fort Laramie, September 3rd, he congratulates with the following passage: "On the 5th the march to Utah will be resumed, and although the accounts of the road as regards grass makes it much more difficult than anything we have yet experienced, I hope to give as favorable a report upon my arrival at the Salt Lake City.

"I may be excused from expressing the pride I feel in the successful accomplishment by my regiment of so much of its first arduous duty, and I confidently express the belief that unless some very unforeseen accident occurs, I will reach the Territory of Utah in a condition of perfect efficiency and discipline."

Meantime a change had come in the disposition of the Expedition, that the Mormons might well consider as fated, both to themselves and the troops; for had that expedition under General Harney reached the Great Salt Lake Valley that year, it certainly must have been after a desperate battle or two with the " Nauvoo Legion" under General Wells; then if the word of Brigham Young had been kept, as faithfully as the burning of the government trains indicated, General Harney, even though a victor, would have found Great Salt Lake City in ashes; and, in his spring campaign, every city in Utah would have shared the same fate, or that United States army would have been baptized in its own blood.

But no sooner had Colonel Alexander started with his advance troops than the Kansas troubles revived. "Bleeding Kansas" had for several years been the national sensation, and "Border Ruffianism" was a real terror to the American mind, while Mormon rebellion was much of a myth, and at its worst was no subject of political terrorism to the nation. The presence of General Harney and the Second Dragoons was now needed in Kansas by this new development of affairs. His supposed fitness, above other generals to command the Utah Expedition, made him more abundantly fit now to grapple with Kansas. Captain Van Vliet sensed the strange fatality of this new development when he said to Brigham Young: "I am anxious to get back to Washington as soon as I can. I have heard officially that General Harney has been recalled to Kansas, to officiate as Governor."

Thus the General who, from his experience in Indian warfare, was supposed to be sufficient to put down the Indians and Mormons combined—that being one of the suppositions of this war—never took command of this expedition, and the dragoons were, therefore, absent from the Plains when they were most required.

General Persifer F. Smith was assigned to the command in the place of General Harney, but he fell ill and died at Fort Leavenworth. The infantry and artillery, with all the quartermaster and commissary stores, were then on the plains, and the command of the expedition, by seniority of rank, devolved upon Colonel Alexander, of the Tenth Infantry. The expedition was, therefore, without any instructions from the Government; all that its commander, Colonel Alexander, knew was its destination. The next link of the strange history is found in the following military order:

"Washington, August 28th, 1857.

"Colonel: In anticipation of the orders to be issued placing you in command of the Utah expedition, the general-in-chief directs you to repair, without delay, to Fort Leavenworth, and apply to Brevet Brigadier General Harney for all the orders and instructions he has received as commander of that expedition, which you will consider addressed to yourself, and by which you will be governed accordingly. You will, make your arrangements to set out from Fort Leavenworth at as early a day as practicable. Six companies of the 2nd Dragoons will be detached by General Harney to escort you and the civil authorities to Utah, to remain as part of your command instead of the companies of the 1st Cavalry, as heretofore ordered. Brevet Major T. J. Porter, assistant adjutant general, will be ordered to report to you for duty before you leave Fort Leavenworth.

"I have the honor to be, colonel, very respectfully, your most obedient servant,
Irvin Mcdowell,
Assistant Adjutant General.

"Colonel Albert S. Johnston,
2nd Cavalry, Washington, D C.

As the army passed the boundary line of Utah, Governor Young's Proclamation was forwarded, with his order to arrest the advance of "the forces now invading Utah Territory." This was the juncture when either General Harney or Colonel Johnston should have been on the spot, with the entire force, to have opened the campaign, but at that very moment Colonel Albert Sidney Johnston was still at Fort Leavenworth, a thousand miles from the army to which he had been appointed, while Colonel Philip St. George Cooke, commanding 2nd Dragoons, and Colonel C. F. Smith commanding Battalion 10th Infantry were also far away from the seat of action. Colonel Cooke in command of six companies 2nd Dragoons commenced his march from Fort Leavenworth, on the 17th of September, and arrived at Fort Bridger November 19. Of his onset he has thus reported: "The regiment has been hastily recalled from service in the field and allowed three or four days only, by my then commanding officer, to prepare for a march of eleven hundred miles over an uninhabited and mountain wilderness; in that time the six companies of the regiment who were to compose the expedition were re-organized; one hundred and ten transfers necessarily made from and to other companies; horses to be condemned and many obtained; the companies paid, and about fifty desertions occurred; the commanders of four of them changed. To these principle duties and obstacles, implying a great mass of writing, were to be added every exertion of experience and foresight to provide for a line of operation of almost of unexampled length and mostly beyond communication. On the evening of the 16th, at the commencement of a rain-storm, an inspector general made a hurried inspection by companies, which could not have been very satisfactory to him or others—the company commanders, amid the confusion of Fort Leavenworth, presenting their new men, raw recruits, whom they had yet scarcely found or seen, under the effects usually following the pay table."

Governor Cumming, also, who should have been at the seat of war to have met Governor Young's proclamation with a counter proclamation, giving to Colonel Alexander the power to act as his posse commitatus, before the winter set in, was under the escort of Colonel Cooke, and did not issue his proclamation before the 21st of November.

Brigham and the Mormons alone were prepared for the issue, notwithstanding the Government had taken every precaution to prevent the news of the projected expedition reaching Utah in advance, by cutting off the postal communication. (It is so charged by Governor Young.) In six days after the news reached the Pioneers of the coming of the army, the Utah militia is ordered out; in twenty-one days the first detachment of the Mormon Life Guards has taken the field, under Colonel Burton; in one month and eleven days Lot Smith has burnt the supply trains of the Expedition.

In May, General Scott's circular was issued for the march of the army; in the latter part of November Colonel Albert Sidney Johnston and Governor Alfred Cumming were at headquarters, Camp Scott, powerless to act, locked out from Salt Lake Valley by the commanding general of the year—inexorable winter.

General Sam Houston had said to the Government at the onset: "If you make war upon the Mormons you will get awfully whipped!" which, when it was told to Brigham Young, he said, "General Sam Houston had it right."

Hearing nothing from his commander, without instructions and fearing everything, Colonel Alexander concentrated his forces at Ham's Fork, until some course should be resolved upon by a council of the officers. It was then the latter part of September; winter was approaching, the stock of forage was rapidly decreasing, and the country was altogether unfitted for winter-quarters.

Every day's delay was disastrous, and threatened the very existence of the expedition, for the mountains were already covered with snow and the daring Mormon cavalry were constantly harassing the supply trains and running off the animals. The troops began to show signs of demoralization; they were in a bleak and barren desert, with an enemy surrounding them that knew every inch of the ground, and who, to all appearance, could easily destroy them without shedding a drop of their own blood.

On the 10th of October the officers of the Expedition held a council of war and determined that the army should advance from Ham's Fork, but to change the route of travel and make Salt Lake Valley, if they could, via Soda Springs, a distance of nearly three hundred miles, and at least a hundred and fifty miles farther than the route through Echo Canyon. The order was issued, and next day the troops commenced a dreary march.

"Early in the morning," says Stenhouse, in his "Rocky Mountain Saints," "the sky was surcharged with dark, threatening clouds, and as they started the snow fell heavily. A few supply-trains were kept together and guarded by the infantry, but the travel was slow, vexatious and discouraging. The beasts of burden were suffering from want of forage, as, in anticipation of this movement, the grass had been burned all along that route. The animals were completely exhausted, and, before they were a week on the new route, three miles a day was all the distance that could be made.

"Another council of war was held, but the only topics of discussion were the suffering, disaster, and heavy losses of the company. The soldiers were murmuring, and dissatisfaction reigned everywhere. Some gallant officers were desirous of forcing an issue with the Mormons, cutting their way through the canyons) and taking their chances of what might come. This course might have afforded some gratification to individuals, but to the company at large it was impracticable: every effort was necessary to save the Expedition from total ruin."

In explanation of the unprecedented slow march, it should be stated that every movement was really a military maneuver. Colonel R. T. Burton, with a force of about 200 Mormon soldiers was. constantly harassing the army, which in return resorted to every strategy to deceive the Mormon soldiers in regard to their real intent.

Every day they moved a short distance but realizing that their movements were constantly watched by the Mormon soldiery, Colonel Alexander was in doubt as to what course to pursue, as while moving north, every means of annoyance without actual warfare was employed by this little body of defenders of their Utah homes. Finally, as the result of this continued vigilance, on the part of the little army of Mormons, Colonel Alexander retraced his steps and counter-marched down stream and went into Winter Quarters.

"In this forlorn condition the new commander was heard from, and the troops were instantly inspired with new life. Colonel Johnston comprehended the situation and ordered the Expedition to retrace its steps. The snow was six inches deep, the grass all covered, the animals starving. The advance had been slow, the retreat was simply crawling. On the 3rd of November they reached the point of rendezvous, and next day Colonel Johnston joined them with a small reinforcement and the remainder of the supply-trains.

"The morale of the army was restored by the presence of an efficient commander with instructions in his pocket, but the difficulties of the Expedition were increasing every hour. The supply-trains were strung out about six miles in length, the animals worrying along till, thoroughly exhausted, they would fall in their tracks and die.

"All this long line of wagons and beef cattle had to be guarded to prevent surprise and the stampede of the animals. The snow was deep on the ground and the weather was bitterly cold. Many of the men were fatally frost-bitten, and the cattle and mules perished by the score. In Colonel Philip St. George Cooke's command fifty-seven head of horses and mules froze to death in one night on the Sweetwater, and from there to Fort Bridger, where the Expedition finally wintered, the road was literally strewn with dead animals. The camp on Black's Fork, thirty miles from Fort Bridger, was named 'The Camp of Death.' Five hundred animals perished around the camp on the night of the 6th of November. Fifteen oxen were found huddled together in one heap, frozen stiff.

"In this perilous situation the expeditionary army to Utah made the distance to Bridger—thirty-five miles—in fifteen days! Often the advance had arrived at camp before the end of the train left. On the 16th of November, the army reached their winter-quarters, Camp Scott, two miles from the site of Fort Bridger and one hundred and fifteen from Salt Lake City."

The official report of Colonel Philip St. George Cooke is still more desolate.

The experience of several days, as noted by the Colonel, will illustrate his report of the march of the Second Dragoons from Fort Leavenworth to Camp Scott: "November 6th, we found the ground once more white and the snow falling, but then very moderately; I marched as usual. On a four-mile hill the north wind and drifting snow became severe; the air seemed turned to frozen fog; nothing could be seen; we were struggling in a freezing cloud. The lofty wall at 'Three Crossings' was a happy relief; but the guide, who had lately passed there, was relentless in pronouncing that there was no grass. The idea of finding and feeding upon grass, in that wintry storm, under the deep snow, was hard to entertain; but as he promised grass and other shelter two miles further, we marched on, crossing twice more the rocky stream, half choked with snow and ice; finally he led us behind a great granite rock, but all too small for the promised shelter. Only a part of the regiment could huddle there in the deep snow; whilst, the long night through, the storm continued, and in fearful eddies from above, before, behind, drove the falling and drifting snow. Thus exposed for the hope of grass, the poor animals were driven, with great devotion, by the men, once more across the stream and three-quarters of a mile beyond, to the base of a granite ridge, but which almost faced the storm; there the famished mules, crying piteously, did not seek to eat, but desperately gathered in a mass, and some horses, escaping the guard, went back to the ford, where the lofty precipice first gave us so pleasant relief and shelter.

"Thus morning light had nothing cheering to reveal; the air still filled with driven snow; the animals soon came driven in, and, mingled in confusion with men, went crunching the snow in the confined and wretched camp, tramping all things in their way. It was not a time to dwell on the fact that from that mountain desert there was no retreat, nor any shelter near; but a time for action. No murmurs, not a complaint was heard, and certainly none saw in their commander's face a doubt or clouds; but with cheerful manner he gave orders as usual for the march.

"November 10. The northeast wind continued fiercely, enveloping us in a cloud which froze and fell all day. Few could have faced that wind. The herders left to bring up the rear with extra, but nearly all broken down mules, could not force them from the dead bushes of the little valley; and they remained there all day and night, bringing on the next day the fourth part that had not frozen. Thirteen mules were marched, and the camp was made four miles from the top of the pass. A wagon that day cut partly through the ice of a branch, and there froze so fast eight mules could not move it empty. Nearly all the tent pins were broken in the last camp; a few of iron were here substituted. Nine trooper horses were left freezing and dying on the road that day, and a number of soldiers and teamsters had been frost-bitten. It was a desperately cold night. The thermometers were broken, but, by comparison, must have marked twenty-five degrees below zero. A bottle of sherry wine froze in a trunk. Having lost about fifty mules in thirty-six hours, the morning of the eleventh, on the report of the quartermaster, I felt bound to leave a wagon in the bushes, filled with seventy-four extra saddles and bridles, and some sabers. Two other wagons at the last moment he was obliged to leave, but empty. The Sharp's carbines were then issued to mounted as well as dismounted men.

"November 11. The fast-growing company of dismounted men were marched together as a separate command by day; the morning of the 12th, a number of them were frost-bitten from not being in motion, although standing by fires.

"November 15. The sick report had rapidly run up from four or five to forty-two; thirty-six soldiers and teamsters having been frosted.

"Fort Bridger, November 19. I have one hundred and forty-four horses and have lost one hundred and thirty-four. Most of the loss has occurred much this side of South Pass, in comparatively moderate weather. It has been of starvation; the earth has a no more lifeless, treeless, grassless desert; it contains scarcely a wolf to glut itself on the hundreds of dead and frozen animals, which for thirty miles nearly block the road; with abandoned and shattered property, they mark, perhaps, beyond example in history, the steps of an advancing army with the horrors of a disastrous retreat."

The winter experience of the troops after their arrival at Camp Scott was quite in keeping with the march to Utah as described by Colonel Cooke. Rations were short, and many articles of daily necessity were altogether unattainable.

Whiskey sold at $12 a gallon; tobacco $3 a pound, and sugar and coffee about the same rate. Flour for a time was a luxury at a very high figure; "'and the possession of a good supply with no other protection than the covering of a tent was as dangerous to its owner as a well-filled purse is to a pedestrian in a first-class city after sunset." The cattle, too, were miserably poor, but their hides furnished moccasins for the soldiers. Every day, all through the winter, bands of fifteen or twenty men might be seen hitched to wagons, trailing for five or six miles to the mountain sides to get loads of fuel for the use of the camp. But the greatest privation of all was caused by the lack of salt. Learning of this distress of the soldiers, and knowing that with poor meat and no vegetables, the craving for salt to season the dish must be almost as intolerable as the burning thirst for water in the desert, Brigham sent a load of salt to Colonel Johnston, accompanied with a letter of gift, which forms one of the Government documents. (See appendix.) But Colonel Johnston ordered the messengers from his camp with every expression of contempt for Brigham Young, the great Mormon "rebel."

"How mutable are human affairs!" comments Stenhouse, noting this incident.

"Five years later, that same Colonel Johnston was himself designated a 'rebel,' and became one of the most distinguished generals in the Confederate army. The Colonel Johnston of Utah became the General Albert Sidney Johnston of Shiloh!"

The salt, however, by indirect means was returned to the camp. Johnston's army, after all, did eat Brigham Young's salt; and the soldiers knew it, but the high-spirited commander shared it not. The Indians, however, soon furnished a supply for the Colonel and his officers and hurried through the snow with their packs of salt and sold it at $5 per pound, but the increase of the supply reduced the price.

Probably Colonel Johnston thought that Brigham Young was wantonly tantalizing the high spirit of himself and officers with a realization of their condition; but, if he had read the following entry in Apostle Woodruffs diary, at a later date, he would probably have revised that opinion.

"I spent the evening at President Young's office (at Provo). He said, 'I am sorry for the army; and thought of sending word to the brethren in Great Salt Lake City to sell vegetables to them. I have also had it in my heart, when peace is established, to take all the cattle, horses and mules, which we have taken from the army, and return them to the officers.'"

Here is another similar entry of a later date: "Colonel Alexander called yesterday and had a short interview; and it was very agreeable. President Young said, 'I was much pleased with him, and am satisfied that, if he had the sole command of the army, and I could have had three hours' conversation with him, all would have been right, and they could have come in last fall as well as now.'"

With this couple Colonel Alexander's statement in his letter, "I have only to repeat my assurance that no harm would have happened to any citizen of Utah, through the instrumentality of the army of the United States in the performance of its legitimate duties without molestation. Together, these simple notes combine a volume of historical explanations. The people of Utah regarded it as an unhallowed crusade not a United States army that they were resisting.

CHAPTER XXI.

THE NAUVOO LEGION ORDERED IN FOR THE WINTER. PICKET GUARD POSTED. MARCH OF THE LEGION TO GREAT SALT LAKE CITY: RECEIVED WITH SONGS OF TRIUMPH. A JUBILANT WINTER IN ZION. SUMMARY OF GOVERNMENT MOVEMENTS FOR THE SPRING CAMPAIGN.

The army having gone into Winter Quarters at "Old Fort Bridger" and "Henry's Fork," the Nauvoo Legion was called in and concentrated at Camp Weber, situated at the mouth of Echo Canyon. As soon as the Territorial troops had all arrived, provisions were made for a picket-guard, consisting of fifty picked men under the command of Captain John R. Winder, to remain at Camp Weber during the winter, and the following order was issued: "Head Quarters Eastern Expedition, Camp Weber, December 4th, 1857.

"Capt. John R. Winder.

"Dear Bro: You are appointed to take charge of the guard detailed to remain and watch the movements of the invaders. You will keep ten men at the lookout station on the heights of Yellow Creek. Keep a constant watch from the highest point during daylight, and a camp guard at night, also a horse guard out with the horses which should be kept out on good grass all day and grained with two quarts of feed per day. This advance will occasionally trail out towards Fort Bridger and look at our enemies from the high butte near that place. You will relieve this guard once a week. Keep open and travel the trail down to the head of Echo, instead of the road. Teamsters or deserters must not be permitted to come to your lookout station. Let them pass with merely knowing who and what they are, to your station on the Weber and into the city. If officers or others undertake to come in, keep them prisoners until you receive further advices from the city. Especially and in no case let any of the would be civil officers pass. These are, as far as I know, as follows: A. Cumming (governor), Eckels (chief justice), Dotson (marshal), Forney (superintendent of Indian affairs), Hockaday (district attorney). At your station on the Weber you will also keep a lookout, and guard the road at night, also keep a camp and horse guard. Keep the men employed making improvements, when not on other duty.

Build a good horse corral and prepare stables. Remove the houses into a fort line and then picket in the remainder. Keep a trail open down the Weber to the citizen's road. Be strict in the issue of rations and feed. Practice economy both in your supplies and time and see that there is no waste of either. Dry a portion of the beef and use the bones in soup with the hard bread, which, as it will not keep equal with the flour, it is desirable to have first used so far as practicable.

"Instruct each mess to save their grease and ashes, and make soap, and wash their own clothes. Dig out troughs to save the soap and learn to be saving in all things. If your lookout party discover any movement of the enemy in this direction, let them send two men to your camp on the Weber, and the remainder continue to watch their movements, and not all leave their station, unless it should prove a large party, but keep you timely advised so that you can meet them at the defenses in Echo, or if necessary render them assistance. Where you can do so at an advantage, take all such parties prisoners, if you can without shooting, but if you cannot, you are at liberty to attack them as no such party must be permitted to come into the city.

Should the party be two strong and you are compelled to retreat, do so after safely caching all supplies; in all cases giving us prompt information by express, that we may be able to meet them between here and the city. Send into the city every week all the information you can obtain, and send whether you have any news from the enemy or not, that we may know of your welfare, kind of weather, depth of snow, etc.

"The boys at the lookout station should not make any trail down to the road, nor expose themselves to view, but keep concealed as much as possible, as it is for that purpose that that position has been chosen. No person without a permit must be allowed to pass from this way to the enemy's camp. Be careful about this. Be vigilant, active and energetic and observe good order, discipline and wisdom in all your works, that good may be the result. Remember that to you is entrusted for the time being the duty of standing between Israel and their foes, and as you would like to repose in peace and safety while others are on the watchtower, so now while in the performance of this duty do you observe the same care, vigilance and activity, which you would desire of others when they come to take your place. Do not let any inaction on the part of the enemy lull you into a false security and cause any neglect on your part.

"Praying the Lord to bless and preserve you in life, health and strength, and wisdom and power to accomplish every duty incumbent upon you and bring peace to Israel to the utter confusion and overthrow of her enemies.

"I remain, your brother in the Gospel of Christ,

[Signed,] DAN'L H. WELLS,

Lieut. Genrl. Comdng."

"P. S. Be careful to prevent fire being kindled in or near the commissary storehouse."

The guard having been selected, the Legion marched to Great Salt Lake City and on arriving there was greeted by the enthusiastic citizens with songs of victory. The poetess, Eliza R. Snow, saluted with her war song, which the following lines will illustrate:

"Strong in the power of Brigham's God,
Your name's a terror to our foes;
Ye were a barrier strong and broad
As our high mountains crowned with snows.
* * *
Then welcome! sons of light and truth.
Heroes alike in age and youth."

in about two weeks Captain Winder reported to Governor Young that a deep snow had fallen in the mountains and he was instructed to release all but ten men. This guard was continued during the winter.

There was no need of scouts or spies to keep the city well posted relative to the army, for all through that winter, so cheerless to the Expedition, deserters and army teamsters were constantly arriving from Bridger, in many instances in a starving and destitute condition. They were kindly treated by the Mormon guard, provided with food and passed on to Great Salt Lake City. Through this channel, Governor Young and General Wells were kept well informed of the condition and contemplated movements of the army.

In December the Utah Legislature met in Great Salt Lake City, and Governor Young delivered his annual message, in which he reviewed the conduct of the Administration towards Utah, and at great length expounded the fundamental principles of the American Confederation. It is a remarkable document and will be read a century hence with deep interest. [See Appendix.] On the 20th of December the Legislature unanimously passed resolutions approving of Governor Young's course, and each member, signing his name to the document, pledged himself to maintain the rights and liberties of the people of Utah.

Notwithstanding that Governor Young and the chief men of the community had been indicted for high treason, in the self-constituted court of Chief Justice Eckels, held at Camp Scott; notwithstanding that Governor Cumming had also issued his proclamation to nullify that of Governor Young; and notwithstanding that the prospects were that before the close of the coming year the cities of Utah would be in ashes, and the Mormon women and children have fled to the "chambers of the mountains," while their husbands, fathers, sons and brothers would be doing battle with a reinforced army; yet the winter of 1857-8 is to this day spoken of as the "gayest winter ever known in Utah." One of the literati of Salt Lake City, writing to a brother scribe in New York City, said: " Peace is enjoyed throughout this Territory by the citizens, from north to south, and every heart beats with the love of liberty—religious, political and social. During the winter festivities were very prevalent, and entertainments of various kinds were enjoyed. Dramatic and literary associations were attended to overflowing; balls and parties were frequent and numerously filled, and every amusement suitable for an enlightened and refined people was a source of profit to the caterer and pleasure and benefit to the patronizers. Indeed, had you seen the manner in which they enjoyed themselves, you would never have surmised for one moment that within a few miles of us there was an army—repugnant to every feeling of the people—who were only waiting to kill, corrupt and debase an innocent and virtuous community."

There is the great sagacity and remarkable common-sense leadership of Brigham Young seen in all this jubilee. He was preparing to make his second exodus, if necessary, and did not intend to play his Moses to a dispirited Israel.

Early in the Spring a large number of the soldiers of the Nauvoo Legion were again in the field, occupying their old camping grounds, where they continued until peace was proclaimed.

Of the state of affairs on the government side Stenhouse thus summarizes: "Notwithstanding the difficulty experienced at that time of traveling across the plains in winter, an express occasionally carried to the Government the unwelcome news of the disaster that had befallen the expedition and the sufferings and privations that ensued. At one time there were grave fears of its ultimate success, but brave men and the unlimited resources of the Government were destined to overcome every obstacle. Captain Marcy with a company of picked men undertook a perilous journey from Fort Bridger to Taos, New Mexico, to obtain provisions, cattle and mules, for the relief of the expedition, and after most terrible suffering and heavy loss of animals, and many disabled men, he reached the point of supply, and was eminently successful.

"The misfortunes that had befallen the troops aroused the Government to a realization of the necessity of rendering every aid, both in men and material, to save the expedition and make it successful. Lieut.-Gen. Scott was summoned to Washington to consult with the Secretary of War, and at one time the project of entering Utah from the west was seriously entertained. The intimation that two regiments of volunteers would probably be called for in the spring met with a ready response from all parts of the Union. It was very evident that the nation was thoroughly dissatisfied with the state of affairs in Utah and wanted to bring the Mormons to a settlement.

"Ready to take advantage of anything which promised wealth, there were multitudes of solicitous contractors seeking to supply the army in the West; and with a prodigality beyond all precedent, the War Department was perfectly reckless. The Sixth and Seventh regiments of infantry, together with the First Cavalry, and two batteries of artillery—about three thousand in all—were ordered to Utah, and every arrangement made for speedy and colossal warfare with the Prophet. Political writers charged to the administration of Mr. Buchanan an utter recklessness of expenditure, intended more for the support of political favorites and for the attainment of political purposes in Kansas than for the overthrow of the dynasty of Brigham. It was estimated in Washington that forty-five hundred wagons would be required to transport munitions of war and provisions for the troops for a period of from twelve to eighteen months, besides fifty thousand oxen, four thousand mules, and an army of teamsters, wagon-masters, and employees, at least five thousand strong. It was very evident that the Government was playing with a loose hand, and the consideration of cost to the national treasury was the last thing thought of. The transportation item for 1858, provided for the expenditure of no less than four and a half millions, and that contract was accorded to a firm in western Missouri, without public announcement or competition.

While all this was occupying the attention of the public, and the Government seemed determined that the war against the Mormons should be carried out with vigor, there was another influence at work to bring " the Utah rebellion" to a peaceful termination.

CHAPTER XXII.

BUCHANAN COERCED BY PUBLIC SENTIMENT INTO SENDING A COMMISSION OF INVESTIGATION. HE SENDS COLONEL KANE WITH A SPECIAL MISSION TO THE MORMONS. ARRIVAL OF THE COLONEL IN SALT LAKE CITY. HIS FIRST INTERVIEW WITH THE MORMON LEADERS. INCIDENTS OF HIS SOJOURN. HE GOES TO MEET GOVERNOR CUMMING AND IS PLACED UNDER ARREST BY GENERAL JOHNSTON. HIS CHALLENGE TO THAT OFFICER. HE BRINGS IN THE NEW GOVERNOR IN TRIUMPH. RETURN OF COLONEL KANE.

The reaction came. The leading papers, both of America and England, declared that President Buchanan had committed a great and palpable blunder.

He had sent an army, before a committee of investigation, and had made war upon one of our Territories for rejecting (?) a new Governor before that Governor had been sent. Brigham Young had clearly a constitutional advantage over the President of the United States—for in those days the rights of the citizen, and the rights of a State or Territory, had some meaning in the national mind. The idea of " Buchanan's blunder" once started, it soon became universal in the public mind. The Mormons were not in rebellion, as they themselves stoutly maintained. They were ready to receive the new Governor with becoming loyalty, but not willing to have him forced upon them by bayonets.

There was nothing more to be said in the case, excepting that by the common law of nature, a man may hold off the hand at his throat to say in good old scriptural language, "Come let us reason together."

All America, and all Europe, "perceived the error," and a storm of condemnation and ridicule fell upon the devoted head of the President. Peace commissioners alone could help him out of the trouble.

At this critical juncture Colonel Kane sought the President and offered his services as mediator. Buchanan wisely recognized his potency and fitness, and without a moment's loss of time the Colonel set out on his self-imposed mission, although in such feeble health that any consideration short of the noble impulse that actuated him at the time would have deterred him from making the attempt. The undertaking was as delicate as it was important. Its success alone could make it acceptable, either to the Mormons or to the nation.

For prudential reasons he registered himself as " Dr. Osborne" among the passengers on board the California steamer, which left New York in the first week of January, 1858. On reaching the Pacific coast, he hastened, overland, to Southern California, there overtaking the Mormons who had just broken up their colony at San Bernardino, re-gathering to Utah for the common defense. An escort was immediately furnished him, and he reached Salt Lake City in the following February.

Governor Young called a council of the Presidency and Twelve, at his house, on the evening of the day of Colonel Kane's arrival, and at 8 o'clock the " messenger from Washington" was introduced by Joseph A. Young, as "Dr. Osborne."

The introduction was very formal. The Colonel had a peculiar mission to fulfill and was evidently desirous to maintain the dignity of the Government.

Moreover, it was more than eleven years since he had met his friends of Winter Quarters. They had, with their people, become as a little nation, and the United States was making war upon them as an independent power. Notwithstanding that his great love for them had prompted him to undertake the long journey which he had just accomplished, at first he must have felt the uncertainty of his mission, and some misgivings as to the regard in which they would hold his mediation. But perhaps no other man in the nation at that critical moment would have been received by the Mormon leaders with such perfect confidence.

The Colonel was very pale, being worn down with travel by day and night. An easy chair was placed for him. A profound silence of some moments reigned. The council waited to hear the mind of the Government, for the coming of Colonel Kane had put a new aspect on affairs, though what it was to be remained to be shaped from that night. With great difficulty in speaking he addressed the council as follows: "Governor Young and Gentlemen: I come as an ambassador from the chief executive of our nation, and am prepared and duly authorized to lay before you, most fully and definitely, the feelings and views of the citizens of our common country, and of the executive towards you, relative to the present position of this Territory, and relative to the army of the United States now upon your borders.

"After giving you the most satisfactory evidence in relation to matters concerning you, now pending, I shall then call your attention, and wish to enlist your sympathies, in behalf of the poor soldiers who are now suffering in the cold and snow of the mountains. I shall request you to render them aid and comfort, and to assist them to come here, and to bid them a hearty welcome into your hospitable valley.

"Governor Young, may I be permitted to ask a private interview for a few moments with you? Gentlemen, excuse my formality."

They were gone about thirty minutes, when they returned to the room. Colonel Kane then informed the council that Captain Van Vliet had made a good report of them at Washington and had used his influence to have the army stop east of Bridger. He had done a great deal in their behalf.

"You all look very well," said the Colonel, "you have built up quite an empire here in a short time."

He spoke upon the prosperity of the people, instancing some of its phases; and then the enquiry came from someone present: "Did Dr. Bernhisel take his seat?" No news whatever of the Utah delegate had yet reached them.

"Yes," he answered, "Delegate Bernhisel took his seat. He was opposed by the Arkansas member and a few others, but they were treated as fools by more sagacious members; for, if the delegate had been refused his seat it would have been tantamount to a declaration of war."

Speaking of the conduct of the Mormons, he said: "You have borne your part manfully in this contest. I was pleased to see how patiently your people took it."

"How was the President's message received?" asked Governor Young.

"The message was received as usual. In his appointments he had been cruelly impartial. So far he has made an excellent President. He has an able cabinet. They are more united, and work together better than some of our former cabinets have done."

"I suppose," observed Governor Young, caustically, "they are united in putting down Utah?"

"I think not," replied the Colonel.

Then came conversations on the affairs of the nation—of Spain, Kansas, the Black Warrior affair, financial pressure, etc.

By this time all restraint between the brethren and their noble friend was gone.

"I wish you knew how much I feel at home," he observed. "I hope I shall have the privilege of 'breaking bread with these, my friends.'"

"I want to take good care of you," returned Governor Young warmly. "I want to tell you one thing, and that is, the men you see here do not look old.

The reason is, they are doing right, and are in the service of God. If men would do right they would live to a great age. There are but few in the world who have the amount of labor to do which I have. I have to meet men every hour in the day. It is said of me that I do more business in an hour than any President, King or Emperor has to perform in a day; and that I think for the people constantly. You can endure more now than you could ten years ago. If you had done as some men have done you would have been in your grave before now." The Colonel replied, "I fear that I can endure more than I could ten years ago. The present life doesn't pay, and I feel like going away as soon as it is the will of God to take me."

"I know, to take this life as it is, and as men make it," answered President Young, "it does not appear worth living, but I can tell you that, when you see things as they are, you will find life is worth preserving, and blessings will follow our living in this life, if we do right."

"Now," continued the President, warming with his subject, "if God should say, I will let you live in this world without any pain or sorrow, we might feel life was worth living for. But this is not in his economy. We have to partake of sorrow, affliction and death; and if we pass through this affliction patiently, and do right, we shall have a greater reward in the world to come. I have been robbed several times of my all in this life, and my property has gone into the hands of my enemies; but as to property, I care no more about it than about the dirt in the streets, only to use it as God wishes. But I think a good deal of a friend —a true friend. An honest man is truly the noblest work of God. It is not in the power of the United States to destroy this people, for they are in the hands of God. If we do right, He will preserve us. The Lord does many things which we would count as small things. For instance, a poor man once came into my office; I felt by the spirit that he needed assistance; I took five dollars out of my pocket and gave to him. I soon after found a five-dollar gold piece in my pocket, which I did not put there. Soon I found another. Many think that the Lord has nothing to do with gold; but he has charge of that as well as every other element. Brother Kimball said in Nauvoo, 'if we have to leave our houses we will go to the mountains, and in a few years we will have a better city than we have here.' This is fulfilled. He also said, 'We shall have gold, and coin twenty-dollar gold pieces.' We came here, founded a city, and coined the first twenty-dollar gold pieces in the United States. Setting the brethren poorly clad, soon after we came here, he said, 'It will not be three years before we can buy clothing cheaper in Salt Lake Valley than in the States.' Before the time was out, the gold-diggers brought loads of clothing, and sold them in our city at a wanton price.

"Friend Thomas," concluded Governor Young, "the Lord sent you here, and he will not let you die—no, you cannot die till your work is done. I want to have your name live to all eternity. You have done a great work, and you will do a greater work still."

The council then broke up, and the brethren went to their homes. The straightforward, noble simplicity of what was thus done and said between Thomas L. Kane and Brigham Young, in the presence of the apostles, cannot but strike the attention of the intelligent investigator.

After the council had ended, word was sent to Elder Wm. C. Staines that a Dr. Osborne, traveling with the company from California, was sick, and desired accommodation at his house; and late in the evening "Dr. Osborne" was duly introduced to, and cordially welcomed by, Elder Staines. The elder had no idea that his guest was other than the person represented, for when Colonel Kane was at Winter Quarters, he (Staines) was among the Indians, with Bishop Miller's camp.

However, in a few days Elder Staines learned who his guest was, and, as a favorable opportunity presented itself, said to him: "Colonel Kane, why did you wish to be introduced to me as Dr. Osborne?"

"My dear friend," replied the Colonel, "I was once treated so kindly at winter quarters that I am sensitive over its memories. I knew you to be a good people then; but since, I have heard so many hard things about you, that I thought I would like to convince myself whether or not the people possessed the same humane and hospitable spirit which 1 found in them once. I thought, if I go to the house of any of my great friends of Winter Quarters, they will treat me as Thomas L. Kane, with a remembrance of some services which I may have rendered them. So I requested to be sent to some stranger's house, as 'Dr. Osborne,' that I might know how the Mormon people would treat a stranger at such a moment as this, without knowing whether I might not turn out to be either an enemy or a spy. And now, Mr. Staines, I want to know if you could have treated Thomas L. Kane better than you have treated Dr. Osborne."

"No, Colonel," replied Elder Staines, "I could not."

"And thus, my friend." added 'Dr. Osborne,' "I have proved that the Mormons will treat the stranger in Salt Lake City, as they once did Thomas L. Kane at Winter Quarters."

In a few days, under the inspiring spirit and affectionate nursing of his host, Colonel Kane was sufficiently recovered to carry out his design of proceeding to the headquarters of the army (Fort Bridger, then called Camp Scott).

Governor Young's policy had changed it nought, excepting in that which was consistent with the improved situation. The Mormons would receive their new Governor loyally but would not have him accompanied by an army into their capital; neither would they allow an army to be quartered in any of their cities. The agent of the administration could ask no more nor desire more. It was the basis of a fair compromise, which would give to President Buchanan a plausible out-come, and at the same time maintain the Mormon dignity.

The visit of Colonel Kane to Camp Scott was attended with a chain of circumstances that give to the narration of it a decidedly dramatic cast. At the worst season of the year, in delicate health, he made his way through the almost impassable snows of the mountains, a distance of 113 miles. Arrived on the 10th of March, in the vicinity of the army outposts, he insisted, out of consideration for the safety of his friendly escort, on entering the lines unaccompanied.

Reaching the nearest picket post, the over-zealous sentry challenged him, and at the same time fired at him. In return, the Colonel broke the stock of his rifle over the sentry's head. The post being now full aroused and greatly excited, Colonel Kane, with characteristic politeness as well as diplomacy, requested to be conducted to the tent of Governor Cumming. The Governor received him cordially.

The Colonel's diplomacy in seeking the Governor, instead of General Johnston, is evident. His business was not directly with the commander, but with the civil chief, whose posse commitatus the troops were. The compromise which Buchanan had to effect, with the utmost delicacy, could only be through the new Governor, and that, too, by his heading off the army sent to occupy Utah.

The General was chagrined. Here was Buchanan withdrawing from a serious blunder as gracefully as possible; but where was Albert Sidney Johnston to achieve either glory or honor out of the Utah war?

Affecting to treat Colonel Kane as a spy, an orderly was sent to arrest him. It was afterwards converted into a blundering execution of the General's invitation to him to dine at head-quarters. The blunder was no doubt an intentional one. Colonel Kane replied by sending a formal challenge to General Johnston.

Governor Cumming could do nothing less than espouse the cause of the 'ambassador," who was there in the execution of a mission entrusted to him by the President of the United States. The affair of honor also touched himself.

He resented it with great spirit, extended his official protection to his guest, and from that moment there was an impassable breach between the executive and the military chief. The duel, however, was prevented by the interference of Chief Justice Eckels, who threatened to arrest all concerned in it if it proceeded further.

The conduct of General Johnston was looked upon by the Mormon leader as very like a bit of providential diplomacy interposed in behalf of his people. With the Governor and the commander of the army at swords' points, the issues of the "war" were practically in the hands of Brigham Young. From that moment he knew that he was master of the situation; and the extraordinary moves that he made thereupon, culminating with the second exodus, shows what a consummate strategist he was, and how complex were his methods of mastering men. He was now not only in command of his own people, who at the lifting of his finger would move with him to the ends of the earth, but substantially dictator both to the Governor and the army. Johnston could only move at the call of the Governor and was hedged about by the new policy of the President, while this shaping of affairs converted the Mormon militia, then under arms, into the Governor's posse commitatus, instead of the regular troops.

The mission of Colonel Kane to the seat of war was to induce the Governor to trust himself through the Mormon lines, under a Mormon escort of honor that would be furnished at a proper point, and to enter immediately upon his gubernatorial duties. The officers remonstrated with the Governor against going to the city without the army, predicting that the Mormons would poison him, or put him out of the way by some other wicked ingenuity; but the camp was now no longer the place for him, and with a high temper and a humane spirit, he trusted himself to the guidance of Colonel Kane.

The Governor left Camp Scott on the 5th of April, en route for Salt Lake City, accompanied by Colonel Kane and two servants. As soon as he had passed the Federal lines, he was met by an escort of the Mormon militia and welcomed as Governor of the Territory with military honors.

On the 12 of April they entered Salt Lake City in good health and spirits, escorted by the mayor, marshal and aldermen, and many other distinguished citizens.

Arrived at the residence of Elder Staines, Governor Young promptly and frankly called upon his successor at the earliest possible moment; and they were introduced to each other by Colonel Kane.

"Governor Cumming, I am glad to meet you!" observed Brigham, with unostentatious dignity, and that quiet heartiness peculiar to him.

"Governor Young, I am happy to meet you, sir!" responded His Excellency warmly, at once impressed by the presence and spirit of the remarkable man before him.

"Well, Governor," said Elder Staines, after the interview was ended, " what do you think of President Young? Does he appear to you a tyrant, as represented?"

"No, sir. No tyrant ever had a head on his shoulders like Mr. Young. He is naturally a very good man. I doubt whether many of your people sufficiently appreciate him as a leader."

The brethren were apprised of the fact that the officers at Camp Scott had warned the Governor that the Mormons would poison him, so it was contrived that Elder Staines and Howard Egan should eat at the same table with him and partake of the same food. Of course he understood the delicate assurance that "death was not in the pot."

Three days after his entrance into the city, Governor Cumming officially notified General Johnston that he had been properly recognized by the people; that he was in full discharge of his office, and that he did not require the presence of troops.

On his part, ex-Governor Young set the public example, and on the Sunday following introduced him to a large assembly as the Governor of Utah.

Thus successfully ended the mission of Col. Kane, who shortly thereafter returned to Washington, to report in person to the President. Journeying by the overland route, a body-guard of Mormon scouts accompanied him to the Missouri River. It is no more than simple justice to here testify of him, that a more gentle and noble man has rarely been found, and for his disinterested kindness toward the Mormon people they will ever hold his name in honorable and affectionate remembrance.

CHAPTER XXIII.

REPORT OF GOVERNOR CUMMING TO THE GOVERNMENT. THE GOVERNMENT RECORDS FOUND NOT BURNED, AS REPORTED BY DRUMMOND. THE MORMON LEADERS JUSTIFIED BY THE FACTS, AND THE PEOPLE LOYAL. GRAPHIC AND THRILLING DESCRIPTION OF THE MORMONS IN THEIR SECOND EXODUS. THE GOVERNOR BRINGS HIS FAMILY TO SALT LAKE CITY. HIS WIFE IS MOVED TO TEARS AT WITNESSING THE HEROIC ATTITUDE OF THE PEOPLE.

Governor Cumming immediately reported the condition of affairs in Utah, and the re-action that it caused in the public mind, both in America and Europe, can well be imagined. It was a new revelation, to the age, of Mormon character and Mormon sincerity. The peculiar people were never understood till then, notwithstanding their previous exodus, for only Missouri and Illinois seemed concerned in their early history and doings; but now that the United States Government was a party in the action, all the world became interested in the extraordinary spectacle of a peculiar, little, unconquerable people, braving the wrath of a mighty nation.

The current events of those days, including the "second exodus," which was begun in anticipation of a breach of faith, on the part of the United States authorities, in this instance, as in the previous case of the State authorities at Nauvoo, are well recounted in the following report of Governor Cumming, addressed to General Cass, then Secretary of State:

"Executive Office, Salt Lake City, U. T., May 2nd, 1858.

"Sir: You are aware that my contemplated journey was postponed in consequence of the snow upon the mountains, and in the canyons between Fort Bridger and this city. In accordance with the determination communicated in former notes, I left camp on the 5th, and arrived here on the 12th ult.

"Some of the incidents of my journey are related in the annexed note, addressed by me to General A. S. Johnston, on the 15th ult:"

"Executive Office, Salt Lake City, U. T., April 15th, 1858.

"Sir: I left camp on the 5th, en route to this city, in accordance with a determination communicated to you on the 3rd inst, accompanied by Colonel Kane as my guide, and two servants. Arriving in the vicinity of the spring, which is on this side of the "Quaking Asp" hill, after night, Indian camp fires were discerned on the rocks overhanging the valley. We proceeded to the spring, and after disposing of the animals, retired from the trail beyond the mountain.

We had reason to congratulate ourselves upon having taken this precaution, as we subsequently ascertained that the country lying between your outposts and the 'Yellow Creek' is infested by hostile renegades and outlaws from various tribes."

"I was escorted from Bear River Valley to the western end of Echo Canyon.

The journey through the canyon being performed, for the most part, after night, it was about 11 o'clock p. m., when I arrived at Weber Station. I have been everywhere recognized as Governor of Utah; and, so far from having encountered insults or indignities, I am gratified in being able to state to you that, in passing through the settlements, I have been universally greeted with such respectful attentions as are due to the representative authority of the United States in the Territory.

"Near the Warm Springs, at the line dividing Great Salt Lake and Davis counties, I was honored with a formal and respectful reception by many gentlemen including the mayor and other municipal officers of the city, and by them escorted to lodgings previously provided, the mayor occupying a seat in my carriage.

"Ex-Governor Brigham Young paid me a call of ceremony as soon as I was sufficiently relieved from the fatigue of my mountain journey to receive company.

In subsequent interviews with the ex-Governor, he has evinced a willingness to afford me every facility I may require for the efficient performance of my administrative duties. His course in this respect meets, I fancy, with the approval of a majority of this community. The Territorial seal, with other public property, has been tendered me by William H. Hooper, Esq., late Secretary pro tem.

"1 have not yet examined the subject critically but apprehend that the records of the United States Courts, Territorial Library, and other public property, remain unimpaired.

"Having entered upon the performance of my official duties in this city, it is probable that I will be detained for some days in this part of the Territory.

"I respectfully call your attention to a matter which demands our serious consideration. Many acts of depredation have been recently committed by the Indians upon the property of the inhabitants—one in the immediate vicinity of this city. Believing that the Indians will endeavor to sell the stolen property at or near your camp, I herewith enclose the Brand Book (incomplete) and memoranda (in part) of stock lost by citizens of Utah since February 25th, 1858, which may enable you to secure the property and punish the thieves.

"With feelings of profound regret I have learned that Agent Hart is charged with having incited to acts of hostility the Indians in Uinta Valley. I hope that Agent Hart will be able to vindicate himself from the charges contained in the enclosed letter from William H. Hooper, late Secretary pro tem., yet they demand a thorough investigation.

"I shall probably be compelled to make a requisition upon you for a sufficient force to chastise the Indians alluded to, since I desire to avoid being compelled to call out the militia for that purpose.

"The gentlemen who are entrusted with this note, Mr. John B. Kimball and Mr. Fay Worthen, are engaged in mercantile pursuits here, and are represented to be gentlemen of the highest respectability and have no connection with the Church here. Should you deem it advisable or necessary, you will please send any communication intended for me by them. I beg leave to commend them to your confidence and courtesy. They will probably return to the city in a few days. They are well known to Messrs. Gilbert, Perry and Burr, with whom you will please communicate.

Very respectfully, your obedient servant,

A. CUMMING, Governor Utah Territory.

To A. S. Johnston, commanding Army of Utah, Camp Scott, U. T.

"The note omits to state that I met parties of armed men at Lost Creek and Yellow Creek, as well as at Echo Canyon. At every point, however, I was recognized as the Governor of Utah, and received with a military salute. When it was arranged with the Mormon officers in command of my escort that I should pass through Echo Canyon at night, I inferred that it was with the object of concealing the barricades and other defenses. I was, therefore, agreeably surprised by an illumination in honor of me. The bonfires kindled by the soldiers from the base to the summits of the walls of the canyon, completely illuminated the valley, and disclosed the snow-colored mountains which surrounded us. When I arrived at the next station, I found the 'Emigrant Road' over the 'Big Mountain' still impassable. I was able to make my way, however, down 'Weber Canyon.' Since my arrival, I have been employed in examining the records of the Supreme and District Courts, which I am now prepared to report as being perfect and unimpaired. This will doubtless be acceptable information to those who have entertained an impression to the contrary.

"I have also examined the Legislative Records, and other books belonging to the Secretary of State, which are in perfect preservation. The property return, though not made up in proper form, exhibits the public property for which W. H. Hooper, late Secretary of State pro tem., is responsible. It is, in part, the same for which the estate of A. W. Babbitt is liable, that individual having died whilst in the office of Secretary of State for Utah.

"I believe that the books and charts, stationery and other property appertaining to the Surveyor-General's office will, upon examination, be found in the proper place, except some instruments, which are supposed to have been disposed of by a man temporarily in charge of the office. I examined the property but cannot verify the matter in consequence of not having at my command a schedule or property return.

"The condition of the large and valuable Territorial library has also commanded my attention, and I am pleased in being able to report that Mr. W. C. Staines, the librarian, has kept the books and records in the most excellent condition. I will, at an early day, transmit a catalogue of this library, and a schedule of the other public property, with certified copies of the records of the Supreme and District Courts, exhibiting the character and amount of the public business last transacted in them.

"On the 21st inst. I left Salt Lake City, and visited Tooele and Rush Valleys, in the latter of which lies the military reserve selected by Colonel Steptoe, and endeavored to trace the lines upon the ground, from field-notes which are in the Surveyor-General's office. An accurate plan of the reserve, as it has been measured off, will be found accompanying a communication, which I shall address to the Secretary of War, upon the subject.

"On the morning of the 26th inst., information was communicated to me that a number of persons who were desirous of leaving the Territory were unable to do so and considered themselves to be unlawfully restrained of their liberties.

However desirous of conciliating public opinion, I felt it incumbent upon me to adopt the most energetic measures to ascertain the truth or falsehood of this statement. Postponing, therefore, a journey of importance which I had in contemplation to one of the settlements of Utah County, I caused public notice to be given immediately of my readiness to relieve all persons who were, or deemed themselves to be, aggrieved, and on the ensuing day, which was Sunday, requested a notice to the same effect to be read, in my presence, to the people in the tabernacle.

"I have since kept my office open at all hours of the day and night, and have registered no less than 56 men, 38 women and 71 children, as desirous of my protection and assistance in proceeding to the States. The large majority of these people are of English birth, and state that they leave the congregation from a desire to improve their circumstances and realize elsewhere more money for their labor. Certain leading men among the Mormons have promised them flour, and to assist them in leaving the country.

"My presence at the meeting in the tabernacle will be remembered by me as an occasion of interest. Between three and four thousand persons were assembled for the purpose of public worship; the hall was crowded to overflowing; but the most profound quiet was observed when I appeared. President Brigham Young introduced me by name as the Governor of Utah, and I addressed the audience from 'the stand.' 1 informed them that I had come among them to vindicate the national sovereignty; that it was my duty to secure the supremacy of the constitution and the laws; that I had taken my oath of office to exact an unconditional submission on their part to the dictates of the law. I was not interrupted. In a discourse of about thirty minutes' duration, I touched (as I thought best) boldly upon all the leading questions at issue between them and the General Government. I remembered that I had to deal with men embittered by the remembrance and recital of many real and imaginary wrongs but did not think it wise to withhold from them the entire truth. They listened respectfully to all I had to say—approvingly, even, I fancied—when I explained to them what I intended should be the character of my administration. In fact, the whole character of the people was calm, betokening no consciousness of having done wrong, but rather, as it were, indicating a conviction that they had done their duty to their religion and to their country. I have observed that the Mormons profess to view the constitution as the work of inspired men and respond with readiness to appeals for its support.

"Thus the meeting might have ended; but, after closing my remarks, I rose and stated that I would be glad to hear from any who might be inclined to address me upon topics of interest to the community. This invitation brought forth in succession several powerful speakers, who evidently exercised great influence over the masses of the people. They harangued on the subject of the assassination of Joseph Smith, Jun., and his friends, the services rendered by the Mormon Battalion to an ungrateful country, their sufferings on 'the Plains' during their dreary pilgrimage to their mountain home, etc. The congregation became greatly excited, and joined the speakers in their intemperate remarks, exhibited more frenzy than I had expected to witness among a people who habitually exercise great self-control. A speaker now represented the Federal Government as desirous of needlessly introducing the national troops into the Territory, 'whether a necessity existed for their employment to support the authority of the civil officers or not;' and the wildest uproar ensued. I was fully confirmed in the opinion that this people, with their extraordinary religion and customs, would gladly encounter certain death rather than be taxed with a submission to the military power, which they considered to involve a loss of honor.

"In my first address I informed them that they were entitled to a trial by their peers; that I had no intention of stationing the army in immediate contact with their settlements, and that the military posse would not be resorted to until other means of arrest had been tried and failed, I found the greatest difficulty in explaining these points, so great was the excitement. Eventually, however, the efforts of Brigham Young were successful in calming the tumult and restoring order before the adjournment of the meeting. It is proper that I should add that more than one speaker has since expressed his regret at having been betrayed into intemperance of language in my presence. The President and the American people will learn with gratification the auspicious issue of our difficulties here. I regret the necessity, however, which compels me to mingle with my congratulations, the announcement of a fact that will occasion great concern.

"The people, including the inhabitants of this city, are moving from every settlement in the northern part of the Territory. The roads are everywhere filled with wagons loaded with provisions and household furniture, the women and children often without shoes or hats, driving their flocks they know not where. They seem not only resigned but cheerful. 'It is the will of the Lord,' and they rejoice to exchange the comforts of home for the trials of the wilderness. Their ultimate destination is not, I presume, definitely fixed upon. 'Going south,' seems sufficiently definite for the most of them, but many believe that their ultimate destination is Sonora.

"Young, Kimball and most of the influential men have left their commodious mansions, without apparent regret, to lengthen the long train of wanderers. The masses everywhere announce to me that the torch will be applied to every house indiscriminately throughout the country, so soon as the troops attempt to cross the mountains. I shall follow these people and try to rally them.

"Our military force could overwhelm most of these poor people, involving men, women and children in a common fate; but there are among the Mormons many brave men, accustomed to arms and horses; men who could fight desperately as guerrillas; and if the settlements are destroyed, will subject the country to an expensive and protracted war, without any compensating results. They will, I am sure, submit to 'trial by their peers,' but they will not brook the idea of trials by 'juries' composed of 'teamsters and followers of the camp,' nor of an army encamped in their cities or dense settlements.

"I have adopted means to recall the few Mormons remaining in arms, who have not yet, it is said, complied with my request to withdraw from the canyons and eastern frontiers. I have also taken measures to protect the buildings which have been vacated in the northern settlements. I am sanguine that I will save a great part of the valuable improvements there.

"I shall leave this city for the South to-morrow. After I have finished my business there, I shall return as soon as possible to the army, to complete the arrangements which will enable me before long, I trust, to announce that the road between California and Missouri may be traveled with perfect security by trains and emigrants of every description.

"I shall restrain all operations of the military for the present, which will probably enable me to receive from the President additional instructions, if he deems it necessary to give them.

Very respectfully, your obedient servant,

A. CUMMING, Governor of Utah.

To Hon. Lewis Cass, Secretary of State, Washington, D. C.

" To the Senate and House of Representatives:

"I transmit the copy of a dispatch from Governor Cumming to the Secretary of State, dated at Great Salt Lake City on the 2nd of May, and received at the Department of State yesterday. From this there is reason to believe that our difficulties with the Territory of Utah have terminated, and the reign of the Constitution and laws has been restored. I congratulate you on this auspicious event.

"I lost no time in communicating this information and in expressing the opinion that there will be no occasion to make any appropriations for the purpose of calling into service the two regiments of volunteers authorized by the Act of Congress approved on the 7th of April last, 'for the purpose of quelling disturbances in the Territory of Utah, for the protection of supply and emigrant trains and the suppression of Indian hostilities on the frontier.' "I am the more gratified at this satisfactory intelligence from Utah, because it will afford some relief to the treasury at a time demanding from us the strictest economy; and when the question which now arises upon every appropriation is, whether it be of a character so important and urgent as to brook no delay, and to justify and require a loan, and most probably a tax upon the people to raise the money necessary for its payment.

"In regard to the regiment of volunteers authorized by the same act of Congress to be called into service for the defense of the frontier of Texas against Indian hostilities, I desire to leave this question to Congress, observing, at the same time, that in my opinion, this State can be defended for the present by the regular troops, which have not yet been withdrawn from its limits.

JAMES BUCHANAN.
Washington City, June 10, 1858.

On the 13th of May, Gov. Gumming started for Camp Scott, for the purpose of moving his family to Salt Lake City. Meanwhile the "exodus" had been quietly going forward, and when the Governor returned he only found a few men who had been left in the city to burn it in case the army attempted to quarter there.

The Governor and his wife proceeded to the residence of Elder Staines, whom they found in waiting with a plentiful cold lunch. His family had gone south, and in his garden were significantly heaped up several loads of straw.

The Governor's wife inquired their meaning, and the cause of the silence that pervaded the city. Elder Staines informed her of their resolve to burn the town in case the army attempted to occupy it.

"How terrible!" she exclaimed. "What a sight this is! I never shall forget it! It has the appearance of a city that has been afflicted with a plague. Every house looks like a tomb of the dead! For two miles I have seen but one man in it. Poor creatures! And so all have left their hard-earned homes?"

Here she burst into tears.

"Oh! Alfred (to her husband), something must be done to bring them back! Do not permit the army to stay in the city. Can't you do something for them?"

"Yes, madam," said he, " I shall do all I can, rest assured. I only wish I could be in Washington for two hours; I am persuaded that I could convince the Government that we have no need for troops."

CHAPTER XXIV.

THE ARRIVAL OF PEACE COMMISSIONERS. EXTRAORDINARY COUNCIL BETWEEN THEM AND THE MORMON LEADERS. A SINGULAR SCENE IN THE COUNCIL. ARRIVAL OF A COURIER WITH DISPATCHES. "STOP THAT ARMY OR WE BREAK UP THE CONFERENCE." "BROTHER DUNBAR, SING ZION!" THE PEACE COMMISSIONERS MARVEL, BUT AT LAST FIND A HAPPY ISSUE. RETROSPECTIVE VIEW OF THE MORMON ARMY

The honorable course of Van Vliet, in protesting against an exterminating war upon a religious people, coupled with the guarantee which Colonel Kane had personally given to the Government for the essential loyalty of the Mormons, made the sending of peace commissioners imperative. An example of the right course once set by the noble Kane, President Buchanan hastened to send Governor L. W. Powell, of Kentucky, and Major Ben McCullough, of Texas, to negotiate a peace. They arrived in the city in June, 1858. Wilford Woodruff's Journal contains the following minute of their first council with the Mormon leaders: "June 11th. The Presidency and many others met with the Peace Commissioners in the Council House. Governor Powell, a Senator-elect from Kentucky, and Major McCullough, from Texas, were then introduced to the assembly, as the Peace Commissioners sent by President Buchanan. Governor Powell spoke to the people and informed us what the President wished at our hands.

President Buchanan has sent by them a proclamation, accusing us of treason and some fifty other crimes, all of which charges are false. Yet he pardons us for all these offenses, if we will be subject to the constitution and laws of the United States, and if we will let his troops quarter in our Territory. He pledged himself that they should not interfere with our people, nor infringe upon any city, and said that he had no right to interfere with our religion, faith or practice.

"The Peace Commissioners confirmed the same. They did not wish to enquire into the past at all but wished to let it all go and talk about the present and the future.

"Reflections. President Buchanan had made war upon us, and wished to destroy us because of our religion, thinking that it would be popular, but he found that Congress would not sustain him in it. He has got into a bad scrape and wishes to get out of it the best he can. Now he wants peace, because he is in the wrong, and has met with a strong resistance from a high-minded people in these mountains, which he did not expect to meet. We are willing to give him peace upon any terms that are honorable; but not upon terms which are dishonorable to us. We have our rights and dare maintain them, trusting in God for victory. The Lord has heard our prayers, and the President of the United States has been obliged to ask for peace."

The naivete of Apostle Woodruff, in his idea of giving peace to James Buchanan, is something amusing, yet is there a severe democratic philosophy in it.

" He wants peace because he is in the wrong and has met with a strong resistance from a high-minded people," is a passage that any President of the United States might profitably lay under his official pillow, whether in his administration towards a Utah or a Louisiana. But Brother Woodruff s emphatic view that the Mormons could only consent to a peace on honorable terms; with his brave assertion that, "we have our rights, and dare maintain them, trusting in God for victory," has in it a touch of sublimity.

That day also witnessed a striking example of Governor Young's tact and resolution: The Peace Commissioners had laid their message before the council. Brigham had spoken, as well as the Peace Commissioners. The aspect of affairs was favorable. Presently, however, a well-known character, O. P. Rockwell, was seen to enter, approach the ex-Governor and whisper to him. He was from the Mormon army. There was at once a sensation, for it was appreciated that he brought some unexpected and important news. Brigham arose; his manner self-possessed, but severe: "Governor Powell, are you aware, sir, that those troops are on the move towards the city?"

"It cannot be!" exclaimed Powell, surprised, for we were promised by the General that they should not move till after this meeting."

"I have received a dispatch that they are on the march for this city. My messenger would not deceive me."

It was like a thunderclap to the Peace Commissioners: they could offer no explanation.

"Is Brother Dunbar present?" inquired Brigham.

"Yes, sir," responded the one called.

What was coming now?

"Brother Dunbar, sing Zion."

The Scotch songster came forward and sang the following soul-stirring lines, by Chas. W. Penrose:

O ye mountains high, where the clear blue-sky
Arches over the vales of the free;
Where the pure breezes blow,
And the clear streamlets flow.
How I've longed to your bosom to flee,
O Zion! dear Zion! land of the free,
My own mountain home, now to thee I have come,
All my fond hopes are centered in thee.
Though the great and the wise all thy beauties despise,
To the humble and pure thou art dear;
Though the haughty may smile
And the wicked revile,
Yet we love thy glad tidings to hear.
O Zion! dear Zion! home of the free;
Thou wert forced to fly to thy chambers on high.
Yet we'll share joy or sorrow with thee.
In thy mountain retreat,
God will strengthen thy feet;
On the necks of thy foes thou shalt tread,
And their silver and gold,
As their prophets have told,
Shall be brought to adorn thy fair head.
O Zion! dear Zion! home of the free;
Soon thy towers shall shine with a splendor divine,

And eternal thy glory shall be.
Here our voices we'll raise, and we'll sing to thy praise,
Sacred home of the prophets of God;
Thy deliverance is nigh,
Thy oppressors shall die,
And the gentiles shall bow 'neath thy rod.
O Zion! dear Zion! home of the free;
In thy temples we'll bend, all thy rights we'll defend,
And our home shall be ever with thee.

The action of Brigham had been very simple in the case, but there was a world of meaning in it. Interpreted it meant—"Gentlemen, we have heard what President Buchanan and yourselves have said about pardoning us for standing up for our constitutional rights and defending our lives and liberties. We will consent to a peace on honorable terms; but you must keep faith with us. Stop that army! or our peace conference is ended. Brethren, sing Zion. Gentlemen, you have our ultimatum!"

With the theme before him, the reader will fully appreciate what the singing of "Zion" meant. There have been times when the singing of that hymn by the thousands of saints has been almost as potent as that revolutionary hymn of France—the Marseillaise. This was such a time.

After the meeting McCullough and Governor Cumming took a stroll together for the purpose of chatting upon the affairs of the morning.

"What will you do with such a people?" asked the Governor, with a mixture of admiration and concern.

"D —— n them! I would fight them if I had my way," answered McCullough.

"Fight them, would you? You might fight them but you would never whip them. They would never know when they were whipped! Did you notice the snap in those men's eyes to-day? No, sir; they would never know when they were whipped!"

At night the Peace Commissioners and the Mormon leaders were again in council, in private session, until ten o'clock.

Next morning, at nine o'clock, the conference again convened, and the doors were thrown open to the public. Elders John Taylor, George A. Smith and Adjt.-Gen. James Ferguson gave expression to their views and feelings, and then President Young spoke at some length, with a will and a purpose in every word.

Woodruff, in his journal, says: "Then the Peace Commissioners heard the roar of the "lion of the Lord."

The following brief synopsis of his speech, furnished by one present, will give the reader an idea of what the "roar of the lion of the Lord" was at that critical moment, when the issue of peace or war was pending:

President Young arose. He said: "I have listened very attentively to the commissioners, and will say, as far as I am concerned, I thank President Buchanan for forgiving me, but I really cannot tell what I have done. I know one thing, and that is, that the people called 'Mormons' are a loyal and a law-abiding people and have ever been. Neither President Buchanan nor anyone else can contradict the statement. It is true, Lot Smith burned some wagons containing Government supplies for the army. This was an overt act, and if it is for this we are to be pardoned, I accept the pardon. The burning of a few U. S. wagons is but a small item, yet for this, combined with false reports, the whole Mormon people are to be destroyed.

"What has the United States Government permitted mobs to do to us? Gentlemen, you cannot answer that question! I can, however, and so can thousands of my brethren. We have been whipped and plundered; our houses burned, our fathers, mothers, brothers, sisters and children butchered and murdered by the scores. We have been driven from our homes time and time again; but have troops ever been sent to stay or punish those mobs for their crimes? No! Have we ever received a dollar for the property we have been compelled to leave behind? Not a dollar! Let the Government treat us as we deserve; this is all we ask of them. We have always been loyal, and expect to so continue; but, hands off! Do not send your armed mobs into our midst. If you do, we will fight you, as the Lord lives! Do not threaten us with what the United States can do, for we ask no odds of them or their troops. We have the God of Israel —the God of battles—on our side; and let me tell you, gentlemen, we fear not your armies. I can take a few of the boys here and, with the help of the Lord can whip the whole of the United States. These, my brethren, put their trust in the God of Israel, and have no fears. We have proven him, and he is our friend. Boys, how do you feel? Are you afraid of the United States? (Great demonstration among the brethren.) No! No! We are not afraid of man, nor of what he can do.

"The United States are going to destruction as fast as they can go. If you do not believe it, gentlemen, you will soon see it to your sorrow. It will be with them like a broken potsherd. Yes, it will be like water spilled on the ground; no more to be picked up.

"Now let me say to you Peace Commissioners, we are willing those troops should come into our country, but not to stay in our city. They may pass through it, if needs be, but must not quarter less than forty miles from us.

"If you bring your troops here to disturb this people, you have got a bigger job than you or President Buchanan have any idea of. Before the troops reach here, this city will be in ashes, every tree and shrub will be cut to the ground, and every blade of grass that will burn shall be burned.

"Our wives and children will go to the canyons and take shelter in the mountains; while their husbands and sons will fight you; and, as God lives, we will hunt you by night and by day, until your armies are wasted away. No mob can live in the homes we have built in these mountains. That's the programme, gentlemen, whether you like it or not. If you want war you can have it; but, if you wish peace, peace it is; we shall be glad of it."

The Commissioners "wished peace;" and the result of their negotiations was embodied in the following note to General Johnston:

"Great Salt Lake City, Utah Ter.,
June 12th, 1858.

"Dear Sir: We have the pleasure of informing you that after a full and free conference with the chief men of the Territory, we are informed by them that they will yield obedience to the Constitution and laws of the United States; that they will not resist the execution of the laws in the Territory of Utah; that they cheerfully consent that the civil officers of the Territory shall enter upon the discharge of their respective duties, and that they will make no resistance to the army of the United States in its march to the valley of Salt Lake or elsewhere.

We have their assurance that no resistance shall be made to the officers, civil or military, of the United States, in the exercise of their various functions in the Territory of Utah.

"The houses, fields and gardens of the people of this Territory, particularly in and about Salt Lake City, are very insecure. The animals of your army would cause great destruction of property if the greatest care should not be observed in the march and the selection of camps. The people of the Territory are somewhat uneasy for fear the army, when it shall reach the valley, will not properly respect their persons and property. We have assured them that neither their persons nor property will be injured or molested by the army under your command.

"We would respectfully suggest, in consequence of the feeling of uneasiness, that you issue a proclamation to the people of Utah, stating that the army under your command will not trespass upon the rights or property of peaceable citizens during their sojourn in or march through the Territory. Such a proclamation would greatly allay the existing anxiety and fears of the people, and cause those who have abandoned their homes to return to their houses and farms.

"We have made inquiry about grass, wood, etc., necessary for the subsistence and convenience of your army. We have conversed with Mr. Ficklin [U. S. deputy marshal] fully on this subject, and given him all the information we have, which he will impart to you.

"We respectfully suggest that you march to the valley as soon as it is convenient for you to do so.

"We have the honor to be, very respectfully, your obedient servants,
L. W. POWELL, B
EN McCULLOUGH, *
Commissioners to Utah.
"To General A. S. Johnston, commanding Army of Utah, Camp Scott, U. T."

To this came the following reply:
"Headquarters, Department of Utah, Camp on Bear River, June 14th, 1858.
"Gentlemen: Your communication from Salt Lake City was received today. The accomplishment of the object of your mission entirely in accordance with the instructions of the President, and the wisdom and forbearance which you have so ably displayed to the people of the Territory, will, I hope, lead to a more just appreciation of their relations to the General Government, and the establishment of the supremacy of the laws. I learn with surprise that uneasiness is felt by the people as to the treatment they may receive from the army. Acting under the two-fold obligations of citizens and soldiers, we may be supposed to comprehend the rights of the people, and to be sufficiently mindful of the obligations of our oaths, not to disregard the laws which govern us as a military body. A reference to them will show with what jealous care the General Government has guarded the rights of citizens against any encroachments. The army has duties to perform here in execution of the orders of the Department of War, which, from the nature of them, cannot lead to interference with the people in their varied pursuits; and if no obstruction is presented to the discharge of those duties, there need not be the slightest apprehension that any person whatever will have any cause of complaint.

"The army will continue its march from this position on Thursday, 17th instant, and reach the valley in five days. I desire to encamp beyond the Jordan on the day of arrival in the valley.

With great respect, your obedient servant,

A. S. JOHNSTON,

"Colonel Second Cavalry and Brevet Brigadier-General United States Army, Commanding.

"To the Hon. L. W. Powell and Major-General McCullough, United States Commissioners to Utah."

Although a minute statement of the Mormon military force and the methods by which it was turned to good account in the "Utah war," might be of interest to many, it will doubtless satisfy the general reader to simply know that only so much of that force was used as was necessary to effectively carry out President Young's policy, 1. e., to harass and retard the advance of the U. S. army until a more peaceful solution of the question at issue could be reached. In the execution of that policy an effective body of scouts was sent forward, with orders of which the following is a sample, which orders were scrupulously obeyed and executed with precisely the results desired: "On ascertaining the locality or route of the troops, proceed at once to annoy them in every possible way. Use every exertion to stampede their animals and set fire to their trains. Burn the whole country before them and on their flanks. Keep them from sleeping by night surprises. Blockade the road by felling trees or destroying the fords when you can. Watch for opportunities to set fire to the grass on their windward, so as, if possible, to envelop their trains.

Leave no grass before them that can be burned. Keep your men concealed as much as possible, and guard against surprise."

They were also ordered to not "shed blood" if it could possibly be avoided, and then only and strictly in self-defense. Although often fired upon by the soldiers, in no single instance did they return the fire.

CHAPTER XXV.

REFLECTIONS UPON THE "UTAH WAR." THE REACTION. CURRENT OPINION, AS EXPRESSED BY THE LEADING JOURNALS OF EUROPE AND AMERICA.

That the Mormons would have fought; that they would, in the language of their leader, have made a "Moscow of Utah, and a Potter's Field of every canyon," had the United States pushed the issue to extermination, there can be little doubt, knowing how terribly so large a number as 75,000 or 80,000 earnest religionists could have avenged themselves, at that day, in those far-off mountains and valleys.

But the opinion expressed to Van Vliet, relative to the reaction which would come in the public mind over Utah affairs, and his fixed resolve, if possible, to prevent the shedding of blood, as declared in that conversation, and still more emphatically pronounced in all his orders to Lieut.-Gen. Wells, best denote what was Brigham's policy and first desire. True, it had been as much as he could do to keep his people from fighting the "enemy," notwithstanding the "enemy"

was the United States. A quarter of a century's injustice had fired them with an indignation that made them feel a superhuman strength. But though the founder of Utah had resolved to conquer the issue, he had no wish to lose the nucleus of a nationality which his people had evolved in their isolation.

Why then this second exodus? Why! It was the very backbone of Brigham's triumph. As great a triumph was in that exodus as in any battle the great Napoleon ever fought. It was in fact the exodus which forced the "reaction."

It carried such an overwhelming power that it became like an irresistible impulse in the public mind. Not only was this so with the American people, but it was so with every nation in Europe. Deep sympathy, blended with a mighty admiration, was felt for a people who could at once dare a war with the United States, in defense of their religious cause, and rise to such a towering heroism as to sanctify their act by a universal offering of their homes for sacrifice. This was no common rebellion. These were no unworthy rebels. No rude defiers of "the powers that be" were they: their act placed them on a level with the men who won the independence of America: their women were fitting mates of the mothers, daughters and sisters of the revolution.

The London Times called the Mormons a nation of heroes. It said: "The intelligence from Utah is confirmatory of the news that came by the last steamer. This strange people are again in motion for a new home, and all the efforts of Governor Cumming to induce the men to remain and limit themselves to the ordinary quota of wives have been fruitless. We are told that they have left a deserted town and deserted fields behind them, and have embarked for a voyage, over 500 miles of untracked desert, to a home, the locality of which is unknown to any but their chiefs. Does it not seem incredible that, at the very moment when the marine of Great Britain and the United States are jointly engaged in the grandest scientific experiments that the world has yet seen, 30,000 or 40,000 natives of these countries, many of them of industrious and temperate habits, should be the victims of such arrant imposition? Does it not seem impossible that men and women, brought up under British and American civilization, can abandon it for the wilderness and Mormonism? There is much that is noble in their devotion to their delusions. They step into the waves of the great basin with as much reliance on their leaders as the descendants of Jacob felt when they stepped between the walls of water in the Red Sea. The ancient world had individual Curiatii, Horatii, and other examples of heroism and devotion; but these western peasants seem to be a nation of heroes, ready to sacrifice everything rather than surrender one of their wives, or a letter from Joe Smith's golden plates."

The following from the New York Times will give a specimen of what the American press generally said upon the subject: "Whatever our opinions may be of Mormon morals or Mormon manners, there can be no question that this voluntary abandonment by 40,000 people of homes created by wonderful industry, in the midst of trackless wastes, after years of hardships and persecution, is something from which no one who has a particle of sympathy with pluck, fortitude and constancy can withhold his admiration.

Right or wrong, sincerity thus attested is not a thing to be sneered at. True or false, a faith to which so many men and women prove their loyalty, by such sacrifices, is a force in the world. After this last demonstration of what fanaticism can do, we think it would be most unwise to treat Mormonism as a nuisance to be abated by a posse commitatus. It is no longer a social excrescence to be cut off by the sword; it is a power to be combated only by the most skillful political and moral treatment. When people abandon their homes to plunge with women and children into a wilderness, to seek new settlements, they know not where, they give a higher proof of courage than if they fought for them. When the Dutch submerged Holland, to save it from invaders, they had heartier plaudits showered upon them than if they had fertilized its soil with their blood. We have certainly the satisfaction of knowing that we have to deal with foemen worthy of our steel. * * * If the conduct of the recent operations has had the effect of strengthening their fanaticism, by the appearance of persecution, without convincing them of our good faith and good intentions, and worse still, has been the means of driving away 50,000 of our fellow-citizens from fields which their labor had reclaimed and cultivated, and around which their affections were clustered, we have something serious to answer for. Were we not guilty of a culpable oversight in confounding their persistent devotion with the insubordination of ribald license, and applying to the one the same harsh treatment which the law intends for the latter alone? Was it right to send troops composed of the wildest and most rebellious men of the community, commanded by men like Harney and Johnston, to deal out fire and sword upon people whose faults even were the result of honest religious convictions? Was it right to allow Johnston to address letters to Brigham Young, and through him to his people, couched in the tone of an implacable conqueror towards ruthless savages? Were the errors which mistaken zeal generates ever cured by such means as these? And have bayonets ever been used against the poorest and weakest sect that ever crouched beyond a wall to pray or weep, without rendering their faith more intense, and investing the paltriest discomforts with the dignity of sacrifice?

* * * We stand on the vantage ground of higher knowledge, purer faith and acknowledged strength. We can afford to be merciful. At all events, the world looks to us now for an example of political wisdom such as few people, now-a-days, are called on to display. Posterity must not have to acknowledge with shame that our indiscretion, or ignorance, or intolerance drove the population of a whole State from

house and home, to seek religious liberty and immunity from the presence of mercenary troops, in any part of the continent to which our rule was never likely to extend."

Reynolds' Newspaper, in an editorial written specially to represent the British Republicans, views of the Mormon community in their great struggle for their religious and social liberties, gave the following strong passages: "It may be that Mormonism has originated in imposture, and that many, if not all, of its peculiar rites and customs are the 'abomination of desolation.' Let this point, though not yet proved, be conceded; still, the social and political problem is by no means solved. After we have demonstrated the fabulousness of the gold tablets, convicted Joseph Smith of all sorts of possible and impossible scoundrelisms, and proved his followers to be a mixed multitude of the gravest knaves and idiots that ever walked the earth, Mormonism still remains a great human fact — perhaps the greatest — certainly the most wonderful fact of this nineteenth century. As such, it is entitled to our earnest and respectful consideration.

"There can be no doubt that, in one thing at least, Mormonism has been eminently successful. It has, in the great majority of instances, really improved the earthly condition of those who have embraced it. More than this, it has inspired with hope and with courage thousands of despairing and heartbroken wretches, who, prior to their conversion, seemed abandoned of God and man.

This new faith has, so to speak, created a soul under the ribs of death. It has given to thousands of once destitute and despised Englishmen something to live for, to fight for, and, if need be, to die for. On this ground, then, were it for nothing else, the Mormons, not as fanatics or sectaries, but as heavily-oppressed, long-suffering, and earnestly struggling men, are entitled to the sympathy of the enslaved classes throughout the world.

"But they have a claim to something more than sympathy. Their heroic endurance and marvelous achievements entitle them to the respect and admiration of their fellow-creatures. Twice were the Mormons driven from their settlements in the United States before they had resolved upon their stupendous pilgrimage to the Valley of the Salt Lake. How that gigantic journey was accomplished; how a thousand miles of untrodden desert—untrodden, save by the wild beast or wilder Indian, where death in a hundred forms had to be encountered and defied—had to be traversed; how the poor, hungered, and toil-worn, but still dauntless pilgrims reached their destination; how they built a city, founded a civil and ecclesiastical polity; how law and order were established; how skill and industry converted barren wastes into fruitful fields, howling forests into smiling gardens, until, under the talismanic wand of Labor, the wilderness was made to blossom as the rose, how their missionaries were employed with startling success in every European country; and how many thousands of the down-trodden and penury-stricken victims of European tyranny were leaving the land of their birth, in order to find in the Mormon territory, that hope and encouragement denied to them in their native countries;—how all this has been accomplished by the reviled followers of Joseph Smith, all Europe and America have heard, and, though hating, admired."

The famous African explorer, Captain Burton, of the British army, closing his description of the great man who took his people successfully through that crisis, gives us the following suggestive passage in his "City of the Saints:"

"Such is His Excellency, President Brigham Young, 'Painter and Glazier' (his earliest craft), prophet, revelator, translator and seer; the man who is revered as king or kaiser, pope or pontiff, never was; who, like the old man of the mountain, by holding up his right hand could cause the death of any man within his reach; who, governing as well as reigning, long stood up to fight with the sword of the Lord, and with his few hundred guerrillas, against the then mighty power of the United States; who has outwitted all diplomacy opposed to him; and, finally, who made a treaty of peace with the President of the great Republic, as though he had wielded the combined power of France, Russia and England."

Substantially, the word of Brigham Young was fulfilled, in that he had said an invading army should not enter the city.

General Johnston and his army came not as conquerors into Zion. The entire chain of circumstances, from the start of their expedition, had been most humiliating to the brave men who deserved better service. Their march had been but a series of disasters and failures.

They were merely permitted to pass through the streets of Salt Lake City on their way to a location in the Territory well removed from the Mormon people.

Zion was a forsaken city that day. The Saints were still south with their great leader. If faith was not kept with them they did not intend to return, and war would have been re-opened in deadly earnest.

It was a sad spectacle to see a community of earnest religionists who could not trust in the parent power, even after the proclamation of the President. But the history of the Mormons in their minds to this hour shows a constant justification of this lack of confidence.

On the 13th of June, the army commenced its movement towards the city!

and, on the morning of the 26th, it might have been seen advancing from the mouth of Emigration Canyon to make what once was expected to have been a triumphal entrance into conquered Zion, with all " the pomp and circumstance of glorious war." Here is a picture of it as it was, from the pen of an army correspondent: "It was one of the most extraordinary scenes that have occurred in American history. All day long, from dawn until after sunset, the troops and trains poured through the city, the utter silence of the streets being broken only by the music of the military bands, the monotonous tramp of the regiments, and the rattle of the baggage wagons'. Early in the morning, the Mormon guards had forced all their fellow religionists into the houses and ordered them not to make their appearance during the day. The numerous flags that had been flying from staffs on the public buildings during the previous week were all struck. The only visible groups of spectators were on the corners near Brigham Young's residence and consisted almost entirely of Gentile civilians. The stillness was so profound that during the intervals between the passage of the columns, the monotonous gurgle of the City Creek struck on every ear. The Commissioners rode with the General's staff. The troops crossed the Jordan and encamped two miles from the city, on a dusty meadow by the river bank."

But the army correspondent did not properly construe the death-like stillness and desertion of the city, when he says the Mormon guard had "forced all their fellow religionists into their houses." They were not in their houses, but in the second exodus. It is estimated that there were no less than 30,000 of the Mormon people from the city and northern settlements in "the move south." They took with them their flocks and herds, their chattels and furniture. When that army marched through the streets of Zion, grass was growing on the sidewalks, and there were only a few of " the boys" left on the watch in the city, to see that the people were not betrayed. Some of the officers were deeply moved by the scene and the circumstances. Lieutenant Colonel Philip St. George Cooke, who had commanded the Mormon battalion in the Mexican war, rode through the city with uncovered head, leading the troops, but forgetting not his respect for the brave Mormon soldiers who had so nobly served with him in their country's cause.

Cedar Valley, forty miles west of the city, was chosen as their permanent camping place, which was named Camp Floyd, in honor of the then Secretary of War.

CHAPTER XXV.

GOVERNOR CUMMING PLEADS WITH THE SAINTS. THEY RETURN TO THEIR HOMES. THE JUDGES. CRADLEBAUGH'S COURT. HE CALLS FOR TROOPS. PROVO CITY INVADED BY THE ARMY. CONSPIRACY TO ARREST BRIGHAM YOUNG. GOVERNOR CUMMING ORDERS OUT THE UTAH MILITIA TO REPEL INVASION. TIMELY ARRIVAL OK A DISPATCH FROM GOVERNMENT STAYS THE CONFLICT. ATTORNEY-GENERAL BLACK'S REBUKE TO THE JUDGES. GENERAL JOHNSTON'S FRIENDS DEMAND THE REMOVAL OF GOVERNOR CUMMING. THE SITUATION RECOVERED BY THE PATRIOTISM OF THOMAS L. KANE, DIVISION IN THE CABINET. PARALLEL OF THE BLAINE REMINISCENCE OF JERE S. BLACK.

Return we now to the Saints in their flight. It had taxed their faith and their means to an absolute consecration of their all and called forth as much religious heroism as did their first exodus from Nauvoo. Gallant old Governor Cumming was almost distracted over this Mormon episode. He was not used to the self-sacrifices and devotion of the peculiar people whom he had taken under his official guardianship. They were more familiar than he with this part of their eventful drama. Familiarity had bred in them a kind of contempt for their own sufferings and privations. So they witnessed their new Governor's concern for them with a stoical humor. They were, indeed, grateful, but amused. They could not feel to deserve his pity yet were they thankful for his sympathy. They sang psalms by the wayside. He felt like strewing their path with tears. He followed them fifty miles south, praying them, as would a father his wayward children, to turn back. But the father whom they knew better was leading them on.

"There is no longer danger. General Johnston and the army will keep faith with the Mormons. Everyone concerned in this happy settlement will hold sacred the amnesty and pardon of the President of the United States! By G d, sirs, Yes."

Such was the style of Governor Cumming's pleadings with the " misguided" Mormons. But Brigham replied with a quiet fixedness of purpose: "We know all about it, Governor. We remember the martyrdoms of the past! We have, on just such occasions, seen our disarmed men hewn down in cold blood, our virgin daughters violated, our wives ravished to death before our eyes. We know all about it, Governor Cumming."

It was a terrible logic that thus met the brave meditation of the fine old Georgian successor of Governor Young, who coupled patriotism with humanity, and believed in the primitive faith that American citizens and American homes must be held sacred.

Brigham Young alone could turn the tidal wave and lead back the Mormon people to their homes. Had he continued onward to Sonora, Central America, anywhere—to the ends of the earth—this people would have followed him.

The Mormon leaders, with the body of the Church, were at Provo on the evening of the 4th of July; General Johnston and his army being about to take up their quarters at Camp Floyd. It was on that evening that Governor Cumming informed his predecessor that he should publish a proclamation to the Mormons for their return to their homes.

"Do as you please, Governor Cumming," replied Brigham, with a quiet smile. "To-morrow I shall get upon the tongue of my wagon, and tell the people that I am going home, and they can do as they please."

On the morning of the 5th, Brigham announced to the people that he was going to start for Salt Lake City; they were at liberty to follow him to their various settlements, as they pleased. In a few hours nearly all were on their homeward march.

But scarcely had the people returned to their homes, ere they had abundant proof how much they could have trusted a united Federal power, in an anti-Mormon crusade, with an army at its service to subvert the civil and religious liberties of the people.

The machinery of the Federal power was soon set in motion. Chief Justice Eckles took up his quarters at Camp Floyd; Associate Justice Sinclair was assigned to the district embracing Salt Lake City; and Associate Justice Cradlebaugh was assigned to the judicial supervision of all the southern settlements; and Superintendent of Indian Affairs, Jacob Forney, and Alexander Wilson, U. S. District Attorney, entered upon the discharge of their duties.

The Governor from the beginning assumed a pacific attitude, in which he was seconded by Superintendent Forney and District-Attorney Wilson. But the three Judges, in concert with the Marshal, united in the prosecution of past offences that had naturally arisen out of the condition of the hostility, just brought to a happy and peaceful issue.

Judge Sinclair convened the First, now the Third Judicial District Court in Great Salt Lake City in November, 1858, and in his charge to the Grand Jury he urged the prosecution of the leading men of the Territory for treason, for intimidation of the courts, and for polygamy. President Buchanan's pardon, the Judge admitted, was "a public fact in the history of the country," but "like any other deed, it ought to be brought judicially by plea, motion or otherwise."

In fine, Judge Sinclair wanted to bring before his court ex-Governor Young, Lieut.-General Daniel H. Wells, and the leading Mormons generally, especially the Apostles, "to make them admit that they had been guilty of treason and make them humbly accept from him the President's clemency." So explains Mr. Stenhouse. But it was something more radical and serious than a vainglorious effort to humble Utah to the footstool of a Federal Judge. It was an attempt to reopen in the courts the entire conflict which had so nearly come to the issue of war. U. S. District Attorney Wilson, however, would not present to the jury bills of indictment for treason, pleading that the Commissioners had presented the pardon, and the people had accepted it, and the Governor had proclaimed that peace was restored to the Territory.

"But the young Judge," relates Mr. Stenhouse, "was more successful in his efforts to bring forward the charge of intimidating the courts. It could not be expected that the charge to the jury on polygamy would secure much attention.

It was regarded little better than a grand farce to ask a Mormon jury to find indictments against their brethren for polygamy. The term of Judge Sinclair's judicial service was a failure, only memorable for one thing—he sentenced the first white man who was ever hanged in Utah, and he was a Gentile, to be executed on a Sunday! Of course, the day had to be changed."

But the most extraordinary judicial action, and that which continues the historical thread of those times, was in the important district assigned to Judge Cradlebaugh. The criminal cases which he sought to investigate were those commonly known as the Potter and Parrish murders at Springville, and the Mountain Meadows Massacre in Southern Utah. On the 8th of March, 1859, at Provo, Judge Cradlebaugh delivered an extraordinary address to the Grand Jury, and commenced extraordinary proceedings, which in their sequel nearly made Salt Lake City the seat of actual war between Johnston's troops and the Utah militia under Governor Cumming, and which was barely prevented by the timely interference of the General Government. The history of Salt Lake City, however, cannot follow in detail the entire history of Utah, only so far as its subject and action find therein its proper center of unity. Suffice here to mark that Judge Cradlebaugh in his investigations and prosecutions aimed chiefly to implicate the leaders of the Mormon Church in all the criminal offenses and deeds of violence done within the Territory. In summing up the evidence in the case of the murders at Springville, the Judge concluded with the following address: "Until I commenced the examination of the testimony in this case, I always supposed that I lived in a land of civil and religious liberty, in which we were secured by the Constitution of our country the right to remove at pleasure from one portion of our domain to another, and also that we enjoyed the privilege of worshipping God according to the dictates of our own conscience. But I regret to say, that the evidence in this case clearly proves that, so far as Utah is concerned, I have been mistaken in such supposition. Men are murdered here: coolly, deliberately, premeditatedly murdered—their murder is deliberated and determined upon by the church council-meetings, and that, too, for no other reason than that they had apostatized from your church and were striving to leave the Territory.

"You are the tools, the dupes, the instruments of a tyrannical church despotism. The heads of your church order and direct you. You are taught to obey their orders and commit these horrid murders. Deprived of your liberty you have lost your manhood and become the willing instruments of bad men.

"I say to you it will be my earnest effort, while with you, to knock off your ecclesiastical shackles and set you free."

It is easily to be seen that with such a grand jury, charged in this manner by such a judge, it was impossible to accomplish the ends of justice;—equally impossible whether they had been "the willing instruments" of a "tyrannical church," or a grand jury of honest, innocent men.

In the course of one of these prosecutions, Judge Cradlebaugh made a requisition upon General Johnston for troops to act as protection to certain witnesses, and also, in the absence of a jail, to serve as a guard over the prisoners. The mayor of Provo (Kimball Bullock) protested that the presence of the military was an infringement upon the liberties of his fellow-citizens; but the judge answered that he had well considered the request before he had made it. A petition was sent to Governor Cumming, and he asked General Johnston to withdraw the troops, asserting that the court had no authority to call for the aid of the military, except through him. The judges interpreted General Johnston's instructions from the War Department adversely to the statement of the Governor, and the troops were continued at Provo. On the 27th of March (1859), the Governor issued a proclamation protesting against the continuance of the troops at Provo, taking open ground against the action of the military commander.

About this time was concocted a conspiracy to arrest Brigham Young. It was proposed that a writ be issued for his apprehension. The officers entrusted with its execution presented themselves at the Governor's office, to request his co-operation. But Governor Camming stoutly resisted the attempted outrage.

He himself afterwards thus related this conspiracy to arrest his predecessor: "They had 'got the dead wood on Brigham Young this time,' so they said, as they unfolded to me their plans. If Brigham resisted, General Johnston's artillery was to make a breach in the wall surrounding his premises, and they would take him by force and carry him to Camp Floyd.

"I listened to them, sir, as gravely as I could, and examined their papers.

They rubbed their hands and were jubilant; they 'had got the dead wood on Brigham Young!' I was indignant, sir, and told them, 'by G—d, gentlemen, you can't do it! When you have a right to take Brigham Young, gentlemen, you shall have him without creeping through walls. You shall enter through his door with heads erect as become representatives of your government. But till that time, gentlemen, you can't touch Brigham Young while I live, by G—d!'"

"Such was the story," says Stenhouse, "told by the Governor to the author a few years later, and as he related it all the fire of his nature was depicted on his countenance and told unmistakably that he would have made good every word with his life."

The officers returned to Camp Floyd discomfited, and immediately the news was circulated that General Johnston would send two regiments of troops and a battery of artillery to enforce the writ for the apprehension of Brigham.

The New York Herald of date May 25, 1859, gave to the country a graphic picture of affairs in Utah at that moment:

OUR SALT LAKE CITY CORRESPONDENCE.
"Great Salt Lake City, U. T., April 23, 1859.

"In my last letter I informed you of the threat of Judge Sinclair that he would hold court in this city during May, with three-fourths of the army now at Camp Floyd, quartered in Union Square, ready to carry out his orders. The apprehension of a collision which that threat inspired measurably died away in the bosoms of the people generally, and the youthful judge was beginning to get credit for idle braggadocio, and his tongue was regarded as having only divulged what was in his heart to do, if he only could get the chance; but, alas! the day after the departure of the last mail from here, rumors of his intentions were in circulation at Camp Floyd, which leaves us no reason to doubt that his threat was no idle boast, but is in reality the fixed determination of his heart, to lead to a collision between the citizens and the troops. Of this Governor Cumming is apparently fully convinced, as also the other officials outside of the judicial clique.

By the departure of the next mail, plans will be better developed, if not even then carried into execution, or at least attempted; and should you then hear of the eagerly-sought-for collision having taken place, it can be witnessed that we have not sought it, but that it is the deep-laid scheme of sutlers, degraded judges, and disappointed officers of our great republican army, for the sake of perishable gold, gratification of personal revenge, and the empty glory of swords to be crimsoned with the blood of fellow-citizens, who so love the liberty bequeathed to them by illustrious sires that they will fight for its maintenance, though their homes should be made desolate and their wives and children left without protectors in the land of freemen's inheritance.

"An express from Camp Floyd arrived here on Sunday night with the intelligence that two regiments were coming to the city to make arrests, and it was expected that they would have orders for forced marches, to come in upon us unawares. Immediately on Governor Cumming being made acquainted with the report and circumstances, which leave no room to doubt of the plans of the judges, he notified General D. H. Wells to hold the militia in readiness to act on orders.

By two o' clock on Monday morning five thousand men were under arms. Had the United States' troops attempted to enter the city, the struggle must have commenced, for the Governor is determined to carry out his instructions. What has deferred their arrival here we know not; but now that this plan is known, a watchful eye is kept on the camp, and the shedding of blood seems inevitable. We have confidence in the overruling care of our heavenly Father; and what" ever does take place, will eventually turn out for good.

"Major told me yesterday that General Johnston was resolved to carry out his orders, and he affirms that they are to use the military on the requisition of the judges, and not on the requisition of the Governor only. I have just learned that 500 soldiers were on the march to Sanpete settlement to arrest persons there whom the judges are seeking after. The judicial-military-inquisitorial farce played at Provo satisfies everybody that it is not violated justice that seeks redress, but the madness of men drunken with whisky and vengeance, that seek satiety in blood. There is not an official in any settlement outside this city but what expects to be handled as were those at Provo; and the only safety they have from judicial vengeance—not personal, but vengeance against the community— is in flight to the mountains. In the south, where the weather has been excellent for early agricultural operations this spring, the fields have been left uncultivated, and the seed that should be fructifying in the soil is still lying in the barn, the end of which must be famine; for unless the Governor has power to restrain the judges from calling the military to act as a posse comitatus, no man of any influence will trust himself at home. We fear no judge of the United States.

The Supreme Judge of all we fear, and in His fear we live, and earthly tribunals have no terror for us: but the insolence of men like Cradlebaugh and Sinclair and the despotism of their military aids drive the iron to our souls. The very latest news now in circulation in the city is that the judges have hired the Indians to scour the mountains in search of the persons that the Marshal and military have been unable to discover at home. What next? Shall a price be offered the red men of the forest for the scalps of our citizens? Oh, my God! what shall we be driven to? My heart sickens at the outrages to which we have been subjected, and I dread the future. Nothing shall be done on our part to hasten hostilities; but if it is impossible to avoid them, the responsibility is theirs.

"Governor Cumming has no disposition, nor has this community any, to screen any man or men from the punishment due for any crime or misdemeanor they may be accused of; but he will not suffer military terrorism to reign in the Territory over which he is Governor, and we are to a man ready to sustain him.

We appeal to the American nation, and ask any man whose soul is not absorbed with the acquisition of perishable pelf only, what can we do more than we have done to preserve peace? and what course is open to us but to defend our rights as citizens of the Union?"

Happily at this juncture an official letter from Washington decided that the military could only be used as a posse on a call from the Governor. This communication from the U. S. Attorney-General is a valuable historical review of Utah affairs at that juncture, by the U. S. Government itself:

"Attorney-General's Office, May 17, 1859.

"Gentlemen—The President has received your joint letter on the subject of the military force with which the Court for the Second District of Utah was attended during the term recently held at Provo City. He has carefully considered it, as well as all other advices relating to the same affair, and he has directed me to give you his answer.

"The condition of things in Utah made it extremely desirable that the Judges appointed for that Territory should confine themselves strictly within their own official sphere. The Government had a district attorney, who was charged with the duties of a public accuser, and a marshal, who was responsible for the arrest and safekeeping of criminals. For the judges there was nothing left except to hear patiently the causes brought before them, and to determine them impartially according to the evidence adduced on both sides. It did not seem either right or necessary to instruct you that these were to be the limits of your interference with the public affairs of the Territory; for the Executive never dictates to the Judicial department. The President is responsible only for the appointment of proper men. You were selected from a very large number of other persons who were willing to be employed on the same service, and the choice was grounded solely on your high character for learning, sound judgment, and integrity. It was natural, therefore, that the President should look upon the proceedings at Provo with a sincere desire to find you in all things blameless.

"It seems that on the 6th of March last, Judge Cradlebaugh announced to the commanding officer of the military forces that on the 8th day of the same month he would begin a term of the District Court at Provo, and required a military guard for certain prisoners, to the number of six or eight, who were then in custody, and would be triable at Provo. The requisition mentions it as a probable fact that 'a large band of organized thieves' would be arrested; but the troops were asked for without reference to them. Promptly responding to this call the commanding-general sent up a company of infantry, who encamped at the Court House, and soon afterwards ten more companies made their appearance in sight and remained there during the whole term of the court. In the meantime, the Governor of the Territory, hearing of this military demonstration upon a town previously supposed to be altogether peaceful, appeared on the ground, made inquiries, and, seeing no necessity for the troops, but believing, on the contrary, that their presence was calculated to do harm, he requested them to be removed. The request was wholly disregarded.

"The Governor is the supreme Executive of the Territory. He is responsible for the public peace. From the general law of the land, the nature of his office, and the instructions he received from the State Department, it ought to have been understood that he alone had power to issue a requisition for the movement of troops from one part of the Territory to another,—that he alone could put the military forces of the Union and the people of the Territory into relations of general hostility with one another. The instructions given to the Commanding-General by the War Department are to the same effect. In that paper a "requisition" is not spoken of as a thing which anybody except the Governor can make. It is true that in one clause the General is told that if the Governor, the judges, or the marshal shall find it necessary to summon directly a part of the troops to aid either in the performance of his duty, he (the General) is to see the summons promptly obeyed. This was manifestly intended to furnish the means of repelling an opposition which might be too strong for the civil posse, and too sudden to admit of a formal requisition by the governor upon the military commander. An officer finds himself resisted in the discharge of his duty, and he calls to his aid first the citizens, and, if they are not sufficient, the soldiers.

This would be directly summoning a part of the troops. A direct summons and a requisition are not convertible terms. The former signifies a mere verbal call upon either civilians or military men for force enough to put down a present opposition to a certain officer in the performance of a particular duty; and the call is to be always made by the officer who is himself opposed upon those persons who are with their own hands to furnish the aid. A requisition, on the other hand, is a solemn demand in writing made by the supreme civil magistrate upon the commander-in-chief of the military forces for the whole or part of the army to be used in a specified service. In a Territory like Utah, the person who exercises this last-mentioned power can make war and peace when he pleases and holds in his hands the issues of life and death for thousands. Surely it was not intended to clothe each one of the judges, as well as the marshal and all his deputies, with this tremendous authority. Especially does this construction seem erroneous when we reflect that these different officers might make requisitions conflicting with one another, and all of them crossing the path of the Governor.

"Besides, the matter upon which Judge Cradlebaugh's requisition bases itself was one with which the Judge had no sort of official connection. It was the duty the marshal to see that the prisoners were safely kept and forthcoming at the proper time. For aught that appears, the marshal wanted no troops to aid him, and had no desire to see himself displaced by a regiment of soldiers. He made no complaint of weakness and uttered no call for assistance. Under such circumstances it was a mistake of the Judge to interfere with the business at all.

"But, assuming the legal right of the judge to put the marshal's business into the hands of the army without the marshal's concurrence, and granting also that this might be done by means of a requisition, was there in this case any occasion for the exercise of such power? When we consider how essentially peaceable is the whole spirit of our judicial system, and how exclusively it aims to operate by moral force, or at most by the arm of civil power, it can hardly be denied that the employment of military troops about the courts should be avoided, as long as possible. *Inter arma silent leges*, says the maxim; and the converse of it ought to be equally true, that *inter leges silent arma*. The President has not found, either on the face of the requisition or in any other paper received by him, a statement of specific facts strong enough to make the presence of the troops seem necessary. Such necessity ought to have been perfectly plain before the measure was resorted to.

"It is very probable that the Mormon inhabitants of Utah have been guilty of crimes for which they deserve the severest punishment. It is not intended by the Government to let anyone escape against whom the proper proofs can be produced. With that view, the district attorney has been instructed to use all possible diligence in bringing criminals of every class and of all degrees to justice.

We have the fullest confidence in the vigilance, fidelity and ability of that officer.

If you shall be of opinion that his duty is not performed with sufficient energy, your statement to that effect will receive the prompt attention of the President.

"It is very likely that public opinion in the Territory is frequently opposed to the conviction of parties who deserve punishment. It may be that extensive conspiracies are formed there to defeat justice. These are subjects upon which we, at this distance, can affirm or deny nothing. But, supposing your opinion upon them to be correct, every inhabitant of Utah must still be proceeded against in a regular, legal, and constitutional way. At all events, the usual and established modes of dealing with public offenders must be exhausted before we adopt any others.

"On the whole, the President is very decidedly of opinion—

"1. That the Governor of the Territory alone has power to issue a requisition upon the commanding-general for the whole or part of the army: "2. That there was no apparent occasion for the presence of the troops at Provo: "3. That if a rescue of the prisoners in custody had been attempted, it was the duty of the marshal, and not of the judge, to summon the force which might be necessary to prevent it: "4. That the troops ought not to have been sent to Provo without the concurrence of the Governor, nor kept there against his remonstrance: "5. That the disregard of these principles and rules of action has been in many ways extremely unfortunate.

"I am, very respectfully, yours, &c, J. S. BLACK.

"Hon. J. Cradlebaugh, Hon. C. E. Sinclair, Associate Judges, Supreme Court, Utah."

A great Constitutional pronouncement like the foregoing from a jurist so distinguished as Attorney-General Jeremiah S. Black, given by the direction of the President of the United States, was too authoritative and potent to be set aside. Governor Cumming had clearly won the victory over his rivals, at least in the Constitutional aspects of his position.

The anti-Mormon influence everywhere was now invoked to have Governor Cumming removed, and for a time this was under consideration in the Cabinet.

The probabilities were all against the Governor being retained, but a fine stroke of strategy, executed by Col. Thos. L. Kane, recovered his position. Stenhouse, who was present as reporter for the New York Herald, relates the circumstance thus: "Soon after the return of Col. Kane to the Eastern States, that gentleman was invited to deliver a lecture before the Historical Society of New York upon 'The Situation of Utah.' Though in very feeble health, and unprepared for such a lecture, his devotion to what he no doubt sincerely believed to be the welfare of the Mormons and the honor of the Government, overcame all impediments, and the lecture was delivered. In that audience were two Mormon elders listening eagerly for a sentence that might help "the cause" in the West. By previous arrangement the agent of the Associated Press was to be furnished with a notice of the lecture, and thus a dispatch next morning was read everywhere throughout the Union to the effect that there was a division among the Mormons, that some were eager for strife, others for peace, but that Brigham Young was on the side of peace and order, and was laboring to control his fiery brethren. This was a repetition of a part of the diplomacy of the Tabernacle. Governor Cumming was complimented by the gallant Colonel as a clear-headed, resolute, but prudent executive, and the very man for the trying position.

"Before such an endorsement, sent broadcast over the Republic, coming from the lips of the gentleman who had warded off the effusion of blood, and saved the nation from the expense and horror of a domestic war, the Cabinet of Mr. Buchanan silently bowed, but they were terribly chagrined."

Apostle George Q. Cannon, who was one of the "two Mormon elders" present at the lecture, relates this singular and quite dramatic episode of Utah history with several additional points, which have a national significance. The story is told in an obituary sketch of Thomas L. Kane, with an affectionate simplicity that gives it a special value in the History:

"As I write, another illustration of his forgetfulness of self and his ardent zeal in behalf of Utah comes to my mind. It was during the Buchanan administration. Governor Cumming, who had been sent out by President Buchanan with the army as Governor of the Territory, did not work harmoniously with the army officers. Differences had arisen between them at the time they were in camp during the winter at Ham's Fork and Fort Bridger.

"These differences increased after they came into the valley, and the influence of the army people was used with the administration to have Cumming removed. President Buchanan was inclined to yield to the pressure of Albert Sidney Johnston's friends. Johnston at that time was quite an influential personage; in fact influences were being used to prepare the way for him to succeed General Winfield Scott as commander of the army of the United States. President Buchanan made inquiries of some of General Kane's friends as to how the removal of Governor Cumming would be received by him. He heard of this, and, though at the time confined to his room with an attack of pleurisy, saw that something must be done to prevent the removal of Governor Cumming, which he viewed at the time as a move that would be unfortunate to Utah. The Historical Society of New York City—a very influential society—had solicited him to deliver a lecture upon Utah affairs; but he had postponed accepting the offer.

He saw that this was the opportune moment to deliver it, and though suffering from severe pain he resolved to go to New York and deliver the lecture. His friends tried to dissuade him from the step, as they felt that he was endangering his life. But he was determined to go, and wrote to the President of the Society, who was pleased to accept the proffer of the lecture. Accompanied by his physician, he traveled from Philadelphia to New York, delivered the lecture, in which he eulogized Governor Cumming, and gave him the praise that was due to him for his conduct after reaching Utah, and the next morning there appeared in all the newspapers of the country, through the associated press, a brief epitome of the lecture, commending Governor Cumming's administration of affairs. It had the effect to turn the scale in Cumming's favor. President Buchanan relinquished the idea of removing him, and he remained Governor until he had served out his full term. I was in the East at the time and familiar with all the circumstances, and I was deeply impressed with the General's conduct on that occasion."

There is to be discerned in these two statements a division growing up in the views and purposes of the members of Buchanan's Cabinet at that critical juncture of our national affairs, which is capitally presented in Mr. Blaine's great book of reminiscences, in which he presents, on the one side, John B. Floyd, Secretary of War with President Buchanan preparing the way for secession; on the other, Gen. Lewis Cass, Secretary of State, and Attorney-General Jeremiah S. Black, taking the alarm both for the Democracy and the Union, and setting their faces against the secession movement, which General Albert Sidney Johnston was fated to represent as one of its chiefest military captains. Mr. Blaine has not intended any reference to Utah, but that which he describes touching a division in the Cabinet, relative to our national affairs, is strangely to be traced at the same moment in the Cabinet over Utah affairs. So far as secession and Secretary Floyd is concerned, the statement of ex-Delegate Cannon suggests a very striking parallel to the Blaine reminiscences of the state of Buchanan's Cabinet at that juncture.

The historical pertinence of the case is the more striking from the fact that it was subsequent to the decision of the Attorney-General against the Judges' and General Johnston's action. After the receipt of that dispatch a mass meeting of Gentiles was held at Camp Floyd, on the 23rd of July, at which the Judges and the Indian Agent—Dr. Garland Hurt—were present, and in which they took a prominent part. An address was penned, rehearsing all the crimes charged to the Mormons, asserting that they were as disloyal after the President's pardon as when they were in arms in Echo Canyon, that the President was deceived and badly advised, and had done a great wrong in withdrawing the protection of the military from the courts.

Thus it would seem that there was before the country, emanating from Johnston and his friends, who were seeking to make him commander-in-chief of the armies of the United States, not only a demand for the removal of Governor Cumming, but a virtual impeachment of the Attorney-General as an ill adviser on Utah affairs, for it was undoubtedly Jeremiah S. Black who had given the new impulse to the Buchanan movement, as represented in General Kane and Governor Cumming, and his Constitutional decision had most likely saved Great Salt Lake City from the "baptism of blood," and made valid the President's pardon. But it seems that he would have failed at last, in his revision of the Buchanan policy touching Utah, had not Thomas L. Kane risen from his couch and, in his noble regard for the honor of his country, made valid the proclamation of peace and pardon which had been granted in the august name of the American Republic.

A supplementary page from Mr. Blaine's great book may be given here to illustrate the reorganization of the Buchanan Cabinet, by Judge Black, and the radical change in its policies, so strongly marked both in the affairs of Utah and the greater affairs of the nation; and a bankrupt U. S. Treasury will be very suggestive of Secretary Floyd's expenditure of from fourteen to twenty millions of dollars on the Utah Expedition: "Judge Black entered upon his duties as Secretary of State on the 17th of December—the day on which the disunion convention of South Carolina assembled. He found the malign influence of Mr. Buchanan's message fully at work throughout the South. Under its encouragement only three days were required by the convention at Charleston to pass the ordinance of secession, and four days later Governor Pickens issued a proclamation declaring ' South Carolina a separate, sovereign, free and independent State, with the right to levy war, conclude peace and negotiate treaties.' From that moment Judge Black's position towards the Southern leaders was radically changed. They were no longer fellow-Democrats. They were the enemies of the Union to which he was devoted, they were conspirators against the Government to which he had taken a solemn oath of fidelity and loyalty.

"Judge Black's change, however important to his own fame, would prove comparatively fruitless unless he could influence Mr. Buchanan to break with the men who had been artfully using the power of his Administration to destroy the Union. The opportunity and the test came promptly. The new ' sovereign, free and independent' government of South Carolina sent commissioners to Washington to negotiate for the surrender of the national forts and the transfer of the national property within her limits. Mr. Buchanan prepared an answer to their request which was compromising to the honor of the Executive and perilous to the integrity of the Union. Judge Black took a decided and irrevocable stand against the President's position. He advised Mr. Buchanan that upon the basis of that fatal concession to the disunion leaders he could not remain in his Cabinet. It was a sharp issue but was soon adjusted. Mr. Buchanan gave way and permitted Judge Black and his associates, Holt and Stanton, to frame a reply for the Administration.

"Jefferson Davis, Mr. Toombs, Mr. Benjamin, Mr. Slidell, who had been Mr. Buchanan's intimate and confidential advisers, and who had led him to the brink of ruin, found themselves suddenly supplanted, and a new power installed in the White House. Foiled and no longer able to use the National Administration as an instrumentality to destroy the national life, the secession leaders in Congress turned upon the President with angry reproaches. In their rage they lost all sense of the respect due to the Chief Magistrate of the nation, and assaulted Mr. Buchanan with coarseness as well as violence. Senator Benjamin spoke of him as 'a senile Executive under the sinister influence of insane counsels.' This exhibition of malignity towards the misguided President afforded to the North the most convincing and satisfactory proof that there had been a change for the better in the plans and purposes of the Administration. They realized that it must be a deep sense of impending danger which could separate Mr. Buchanan from his political associations with the South, and they recognized in his position a significant proof of the desperate determination to which the enemies of the Union had come.

"The stand taken by Judge Black and his loyal associates was in the last days of December, 1860. The reorganization of the Cabinet came as a matter of necessity. Mr. John B. Floyd resigned from the War Department, making loud proclamation that his action was based on the President's refusal to surrender the national forts in Charleston Harbor to the secession government of South Carolina. This manifesto was not necessary to establish Floyd's treasonable intentions towards the Government; but, in point of truth, the plea was undoubtedly a pretense, to cover reasons of a more personal character which would at once deprive him of Mr. Buchanan's confidence. There had been irregularities in the War Department tending to compromise Mr. Floyd, for which he was afterwards indicted in the District of Columbia. Mr. Floyd well knew that the first knowledge of these shortcomings would lead to his dismissal from the Cabinet. Whatever Mr. Buchanan's faults as an Executive may have been, his honor in all transactions, both personal and public, was unquestionable, and he was the last man to tolerate the slightest deviation from the path of rigid integrity.

"Mr. Thompson, the Secretary of the Interior, followed Mr. Floyd after a short interval. Mr. Cobb had left the Treasury a few days before General Cass resigned from the Cabinet and had gone to Georgia to stimulate her laggard movements in the scheme of destroying the Government. His successor was Philip Francis Thomas, of Maryland, who entered the Cabinet as a representative of the principles whose announcement had forced General Cass to resign. The change of policy to which the President was now fully committed forced Mr. Thomas to retire after a month's service. He frankly stated that he was unable to agree with the President and his other advisers 'in reference to the condition of things in South Carolina,' and therefore tendered his resignation. Mr. Thomas adhered to the Union and always maintained an upright and honorable character; but his course at that crisis deprived him subsequently of a seat in the United States Senate, though at a later period he served in the House as Representative from Maryland.

"Mr. Cobb, Mr. Floyd and Mr. Thompson had all remained in the Cabinet after the Presidential election in November, in full sympathy, and so far as possible in co-operation with the men in the South who were organizing resistance to the authority of the Federal Government. Neither those gentlemen, nor any friend in their behalf, ever ventured to explain how, as sworn officers of the United States, they could remain at their posts consistently with the laws of honor—laws obligatory on them not only as public officials who had taken a solemn oath of fidelity to the Constitution, but also as private gentlemen, whose good faith was pledged anew every hour they remained in control of the departments with whose administration they had been entrusted. Their course is unfavorably contrasted with that of many Southern men (of whom General Lee and the two Johnstons were conspicuous examples), who refused to hold official positions under the national Government a single day after they had determined to take part in the scheme of disunion.

"By the reorganization of the Cabinet the tone of Mr. Buchanan's administration was radically changed. Judge Black had used his influence with the President to secure trustworthy friends of the Union in every department. Edwin M. Stanton, little known at the time to the public, but of high standing in his profession, was appointed Attorney-General soon after Judge Black took charge of the State Department. Judge Black had been associated with Stanton personally and professionally and was desirous of his aid in the dangerous period through which he was called to serve.

"Joseph Holt, who, since the death of Aaron V. Brown in 1859, had been Postmaster-General, was now appointed Secretary of War, and Horatio King, of Maine, for many years the upright first assistant, was justly promoted to the head of the Post-office Department. Mr. Holt was the only Southern man left in the Cabinet. He was a native of Kentucky, long a resident of Mississippi, always identified with the Democratic party, and affiliated with its extreme southern wing.

Without a moment's hesitation he now broke all the associations of a lifetime, and stood by the Union without qualification or condition. His learning, his firmness and his ability were invaluable to Mr. Buchanan in the closing days of his administration.

"General John A. Dix, of New York, was called to the head of the Treasury.

He was a man of excellent ability, of wide experience in affairs, of spotless character and a most zealous friend of the Union. He found the Treasury bankrupt, the discipline of its officers in the South gone, its orders disregarded in the States which were preparing for secession. He at once imparted spirit and energy into the service, giving to the administration of this department a policy of pronounced loyalty to the Government. No act of his useful and honorable life has been so widely known or will be so long remembered as his dispatch to the Treasury agent at New Orleans to take possession of a revenue cutter whose commander was suspected of disloyalty and of a design to transfer his vessel to the Confederate service. Lord Nelson's memorable order at Trafalgar was not more inspiring to the British Navy than was the order of General Dix to the American people, when, in the gloom of that depressing winter, he telegraphed South his peremptory words: 'If any man attempts to haul down the American flag, shoot him on the spot.' "Thus reconstructed, the Cabinet as a whole was one of recognized power, marked by high personal character, by intellectual training, by experience in affairs, and by aptitude for the public service. There have been Cabinets perhaps more widely known for the possession of great qualities; but, if the history of successive administrations from the origin of the Government be closely studied, it will be found that the reorganized Cabinet of President Buchanan must take rank as one of exceptional ability."

CHAPTER XXVI.

JUDGE CRADLEBAUGH DISCHARGES THE GRAND JURY AND TURNS SOCIETY OVER TO LAWLESS RULE. THE INDIANS ENCOURAGED TO DEPREDATIONS ON THE SETTLEMENTS. A DARK PICTURE OF SALT LAKE SOCIETY. WHY GOVERNOR CUMMING DID NOT INVESTIGATE THE MOUNTAIN MEADOWS MASSACRE.

Having failed to obtain the indictment of the leaders of the Mormon Church, the judges resolved that they would close their courts and give society into the hands of the numerous desperadoes with which the Territory now abounded. In discharging the grand jury, Judge Cradlebaugh uttered one of the most remarkable passages to be found in the whole history of criminal jurisprudence: "If it is expected," he said, "that this court is to be used by this community as a means of protecting it against the peccadilloes of Gentiles and Indians, unless this community will punish its own murderers, such expectations will not be realized. It will be used for no such purpose. When the people shall come to their reason and manifest a disposition to punish their own high offenders, it will then be time to enforce the law also for their protection. If this court cannot bring you to a proper sense of your duty, it can at least (urn the savages held in custody loose upon you." Accordingly Judge Cradlebaugh dismissed the prisoners and adjourned his court "without day."

On his part D. Hurt, the Indian agent, had, both before and after the entrance of Johnston's troops, spent his official service in inciting hostile Indians to commit depredations upon the Mormon settlements. This, indeed, was the specific charge which Governor Cumming reported to Secretary Cass against Indian Agent Hurt, both as inimical to the peace of the Territory and interruptive of his own executive duties representing the Federal Government. Upon this Indian line of the history, George A. Smith, just prior to the entrance of Johnston's troops, writing to T. B. H. Stenhouse, said: "It has been the policy of Governor Young and our people to keep the Indians neutral, should a contest ensue. I read in the last papers received from the States loud boasts of having secured the Utah and other Indians as allies against the Mormons. Strange as it may seem to civilized persons, all the reckless and unprincipled Indians of the mountains have been hired, with new guns, blankets, clothing, ammunition, paint, etc., to steal, rob, murder, and do anything else that can be done to destroy the Mormons. Indian agents have sent messengers to all the peaceable Indians to incite them to deeds of rapine and bloodshed. A number of scattering settlements have been attacked, and innocent blood stains the skirts of the present administration, whose agents have procured the murders.

"I am an American, as you well know. I love my country and hate to see her rulers trample under foot her glorious institutions and re-enact barbarism more cruel than that inflicted by the King of Great Britain, through the hands of the red men upon the scattered settlements of the colonies, in the war of independence. We wish 'life, liberty, and the pursuit of happiness.' "With 3,500 bayonets, rifles, revolvers, and heavy ordnance pointed at us, and within three days' march of our city, 4,500 more en route to reinforce them, carte blanche on the United States treasury, would seem enough to satisfy our most bitter persecutors, without hiring as allies the savage hordes of the deserts and mountains to murder, scalp, roast, and eat their fellow-citizens, because they forsooth differed on the subject of religion.

'Who can believe it!— the cause is rather odd—
Men hate each other for the love of God!'

"You are aware that all the outrages in the country, heretofore, have been caused by men who are enemies to the inhabitants of this Territory—who have passed through our borders and recklessly shot at and otherwise abused the Indians.

"Experience shows that Indians, like Congressmen and Government officials, have their price."

Mr. William G. Mills, writing to the same person, who at that time was a special attaché of the New York Herald on Utah affairs, said:

"The officials and others among the troops are employing their influence and means to bribe the Indians to steal the cattle, and horses, and mules from the settlers here; and already some have succeeded in stealing and have mas sacred several persons in the outer settlements. The cattle will be conveyed to the army. One poor fox skin from an Indian will be paid for with a quantity of powder, lead, caps, blankets, and shirts—more than a hundred times its value— in order to buy over the rude savages to rob from and murder those who have hitherto fed and clothed them. This is done whenever an Indian visits them. It is not, of course, bribing or buying the Indian—it is only paying for the fox or buckskin; and significant nods, winks, and signs accompanying the gift are easily interpreted, and robbery and murder are the result. Dr. Hurt, the Indian agent, who decamped from the Indian farm, to create an excitement in his favor, in pretense for personal safety—'The wicked fleeth when none pursueth '—has collected a band of Indians in Uintah Valley, among whom is the murderer Tintic, and placed himself as their chief at their head, to make an attack on the southern settlements, and promising not only blankets, powder, etc., but a share of the pillage, as the reward of their nefarious acts. Murder in the north is to be responded to by murder of quiet and peaceable citizens in the south. Every mule and horse that the Indians steal is blamed on the Mormons, though the latter may be a hundred miles from the scene of action. A good supply of whisky is furnished to the Indians by the officers and others, and they seem to enjoy themselves well together. Drinking among the troops was carried on to excess during the winter, which was calculated to excite their bitterest feelings and to enter in every scheme to annoy and kill the citizens. White men and murderous Indians are 'hail fellows well met.' "The Indians, by the presence of the troops, are emboldened to annoy the various settlements, because the Mormons would rather not fight. In Tooele County—the most westerly in the Territory—those Indians who were hitherto friendly have become excited by the conversations and bribes of the army and have stolen about one hundred and fifty head of cattle and sixty horses and fired upon the men who were guarding. At Salmon River settlement, two hundred and fifty head of cattle were stolen about the 4th of March, and several Mormons killed and scalped, and again attacked subsequently. It is expected that Dr. Hurt and his tribe will make an attack soon upon the southern settlements; but the people are prepared for every emergency and will repulse them.

"The war chiefs of several tribes of Indians, during the time of the excitement last fall and winter, applied personally to Governor Young for his advice and permission to go out with their tribes and 'use up' the soldiers, which they deemed themselves amply capable to do; but he, in every instance, told them to keep away from the army and show no bad feelings whatever, and requested them to avoid killing the white men. I have seen the chiefs exhibit sanguine feelings in relation to killing the soldiers, but entirely softened down by the counsel and expressions of Governor Young. He wrote to Ben Simons, the Delaware Indian, chief of the Weberites, in reply to a letter, to stand in a neutral position, neither take part with the Mormons nor the soldiers, in the event of a collision, and has always endeavored to suppress that bloodthirsty spirit of the treacherous red men."

The action of the judges, in suspending altogether the administration of justice, and by semi-proclamation turning loose upon society the desperadoes, produced such a condition of things, compared with which the history of Great Salt Lake City was stainless before the onset of the Buchanan Expedition.

Mr. Stenhouse in his Rocky Mountain Saints has painted the dark picture of those times thus outlined and colored: "With such a large body of troops there were, as usual, numerous camp followers plying their petit industries, gambling, thieving, and drinking. General Johnston, with strict surveillance and severe military punishment, had been able to control them on the march and at Camp Scott; but when they found in the valleys of the Saints a wider and safer field for operations, they gave rein to their vilest passions, and a worse set of vagabonds never afflicted any community with their presence than did the followers of Johnston's army the inhabitants of the chief city of Zion. Quite a number of young Mormons—and some not -so young—became as reckless and daring as any of the imported Gentiles, and life and property for a time were very insecure in Salt Lake City.

"The programme of the police authorities seemed to be to give the desperadoes the largest liberty, so that they might, in their drunken carousals, 'kill off each other,' and what they left undone invisible hands readily accomplished.

During the summer and fall of 1859 there was a murder committed in Salt Lake City almost every week, and very rarely were the criminals brought to justice.

"The Mormon leaders taught the people to attend to their fields and workshops, keep out of 'Whisky Street,' and let 'civilization' take its course. They had plenty of hard work to engage their attention, and no money, so that the business street was seldom visited by them, and they saw little of what was transpiring in their midst. The Church weekly paper took pride in reporting, as it occurred, 'another man for breakfast,' and with that 'the people of God' were satisfied that 'the good work was rolling on.' Israel would one day be free from his oppressors.

"The rioting and killing that were traceable occupied little more than passing attention, but the midnight work of invisible hands created a sensation of terror in the minds of all who were inimical to the priesthood. The Valley Tan, notwithstanding its true boldness, felt the danger of the hour, and in one of its doleful wails ejaculated: 'How long, oh! how long are scenes like this to continue? * * * It would seem as if the insatiable demon and enemy of man must himself be gorged with the flow of human blood in our midst.' * * * 'No man's life is secure as long as the scenes of violence and bloodshed, which have been of such frequent occurrence among us for months past, continue to be repeated, and the perpetrators escape unpunished or not detected.' "The bloody work continued, and finally terminated with the murder of Brewer and Joaquin Johnston, two intimate friends, who were shot at the same instant as they were walking home together. The author well remembers seeing very early the next morning the marshal of the city and the chief of police who gravely informed him of the 'sad news'—'Johnston and Brewer had quarreled and killed each other!' This story was feeble enough, but no one cared to question it: the people had got used to the record of scenes of blood.

"In the 'swift destruction' that fell upon the desperadoes, there was no mitigation of punishment on account of faith or family relationship, and very respectable Mormon families had to mourn the untimely end of boys who, before the entrance of the army, gave promise of lives of usefulness and honor. All the bad and desperate Mormons were not brought to judgment, but the pretext alone was wanting for carrying more extensively into execution the general programme. Resistance to an officer, or the slightest attempt to escape from custody, was eagerly seized, when wanted, as the justification of closing a disreputable career, and in more than one case of this *legal* shooting, there is much doubt if even the trivial excuse was waited for. The Salt Lake police then earned the reputation of affording every desperate prisoner the opportunity of escape, and, if embraced, the officer's ready revolver brought the fugitive to a 'halt,' and saved the country the expenses of a trial and his subsequent boarding in the penitentiary. A coroner's inquest and cemetery expenses were comparatively light.

"With the troops themselves there was no collision. The Governor had requested General Johnston to withhold furlough from the soldiers, and few of them ever had the opportunity of visiting the City of the Saints. With some officers there had been, in the city, slight difficulties, which were, however, easily settled. Only one serious affair occurred, ending in the death of Sergeant Pike.

This person was charged with violently assaulting a young Mormon and cracking his skull with a musket. During the Sergeant's trial in Salt Lake City, while on the public street at noon, passing to his hotel, a young man shot him down, and shortly afterward he died. The young man, with the aid of others, escaped, and was never arrested. There was great excitement at Camp Floyd, but the Sergeant's comrades were too far away to retaliate.

"From the time of the arrival of the troops in the valley, Brigham was personally very cautious, and never exposed himself to attack. For a long time he absented himself from the public assemblies, kept an armed door-keeper at the entrance of his residences, and by night was protected by an armed guard of the faithful. Every ward in the city took its turn in watching over the Prophet, and the floors of his offices were nightly covered with a guard, armed and equipped, and ready at a moment's notice to repulse the imaginary foe.

"During the day, when Brigham ventured beyond the outer walls of his premises, half a dozen friends always accompanied him wherever he went. It is pleasing to add that no one ever so much as said to him an unbecoming word."

In this condition of society, and the antagonistic complication of affairs existing between the Governor and General Johnston and the Judges, is to be found the exact historical exposition why the Mountain Meadow Massacre was not brought to judgment and avenged years before the execution of John D. Lee.

Ex-Governor Young has often, yet most senselessly been reproved and held guilty for not causing an investigation of the tragedy in question and bringing its executors to justice immediately after the bloody deed was done. One of the questions and its answer from the deposition of Brigham Young, taken at the trial of Lee, bears directly upon this point:

"Q. Why did you not as Governor institute proceedings forthwith to investigate the massacre and bring the guilty authors to justice?

"A. Because another Governor had been appointed by the President of the United States and was then on the way here to take my place, and I did not know how soon he might arrive; and because the United States Judges were not in the Territory. Soon after Governor Cumming arrived I asked him to take Judge Cradlebaugh, who belonged to the Southern District, with him, and I would accompany them with sufficient aid to investigate the matter and bring the offenders to justice."

But the action of the Judges, at the very onset, made it impossible for ex-Governor Young or Governor Cumming to move far in the matter. Though Brigham Young had been Justice personified, had he proceeded he must have walked into the death-trap set for him.

The following editorial excerpt from the New York Tribune, July 3rd, 1858, describes the case of Governor Cumming before the entrance of the troops, which was more abundantly illustrated afterwards: "The latest accounts from Utah present the affairs of that Territory in rather a queer light. All the correspondents of the newspapers who write from Camp Scott most zealously contend that Governor Cumming, in representing the Mormons as having submitted to his authority, has either been grossly deceived himself, or else is seeking to deceive the Government and the country. Possibly, as to this matter, the good people of Camp Scott, civil and military, judge the Mormons a little too much by themselves. If the disposition to obey the Governor and to second and sustain him in the exercise of his office is not greater within the valley than it seems to be at Camp Scott and Fort Bridger, the extent of the Governor's authority is certainly limited enough. Whether or not Brigham Young and his people have combined together, while seeming to acknowledge Cumming as Governor—in fact to set aside and override his authority, at least it is very certain that such a combination exists in full force at Camp Scott, with Mr. Chief Justice Eckles at its head. Perhaps there is something in the air of Utah that stimulates to treason, rebellion, and resistance to authority.

Whether that be so or not, the authority of Cumming as Governor seems just now quite as much in danger from the Chief Justice, the civil officers, and the army sent to Utah at such an expense to place him and sustain him in the Governor's chair, as from those whose anticipated opposition to his authority led to such costly preparations to uphold it. In fact, it would seem that, on the question of due respect to Cumming's gubernatorial authority, the people inside the valley and those out of it had completely changed ground. The resistance to Governor Cumming is not now on the part of Brigham Young and the Mormons generally, but on the part of Chief Justice Eckels, Marshal Dotson, General Johnston, the camp, and the camp-followers.

"In this resistance to the authority of Governor Cumming and combination to reduce him, if possible, to a cipher, the recently arrived Peace Commissioners, according to all accounts, have joined, actuated possibly by a feeling of jealousy that they should have been anticipated by Governor Cumming and the work of pacification taken out of their hands. Nor, if we are to believe the letters from the camp, do these gentlemen confine themselves merely to thwarting the policy of Governor Cumming and nullifying his authority as Governor.

They go, indeed, much further than that. The President's proclamation, of which they are the bearers, does not meet their approbation, or appear to them adapted to the exigencies of the case. They harmonize completely, we are told, with Judge Eckles and General Johnston, and not content with upsetting and overriding the Governor, are resolved to upset and override the President too. The proclamation is, therefore, to be construed—by the help, we suppose, of that profound jurist, Judge Eckles—in conformity to their ideas. In other words, it is to be nullified and set aside.

"We have heard a great deal heretofore about the danger of personal violence and loss of property to which the Gentiles in the Territory of Utah have been exposed on the part of the Mormons. At present, the danger seems to be entirely the other way. Nothing can exceed the rancorous and even ferocious feelings against the Mormons with which the army at Camp Scott appears to be penetrated. They regard themselves as engaged not so much in a public service as in the prosecution of a private quarrel. They regard the Mormons as having subjected them to all the hard service of this campaign—as having kept them encamped all winter on short rations amid the mountains—as having derided, maligned, and insulted them; and even the very common soldiers are represented as having put on an air of offended dignity at the idea that the Peace Commissioners had arrived to snatch their intended victims from their revengeful grasp.

This state of feeling on the part of the soldiers affords an abundant justification for Governor Cumming's objections to their entry into the valley and for the dread and horror with which the Mormons regard their presence there. If it be deemed proper or necessary to station troops in Utah, they ought to be some fresh corps, and not a body of men filled with such hatred and prejudice. Let some of the troops now on their march across the plains be employed in this service, and the force now collecting under General Johnson be sent in some other direction. That officer, however, would seem bent upon entering the valley, in spite of the remonstrances of Governor Cumming, whose authority over the troops he denies, with the very object, it would seem, of driving the Mormons to destroy their houses and to prevent them from gathering their crops, thus subjecting thousands of women and children to the danger of starvation."

The Peace Commissioners, however, in the sequel accomplished their mission, but the breach between Governor Cumming and General Johnston and the Judges, extended, as we have seen, to the impeachment of his course and a demand from Camp Floyd for his removal.

But his inability to investigate and bring to justice the authors of the Mountain Meadow Massacre, during his term of office, is known to have been a thorn in Governor Cumming's side. After him no Governor could be specially held responsible; and thus justice tarried long, impeded at the onset by the Judges themselves, which is the unmistakable import of Attorney-General Black's rebuke to them.

CHAPTER XXVII.

AFTER THE UTAH WAR. CELEBRATION OF THE FOURTH OF JULY. BENEFITS OF CAMP FLOYD TO THE COMMUNITY. TRADE WITH THE CAMP. THE PONY EXPRESS. THE BULK OF THE TROOPS MARCH FOR NEW MEXICO AND ARIZONA. JOHNSTON LEAVES FOR WASHINGTON. THE DEPARTURE OF GOVERNOR CUMMING. THE REMNANT OF THE ARMY ORDERED TO THE STATES. SALES OF CAMP FLOYD. GOODS WORTH FOUR MILLION DOLLARS SOLD FOR ONE HUNDRED THOUSAND. DESTRUCTION OF ARMS AND AMMUNITION. LINCOLN'S NEW APPOINTMENTS FOR UTAH. COMPLETION OF THE TELEGRAPH LINE. FIRST MESSAGE FROM EX-GOVERNOR YOUNG-" UTAH HAS NOT SECEDED." THE GOVERNOR TO PRESIDENT LINCOLN AND HIS RESPONSE. UTAH'S MANIFESTO ON THE CIVIL WAR.

Soon after the attempt of the military, instigated by the Judges, to arrest Brigham Young, the Lieut.-General of the Utah militia issued the following:

"Special Order no. 2.

"Headquarters Nauvoo Legion,

Adjutant-General's Office, G. S. L. City, July 1st, 1859.

"Monday, the 4th, will be the eighty-third anniversary of the birth of American freedom. It is the duty of every American citizen to commemorate the great event; not in a boisterous revelry, but with hearts full of gratitude to Almighty God the Great Father of our rights.

"The Lieutenant-General directs for the celebration in the city as follows:

"1st.—At sunrise a salute of thirteen guns will be fired, commencing near the residence of His Excellency the Governor, to be answered from a point on South Temple Street, near the residence of President Brigham Young.

"The national flag will be hoisted at the signal from the first gun, simultaneously at the residences of Governor Cumming and President Young, at the office of the Territorial Secretary, and the residence of the United States Attorney. Captain Pitt's band will be stationed at sunrise opposite the residence of Governor Cumming, and Captain Ballo's band opposite the residence of President Young.

"At the hoisting of the flags the bands will play the 'Star Spangled Banner.'

"2nd.—After the morning salute the guns will be parked at the Court House till noon, when a salute of 33 guns will be fired.

"3rd.—At sunset a salute of five guns, in honor of the Territories, will be fired, and the flags lowered.

"4th.—For the above service Lieutenant Atwood and two platoons of artillery will be detailed. Two six-pounder iron guns will be used for the salutes. Also a first lieutenant and two platoons of the 1st cavalry will be detailed as a guard, and continue on guard through the day. The whole detachment will be dismissed after the sunset salute.

"5th.—Col. J. C. Little, of the General's staff, will perform the duties of marshal of the day, with permission to select such deputies as he may require to assist him. The Declaration of Independence will be read by him from the steps of the Court House at noon.

"6th.—The bands and the services to be performed by them will be under the direction of Col. Duzette.

"By order of Lieut.-Gen. DANIEL H. WELLS.

Adjt.-Gen. JAMES FERGUSON."

When the danger of conflict between Camp Floyd and Salt Lake City was passed, the citizens began to realize many material benefits from the camp.

The famine of 1855-6 had impoverished the Territory in its agricultural resources; the handcart emigration had brought to the country several thousand poor people, destitute, after their terrible journey, of even the barest clothing, whereas in former years the "Independent Companies," and the "Ten-pound ox-team companies," had brought moderate, and in some cases rich and plentiful supplies, which had lasted the emigrants several years before they were entirely exhausted. But now for a long while the common sources of supplies had been stopped; and commerce with the east had been suspended by the expedition itself. The Gentile merchants had broken up their houses at the approach of the army, and General Johnston on his joining his army issued orders that no trains of merchandise bound for Great Salt Lake City should be allowed to pass his lines.

Thus the community had become utterly destitute of almost everything necessary to their social comfort. The people were poorly clad, and rarely ever saw anything on their tables but what was prepared from flour, corn, beet molasses, and the vegetables and fruits of their gardens. They were alike destitute of implements of industry, and horses, mules, and wagons for their agricultural operations. Utah was truly very poor at that period; indeed, never so poor since the Californian emigrants poured into Great Salt Lake City in 1849.

The presence of the army soon changed the condition of the community.

It was not to be expected that the leaders of the Church would from the Tabernacle encourage much intercourse between the camp and the citizens, but quite a number of the self-reliant men, who have since represented the business and commerce of the Territory, sought directly the intercourse of trade with the camp, while the more cautious furnished these middle men with the native supplies of the country, by which the trade was sustained. In this way money was gathered in freely by the Gentiles and the bold Mormon traders, and the people generally were thus indirectly clothed and supplied with the delicacies of tea, coffee and sugar, in return for the produce of the field, the dairy and the chicken-coop.

It was at Camp Floyd, indeed, where the principal Utah merchants and business men of the second decade of our history may be said to have laid the foundation of their fortunes, among whom were the Walker Brothers. Nor should it be made to appear that this commerce with Camp Floyd marked the rising of an apostate wave in Utah society. It signified simply the desire of each to better his own condition and that of society at large. And thus commercial intercourse and mutual benefits softened the feelings of hostility between the citizens and the soldiers, and the Utah Expedition became transformed into a great blessing to Utah, and especially to the Mormon community. A passage here, from the New York Herald's Utah special correspondent, of the novelties of the Camp Floyd trade, must be quoted for its striking illustration: "Among the rascalities of those times, contracts were awarded to certain political hucksters at Washington for an enormous quantity of flour to be supplied at $28.40 per 100 pounds, which in the course of time was furnished by the

Prophet at $6 in the City of the Saints. That contractor also managed to get an order from the Secretary of War for the specie at Camp Floyd, failing which he was to be paid in mules, and of these he had his choice, at figures ranging from £100 to $150 each. Great bands of these animals were driven to California and sold on the Pacific at nearly six times their Camp Floyd prices. With such and many other flagrant facts, it is not surprising that the Prophet and the Apostles designated Mr. Buchanan's expedition to Utah in 1857, 'The Contractors' War!'"

The experiment of the Pony Express from the Missouri River to the Pacific Ocean was made in the spring of 1860. The Deseret News of date April 11th, made note: "The first Pony Express from the west left Sacramento City at 12 m., on the night of the 3rd instant, and arrived in this city at 11:45 of the 7th, inside of the prospectus time. The express from the east left St. Joseph, Missouri, at 6:30 on the evening of the 3rd, and arrived in this city at 6:25 on the evening of the 9th. This brings us within six days' communication from the frontier and seven from Washington—a result which we Utonians, accustomed to receive news three months after date, can well appreciate."

Among the first news brought was that a bill was before the House to amend the organic act of this Territory, remove the seat of government from Great Salt Lake City to Carson Valley, and change the name from Utah to Nevada. The object stated was to take the controlling power out of the hands of the Mormons of Utah and give it into the hands of the Gentiles of Nevada.

In May of this year the mass of the troops from Camp Floyd took up their march for New Mexico and Arizona. Only a few were left to perform the requisite duties of the garrison.

Just previous, General Albert Sidney Johnston left Camp Floyd for Washington, via the southern route to California. He never visited Great Salt Lake City after he passed through it with his army. General Johnston and Brigham Young therefore never met. After his departure the command devolved upon Colonel Philip St. George Cooke, who by a general order February 6th, 1861, changed the name of Camp Floyd to Fort Crittenden. The intent was understood to disconnect the fort from the name of Secretary Floyd, whose plot for secession was exposed, and his Utah Expedition, sinking twenty millions of the nation's money, considered to be a part of that secession plot.

In May, 1861, just previous to the outbreak of our great civil war, Governor Cumming and his lady departed from Great Salt Lake City with no expectation of returning. He had entered the city amid great display of welcome, and fain had the city shown him and his lady like honors in their retirement, but it was against his wish; so his departure was not generally known until it was announced in the Deseret News, in which the thanks of a grateful community were sent after him for the faithful performance of his service towards them and to the General Government.

The remainder of Johnston's army was ordered to the States to participate in the war; and the order was given to destroy the best equipped military post ever established in the West. But before the evacuation and destruction of arms, public sales were announced of provisions and army stores of every kind. Many went from Great Salt Lake City and the nearer settlements to purchase these valuable supplies, which were sold by auction, and consisted of flour, bacon, groceries of all kinds, hardware, carpenters' tools, blacksmiths' tools, wagons, harness, tents, medical stores, clothing, and, in fine, everything the settlers most needed.

It was estimated that four million dollars' worth of goods were sold for $100,000. Flour sold for 52 cents per sack of 100 lbs. in double sacks, for which the Government had paid $28.40. Everything else was in proportion.

President Young sent his business manager, Mr. H. B. Clawson, to purchase all kinds of supplies most needed for his numerous family, dependents and workmen. He bought about £40,000 worth, among which was the Government safe, where had been deposited 580,000 in gold, which the Government had freighted to Camp Floyd in an ox team.

But the most historical article was the flagstaff, which was transplanted from Camp Floyd to the brow of the hill on the east of Brigham's mansion, where for many years it stood, though now seen no more.

During the sale Mr. Dawson, in his character of ex-Governor Young's business manager, became familiarly acquainted with Quartermaster Col. H. G. Crossman and other officers, to whom he extended a courteous invitation to visit President Young before their departure from the Territory. They politely accepted and seized the opportunity to present to the Founder of Utah the flagstaff which had borne aloft the national banner at Camp Floyd. At such a moment of secession, the gift was a magnificent compliment to the ex-Governor, and, indeed, to the Mormon people also; but Philip St. George Cooke, the commander of the Mormon Battalion, was in command after the departure of General Johnston, and perhaps he and others of the officers had revised their views of the "Utah rebellion."

After the sales were over, the arms and ammunition were taken to a distance and piled up in pyramids; long trains of powder were then properly arranged, and at a given signal the fusee was touched and the work of destruction accomplished. Several pieces of ordnance that could not be exploded were consigned to deep wells; but it is said that they were recovered and that they have often since done good service in the celebration of the Fourth of July, in honor of the national birth, and of the Twenty-fourth of July, in honor of the arrival of the Pioneers into these valleys and the founding of Great Salt Lake City. In the early autumn of 1861 the troops marched Eastward, and thus ended the famous Utah expedition.

The change of Federal administration incident to the election of Abraham Lincoln, also, in due course of time gave to Utah a new set of Federal officials. Excepting the Governor, these proved to be more acceptable to the people than their predecessors had been. Secretary Wooton, after the departure of Governor Cumming, on the first announcement of secession sent in his resignation to President Lincoln. John W. Dawson, of Indiana, was then appointed Governor; Frank Fuller, of New Hampshire, Secretary; John F. Kinney, who had already been Chief Justice of this Territory, replaced Chief Justice Eckles; and Associate Justices Crosby and Flenniken were appointed to succeed Sinclair and Cradlebaugh. Secretary Fuller arrived before Governor Dawson, and, on the retirement of Mr. Wooton, Fuller also became acting Governor. James Duane Doty was Superintendent of Indian Affairs. It was said that these appointments were designed by President Lincoln to conciliate ex-Governor Young and the Mormons at the outbreak of our civil war. Whether this was so or not, it is no more than just to here record that, notwithstanding the anti-

Mormon attitude of the party that elevated Mr. Lincoln to the Presidency, his course towards Utah was uniformly considerate.

Governor Dawson arrived and entered happily upon his official duties, but he soon fell into temptation, and his gallantries towards a lady of the city becoming exposed, he hastily departed, and Secretary Fuller a second time became the acting Governor.

About the middle of October, 1861, the eastern portion of the Pacific Telegraph Line was completed to Great Salt Lake City. The following record of the event is from the Deseret News of October 23: "On Thursday afternoon the 'operator' connected with the eastern portion of the telegraph line informed the visitors who had gathered around his table to witness the first operations in communicating with the Eastern States, that the Mine was built," but for some reason there was no through message either sent or received till the following day.

"The first use of the electric messenger being courteously extended to President Young, he forwarded the following congratulations to the President of the Company:

"Great Salt Lake City, U. T., Oct. 18, 1861.

"Hon. J. H. Wade, President of the Pacific Telegraph Company, Cleveland, Ohio.

"Sir—Permit me to congratulate you on the completion of the Overland Telegraph line west to this city, to commend the energy displayed by yourself and associates in the rapid and successful prosecution of a work so beneficial, and to express the wish that its use may ever tend to promote the true interests of the dwellers upon both the Atlantic and Pacific Slopes of our continent.

"Utah has not seceded but is firm for the Constitution and laws of oar once happy country and is warmly interested in such useful enterprises as the one so far completed.

BRIGHAM YOUNG."

On Sunday morning the following very becoming reply was received:

"Cleveland, Oct. 19, 1861.

"Hon. Brigham Young, Prest., Great Salt Lake City:

"Sir—I have the honor to acknowledge the receipt of your message of last evening, which was in every way gratifying, not only in the announcement of the completion of the Pacific Telegraph to your enterprising and prosperous city, but that yours, the first message to pass over the line, should express so unmistakably the patriotism and union-loving sentiments of yourself and people.

"I join with you in the hope that this enterprise may tend to promote the welfare and happiness of all concerned, and that the annihilation of time in our means of communication may also tend to annihilate prejudice, cultivate brotherly love, facilitate commerce and strengthen the bonds of our once and again to be happy union.

"With just consideration for your high position and due respect for you personally,

"I remain your obedient servant,

J. H. WADE,

Prest. Pac. Tel. Co."

Acting-Governor Fuller made early use of the wire to extend salutations to President Lincoln, of which the following are copies of the congratulations and the acknowledgment:

"G. S. L. City, Oct. 18, 1861.

"To the President of the United States: "Utah, whose citizens strenuously resist all imputations of disloyalty congratulates the President upon the completion of an enterprise which spans a continent, unites two oceans, and connects with nerve of iron the remote extremities of the body politic, with the great governmental heart. May the whole system speedily thrill with the quickened pulsations of that heart, as the paracide hand is palsied, treason is punished, and the entire sisterhood of States joins hands in glad reunion around the National fireside.

FRANK FULLER,
Acting Governor of Utah Territory."

"Washington, D. C, Oct. 20, 1861.

"Hon. Frank Fuller, Acting Governor of Utah:

"Sir—The completion of the telegraph to Great Salt Lake City, is auspicious of the stability and union of the Republic. The Government reciprocates your congratulations.

ABRAHAM LINCOLN."

"During the business hours on Friday there was quite an interest in the performances of the electricity, and congratulations over the wire to distant friends were extended in every direction. The day throughout was quite an occasion for the moving celebrities of Main Street.

"The western line, as reported to us, was to have been finished on Monday evening or yesterday morning—a much earlier day than the most sanguine friends of Mr. Street anticipated. The last poles being set to the west of Fort Crittenden, Mr. Street has consequently been detained there, but was expected in this morning, and will doubtless open his battery on the inhabitants of the Pacific during the course of to-day; and thus the inhabitants of the Pacific and Atlantic States will be united in electric bonds.

"Having expressed our sentiments on the building of the telegraph line through the Territory in a recent number of the *News*, we will now only say that the hope is entertained that at no distant day the 'iron horse' may have a track prepared for it across the continent."

As might be expected, the great civil war between the North and the South gave to Utah the opportunity for a unique example in her conduct. She had herself just been "in rebellion"; how would she now act? This was a most natural question, and, strange to say, her answer was almost the reverse of the general pronouncement of what she would do.

And here it might be said that it matters not to the integrity of history whether or not the Mormons be understood by others, as long as they act consistently with themselves, and their own faith in their religious and national mission. We have just seen that on the very first occasion after the "Utah rebellion," as we will style it to illustrate the example, they made haste to re assert their faith in the Constitution and the Union, by celebrating the day of American independence very much with the same intention as though they had sent a manifesto to the States of their views and conduct. And just in keeping with this was the pronouncement of the Mormon leaders upon secession at its very birth, as the accompanying Fourth of July military order will suggest:

Headquarters Nauvoo Legion,
G. S. IL. City, June 25th, 1861.

GENERAL ORDERS, NO. I.

1. Thursday, the Fourth of July, being the eighty-fifth anniversary of American independence; notwithstanding the turmoil and strife which distress the nation established on that foundation, the citizens of Utah esteem it a privilege to celebrate the day in a manner becoming American patriots and true lovers of the Constitution of their country.

2. The Lieut.-General directs that district commanders throughout the Territory will conform, as far as practicable, to the requisitions of the various committees of arrangements for details.

3. In Great Salt Lake City, at the request of the committee of arrangements, the following details will be made, and placed under the direction of Major John Sharp, marshal of the day, viz: One company of the 1st, and one of the 3rd regiments of infantry.

One company of light artillery and two guns.

Two brass bands and one martial band.

By order of

Lieut.-Gen. D. H. Wells,

James Ferguson, Adjt.-Gen.

This military manifesto, just after the national flag had been fired upon at Fort Sumter, meant simply that Utah was going to stand by the Union.

CHAPTER XXVIII.

MORMON SERVICE ON THE OVERLAND MAIL LINE. PRESIDENT LINCOLN CALLS ON BRIGHAM YOUNG FOR HELP. THE EX-GOVERNOR'S RESPONSE. BEN HOLLADAY THANKS BRIGHAM. LOT SMITH'S COMMAND. REPORT OF THE SERVICE. GENERAL CRAIG COMPLIMENTS THE MORMON TROOPS.

In the spring of 1862 the Indians were troublesome on the Overland Mail Route and stopped the mails. They destroyed nearly every mail station between Fort Bridger and North Platte, they burned the coaches and mail bags, ran off the stock, and killed the drivers.

Acting-Governor Fuller, Chief Justice Kinney, and six other gentlemen connected with the mail and telegraph lines, joined in recommending to Secretary Stanton to authorize the Superintendent of Indian Affairs, James Duane Doty, to raise and put in service immediately, "a regiment of mounted rangers from the inhabitants of the Territory, with officers to be appointed by him," etc.

But Acting-Governor Fuller and Chief Justice Kinney had over-rated the Federal power in Utah, as embodied in themselves, for such a service, when they overlooked ex-Governor Young, Lieutenant-General Wells and the Utah militia.

Three days after the dispatch of Governor Fuller and others to Secretary Stanton, Brigham Young telegraphed to the Utah Delegate at Washington a corrected statement in which he said, "the militia of Utah are ready and able, as they ever have been, to take care of all the Indians, and are able and willing to protect the mail line if called upon to do so."

But ex-Governor Young, however, did not wait even to be called upon for help. The need of the service was too imperative to linger for official etiquette, and to Colonel Robert T. Burton the Commanding-General issued the following

"INSTRUCTIONS.
"G. S. L. City, April 24, 1862.
"Col. Robert T. Burton and the detachment to guard the mail stage under you:
"You are detailed for this special service, and will proceed from this place in company with Captain Hooper, General C. W. West, Judge Kinney, and probably other passengers in the mail coach for the Eastern States, as a guard to protect them against the depredations of Indians, who are said to be hostile; and continue in their company on the route as far as it may be deemed necessary by yourself and Captain Hooper for their safety. In traveling, the stage must correspond to your time, as it cannot be expected that without change of animals your detachment can keep pace with the stage, especially where the roads are good.

You will obtain grain for your animals, and some provisions for your command at the mail stations, for which you will give a receipt to be paid in kind, keeping a copy of each receipt, and advising President Young by telegraph, so that we can forward the amounts by the teams going to the States, which are expected to start in a few days. In traveling be cautious, and vigilant, and keep together and allow no straggling from camp, either night or day. There must not be any drinking of spirituous liquors, neither swearing, or abusive language of any kind, and treat everybody with courtesy, and prove there is no necessity of trouble with the Indians, when white men act with propriety.

"If you can get to speak with Indians, treat them kindly, showing them you are their friends; and so far as you are able, investigate the cause and origin of the present difficulties.

"You had better have one or two friendly Indians to accompany you, through whose agency you may be able to communicate with others, and thus become apprised of their intentions.

"When you meet the troops from the East said to be on their way, you can return, but you will remain in the vicinity of the threatened difficulties until relieved, or so long as it may be necessary.

"* * * Keep a journal of every day's proceedings, and a strict account of every business transaction, as well of the causes leading to the disturbances, if obtainable.

"Send by telegraph to President Young from every station giving us in short the current news, and prospects of Indians, state of the roads, weather, and other matters of interest.

"When you arrive at or near the scene of disaster, feel your way before you, proceed so that you may not be surprised by a concealed or sudden movement of the Indians, or other evil-disposed persons.

"May God bless, prosper and preserve you all.
DANIEL H. WELLS,
"Lieut.-General Commanding N. L. Militia of Utah Territory."

A day later Acting-Governor Fuller made an official requisition for the escort, and the Lieut.-General issued a supplemental order:

"SPECIAL ORDERS, NO. 2.
"Headquarters Nauvoo Legion,
"G. S. L. City, April 25th, 1862.

"1st. In compliance with the requisition this day made by His Excellency Frank Fuller, Acting-Governor Utah Territory, Col. R. T. Burton will forthwith detail twenty men, properly armed and equipped, and mounted on good and efficient animals, provided with thirty days' rations and grain for animals, and wagons sufficient to carry grain, rations and bedding, and proceed East on the overland mail route, guarding mails, passengers, and property pertaining thereto.

"2nd. It is expected that to have the protection of the escort, the mail coaches will travel with it, as it cannot be expected that without change of animals it can keep pace with the mail coaches, especially when the roads are good.

"3rd. Colonel Burton will immediately offer his services to said Mail Company, and then proceed upon his journey, and remain on the line until relieved by the troops said to be coming up from the East, or so long as it may be necessary to quiet the Indians, who are said to be hostile, and the road considered safe from their depredations.

"God bless and prosper you all.
DANIEL H. WELLS,
Lieut.-General Commanding N. L. Militia Utah Territory."

But the historical mark extraordinary of this service is seen in the call of President Lincoln on Brigham Young for help, and his authorizing of him to raise a company, just as though he had been still the Governor of Utah:

"ORDER.
"Washington, April 28th, 1862.
"Mr. Brigham Young, Salt Lake City: "By express direction of the President of the United States, you are authorized to raise, arm and equip one company of cavalry for ninety (90) days' service.

"This company will be organized as follows: One captain, one first lieutenant, one second lieutenant, one first sergeant, one quartermaster sergeant, four (4) sergeants, and eight (8) corporals, two (2) musicians, two (2) farriers, one saddler, one wagoner, and fifty-six (56) to seventy-two (72) privates.

"The company will be employed to protect the property of the Telegraph and Overland Mail Companies, in or about Independence Rock, where depredations have been committed, and will continue in service only until the U. S. troops can reach the point where they are so much needed. It may therefore be disbanded previous to the expiration of ninety (90) days.

"It will not be employed for any offensive operations other than may grow out of the duty herein assigned to it. The officers of the company will be mustered into the U. S. service by any civil officer of the U. S. at Salt Lake City competent to administer an oath. The men employed in the service above named will be entitled to receive no other than the allowance authorized by law to soldiers in the service of the U. S. Until the proper staff officers for substituting these men arrive, you will please furnish subsistence for them yourself, keeping an accurate account thereof for future settlement with U. S. Government.

"By order of the Secretary of War.
L. THOMAS, Adjutant General."

This telegram was received at 9 o'clock at night, April 28; but, within the hour, the following was issued and immediately in the hands of Major Lot Smith:

"Headquarters Nauvoo Legion,
"Great Salt Lake City, April 28th, 1862.
"SPECIAL ORDERS, NO. 3.
"1st. Pursuant to instructions received this day from ex-Governor Brigham Young, and in compliance with a requisition from the President of the United States, Major Lot Smith of the Battalion of Life Guards is hereby directed to enlist by voluntary enrollment for the term of ninety days a company of mounted men, to be composed as follows, to-wit: One captain, one first lieutenant, one second lieutenant, one quartermaster sergeant, one first sergeant, four sergeants, eight corporals, two musicians, two farriers, one saddler, one wagoner, and seventy-two privates. Major Smith is hereby assigned to the command of the company with rank of captain, and on mustering the men into service, will administer the proper oath agreeably to instructions herewith accompanying.

"2nd. The object of this expedition, to which this company is assigned, as instructed and authorized by the President, is the protection of the property of the

Overland Mail and Telegraph Companies, at or about Independence Rock, and the adjoining country. Captain Smith will, therefore, as soon as his company is completed proceed at once to the above-named vicinity and patrol the road so as to render all necessary aid as contemplated by the instructions. It is not anticipated that the company, or any portion of it will camp so near any of the mail stations, as to give trouble or inconvenience; but sufficiently adjacent to render prompt and ready aid when required. Captain Smith is enjoined to preserve strict sobriety in his camp and prevent the use of all profane language or disorderly conduct of any kind. No apprehension is entertained by the General commanding, but that the best and most praiseworthy deportment will characterize the expedition, the officers and men having been selected with care, and with a view to their ability to render good and efficient service.

"3rd. Judging from advices received from the President of the United States, troops may soon be expected on the road to relieve the company now ordered out; the commander of the detachment will receive the necessary instructions in proper time and will remain on duty with his command until so instructed.

"4th. It is desirable to cultivate as far as practicable friendly and peaceful relations with the Indians.

"5th. The service to be expected from the horses and mules on the expedition will be a sufficient argument in favor of great care in marching and feeding, as well as vigilant guarding and precaution against surprises. The greatest economy must be used with ammunition; none should be heedlessly wasted.

DANIEL H. WELLS.
"Lieut.-General Commanding
Nauvoo Legion, Militia of Utah Territory."

BRIGHAM YOUNG'S TELEGRAM TO ADJT.-GENERAL L. THOMAS, WASHINGTON, D. C.

"Great Salt Lake City, May 1st, 1862.

"Adjt.-Gen. L. Thomas, U. S. A., Washington City, D. C: "Immediately on the receipt of your telegram of the 28 ult., at 8:30 p. m., I requested General Daniel H. Wells to proceed at once to raise a company of cavalry to be mustered into the service of the United States for ninety days, as per your aforesaid telegram. General Wells forthwith issued the requisite orders, and yesterday the captain and other officers were sworn by Chief Justice J. F. Kinney, the enrolling and swearing in the privates attended to, and the company went into camp adjacent to this city.

"To-day the company, seventy-two (72) privates, officered as directed, and ten (10) baggage and supply wagons, with one assistant teamster deemed necessary, took up their line of march for the neighborhood of Independence Rock.

BRIGHAM YOUNG."

It will be noticed that about a day and a half had elapsed before the return telegram of the ex-Governor was sent answering the call of President Lincoln.

At first it might seem that there was a missing link—that a previous answer must have been sent to the effect that the call would be responded to at the earliest moment; but the feature of the case is eminently like the character of Brigham Young. He answered the moment he could say to the President of the United States,

Your order is obeyed; the company is on the march! Abraham Lincoln was just the man to appreciate such a telegram and such executive business; so was also the great mail contractor Ben Holladay, who became assured the moment he knew that Brigham Young was moving in the service and thus acknowledged:

"New York, May 2, 1862.

"To Gov. Brigham Young: "Many thanks for your prompt response to President Lincoln's request. As soon as the boys can give protection, the mails shall be resumed. I leave for your city Sunday next.
BEN HOLLADAY."

As a link of the history may be given Chief Justice Kinney's certificate.

"I, John F. Kinney, Chief Justice of the Supreme Court of the United States for the Territory of Utah, do hereby certify, that in pursuance of the following order from the War Department, I mustered into service of the United States for the period of ninety days, unless sooner discharged, the following officers, whose names appear to the certificate by administering the usual oath, and the oath provided by the act of Congress August 6th, 1861."

The following extracts from Major Lot Smith's letters to Brigham Young, give a touch of the performance of the service:

"Pacific Springs, June 15th, 1862.

" Prest. Brigham Young: "Dear Sir—I had an interview with Brig.-Gen. Craig, who arrived by stage at this point. He expressed himself much pleased with the promptness of our attention to the call of the General Government, also the exertions we had made to overcome the obstacles on the road, spoke well of our people generally; he also informed me he had telegraphed to President Lincoln to that effect, and intended writing him at a greater length by mail. I received written instructions to the effect that he had placed the whole of Nebraska Territory under martial law; Utah, he remarked, was perfectly loyal, and as far as he knew always had been.

He also remarked, we were the most efficient troops he had for the present service and thought as we had broke into our summer's work, of recommending President Lincoln to engage our services for three months longer."

"Pacific Springs, June 27th, '62.

"President Young: "Dear Sir—I have just received orders from General Craig through Colonel Collins to march my command to Fort Bridger to guard the line from Green River to Salt Lake City and start from here to-morrow morning.

"Lieut. Rawlings and command arrived here yesterday; owing to neglect of the mail, my orders to Lieut. Rawlings did not reach him until eight days after they were due, consequently there has been no detail left at Devil's Gate.

"There has been built by the command at the former place a log house 20 feet by 16 feet, with bake houses and detached also a commodious corral.

"Lieut. Rawlins has left the above station of Major O'Farral, Ohio volunteers, but occupied by Messrs. Merchant and Wheeler, traders, who formerly owned the station that was destroyed there; the property is subject to our order at any time. The command also made a good and substantial bridge on Sweetwater; three of our teams crossed over; the mail bridge would have been $200 per wagon, this bridge is free, and also in charge of Major O'Farral. Several emigration companies crossed during the time the command was there, free. One company presented us with a good wagon, which Lieut. Rawlins handed over to Captain Harmon. "

"I have had frequent interviews with Col. Collins and officers; they have behaved very gentlemanly, and expressed themselves much pleased with our exertions, and seemed disposed to render us every assistance to contribute to our comfort.

"Col. Collins is decidedly against killing Indians indiscriminately, and will not take any general measures, save on the defensive, until he can ascertain satisfactorily by whom the depredations have been committed, and then not resort to killing until he is satisfied that peaceable measures have failed.

"Col. Collins and officers all allow we are best suited to guard this road, both men and horses; they are anxious to return, and if they have any influence, I imagine they will try to get recalled and recommend to Utah to furnish the necessary guard. The Colonel has just left our camp, he has sent for Washakie, chief of the Snakes, with a view to make treaty or obtain information. No sickness at all in camp at present. We are attached to Col. Collins' regiment, Gen. Craig's division, and furnish our muster, descriptive and other returns to that command. Should General Wells require duplicates, we will forward them.

I am sir, yours respectfully,
LOT SMITH."

"Deer Creek, May 16, 1862.
"Governor Fuller—My detachment arrived here yesterday at 3 p.m., encountering no difficulty, save that caused by the mud, snow, etc. We have seen no Indians on the route; found all the mail stations from Green River to this point deserted, all stock having been stolen or removed, and other property abandoned to the mercy of the Indians or white men. We found at the Ice Spring station, which had been robbed on the night of the 27th, a large lock mail—twenty-six sacks, a great portion of which had been cut open and scattered over the prairie. Letters had been opened and pillaged, showing conclusively that some renegade whites were connected with the Indians in the robbery. The mail matter, after being carefully collected and placed in the sacks, I have conveyed to this point, also ten other sacks of lock mail, from the Three Crossings: all of which will be turned over to the mail agent at Lapariel. Twenty miles from this, we will meet men from the East for this purpose. The United States troops from the East will be in this vicinity to-morrow; and, unless otherwise directed by yourself or General Wells, I will return immediately, halting on the Sweet Water to investigate still further the causes of the difficulty, as I have not been able to learn who or what Indians positively have been engaged in the matter; but suppose it to be about thirty renegade Snakes and Bannacks from the north. Some of the party spoke English plainly, and one the German language. Hon. W. H. Hooper and Mr. C. W. West will take passage in the coach that comes for the mail.

R. T. BURTON, Commanding."

General Burton supplements this with the following:

"This year (1862) will be remembered as the season of the highest water ever experienced in the mountains; as a consequence travel (over the mountains) was almost impossible. Some idea may be formed of this matter from the fact that it took this command, with all their energy and exertion, nine days to go to Fort Bridger, a distance of only 113 miles from Salt Lake. Most of our wagons had to be dispensed with at Fort Bridger, at which point we proceeded mainly with pack animals. It is proper, also, to state that we received from the Government officers stationed at the military fort at Fort Bridger, provisions, tents, camp equipage, etc., all that was within their power to grant. From this point (Fort Bridger) all the mail stations were abandoned, many of them burned, some of the coaches still standing upon the road riddled with bullet holes from the attack made by the Indians at the time the drivers and passengers were killed. In some of the mail stations west of the Devil's Gate we found large numbers of mail sacks which had been cut open by Indians and the contents scattered over the ground, which were carefully picked up by my company and carried on to the North Platte and turned over to the mail contractor at that point. The coaches were enabled to come west as far as Lapariel Station, a distance of some thirty miles east of the Platte.

"The expedition was one of the most hazardous and toilsome we were ever called upon to perform but succeeded admirably without the loss of a man or animal. Returned to Salt Lake City thirty days from the time of starting and were mustered out of service by Governor Fuller."

CHAPTER XXIX.

UTAH AGAIN ASKS ADMISSION INTO THE UNION AS A STATE. THE HISTORY AND PASSAGE OF THE ANTI-POLYGAMIC BILL IN THE HOUSE AND SENATE. THE BILL SIGNED BY ABRAHAM LINCOLN. PRESENTATION TO CONGRESS OF THE CONSTITUTION OF THE "STATE OF DESERET."

At this juncture, in the spring of 1862, it is worthy of special notice that Utah was again asking admission into the Union. The Legislature of the proposed "State of Deseret" was then in session. Hons. Wm. H. Hooper and George Q. Cannon were elected senators; the former with the memorial and constitution, went east under the escort of Colonel Burton and his troop; and a dispatch was sent to Apostle Cannon, who was then in England, requesting him to join Mr. Hooper in Washington early in June, which he did. The senators-elect labored diligently in Washington during the remainder of that session of Congress, and, notwithstanding that Utah was not admitted to statehood, she provoked much respect from members of Congress over her conduct at that moment, when it was thought by no inconsiderable portion of the world that the issues of the war would be won by the South. It was universally understood at that time that the sympathies of France and England were with the Southern Confederacy.

It is due to the history to here affirm something of the political views of Utah relative to the Union. Delegate Hooper, December 16th, 1860, in a letter to Apostle George Q. Cannon, said: "I think three-quarters of the Republicans of the House would vote for out admission; but I may be mistaken. Many say they would gladly 'swap' the Gulf States for Utah. I tell them that we show our loyalty by trying to get in, while others are trying to get out, notwithstanding our grievances, which are far greater than any of the seceding States; but that I consider we can redress our grievances better in the Union than out of it."

Now it was with just this view before them that the people of Utah again sought admission into the Union as a State in the spring and summer of 1862.

Ex-Governor Young and his compeers who were proud that so many of their sires were among the men who founded this nation, and then, in a later generation, won for it independence, held, as we see in every view, that the South committed a grave error in seceding. They affirmed that the Southern States should have fought out their issue inside the Union, and under the sanction of the Constitution. They did wrong, the people of Utah thought, in setting up a new confederacy, and firing upon the old flag, thus tarnishing the bright integrity of their cause.

The Mormon view of the great national controversy then, was, that the Southern States should have done precisely what Utah did, and placed themselves on the defensive ground of their rights and institutions, as old as the Union. And it is worthy of special note in the political record of Utah that her Delegate advocated the Union doctrine at the capitol and condemned secession, during the term of the last Congress preceding the dissolution, offering Utah as a political example with words that deserve to be imperishable in history: "We can redress our grievances better in the Union than out of it."

In the House of Representatives, April 8, 1862, Mr. Morrill, of Vermont, by unanimous consent, introduced a bill to punish and prevent the practice of polygamy in the Territories of the United States, and for other purposes, and to disapprove and annul certain acts of the Legislative Assembly of the Territory of Utah; which was read a first and second time, and referred to the Committee on Territories.

April 28.—Mr. Ashley, from the Committee on Territories, reported back, with a recommendation that it do pass, a bill (H. R. No. 391) to punish and prevent the practice of polygamy in the Territories of the United States and other places, and disapproving and annulling certain acts of the Territorial Legislature of Utah.

The bill was read.

Mr. Morrill, of Vermont. I desire to say to the House that this is the identical bill passed about two years ago, when there was an elaborate report made by a gentleman from Tennessee, Mr. Nelson, and when it received the almost unanimous support of the House. The only difference between the two bills is this: that bill excepted from its provisions the District of Columbia, and that exception is stricken out in this bill. I presume there is no member of the House who is desirous to discuss this measure, and I move the previous question.

Mr. Maynard. I ask the gentleman from Vermont to allow me to suggest a single verbal amendment, rather a matter of taste than otherwise.

Mr. Morrill, of Vermont. I will hear the suggestion.

Mr. Maynard. It is to strike out the word "nevertheless" in the proviso to the first section. It has no business there; it is surplusage.

Mr. Morrill, of Vermont. Well, if the gentleman from Tennessee says that "nevertheless" has no business there, I presume he is right; and I have no objection to the amendment.

Mr. Maynard. I offer the amendment. I have no speech to make about it.

The amendment was agreed to.

Mr. Cradlebaugh. I ask the gentleman from Vermont to allow me to offer an amendment.

Mr. Morrill, of Vermont. I prefer to have the bill pass as it is.

Mr. Cradlebaugh. I think if the gentleman understood the character of the amendment he would not object. It is merely to correct the bill, and not for the purpose of throwing any impediments in the way of its passage. The bill, in its present shape, does not amount to anything.

The Speaker. Does the gentleman withdraw the demand for the previous question?

Mr. Morrill, of Vermont. I decline to do so.

The previous question was seconded, and the main question ordered.

The bill was ordered to be engrossed, and read a third time; and being engrossed, it was accordingly read the third time.

Mr. Morrill, of Vermont. I move the previous question on the passage of the bill.

Mr. Biddle. Is all debate necessarily cut off at this time?

The Speaker. It will be if the previous question is sustained.

Mr. Biddle. There are some of us who would like to hear debate, if not to participate in it.

The Speaker. Does the gentleman withdraw the demand for the previous question?

Mr. Morrill, of Vermont. I decline to do so and call for tellers.

Tellers were ordered; and Messrs. Cox and Chamberlain were appointed.

The House divided; and the tellers reported—ayes sixty-five, noes not counted. So the previous question was seconded.

The main question was ordered to be put; and being put, the bill was passed.

In the Senate, June 3rd— Mr. Bayard. I move to take up House bill No. 391. It was reported back from the Committee on the Judiciary, with amendments, about three weeks ago.

It is a bill that ought to be acted upon.

The motion was agreed to; and the bill (H. F. No. 391) to punish the practice of polygamy in the Territories of the United States, and other places, and disapproving and annulling certain acts of the Legislative Assembly of the Territory of Utah, was considered as in committee of the Whole.

The amendment of the Committee on Judiciary was to strike out all after the enacting clause, and insert, as a substitute: That every person having a husband or wife living, who shall marry any other person, whether married or single, in a Territory of the United States, or other place over which the United States have exclusive jurisdiction, shall, except in the cases specified in the proviso to this section, be adjudged guilty of bigamy, and upon conviction thereof, shall be punished by a fine not exceeding $500, and by imprisonment for a term not exceeding five years: Provided nevertheless, That this section shall not extend to any person by reason of any former marriage whose husband or wife by such marriage shall have been absent for five successive years without being known to such person within that time to be living; nor to any person by reason of any former marriage which shall have been dissolved by the decree of a competent court; nor to any person by reason of any former marriage which shall have been annulled or pronounced void by the sentence or decree of a competent court on the ground of nullity of the marriage contract.

Sec. 2. And be it further enacted, That the following ordinance of the provisional government of the State of Deseret, so called, namely: "An ordinance incorporating the Church of Jesus Christ of Latter-day Saints," passed February 8, in the year 1851, and adopted, re-enacted, and made valid by the Governor and Legislative Assembly of the Territory of Utah, by an act passed January 19, in the year 1855, entitled, "An act in relation to the compilation and revision of the laws and resolutions in force in Utah Territory, their publication and distribution," and all other acts and parts of acts heretofore passed by the said Legislative Assembly of the Territory of Utah, which establish, support, maintain, shield, or countenance polygamy, be, and the same hereby are, disapproved and annulled: Provided, That this act shall be so limited and construed as not to affect or interfere with the right of property legally acquired under the ordinance heretofore mentioned, nor with the right "to worship God according to the dictates of conscience," but only to annul all acts and laws which establish, maintain, protect, or countenance the practice of polygamy, evasively called spiritual marriage, however disguised by legal or ecclesiastical solemnities, sacraments, ceremonies, consecrations, or other contrivances.

Sec. 3. And be it further enacted, That it shall not be lawful for any corporation or association for religious or charitable purposes to acquire or hold real estate in any Territory of the United States during the existence of the Territorial government of a greater value than $100,000; and all real estate acquired or held by any such corporation or association contrary to the provisions of this act, shall be forfeited and escheat to the United States: Provided, That existing vested rights in real estate shall not be impaired by the provisions of this section.

Mr. Bayard. I will state, very briefly, the difference between the bill as proposed to be amended by the Judiciary Committee, and the bill as passed by the House of Representatives. The bill of the House is intended to punish the crime of polygamy, or bigamy properly speaking, when committed in any Territory of the United States; but, in point of fact, it goes beyond that—it punishes cohabitation without marriage. The committee, in their amendments, have so altered the first section as to provide for the punishment of the crime of bigamy, leaving the punishment for a similar offense, where marriage had been contracted elsewhere, to the State where it was contracted. We thought that clearly preferable, and that it would be of no utility to carry the act beyond the evil intended to be remedied, which was to put down polygamy, as a part of the recognized legal institutions of Utah.

There is a mistake in printing as to the second section. The second section of the bill is not altered at all; we leave it precisely the same as it was in the original bill. It repeals the ordinance of Utah, commonly called "An ordinance incorporating the Church of Jesus Christ of Latter-day Saints." It is precisely in words like the second section of the House bill, which is not altered in any respect.

The third section is an amendment of the committee, and it is in the nature 01 a mortmain law. The object is to prevent the accumulation of real estate in the hands of ecclesiastical corporations in Utah. Though that Territory is large, the value of real estate is not of large amount; and the object of the section is to prevent the accumulation of the property and wealth of the community in the hands of what may be called theocratic institutions, inconsistent with our form of government. In my own judgment it would be wiser to limit the amount of real estate that could be held by any corporation of that character in a Territory, to the value of $50,000, I think $100,000 is too much. I am satisfied that there is great danger in that Territory, under its present government, that the ecclesiastical institutions which prevail there will ultimately become the owners in perpetuity of all the valuable land in that Territory, and so afford a nucleus for the permanence of their general institutions unless a stop be put to it by act of Congress.

I have now stated the provisions of the amendment as proposed by the committee. The first section of the bill is altered so as to punish the crime of bigamy but leaving the question of cohabitation or mere adultery apart from the crime of bigamy, without reference to any action of Congress. The second section is exactly the same as the section in the House bill. The third section is a new one, the object of which is to operate in the nature of a mortmain law, to prevent the entire property of that Territory being accumulated in perpetuity in the hands of a species of theocratic institutions.

The amendment was agreed to.

Mr. Hale. I shall probably vote tor the bill; but I should like to know from the chairman of the committee if its provisions are not inconsistent with ——

Mr. Bayard. I move to strike out "$100,000" and insert "$50,000," in the third section.

Mr. Hale. I will wait until that is decided.

Mr. Bayard. I make that motion.

The Vice President. The Senator's motion is not now in order, the amendment of the committee having been adopted. It will be in order when the bill shall have been reported to the Senate.

Mr. Hale. I was only going to say that I had been looking at a decision of the Supreme Court in which the rights of Congress over the Territories are examined with some care, and it occurred to me that possibly the provisions of this bill might be inconsistent with some of the doctrines and dogmas of that decision.

I refer to a case decided in the Supreme Court at the December term of 1856, entitled, "Dred Scott vs. Sandford," and the doctrine was pretty thoroughly gone over in that decision as to how far the powers of Congress extended over the Territories It strikes me that by analogy this bill infringes upon that decision, for I remember that one of the exponents of the true faith on this floor used to illustrate this dogma at least as often as once a month by saying that the same law prevailed as to the regulation of the relations of husband and wife, parent and child, and master and servant. I think at least once a month for years that was proclaimed to be the law. If the national Legislature have no more power over the relations of husband and wife—and that seems to be the one touched here—than over master and slave, it seems to me that if we mean to maintain that respect which is due to so august a tribunal as the Supreme Court of the United States, we ought to read the Dred Scott decision over again, and see if we are not in danger of running counter to it. It strikes me decidedly that we are; and at this time when there is so much necessity for invoking all the reverence there is in the country for the tribunals of the country, it seems to me we ought to tread delicately when we trench upon things that have been so solemnly decided by the Supreme Court as this has. But, as the gentleman who reports the bill is a member of the Judiciary Committee, if it is clearly his opinion that we can pass this bill without trenching upon the doctrine of the Dred Scott decision, I shall inter pose no objection.

Mr. Bayard. I will not be drawn into any argument. It is sufficient to say that I have read the decision to which the honorable Senator alludes, I think with some care, and in my judgment this bill is entirely within its principles as well as within the decision itself. I cannot see the contrariety. I shall not enter into the argument now. To me it is very palpable that the bill is within the power of Congress and is necessary legislation.

The bill was reported to the Senate.

Mr. Bayard. I propose now in the fifth line of the third section to strike out "one hundred" and insert "fifty," so as to make the limitation of real estate held by an ecclesiastical corporation, $50,000.

The amendment to the amendment was agreed to.

The amendment made as in the Committee of the Whole, as amended, was concurred in.

Mr. McDougall. It may not be considered a very judicious thing to object to this measure here, but I feel called upon to do it. There is no Senator, I think, who objects more strongly than I do to the vicious practice that obtains in the Territory of Utah; but I think we have just at this time trouble enough on our hands without invoking further trouble. We have had our communication with California cut off by the Indians on the line of communication. We have already had a Utah war that cost the Government a large amount of money. We are to have a controversy with them as to their admission as a State. They are clamoring for that now. In my judgment, no particular good is to be accomplished by the passage of this bill at present. When the time does come that our communication across the continent is complete, then we can take jurisdiction where we have power, and can employ power for the purpose of correcting these abuses. I suggest to gentlemen, in the first place, that they cut off most likely the communication across the continent to our possessions on the Pacific by a measure of legislation of this kind, which will be well calculated to invite, certainly will invite, great hostility, and interfere with the general interests of the country. It will cost the Government a large amount if communication is interfered with and do no substantial good. I do not think the measure at this time is well advised. It is understood its provisions will be a dead letter upon our statute-book. Its provisions will be either ignored or avoided. If Senators will look the question fairly in the face, and consider how important it is that we should have no difficulties now on our western frontier between us and the Pacific, how poorly we can afford to go into the expenditure of a large amount of money to overcome difficulties that will be threatened on the passage of this bill, and then consider the little amount of substantial good which will result from it, I think they will hesitate before they pass it. The impolicy of its present passage will cause my colleague and self, after consultation, to vote against the bill.

The amendment was ordered to be engrossed, and the bill to be read a third time.

Mr. Howard. 1 ask for the yeas and nays on the passage of the bill.

Mr. Sumner. I was about to make the same request.

The yeas and nays were ordered, and being taken, resulted—yeas 37, nays 2: as follows: Yeas—Messrs. Anthony, Bayard, Browning, Chandler, Collamer, Cowan, Davis, Dixon, Doolittle, Fessenden, Foot, Foster, Grimes, Hale, Harlan, Harris, Howard, Howe, King, Lane of Indiana, Lane of Kansas, Morrill, Rice, Saulsbury, Sherman, Simmons, Stark, Sumner, Ten Eyck, Thomson, Trumbull, Wade, Wilkinson, Willey, Wilmot, Wilson of Massachusetts, and Wright—37.

Nays—Messrs. Latham and McDougall—2.

So the bill was passed.

The title was amended so as to read, "A bill to punish and prevent the practice of polygamy in the Territories of the United States and other places and disapproving and annulling certain acts of the Legislative Assembly of the Territory of Utah."

In the House of Representatives, June 5, 1862— Mr. Morrill, of Vermont. I ask the unanimous consent of the House to take up and consider at this time the amendments of the Senate to an act (H. R No. 391) to punish and prevent the practice of polygamy in the Territories of the United States and other places and annulling certain acts of the legislative Assembly of the Territory of Utah.

Objection was made.

Mr. Moorhead. I ask the unanimous consent of the House to introduce a resolution of inquiry.

Mr. Wickliffe. I object.

Mr. Bingham. I call for the regular order of business.

In the House of Representatives, June 17, 1868— The Speaker laid before the House bill of House (No. 391) to punish and prevent the practice of polygamy in the Territories of the United States and other places, disapproving and annulling certain acts of the Legislative Assembly of the Territory of Utah—reported from the Senate with amendments.

The Speaker. The bill and amendments will be referred to the Committee on Territories.

Mr. Morrill, of Vermont. I object to these bills being taken up for reference. There is no necessity for the reference of this bill.

The Speaker. The order has been made.

Mr. Morrill, of Vermont. I move to reconsider the vote by which the order was made; and on that motion I demand tellers.

Tellers were ordered; and Messrs. Morrill, of Vermont, and Olin were appointed.

The tellers reported—ayes sixty-eight, noes not counted.

So the motion to reconsider was agreed to.

In the House of Representatives, June 17— The next bill taken up was (H. R. No. 391) to punish the practice of polygamy in the Territories of the United States and other places and disapproving and annulling certain acts of the Legislative Assembly of the Territory of Utah, with Senate amendments.

The amendments were read.

Mr. Phelps, of Missouri, I think, Mr. Speaker, that this is rather hasty legislation. I should not be at all surprised if it were ascertained that the Catholic Church in the city of Santa Fe owns real estate to the amount of more than fifty thousand dollars under grants made by the Mexican Government. I was about to submit a motion that the bill be referred to the Committee on the Judiciary. I recollect very well that, in the hurry and haste of legislation, a bill passed the House to prohibit polygamy in the Territories, which indirectly sanctioned it within the District of Columbia, or inflicted no punishment for it here. I desire that this matter shall be critically examined, and therefore I think it should be referred to the Judiciary Committee.

Mr. Morrill, of Vermont. I am perfectly willing that the bill shall be passed over informally until the gentleman from Missouri can inform himself on the subject.

Mr. Phelps, of Missouri. I have no objection to letting the bill remain on the Speaker's table. Let the amendments be printed and let us know what we are legislating upon.

Mr. Morrill, of Vermont. I have no objection to that.

It was so ordered.

In the House of Representatives, June 24, 1862— An act, (H. R. No. 391) to punish the practice of polygamy in the Territories of the United States and other places and disapproving and annulling certain acts of the Legislative Assembly of the Territory of Utah, with Senate amendments thereon.

Mr. Morrill, of Vermont. I desire to say, in reference to the objection made by the gentleman from Missouri [Mr. Phelps] last week, to one of the provisions of this bill, that I understand the Roman Catholic church at Santa Fe has property exceeding $50,000 in amount, but that is protected under treaty stipulations. His objection, therefore, is not valid. I now move the previous question on concurring with the Senate amendments.

The previous question was seconded, and the main question ordered.

The amendments were read.

The amendments of the Senate were concurred in. Mr. Morrill of Vermont moved to reconsider the vote by which the amendments were concurred in; and also moved to lay the motion to reconsider on the table.

The latter motion was agreed to.

In the House of Representatives, June 30, 1862— Mr. Granger, from the Committee on Enrolled Bills, reported as a truly enrolled bill an act (H. R. No. 391) to punish and prevent the practice of polygamy in the Territories of the United States and other places, and disapproving and annulling certain acts of the Legislative Assembly of the Territory of Utah.

In the House of Representatives, July 2, 1862— A message was received from the President of the United States, informing the House that he had approved and signed an act (H. R. 391) to punish and prevent the practice of polygamy in the Territories of the United States and other places, and disapproving and annulling certain acts of the Legislative Assembly of the Territory of Utah.

In the House of Representatives, on the 9th of June, 1862, Hon. J. M. Bernhisel, Delegate from Utah, presented the Constitution of the State of Deseret and the memorial accompanying it, asking for admission into the Union on an equal footing with the original States, which were received and referred to the Committee on Territories. On the 10th the Vice-President presented the same in the Senate, when Mr. Latham, of California, moved to print the constitution and memorial, and to admit the senators-elect, Messrs. W. H. Hooper and George Q. Cannon to the floor of the Senate, which motion was referred to the committee on Territories, in that branch of the National Legislature. The next day Mr. Latham offered a resolution to admit Messrs. Hooper and Cannon, claiming to be senators from Deseret, to the floor of the Senate, which was laid over.

CHAPTER XXX.

FOURTH OF JULY PROCLAMATION BY THE CITY COUNCIL. THE CITY'S LOYALTY. THE TWO GOVERNORS. GREAT SPEECH OF GOVERNOR HARDING. THE CITY HONORS THE CALIFORNIA SENATOR. THANKSGIVING PROCLAMATION. A CHANGE IN GOVERNOR HARDING'S CONDUCT.

Great Salt Lake City this year deemed it a duty to make special call for the Fourth of July, whereas, formerly, either the Governor of the Territory, or the Lieutenant-General of the militia, made proclamation and gave the order of the day. It signified that Salt Lake City was, with well-considered formality, making a record that it upheld the Union as an everlasting covenant of the American States. The following Preamble and Resolutions were passed by the City Council of Salt Lake City, June 28th, 1862: "Whereas, While we lament the deplorable condition of our once happy country, the independence of which was purchased by the best blood of our sires, we hail with pleasure the approaching anniversary of the birthday of the Nation, and in view of perpetuating our free and liberal institutions which have for so long a time inspired the patriotism of every true American citizen, and the strangers of other climes, who have sought an asylum under the protecting aegis of our glorious Constitution; therefore,

"Resolved, That we will celebrate the eighty-sixth anniversary of our National independence.

"Resolved, That a committee of five be appointed, in behalf of the City Council, to arrange the programme and order of celebration.

"Resolved, That Lieutenant-General Wells and staff be respectfully solicited to co-operate in the celebration of the day, with such of the military of the district, and the several bands, as may be deemed proper.

"Resolved, That the State, Federal, Territorial and County officers be invited to take part in the celebration and join in the procession, and that the invitation be extended to strangers and citizens generally, to participate in the ceremonies at the Bowery.

"The following appointments for the occasion were then made, viz: "Committee of Arrangements: Messrs. Wm. Clayton, J. C. Little, Theodore McKean, Enoch Reese, and Nathaniel H. Felt.

"Furnishing Committee: Alonzo H. Raleigh, Elijah F. Sheets, and Isaac Groo.

"Marshals of the Day: Col. Robert T. Burton and Majors John Sharp and Andrew Cunningham.

ROBERT CAMPBELL, City Recorder."

On the 7th of July Stephen S. Harding of Indiana, the new Governor of Utah Territory, arrived in the city and received a hearty welcome; Judges Waite and Drake arrived a few days later.

The Pioneer Day of this year was celebrated with a grand pageantry and extraordinary enthusiasm. The procession halted in front of ex-Governor Young's mansion, where with his counselors, H. C. Kimball and Daniel H. Wells, he joined it, accompanied by Governor Harding, Secretary Fuller, Judges Waite and Drake,

Superintendent Doty, Mr. Fred Cook, assistant treasurer of the Overland Mail Co., Mr. James Street, of the U. P. Telegraph Co., and H. S. Rumfield, Esq. It may be said that the "forces of the Gentiles" united this year to celebrate the anniversary of the Utah Pioneers. It was computed that there were under the branches of the "Old Bowery" five thousand persons, besides the thousands congregated outside. The most unique feature of the day was the introduction and speech of Governor Harding.

Governor Young invited Governor Harding to address the people; and on the two Governors taking the stand, there was a perfect stillness in the vast assembly; but, on Governor Young saying, "I have the pleasure of presenting Governor Harding, who will make a speech," the stillness of the multitude was broken and the Governor was greeted with cheering.

SPEECH OF GOVERNOR HARDING.

"Fellow Citizens—And in that word, I mean all of you, of all ages, sexes and conditions—I am pleased at being with you to-day, and of being introduced in the agreeable manner you have just witnessed. I have desired the opportunity of looking upon such a vast concourse of the people of Utah, at one time; and, as such an occasion now presents itself, it u right and proper that I should say a few things to you.

"You have doubtless been informed before now that the President of the United States, by and with the advice and consent of the Senate, has appointed me to the office of Governor of this Territory. I have come amongst you to enter upon the discharge of the high and important duties that have devolved upon me, and when I greatly distrust my own ability, yet I cannot but hope that, with your assistance, I shall be able to discharge those duties to your satisfaction, and with strict fidelity to the Government, whose servant I am.

"If I know my own heart, I come amongst you a messenger of peace and good will. I have no wrongs—either real or imaginary, to complain of, and no religious prejudices to overcome—[applause]. Believing, as I do, that the Constitution of the United States secures to every citizen the right to worship God according to the dictates of his own conscience; and holding, further, that the Constitution itself is dependent for its support and maintenance on the preservation of that sacred right, it follows, as a corollary, that, under no pretext whatever, will I consent to its violation in this particular, by any official act of mine, whilst Governor of this Territory—[tremendous applause.] "In a Government like ours, based upon the freest exercise of conscience, religion is a matter between man and his Maker, and not between man and the Government, and for the honest exercise of duties inculcated by his religious faith and conscience, so long as he does not infringe upon the rights of others, equally as sacred as his own, he is not responsible to any human tribunal, other than that which is found in the universal judgment of mankind [hear hear]. If the right of conscience of the minority depended upon the will of the majority, then, in a government like ours, that same minority in a future day might control the conscience of the majority of to-day—when by superior cunning and finesse a political canvass had been won in its favor, and thus alternately would it be in the power of either when elevated to the seat of the law-makers to impose a despotism upon the conscience of its adversary only equaled by the 'Index Expurgatoris' against which the Protestant world so justly complained [applause].

"It has long been a maxim and accepted as true by our people, 'That it is safe to tolerate error, so long as truth is left free to combat it.' Who are in error, and in what that error consists in matters of speculative theology, are questions only cognizable at the bar of heaven. It has been the fate of propogandists of new ideas and religious dogmas, without regard to their truth or falsity, to meet with opposition, often ending in the most cruel persecution.

Hoary-headed error, claiming for itself the immunity of ages, glares with jaundiced eyes upon all new ideas, which refuse to pay to it its accustomed homage.

I know of no law of the human mind that makes this age an exception to the rule. Nevertheless, he who founds his ideas and theories on truth, correlative with his physical and spiritual being, and consequently in harmony with the law of nature, must ultimately succeed; whilst he who builds upon falsehood roust share the fate of him who built his house upon the sand. This is not only a declaration of divine truth but is in accordance with all human experience. The great highway of man's civilization and progress is strewn with the wrecks of a thousand systems—once the hope of their founders and challenging the confidence of mankind [hear, hear]. But I must limit this dissertation and will sum up in a few words what I have intended to say on this branch of the subject.

"The founders of our Constitution fully comprehended these ideas which I have so briefly glanced at, and they clothed the citizen with absolute immunity in the exercise of his rights of conscience, and thence the protecting shield of the Constitution around him, and over him, in all the diverging paths that lead the enquirer in his researches after truth in the dim unknown of speculative theology.

"But I must not detain you, I leave this part of the subject, and address myself to the occasion that has called together this mighty multitude.

"On every hand I behold a miracle of labor. Fifteen years ago to-day, and your Pioneers, by their heroism and devotion to a principle, consecrated this valley to a civilization wonderful 'to the stranger within your gates,' and in the developments of which a new era will be stamped not only upon the history of our own country, but on the world. You have indeed 'caused the desert to blossom as the rose.' Waving fields of gold; gardens containing all that is necessary for the comfort of civilized man; 'shrubberies that a Shenstone might have envied;' orchards bending beneath the promise of most luscious fruit,—now beautify the fields which your industry has filled with new life, and where but fifteen years ago the genius of solitude, from yon snowcapped peak, stood marking on her rocky tablets the centuries of desolation and death that rested on these same fields, since the upheaval force of nature formed the mighty zone that separates the two oceans that wash the shores of our continent.

"Wonderful progress! wonderful people! If you shall be content, as I doubt not you will be, to enjoy the blessings with which you are surrounded, and abide your time, and enjoy your privileges under a benign and just government, 'Imperium in Imperio' and not attempt to reverse this order of things absolutely necessary under our form of government; and above all things, if you will act up to the line of your duty contained in that one grand article of your faith, 'We believe in being honest, true, chaste, temperate, benevolent, virtuous and upright, and in doing good to all men,' you cannot fail to obtain that ultimate success [applause] which is the great desideratum of your hopes. Honestly conform to the standard of your creed and faith, and though you may for a time be 'cast down,' you cannot be destroyed [great applause]; for the power of the Eternal One will be in your midst, though no mortal eye may behold the ' pillar of cloud and of fire' [applause]. As the Great Master of sculpture gathered and combined all the perfections of the human face into one divine model, so you, in that one grand article, have bound into one golden sheaf, all the Christian virtues that underlie our civilization.

"But this must suffice. I, perhaps, have said more than I ought to have said, and yet I cannot see how I could have said less. If my words shall be as kindly received by you as they have been honestly and frankly uttered by me, and we will act accordingly, my mission among you cannot fail of being alike profitable to you and to the government that I represent [hear, hear].

"This is the hour when your loyalty to our common country is most acceptable and grateful to the heart of every patriot. Be but content and abide your time, and your reward will be as great as it is certain. Duty to ourselves, to our God and our country calls upon us to cast aside every prejudice and to rally around the Constitution and the flag of our fathers, and if need be, to baptize them anew with our own blood. The Constitution will not perish, that flag will not trail in the dust, but they will both come out of the present fiery ordeal, redeemed, regenerated, and disenthralled, by the genius of universal liberty and justice [great applause]."

In view of Governor Harding's subsequent course the foregoing speech will presently assume the character of a page of Utah history.

Senator Milton S. Latham, of California, passed through the city early in November on his way to Washington. The City Council in its session on the evening preceding his arrival, adopted a preamble and resolutions tendering him the hospitality of the city during his sojourn here. The Senator was waited upon by Councilors Little, Felt and Groo, to whom he returned his thanks for the complimentary resolutions of the Council, but his short stay prevented his acceptance. Latham and McDougall, California's two Senators, were the only ones who voted "nay" on the passage of the anti-polygamic bill of 1862. The honor shown to Senator Latham signified that Great Salt Lake City was returning thanks to California for her minority vote in protest of the bill.

Towards the close of the year 1862, an entire change of feeling came over Governor Harding towards "his Mormon people," especially those of the leaders; and singularly enough it began with his following

THANKSGIVING PROCLAMATION:
"Man, in all ages of the world, in the development of his moral nature, has demonstrated that he is not less a religious than a social being.

"Whether we study his attributes at the shrine of Isis in her ancient temples; at the rude altar of the wandering Hebrew amidst his flocks and herds; in the fierce games of the warlike Greek and Roman, or in that simple and more touching act of the Hindoo husbandman, as he lays a portion of his harvest at the feet of his rude idol, still do all these acts of devotion, rude and unseemly as they may appear to us, demonstrate his character as a devotional being—that his spiritual nature cannot be satisfied 'with bread alone,' but requires 'that manna of consolation that comes down from above.' "That without this, the soul is ever crying out like a wandering outcast,"

' Oh, Father of Life, withhold not thy mercies from me.'

"If these manifestations have been in all ages of the world, ere the shepherds of Galilee heard the song of 'Peace and good will to men,' much more should we feel it to be our duty, as a Christian people, to inculcate even a higher spirit of devotion, and manifest by our acts, our dependence upon God, the God of our fathers, the Supreme Ruler of the Universe, from whose bounteous hands 'proceed every good and perfect gift.' "He has kept the people here, guarded by His eternal ramparts, as in the 'hollow of His hand.' He has said Peace, Peace, and the troubled elements became still. The angel of his mercy has stretched out her burning scepter, and the elements became purified; disease and mildew and blight vanished to their silent caves, and Plenty poured out upon you from her abundant horn. Your granaries are full to overflowing; no scourge has fallen upon you, but the God of Peace has reigned triumphantly in your midst, while in other and fairer portions of the land, the Demon of Civil War has driven his blood-stained chariot over desolated fields and deserted cities—the plowshare has been beaten into a sword, and the pruning-hook into the murderous knife, and waving harvests, ready for the reaper, have not been gathered into barns, but ' plowed under"

' By gory felloes of the cannon's wheels.'

"It is meet that at such a time as this, that the good people of this Territory, following, not only the examples of their fathers, but a precedent set by its first Governor, should dedicate, and set apart at least one day in the year, for thanksgiving and praise to Almighty God for the manifold mercies and blessings that he has vouchsafed unto us, and that He will continue his mercies. That He will put it into the hearts of our rulers to rule in righteousness, and that 'Judgment may not be turned aside in the streets.' That peace may again return to our bleeding country, and that the institutions of our fathers may come forth purified from the sins which have weighed down a nation and brought the keen displeasure and wrath of God upon us.

"Therefore, I, Stephen S. Harding, Governor of the Territory of Utah, do hereby set apart Thursday, the first day of January, proximo, as a day of Thanksgiving and Praise to Almighty God, for all His mercies to us as a people, and recommend and request a general observance of it to that end, that here, on the threshold of a New Year, we may manifest in a proper spirit our dependence on Him, and supplicate His Omnipotent Power to continue to protect and guard us from future evils, as a nation and people.

"In testimony whereof, I have hereunto set my hand, and caused [L.S.] the seal of said Territory to be affixed.

"Done at Great Salt Lake City, in the Territory of Utah, this second day of December, in the year of our Lord one thousand eight hundred and sixty-two.

(Signed) STEPHEN S. HARDING.

"By the Governor, Frank Fuller, Secretary."

This proclamation, which greeted Great Salt Lake City with a classic swell, was passed unheeded, not only by our city, but by the entire Territory. Governor Harding took the non-response of the citizens, not only as marked personal slight to himself, but also as a scoff at the Federal power embodied in his Excellency, Stephen S. Harding. But the citizens, in not holding high "temple service for Thanksgiving and

Praise to Almighty God," on the day appointed by Governor Harding, intended no personal slight towards him or scoff at Federal authority.

But the salient point of the history to the secular mind would be that, the non-observance of this Thanksgiving Day, brought Stephen S. Harding to the full realization of the fact that, though he was Governor of Utah, Brigham Young was still Governor of the Mormon people. Therein was the intolerable offence to his Excellency.

A few days afterwards the Utah Legislature met. In the State House, Stephen S. Harding could teach the people that he, and not Brigham Young, was their Governor. At least such was the intent of the lesson conveyed in his message. Mr. Stenhouse notes the example thus: "The Governor's message to the Legislature, in December, was the tocsin of war, and was considered a very offensive document. He referred to the passage of the anti-polygamic law of July of that year and warned the people against the pernicious counsels of the apostles and prophets who had recommended it "to be openly disregarded and defied." The manner of the delivery of the message was worse than the matter, and probably no Legislature ever felt more humiliated and insulted. It was painful to observe the legislators, as they sat quiet and immovable, hearing their faith contemned. It was interpreted as an open and gratuitous insult on the part of the Executive."

CHAPTER XXXI.

THE CALIFORNIA VOLUNTEERS ORDERED TO UTAH. SKETCH OF GENERAL CONNOR. HIS FIRST MILITARY ORDER. INTERESTING LETTER FROM THE COMMAND. PETITION OF THE VOLUNTEERS TO GO TO THE POTOMAC. MARCH FROM FORT CRITTENDEN TO SALT LAKE. PREPARATIONS FOR BATTLE AT THE JORDAN. ZION AT PEACE. SURPRISE OF THE TROOPS. THE HALT AT THE GOVERNORS MANSION HIS ADDRESS TO THE TROOPS. CAMP DOUGLAS.

Although the Utah militia had been offered for the protection of the Overland Mail and Telegraph line, Secretary Stanton deemed it prudent to entrust the permanent service to the California Volunteers rather than to the Utah militia.

Utah was placed under a military surveillance during the war, and California was made her sister's keeper. At least, such was the interpretation placed upon the military mission of General Connor and his command, to whom is devoted the following historical sketch, quickly connecting as it does with the main branch of the history of Great Salt Lake City.

General Patrick Edward Connor was born in the south of Ireland, March 17, 1820. At an early age he emigrated with his parents to New York City, where he was educated. In 1839 he entered the regular army, at the age of 18, during the Florida war. He left the service in November of 1844, and returned to New York, where he entered into mercantile business; but in the early part of 1846 emigrated to Texas. The war with Mexico broke out that year, and young Connor, as Captain of the Texas Volunteers, was the second volunteer officer mustered into service, in the regiment of Albert Sidney Johnston, whom they elected Colonel.

Connor was with his company at the battles of Palo Alto, Resaca de la Palma, and Buena Vista. In the latter battle he was severely wounded, being the first officer who bore the scars of war, for which honor he now draws a full Captain's pension.

Shortly after the close of the Mexican war, Captain Connor emigrated to California, where he engaged in business till the breaking out of our great civil war. Immediately the gallant officer tendered his services to the Governor of California and was appointed by him Colonel of the Third California Infantry.

The California Volunteers entered the service with the full expectation of being called directly to the theatre of war, for both officers and men were fired with a martial spirit becoming California in the nation's crisis. It is doubtful, indeed, if this military fervor would have been kindled had the Volunteers known that they were about to be ordered to Utah by the Government, to watch the Mormons, lest their leaders should take advantage of our national calamity and proclaim a rebellion. Some of the officers and men, it is understood, gave way to occasional fits of ill-humor, very pardonable in men who, panting for military glory, as well as inspired by patriotism, had offered their lives in defense of the Union, only to find themselves, in the sequel, transported to our then Rocky Mountain isolation.

It was in May, 1862, that Colonel Connor was ordered with his regiment to Utah. His command consisted of the Third California Infantry and a part of the Second California Cavalry. He took up his line of march in July, 1862.

On assuming command of the Military District of Utah, Colonel Connor issued the following military order:

"Headquarters, District of Utah, Fort Churchill, August 6th, 1862.

"Order No. 1.—The undersigned, pursuant to orders from Department Headquarters, hereby assumes command of the Military District of Utah, comprising the Territories of Nevada and Utah.

"In assuming command of the district I especially enjoin upon all disbursing officers the necessity of being particularly attentive, careful and economical in their disbursements of the public funds; and that they in no instance purchase from persons who have at any time, by word or act, manifested disloyalty to the Federal Government.

"Being credibly informed that there are in this district persons who, while claiming and receiving protection to life and property, are endeavoring to destroy and defame the principles and institutions of our Government under whose benign influence they have been so long protected, it is therefore most rigidly enforced upon all commanders of posts, camps and detachments, to cause to be promptly arrested and closely confined until they have taken the oath of allegiance to the Government of the United States, all persons who from this date shall be guilty of uttering treasonable sentiments against the Government; and upon a repetition of the offense to be again arrested and confined until the fact shall be communicated to these headquarters. Traitors shall not utter treasonable sentiments in this district with impunity, but must seek some more genial soil, or receive the punishment they so richly merit. By order of

P. EDWARD CONNOR,
Col. 3rd Infantry, C. V., Com. Dist. of Utah.
"James W. Stillman, A. A. A. General."

The Deseret News of September 10, notes: "Col. P. E. Connor, commanding the California Volunteers, arrived in the city yesterday afternoon. The Volunteers remain at Ruby Valley till the Colonel's return, when they will afterwards advance to the place that will be selected as a military post. The Colonel took a stroll about town and looked around with an air of familiarity that indicated that after all Salt Lake City was something of a place, and might not be unpleasant, notwithstanding its desert surroundings."

A correspondent writing to the San Francisco Bulletin in behalf of his comrades, gives a very interesting and suggestive page of history:

"Headquarters Utah District, Ruby Valley, N. T., September 24, 1862.

"The Third Infantry California Volunteers wants to go home—not for the purpose of seeing the old folks, but for the purpose of tramping upon the sacred soil of Virginia, and of swelling the ranks of the brave battlers for the brave old flag. The action of the San Francisco" Quartette and the glory which awaits the California regiment that first lands on the Atlantic coast, combined to make the 700 hearts camped in Ruby Valley pulse vigorously with the patriotic desire to serve their country in shooting traitors instead of eating rations and freezing to death around sage-brush fires, which two are the only military duties to be performed hereabouts. Accordingly a meeting of the officers was called on Tuesday night. A committee was appointed to draft a dispatch to be sent to Gen. Halleck; and each captain was requested to draw up a paper to the purport that the subscriber would authorize the paymaster to withhold from his pay the amount subscribed by him, on the condition, and no other condition, that the regiment be ordered east. Each captain was requested to present this document to his company and report at an adjourned meeting.

"To-day, at 1 p. m., the following sums had been subscribed by the privates and company officers: "Company I, Capt. Lewis, $3,430; Company K, Capt. Hoyt, $3,475; Company H, Capt. Black, $2,550; Company F, (part absent on detailed duty) Capt. Potts, $600; Company C, Capt. May, $3,260; Company E, Capt. Tupper, $4,674; Company G, Capt. Urmy, $7,431.

"That is excellent evidence of the earnest patriotism of our 700 men. In addition to packing a musket, eating salt pork, and tramping over these abominable deserts, they are willing, and actually do, out of their $13 per month, subscribe $25,000 for the privilege of going to the Potomac and getting shot. If California is not proud of them, the God of Washington is; and that is quite as satisfactory. But California cannot help appreciating such a sacrifice upon the part of men who, after giving their time, labor, and if need be, their lives, to their country, now give the last mite of their small pittance. Private Goldthaite, of Company G, alone, subscribed $5000, while the majority of the men gave every cent of their pay.

"The company officers ranged about thus: Second lieutenants, $100 to $200; first lieutenants, $200 to $300; captains, $300 to $500. In some instances that takes more than their pay. The staff officers have not yet pungled, as they are waiting to see what amount will remain to be raised.

"The three companies at Stockton would most undoubtedly equal their comrades. Should they do so, at the average of $3,000 per company the funds would reach upwards of $36,000.

"The following dispatch was sent to Gen. Halleck, with the consent of Gen. George Wright: "' Major General Halleck, Secretary of War, Washington, D. C.

"The Third Infantry, Cal. Vols., has been in service one year, and marched 600 miles; it is well officered and thoroughly drilled; is of no service on the Overland Mail route, as there is cavalry sufficient for its protection in Utah District. The regiment will authorize the Paymaster to withhold $30,000 of pay now due if Government will order it East; and it pledges Gen. Halleck never to disgrace the flag, himself or California. The men enlisted to fight traitors and can do so more effectively than raw recruits; and ask that they may be placed at least on the same footing in regard to transportation East. If the above sum is insufficient, we will pay our own passages from San Francisco to Panama.

"' By request of the regiment.
P. EDW. CONNOR,
"' Col, Commanding.
"' Ruby Valley, N. T., September 24, 1862.'"

"So far as anybody can see, there is not a bit more use for infantry out here than there is for topographical engineers. Cavalry is the only efficient arm against Indians, and the companies of the 2nd regiment, in the district, are fully competent to chastise all offenders. Brigham Young offers to protect the entire line with 100 men. Why we were sent here is a mystery. It could not be keep Mormondom in order, for Brigham can thoroughly annihilate us with the 5,000 to 25,000 frontiersmen always at his command."

Towards the middle of October the Volunteers reached the former encampment of U. S. troops at Camp Floyd. Parties who would have been financially benefitted by the Volunteers occupying the vacated quarters at Camp Floyd tried to induce the Colonel to remain there, and, failing that, they sought to intimidate him with the intelligence that the Mormon intended to dispute the passage of the Californians over the Jordan. At the same time, a story was current among the Volunteers that Brigham Young, on hearing of their advance, had out of contempt for them and the nation, cut down the United States flag-staff at Camp Floyd and left it lying on the public road, over which they had to travel.

There was no truth in this reported threat of Mormon resistance; and, as already told, the flag-staff was presented to ex-Governor Young by the officers at Camp Floyd.

A few days after the establishment of Camp Douglas the San Francisco Bulletin published, from the correspondent already noticed, the following very interesting details of the march of the Volunteers from Fort Crittenden and their passage through Great Salt City:

"Jordan Springs, U. T., Saturday, October, 18, 1862.

"The Salt Lake Expedition, numbering 750 men, is within twenty-five miles of the City of the Saints, having marched twenty miles north of Fort Crittenden to-day. From the slope on which our camp is pitched we can discern the white specks which constitute the residences of the modern apostles; but at present we are more interested in the designs and doings of said apostles than in the general appearance of their habitations. I closed yesterday's letter [see Bulletin of 30th October] by mentioning a camp rumor, to the effect that the Mormons would prevent a nearer approach of our troops to the city than Fort Crittenden, and that the banks of the narrow stream called Jordan, which empties the waters of Lake Utah into Great Salt Lake, would form the field of battle. At the time it caused no further thought than as the starting point of rambling conversations respecting Mormondom and the mission which the command has been detailed to execute—both subjects upon which we have but little information. However, at the present writing—sundown— reliable advices received tend to establish the probable truthfulness of the report. When information reached the city, as it did last night, that Col. Connor would not purchase the buildings erected by Johnson's command in 1858 at what was then Camp Floyd, now Fort Crittenden, and that he designed to occupy some locality within striking distance of the heart of Mormondom, the most intense excitement is said to have prevailed. The leaders are represented to be in conclave, meditating upon the question and striving to arrive at a determination, while the people were in a high state of expectancy as to what the leaders would do, what the troops would do, and what they themselves would be called upon to do. The Chief of the Danites—better known perhaps as the Destroying Angels, whose duty it is, if report be true, to place parties odious to the leaders of the Church where they can never tell tales, is represented as riding through the streets offering to bet $500 that we could and should not cross the river Jordan, the bet being untaken. Furthermore, not a single camp rumor, but reliable parties assert that Brigham Young would, when we near Jordan, have us met by commissioners empowered to inform us that the Mormons objected to our close proximity to their city and would forcibly resist an attempt on our part to cross that stream.

"How much truth there may be in these advices, or how much the real state of affairs in Salt Lake is exaggerated I know not. As a faithful correspondent it is only my province to inform you of the exact condition and operations of this command, but further than that I cannot go, and, of course, will not be held responsible for the correctness or incorrectness of the rumors which reach this command. Be they, however, true or untrue, and be the opinion entertained by our Colonel what it may, certain it is that he is moving with the utmost prudence, that thirty rounds of ammunition have just been issued to each man, and that the two 6-pounders are abundantly furnished with destructive missiles, and the 12-pound mountain howitzer amply supplied with shells, that the camp is so pitched upon an open plain that no force can get to it without a fair fight; in short, that every preparation for war that can be made is made, and equally certain is it that on to-morrow we will cross the river Jordan if it lies within our power.

"Col. Connor sent word to-day to the above-mentioned chief of the Danites that he would 'cross the river Jordan if hell yawned below him;' and the battle-fields of Mexico testify that the Colonel has a habit of keeping his word.

"Thus you see that whether we are to have a fight or not rests entirely with the Mormon rulers. And if it be true that United States troops, when ordered by Government to occupy United States territory, are to be forcibly prevented by those living upon United States lands, from executing the order—if this principle is to constitute the national policy, then the nation has ceased to be a live nation, and the sooner it recognizes the Southern Confederacy the better.

But if our troops are to march on United States territory wherever Government sends them, and those who resist their march, because of polygamy, are as really traitors as those who resist because of slavery and are to be dealt with as such. This command, from the highest to the lowest, is disposed to treat the Mormons with true courtesy and the strictest justice, so long as they remain friendly to the Government; but the moment they become traitors the river Jordan will be as acceptable to us as the river Potomac, for we shall be fighting for the same precise principle—the flag and national existence—as are our eastern brethren; and even should annihilation be our fate, of which we have no fears, the belief that our countrymen would think of our graves as they do of those in Virginia, and that the Union men of California, our old friends, would swarm forth by the thousand to avenge us—such a hope and belief would nerve us for death.

"Nevertheless, unless he fails to exercise his statesmanship, universally accorded to him, Brigham Young cannot but foresee the results which would flow from a war of his beginning. Admitting him to have an army of 8,000 well drilled and effective men, or, for that matter, one of 50,000—and admitting him to be able to capture our force and all the forces which California could send hither, yet, in the course of one, or two, or three years, the Government could flood his valley with regiments, and sweep it with a gulf stream of bayonets.

That he is prepared to initiate a movement which cannot fail to bring upon his people the full power of the nation I do not believe; and yet there may be hot heads over whom he has but partial control. A small spark can ignite the powder of a vast magazine.

"Having given you the prevalent opinion of the camp, there should also be given what probably may turn out to be the cause why some, if not most, of the rumors currently in Salt Lake were set afloat. When Floyd after expending $5,000,000 in the erection of quarters in Camp Floyd ordered the disgraceful and outrageous sale of the same, the buildings were bought for a mere song by private parties.

"On several occasions, in fact during the whole march, Col. Connor has been solicited by the agents of owners to repurchase them. He did not see fit to do so; but it was expected that the smallness of the command, and the avowal that the Mormons would not permit him to locate near the city, taken in connection with the fact that his arrival so late in the season would prevent him from erecting winter quarters, it was expected, I say, that these and other prudential reasons would induce him to effect the purchase of Fort Crittenden; and it is more than probable that his refusal of the offers was regarded as a financial maneuver by which to secure the property at low figures. Hence the idea that we really would not winter at that point has never been realized by them, and so thoroughly has the belief that we would winter there pervaded the Mormon people, that when we marched beyond it they—unable to understand the object of the expedition, and fearful that the real, and to them a hostile, design, is hidden under the avowed one—have their fears a thousand fold quickened and imagine an attack upon the city possible. In addition it appears that the chief of the Danites is the principal owner of the buildings and decidedly anxious to sell and that the agents have from time to time assured him of the certainty of his prospects. Up to the hour that Col. Connor's decision was unknown at Fort Crittenden, the city is reported to have been perfectly quiet, but in about the time it would take to telegraph his refusal to Salt Lake, the excitement is said to have begun. There can, therefore, be little doubt that the already aroused suspicions of the Mormons have been worked upon by parties interested in the sale of the property, and who, failing to persuade Col. Connor into buying, now seek to frighten him therein by threats of forcible resistance, and mayhap a display of military power. In this they will most signally fail, for I must say that he is a blessed hard man to scare. At the same time, if it is the settled Mormon policy to resist the Federal Government, and if the people have been toned up to the Union pitch, a few leaders actuated by selfish motives, can easily indicate its execution. A courier will arrive late to-night with authentic intelligence, which I will endeavor to obtain.

"Salt Lake City, October 20, 1862.

"When Sunday's reveille awoke the command, it awoke expectant of battle ere another one should roll out upon the grey day-break. Blankets were never got out from under and compactly strapped in knapsacks more promptly; cooks never prepared steaming breakfast with greater alacrity, and upon the principle that the aggregate stomach of a regiment has a great deal to do with the aggregate prowess of a regiment, they never prepared a more bountiful repast. Upon the same principle, no breakfast during the whole march was stowed away in a more cool, nonchalant, jovial manner. The routine of months was dissipated, and, doubtless each man's curiosity to know how he would personally stand fire, and the more general question which side would whip, made everybody happy. The first scene which met my eyes was Colonel Connor seated upon a log, calmly engaged in loading his pistols, and playing with his toddling child. In some directions were heard the popping of muskets and the thud of ramrods, as the men made sure of their pieces, while in others could be seen individuals seated on the ground, vigorously burnishing up their already glittering muskets and brasses— determined no doubt to die according to regulations, if die they must. No difference what thoughts raged within each breast, the exterior seemed calm and determined.

"An incident at the hospital will serve as a criterion of the general animus.

Five men were sick in the hospital and thirty-six sick in quarters. At sick-call Surgeon Reid, who had been arranging his abominable knives, saws and probes, said that this was a day when every man able to carry a musket should do so, and one that would determine who were loafers and who were soldiers. Twenty-eight out of the forty-one, many of whom were really unfit for service, shouldered their pieces, and the remainder did not only because they could not.

"A strong force of cavalry preceded the staff, and the command moved forward in so compact a body, and with such a steady, springing step, that General Wright's heart would have rejoiced at the sight. The fact that the carriages formed behind the staff as usual was an intimation to the men that a fight was improbable, and word presently passed that a courier had arrived with information that no resistance would be made at the bridge. Before it did so, however, as the Colonel passed the artillery, he put several questions to Lieutenant Hunneyman, commanding, respecting the quantity and kind of ammunition in the caissons, and also the numbers of the ammunition wagons. When through, the Lieutenant, who has seen service, said, 'Colonel, if you expect an attack to-day, I will overhaul those wagons and take more cannister,' with the same air that one calls for fried oysters in a restaurant. The reply was, 'Not to day; but to-morrow do so.' There were other incidents of the same kind, but I did not happen to see them.

"After a speedy march of fifteen miles—during which not one of the usual stragglers fell back from his position—we crossed the Jordan at 2 p. m. and found not a solitary individual upon the eastern shore. It was a magnificent place for a fight, too, with a good-sized bluff upon the western side from which splendid execution could have been done; but all were glad that no necessity existed therefor, as we heartily desire to avoid difficulty with the loyal citizens.

"While camped for the night, it was definitely ascertained that, although there had been some excitement in the laity, yet it was far from general, and was instigated by parties interested in selling the Fort Crittenden buildings. Furthermore, that the mass of the people were glad of our near location, as it would bring many a dollar into the city circulation. Bishop Heber Kimball, who, I am told, ranks next to President Young, is reported to have spoken thus in his sermon .at the temple: 'Letters have been written to Colonel Connor's command, to California and the East, that we are opposed to the coming of the troops; that we are disloyal to the Government and sympathizers with Secessionists. It is all a d—d lie." This certainly was a gratifying assurance, though not mildly expressed.

"This morning, Monday, we resumed the line of march, thoroughly ignorant of the spot that "would next receive our tents, but decidedly hopeful that it would receive them permanently. That it was to be near the city we knew; that the leading Mormons objected to its proximity because of the danger of difficulties between the soldiers and citizens, we knew; that in 1858 they had resisted the now traitor Johnston's 10,000 men, and after compelling him to winter in the mountains, had, late in the Spring, forced him into a treaty by which he bound himself not to locate within 40 miles of Salt Lake, we knew; that they were far stronger and better armed now than they then were, we knew; and that more than one of their leading men—among them a Bishop—had offered to bet that we would not come within twenty miles of the Temple, we also knew. A large and influential party was avowedly opposed to any near approach, and, in view of the advice received by our commander—which were from reliable sources—the precise animus of the people and the treatment that would meet us, we did not know. That, should they see fit, it was in their power to vastly outnumber and in all probability annihilate us, was more than possible, and that we were 600 miles of sand and draught from reinforcements, was certain. All of these certainties and uncertainties conspired to create the same excitement that passengers in olden days felt when two Mississippi steamers lapped guards, burned tar, and carried the engineer as a weight on the safety valve. We had generally supposed, and the people had universally supposed, that the command would pass around the city, or at the most but through the outer suburbs, which course, under all the circumstances, was considered decidedly bold, and upon the whole, not so conciliatory a policy as had been adopted by General Johnston's thousands.

"Accordingly, when some two miles out, a halt was sounded and the column formed as follows: Advance guard of cavalry, Colonel Conner and staff; cavalry brass band; Cos. A and M of 2nd Cavalry, C. V., light battery; infantry field band; 3rd Infantry Battalion; staff, company quarters and commissary wagons; rear guard of infantry.

"You may imagine our surprise—strive to imagine the astonishment of the people, and the more than astonishment of the betting bishop—as the column marched slowly and steadily into a street which receives the overland stage, up it between the fine trees, the sidewalks filled with many women and countless children, the comfortable residences, to Emigration Square, the Theatre and other notable landmarks were passed, when, about the center of the city, I should think, it filed right through a principal thoroughfare to Governor Harding's Mansion—on which, and on which alone waved the same blessed stars and stripes that were woven in the loom of '76. Every crossing was occupied by spectators, and windows, doors and roofs had their gazers. Not a cheer, not a jeer greeted us. One little boy, running along close to the staff, said—" You are coming, are you?" to which it was replied that we thought we were. A carriage, containing three ladies, who sang "John Brown" as they drove by, were heartily saluted. But the leading greeting was extended by Governor Harding, Judges Waite and Drake, and Dr. ——— , who met us some distance out. Save these three instances, there were none of those manifestations of loyalty that any other city in a loyal Territory would have made.

"The sidewalk by the mansion was thoroughly packed with Mormons, curious to know what would be the next feature. It was this: The battalion was formed into two lines, behind them the cavalry, with the battery resting upon their right, in front of the Governor's residence.

"After giving the Governor the salute due his rank he was introduced by Col. Connor to the command, and, standing in his buggy, spoke precisely thus: "Soldiers and Fellow Citizens: "It is with pleasure that I meet you all here to-day. God forbid that ever I shall live to see the day that I will not be rejoiced to see the flag of my country in hands that are able and worthy to defend it. When I say this, I am conscious, soldiers, that your mission here is one of peace and security, not only to the government that gives you employment, but to every individual who is an inhabitant of this Territory.

"The individual, if any such there be, who supposed that the Government had sent you here that mischief might come out of it, knows not the spirit of our Government, and knows not the spirit of the officers who represent it in this Territory. When I say this, I say what is strictly true; and I say it that it may be impressed upon your minds as true, as well as upon the minds of every individual who hears me upon this occasion. Never let it be said that an American soldier, employed under the glorious flag of his country, that emblem of beauty and glory, has disgraced it by conduct not in accordance with his duty, and the discipline of the United States army. The duty of a soldier is a plain and stern duty; and yet it is one that redounds to the glory and happiness of himself, and to the happiness of every true and loyal individual in whose midst he may be placed. If, however, he should break over the bounds of his discipline—if he should run wild in the riot of the camp, then, indeed, his presence will be a curse everywhere, and not a security to the institutions of the Government, which it is his duty to maintain with his life's blood.

"I confess that I have been disappointed, somewhat, in your coming to this city. I have known nothing of the disposition that has been made of you; and for the truth of this assertion, I appeal to your commander, and to every individual with whom I have had communication on this subject. But you are here, and I can say to you, God bless you, and God bless the flag you carry; God bless the Government you represent; and may she come out of her present difficulties unscathed; and may the fiery ordeal through which she is passing purge her of her sins; may her glorious institutions be preserved to the end of time; may she survive these troubles, and be redeemed, and disenthralled from the causes of the difficulties and calamities through which she is passing, and through which she may be yet called to pass.

"I do not know now what disposition is to be made of you, but I suppose you will be encamped somewhere, I know not where, but within a short distance of this city. I believe the people you have now come amongst will not disturb you if you do not disturb them in their public rights and in the honor and peace of their homes; and to disturb them you must violate the strict discipline of the United States Army which you must observe, and which you have no right to violate. In conforming thus to your duty, you will have my countenance and support, and every drop of blood in my veins if necessary for the maintenance of your rights and the Government I represent. But if on the contrary you for any reason whatever should run wild in the riot of the camp—should break over the bounds of propriety, and disregard that discipline that is the only possible safety for yourselves, then shall I not be with you; but in the line of your duty, God being my helper, I will be with you to the end, and to death. I thank you."

"At the conclusion of the speech, Colonel Connor called for three cheers for our Country and Flag, and three more for Governor Harding, all of which would have drawn forth the admiration of your Fire Department. Thereupon the march through the city was resumed, the bands continuing their flood of music, and a tramp of two and a half miles east brought us to the slope between Emigration and Red Butte Canyons, where a permanent post will probably be established.

"I have very astutely discovered that we could have reached the spot by a much shorter road, and that we marched over six miles for the purpose of passing through the well-built metropolis of the modern Saints. There is no reason why we should not do it that is recognized by the United States Government, and I for one was curious to see rosy cheeks and sparkling eyes.

"And so ended the long tramp from your good State, and the attempts to frighten Colonel Connor into the purchase of Fort Crittenden.

CHAPTER XXXII.

BATTLE OF BEAR RIVER. CONNOR'S REPORT TO THE DEPARTMENT HISTORY OF THE BATTLE. CONGRATULATIONS OF THE COLONEL TO HIS TROOPS. BURIAL OF THE DEAD. OUR CITIZENS AT THE FUNERAL, THE BATTLE AS RECORDED IN THE MILITARY HISTORY OF CACHE VALLEY

Soon after his arrival in Utah, Colonel Connor, on the 29th of January, 1863, fought the celebrated battle of Bear River, against the Snake end Bannock Indians under Bear Hunter and other chiefs. There they killed and captured of the Indians nearly 400. The cemetery of Camp Douglas was consecrated to receive the relics of the heroes who fell in that battle; but there was compensation for their loss, as that famous victory forever put a quietus to Indian hostilities in Northern Utah and Southern Idaho.

The following official report of the battle from Colonel Connor is a valuable page of Utah history:

"Headquarters District of Utah,
Camp Douglas U. T., Feb. 6th, 1863.

" Colonel: "I have the honor to report that from information received from various sources of the encampment of a large body of Indians on Bear River, in Washington Territory, one hundred and forty miles north of this point, who had murdered several miners, during the winter, passing to and from the settlements in this valley to the Beaver Head mines, east of the Rocky Mountains, and being satisfied that they were part of the same band who had been murdering emigrants on the overland mail route for the past fifteen years and the principal actors and leaders in the horrid massacres of the past summer, I determined although the season was unfavorable to an expedition, in consequence of the cold weather and deep snow, to chastise them if possible. Feeling that secrecy was the surest way to success, I determined to deceive the Indians by sending a small force in advance, judging, and rightly, that they would not fear a small number.

"The chiefs, Pocatello and Sanpitch, with their bands of murderers, are still at large. I hope to be able to kill or capture them before spring.

"If I succeed, the overland route west of the Rocky Mountains will be rid of the Bedouins who have harassed and murdered emigrants on that route for a series of years.

"In consequence of the number of men left on the route with frozen feet and those with the train and howitzers and guarding the cavalry horses, I did not have to exceed two hundred men engaged.

"On the 22nd ultimo, I ordered Co. K. Third California Volunteers, Capt. Hoyt; two howitzers under command of Lieut. Honeyman and twelve men of the Second California Cavalry with a train of fifteen wagons, conveying twelve days' supplies, to proceed in that direction. On the 24th ultimo, I proceeded with detachments from companies A, H, K, and M. Second California Cavalry, numbering two hundred and twenty men, accompanied by Major McGarry, Second California Cavalry; Surgeon Reid, Third California Volunteers; Captains McLean and Price, and Lieutenants Chase, Clark, Quinn and Conrad, Second California Cavalry. Major Gallager, Third

California Volunteers and Capt. Berry, Second California Cavalry, who were present at this post attending general court martial as volunteers.

"I marched the first night to Brigham City about sixty-eight miles distant; and the second night's march from Camp Douglas, I overtook the infantry and artillery at the town of Mendon and ordered them to march again that night. I resumed march with the cavalry and overtook the infantry at Franklin, W. T., about twelve miles from the Indian encampment. I ordered Capt. Hoyt, with the infantry, howitzers and train not to move until after 3 o'clock a. m., I moved the cavalry in about an hour afterward, passing the infantry, artillery and wagons about four miles from the Indian encampment. As daylight was approaching 1 was apprehensive that the Indians would discover the strength of my force and make their escape. I therefore made a rapid march with the cavalry and reached the bank of the ravine shortly after daylight, in full view of the Indian encampment, and about one mile distant, I immediately order Major McGarry to advance with the cavalry and surround, before attacking them, while I remained a few minutes in the rear to give orders to the infantry and artillery. On my arrival on the field I found that Major McGarry had dismounted the cavalry and was engaged with the Indians, who had sallied out of their hiding places on foot and horseback and, with fiendish malignity, waved the scalps of white women, and challenged the troops to battle, at the same time attacking them. Finding it impossible to surround them, in consequence of the nature of the ground, he accepted their challenge.

"The position of the Indians was one of strong natural defense, and almost inaccessible to the troops, being in a deep dry ravine from six to twelve feet deep, and from thirty to forty feet wide, with very abrupt banks and running across level table land, along which they had constructed steps from which they could deliver their fire without being themselves exposed. Under the embankment they had constructed artificial courses of willows, thickly wove together, from behind which they could fire without being observed.

"After being engaged about twenty minutes, I found it was impossible to dislodge them without great loss of life. I accordingly ordered Major McGarry, with twenty men, to turn their left flank which was in the ravine where it entered the mountain. Shortly afterward Capt. Hoyt reached the ford, three fourths of a mile distant, but found it impossible to cross footmen, some of whom tried it, however, rushing into the river but finding it deep and rapid, retired.

I immediately ordered a detachment of cavalry with led horses, to cross the infantry, which was done accordingly and upon their arrival on the field I ordered them to the support of Major McGarry's flanking party who shortly afterward succeeded in turning the enemy's flank.

"Up to this time, in consequence of being exposed on a level and open plain, while the Indians were under cover they had the advantage of us, fighting with the ferocity of demons. My men fell thick and fast around me, but after flanking them we had the advantage and made good use of it. I ordered a flanking party to advance down the ravine on either side, which gave us the advantage of an enfilading fire and caused some of the Indians to give way and run towards the mouth of the ravine. At this point I had a company stationed who shot them as they run out. I also ordered a detachment of cavalry across the ravine to cut off the retreat of any fugitives who might escape the company (Capt. Price) at the mouth of the ravine. But few, however, tried to escape, but continued fighting with unyielding obstinacy, frequently engaging hand to hand with the troops until killed in their hiding-places. The most of those who did escape from the ravine were afterward shot in attempting to swim the river or killed while desperately fighting under cover of the dense willow thicket which lined the river banks. To give you an idea of the desperate character of the fight, you are respectfully referred to the list of killed and wounded transmitted herewith. The fight commenced at about six o'clock in the morning and continued until ten. At the commencement of the battle the hands of some of the men were so benumbed with cold that it was with difficulty that they could load their pieces. Their suffering during the march was awful beyond description, but they steadily continued without regard to hunger, cold or thirst, not a murmur escaping them to indicate their sensibilities to pain or fatigue. Their uncomplaining endurance during their four nights' march from Camp Douglas to the battle field is worthy the highest praise. The weather was intensely cold and not less than seventy-five had their feet frozen and some of them, I fear, will be crippled for life.

"I should mention here that in my march from this post no assistance was rendered by the Mormons, who seemed indisposed to divulge any information regarding the Indians and charged enormous prices for every article furnished my command. I have also to report to the General commanding, that previous to my departure, Chief Justice Kinney, of Salt Lake City, made a requisition for the purpose of arresting the Indian Chiefs, Bear Hunter, Sanpitch and Sagwitch.

I informed the Marshal that my arrangements for an expedition against the Indians were made and that it was not only my intention to take any prisoners, but that he could accompany me. Marshal Gibbs accordingly accompanied me and rendered efficient aid in caring for the wounded.

"I have great pleasure in awarding to Major McGarry, Major Gallagher and Surgeon A. K. Reid the highest praise for their skill, gallantry and bravery throughout the engagement. And to the company officers the highest praise is due, without invidious distinction for their courage and determination evinced throughout the engagement; their obedience to orders, attention, kindness and care for the wounded are no less worthy of notice. Of the good conduct and bravery of both officers and men, California has reason to be proud.

"We found 224 bodies in the field, among which were those of the chiefs Bear Hunter, Sagwitch and Lehi. How many more were killed than stated I am unable to say; as the condition of the wounded rendered their immediate removal a necessity, I was unable to examine the field. I captured 175 horses, some arms, destroyed over seventy lodges, and a large quantity of wheat and other provisions which had been furnished them by the Mormons. I left a supply of provisions for the sustenance of 160 captive squaws and children who were released by me on the field.

"The enemy had about three hundred warriors, mostly all armed with rifles and having plenty of ammunition, which rumor says they received from the inhabitants of this Territory in exchange for property of massacred emigrants. The position of the Indians was one of great natural strength and had I not succeeded in flanking them the mortality of my command would have been terrible. In consequence of the deep snow the howitzers did not reach the field in time to be used in the action.

"I have the honor of remaining, very respectfully,
Your obedient servant, (Signed)

P. Ed. Connor, Colonel 3rd Cal. Vol., Cont'd. District.
"To Lt. Col. R. C. Drum, Asst. Adjt. Gen. U. S. A., Department of the Pacific:'

"Headquarters of the Army,
Washington, D. C, March 29th, 1863.
"Brig.-General Geo. Wright,
Comd'g Deft of the Pacific, San Francisco, Cal.
"General: "I have this day received your letter of February 20th, inclosing Col. P. Ed. Connor's report of his severe battle and splendid victory on Bear River, Washington Territory. After a forced march of one hundred and forty miles in midwinter and through deep snows, in which seventy-six of his men were disabled by frozen feet; he and his gallant band of only two hundred, attacked three hundred warriors in their stronghold and after a hard-fought battle of four hours, destroyed the entire band, leaving 224 dead upon the field. Our loss in the battle was fourteen killed and forty-nine wounded. Colonel Connor and the brave Californians deserve the highest praise for their gallant and heroic conduct.
Very respectfully,
Your obedient servant,
(Signed) H. W. Halleck,
General-in-chief.

The following order, bearing the same date as that of Col. Connor's letter to the Department of the Pacific, was read to the volunteers, while on dress parade, by Adjutant Ustick:

"Headquarters District of Utah, Camp Douglas, U. T., Feb. 6, 1863.
"The Colonel commanding has the pleasure of congratulating the troops of this Post upon the brilliant victory achieved at the battle of Bear River, Washington Territory.

"After a rapid march of four nights in intensely cold weather, through deep snow and drifts, which you endured without murmur or complaint, even when some of your number were frozen with cold, and faint with hunger and fatigue, you met an enemy who have heretofore, on two occasions, defied and defeated regular troops, and who have for the last fifteen years been the terror of the emigrants, men, women and children and citizens of those valleys, murdering and robbing them without fear of punishment.

"At daylight on the 29th of January, 1863, you encountered the enemy, greatly your superior in numbers, and had a desperate battle. Continuing with unflinching courage for over four hours, you completely cut him to pieces, captured his property and arms, destroyed his stronghold and burnt his lodges.

"The long list of killed and wounded is the most fitting eulogy on your courage and bravery. The Colonel commanding returns you his thanks. The gallant officers and men who were engaged in this battle, without invidious distinction, merit the highest praise. Your uncomplaining endurance and unexampled conduct on the field, as well as your thoughtful care and kindness for the wounded, is worthy of emulation. While we rejoice at the brilliant victory you have achieved over your savage foe, it is meet that we do honor to the memory of our brave comrades, the heroic men who fell fighting to maintain the supremacy of our arms.

"While the people of California will regret their loss, they will do honor to every officer and soldier who has by his heroism added new laurels to the fair escutcheon of the State.

"By order of Colonel Connor.

(Signed) WM. D. Ustick

"First Lieutenant and Adjutant, Third Infantry, C. V.,

Acting Assistant Adjutant General."

The burial of the dead who fell in the battle of Bear River was a solemn occasion to the city as well as to the camp. The day was cold and raw, yet a large number of our citizens were present at the burial. Up to this time scarcely any of the citizens had set foot within the encampment, but now there was quite a score of carriages from the city, many equestrians and a large concourse of people on foot, and had it been generally known, thousands from the city would have paid reverent tribute to the slain, for it was duly appreciated that they had fallen in the service of Utah.

"Up to 1 p. m. the sixteen coffins lay side by side in the Quartermaster's storeroom, where the dead were visited by their surviving comrades. ' At that hour the entire command formed in procession and escorted the bodies to the military graveyard, where Parson Anderson officiated in the burial service. Three volleys were fired over the bodies as they were laid in their graves, and the last solemn rites were ended. The band, that before led the measured, solemn step of the procession to the funeral dirge and Dead March, now moved away gaily, reviving the thoughtful, and recalling to the duties and obligations of life those who had not yet finished their page of history.

"The remains of Lieutenant Chase were consigned to their resting-place by the brethren of the Masonic fraternity attached to the command, together with a few from the city. The deceased was a Royal Arch Mason, but the small number of that grade in attendance rendered the adoption of the Master Mason's burial service necessary. At the solicitation of the brethren, Sir Knight Frank Fuller, Secretary of the Territory, officiated as W. M., and Colonel Evans, of the Second Cavalry, as Marshal, Chief Justice Kinney and United States Marshal Gibbs walked in the procession, which consisted altogether of some twenty members.

The services at the grave were of a highly impressive character and were witnessed by nearly the whole of the command, together with numerous citizens. At the close of the solemnities, the fraternity changed their position while a dirge was performed by the band, and gave place to a detail of forty-eight soldiers, who fired three volleys over the grave. The procession then returned to camp in reversed order."

It may be noted that Lieutenant Darwin Chase in his youth was one of the most promising of the Mormon Elders; his name and labors in the ministry was often associated with Apostle Erastus Snow. It was supposed that the Indians mistook Lieutenant Chase for Colonel Connor and made him a particular mark.

The Lieutenant's horse had more attractive trappings, which drew the attention of the Indians towards him and away from the real commander, who is said to have "sat almost motionless on his charger, within easy distance of the Indians' rifles, watching the progress of the fight and giving his orders."

For the integrity of history, it must be noted that Colonel Connor in his report to the War Department did an injustice to the people of Cache Valley when he said: "I should mention here that in my march from this post no assistance was rendered by the Mormons, who seemed indisposed to divulge any information regarding the Indians, and charged enormous prices for every article furnished my command."

Accompany the above with an historical note in the Logan Branch records, from which the author himself copied it: "Jan. 28th, 1863, Colonel Connor passed through Logan with a company of 450 soldiers, and on the 29th he came upon and attacked a band of Indians in a deep ravine through which a small creek runs west of Bear River and twenty miles north of Franklin. The Indians resisted the soldiers and a severe battle ensued which lasted four hours, in which eighteen soldiers were killed and [many] wounded. About 200 Indians were killed and a great many wounded. Colonel Connor captured about 150 Indian ponies and returned through Logan on Jan. 31.

The weather was so intensely cold that scores of his men had their feet and hands frozen. We, the people of Cache Valley, looked upon the movement of Colonel Connor as an intervention of the Almighty, as the Indians had been a source of great annoyance to us for a long time, causing us to stand guard over our stock and other property the most of the time since our first settlement."

This historical minute was made early in 1863, just after the battle of Bear River. Notice the striking proof of this in the naming of Connor's rank— "Colonel Connor." He was not yet created Brigadier-General, for fighting that battle, when Secretary Farrell made that minute. Records are invaluable! This one justifies Cache Valley. A misrepresentation of the Mormon people was made to the War Department, though we are quite as confident that "Colonel Connor" was too honorable to so design his report. The above will show General Connor's views of the Mormon people at the date of the writing of his official letter, and of the sympathy of the people of Cache Valley with the Indians. The records of Cache speak of the absolute sympathy of the entire people of Cache with the California Volunteers, and their gratitude to them for redeeming them from Indian depredations.

Col. Martineau, in his most interesting sketch of the military history of Cache Valley, gives the following account of the battle: "In January, 1863, Col. P. E. Connor, with about 400 United States troops, fought the battle of Bear River, about twelve miles north of Franklin. This action, though more properly belonging to the annals of the United States army, we think should be noticed in this connection, as it had an immense influence in settling Indian affairs in Northern Utah, and especially in Cache County. Indian outrages against settlers and travelers had grown more and more frequent and audacious, until they became unbearable, and Colonel Connor determined to put an end to them. Making forced marches from Camp Douglas to Franklin during an intensely cold winter and through deep snow, his command left Franklin some hours before daylight, and after a march of twelve miles, found the Indians, numbering about 400 warriors, very strongly posted in the deep ravine through which Battle Creek enters Bear River. To attack this natural fortress the troops had to cross an open plain about half a mile in width, in plain view of the Indians, who were hidden behind the steep banks of the stream. The troops reached Bear River early in the morning of an intensely cold day. The river was full of running ice, but was gallantly forded, many of the men getting wet and afterwards having their feet and legs frozen.

"As the troops advanced they met a deadly fire from the Indian rifles; but without wavering pressed steadily on, and after a bloody contest of some hours, in which the Indians fought with desperation, the survivors, about 100 in number, fled. Pocatello and Saguich, two noted chiefs, escaped, but Bear Hunter was killed while making bullets at a camp fire. When struck he fell forward into the fire and perished miserably. For years he had been as a thorn to the settlers, and his death caused regret in none. A simultaneous attack in front and on both flanks finally routed the Indians, whose dead, as counted by an eye-witness from Franklin, amounted to 368, besides many wounded, who afterwards died. About ninety of the slain were women and children. The troops found their camp well supplied for the winter. They burnt the camp and captured a large number of horses. The troops suffered severely in killed and wounded, besides a great number who had their feet and legs frozen by fording Bear River. The morning after the battle and an intensely cold night, a soldier found a dead squaw lying in the snow, with a little infant still alive, which was trying to draw nourishment from her icy breast. The soldiers, in mercy to the babe, killed it. On their return the troops remained all night in Logan, the citizens furnishing them supper and breakfast, some parties, the writer among the number, entertaining ten or fifteen each. The settlers furnished teams and sleighs to assist them in carrying the dead, wounded and frozen to Camp Douglas. In crossing the mountains between Wellsville and Brigham City the troops experienced great hardships. They toiled and floundered all day through the deep snow, the keen, whirling blasts filling the trail as fast aa made, until, worn out, the troops returned to Wellsville. Next day Bishop W. H. Maughan gathered all the men and teams in the place and assisted the troops through the pass to Salt Lake Valley.

"The victory was of immense value to the settlers of Cache County and all the surrounding country. It broke the spirit and power of the Indians and enabled the settlers to occupy new and choice localities hitherto unsafe. Peter Maughan, the presiding bishop of the County, pronounced it an interposition of Providence in behalf of the settlers; the soldiers having done what otherwise the colonists would have had to accomplish with pecuniary loss and sacrifice of lives illy spared in the weak state of the settlements. This was the universal sentiment of the County. It made the flocks and herds and lives of the people comparatively safe; for though the survivors were enraged against the people of the County, whom they regarded as in a manner aiding and abetting the troops, they felt themselves too weak to forcibly seek revenge."

CHAPTER XXXIII.

GREAT MASS MEETING OF THE CITIZENS TO PROTEST AGAINST THE CONDUCT OF GOVERNOR HARDING AND JUDGES WAITE AND DRAKE. THE READING OF HIS MESSAGE TO THE LEGISLATURE. DEEP INDIGNATION OF THE PEOPLE. STIRRING DENUNCIATIONS BY THE LEADERS OF THE PEOPLE. RESOLUTIONS. PETITION TO ABRAHAM LINCOLN FOR THE REMOVAL OF THE GOVERNOR AND JUDGES. A COMMITTEE APPOINTED TO WAIT UPON THEM AND ASK THEIR RESIGNATION IN THE NAME OF THE PEOPLE. THE COMMITTEE'S REPORT.

In the Spring of 1863 there occurred a demonstration of the people of Great Salt Lake City over the conduct of Governor Harding and Judges Waite and Drake. An immense mass meeting was held in the city on the 3rd of March As a prelude to the proceedings Captain Thomas' brass band played " Hail Columbia," after which the meeting organized with the Hon. Daniel Spencer, chairman. Next came a prayer from the chaplain, Joseph Young, for divine guidance in their important business, followed by the band playing the "Star Spangled Banner," after which the Hon. John Taylor arose and briefly stated the object of the meeting. They had met together, he said, for the purpose of investigating certain acts of several of the United States officials now in the Territory.

It was a mass meeting of the citizens, and he, for one, desired to hear a proper statement of the course of the persons alluded to, so far as that affected the citizens of the Territory, laid before the people, and that such action might be adopted as they thought proper, and as the circumstances demanded.

The time had come for certain documents to be placed before the people and before the country, and on which they could not avoid taking action.

Though the Legislature was under no obligation at the opening of the session to publish the Governor's message—as such action on their part was purely complimentary—they did at first contemplate doing so, but on reflection, considered that the character of that message was such that they could not with respect to themselves and to the community do so, and many were of opinion that its publication at that time might have subjected his Excellency to the insult which his intemperate language had provoked. Mr. Taylor then gave place to the Hon. Albert Carrington, who read the message from the printed Journals of the Legislature.

"Gentlemen of the Council and House of Representatives of the Territory of Utah: "

Since the adjournment of the eleventh annual session of this body, the office of Governor of this Territory has been conferred upon me according to law. On the 7th day of July last I arrived in this city and assumed the duties of my office. I had heard much of the industry and enterprise of the people of Utah, but I must admit that my most sanguine expectations were more than realized upon my arrival here. A few years since this Territory was only known as a desert. I found it the home of a large and thriving population, who have accomplished wonders in the short period that it has been settled; and under the steady progress of labor, protected in its indefensible rights, the whole area embraced in the Organic Act establishing this Territory must present a spectacle to the people of the United States as satisfactory to them as it is creditable to yourselves.

"The present season has been one of unusual abundance, not only here, but throughout the entire Union; and, notwithstanding civil war has made desolate many of the fairest districts which have ever been the abode of a civilized people; yet He who has promised 'seed time and harvest,' and ' the rain to fall upon the unjust as well as the just,' has still remembered the whole American people with superabundant mercies. If the harmony of the world has been marred, it has not been through the withholding of His kindness from the nation.

"It is not necessary for me to dwell upon the causes which have superinduced the unhappy troubles now existing in the States of the American Union.

That African slavery, and the unnatural antagonisms which grow out of that relation, lie at the foundation, I have no doubt. I am aware that other reasons have been assigned, but such reasons are confined to but very few in comparison to the many who will agree with me in my proposition. That it is the duty of every lover of human-liberty and friend of republican institutions on this continent to stand by the Government in its present trials is, to my mind, a proposition too clear for argument. Notwithstanding organized treason is still making gigantic efforts to carry out its purpose of the destruction of the Union, yet I am happy in the belief that the rebellion has culminated; that it can never be as strong again as it has been for a few months past. The extremest measures have been resorted to in the rebel States to put the last man in the field for the purpose of sustaining the rebel flag; nevertheless, that flag has been compelled to retreat step by step before the victorious legions of the Union, and still there are millions of men to be called into the field, if it shall hereafter be found that those millions are needed.

"*Conservatism of the administration.*

"The most conservative advocate of the Union, no matter what his opinions heretofore may have been on the question of slavery, cannot complain of the policy of the Administration of President Lincoln in dealing with this question.

While it was known to all men that 4,000,000 of chattel slaves were supplying their rebel masters with means to prosecute their work of ruin to the Government, and for the overthrow of the Constitution—the joint labors of our common ancestors; yet that same Government, through its civil ministers and military commanders, it must be confessed, hesitated long to strike the rebel interests where its blows could be made to tell with most terrible effect.

"*Objects of the war.*

"The present war has not been prosecuted by the Federal Government because of any hostility towards the institutions of the Southern States, but to preserve the union of the great family of States. The question of emancipation, or no Union, has been thrust upon the President. In meeting that question he has shown a patriotic wisdom worthy the head of a great nation. If the Union could have been preserved and slavery still suffered to remain intact, that institution would never have been disturbed by the American people, but would have been suffered to expand its malign influences in the impoverishment of the soil where it exists, until finally it must have perished by the inexorable law of retribution, which, like an avenging Nemesis, is ever following in the track of wrong.

But no matter when or how the present difficulties may be settled, slavery is doomed—it must perish, from the very nature of things.

"*Proclamation of emancipation.*

"On the first day of January, proximo, the time given by the President to the slave masters of the rebel States will have expired. If madness shall still rule la their councils and no returning sense of duty or patriotism shall have been awakened in their hearts, and they shall still refuse to return to that allegiance which is their plainest duty, then the President, exercising that power which he holds as commander-in-chief, and which, as a war power, no man, whose opinions are entitled to the least respect, has ever denied, will by proclamation declare the freedom of every slave in the States or districts of States, where such rebellion shall then exist. This new order of things may for a time jostle the commercial interests of not only this country, but of the whole civilized world; but order and harmony will soon be restored, and our system of Government will still be preserved, with no disturbing element remaining—a beacon-light to the nations, and a refuge to countless millions who will come after us.

"ADMISSION OF THE STATE OF DESERET INTO THE UNION.

"After the adjournment o(the last session of this body, in accordance with a joint resolution emanating therefrom, the people of this Territory proceeded to elect delegates to form a Constitution for the State of Deseret; and after such Constitution was formed and adopted, the people proceeded to elect a Governor, Lieutenant-Governor, and other officers, amongst which was a representative to Congress; and also two United States Senators were elected. One of the gentlemen elected as a United States Senator proceeded to Washington City and caused to be laid before Congress the object of his mission. He was treated with that courtesy to which a gentleman on so grave a mission should ever be entitled.

He was permitted to occupy a seat within the bar of the Senate chamber,' and was otherwise received with the kindest consideration. In consequence of the lateness of the session, it could not be expected that more would have been done than was in the premises. The Constitution and other documents were referred to the appropriate committee, where the matter now rests. That the question will be taken up at the approaching session of Congress and acted on in that spirit of fairness that becomes a great and generous nation, I have no doubt.

"I am sorry to say that since my sojourn amongst you I have heard no sentiments, either publicly or privately expressed, that would lead me to believe that much sympathy is felt by any considerable number of your people in favor of the Government of the United States, now struggling for its very existence ' in the valley and shadow' through which it has been called to pass. If I am mistaken in this opinion no one will rejoice more than myself in acknowledging my error.

I would, in the name of my bleeding country, that you, as the representatives of public sentiment here, would speedily pass such a resolution as will extort from me, if necessary, a public acknowledgment of my error, if error I have committed.

"I have said this in no unkind spirit; I would much rather learn that the fault has been on my part and not on yours.

"I regret also to say, I have found in conversing with many gentlemen of social and political influence, that because the question of the admission of this Territory into the Union was temporarily postponed, distrust is entertained in regard to the friendly disposition of the Federal Government, and expressions have been used amounting to innuendoes at least, as to what the result might be in case the admission should be rejected or postponed. Every such manifestation of spirit on the part of the objectors is, in my opinion, not only unbecoming, but is based on an entire misconception of the rights of the applicant, and the duties of the representatives of the States composing the Union.

"The Constitution of the United States provides, in Art. 4, and Sec. 3, 'that new States may be admitted by Congress in this Union,' etc. The question properly arises, when and how are they to be admitted? Not, surely, upon the demand of the people of the Territory seeking to be admitted, but upon the consent of Congress. When that consent becomes a right to be demanded, depends on circumstances. It is doubtless the interest and policy of the Federal Government to admit the Territories belonging to it to the status and condition of States whenever there is a sufficient population to warrant it, and they apply to Congress with a Constitution republican in spirit and form.

"But still the Congress has not only the right but it is one of their gravest duties, to see that this great boon is not conferred upon a people unprepared to enter into the great political family on a basis that is unjust to other members of the Union. Amongst the first inquiries is that in relation to the population of the Territory knocking for admission. Is it such as to entitle a State to a member in the House of Representatives? If such is the case, and the Constitution which has been adopted as the organic law is such as the Constitution of the United States contemplates; if the same has been adopted in good faith, and the people are loyal to the Constitution and the laws, and desire the welfare of the Federal Government, then it becomes not only the duty of the Congress to admit such applicant, but the latter has a right morally and politically to demand such admission. But on the other hand, if it is not clearly shown that there is a sufficient population, that the Constitution is republican in form and spirit, that the same has been adopted in good faith, and that the people are loyal to the Federal Government and to the laws, then the right to make such demand does not exist, nor should the application be entertained after these facts appear.

"The admission of a new State into the Union is, or ought to be, attended with gravest consideration. For instance, suppose the population of the Territory is known to fall far short of the number that entitles the present members of the Union to a representation in Congress, should it be thought hard or strange that objections should be made? Is it thought a hardship that the people of the State of New York, comprising 4,000,000, are not willing that their voices should be silenced in the Senate of the United States by 60,000 or 80,000 in one of the Territories? I am aware that precedents may be cited in some few instances, where these reasons have been overlooked and disregarded, but that fact does not affect the question under consideration. The reasons which controlled Congress at the time referred to were never good and sound ones, but we found in the wishes and ambition of political parties, anxious to control the vote in the electoral college, for chief magistrate. If the precedent was a bad one, the sooner it is changed the better for all parties concerned.

"In connection with this subject, I respectfully recommend the propriety of passing an act whereby a correct census may be taken of the population of the Territory. If it shall be found that the population is sufficient to entitle it to one representative in Congress, on the present basis, I shall be most happy in aiding you to the extent of my humble abilities, in forwarding any movements having for their end, the admission of the Territory into the Union as a State.

"*Polygamy.*

"It would be disingenuous if I were not to advert to a question, though seemingly it has nothing to do with the premises, is yet one of vast importance to you as a people, and which cannot be ignored—I mean that institution which is not only commended but encouraged by you, and which, to say the least of it, is an anomaly throughout Christendom—I mean polygamy, or, if you please, plural wives. In approaching this delicate subject, I desire to do so in no offensive manner or unkind spirit; yet the institution, founded upon no written statute of your Territory, but upon custom alone exists. It is a patent fact, and your own public teachers, by speech and pamphlet, on many occasions, have challenged its investigation at the bar of Christendom. I will not on this occasion be drawn into a discussion either of its morality or its Bible authority; I will neither affirm or deny any one of the main proceedings on which it rests. That there is seeming authority for its practice in the Old Testament Scripture, cannot be denied.

"But still there were many things authorized in the period of the world when they were written which could not be tolerated now without overturning the whole system of our civilization, based, as it is, on the new and better revelation of the common Savior of us all. While it must be confessed that the practice of polygamy prevailed to a limited extent, yet it should be remembered that it was in that age of the world when the twilight of a semi-barbarism had not yielded to the effulgence of the coming day, and when the glory and fame of the kings of Israel consisted more in the beauty and multitude of their concubines than in the wisdom of their counselors. "An eye for an eye, and a tooth for a tooth," was once the *lex talionis* of the great Jewish law-giver. So capital punishment was awarded for Sabbath breaking; and there were many other statutes and customs which at this age of the world, if adopted, would carry us backward into the centuries of barbarism.

"I lay it down as a sound proposition that no community can happily exist with an institution as important as that of marriage wanting in all those qualities that make it homogenic with institutions and laws of neighboring civilized communities having the same object. Anomalies in the moral world cannot long exist in a state of mere abeyance; they must form the very nature of things, become aggressive, or they will soon disappear from the force of conflicting ideas. This proposition is supported by the history of our race and is so plain that it may be set down as an axiom. If we grant this to be true, we may sum up the conclusion of the argument as follows: either the laws and opinions of the community by which you are surrounded must become subordinate to your customs and opinions, or, on the other hand, you must yield to theirs. The conflict is irrepressible.

"But no matter whether this anomaly shall disappear or remain amongst you, it is your duty at least, to guard it against flagrant abuse. That plurality of wives is tolerated and believed to be right, may not appear so strange. But that a mother and her daughter are allowed to fulfill the duties of wives to the same husband, or that a man could be found in all Christendom who could be induced to take upon himself such a relationship, is perhaps no less a marvel in morals than in matters of taste. The bare fact that such practices are tolerated amongst you is sufficient evidence that the human passions, whether excited by religious fanaticism or otherwise, must be restrained and subject to laws, to which all must yield obedience. No community can long exist without absolute social anarchy unless so important an institution as that of marriage laws is regulated by law.

It is the basis of our civilization, and in it the whole question of the descent and distribution of real and personal estate is involved.

"Much to my astonishment, I have not been able to find any laws upon the statutes of this Territory regulating marriage. I earnestly recommend to your early consideration the passage of some law that will meet the exigencies of the people.

"Act of congress against polygamy.

"I respectfully call your attention to an Act of Congress passed the first day of July, 1862, entitled "An Act to punish and prevent the practice of polygamy in the Territories of the United States, and in other places, and disapproving and annulling certain Acts of the Legislative Assembly of the Territory of Utah." (Chap. CXXVII. of the Statutes at Large of the last Session of Congress, page 501.) I am aware that there is a prevailing opinion here that said Act is unconstitutional, and therefore it is recommended by those in high authority that no regard whatever should be paid to the same—and still more to be regretted, if I am rightly informed, in some instances it has been recommended that it be openly disregarded and defied, meanly to defy the same.

"I take this occasion to warn the people of this Territory against such dangerous and disloyal counsel. Whether such Act is unconstitutional or not, is not necessary for me either to affirm or deny. The individual citizen, under no circumstances whatever, has the right to defy any law or statute of the United States with impunity. In doing so, he takes upon himself the risk of the penalties of that statute, be they what they may, in case his judgment should be in error. The Constitution has amply provided how and where all such questions of doubt are to be submitted and settled, viz: in the courts constituted for that purpose. To forcibly resist the execution of that Act would, to say the least, be a high misdemeanor, and if a whole community should become involved in such resistance, would call down upon it the consequences of insurrection and rebellion.

I hope and trust that no such rash counsels will prevail. If, unhappily, I am mistaken in this, I choose to shut my eyes to the consequences.

"Liberty of conscience.

"Amongst the most cherished and sacred rights secured to the citizens of the United States, is the right 'to worship God according to the dictates of conscience.' It would have been, strange indeed, if the founders of our Government had not thrown around the citizen this irrevocable guaranty, when it is remembered that so many of the framers of the Constitution must have been familiar with the acts of the British Parliament against 'non-conformists,' and had witnessed the injustice and hardship resulting therefrom. They had seen men of the most exalted abilities and virtues excluded from places of public trust for no other reason than that they would not subscribe to all of the dogmas of a church established by law. They had witnessed, at the same time, other men of the most questionable integrity and morality clothed in the robes of prelate and bishop, exacting without stint or mercy, enormous revenues from an unwilling people, and spending the same in the pursuit of an unholy ambition, and in a luxury that better befitted some Eastern satrap than the followers of 'the meek and lowly Jesus,' in whom they professed to believe. In the light of their past experience and inspired by the great primal truths of the

Declaration, the 'indefeasible rights of man to the enjoyment of life, liberty and the pursuit of happiness' still sounding in their ears, they founded a government on the basis of religious toleration, before unknown to mankind. This could not well have been otherwise, from the very nature of things. It was the inevitable corollary that proceeded from the premises, and thus was it that religion was made a matter between man and his Maker, and not between man and the Government.

"But here arises a most important question, a question perhaps that has never yet been asked or fully answered in this country—how far does the right of conscience extend? Is there any limit to this right? and, if so, where shall the line of demarcation be drawn, designating that which is not forbidden from that which is? This is indeed a most important inquiry, and from the tendency of the times, must sooner or later be answered. I cannot and will not on this occasion pretend to answer this question but will venture the suggestion that when it is answered the same rules will be adopted as if the freedom of speech and of the press were involved in the argument.

"Let us refer to this provision of the Constitution; it is found in the first article of the amendments: 'Congress shall make no laws respecting the establishment of religion, or prohibiting the free exercise thereof, or abridging the freedom of speech or of the press' Can we logically infer from the above provision that these rights are not co-relative, or that they do not rest on the same principles? that one of these rights is of more importance to the citizen than the other, and that his duty in their ' free exercise' is not the same? I think not.

"Let us briefly examine this proposition. Because 'the freedom of speech and of the press' is guaranteed, can the citizen thereby be allowed to speak slanderously and falsely of his neighbor? Can he write and print a libel with impunity? He certainly cannot; and his folly would almost amount to idiocy if he should appeal to the Constitution to shield him from the consequences of his acts. But the question may be asked—why not? The answer is at hand. Simply because he is not allowed to abuse these rights. If, upon a prosecution for slander or libel, the defendant should file his plea setting up that provision of the Constitution as a matter of defense, the plea would not only be bad on demurrer, but the pleader would be looked upon as a very bad lawyer. Will any one inform me why the same parity of reasoning should not apply in one case as the other?

"That if an act, in violation of law and repugnant to the civilization in the midst of which that act has been committed, should be followed by a prosecution, could be justified under the guaranty of the Constitution securing the 'free exercise of religion' more than in the case above cited? I shall pause for an answer. There can be no limits beyond which the mind cannot dwell, and our thoughts soar in their aspirations after truth. We may think what we will, believe what we will, and speak what we will, on all subjects of speculative theology. We may believe with equal impunity the Talmud of the Jew, the Bible of the Christian, the Book of Mormon, the Koran, or the Veda of the Brahmin.

We cannot elevate, other than by moral forces, the human soul from the low plane of ignorance and barbarism, whether it worships for its God, the Llama of the Tartars, or the Beetle of the Egyptians. But when religious opinions assume new manifestations and pass from mere sentiments into overt acts, no matter whether they be acts of faith or not, they must not outrage the opinions of the civilized world, but, on the other hand, must conform to those usages established by law, and which are believed to underlie our civilization.

"But, the question returns—Is there any limit to the 'free exercise of religion?' If there is not, then in the midst of the nineteenth century, human victims may be sacrificed as an atonement for sin, and "widows may be burned alive on the funeral pile." Is there one here who believes that such shocking barbarisms could be practiced in the name of religion, and in the 'free exercise thereof in any State or Territory of the United States? If not, then there must be a limit to this right under consideration, and it only remains for the proper tribunal at the proper time to fix the boundaries, as each case shall arise involving that question.

"*Powers vested in the governor by the organic act.*

"The Act of Congress organizing the Territory of Utah, and providing a Government therein, defined with sufficient certainty the duties of each department in said Government. These several departments were made to consist of the Executive, the Legislative and the Judicial. Amongst the duties imposed upon the Governor, is that of nominating certain officers, by and with the advice and consent of the Council. The first question that arises under this head is, what officers are to be nominated by the Governor? The seventh section of said Act is in the following words: 'And be it further enacted, that all township, district and county officers, not herein otherwise provided for, shall be appointed, or elected, as the case may be, in such manner as shall be provided for by the Governor and Legislative Assembly of the Territory of Utah.' The Governor shall nominate, and by and with the advice and consent of the Legislative Council (not Assembly) appoint all officers not herein otherwise provided for, etc. Township, district and county officers are to be appointed or elected, as the case may be, in such manner as the Governor and Legislative Assembly may direct. It is clear to my mind that the Organic Act contemplates two classes of officers, viz.; township, district and county, and another class not included in the former, which embraces all officers strictly Territorial, such as attorney-general for the Territory, marshal, auditor, treasurer, etc.

"I cannot arrive at any other conclusion in the examination of the Act, than that the officers not included in the first class must be appointed by the Governor, by and with consent of the Legislative Council, and cannot be elected, as in the former instance, by joint ballot of the Legislative Assembly, have held such offices contrary to law and have been removed upon the prosecution of a writ of *quo warranto*. It follows further, that if such officers acted without authority of law their acts were void and are not binding upon the citizens. This becomes a question of much importance when we consider the hardship and inconvenience that may hereafter grow out of the same. I respectfully submit for your consideration, whether it would not be safer either to pass some law legalizing the acts of such persons, while in the supposed discharge of their duties, or it may be that it would require an Act of Congress legalizing such assumed official acts.

"Before dismissing this part of my subject, I feel it to be my duty to suggest to you whether a very grave question may not hereafter arise as to the authority of the Legislative Assembly to elect by joint ballot any of the officers denominated as ' township, district or county officers.' I have been unofficially advised that the word 'election' as used in the Organic Act, might be held to refer to the people, and not to the Legislative Assembly. If such a question should hereafter arise, and such a possible view should be taken in deciding this question, it would involve the most serious consequences. I will express no opinion on the subject. I only raise the question for your consideration.

"Revision and codification of the statutes.

"I respectfully call your attention to the necessity of a thorough revision and codification of the statutes of this Territory. I am aware that something was attempted at your last session in that direction; but it seems to me that the committee which had that duty under their charge stopped far short of what was required at their hands. It is the duty of the law makers to leave the statutes by which the people are to be governed so plain in their several requirements that the stranger cannot be misled. It is extremely difficult to ascertain what precise statutes are in force on many subjects in this Territory. Besides this, there are many provisions in the statutes manifestly unjust, and whilst they remain must be considered anomalies. I will not consume time in any argumentation on this subject, believing that i: will be only necessary to call your attention to the facts as they exist.

"Amongst the most objectionable of these provisions, may be found the following in the revised statutes of 1855, and which are still in force: "Chap, s, relating to justices of the peace. Sees. 8, 15, 19.

"Chap. 3, relating to the procedure in civil cases. Sec. 28.

"Chap. 6, relating to attorneys-at-law. This whole chapter should be repealed.

"Chap. 12, relating to estates of decedents. Sees. 14, 24, 25, 26. The great objection to these sections is, that no limit whatever is fixed to the value of the estate, thereby cutting off claims which ought to be paid, when there is enough to do so, and still the family will be left in comfortable circumstances.

"Chap. 18, in relation to divorces. There should be a specified time when such notice of the pendency of the application should be given to the defendant.

Sec. 18, in the same chapter, gives the probate judge power too plenary. In questions of so much importance, the party should have the benefit of a trial by jury.

"Chap. 32 should be stricken from the statute. No such crime as treason against a Territory is known to the laws.

"I call your attention especially to sections 112 and 113, under the title of 'Justifiable Killing, and the Prevention of Public Offences.' These provisions are too palpably unjust to stand a day on your statutes. It would be an easy matter for a man to be murdered, and yet under these provisions his murderer could escape under the plea that the circumstances were such as to excite his fears that certain acts either would be done or had been, for which he claimed the immunity of the statute. If your laws against the offenses therein named are not sufficiently penal, make them so; but to authorize by a public statute the killing of a man on mere suspicion that he has committed or will commit certain acts, which are less than capital upon his conviction after a fair trial, seems to be most cruel and unjust. In China, it is said that a high Mandarin of the ' blue button' may kill with impunity a person suspected of stealing rice and cut open his stomach to find the evidence of his guilt. In no other instance have I been able to find any statute or custom analogous to the one under consideration. No community can adopt the principles contained in that statute without soon becoming (dropping the figure) 'as a whitened sepulcher filled with dead men's bones.

"Voting by ballot.

"I respectfully call your attention to Chap. 47, Sec. 5, in relation to voting at elections by ballot. Said section is as follows: 'Each elector shall provide himself with a vote containing the names of the persons he wishes elected, and the offices he would have them fill, and present it neatly folded to the judge of the election, who shall number it and deposit it in the ballot-box. The clerk shall then write down the name of the elector opposite the number of his vote.' Why the elector should be required to provide himself a vote and present it neatly folded, perhaps can be satisfactorily explained; but I confess that the object of voting by ballot is completely defeated by the above provisions. Why not vote viva voce at once. The great object to be obtained in voting at our popular elections is absolute freedom of the elector in depositing his vote. Hence it is that in most, if not all the States, the right of voting by secret ballot is secured to the elector by stringent laws. The reason is obvious. A thousand circumstances might so completely surround the elector that he would be compelled oftentimes to vote against the convictions of his judgment, and yet could not, if interested and powerful parties were permitted to exercise their control over him in the discharge of one of his most sacred duties.

"In connection with this subject, I take pleasure in adopting the language of my worthy predecessor, Governor Cumming, as being eminently fit and proper: 'Many of the laws now on the statute book were passed under a condition of things which will soon cease to exist. You cannot reasonably anticipate a continuance of the partial isolation which has characterized your early history in this region. It must be borne in mind, that you are situated upon the great highway between the oceans, which is already traversed by expresses and telegraphs, and is soon to witness the establishment of a railroad transporting through your valleys the commodities of the world. It would be well that you make timely preparation for changes that are fast approaching you and are ultimately inevitable. New relations between yourselves and the outer world must occur. I would therefore urge upon you that you appoint a committee to prepare a code of laws suitable for the present and future requirements of this community. The judges are constituted your legal advisers in these matters—to them I refer you.' If this was true in 1860, how much more is it true to-day? The constantly increasing travel over the great Overland Mail route, the thousands of emigrants passing yearly through your Territory, many of whom become permanent citizens, admonish all of us that your days of isolation from the outside world have forever passed. Even if it were desirable, you cannot longer remain isolated and walled in by these natural ramparts around you.

Every canyon susceptible of improvement will be converted into some thoroughfare where the never-ceasing tide of our population will be poured along. Every nook and valley, which for ages have been trodden by wild beasts or savage men, will become the home of some enterprising citizen whose right it will be to claim the protection of just and wholesome laws.

"Financial.

"I herewith annex the auditor's and treasurer's reports for the year 1862.

They have been made out with so much clearness in their details that it is only necessary for me to refer them to you, accompanying the former with a few brief suggestions. By reference to appended statement "A" in the auditor's report, it will be seen that the aggregate amount of taxable property assessed within the said

Territory for the year 1862 is $4,779,518; and the same statement shows a tax due the Territorial treasury for the current year, estimated at one per cent., of $47,795,18, from which will have to be taken, for cost of assessing, collecting and remittances by county courts, at least 12 per cent.; leaving a probable net revenue of $42,059.76.

"The whole Territorial liability, including the direct tax assessed by the United States, and assumed by the Territorial Legislature, January 17, 1862, amounts to the aggregate sum of $40,199.31. The assets out of which this sum is to be paid, by reference to the same report, amounts to the sum of $50,612.10, leaving a balance still in the treasury on the 1st day of November, 1862, of J 10,412.99. The above result cannot fail in being satisfactory to you. The report of the treasurer is so clear and concise that it is not necessary for me to add one word more than what is contained in the report itself.

"Before dismissing the subject I call your attention especially to the auditor's report for the year 1861, in regard to the aggregate value of taxable property within this Territory for that year. By examining the same you will find that such aggregate amount was $5,032,184—thereby showing the strange fact that since that assessment was made there has been a falling off in the value of taxable property within this Territory in a single year of $252,666, and what is still more remarkable, this apparent loss in Great Salt Lake County alone has been $140,280, whilst, on the other hand, in the County of Davis, there has been an apparent gain of $410,514. I am advised that the cutting off a portion of this Territory, and adding the same to that of Nevada, cannot account for this phenomenon.

"If there is no mistake in these computations it presents a most remarkable fact indeed. I shall not attempt to account for it here, but call your attention to the same, merely adding that in the absence of great local calamities, which affect in their nature whole communities, I question whether such an instance can be found in the history of any people. But it remains with you to account for this phenomenon. This city is the heart and center of the county where so remarkable a deficiency has developed itself, and yet there certainly has been no natural causes for this condition of things. Not only have the people stood still in all of their industrial pursuits, absolutely earning nothing over and above their current expenses that goes to swell the aggregate wealth, but there has been a positive loss, if we are to be governed by these data, in Great Salt Lake County alone, in one year, of $140,280. Can this be so, when we take into consideration that the present year has been one of unusual prosperity, while the labors of the husbandman have been most bountifully paid, and on every hand of this thriving city unmistakable evidences of prosperity are apparent? This result can only be accounted for on one hypothesis, viz: in former years the valuation of property has been too high, or the present year it has been too low. These fluctuations to some extent will always exist from factitious causes alone, in spite of the greatest precaution; but it is the duty of the Legislature to guard not only the people but the treasury, against abuses of the kind, if any exist. There can be no wrong to the people in the collection of an ad valorem tax, providing the property has been fairly assessed and its value fairly determined. The revenue is the common fund of the people, and there should be no favoritism in the collection of the same. No matter whether the individual property-holder possesses ten, twenty or a hundred thousand dollars' worth, he should submit to the same rules in determining its value, as if he was the owner only of one hundred or ten hundred dollars' worth.

"*Miscellaneous.*

"On the 29th of October last the Secretary of the Interior addressed me a letter informing me that he had designated me to receive for the Territorial Library here, two sets of the documents of the 2nd session of the 36th Congress; that by the Act approved the 14th March, 1862, making appropriations for the Legislative, Executive and Judicial expenses for the Government for the year ending 30th June, 1862, there is the following provision: 'Provided, that the said journals and documents shall be sent to such libraries and public institutions only as shall signify a willingness to pay the cost of transportation of the same.' Upon inquiry I find that no funds were at my disposal with which to pay for such transportation, and I notified the Department accordingly.

"There will doubtless be other important documents to be distributed on the same terms hereafter, and I recommend that you provide the necessary means whereby you can avail the people of this Territory of the benefits of these donations.

"I am advised that the penitentiary of this Territory is in a dilapidated condition, and that some repairs are absolutely necessary in order to make the same a safe or proper receptacle for public offenders. I recommend that you memorialize Congress upon that subject.

"I have not been able to find any law upon your statutes inaugurating a common school system, or that any money has been appropriated with a view to that end, although you have appropriated money to other objects of much less importance, for instance, in keeping up a quasi-military establishment at a considerable expense to the people. As much as this condition of things at one period of your history may have been required, it seems to me that the time has passed when the Territorial fund should be used for that purpose at the expense of so important a measure as that which looks to the education of the rising generation amongst you. I need not dwell here upon the importance of common schools; your intelligence must supply any argumentation on my part.

"The condition of the militia of this Territory is unknown to me. Although the statute organizing the same makes it the duty of the lieutenant-general commanding to report to the Governor, who is recognized as commander-in-chief, on or before the 1st day of December, annually; yet no such report has been made to me, and therefore I am wholly uninformed on the subject. If I shall hereafter deem it my duty, I may require that such report be made.

"There are many other topics to which, perhaps, I ought to refer, but I have no data from which to draw conclusions. If reports on any of these subjects shall hereafter be made to me I will communicate them to you, with such suggestions as I shall deem proper.

"*Indian troubles.*

"Complaints have been frequently made to me during the past summer and up to a recent period by immigrants who have suffered great loss and violence from hostile Indian bands who infest some parts of this and adjoining Territories, whilst peacefully pursuing their travel to such points of destination as was their right to do; and from statements which I believe to be reliable, certain residents of this Territory have been known openly to barter and trade with the Indians for clothing and other articles which they at the time must have known were the spoils and plunder from murdered citizens. These practices have, in my opinion, a direct tendency to encourage these outrages against humanity. I respectfully suggest for your consideration whether any legislation is demanded at your hands to prevent these outrages in the future. The presence of a military command here will doubtless have a tendency to prevent many of these horrors.

"I am glad that I am enabled to inform you that the Federal Government has made arrangements to hold treaties with some if not all the tribes of Indians that have so long infested this and neighboring Territories, and it is to be hoped that this will be done at an early day, and the Indian title to the lands therein be speedily extinguished, and such disposition will be made of their former occupants as becomes a great, generous and just Government.

"*Homestead act.*

"On the 1st day of January, 1863, the Homestead Act passed on the 20th May last will go into effect, thereby enabling any person who is of the age of 21 years, or who is the head of a family, or who has performed service in the army or navy of the United States, and who has not been in arms against the United States, or given aid or comfort to the enemies thereof, and has declared his intention to become a citizen of the fame, to enter on and take possession of 160 acres of any of the public lands not otherwise appropriated, and by cultivating the same for the term of five years, and paying $ 10, will, upon the compliance with these conditions, be entitled to a patent for the same. Thus will it be in the power of every loyal citizen to possess a homestead of 160 acres of land, secured from all liabilities from any debts which he may have contracted prior to his patent for the same. When it is remembered that the beneficent act was intended to secure a home to every loyal citizen, on terms so easy and just, its consequences for good cannot well be estimated to the present and future generations. What patriotic devotion does the recipient of this great boon not owe to the Government that thus shields himself and his family from the possibility of want, if he will make use of the means that God and nature have given him! What should be the character of that loyalty due from the citizens from such a Government— a Government which enables him at one bound, although ruined in his fortunes, to spring from indigence and poverty to comparative ease and independence?

The Indian title to the lands in our vast territories will soon be extinguished, and they will be open to settlement on the terms above presented. What inducements are there which are not held out to those just beginning life, and who may reasonably hope to witness thriving cities springing up where the wild Indian now lights his camp fires and pitches his rude lodge!

"When it is also remembered that every rood of land in this Territory will be open to the citizens, upon no harder terms than that they will occupy and cultivate it, and remain loyal to our common Government, who should doubt for a moment that such a golden opportunity shall be offered in vain, or that one link shall be stricken from the chain of sympathy that should ever bind us alike in interest, in body and soul, to that same benign and just Government?

"I have felt it my duty to urge upon your earnest consideration the suggestions and measures herein recommended; at the same time I felt that I would be wanting in proper respect to you were I to accompany each of these recommendations with an assignment of all the reasons which might be urged in their favor.

I am accountable to the Government of our common country for these recommendations. You too are accountable to the same tribunal and to your immediate constituents for the disposition that you make of them. It is your province and duty to consider and discuss them, and either adopt or reject them as your wisdom shall determine.

"I desire to assure you, gentlemen, that nothing in my power shall be wanting to demonstrate my honest regard for the interest and welfare of the people of this Territory. They deserve much at the hands of the Federal Government for their persevering industry; and, so far as my humble efforts may contribute to that end they shall never be wanting. No matter what differences of opinion may exist between us on many subjects, I will endeavor to convince you of my sincerity by the uprightness of my conduct and shall always be satisfied with the discharge of my official duties, when I know that they stand approved by the general voice of the people.

"May each one of you be clothed with wisdom from on high, in the discharge of the important duties which devolve upon you, and may your deliberations be such as not only to secure the lasting peace, happiness and prosperity of the people of this Territory, but also redound to the welfare and glory of our common county.
STEPHEN S. HARDING.
"Great Salt Lake City, U. T., December 8, 1862."

The reading of the message was listened to with great attention, and at its conclusion, the audience unmistakably indicated their uneasiness over the insult offered to their representatives, who had been forced to listen to its delivery by the Governor in person. There was one deep feeling of contempt manifest for its author. Mr. Carrington then alluded to the inconsistences of the Governor's professions and his actions. He said his Excellency reminded him of the man and his cow. He commenced with sweet apples and at every opportunity threw in the onions. The Governor commenced with admitting that the Constitution debarred him from interfering with their religious rights, and at every opportunity throughout the message he attacked them. He said he would neither affirm nor deny with regard to the question of polygamy, yet at the same time, he held it up to ridicule and obloquy, and everywhere affirming that it was not only contrary to civilization, but anomalous, and that it could not be endured, was contrary to the law and unconstitutional, while at the same time he conceded that it was a religious rite and a matter of faith with the people. These were, he said, a few of the reasons which induced the Legislative Assembly to waive the complimentary publication of the message, in hopes that his Excellency might consider his folly, mend his ways and pursue the course which he promised in the latter part of his message; but how consistently he had acted since that time, the audience would be able to judge after the reading of other documents during the meeting.

IMPORTANT DOCUMENTS FROM WASHINGTON.

Mr. Carrington then read correspondence from Hon. John M. Bernhisel, Delegate to Congress, and from the Hon. Wm. H. Hooper, Senator-elect, in which the unjustifiable proceedings of Governor Harding and the Associate-Justices Wane and Drake were exposed. Mr. Carrington read an extract from a letter, dated

Washington, 2nd January, in which Governor Harding was represented to have communicated to the Hon. Hannibal Hamlin, Vice-President of the United States and President of the Senate, his message, accompanied by a letter stating that the message had been suppressed through the influence of one of our prominent citizens, referring, unquestionably, to Governor Young. The following is the last paragraph of the letter referred to: "I entertain strong hopes that we shall be able to obtain, before the termination of the session, an appropriation to liquidate your Indian amounts, unless prevented by Governor Harding's insinuation of the disloyalty of our people."

The following is an extract from a letter, dated Washington, February, 1863: "On the 11th of December last, Senator Browning introduced a bill in the Senate, which was referred to the Committee on the Judiciary. This bill was prepared at Great Salt Lake City, and its enactment by Congress, recommended by Governor Harding and Judges Waite and Drake. The leading and most exceptional features of this bill are the following: 1st: It limits the jurisdiction of the Probate Court to the probate of wills, to the issue of letters of administration and the appointment of guardians. 2: It authorizes the Marshal to summon any persons within the district in which the court is held that he thinks proper as jurors. 3: It authorizes the Governor to appoint and commission all militia officers, including Major-General, and remove them at pleasure. It also confers on the Governor authority to appoint the days for training."

On the 27th of January, the Hon. Wm. H. Hooper writes from Washington that "Governor Harding is, of course, doing all he can by letters" against the people of Utah. His letter was chiefly occupied with the bill presented by Mr. Browning. The Senator's letter was entirely confirmatory of those from the pen of our Delegate. He says: "The bill has been presented and referred back. There does not appear to have been any action on it. It has not been printed; should it be, I will forward a copy. The bill was drawn up at Salt Lake City and attached with eyelets. Also attached was as follows: "The bill should be passed." Signed: S. S. Harding, Governor; Waite and Drake, Associate Justices."

The reading of these extracts created quite a sensation. When the insinuation of the disloyalty of the people was read, there was a loud murmur of dissatisfaction throughout the audience. Mr. Carrington's sarcastic reference to the Governor's promise "to help us" and his allusion to His Excellency's private room being a new place for drafting bills for the action of Congress, had a telling effect upon the meeting.

SPEECH OF HON. JOHN TAYLOR.

After the applause had subsided, which greeted his rising, Mr. Taylor said, "It has already been stated that these documents speak for themselves. They come from those who are ostensibly our guardians and the guardians of our rights. They come from men who ought to be actuated by the strictest principles of honor, truth, virtue, integrity, and honesty, and whose high official position ought to elevate them above suspicion, yet w, at are the results?

"In relation to the Governor's Message, enough perhaps has already been said. We are not here to enter into any labored political disquisitions, but to make some plain matter-of-fact statements, in which are involved the vital interests of this community. There is one feature, however, in that document which deserves a passing notice. It would seem that we are by direct implication accused of disloyalty. He states that he has not heard any sentiments expressed, either publicly or privately, that would lead him to believe that much sympathy is felt by any considerable portion of this people in favor of the Government of the United States. Perhaps we may not be so blatant and loud-spoken as some people are; but is it not patent to this community that the Legislature, during the session of 1861-2, assumed the Territorial quota of taxation, and at the very time that his Excellency was uttering this infamy, a resolution passed by the House, lay on the table, requesting the secretary to place a United States flag on the State House during the session. This was a small affair, yet significant of our feelings.

"It is not a matter of very grave importance to us generally what men may think of us, whether they be Government officials or not; but these allegations assume another form, and their wickedness is now rendered vindictive from the peculiar circumstances in which our nation at the present time is placed. When treason is stalking through the land, when all the energies, the wealth, the power of the United States have been brought into requisition to put down rebellion, when anarchy and distrust run riot through the nation; when, under these circumstances, we had a right to look for a friend in our Governor, who would, at least, fairly represent us, we have met a most insidious foe, who, through base insinuations, misrepresentations and falsehood, is seeking with all his power, privately and officially, not only to injure us before Government, but to sap the very foundations of our civil and religious liberty; he is, in fact, in pursuit of his unhallowed course, seeking to promote anarchy and rebellion, and dabbling in your blood. It is then a matter of no small importance (hear, hear). Such it would seem were Governor Harding's intentions when he read this message, such were his feelings when he concocted it. The document shows upon its face that it was not hastily written; it has been well digested and every word carefully weighed. It most assuredly contains the sentiments of his heart (hear, hear), of which his Washington letters are proof positive in relation to our alleged disloyalty.

"We are told about the generous reception of our senators-elect; of this we are most profoundly ignorant. Their reception was not so gracious as he would represent. He labors under error, for which we do not feel to reproach him; but what are we to think of his official letters to Washington? They are facts. What of his gracious acts of kindness to this people and to their representatives. From the statements of our representatives in Congress, he is the most vindictive enemy we have. The only man, it would seem, who is insidiously striving to sap the interests of the people, and to injure their reputation, yet he is our Governor, and professes to represent our interests and to feel intensely interested in our welfare. Let us investigate for a short time the results of his acts, should his designs be successful, leaving the allegations of treason out of the question.

"We have been in the habit of thinking that we live under the auspices of a republican government; that we had the right of franchise; that we had the privilege of voting for whom we pleased, and of saying who should represent us; but it may be that we are laboring under a mistake, a political illusion. We have thought too that if a man among us was accused of crimes, that it was his privilege to be tried by his peers; by people whom he lived among, who would be the best judges of his actions. We have farther been of the opinion that, while acting in a military capacity, when we were called to muster into service, to stand in defense of our country's rights, we had a right to the selection of our own officers. It is a republican usage—we have always elected our own militia officers; but if the plotting of Governor Harding and our honorable Judges should be carried into effect we can do so no more; we shall be deprived of franchise, of the rights of trial by an impartial jury, and shall be placed in a military capacity, under the creatures of Governor Harding or his successors' direction; in other words, we shall be deprived of all the rights of freemen, and placed under a military despotism; such would be the result of the passage of this act. Let us examine it a little. An act already framed by the Governor and Judges, passed in the congress of Governor Harding's sitting room, is forwarded to Washington with a request that it be passed. Now suppose it should, what would be the result? As I have stated, we suppose that we possess the rights of franchise; that is a mistake, we do not, we only think we do. The Governor has already taken that from us. How so? Have we not the privilege of voting for our own legislators, our own representatives in the Legislative Assembly? Yes. But the Governor possesses the power of veto. This old relic of Colonial barbarism ingrafted into our Territorial organization was always in existence among us, but never was so foully abused as in the person of our present Governor; he has done all he could to stop the wheels of government, and to produce dissatisfaction, and has exercised his veto to the fullest extent of his power. As an instance of this, there were twenty laws passed the Legislative Assembly, only six of which are approved; two of those were resolutions, one changing the place of meeting from the Court House to the State House, and the other the adjournment to next session. The other four are matters of minor importance, while everything connected with the welfare of the community, fourteen acts, are just so much waste paper. Now, I ask, where is your franchise? In Governor Harding's pocket, or stove.

"Again, in regard to juries, already referred to, you know what the usage has been, in relation to this matter. Governor Harding and the Judges want to place in the hands of the United States Marshal the power of selecting juries whom he pleases, no matter whither they come, or who they are. This is what our honorable Judges and Governor would attempt. Your liberties are aimed at, and your rights as freemen; and then, if you do not like to be disfranchised, and jog your liberties trampled under foot by a stranger—if you do not like to have blacklegs and cutthroats sit upon your juries. Mr. Harding wants to select his own military, and choose his own officers to lead them, and then if you will not submit, 'I will make you' [voices all over the house, 'Can't do it,' with loud applause.] We know he cannot do it, but this is what he aims at. [Clapping and great applause.] When these rights are taken from us, what rights have we left? [Cries of 'None.'] It could scarcely be credited that a man in his position would so far degrade himself as to introduce such outrageous principles, and it is lamentable to reflect upon, that men holding the position of United States' Judges could descend to such injustice, corruption and depravity [applause].

These things are so palpable that any man with five grains of common sense can comprehend them; 'he that runneth may read.' It is for you to judge whether you are willing to sustain such men in the capacity they act in or not. [One unanimous cry of 'No!' and loud clapping].

"GOVERNOR YOUNG'S SPEECH.

"On Governor Young responding to the invitation to address the meeting, and approaching the speaker's desk, he was greeted with prolonged deafening applause. He stated that he had no intention of delivering a lengthy address, but while he spoke he would solicit the quiet of the assembly. He knew well the feelings of his auditory; but would prefer that they should suppress their demonstrations of applause to other times and places, when they might have less business and more leisure. On the resumption of perfect silence, he said that they had heard the message of the Governor to the last Legislature of Utah. They would readily perceive that the bread was buttered, but there was poison underneath. It seemed to him that the enemies of the Union, of the Constitution and of the nation, were determined to ruin if they could not rule. A foreseeing person might suppose that they conspired to bring about a revolution in the west, so as to divide the Pacific from the Atlantic States, for their acts tended to that end. He believed that no true Democrat, no true Republican desired to see the nation distracted as it now was, but the labors of fanatics, whether they had plans which they comprehended or not, were in that direction. When Governor Harding came to this Territory last July, he sought to ingratiate himself into the esteem of our prominent citizens, with whom he had early intercourse, by his professed friendship and attachment to the people of Utah. He was then full of their praises, and said that he was ready to declare that he would stand in the defense of polygamy, or he should have to deny the Bible, and that he had told the President of the United States before he left Washington, that if he was called upon to agitate the question, he would have to take the side of polygamy, or he should have to renounce the Bible. He said, in the Bowery, on the 24th of July, and at other places and at other times that if he ever learned that he was obnoxious to the people, and they did not wish his presence, he would leave the Territory.

[Voices everywhere, 'He had better go now.'] "He was not aware whether the two Associate Judges were tools operating with him, or whether they knew no better. The success sought in their schemes was the establishment of a military government over the Territory, in the hopes of goading on the people to open rupture with the general government. Then, they would call out that Utah was disloyal! He was aware that nothing would please such men better than the arrest of all progress Westward; they would, no doubt of it, be delighted to see the stoppage of travel across the plains and all intercourse by mail or telegraph destroyed. Any amount of money had been employed by parties interested in mail transportation and passenger travel to the Pacific, by way of Panama, to destroy the highway across the plains; and there were men among them not above operating to the accomplishment of that end, under the pretense of other purposes.

"He then alluded to the law that was drafted in this city and sent to Washington for adoption by Congress, to take from the people their rights as free American citizens and portrayed the despotism that would follow placing the power of selecting jurors in the hands of a United States Marshal. Any such power could in the hands of designing men, destroy and subvert every right of free citizens. For that purpose, any class of disreputable men could at any time be imported into the Territory, and with a residence of a few hours be the ready tools for the accomplishment of any purpose. When their rights and the protection of their liberties were taken from them, what remained? [Voices, ' Nothing, nothing.'] Yes, service to tyrants, service to despots!

"He concluded his address by expressing that his feelings were that the nation might be happy and free as it had been, and exhorted the people to be true to themselves, to their country, to their God, and to their friends. Governor Young resumed his seat amidst great applause and cheering.

"Wm. Clayton, Esq., then read the following

"RESOLUTIONS:

"Resolved, That we consider the attack made upon us, by his Excellency Governor Harding, wherein our loyalty is impugned, as base, wicked, unjust and false; and he knew it to be so when uttered.

"Resolved, That we consider the attempt to possess himself of all military authority and dictation, by appointing all the militia officers, as a stretch at military despotism hitherto unknown in the annals of our Republic.

"Resolved, That we consider his attempt to control the selection of juries, as so base, unjust and tyrannical, as to deserve the contempt of all freemen.

"Resolved, That we consider the action of Judges Waite and Drake, in assisting the Governor to pervert justice and violate the sacred palladium of the people's rights, as subversive of the principles of justice, degrading to their high calling, and repulsive to the feelings of honest men.

"Resolved, That we consider that a serious attack has been made upon the liberties of this people, and that it not only affects us as a Territory, but is a direct assault upon Republican principles, in our own nation, and throughout the world; and that we cannot either tamely submit to be disfranchised ourselves, nor witness, without protest, the assassin's dagger plunged into the very vitals of our national institutions.

"Resolved, That while we at all times honor and magnify all wholesome laws of our country, and desire to be subservient to their dictates and the equitable administration of justice, we will resist, in a proper manner, every attempt upon the liberties guaranteed by our fathers, whether made by insidious foes, or open traitors.

"Resolved, That a committee be appointed, by the meeting, to wait upon the Governor and Judges Waite and Drake, to request them to resign their offices and leave the Territory.

"Resolved, That John Taylor, Jeter Clinton and Orson Pratt, Senior, be that committee.

"Resolved, That we petition the President of the United States to remove Governor Harding and Judges Waite and Drake, and to appoint good men in their stead.

"The Chairman called upon the meeting for an expression of their wishes and the building rang with a glorious 'Aye' for their adoption.

"The following petition was likewise read and committed to the people for their action:

THE PETITION TO PRESIDENT LINCOLN.

"To his Excellency, Abraham Lincoln, President of the United States:

"Sir—We, your petitioners, citizens of the Territory of Utah, respectfully represent that: "Whereas, From the most reliable information in our possession, we are satisfied that his Excellency Stephen S. Harding, Governor, Charles B. Waite and Thomas J. Drake, Associate Justices, are strenuously endeavoring to create mischief and stir up strife between the people of the Territory of Utah and the troops now in Camp Douglas (situated within the limits of Great Salt Lake City,) and, of far graver import in our Nation's present difficulties, between the people of the aforesaid Territory and the Government of the United States.

"Therefore, We respectfully petition your Excellency to forthwith remove the aforesaid persons from the offices they now hold, and to appoint in their places men who will attend to the duties of their offices, honor their appointments, and regard the rights of all, attending to their own affairs and leaving alone the affairs of others; and in all their conduct demeaning themselves as honorable citizens and officers worthy of commendation by yourself, our Government and all good men; and for the aforesaid removals and appointments your petitioners will most respectfully continue to pray.

"Great Salt Lake City, Territory of Utah, March 3, 1863."

The same unanimous approval followed the reading of the petition. The band then played " The Marseillaise," and the chairman dissolved the meeting. The News says—

"By way of conclusion, we must add that we never saw a more earnest, yet calm and deliberate assembly in Utah or elsewhere; the rights of the people were threatened, and they solemnly entered their protest, leaving the results for the future in the hands of an overruling Providence. Before eight o'clock last evening, upwards of 2,100 signatures were affixed to the petition, and, no doubt, there will be a large addition to that number in the course of to-day."

The following is the report of the committee:

"G. S. L. City, March 5, 1863.

"To the citizens of Great Salt Lake City: "Gentlemen: "Your committee, appointed at the mass meeting held in the Tabernacle on the 3rd inst., waited upon his Excellency Governor Harding and their Honors Judges Waite and Drake, on the morning of the 4th.

"Governor Harding received us cordially, but, upon being informed of the purport of our visit, both himself and Judge Drake, who was in the Governor's office, emphatically refused to comply with the wishes of the people, notwithstanding the Governor had repeatedly stated that he would leave whenever he learned that his acts and course were not agreeable to the people.

"Upon being informed that, if he was not satisfied that the action of the mass meeting expressed the feelings of the people, he could have the expression of the whole Territory, he replied, 'I am aware of that, but that would make no difference.'

"Your committee called at the residence of Judge Waite, who, being absent at the time, has since informed us, by letter, that he also refuses to comply with the wishes of the people.

JOHN TAYLOR, JETER CLINTON, ORSON PRATT, Sen."

CHAPTER XXXIV.

A COUNTER PETITION FROM CAMP DOUGLAS TO PREST. LINCOLN. IMPENDING CONFLICT BETWEEN CAMP DOUGLAS AND THE CITY. A SUPPOSED CONSPIRACY TO ARREST BRIGHAM YOUNG AND RUN HIM OFF TO THE STATES. JUDGES WAITE AND DRAKE HOLD UNLAWFUL COURTS IN JUDGE KINNEY'S DISTRICT. THE CHIEF JUSTICE INTERPOSES WITH A WRIT TO ARREST BRIGHAM YOUNG FOR POLYGAMY. IT IS SERVED BY THE U. S. MARSHAL INSTEAD OF A MILITARY POSSE. THE CITY IN ARMS. EXPECTING A DESCENT FROM CAMP DOUGLAS. THE WARNING VOICE OF CALIFORNIA HEARD. BOOMING OF THE GUNS OF CAMP DOUGLAS AT MIDNIGHT. THE CITY AGAIN IN ARMS. FALSE ALARM. CONNOR CREATED BRIGADIER-GENERAL.

A counter petition signed by the officers of Camp Douglas and the non-Mormons of Salt Lake City was sent to President Lincoln urging the retention of Governor Harding, and Judges Drake and Waite.

The issue of affairs had now reached the condition of impending war between the camp and the city, while Chief Justice John F. Kinney occupied a similar position in the case to that of Governor Cumming, when the conflict was threatened between the city and Camp Floyd. It was the prevailing opinion of the citizens that a descent upon the city by Colonel Connor and his troops to arrest Brigham and his counselors might be expected at any moment. It was also further believed that could this be accomplished, by a dashing "surprise," the intention was to run these Mormon leaders off to the States for trial. General Connor and his officers have indignantly denied any such intentions on the part of Camp Douglas; but, it is certain, that the citizens thus viewed the prospect in those days, which to them signified the prospect of a fierce conflict and the shedding of much blood; for the citizens never would have permitted Brigham Young to have been taken to Camp Douglas, and held under military guard, as the Mayor of Great Salt Lake City was a decade later. No mere historical summary could harmonize the views of the camp and the city; but for an appreciation of the situation and the excited condition of the then public mind, both of California and Utah, we must cull from the chronicles of those times. The first presented is from the Deseret News of March 11, 1863: "We have been aware for a number of days that the issuance of writs against President Young was in contemplation. There has been an unusual stir at Camp Douglas, the most ample preparations made for the purpose of making a descent with an armed force upon the President, whenever those writs should be placed in the hands of the marshal. It was vainly and foolishly supposed that he would resist the service of a writ issued under the act referred to. Persons desiring collision were anxious to make the pretext of an armed military force in executing this process, the excuse for gratifying their wicked purposes. But in this they have been disappointed. As a people we believe in and have ever taught obedience and submission to the laws of the land. No one has more earnestly taught this than the President of this church. It is well known that in his private and public teachings he has taken the position of obedience to any legal writ emanating from proper authority, whether against him or any of the people under this or any other law.

"On the 10th inst., an affidavit w.is made before His Honor Chief Justice J. F. Kinney, charging Brigham Young with having violated the act of Congress, by taking another wife. Judge Kinney promptly issued a writ for his arrest and placed it in the hands of Mr. Gibbs, United States marshal. The marshal adopted the very prudent course of serving the writ himself, without calling a "posse," and accordingly waited upon the President, only fortified by the process and with such civil authority as the law invested him.

"An immediate response was made to the writ, by the prompt appearance of the defendant before Judge Kinney at the State House, accompanied by two or three of his immediate friends. An investigation was made of the facts charged in the affidavit, by the introduction of evidence, resulting in the Judge holding the defendant to bail in the sum of two thousand dollars, for his appearance at the next term of the United States Court for the Third Judicial District.

"The sureties were required to justify under oath, when it appeared that they were worth some twenty thousand dollars.

"We have no fault to find with Judge Kinney for issuing the process, or his determination upon the testimony. As the judge of this district, he can make no distinction, and it is his duty to magnify all constitutional law, as we trust it will ever be the pleasure of the people to submit to and obey the authority with which such law invests him."

Of simultaneous date the California press on Utah affairs gives the following pungent views:

[From the Daily Alta California, March 11.]

"We have some strange news to-day from Salt Lake, via New York. It is to the effect that there is danger of a collision between the Mormons and our troops there. The dispatch goes so far as to state that Governor Harding and Associate Justices Waite and Drake have called upon Col. Connor to arrest Brigham Young and some of the Mormon leaders. It is strange that we have heard nothing on this side of these important events, and that the first intimation we should have of what is going on should reach us via New York. We had, to be sure, a report, recently of some angry meetings which had taken place there, but we had no idea that anything serious was going on.

"To get at the facts of the case we telegraphed to Salt Lake last night. The telegram which we received does not clear up matters fully. Our correspondent speaks of an anti-bigamy law as the cause of the trouble. We do not know of any except the one providing for the admission of Utah as a State, provided polygamy was abolished. The whole affair therefore is still enveloped in some confusion. There is one thing, however, that we do know; Colonel P. Edward Connor and his regiment were sent across the mountains to protect the telegraph and the overland mail, and to fight the Indians, and not to kick up trouble with the Mormons or any other class of persons The Government has enough of fighting now on its hands and there is no necessity for increasing it. Perhaps an expenditure of a few more millions of dollars in a Utah war is deemed necessary to promote the happiness of somebody behind the scenes."

[From Sacramento Daily Union, March 12.]

"It seems that matters at Salt Lake are in an unsettled and uncertain state. Some difficulty has grown up between the Governor, the United States Judges, and the head of the Mormon Church, which may—though we hope not—terminate in a collision. We never deemed it particularly an act of wisdom to order a single regiment to Salt Lake. It was not needed there for protection, and in the event of a collision was to weak too be of any particular use. We fear, too, that the Governor has been imprudent. The Mormons should, of course, submit to the laws, but laws ought not be forced upon them which are repugnant to a very large majority of that singular people. A conflict at this time would prove a great misfortune to California. It would also prove fatal to the Mormons, and hence we reason that they will avoid any hostile demonstrations except in self-defense. The pretty-much let-alone policy is the one which should be adopted toward the Mormons."

[From the Daily Alta California, March 14.]

"In our columns to-day will be found an interesting letter from Salt Lake.

It gives an account of the commencement of the troubles there. Our next will, in all probability, bring down the narrative to the late proceedings. Mr. Lincoln, it must be admitted, has been very unfortunate in the selection of officeholders. If his intention in sending Harding to rule over the Mormons was to kick up a row there, he has succeeded. The policy of such a proceeding, just at this juncture, however, may very well be doubted. We have enough of fighting on hand at present."

It will be observed, from the above editorial passages, that the two great journals of San Francisco and Sacramento, speaking for California, manifested a decided agreement with the judgment of California's senators, as stated by Senator McDougal in his speech opposing the passage of the anti-polygamic bill and emphasized by the votes of himself and colleague, Senator Latham. Neither of these statesmen favored polygamy, much less did they intend to imply by their solitary "nays" against both Houses of Congress that Utah could continue the practice of polygamy with the consent of California. Senator McDougal's words very sagely but simply expounded the case and the situation.

Only a few months had elapsed since the passage of the anti-polygamy bill of '62 and California and Utah were now nearly brought into a conflict over an improper attempt at its execution, for it is apparent that had a conflict ensued between the Utah militia and the California Volunteers, these "sister States of the Pacific"

must themselves have been brought into the conflict. The warning passage from the Sacramento Daily Union was very pointed: "A conflict at this time would prove a great misfortune to California. It would also prove fatal to the Mormons."

This with the stinging passage from the Daily Alta doubtless had the desired effect, both upon the Volunteers and the people of Great Salt Lake City. Colonel Connor and his officers could not with indifference read California's reminder to them that they were sent across the mountains to protect the overland mail and to fight the Indians "and not to kick up trouble with the Mormons."

But in the foregoing excerpts from the Deseret News and the California press there are merely a few points of detail of the stirring events which came nigh to the very pitch of battle.

It must be told for a comprehension of the alarm of those times that not only had Governor Harding vetoed nearly every act passed by the Legislature of that year, as he soon afterwards overrode nearly all the judicial decisions of the Chief Justice by wholesale pardons, which whether deserved or not leaves the sequence of events the same, but Judges Waite and Drake were also setting aside the Chief Justice in his own district, where they presumed unlawfully to hold courts, and that, too, while he was holding his regular term with a grand jury at business daily bringing in their indictments. The Deseret News commenting upon "Judge Waite and his judicial presumption " said: "We are not a little astonished at His Honor Judge Waite assuming the prerogative of holding court in the third district, when the Legislature had assigned him to the second.

"We confess we were prepared to witness almost anything from the disaffected Judge, but hardly ready to behold so strange a spectacle as a Judge assuming judicial authority in defiance of law.

"The ninth section of the Organic Law provides as follows: '"The Territory shall be divided into three judicial districts, and a district court shall be held in each of said districts by one of the justices of the supreme court, at such time and place as shall be prescribed by law, and the judges shall, after their appointment, respectively reside in the districts which shall be assigned them.' "This is a plain, unequivocal provision and should be complied with by those whose duty it is to administer the law. Two months have elapsed since the Legislature assigned Judge Waite to the second district, and yet, in place of submitting to and obeying the law, which His Honor has sworn to support, we find him still in this city issuing writs and holding an examining court.

"Aside from the illegality of the proceeding, common courtesy, it seems to us, if His Honor had no regard for the law, should have operated to deter the Judge from assuming judicial power in Judge Kinney's district."

There had been no alarm in the city over a proper warrant of arrest of Brigham Young, to test in his person the constitutionality of the anti-polygamy bill of 1862, or its operative powers, which latter it may be said was at that time as nothing with a polygamic grand jury, who believed that bill to be unconstitutional and that it would be so decided when it came before the Supreme Court of the United States. The alarm was at the prospect of the issuance of a writ for the arrest of President Young through the same associate Justice Waite who, it was believed, for this and similar purposes was with Associate Justice Drake administering in the district of the Chief Justice. It was with this view that the Deseret News noted: "We have been aware for a number of days that the issuance of writs against President Young was in contemplation ;" and further, "there has been an unusual stir at Camp Douglas, the most ample preparations made for the purpose of making a descent with an armed force upon the President whenever those writs should be placed in the hands of the marshal." In fine, the writ which was issued by Chief Justice Kinney, upon an affidavit made by one of the citizens, charging Brigham Young with violating the act of Congress prohibiting polygamy, was designed to prevent the arrest of Brigham Young by those other improper writs in contemplation to be executed by military force. The further note on the execution is like a volume of history of the case: "Judge Kinney promptly issued a writ for his arrest and placed it in the hands of Mr. Gibbs, United States marshal. The marshal adopted the very prudent course of serving the writ himself, without calling for a posse, and accordingly waited upon the President, only fortified by the process and with such civil authority as the law invested him." Thus was a very different result obtained from that of the arrest of Brigham Young by the "descent of an armed force," as a " posse" to execute a writ issued by Judge Waite to bring the prisoner before his court, to be held at Camp Douglas or wherever it might have pleased him and his Associate Judge Drake and Governor Harding. Here may be told a part of the story of those times by Mr. Stenhouse, from his Rocky Mountain Saints, though in some respects it is different from his " interesting letters," published in the San Francisco Alta, the Sacramento Union, and in the New York Herald, which gave the current views of Utah affairs to the American public, east and west: "Colonel Connor had visited Judge Waite, and, on leaving his house, one of the elders, who was loitering about, believed that he overheard the colonel say: 'These three men must be surprised.' That was sufficient. Instantly the eavesdropper flew to Brigham. The Prophet believed the story, hoisted a signal to rally the militia, and in half an hour a thousand armed men surrounded his premises, and within an hour another thousand were armed and on duty. The city was in commotion, and rifles, lead, and powder, were brought out of their hiding places. On the inside of the high walls surrounding Brigham's premises, scaffolding was hastily erected in order to enable the militia to fire down upon passing Volunteer? The houses on the route which occupied a commanding position where an attack could be made upon the troops were taken possession of, the small cannon were brought out and the brethren prepared to protect the Prophet.

"There was no truth in the rumor of an intended arrest of Brigham and his counsellors. The Mormon leaders, all the same, believed it to be true, and they were cautious and watchful. A powerful telescope was placed on the top of Brigham's 'Beehive' residence, and every move of the Volunteers in Camp Douglas was watched with great care. Night and day, for several weeks, there was a body of armed men around the Prophet, and signals agreed upon, by which the whole people could be rallied by night or by day.

"The Volunteers were not numerous enough to ' overawe' the Mormons, and their presence was on that account, all the more irksome. To know that they 'could use them up any morning before breakfast,' and yet be forced to tolerate their presence on the brow of a hill, like a watch-tower, was irritating to the Prophet's mind. The Tabernacle resounded with fierce denunciations every Sunday. Mischief-makers poured into the ears of the Prophet every story that could increase his prejudice against Colonel Connor; and the latter heard quite as much to incense him against Brigham. A collision for a long time seemed inevitable.

"Providing for the possibility of a rupture at any moment, it was agreed that, if the struggle came by night, the citizens were to be summoned to arms by firing cannon from the hill-side, at the east of Brigham's residence; and, if the difficulty began during the day, the flag was to be hoisted over his Bee-Hive residence. To the latter signal the citizens had once responded; and it was believed that their readiness to fight for the Prophet had intimidated the commander of the Volunteers, so that he would be unlikely to make an attack by day. At that time, it was believed that Colonel Connor, having been foiled in this first attempt, entertained the idea of making a dash upon the Prophet's bed-room 'in the dead of night,' seizing him, and running him off to the States before the Mormons could learn of his situation, and render him any assistance.

"General Connor never had orders to arrest Brigham Young, or he would have done so—or tried. At the time of the conversation with Judge Waite, already referred to, which created the panic and the assembling of the Mormons in arms, the Prophet was not the subject of consideration. One of the brethren had married the three widows of a wealthy merchant within sight of Judge Waite's residence, and as that was an excellent case in which to try the application of the Anti-Polygamic Law, the General replied to the Judge that he would arrest him if the court furnished the order. The anticipation that difficulty would arise, from Judge Waite acting within Judge Kinney's judicial district while the latter was present, was the only thing that prevented the arrest.

"On the night of the 29th of March, the citizens were aroused by the booming of cannon. As hastily as garments could be thrown on, and arms could be seized, the brethren were seen hurrying from their homes towards the Prophet's residence. The struggle was apparently at hand. The signal cannon had been distinctly heard, and, as there was a gentle current of air from the east, those who lived west of the Prophet could hear the very music to which the Volunteers were supposed to be marching into the heart of the city!

"For his great victory over Bear Hunter and other Indian chiefs, in a desperate battle in the depth of winter, two months before, Colonel Connor had now been promoted to the rank of Brigadier-General, and the news had only just reached Camp Douglas! The military band had been called out to serenade the promoted commander, and the cannon was roaring over the mountains in honor of the victor!

"Fortunately for those concerned, Elder A. O. Smoot, and not some mad fanatic, was mayor of the city of the Saints in those troublesome times."

CHAPTER XXXV.

TRIAL OF THE MORRISITES. SENTENCE OF THE PRISONERS. THEY ARE IMMEDIATELY PARDONED BY GOVERNOR HARDING. COPIES OF THE EXTRAORDINARY PARDONS. THE GRAND JURY DECLARES THE LAW OUTRAGED AND PRESENTS GOVERNOR HARDING IN THE THIRD U. S. DISTRICT COURT FOR JUDICIAL CENSURE. THEIR HISTORY OF THE MORRISITE DISTURBANCE. THE COURT SUSTAINS THE CENSURE.

At the March term of the Third U. S. District Court the famous Morrisite trial took place with Chief Justice John F. Kinney presiding. Ten of the prisoners were indicted for killing two of the U. S. posse sent to enforce the law which the Morrisite community openly defied; several of these were convicted, one "nolled," and two were acquitted. Sixty-six others were fined one hundred dollars each for resisting the posse. Of the seven convicted of " murder in the second degree" one was sentenced to fifteen years' imprisonment, one to twelve years, and five to ten years each. Immediately after the passing of the sentence the following pardons were granted by Governor Harding, embracing the whole of the Morrisite prisoners.

"Utah Territory, Executive Department.

To all to whom these presents shall come greeting: "Whereas, at the March term of the District Court for the Third Judicial District in said Territory, A. D. 1863. The Honorable John F. Kinney presiding.

Peter Klemgard, Christen Nielsen, Gens Christensen, Kadrup Nielsen, Abraham Taylor, Andrew Lee, and Andrew M. Mason were convicted of murder in the second degree, and sentenced each for a term of years, at hard labor in the Penitentiary.

"Now, know ye, that I, Stephen S. Harding, Governor of the Territory of Utah, divers good causes me thereto moving, by virtue of the power in me vested, have given and granted, and by these presents do give and grant unto the said Peter Klemgard, Christen Nielsen, Gens Christensen, Kadrup Nielsen, Abrar ham Taylor, Andrew Lee, and Andrew M. Mason, and to each of them, full and perfect pardon for the offense aforesaid, of which they stand convicted, and they are, and each of them is, hereby forever exonerated, discharged, and absolved from the punishment imposed upon them or either of them, in pursuance of said conviction.

"In testimony whereof I have hereunto set my hand, and caused the [L.S.] Great Seal of the Territory of Utah to be affixed at Great Salt Lake City this 31st day of March, A. D. 1863.

STE. S. HARDING.
Gov. of Utah Territory.
"By the Governor: Frank Fuller, Secretary."

"Utah Territory, Executive Department.

" To all to whom these presents shall come greeting; "Whereas, at the March term of the District Court for the Third Judicial District in said Territory, A. D. 1863. The Honorable John F. Kinney presiding.

Richard Cook, John Parson, Edward Moss, Daniel Smith, John B. Ledgeway, John O. Mather, James Mather, Richard D. Aloey, Alexander Warrender, William

McGhie, Elijah L. Chappel, John E. Jones, John Cook, David Thomas, Peter John Moss, Joseph Taylor, Mathew Mudd, James Bowman, Robert E. Farley, William W. Thomas, Alexander Dow, John Keehorn, John C. Edwards, John Gray, Joseph Dove, Thomas L. Williams, William Davis, Alonzo Brown, Edward Lloyd, Samuel Halse, Elijah Clitford, George Thompson, Goodman Goodmunsen, Charles Higham, John E. Reese, Soren Peter Gould, Jorjen Jensen, Soren Willissen, Lars Christen Hanson, Andres Jensen, Swen Hagg, Soren Peter Rasmussen, Hans Peterson, Peter Peterson, John Peter Sorensen, Neils Larsen, Neils Andersen, Michael Christen Christiansen, Gens Paulsen, Neils Peterson, Lars Christen Larsen, Hans Aggerson, John G. Looselary, Lebrecht Barr, John Neilsen, Nels Rasmussen Beck, Christen Jensen, Peter Swenson, Neils Magnus Jorensen, Rasmus Rasmussen, James Peterson, Lars Olsen, Gens Christian Senensen, Hans Peter Smith, Andres Anderson, Andres Christopherson, Hans Hanson, Ole Rosenblade, and Peter Sorenson were convicted of the charge of resisting an officer in the service of process, and sentenced each to pay a fine of one hundred dollars.

"Now know ye, that I, Stephen S. Harding, Governor of the Territory of Utah, divers good causes me thereto moving, by virtue of the power and authority in me vested have given and granted, and by these presents do give and grant unto the said Richard Cook, etc., etc., (all of the aforementioned,) and to each of them full and perfect pardon for the offence of which they stand convicted, and they are, and each one of them is, hereby forever exonerated, discharged and absolved from the fine, costs and charges imposed upon them, or either of them, in pursuance of said conviction.

"In testimony whereof I have hereunto set my hand, and caused the [L.S.] Great Seal of the Territory of Utah to be affixed at Great Salt Like City this 31st day of March, A. D. 1863.

STE. S. HARDING, Gov. Utah Territory.

"By the Governor: Frank Fuller, Secretary."

Of the relative merit or demerit of the action of the United States and Territorial authorities concerned in the Morrisite affair the historian does not presume to touch, further than to present the record itself and its significance. The Chief Justice and the Grand Jury considered the law outraged, as set forth in the following presentment of Governor Harding for judicial censure and the very plain passage of censure by the Chief Justice in court: "We trust the court will pardon the Grand Jury for briefly referring to the facts connected with the arrest and trial of the men the Governor has seen proper, in such hot haste, to pardon and turn loose upon the community.

"They are as follows: On the 22nd day of May, A. D. 1862, a petition was filed before Hon. John F. Kinney, the Judge of the Third Judicial District, for a writ of habeas corpus, alleging that three men were unlawfully imprisoned at South Weber, in Davis County, and kept in close confinement, heavily ironed, without any process or authority of law. It may be well to state that, at the place mentioned in the petition, a body of some two hundred men with their families had congregated in what is known as Kington Fort, and for more than a year had remained without cultivating the soil or following any industrial pursuit. What little property they had was owned in common, and this from time to time was disposed of to procure the bare necessaries of life.

"At this place and by these men were the prisoners confined (mentioned in the petition for the writ of habeas corpus). The writ was issued and served upon those who had the prisoners in custody, on the 24th day of May. No attention was paid to it by defendants. The authority of the court was openly contemned and placed at defiance. Judge Kinney, after waiting for the defendants to produce the prisoners from the 24th day of May till the 11th day of June (some eighteen days) issued, upon another affidavit, a writ for false imprisonment, another writ of habeas corpus, and a writ for contempt for disobedience to the first writ. These writs were placed in the hands of the Territorial marshal, who, being well advised that armed resistance would be made to the service of any process in said fort, called upon Acting-Governor Fuller, who furnished the officer with a military posse to enable him to execute the mandates of the court. On the morning of the 13th day of June, the marshal with his posse arrived near the fort and sent the following proclamation under a flag, which was received and read by Banks and others, the parties named in said writs, and to whom said proclamation was directed:

"'Headquarters Marshal's Posse, Weber River, June 13, 1862.
"'To Joseph Morris, John Banks, Richard Cook, John Parsons and Peter Klemgard:'" Whereas, you have heretofore disregarded and defied the judicial officers and the laws of the Territory of Utah; and whereas, certain writs have been issued for you from the Third Judicial District Court of said Territory, and a sufficient force furnished by the Executive of the same to enforce the law: This is therefore to notify you to peaceably and quietly surrender yourselves and the prisoners in your custody forthwith.

"' An answer is required in thirty minutes after the receipt of this document; if not, forcible measures will be taken for your arrest.

"'Should you disregard this proposition and place your lives in jeopardy, you are hereby required to remove your women and children; and all persons peaceably disposed are hereby notified to forthwith leave your encampment, and are informed by this proclamation that they can find protection with this posse.
H. W. LAWRENCE, Territorial Marshal.
"'Per R. T. Burton and Theodore McKean, Deputies.'"

"This was unheeded and disregarded. Additional time was given after the expiration of the thirty minutes for the delivery of the persons called for by the writ; still no attention was paid to the demands of the officer. At length fire was opened and for three days, almost continuously, did the belligerents within the fort keep up a fire on the marshal and his posse, killing on the first day a man by the name of Jared Smith, and on the third day another man attached to the marshal's posse. On the evening of the 15th the rebellion was subdued by the surrender of the men, and one hundred stand of arms. Parties on both sides had been killed in consequence of the defiant position taken against the enforcement of the law, and in defending the position thus unlawfully assumed by more than one hundred well-armed men.

"The disloyal men thus found in arms, fighting against the service of process, were taken prisoners, taken before Judge Kinney, in chambers, who admitted all but two to bail for their appearance at the next March term of the court— said two being committed to await their trial for murder. At the recent sitting of the Territorial

Court, Judge Kinney presiding, some ninety or more were indicted under the statute for resisting an officer, and ten of the principle men for the murder of Jared Smith, who was shot dead on the first day of the resistance.

Sixty-six appeared and were tried for resisting the officer, the others having left the country. After a long, patient and entirely satisfactory trial to the defendants, the jury assessed a fine of one hundred dollars against each of them—the lowest sum allowed by the statute and when the law authorized them to fine not exceeding one thousand dollars and imprisonment not exceeding one year. The least punishment allowed by the statute was meted out to the prisoners, and that, too, when the testimony of their guilt was overwhelming of the ten indicted for murder, one was nulled, two acquitted and seven convicted of murder in the second degree.

The punishment for murder in the second degree is imprisonment not less than ten years and may be during natural life; still the jury actuated by feelings of humanity and mercy, affixed the punishment of five of the prisoners to imprisonment for the period of ten years each, one for twelve and one for fifteen years.

****

"But, the Governor, clothed with the pardoning power, interposes to prevent the punishment due to rebels against the law. He sanctions and sustains their rebellion and, by pardoning them, proclaims to the world that they have acted rightly, wisely and lawfully. Na time is allowed for investigation, none for repentance or reformation; but in less than three days from the time of the sentence of the court, are all of them pardoned by the Executive, to renew their armed resistance against the power of the Government—a pardon which not only seeks to release them from fine and punishment, but the costs due to the officers and witnesses.

******** '

"Therefore, we the United States Grand Jury for the Third judicial District for the Territory of Utah, present his 'Excellency' Stephen S. Harding, Governor of Utah, as we would an unsafe bridge over a dangerous stream—jeopardizing the lives of all who pass over it, or, as we would a pestiferous cesspool in our district, breeding disease and death.

"Believing him to be an officer dangerous to the peace and prosperity of this Territory; refusing, as he has, his assent to wholesome and needed legislation; treating nearly all the Legislative acts with contumely; and last of all, as the crowning triumph of his inglorious career, turning loose upon the community a large number of convicted criminals.

"We cannot do less than present his Excellency as not only a dangerous man, but also as one unworthy the confidence and respect of a free and enlightened people.

"All of which is respectfully submitted.

"George A. Smith, Franklin D. Richards, Elias Smith, William S. Muir, Samuel F. Atwood, Philip Margetts, John Rowberry, Claudius V. Spencer, Chas. J. Thomas, John W. Myers, Alfred Cordon, George W. Ward, Horace Gibbs, Lewis A. West, Leonard G. Rice, Isaac Brockbank, George W. Bryan, James Bond, John B. Kelley, Gustavus Williams, Wells Smith, John D. T. McAllister, Andrew Cunningham.

His Honor directed, that in accordance with the request, they be spread upon the records of the court.

The foreman of the Grand Jury then stated that they had concluded their labors, and had no further business before them, whereupon the Judge addressed them as follows: " Gentlemen of the Grand Jury: "The paper just read by the clerk, is one of great responsibility, presenting the Governor of this Territory as unworthy the confidence and respect of the people.

"I trust you have fully considered the importance of the step which you as a Grand Jury have felt called upon, under the oaths of your office, to take.

"I am well persuaded that in no spirit of malice or undue prejudice have you been induced to call the attention of the Court and people to what you regard as the official misconduct of the Executive, but only as the deliberate result of your investigations for the public good.

"I am perfectly familiar with the facts referred to by you in relation to the armed resistance to the law in the service of process. Upon affidavit made before me were the writs issued, the service of which was attempted to be resisted by an armed rebellion.

"The trial of men thus found in arms very recently took place in the Court over which I have the honor to preside, and the trial, as you state, was conducted with deliberation, and the verdict of the jury in each of the cases for resisting the officer and for murder were such as met with the approval of the court.

"The law and its authority were fully vindicated by the verdicts, but, as you state, the Governor has granted an unconditional pardon.

"What effect this may have upon the minds of evil disposed persons I know not, but leave the responsibility where it belongs, with the Governor, who, in the exercise of a naked power, has seen proper to grant executive clemency.

"You have now, as you state, concluded your labors and before discharging you I desire to tender to you the commendations of the Court for your attention and diligence in the discharge of your duties.

"Your labors have resulted in the presentation of a number of indictments for crime—some of the prisoners charged by you having been tried and convicted, and others are awaiting their trial.

"It is only by a grand jury discharging their duty faithfully and fearlessly that crime can be suppressed, and offenders punished, for all persons must pass the ordeal of your body, before they can be introduced by the Government into this Court for trial and punishment.

"It is possible, and highly probable, that this is the last court over which I shall have the honor to preside in your Territory. Such are the indications. I have been the Chief Justice of the Supreme Court of Utah, and Judge of this district most of the time since 1854—having come among you a stranger, but I was treated with kindness, and my authority with consideration and respect.

"Appointed by Mr. Pierce in 1853, and reappointed in 1860 by Mr. Buchanan, and continued in office by Mr. Lincoln, and having held many courts, tried many cases, both civil and criminal, of an important character, I am happy in being able to state that I have found no difficulty in Utah in administering the law, except where its administration has been thwarted by Executive interference.

"Let honesty, impartiality and ability be the characteristic qualifications of the Judge, and a fearless discharge of duty, and he will be as much respected in this Territory, and his decisions as much honored, as in any State or Territory of the Union. And to use an odious distinction, attempted to be made between 'Mormon' and 'Gentile,' I am also happy in being able to state, that while these parties, differing so widely as they do in their religious faith, have been suitors in my court, the so-called Gentile, has obtained justice from the verdict of a so-called ' Mormon' jury.

"I repeat gentlemen, that the law is, and can be maintained in this Territory, and that there is more vigilance here in arresting and bringing criminals to trial and punishment than in any country where I have ever resided.

"In the discharge of my judicial duties, I have endeavored to be actuated by a sense of the responsibility of my position; ever keeping constantly in mind that I was among a civilized and enlightened people, who were entitled to the same consideration from the court, as the people of any other Territory; and that the court here, as well as elsewhere, should be free from bias and prejudice.

"Gentlemen, accept my thanks for your co-operation, in support of my efforts to maintain and enforce the law.

"To the Petit Jurors I will say, that I have been well sustained by them in the trial of causes and can only hope that when I retire from the bench my successor will be an able, honest judge, and have no more difficulty in discharging his duties than I have had.

"With these remarks, gentlemen, I dismiss you from further attendance upon the court."

Mr. Ferguson moved that as the Grand Jury were discharged without finding an indictment against Brigham Young, that he be discharged from his recognizance.

CHAPTER XXXVI.

REMOVAL OF GOVERNOR HARDING, SECRETARY FULLER, AND CHIEF JUSTICE KINNEY. LINCOLN'S POLICY TO "LET THE MORMONS ALONE." STARTING OF THE UNION VEDETTE. OPENING OF THE UTAH MINES. MILITARY DOCUMENTS, CREATION OF A PROVOST MARSHAL OF GREAT SALT LAKE CITY.

The counter petitions to the President of the United States from the city and camp, one for the removal and the other for the retention of Governor Harding, were responded to by concessions to both parties. Governor Harding, Secretary Fuller and Chief Justice Kinney were removed; James Duane Doty was appointed Governor; Amos Reed, Secretary; and John Titus of Pennsylvania, Chief Justice.

The official decapitation of the Governor was clearly in answer to the petition of the citizens, while the removal of Chief Justice Kinney and Secretary Fuller was in consideration of the charge made against them—that they had been "subservient to the will of Brigham Young." The Chief Justice had for months felt that in maintaining the integrity of the judicial department he was placing himself upon the altar of sacrifice, as shown in his parting words to the grand jury; but his official relations with Utah were not permitted to end with his removal, for at the next election, in August, 1863, he was sent to Congress as Delegate from Utah.

The following noteworthy passage of a letter from President Brigham Young to Elder George Q. Cannon, then in England, expresses the policy of the Government towards Utah during the remainder of President Lincoln's life:

"Great Salt Lake City, U. T., June 25, 1863.

" President Cannon: "Dear Brother— * * * Since Harding's departure on the 11th inst., without the least demonstration from any party, and only one individual to bid him good-bye, the transient persons here continue very quiet, and apparently without hope of being able to create any disturbance during the present Administration. They certainly will be unable to, if President Lincoln stands by his statement made to Brother Stenhouse on the 6th inst., viz: 'I will let them alone if they will let me alone.' We have ever been anxious to let them alone further than preaching to them the gospel and doing them good when they would permit us, and if they will cease interfering with us unjustly and unlawfully, as the President has promised, why of course they will have no pretext nor chance for collision during his rule. * * *

"Your brother in the gospel,
BRIGHAM YOUNG."

On the 20th of November, 1863, the first number appeared of The Union Vedette, published, as announced, "by officers and enlisted men of the California and Nevada Territory Volunteers."

The initial number of the Vedette contains the following circular letter from General Connor, relative to mines and mining interests in this Territory:

"Headquarters, District of Utah,
Great Salt Lake City, U. T. November 14, 1863.

"Colonel: "The general commanding the district has the strongest evidence that the mountains and canyons in the Territory of Utah abound in rich veins of gold, silver, copper and other minerals, and for the purpose of opening up the country to a new, hardy, and industrious population, deems it important that prospecting for minerals should not only be untrammeled and unrestricted, but fostered by every proper means. In order that such discoveries may be early and reliably made, the general announces that miners and prospecting parties will receive the fullest protection from the military forces in this district, in the pursuit of their avocations; provided, always, that private rights are not infringed upon. The mountains and their now hidden mineral wealth, are the sole property of the nation, whose beneficent policy has ever been to extend the broadest privileges to her citizens, and, with open hand, invite all to seek, prospect and possess the wonderful riches of her wide-spread domain.

"To the end that this policy may be fully carried out in Utah, the General commanding assures the industrious and enterprising who may come hither, of efficient protection, accorded as it is by the laws and policy of the nation, and enforced, when necessary, by the military arm of the Government.

"The General in thus setting forth the spirit of our free institutions for the information of commanders of posts within the district, also directs that every proper facility be extended to miners and others in developing the country; and that soldiers of the several posts be allowed to prospect for mines, when such course shall not interfere with the due and proper performance of their military duties.

"Commanders of posts, companies and 'detachments within the district are enjoined to execute to the fullest extent the spirit and letter of this circular communication, and report, from time to time, to these head-quarters the progress made in the development of the Territory, in the vicinity of their respective posts or stations.

"By command of Brig.-Gen. Connor:
CHAS. H. HEMPSTEAD,
Capt. C. S. and A. A. A. Gen'l."

In March, 1864, another circular was issued by General Connor which was considered to be very pronounced and threatening towards the leaders of the Mormon community:

"Headquarters, District of Utah,
Camp Douglas, U. T., March 1st, 1864.

" Circular: "The undersigned has received numerous letters of complaint and inquiry from parties within and without the district, the former alleging that certain residents of Utah Territory indulge in threats and menaces against miners and others desirous of prospecting for precious metals, and the latter asking what, if any, protection will be accorded to those coming hither to develop the mineral resources of the country.

"Without giving undue importance to the thoughtless or reckless words of misguided, prejudiced, or bad-hearted men who may be guilty of such threats as those referred to, and indulging the hope that they are but individual expressions rather than menaces, issued by any presumed or presumptuous authority whatsoever, the undersigned takes occasion to repeat what no loyal citizen will gainsay, that this

Territory is the public property of the nation, whose wish it is, that it be developed at the earliest possible day, in all its rich resources, mineral as well as agricultural, pastoral and mechanical. To this end, citizens of the United States, and all desirous of becoming such, are freely invited by public law and national policy, to come hither to enrich themselves and advance the general welfare from out the public store, which a bountiful Providence has scattered through these richly laden mountains and fertile plains. The mines are thrown open to the hardy and industrious, and it is announced, that they will receive the amplest protection in life, property and rights, against aggression from whatsoever source, Indian or white.

"The undersigned has abundant reason to know that the mountains of Utah north, south, east and west, are prolific of mineral wealth. Gold, silver, iron, copper, lead and coal, are found in almost every direction, in quantities which promise the richest results to the adventurous explorer and the industrious miner.

"In giving assurance of entire protection to all who may come hither to prospect for mines, the undersigned wishes at this time most earnestly, and yet firmly, to warn all, whether permanent residents or not of this Territory, that should violence be offered, or attempted to be offered to miners, in the pursuit of their lawful occupation, the offender or offenders, one or many, will be tried as public enemies, and punished to the utmost extent of martial law.

"The undersigned does not wish to indulge in useless threats, but desires most fully and explicitly to apprise all of their rights, and warn misguided men of the inevitable result, should they seek to obstruct citizens in their rights, or throw obstacles in the way of the development of the public domain. While miners will be thus protected, they must understand, that no interference with the vested rights of the people of the Territory will be tolerated, and they are expected to conform in all things to the laws of the land which recognize in their fullest extent the claims of the bona fide settler on public lands.

"While the troops have been sent to this district to protect from a savage foe the homes and premises of the settlers, and the public interests of the nation, they are also here to preserve the public peace, secure to all the inestimable blessings of liberty, and preserve intact, the honor, dignity and rights of the citizen, vested by a free Constitution, and which belong to the humblest equally with the highest in the land. This, their mission, it is the duty of the undersigned to see fulfilled by kindly and warning words, if possible, but if not, still to be enforced at every hazard and at any cost. He cannot permit the public peace and the welfare of all to be jeoparded by the foolish threats or wicked actions of a few.

P. EWD. CONNOR,
Brig. Gen., U. S. Vol., Comd'gDist."
In June a special order was issued creating a

Provost marshal of Great Salt Lake City.
"Headquarters District of Utah,
Camp Douglas, Utah Territory,
Near Great Salt Lake City, July 9th, 1864.
"SPECIAL ORDER NO. 53.
"1st. Capt. Chas. H. Hempstead, Commissary of Subsistence, U. S. Vol's, is hereby appointed Provost Marshal of Great Salt Lake City, U. T., and will

immediately enter upon the duties of his office. He will be obeyed and respected accordingly.

"2nd. Company L, 2nd Cav. C. V., Capt. Albert Brown, is hereby detailed as Provost Guard, and will immediately report to Capt. Chas. H. Hempstead, Provost Marshal, Great Salt Lake City, for duty.

"3rd. The Quartermaster's Department will furnish the necessary quarters, offices, etc.

"By command of
BRIG.-GEN. CONNOR.

"Chas. H. Hempstead, Capt. C. S. U. S. Vol's, and A. A. A. Genl."

This series of circulars was climaxed by the following letter to the War Department (a copy of which has been furnished to the author by the General himself), setting forth his views and policy concerning Utah.

Headquarters District of Utah, Camp Douglas, Utah Territory, Near Great Salt Lake City, July 21st, 1864.

"Colonel: " Having had occasion recently to communicate with you by telegraph on the subject of the difficulties which have considerably excited the Mormon community for the past ten days, it is perhaps proper that I should report more fully by letter relative to the real causes which have rendered collision possible.

"As set forth in former communications, my policy in this Territory has been to invite hither a large Gentile and loyal population, sufficient by peaceful means and through the ballot-box to overwhelm the Mormons by mere force of numbers, and thus west from the Church—disloyal and traitorous to the core—the absolute and tyrannical control of temporal and civil affairs, or at least a population numerous enough to put a check on the Mormon authorities, and give countenance to those who are striving to loosen the bonds with which they have been so long oppressed. With this view, I have bent every energy and means of which I was possessed, both personal and official, towards the discovery and development of the mining resources of the Territory, using without stint the soldiers of my command, whenever and wherever it could be done without detriment to the public service. These exertions have, in a remarkably short period, been productive of the happiest results and more than commensurate with my anticipations. Mines of undoubted richness have been discovered, their fame is spreading east and west, voyageurs for other mining countries have been induced by the discoveries already made to tarry here, and the number of miners of the Territory steadily and rapidly increasing. With them, and to supply their wants, merchants and traders are flocking into Great Salt Lake City, which by its activity, increased number of Gentile stores and workshops, and the appearance of its thronged and busy streets, presents a most remarkable contrast to the Salt Lake of one year ago. Despite the counsel, threats, and obstacles of the Church, the movement is going on with giant strides.

"This policy on my part, if not at first understood, is now fully appreciated in its startling effect, by Brigham Young and his coterie. His every efforts, covert and open, having proved unequal to the task of checking the transformation so rapidly going on in what he regards as his own exclusive domain, he and his Apostles have grown desperate. No stone is left unturned by them to rouse the people to resistance against the policy, even if it should provoke hostility against a government he hates and daily reviles. It is unquestionably his desire to provoke me into some act savoring of persecution, or by the dexterous use of which he can induce his deluded followers into an outbreak, which would deter miners and others coming to the Territory. Hence he and his chief men make their tabernacles and places of worship resound each Sabbath with the most outrageous abuse of all that pertains to the Government and the Union—hence do their prayers ascend loudly from the housetops for a continuance of the war till the hated Union shall be sunk—hence the persistent attempt to depreciate the national currency and institute a "gold basis" in preference to "Lincoln skins," as treasury notes are denominated in Sabbath day harangues.

"Hence it was that the establishment of a provost guard in the city was made the pretext for rousing the Mormon people to excitement and armed assembling, by the most ridiculous stories of persecution and outrage on their rights, while the fanatical spirit of the people, and the inborn hatred of our institutions and Government were effectually appealed to, to promote discord and provoke trouble. I am fully satisfied that nothing but the firmness and determination with which their demonstrations were met, at every point, prevented a collision, and the least appearance of vacillation on my part would surely have precipitated a conflict. I feel that it is not presumptuous in me to say that in view of what has already been accomplished in Utah, that the work marked out can and will be effectually and thoroughly consummated if the policy indicated be pursued and I am sustained in my measures at department headquarters. I am fully impressed with the opinion that peace is essential to the solving of the problem, but at the same time conscious that peace can only be maintained by the presence of force and a fixed determination to crush out at once any interference with the rights of the Government by persons of high or low degree. While the exercise of prudence in inaugurating measures is essential to success, it should not be forgotten that the display of power and the exhibition of reliance on oneself have the most salutary restraining effect on men of weak minds and criminal intent. Deeply as Brigham Young hates our Government, malignant and traitorous as are his designs against it, inimical as he is against the policy here progressing of opening the mines to a Gentile populace, and desperate as he is in his fast-waning fortunes, he will pause ere he inaugurates a strife, so long as the military forces in the Territory are sufficiently numerous to hold him and his deluded followers in check. The situation of affairs in Utah is clear to my own mind, and, without presumption, I have no fear for the result, if sustained by the department commander as indicated in this and former communications. Desirous as I am of conforming strictly to the wishes and judgment of the Major-General commanding the department, and having thus fully set forth my views and the facts bearing on the case, I beg leave respectfully to ask from the department commander an expression of opinion as to the policy of the course pursued, and such suggestions or instructions as he may deem proper, as a guide in the future.

"Very respectfully, your obedient servant,
P. EDW. CONNOR,
"Brig.-Genl. U. S. Vol., Commanding District.
"Lieut-Col. R. C Drum, Asst. Adjt.-Genl. U. S. A., San Francisco, Cal."

The foregoing documents show that General Connor designed with his troops to reconstruct Utah. In pursuance of that design undoubtedly the provost guard was established in Great Salt Lake City and his report to the Department seems a very decided asking of the Government for the mission of a semi-military dictatorship over Utah. A few years later the mines of Utah were everywhere opened and thousands of a Gentile population poured into the Territory without provoking even a desire of hindrance from the Mormon people. The General's report, though a true expression of his then views, does not accord with the actual history as since developed. And it is very suggestive to note that the Provost Marshal of our city of 1864, was Brigham Young's legal counsellor and advocate in 1872, and that General Connor offered to go bail for Brigham Young in the sum of $100,000 when he was on trial in the court of Chief Justice James B. McKean.

CHAPTER XXXVII.

HAPPY CHANGE IN THE RELATIONS BETWEEN THE CITY AND THE CAMP. GRAND INAUGURAL CELEBRATION OF LINCOLN BY THE MILITARY AND CITIZENS. CONNOR GREATLY MOVED BY THE LOYALTY OF THE MASSES, OF THE MORMON PEOPLE. THE BANQUET AT NIGHT: THE CITY GIVES A BALL IN HONOR OF GENERAL CONNOR. THE CITY IN MOURNING OVER THE ASSASSINATION OF PRESIDENT LINCOLN. FUNERAL OBSEQUIES AT THE TABERNACLE.

The year 1865 saw a most happy change in the relations between the city and the camp. It was brought about by a hearty mutual disposition to celebrate the victories of the Union, and the inauguration of Abraham Lincoln on his second term.

An enthusiastic meeting of the officers of Camp Douglas and prominent citizens was held in the city, at Daft's Hall, on the 28th of February, 1865, and the following committees were appointed.

Committee of Arrangements: Wm. Gilbert, D. F. Walker, Samuel Kahn, Lieut.-Col. Milo George, Capt. M. G. Lewis, John Meeks. Committee on Finance: Frank Gilbert, Charles B. Greene. Committee on Exercises: Capt. C. H. Hempstead, Col. O. M. Irish, Richard A. Keyes.

The committee on arrangements selected S. S. Walker, Esq., to act as Grand Marshal who chose as his aids: Richard A. Keyes, G. W. Carleton, Charles King, Thos. Stayner, Samuel Serrine and John Paul.

On the 2nd of March the grand marshal published by order of the committee of arrangements the

PROGRAMME OF THE DAY.

The procession will form at 11 a. m., at the eastern end of Market Street (First South Temple Street) where it will be joined by the military from Camp Douglas.

Escort—Provost Guard—Co. "D." 3rd Infy C. V., Capt. W. Kettredge commanding; Grand Marshal—Sharp Walker, Esq., and Aids; band; His Excellency the Governor of Utah and General Commanding the District; District Staff; Chaplain—Rev. N. McLeod; Orator of the day—Hon. Chief Justice John Titus; Federal Officers; Mayor, City and County Officers; Civic Societies and Citizen Military Organizations; Citizens in vehicles; Citizens on horseback; Citizens on foot; band; Lieut. Col. Milo George, 1st Cav. N. Vols, and staff; Detachments from Co.'s A, B, and D 3rd Inft'y Bat. C. V. Artillery; Detachments from Co's. C, and F, 1st Cav. Nev. Vols.

A Federal salute (13 guns) will be fired by the artilery at meridian.

The procession will march under the command of the Grand Marshal through the principal streets of Salt Lake City, and assemble at the State House, corner of Main and South Temple Streets. After appropriate exercises, a national salute of 36 guns will be fired by the artillery.

All loyal citizens of Great Salt Lake City and vicinity are cordially invited to participate in the procession and exercises, and the merchants, bankers and others are requested to close their places of business and take part in the ceremonies.

By order of the committee on arrangement.
SHARP WALKER,
Grand Marshal.

On the same day the City Council issued the following:

"City Council Chamber, Great Salt Cut, March 2nd, 1865.
"Whereas, Saturday, the 4th instant, being the day of inauguration of the President of the United States, and "Whereas, also, by reason of the many recent victories of the armies of our country; therefore be it "Resolved, by the City Council of Great Salt Lake City, that we cheerfully join in the public celebration and rejoicings of that day throughout the United States, and that we cordially invite the citizens, and organizations, military and civil, of the Territory, county and city, to unite on that occasion. Be it further "Resolved, that a committee of three be appointed to confer with the Grand Marshal of the day and make the necessary arrangements to join in the general celebration.
A. O. SMOOT,
Mayor.
"Attest: Robert Campbell, City Recorder."

The committee appointed by the City Council consisted of John Sharp, Enoch Reese and Theodore McKean. Colonel Robert T. Burton of the Utah militia was appointed Marshal. On learning of this action the following correspondence was had between the chairmen of committees:

"Great Salt Lake City, U. T., March 3rd, 1865.
"Messrs. John Sharp, Enoch Reese and 7. McKean, Esqs., Com. of the Common Council: "Gentlemen: "The undersigned, chairman of committee on exercises on the 4th inst., appointed at mass meeting of citizens, having selected the Hon. John Titus, Chief Justice of Utah to deliver an oration on the occasion of the proposed national celebration, begs leave to say that as the exercises will be brief, the committee would be pleased to tender the stand and the occasion to some gentlemen, to be selected by yourselves, to address the concourse at the close of the oration.
"I have the honor to remain, gentlemen, very respectfully,
Your obedient servant,
CHAS. H. HEMPSTEAD,
Chairman Committee on Exercises."

"Great Salt Lake City, March 3rd, 1865.
"Hon. Chas. H. Hempstead, Chairman Committee on Exercises: "Sir—Your communication of to-day has been received. The committee tender their thanks, and accept the proposition, and beg leave to name Hon. Wm. H. Hooper to deliver the closing address.
Very respectfully,
JOHN SHARP,
Chairman Com. on Arrangements."

Of the celebration the Vedette said: "This was decidedly a notable occasion in Utah. The demonstrations were so entirely different from anything which has come within the range of our experience here, that it deserves special notice at our hands as an important event in the history of this Territory. * * * * "The whole procession was about one mile in length and presented a very imposing appearance. As it moved along the streets, broad and straight, of the Mormon Capital, the sidewalks, wherever it passed, the windows and even the housetops being thronged by eager, and in some instances, enthusiastic lookers on.

The bands awoke the wintry echoes with inspiring strains of music, appropriate to the occasion, and, what with the profusion of flags floating from many buildings and ornamenting the teams and sleighs in the procession, or borne by the occupants, the rosettes, streamers, and the thousand and one other devices, in all of which red, white and blue were the pervading colors, the city wore a gala appearance, which seemed to be participated in by all parties, and it was evidently the determination, on all hands, to make it a day of general rejoicing.

"Having completed its perambulations, the immense concourse assembled at the stand, prepared for the purpose, in front of the market, the provost guards which had acted as escort, formed in front facing the stage, the citizen companies in their rear, stretching along the streets, and the troops from this post drawn up in four ranks on the right and with all arms at rest. Around, and on all sides, completely filling the streets, covering the roofs and hanging out of the windows, was a dense mass of humanity silent and attentive to the proceedings.

"The stand was occupied by Governor Doty, General Connor and staff, Chief Justice Titus, orator of the day, the Reverend Norman McLeod, chaplain of the day, and various of the city authorities and prominent citizens among whom were Mayor Smoot, Hon. George A. Smith, and Captain Hooper, who delivered the closing address.

"Capt. Hempstead opened the ceremonies with some brief and patriotic remarks, and on behalf of the Committee of Arrangements, announced His Excellency J. Duane Doty, Governor of Utah, as the presiding officer of the day.

The Chaplain of the day then delivered an appropriate and impressive prayer, followed by Chief Justice Titus in a most able and exceedingly eloquent oration.

Capt. W. H. Hooper then delivered a brief and patriotic address, relating some interesting incidents attending the opening scenes of rebellion at Washington in 1860-1. The bands discoursed most excellent music in the intervals of the several exercises, and both the oration and address were received by the attentive multitude with rousing cheers and demonstrations of applause.

"At the conclusion of the interesting ceremonies at the stand, the vast concourse dispersed amid rousing cheers and salvos of artillery. The United States forces from Camp Douglas were placed in line, and the citizen cavalry of Great Salt Lake City, under Colonel Burton, escorted them on the road to camp.

Afterwards, about four o'clock, Col. George and staff, of Camp Douglas, were invited to partake of an elegant repast provided by the City Council at the City Hall. The Mayor presided, and after the cloth was removed the era of toasts, speeches, and good things generally, seemed to have arrived. Mayor Smoot opened the ball by proposing the health of President Lincoln, and success to the armies of the Union. Capt. Hempstead responded at some length and closed by a toast to 'Our hosts, the

Mayor and civic authorities of Great Salt Lake City.' "This was met in most happy style by a toast to General P. E. Connor, District Commander—responded to on behalf of the General by a member of his staff. Then came the health of 'Our guests, Colonel George and staff,' neatly replied to by the Colonel in a patriotic speech, followed by a toast to 'the Judiciary, the mainstay of republican institutions.' This called out Judge Smith, who retorted most admirably and appropriately on 'his friends the military, the right arm of the Government.' "On the whole, the proceedings at the City Hall were an appropriate culmination of the day's proceedings. It was free, easy, hospitable and a most kindly interchange of loyal sentiment among gentlemen not wont often to meet over the convivial board. Like the procession, it was a union of the civil and military authorities of Utah and passed off with eminent satisfaction to all concerned.

"Among those present we noticed Mayor Smoot, the members of the City Council, Judge Smith, Judge Clinton, John Taylor, John Sharp, Councilor Woodruff, George Q. Cannon, Col. Burton, Wm. Jennings, Mr. Lawrence and others, Col. George and staff, Major O'Neil and a host too numerous to mention in detail. Nearly everybody present responded to a toast most patriotically and frequently most eloquently.

"At a late hour the whole party rose and adjourned to meet at the Theatre. It was a source of very general regret that General Connor was not present, but as the whole affair was somewhat impromptu, the General was called to camp before the committee could meet him, and the members of his staff were constrained to respond in his name to the sentiments proposed in his honor.

"In the evening, fire-works and general rejoicings testified, to a late hour, the universal feeling, and the day closed after a general and patriotic jubilee rarely, if ever before seen in Utah."

Stenhouse says: "General Connor was greatly moved at the sight of the tradesmen and working people who paraded through the streets, and who cheered most heartily—and no doubt honestly—the patriotic, loyal sentiments that were uttered by the speakers. He wanted differences to be forgotten, and, with gentlemanly frankness, approached the author with extended hand, and expressed the joy he felt in witnessing the loyalty of the masses of the people."

General Connor having been called to take command of the Department of the Platte, a ball was given by the city authorities at the Social Hall in honor of the General, preceding his departure.

Within two months after the celebration of his inaugural day the city and camp were called to unite in deep mourning over the martyrdom of Abraham Lincoln, which struck the soldier and the loyal citizen alike with horror. At the receipt of the dreadful news some of the soldiers of the provost guard established in the city seemed ready to vent their vengeful fury on the citizens, but even the rudest of them appreciated that for once they had done injustice to the Mormons, both leaders and people, in imagining that they would sympathize with that crowning infamy. The Mormons too keenly felt the memory of their own martyrs not to be most genuinely affected by the stroke which had given to the nation a martyr so pure in his life and patriotism, as was Abraham Lincoln.

The Vedette quickly did the city justice and noted:

"The merchants, bankers, saloon keepers, and all business men of Salt Lake City, closed their places of business at 10 a.m. on Saturday. The flags on all the public buildings, Brigham Young's residence, stores, etc., were displayed at half-mast, with crape drooping over them. Many of the principal stores and private residences were dressed in mourning. Brigham Young's carriage was driven through town covered with crape. The theatre was closed for Saturday evening, the usual night of performance, and every respect was shown for the death of our honored President. On Sunday the Tabernacle pulpit, Salt Lake City, was covered with crape, and everyone throughout the city, that is, of the rightminded class, manifested the deepest sorrow at the horrible news conveyed by the telegraph."

At a meeting of the Federal, civil and military officials of Utah, held at the Executive, in Great Salt Lake City, April 18th, at 2 p. m., Hon. J. Duane Doty, Governor, was called to the chair, Capt. C. H. Hempstead and T. B. H. Stenhouse, Esq., appointed secretaries.

After preliminary consultation and expression of feeling over the sad event which called this meeting together, resolutions were presented by the Hon. Chief Justice Titus, which were unanimously adopted. We cull the following: "Resolved, that a committee of five be appointed on the part of the Federal officers to confer with a committee of like number on the part of the city authorities, to made arrangements for suitable religious exercises to be held at the Tabernacle, April 19, at 12 o'clock m.

Col. J. C. Little informed the meeting that Elder Amasa M. Lyman had been selected by the city authorities to deliver an address at the Tabernacle.

"On motion, it was unanimously resolved that Rev. Norman McLeod be also invited to deliver an eulogium on the life, character and illustrious services of the late President, on the same occasion and at the same place.

"In accordance with the foregoing resolutions the following gentlemen were appointed by the chair as the committee of arrangements, viz: Hon. Chief Justice John Titus, Col. O. H. Irish, Capt. Chas. H. Hempstead, Col. Robt. T. Burton, and Col. J. C. Little.

"Following is the committee appointed on behalf of the city authorities, viz: Hon. Mayor Smoot, Alderman Sheets, Alderman Raleigh, Theo. McKean and N. H. Felt, Esqs.

"On motion, the secretaries were instructed to transmit a copy of the proceedings of this meeting to the City Council, and that public notice be given of the exercises at the Tabernacle.

J. DUANE DOTY,
President.
"T. B. H. Stenhouse, Chas. H. Hempstead, Secretaries.

Of the funeral obsequies in the Tabernacle the Vedette says: "On Wednesday, pursuant to notice, all business was suspended in Great Salt Lake City, the stores, public and private buildings were draped in mourning, and long before the hour named—12 M.—throngs of citizens were wending their way to the Tabernacle to render the last sad, solemn, and heartfelt tribute to the great departed and deeply mourned dead. The Tabernacle was more than crowded, and upwards of three thousand people were present. The vast assemblage was called to order by City Marshal Little, in the name of the mayor, immediately after the entrance of the orators, civil and military functionaries, and a large body of prominent citizens, who occupied the platform. The scene was impressive and solemn, and all seemed to partake of the deep sorrow so eloquently expressed by the speakers on the occasion. The stand was appropriately draped in mourning, and the exercises were opened by an anthem from the choir. Franklin D. Richards delivered an impressive prayer. The address of Elder Amasa M.

Lyman was an earnest and eloquent outburst of feeling, and appropriate to the occasion. He spoke for forty-five minutes and held the vast audience in unbroken silence and wrapped attention.

"The address did credit to Mr. Lyman's head and heart. After another anthem from the choir, Rev. Norman McLeod, Chaplain of Camp Douglas was introduced, and delivered one of the most impressive and burning eulogiums on the life, character, and public services of President Lincoln which it was ever our pleasure to hear."

CHAPTER XXXVIII.

VISIT OF THE COLFAX PARTY TO SALT LAKE CITY. A TELEGRAM FROM THE MUNICIPAL COUNCIL MEETS THEM ON THE WAY WITH TRIBUTE OF THE CITY'S HOSPITALITIES. THEY ACCEPT THE WELCOME. ENTRANCE INTO THE CITY UNDER ESCORT. ENTHUSIASM OF THE PARTY OVER THE BEAUTIES OF THE ROCKY MOUNTAIN ZION. GRAND SERENADE AND SPEECHES. FORECAST OF THE GREAT FUTURE OF SALT LAKE CITY.

The visit of Schuyler Colfax and party to Great Salt Lake City commences a new epoch in the history both of our city and Territory. The party consisted of Hon. Schuyler Colfax, the then speaker of the House of Representatives, Lieutenant-Governor Bross, of Illinois, Samuel Bowles, editor of the Springfield (Mass.) Republican, and Albert D. Richardson, of the New York Tribune.

Speaker Colfax undoubtedly came in a semi-official capacity. Indeed, in his address to the people of the West, he told them specifically that President Lincoln, just previous to his assassination, charged him specially to thoroughly investigate the affairs and interests of the Pacific States and Territories, for the Nation's purposes, and that Mr. Lincoln had entertained an extraordinary faith in the destiny of the great West, believing it would become the treasure-house of the Nation. In this view Utah was particularly an object of interest, not only for her prospects as a great silver mining Territory, but extraordinarily because of her peculiar social and domestic institutions. It was inferred that President Lincoln had designed some adequate legislation on Utah, consonant with his aims and spirit in the reconstruction of the South. This was to be gathered from the utterances of his envoy to the West—the character which Mr. Colfax certainly assumed. It is true that early in the war period President Lincoln had said to a representative of Brigham Young—" that if the Mormons would let him alone he would let them alone;" but the Republican party which had elected him to supreme power, and in their initial platform coupled Utah and the South in a common and final settlement, now expected of him to adjust the affairs of Utah simultaneously with those of the "conquered South," and in accordance with the " Chicago platform," which had declared "Slavery and Polygamy twin relics of barbarism."

Such was the significance of the Colfax visit to Utah; and, though the contemplated "settlement of Utah affairs " by special legislation was interrupted by the assassination of President Lincoln, and further interrupted by the great controversy which took place between the leaders of Congress and President Andrew Johnson, the original design of legislation for Utah quickly came up again when Colfax was elected vice-president, when it further assumed quite a war aspect. As this first visit of Mr. Colfax and party is the beginning of a chain of events and circumstances which have an unbroken continuance from the rise of General Grant and Mr. Colfax to the control of the nation, and perchance may be continued for the next quarter of a century, the narrative of this Colfax visit, and a digest of the salient points of the speeches and utterances of the party in public to the citizens, and in private conversations with the Mormon leaders, may be preserved as a unique and very suggestive chapter of Utah's history.

Along the journey from Atchison to San Francisco, the public was kept posted and alive with the movements and utterances of the Speaker and his companions, through the medium of the telegraph and Mr. Bowles' letters; and, at every stage of the journey, the national importance of this visit to the great West was made the universal topic throughout the land.

Mr. Bowles in closing his letters from Denver announced: "Our week in Colorado is ended; we are off this morning for the seven days' stage ride north and west along the base of the Rocky Mountains, and through them at Bridger's Pass, to Salt Lake City, where we expect to worship with Brigham Young in his Tabernacle on Sunday week."

In this same letter Mr. Bowles gives a description of Mr. Colfax's person, life, and public character, in which he said: "Without being, in the ordinary sense, one of the greatest of our public men, he is certainly one of the most useful, reliable and valuable, and in any capacity, even the highest, he is sure to serve the country faithfully and well.

He is one of the men to be tenaciously kept in public life, and I have no doubt he will be. Some people talk of him for president; Mr. Lincoln used to tell him he would be his successor; but his own ambition is wisely tempered by the purpose to perform present duties well. He certainly makes friends more rapidly and holds them more closely than any public man I ever knew; wherever he goes, the women love him, and the men cordially respect him; and he is sure to always be a personal favorite, even a pet, with the people."

In the very nature of things, the heralded visit of such a personage to the Rocky Mountain Zion created an uncommon interest here; and the City Fathers hastened to meet him on the way with the following telegram:

"Great Salt Lake City, Utah, June 7th, 1865.

"Hon. Schuyler Colfax and Traveling Companions, at Fort Bridger:

"Gentlemen:—The undersigned committee, appointed by the city council of Great Salt Lake, take pleasure in informing you that the city council have unanimously passed a resolution tendering to you the hospitalities of the city during your sojourn in our midst.

Being appointed to notify you of this resolution, we beg to add that a committee of gentlemen have been also appointed by that body, to meet you before arrival in the city, and to conduct you to apartments prepared for your use.

"Not being fully acquainted with the names of the gentlemen in the party, we ask excuse for the omission, by extending a warm invitation to them all.

"We are, gentlemen, yours very respectfully.

W. H. Hooper,

J. H. Jones,

William Jennings,

T. B. H. Stenhouse, Committee."

"W. H. Hooper, Committee:—Our party accept. We leave here this morning about ten o'clock and expect to reach Salt Lake City, on Sabbath morning about eight o'clock.

Schuyler Colfax."

The committee appointed by the Mayor and city council, to receive Speaker Colfax and friends, met them as they descended the hill entering the city, about eight o'clock on Sunday morning. As the stage halted, Captain Hooper, the chairman of the committee, exchanged salutations with Mr. Colfax, and simultaneously both parties descended from their carriages and shook hands. The chairman of the committee then made a cordial address of welcome to Mr. Colfax and friends in the city's name, in which he said: "In tendering you, and your traveling companions, Mr. Colfax, the hospitality of our mountain home, I do so with pride, that I am able to present to you a monumental evidence of what American people can do.

"Seventeen years ago, this people, the citizens of Utah, immigrated to these distant parts, and were the first to unfurl the flag of the United States, when they fixed their camp where the city now stands, and to-day we are surrounded with the solid comforts and with many of the luxuries of life.

"While I bid you welcome, sir, we think of the many services you have rendered us, and of the great good we have derived therefrom, for we are sensible that no man has done more to establish postal facilities on the great overland route to the Pacific. No people can appreciate those services more sensibly than the citizens of Utah, for we have often passed many months in the year without any communication whatever with our parent government. You, sir, were one of the first to stretch forth your hand to remedy this evil, and now instead of waiting months for news from the East, we receive it almost daily, by means of this service; and thousands are blessed in the benefits of that great measure you have so faithfully advocated.

"The great enterprise of establishing the telegraph wire across the continent, from which we have derived hourly communication with our sister States and Territories, is truly a great blessing, and to no one I am sure, Mr. Colfax, is the country indebted more than to yourself, for its erection. The active support which you gave the measure, contributed much to the establishment of the line, a medium through which time and space are nearly annihilated.

"We take pride in introducing you to our city, in calling your attention to the improvements with which it is surrounded, as well as those of our settlements, reaching five hundred miles north and south and two hundred miles east and west.

We take pleasure as well as pride, in alluding to our mills, woolen, cotton and paper factories, orchards, vineyards and fields of cotton and grain, and to every branch of our home industry introduced to multiply among ourselves, from the facilities which our country offers, every means of social and national comfort and independence. We present you these as the result of our industry and of our perseverance, against almost insurmountable obstacles.

"To you editorial gentlemen, who not only govern, but in a sense manufacture, public opinion, we offer a hearty welcome. We had the pleasure, some years ago, of a visit from Mr. Greeley, of the Tribune, who spent some time in our midst, and I can say with truth that in him we have always found a gentleman ready and willing at all times to lend his influence in the cause of human progress. In conclusion, gentlemen, I again say, welcome."

Mr. Colfax made a fitting reply to the " welcome," and the guests and committee were then formally introduced to each other. Mr. R. Campbell, city recorder, read the resolutions passed by the city council, tendering to Speaker Colfax and party the hospitalities of the city, after which the guests stepped into the carriages provided by the committee and were escorted by them into the city.

Letter VIII. in Bowles' Book—"Across the Continent"—gives a graphic touch of the feelings and views of the Colfax party on their entrance into the Mormon Zion, amid the hearty welcomes of our citizens, both Mormon and Gentile. It-is his first letter to the Springfield Republican from Great Salt Lake City, and is dated June 14, 1865: "Leaving Fort Bridger for our last day's ride hither," wrote the pen of the Colfax party, "we leave the first Pacific slopes and table lands of the Rocky Mountains, drained to the south for the Colorado River, and to the north for the Columbia, and go over the rim of the basin of the Great Salt Lake, and enter that continent within a continent, with its own miniature salt sea, and its independent chain of mountains, and distinct river courses; marked wonderfully by Nature, and marked now as wonderfully in the history of civilization by its people, their social and religious organization, and their material development. This is Utah—these the Mormons. I do not marvel that they think they are a chosen people; that they have been blessed of God, not only in the selection of their home, which consists of the richest region, in all the elements of a State, between the Mississippi Valley and the Pacific Shore, but in the great success that has attended their labors, and developed here the most independent and self-sustaining industry that the western half of our continent witnesses. Surely great worldly wisdom has presided over their settlement and organization; there have been tact and statesmanship in their leaders; there have been industry, frugality and integrity in the people; or one could not witness such varied triumphs of industry and ingenuity and endurance as here present themselves. * * * * "Early 'sun-up' brought us to the last station, kept by a Mormon bishop with four wives, who gave us bitters and breakfast—the latter with green peas and strawberries—and then, leaving number one at his home, went on with us to the city for parochial visits to the other three, who are located at convenient distances around the Territory.

"Finally we came out upon the plateau—or 'bench,' as they call it here— that overlooks the valley of the Jordan, the valley alike of Utah Lake and the Great Salt Lake, and the valley of the intermediate Great Salt Lake City. It is a scene of rare natural beauty. To the right upon the plateau lay Camp Douglas, the home of the soldiers and a village in itself; holding guard over the town and within easy cannon range of tabernacle and tithing-house; right beneath, in an angle of the plain—which stretched south to Utah Lake and west to the Salt Lake—"and Jordan rolled between"—was the city, regularly and handsomely laid out, with many fine buildings, and filled with thick gardens of trees and flowers, that gave it a fairy-land aspect; beyond and across, the plain spread out five to ten miles in width, with scattered farm-houses and herds of cattle; below, it was lost in the dim distance; above, it gave way, twenty miles off, to the line of light that marked the beginning of the Salt Lake— the whole flat as a plain, and sparkling with river and irrigating canals, overlooked on both sides by hills that mounted to the snow line, and from which flowed the fatness of water and soil that makes this once desert valley blossom under the hand of industry with every variety of verdure, every product of almost every clime.

"No internal city of the Continent lies in such a field of beauty, unites such rich and rare elements of nature's formation, holds such guarantees of greatness, material and social, in the good time coming of our Pacific development. I met all along the plains and over the mountains, the feeling that Salt Lake was to be the central city of this West; I found the map, with Montana, Idaho, and Oregon on the north, Dakota and Colorado on the east, Nevada and California on the west, Arizona on the south, and a near connection with the sea by the Colorado River in the latter direction, suggested the same; I recognized it in the Sabbath picture of its location and possessions; I am convinced of it as I see more and more of its opportunities, its developed industries and its unimproved possessions.

"Mr. Colfax's reception in Utah was excessive if not oppressive. There was an element of rivalry between Mormon and Gentile in it, adding earnestness and energy to enthusiasm and hospitality. First a troop cometh, with band of music, and marched us slowly and dustily through their Camp Douglas. Then, escaping thus, our coach was waylaid, as it went down the hill, by the Mormon authorities of the city. They ordered us to dismount; we were individually introduced to each of twenty of them; we received a long speech; we made a long" one— standing in the hot sand with a sun of forty thousand lens power concentrated upon us, tired and dirty with a week's coach ride: was it wonder that the mildest tempers rebelled? Transferred to other carriages, our hosts drove us through the city to the hotel; and then—bless their Mormon hearts—they took us at once to a hot sulphur bath, that nature liberally offers just on the confines of the city, and there we washed out all remembrance of the morning suffering and all the accumulated grime and fatigue of the journey, and came out baptized in freshness and self-respect. Clean clothes, dinner, the Mormon Tabernacle in the afternoon, and a Congregational (Gentile) meeting and sermon in the evening, were the proceedings of our first day in Utah.

"Since and still continuing, Mr. Colfax and his friends have been the recipients of a generous and thoughtful hospitality. They are the guests of the city; but the military authorities and citizens vie together as well to please their visitors and make them pleased with Utah and its people. The Mormons are eager to prove their loyalty to the government, their sympathy with its bereavement, their joy in its final triumph—which their silence or their slants and sneers heretofore had certainly put in some doubt—and they leave nothing unsaid or undone now, towards Mr. Colfax as the representative of that government, or towards the public, to give assurance of their right mindedness. Also they wish us to know that they are not monsters and murderers, but men of intelligence, virtue, good manners and line tastes. They put their polygamy on high moral grounds; and for the rest, anyhow, are not willing to be thought otherwise than our peers. And certainly we do find here a great deal of true and good human nature and social culture; a great deal of business intelligence and activity; a great deal of generous hospitality—besides most excellent strawberries and green peas, and the most promising orchards of apricots, peaches, plums and apples that these eyes ever beheld anywhere."

Passing from Mr. Bowles' gushing description of the entrance of the Colfax party to the Mormon Zion, we come to the grand serenade and welcome given to them, on the Monday evening, by the citizens generally.

At an early hour crowds of citizens assembled on Main Street, in front of the Salt Lake House. After dusk the assemblage grew immense, and anxious silence was enlivened by patriotic airs from the city brass band, under Captain Charles J. Thomas. On the appearance of the distinguished visitors on the balcony, escorted by the city authorities, Mayor A. O. Smoot was unanimously called to the chair. Hon. John F.

Kinney, the then delegate of Utah to Congress, made some prefatory remarks, introducing Speaker Colfax, who came forward and favored the gathered thousands with a speech, in the capacity of a social talk at times, and anon exalting into the realms of patriotism and eloquence. The points touching on our city and its people will form links in the chain of history. Speaker Colfax thus addressed the Mormon people: "Fellow citizens of the Territory of Utah: Far removed as I am to-night from my home, I feel that I have a right to call every man that lives under the American flag in this wide-spread republic of ours, by the name of fellow citizen.

I come before you this evening—introduced by your delegate in so complimentary a manner, fearing that you will be disappointed by the speech to which you have to listen. I rise to speak to you of the future of this great country of ours, rather than of the past, or of what has been done for it in the progress of this great republic.

"I was gratified when, on this long journey which my companions and myself are taking, we were met at the gates of your city, and its hospitality tendered to us; although I must confess I would far rather have come among you in a quiet way, travelling about, seeing your city and Territory, and making observations, without subjecting your official dignitaries to the trouble and loss of time that our visit seems to have entailed upon them, but which they insist is a pleasure. Yet when they voluntarily, and unexpectedly to us, offered us officially this hospitality, we felt that it should be accepted as promptly as it was tendered. I accept it the more cordially because I know that every one of you who knows anything about me and my companions, is sure that, reared as we have been in a different school from what you have been, and worshipping on a different altar, we are regarded as gentiles; yet, despite of all this, you have seen fit to request us to stop, on this journey to the Pacific, to receive the hospitalities which we have had lavished on us =o boundlessly during the two days we have been in your midst. I rejoice that I came to you in a time like this, when the rainbow of peace spans our entire horizon from ocean to ocean, giving the assurance that the deluge of secession shall not again overwhelm this fair land of ours. (Cheers). I come to you rejoicing, and I was glad to hear from my old friend, Capt. Hooper, your former delegate to Congress, when he made his welcoming speech on Sabbath morning in the suburbs of your city, that you too rejoiced in the triumph of this great republic of ours over the enemies who sought to bayonet the prostrate form of liberty, and to blot this great country from the map of the world. Thank God, who rules in the heavens, who determined that what he joined together on this continent, man should not put asunder; the republic lives to-day and will live in all the coining ages of the future. (Cheers). There may be stormy conflict and peril; there may be a foreign war, but I trust not; I am for peace instead of war, whenever war can be honorably avoided. I want no war with England or France. I want the development and mighty sweeping forward of our giant republic, in its march of progress and power, to be, as it will be, the commanding nation of the world, when it shall lift its head like your Ensign Peak, yon tall clift that lifts its mighty form swelling over the valley, laughing at the rolling storm clouds around its base, while the eternal sunshine settles on its head. *****

"I came here to-night, my friends, to speak to you frankly about the object of our visit in your midst. I know it is supposed, it is almost a by-word, that we of the sterner sex have adopted, that the ladies, the other sex, are the most inquisitive. Having a profound reverence for woman, for I believe that mother, wife, home and heaven are the four noblest words in the English language, I have never believed this to be true; but from long experience and observation, am persuaded that our own sex is quite as inquisitive as the other. I can give you some proof of this: there has not been a single lady in Salt Lake City that has asked, 'what have you come out here for?' While there have been several gentlemen who have inquired, very respectfully, it is true, 'what was the object of your coming to Utah?' (Cheers and laughter.) Now I am going to tell you frankly all about it, so that your curiosity shall be entirely allayed.

"I will begin by telling you what we did not come for. In the first place, we did not come here to steal any of your lands and possessions, not a bit of it. In the second place we did not come out here to make any remarkable fortune by the discovery of any gold or silver mines just yet. In the third place, we did not come out here to take the census of either sex among this people, and to this very hour I am in blissful ignorance as to whether the committee that met me in the suburbs of the city, are, like myself, without any wife, or whether they have been once or twice married, except your two delegates to Congress—they told me they only had a wife apiece. (Laughter.) In the fourth place, we did not come out here to stir up strife of any character; we came here to accept the hospitality of everybody here, of all sects, creeds and beliefs who are willing to receive us, and we have received it from all. Well, now, you see we could not have any ulterior design in coming here.

* * * *

"Now, you who are pioneers far out here in the distant West, have many things that you have a right to ask of your government. I can scarcely realize, with this large assembly around me, that there is an almost boundless desert of 1,200 miles between myself and the valley of the Mississippi. There are many things that you have a right to demand; you have created, however, many things here for yourselves. No one could traverse your city without recognizing that you are a people of industry. No one could look at your beautiful gardens, which charmed as well as astonished me, for I did not dream of any such thing in the city of Salt Lake when I came here, without realizing that you, or many of you, are a people of taste. If anybody doubt that, I think that one of your officers on the hill, who turned us loose into his strawberries today, realized that he had visitors of taste. (Cheers and laughter.) I regret yet that I left it; but I was full, and the truth is I was too full for utterance, therefore I cannot make much of a speech to night.

"In the first place, to speak seriously, coming out here as you had, so far from the old States, you had a right to demand postal communication. I heard something that surprised me, it must be an exaggeration of the truth—that at one time in your early settlement of this place, you were so far removed from postal communication, that you never heard of the nomination of President Pierce until he was elected and inaugurated as President. (A voice, 'that's so.') That was some six or eight months— that was a slow coach, and I don't see how anyone who had been in the habit of reading a newspaper ever could get along at all; he must have read the old ones over and over again.

"It happened to be my fortune in Congress to do a little towards increasing the postal facilities in the West; not as much as I desired, but as much as I could obtain from Congress. And when it was proposed, to the astonishment of my fellow-members, that there should be a daily mail run across these pathless plains and mighty mountains, through the wilderness of the West to the Pacific, with the pathway lined with our enemies, the savages of the forest, and where the luxuries and even the necessaries of life in some parts of the route are unknown, the project was not considered possible; and then, when in my position as chairman of the post office committee, I proposed that we should vote a million dollars a year to put the mail across the continent, members came to me and said, 'You will ruin yourself.' They thought it was monstrous—an unjust and extravagant expenditure. I said to them, though I knew little of the West then compared to what I have learned in a few weeks of this trip, I said, ' the people on the line of that route have a right to demand it at your hands, and in their behalf I demand it.' (Cheers.) Finally the bill was coaxed through, and you have a daily mail running through here, or it would run with almost the regularity of clockwork, were it not for the incursions of the savages. * * *

"You had a right to this daily mail, and you have it. You had a right, also, to demand, as the eastern portion of this republic had, telegraphic communication—speeding the messages of life and death, of pleasure and of traffic; that the same way should be opened up by that frail wire, the conductor of Jove's thunderbolts, tamed down and harnessed for the use of man. And it fell to my fortune to ask it for you; to ask a subsidy from the government in its aid. It was but hardly obtained; yet now the grand result is achieved, who regrets it,—who would part with this bond of union and civilization? There was another great interest you had a right to demand. Instead of the slow, toilsome and expensive manner in which you freight your goods and hardware to this distant Territory, you should have a speedy transit between the Missouri Valley and this intermountain basin in which you live. Instead of paying two or three prices,'—sometimes overrunning the cost of the article,—you should have a railroad communication, and California demands this. I said, as did many others in Congress, 'This is a great national enterprise; we must bind the Atlantic and Pacific States together with bands of iron; we must send the iron horse through all these valleys and mountains of the interior, and when thus interlaced together, we shall be a more compact and homogenous republic' And the Pacific Railroad bill was passed.

This great work of uniting three thousand miles, from shore to shore, is to be consummated; and we hail the day of peace, because with peace we can do many things as a nation that we cannot do in war. This railroad is to be built—this company is to build it; if they do not the government will. It shall be put through soon; not toilsomely, slowly, as a far distant event, but as an event in the decade in which we live. * * * * "And now, what has the government a right to demand of you! It is not that which Napoleon exacts from his officers in France,—which is allegiance to the constitution and fidelity to the emperor. Thank God, we have no emperor nor despot in this country, throned or unthroned. Here every man has the right, himself, to exercise his elective suffrage as he sees fit, none molesting him or making him afraid. And the duty of every American citizen is condensed in a single sentence, as I said to your committee yesterday,—not in allegiance to an emperor, but allegiance to the constitution, obedience to the laws, and devotion to the Union. (Cheers.) When you live to that standard you have the right to demand protection; and were you three times three thousand miles from the national capital, wherever the starry banner of the republic waves and a man stands under it, if his rights of life, liberty and property are assailed, and he has rendered this allegiance to his country, it is the duty of the government to reach out its arm, if it take a score of regiments, to protect and uphold him in his rights. (Cheers.) "I rejoice that I came into your midst. I want to see the development of this great country promoted. I would now touch on a question which I could allude to at greater length—that is about mining—but I find that our views differ somewhat with the views of some whom you hold in great respect here, therefore I will not expand on this subject as in Colorado or Nevada. But I would say this, for the truth compels me to say it, that this great country is the granary of the world everybody acknowledges, at home and abroad. When five of the Slates in the Northwest produce three hundred and fifty million bushels of grain per year—when you can feed all your own land, and all the starving millions of other lands besides, with an ordinary crop, then you are indeed the granary of the world. But this country has a prouder boast than that—it is the treasury of the world. God has put the precious metals through and through these Rocky Mountains, and all these mountains in fact, and I only say to you that if you, yourselves, do not develop it, the rush and tide of population will come here and develop it and you cannot help it. (Cheers.) The tide of emigration from the old world, which even war with all its perils did not check, is going to pour over all these valleys and mountains, and they are going to extend the development of nature, and I will tell you if you do not want the gold they will come and take it themselves. (Cheers.) You are going to have this Territory increase in population, then there will not be much danger about this State matter.

"Now, with the bright stars looking down upon us here, as they do on our friends in distant States, I thank you for the kind attention with which you have listened to me; and while I hold the stand I ask you to join with me, if you will, in three hearty hurrahs for that Union which is so dear to our hearts, the very ark of our covenant, which may no unhallowed hand ever endanger in the centuries yet to come."

The assembled throng joined with the speaker and gave three hearty cheers, which were followed with three cheers "for Colfax."

Next came Lieutenant-Governor Bross of Illinois, editor of the Chicago Tribune, whose speech (given entire) is one of the most hearty, genuine tributes ever uttered or penned in honor of the early settlers of Utah: "Fellow citizens: I have no doubt at all but that I could make a very good speech, if the Honorable Speaker of the House of Representatives of this great nation had not taken all the wind out of my sails, and left me nothing to say.

(Laughter.) But it is just like him, for though he and I are neighbors, close neighbors, as he lives in the State of Indiana and I in the State of Illinois, yet that is the concession I am always obliged to make to the honorable gentleman.

But I can only join my testimony to what the honorable Speaker has said, of my amazement at the development which 1 witness around me.

"To see what I have seen to day—your beautiful gardens; where, less than twenty years ago, sage brush held undisturbed possession of the soil, now side by side, grow in luxuriance and tempting sweetness the peach, the apple and the strawberry, is a matter of astonishment to me beyond anything I ever saw before in my life, (Cheers.) And it shows to me, my fellow-citizens, because we are all citizens of this great and glorious republic, what industry and energy, guided by intelligence, can do for this broad land, (cheers.) I can look back over those wastes of sage brush, over which we have passed in our travel, and wherever there is a mountain current to water the soil,

I see before me in this great city what can be realized on every acre of the broad plains between the Missouri and this beautiful valley. And I know that American energy and American enterprise will soon redeem large tracts of this land through which we have passed, and soon, instead of being a vast desert, it will bloom and blossom like the rose, as your city does to-day. (Hear, hear.) "I have always been a western man, though living down east. I have always felt that the West was soon to be the center of wealth and power to this great nation.

When but a boy I studied its geography; when I grew to manhood, I studied its resources; now I am here to witness with my own eyes what American enterprise can do in the center of the continent. And representing as I do, the great State of Illinois, that State that can furnish food for the nation, and that city that sits as a queen at the head of Lake Michigan, ready with open arms to grasp the wealth of this North-west, and to pour back her wealth upon it, I feel here to-night, as if I had an interest in you, and in the progress and development of this Territory and every other Territory between the lakes and the Pacific. And whatever lean do, as editor of what is recognized as one of the chief newspapers in the city of Chicago, to advance the interests of this North-west, you may calculate I shall do for your benefit. (Cheers.) "Among those things which I shall advocate is the necessity of the further development and the pushing forward of those great lines of communication which are to make us neighbors; and then, instead of rolling along in one of Mr. Holladay's fine coaches, for fine they certainly are, with our good friend Otis, I expect to have him by the hand, and taking our seat in the cars, come to Salt Lake City to eat strawberries with you in the short space of three days. (Cheers.) "I have seen a stage coach and the men who drive these stages across these great plains and mountains, and I wish to add my tribute of respect not only to Ben Holladay, but to the humblest stage driver between here and the Missouri. (Cheers.) They are brave men all, noble men all, everywhere in these stations.

Passing along from one to the other, we found intelligence and that which charmed us; and from my position here before you to-night, you can see I must have fared very well, and in Salt Lake City they have not starved me. (Laughter.) I can say, from my experience here, I have tested the capacity of man's system to contain strawberries and I find it large, but it did not equal the capacity of our friend's strawberry bed."

"My fellow citizens, let me here repeat that in this excursion we have found a great many things to interest us. I have made a great many discoveries which I intend to send down home for the benefit of those who shall come here in the stage coach, for that is an institution I have learned to value. I reverence the stage coach; there is no such place to sleep in as the stage coach when running over the rocks and through chuck-holes. A man can sleep in a stage coach, and four hour's sleep there is worth a whole night's sleep in a bed. I have engaged of our good friend Otis one of his stage coaches, and I intend to have it sent right down to Chicago, and have some of Gates' machinery to work it, and I shall sleep in it the rest of my life. (Laughter.) "I say, therefore, go on developing this valley as you have done. Build your canal from Utah Lake, cut your canal the other side of Jordan; they say it is a hard road to travel, but I have not found it so. Cut your canals and water this whole land, that it may bud and blossom and bring forth abundantly. I have seen here such an evidence of wealth, cultivation and progress as would surprise any man, let him come from where he will; even if he be a western man, it will surprise him.

"So far as the railroad is concerned, and my friend Colfax has run the engine pretty well, I want to say to you, that we here, connected with the newspapers back east, I and my associates of the quill, will do all that we can do; we will concentrate our energies for the accomplishment of that great enterprise, to push it through to the Pacific—we will do all we can for you, we will do all we can to lessen the expense, the vast expanse, of drawing your goods all the way from the Missouri to Salt Lake City. You want the railroad—you want it for its intelligence; you want it from the fact that it mixes up a people and enlightens them and gives them broader and more liberal views. It will place within your reach here many of the facilities and conveniences of life, now enjoyed by other sections of the nation. I say, my fellow citizens, let us all feel, in the great work of developing this continent, that each one must do his share.

"I will say here, and ever hereafter, that, so far as you citizens of Utah are concerned, you have done your full share in developing the resources of this Territory. (Cheers.) If seventeen years, that is the exact time you have been here, has accomplished what it has, what will not the seventeen years to come accomplish, or a quarter or half a century, for this magnificent valley? You will have these hills swarming with the denizens of New York and Chicago—gentlemen coming to spend the summer angling on the lakes, and to see what wonders you have developed among the mountains, as we are doing in our stay during the week.

To-morrow we go down to Salt Lake, to enjoy ourselves the best possible. And when we go home, we will tell the people what we have seen. We are accustomed to tell the truth. The newspaper is not what it once was. We hold this, that the truth in a newspaper is as essential to its success, as is the truth in social life, (cheers) and that nothing but the truth, plainly told, will tell on the interests of this Territory and of this great Northwest, and so far as I am concerned I will tell nothing but the truth about you. (Cheers.) "Now, passing over the things in which we differ, leaving time and circumstances to bring us together, let me say that I believe in the great principles that our Creator has established. I believe that the principles of commerce, the principles of our holy religion, will in the end fuse mankind together and make us all love each other as brothers. (Cheers.) I believe in a higher civilization, in a higher Christianity, being developed in the progress of human events, and such as shall make all men feel that all men are brothers. (Cheers.) Now, my fellow-citizens, wishing you all prosperity and happiness, and thanking you for your kind reception which you have given to us individually, I bid you good evening."

Mr. Albert D. Richardson, of the New York Tribune, closed the speeches of the evening in a strain congenial to that of his companions.

* * * " I am impressed," he said, "with gratification and pleasure at your kind reception and warm and pleasant hospitalities, with wonder at the natural beauties of your surroundings, and at the artificial beauties which your skill and perseverance have given to your young and flourishing city. To me they are full of material for thought, full of suggestiveness.

"The last four years have taught us and the world a great lesson—the lesson that any community, that any section of States under this government which attempts to resist the laws, will be ground to dust, under the authority of the American people.

The next four years will teach a lesson, equally impressive, that peace hath her victories no less renowned than war. * * * "There is to be a tide of migration towards the West, such as the world has never seen before—there is to be a rapid development, such as the world has never seen before. There are boys here to-night who are to see the great regions of the West, from the Alleghanies to the Pacific, teeming with the life of a hundred millions of people. There are old men here to-night who will live to see the accomplishment of that grandest of material enterprises—such a one as the world has never seen—the Pacific Railroad, to see people from New York and San Francisco, London and China, stopping on the great plains to exchange greetings and newspapers, while their respective trains are stopping for breakfast.

"It is only in the grand material development of the country—the building of cities and railroads, the commerce on the river, the establishment everywhere of farms, that the greatest pride of American development is to consist, but that, by and bye, when all these mingling and divers nationalities are blended into one, America is to give the world the best men, the highest average men, the most intelligent men, of the purest integrity, of the most varied accomplishments, that the world has ever seen.

"But what is all this specially to you? In my judgment it is a great deal— it is everything, because your location is in the very heart, the very focal point of the new States which are to spring up here. Here is the line of travel, here are the fields of settlement, here is the path of empire. Here is such a site for a city as no commercial metropolis in the whole world occupies. I am dazzled at the thought of the future which may be before it, and of the future which may be before your people.

"The government of the United States, I believe, will do its part to help you. The people of the United States, through their pioneer instinct to move westward, to plant themselves, to build new regions, will help you. Will you do your part of the work? (Yes, yes.) It is with the profoundest interest that, during the few days that I have been in your Territory, I have been studying its features and its developments. I have been in many of your ranches, in your green fields, in many of your gardens, your residences, your business houses, and I have looked with wonder at the almost miracles you have performed in the few years you have been here. And I will tell you, gentlemen, what the development which I have seen means, what it means to me. When I think of the vast labor you had to perform, of this terrible journey from the river here, and when I see what you have done, I am full of wonder and admiration; they mean to me industry; they mean to me integrity and justice in your dealings with each other.

(Cheers.) Because I know enough of pioneer life, I know enough from practical observation and experience of the difficulties that environ and constantly beset new communities, to know this could not have been done by an idle people, by a volatile people, by a people who do not deal fairly and justly among themselves and with each other.

"That to me is a grand augury for your future; if you display in the future the same industry you have displayed during these pioneer years, and then adjust yourselves, as you will be compelled to, to the wants, necessities, and associations of the great communities that will flow in here upon you, to become a part of yourselves; if you perform your duties, as I doubt not you will, to our common country, right here in this beautiful valley, in this great basin, is to be one of the richest and most populous portion of our nation.

"I wish I could paint your coming horizon ; I wish I could cast the horoscope of your future; but I think it cannot be many years before the new star of Utah will sail up our horizon to take her place among the other members of our American constellation, (cheers) which we fondly hope, like the stars that light us tonight, shall 'haste not nor rest not, but shine on forever.'"

CHAPTER XXXIX.

THE CITY FATHERS TAKE THE PARTY TO THE GREAT SALT LAKE. MEETING OF THE SPEAKER OF THE HOUSE AND THE FOUNDER OF UTAH. THE NATION DINES WITH THE CHURCH. THE PRESIDENT PREACHES IN THE TABERNACLE AT THE REQUEST OF THE SPEAKER, WHO IN TURN TREATS THE SAINTS WITH HIS EULOGY ON LINCOLN. ADVICE TO THE FATHERS OF THE CHURCH TO ABOLISH POLYGAMY. BY A NEW REVELATION, IN EXCHANGE FOR A STATE. THE COLFAX CLOSET VIEWS. ADIEU TO THE MORMON ZION. DEATH OF GOVERNOR DOTY. A TALK ON POLYGAMY WITH THE CHAIRMAN ON TERRITORIES.

Next day Speaker Colfax, Gov. Bross, Messrs. Bowles and Richardson, accompanied by the city council and some of the leading merchants, drove over to the Great Salt Lake. "We have" wrote Mr. Bowles, "been taken on an excursion to the Great Salt Lake, bathed in its wonderful waters, on which you float like a cork, sailed on its surface, and picknicked by its shore,—if picnic can be without women for sentiment and to spread table cloth, and to be helped up and over rocks. Can you New Englanders fancy a stag picnic? We have been turned loose in the big strawberry patch of one of the Saints, and we have had a peep into a moderate Mormon harem, but being introduced to two different women of the same name, one after another, was more than I could stand without blushing."

But the meeting of President Brigham Young and Speaker Colfax and party was the crowning circumstance of the visit.

The Speaker of the House stood upon his dignity. Esteeming himself a chief representative of the nation, he did not think it becoming his national importance to first call on Brigham Young. This was expressed, and President Young was fully informed of the mountain of etiquette that burdened the spirit of the honorable Speaker. There could be no doubt that he wished to see the Prophet. To have gone away without seeing him would have taken away half the relish of the visit. So Brigham (who was matchless when he undertook to play the character of simple native greatness) humored him, and went down from his "Lion House," in company with several apostles and leading men of the city, to call upon the nation in the person of Mr. Colfax. The circumstance is told by Mr. Bowles, but with an evident effort to poise the Speaker of the House well as the principal figure in his meeting with the Mormon Moses.

"In Mormon etiquette," he wrote, "President Brigham Young is called upon; by Washington fashion the Speaker is called upon, and does not call; there was a question whether the distinguished resident and the distinguished visitor would meet; Mr. Colfax, as was meet under the situation of affairs here, made a point upon it, and gave notice he should not call; whereupon President Brigham yielded the question and graciously came to-day with a crowd of high dignitaries of the church, and made, not one of Emerson's prescribed ten minute calls, but a generous, pleasant, gossiping silting of two hours long. He is a very hale and hearty looking man, young for sixty-four, with a light grey eye, cold and uncertain, a mouth and chin betraying a great and determined will—handsome perhaps as to presence and features, but repellent in atmosphere and without magnetism. In conversation he is cool and quiet in manner but suggestive in expression; has strong and original ideas but uses bad grammar. He was rather formal, but courteous, and at the last affected frankness and freedom, if he felt it not. To his followers, I observed he was master of that profound art of eastern politicians, which consists in putting the arm affectionately around them and tenderly enquiring for health of selves and families; and when his eye did sparkle and his lips soften, it was with most cheering, though not warming effect— it was pleasant but did not melt you."

There were present at this interview, Speaker Colfax, Governor Bross, and Messrs Richardson and Bowles—the party of distinguished visitors;—Presidents Brigham Young and Heber C. Kimball, Apostles John Taylor, Wilford Woodruff, George A. Smith, F. D. Richards, George Q. Cannon, Hons. John F. Kinney, J. M. Bernhisel, Wm. H. Hooper, Mayor Smoot, Marshal J. C. Little; Bishops Sharp and Hardy, Wm. Jennings, John W. Young, N. H. Felt, and George D. Watt, Esqrs.

The Colfax party made a trip to Rush Valley, and on their return to Salt Lake City, on Friday, June 16th, they were the guests of Hon. W. H. Hooper. Next day they visited President Young, and afterwards were the guests of Wm. Jennings, Esq., dining in company with Presidents Young and Kimball; Apostles George A. Smith and George Q. Cannon; Hons. J. F. Kinney and Wm. H. Hooper; Col. Irish, Mayor Smoot, Marshal J. C. Little, and Charles H. Hapgood, John W. Young, J. F. Tracy, H. S. Rumfield and T. B. H. Stenhouse, Esqrs. Of this dinner Mr. Bowles wrote: "In the early years of the Territory, there was terrible suffering for want of food; many were reduced to roots of the field for sustenance; but now there appears to be an abundance of the substantial necessaries of life, and as most of the population are cultivators of the soil, all or nearly all have plenty of food. And certainly, I have never seen more generously laden tables than have been spread before us at our hotel or at private houses. A dinner to our party this evening by a leading Mormon merchant, at which President Young and the principal members of his council were present, had as rich a variety of fish, meats and vegetables, pastry and fruit, as I ever saw on any private table in the east; and the quality and the cooking and the serving were unimpeachable. All the food too was native in Utah. The wives of our host waited on us most amicably, and the entertainment was, in every way, the best illustration of the practical benefits of plurality, that has yet been presented to us.

"Later in the evening we were presented to another, and perhaps the most wonderful, illustration of the reach of social and artificial life in this far off city of the Rocky Mountains. This was the Theatre, in which a special performance was improvised in honor of Speaker Colfax. The building is itself a rare triumph of art and enterprise. No eastern city of one hundred thousand inhabitants,— remember Salt Lake City has less than twenty thousand,—possesses so fine a theatrical structure. It ranks, alike in capacity and elegance of structure and finish, along with the opera houses and academies of music of Boston, New York, Philadelphia, Chicago and Cincinnati. In costumes and scenery it is furnished with equal richness and variety, and the performances themselves, though by amateurs, by merchants and mechanics, by wives and daughters of citizens would have done credit to a first-class professional company. There was first a fine and elaborate drama, and then a spectacular farce, in both of which were introduced some exquisite dancing, and in one some good singing also. I have rarely seen a theatrical entertainment more pleasing and satisfactory in all its details and appointments. Yet the two principal characters were by a day laborer and a carpenter; one of the leading parts was by a married daughter of Brigham Young, herself the mother of several children; and several other of his daughters took part in the ballet, which was most enchantingly rendered, and with great scenic effect.

The house was full in all its parts, and the audience embraced all classes of society from the wives and daughters of President Young—a goodly array—and the families of the rich merchants, to the families of the mechanics and farmers of the city and valley, and the soldiers from camp."

Next day being Sunday, the Colfax party attended the Tabernacle to hear President Young, who had been asked by Mr. Colfax "to preach upon the distinctive Mormon doctrines." "Brigham's preaching to-day," wrote Mr. Bowles, "was a very unsatisfactory performance. There was every incentive in him to do his best; he had an immense audience spread out under the 'bowery' to the number of five or six thousand; before him was Mr. Colfax, who asked him to preach upon the distinctive Mormon doctrines; around him were all his elders and bishops, in unusual numbers; and he was fresh from the exciting discussion of yesterday on the subject of polygamy." The writer continues and gives with great disgust the subject matter of Brigham's sermon, thus closing his review: "Brigham Young may be a shrewd business man, an able organizer of labor, a bold brave person in dealing with all the practicalities of life,—he must, indeed, be all of these for we see the evidence all around this city and country; but he is in no sense an impressive or effective preacher, judging by any standard that I have been accustomed to. His audience, swollen by one or two thousand more, could not have helped drawing a sharp contrast,—dull in comprehension and fanatically devoted to him as most of them probably are,—between his speech and his style, and those of Mr. Colfax, who at a later hour this evening, delivered in the same place, by invitation of the church and city authorities, his Chicago eulogy on the Life and Principles of President Lincoln. He spoke it with tut notes, and with much freedom to an audience unused to so effective and eloquent a style, and more unused, we fear, to such sentiments; and he received rapt attention and apparently delighted approval throughout the whole."

But, if the Colfax party was greatly disgusted with Brigham's sermon of that Sabbath morning, the "unusual numbers" of "his elders and bishops around him" were as greatly amused by Brigham's signal failure. It was the talk of the following week, among some of his friends, that the President, on the Sunday, had treated Speaker Colfax and party to the worst sermon he had ever preached.

They were "glad of it," they said. "The Lord intended to read his servant Brigham a lesson." "The Lord didn't want him to show off before the Speaker of Congress." There was considerable common sense in this view of the matter which the Saints took, and though at first, perhaps, somewhat disappointed with himself probably the "Prophet Brigham " appreciated the "Lord's lesson" to him in the same spirit—glad that he had not been allowed to show off before the Speaker of the House.

Brigham Young and Schuyler Colfax were measured that day by two different standards: the one was a great colonizer, and already the founder of a hundred cities; the other the eloquent Speaker of the House of Representatives.

This is the only salient point of the "sharp contrast " between Brigham's bungling sermon on Mormonism, and Colfax's magnificent "eulogy on the Life and Principles of President Lincoln."

But the chief subject of interest, of that time as well as of all times, till the peculiar and distinguishing marriage institution of the Mormons shall have been either reformed or more firmly established, was brought up between Mr. Colfax and his party, as representative of the Nation, and President Young and the apostles, as representative of the Mormon Church, in their second interview on the Saturday when Mr. Colfax and his companions called upon President Young at his office. Mr. Bowles is the most proper person to relate the conversation.

He wrote: "Mr. Colfax and his friends have also had two long interviews with Brigham Young and other leaders of the Church, in one of which the peculiar institution of the people was freely and frankly but most earnestly discussed by all.
* * * * *

"The conversation I have alluded to with Brigham Young and some of his elders, on this subject of polygamy, was introduced by his enquiry of Mr. Colfax what the Government and the people East proposed to do with it and them, now they had got rid of the slavery question. The Speaker replied that he had no authority to speak for the Government; but for himself, he might be permitted to make the suggestion, he had hoped ihe Prophets of the Church would have a new revelation on the subject, which should put a stop to the practice. He added, further, he hoped that, as the people of Missouri and Maryland, without waiting for the action of the general government against slavery, themselves believing it to be wrong and an impediment to their prosperity, had taken measures to abolish it, so he hoped the people of the Mormon Church would see that polygamy was a hindrance and not a help, and move for its abandonment. Mr. Young responded quickly and frankly that he should readily welcome such a revelation; that polygamy was not in the original book of the Mormons; that it was not an essential practice in the Church, but only a privilege and a duty, under special command of God; that he knew it had been abused; that people had entered into polygamy who ought not to have done so, and against his protestation and advice.

At the same time, he defended the practice as having biblical authority, and as having, within proper limits, a sound moral and philosophical reason and propriety.

"The discussion, thus opened, grew general and sharp, though very good natured.
* * * *

"In the course of the discussion, Mr. Young asked, suppose polygamy is given up, will not your government then demand more,—will it not war upon the Book of the Mormons, and attack our church organization? The reply was emphatically, No, that it had no right, and could have no justification to do so, and that we had no idea there would be any disposition in that direction.

"The talk, which was said to be the freest and (rankest ever known on that subject in that presence, ended pleasantly, but with the full expression, on the part of Mr. Colfax and his friends, of their hope that the polygamic question might be removed from existence, and thus all objection to the admission of Utah as a State be taken away; but that until it was, no such admission was possible, and that the government could not continue to look indifferently upon the enlargement of so offensive a practice. And not only what Mr. Young said, but his whole manner left us with the impression that, if public opinion and the government united vigorously, but at the same time discreetly, to press the question, there would be found some way to acquiesce in the demand and change the practice of the present fathers of the church."

Still more important than this conversation, as a connecting vein of history is the exposition of the Colfax closet views and forecast of national policy concerning the Mormons and their institutions—views and policy matured while on this very visit to Salt Lake City, next quickly infused into the public mind on his return East, and finally brought into sharp administrative action, when he became Vice-President of the United States. And what is exceedingly significant is that, when this exposition and forecast of Mr. Colfax's views and national policy was sent to the American public, in Mr. Bowie's last letter from Salt Lake City to the Springfield Republican, the expectation was that Schuyler Colfax would be the next President of the United States—the regular "successor of Abraham Lincoln" after Andrew Johnson had filled the unexpired term. In the dedication of his "Across the Continent," to the then prospective President of the United States, Mr. Bowles said. "Besides the book is more yours than mine;" so the following from the same letter, which relates the conversation with Brigham Young on polygamy, may be read as from Mr. Colfax himself on Utah policy.

"The result of the whole experience has been to increase my appreciation of the value of their material progress and development to the nation; to evoke congratulations to them and to the country for the wealth they have created and the order, frugality, morality and industry that have been organized in this remote spot in our Continent; to excite wonder at the perfection of their Church system, the extent of its ramifications, the sweep of its influence; and to enlarge my respect for the personal sincerity and character of many of the leaders in the organization; also, and on the other hand, to deepen my disgust at their polygamy, and strengthen my convictions of its barbaric and degrading influences.

They have tried it and practiced it under the most favorable circumstances, perhaps under the mildest forms possible, but now, as before, here as elsewhere, it tends to and means only the degradation of woman. By it and under it, she becomes simply the servant and serf, not the companion and equal of man; and the inevitable influence of this upon society need not be depicted.

"But I find that Mormonism is not necessarily polygamy; that the one began and existed many years without the other; that not all the Mormons accept the doctrine, and not one-fourth, perhaps not one-eighth, practice it; and that the nation and its government may oppose it and punish it without at all interfering with the existence of the Mormon Church, or justly being held as interfering with the religious liberty that is the basis of all our institutions. This distinction has not been sufficiently understood heretofore, and it has not been consistently acted upon by either the government or the public of the East. Here, by the people, who are coming in to enjoy the opportunities of the country for trade and mining, and there by our rulers at Washington and by the great public, this single issue of polygamy should be pressed home upon the Mormon Church,—discreetly and with tact, with law and with argument and appeal, but with firmness and power.

"Ultimately, of course, before the influences of emigration, civilization and our democratic habits, an organization so aristocratic and autocratic as the Mormon Church now is must modify its rule; it must compete with other sects and take its chances with them. And its most aristocratic and uncivilized incident or feature of plurality of wives must fall first and completely before contact with the rest of the world, —marshalled with mails, daily papers, railroads and telegraphs —ciphering out the fact that the men and women of the world are about equally divided and applying to the Mormon patriarchs the democratic principle of equal and exact justice. Nothing can save this feature of Mormonism but a new flight and a more complete isolation. A kingdom in the sea, entirely its own, could only perpetuate it; and thither even, commerce and democracy would ultimately follow it. The click of the telegraph and the roll of the overland stages are its death-rattle now; the first whistle of the locomotive will sound its requiem; and the pickaxe of the miner will dig its grave. Squatter sovereignty will speedily settle the question, even if the Government continues to coquette and humor it, as it has done.

"But the Government should no longer hold a doubtful or divided position towards this great crime of the Mormon Church. Declaring clearly both its want of power and disinclination to interfere at all with the Church organization as such, or with the latter's influence over its followers, assuring and guaranteeing to it all the liberty and freedom that other religious sects hold and enjoy, the Government should still, as clearly, and distinctly, declare, by all its action, and all its representatives here, that this feature of polygamy, not properly or necessarily a part of the religion of the Mormons, is a crime by the common law of the Nation, and that any cases of its extension will be prosecuted and punished as such. Now half or two-thirds the Federal officers in the Territory are polygamists; and others bear no testimony against it. These should give way to men who, otherwise equally Mormons it may be, still are neither polygamists nor believers in the practice of polygamy. No employees or contractors of the Government should be polygamists in theory or practice.

"Here the Government should take its stand, calmly, quietly, but firmly, giving its moral support and countenance, and its physical support if necessary to the large class of Mormons who are not polygamists, to missionaries and preachers of all other sects, who choose to come here, and erect their standards and invite followers; and to that growing public opinion, here and elsewhere, which is accumulating its inexorable force against an institution which his not inaptly been termed a twin barbarism with slavery. There is no need and no danger of. physical conflict growing up; only a hot and unwise zeal and impatience on the part of the Government representatives, and in the command of the troops stationed here, could precipitate that. The probability is, that, upon such a demonstration by the Government, as I have suggested, the leaders of the Church would receive new light on the subject themselves, perhaps have a fresh revelation, and abandon the objectionable feature in their polity. No matter if they did not—it would soon, under the influences now rapidly aggregating, and thus reinforced by the Government, abandon them.

"In this way, all violent conflict would, I believe, be successfully avoided; and all this valuable population and its industries and wealth may be retained in place and to the Nation, without waste. Let them continue to be Mormons, if they choose, so long as they are not polygamists. They may be ignorant and fanatical, and imposed upon and swindled even by their church leaders; but they are industrious, thriving, and more comfortable than, on an average, they have ever been before in the homes from which they came hither; and there is no law against fanaticism and bigotry and religious charlatanry. All these evils of religious benightment are not original in Utah, and they will work out their own cure here as they have elsewhere in our land. We must have patience with the present, and possibly forgiveness for supposed crimes in the past by their leaders, because we have heretofore failed to meet the issues promptly and clearly and have shared, by our consent and protection to their authors, in the alleged wrongs."

In closing his letters from Salt Lake City Mr. Bowles gives a very notable adieu to our city: "But adieu to Salt Lake and many-wive-and-much-children-dom; its strawberries and roses; its rare hospitality; its white crowned peaks; its wide spread valley; its river of scriptural name; its lake of briniest taste. I have met much to admire, many to respect, worshipped deep before its nature,—found only one thing to condemn. I shall want to come again when the railroad can bring me and that blot is gone."

During the visit of the Colfax party to our city, Governor James Duane Doty died, whereupon the following order was issued by the city authorities:

"Mayor's Office, Great Salt Lake City, June 14th, 1865."

"Whereas, intelligence has reached me of the sudden death of Governor James Duane Doty, who departed this life on the 13th inst., at 9 o'clock, "Therefore, in token of respect for the dead, I do hereby request that all secular business in the city be suspended; that all business houses be closed, and that the flags be draped at half-mast until after the funeral ceremonies.

By order of A. O. Smoot, Mayor.

J. C. Little, Marshal.

On Thursday morning, June 15th. at ten o'clock, the citizens assembled in large numbers around the residence of the late governor of Utah, and punctually the ostentatious funeral service was performed by the Rev. Norman McLeod before the corpse left the house. The coffin was carried to the hearse by the Hon. Schuyler Colfax, Governor Bross, Chief Justice Titus, Associate Justice Drake, Superintendent Irish, and U. S. Marshal Gibbs. The carriages of the citizens and families of the military command formed in a long procession, and moved northward, thence east by South Temple Street, preceded by the Provost Guard and the military band to the cemetery at Camp Douglass. "All business was suspended in the city, the flags at half-mast were draped in crape, drooping in the air, while the unusual somber clouds lent a sadness to the scene that faithfully depicted the heart-felt sadness of the people."

About two weeks later the Honorable Jas. M. Ashley, of Ohio, then chairman of the Committee on Territories, visited Salt Lake City. President Brigham Young met the gentleman frankly, and in the parlor of Delegate Hooper there was a free conversation upon the probable future relations between the Government and the Mormons. The first question from Brigham was: Well, Mr. Ashley, are you, also, going to recommend us to get a new revelation to abolish polygamy, or what are you going to do with us? * * * *

"Now, Mr. President, I don't know what we can do with you. Your situation reminds me of an experience of Tom Corwin, In the days of Tom's poverty, somewhere in Ohio, he thought he would hang out a lawyer's shingle and catch a share of business. One day a smart fellow solicited his legal services; he wanted Tom to defend him and proposed to give him a fee of fifty dollars.

That was a big sum to Tom then; but when he heard the situation of his client he stated that he was under professional obligations to say he could be of no service to him. The client insisted that Tom should make a speech in court, and that was all he wanted. The case came on: the evidence was clear, witnesses had seen the prisoner steal some hams, carry them to a house, and there the hams were found in the client's possession. It was a clear case of theft, the evidence was incontestable, and the prosecutor thought it needless to address the jury. The defendant, however, insisted that Tom should make his speech. A brilliant effort was made, the jury retired, and in a few minutes returned with a verdict of 'not guilty." The judge, the prosecutor and Tom were perfectly confounded. They glanced at each other a look of inquiry. Nothing more could be done, and the prisoner was discharged. As they retired from the court the lawyer said to the thief: 'Now old fellow, I want you to tell me how that was done!' 'Your speech did it,' was the reply. No, it didn't and I want to know how *you* did it?' 'Well, if you will not speak of it till I get out of the State, I shall tell you.' Tom accorded to this, and in perfect confidence his client whispered: 'Well, eleven of the jurors had some of the ham.'"

Brigham roared and laughed. It was Mr. Ashley's pleasant incarnation that with a Mormon jury the institution was perfectly secure. The story is told by T. B. H. Stenhouse who was present at the interview between the Mormon President and the chairman of the Committee on Territories.

CHAPTER XL.

BEGINNING OF THE ANTI-MORMON CRUSADE. THE CHANGE IN THE COLFAX VIEWS. INITIAL OF THE ACTION AGAINST THE UTAH MILITIA. URGING THE ADMINISTRATION. CORRECTED VIEWS CONCERNING THE MILITIA.

Out of this Colfax visit to Salt Lake City directly grew what the Mormons call the crusades against their religion, or as Chief Justice James B. McKean described it, the prosecution of "Polygamic Theocracy." It began immediately on the return of the Colfax party from their tour of investigation of the Great West, first in the agitation of the public mind by the speeches and expositions of Speaker Colfax relative to the Pacific States and Territories, in which polygamic Utah came in constantly for a sharp and special treatment. Until this Colfax movement commenced to stir up the Nation upon Utah affairs, there had been no "crusade" of the Government and Congress against Mormon polygamy. In the causes presented to Congress by the Buchanan administration, for the sending out of the Utah Expedition, polygamy was not even named. General Winfield Scott, in issuing his orders to General W. S. Harney, named the specific cause: —"The community and, in part, the civil government of Utah Territory are in a state of substantial rebellion against the laws and authority of the United States." Neither had the action of the Government against polygamy entered into the early differences between the Gentile part of the Federal officers and the Mormon community, though Judge Brocchus did offensively rebuke in their public assembly, the community relative to their polygamic institutions. It was not until the Grant-Colfax administration that Government took any action at all against Utah, touching polygamy. It is true there had been the passage of the anti-polygamic law by Congress in 1862; but it was generally understood to be inoperative and as a dead letter on our statute books. Indeed the Senators from California—Latham and McDougall—voted against the passage of the bill, —McDougall opposing it in a speech in which he said, "I do not think the measure at this time is well advised. It is understood its provisions will be a dead letter on our statute book. Its provisions will be either ignored or avoided. * * The impolicy of its present passage will cause my colleague and self, after consultation, to vote against the bill." And a year after the passage of that bill, though President Lincoln signed it, he sent private word, as already noted, to Ex-Governor Young concerning the Mormon polygamists with this assurance: "I will let them alone if they will let me alone."

But with the return of Speaker Colfax, from his visit of observation of the Pacific Static and Territories, the plan and policy over Utah affairs was entirely changed from a dead letter to a live action, and Government itself became the prime mover against polygamic Utah, until finally it grew into an administrative and congressional "crusade" against them as a religious community. This was inspired by Mr. Colfax and sustained by President Grant with all the determination of the man who had conquered secession in the South and finished with the sword what President Lincoln had begun in his proclamation abolishing slavery.

Brigham Young's inquiry of Mr. Colfax as to "what the Government and people of the East proposed to do with polygamy and the Mormons, now that they had got rid of the slavery question," was a most pertinent question. It was substantially the same enquiry which met Mr. Colfax everywhere on his return to the Eastern States with his expositions and policy relative to the Pacific States and Territories. All his speeches dealt with Utah consonant with the foregoing expositions of views and policy contained in Mr. Bowies' closing Salt Lake letter.

The warm genuine hospitality which Salt Lake City had extended to Mr. Colfax and his friends; the admiration expressed by all touching what the Mormons had done in these once desert places, and their value as a community to the Nation; and, above all, the free and cordial interviews and conversations which took place between the Colfax party and Brigham and his friends, seemed to promise a happy union between the general Government and the Mormon leaders, in the adjustment of the affairs in question. But, when on his return from the West, to speak with a permitted national voice of its affairs, the enquiry which Brigham Young had put came sharply from the public, "what does the Nation intend to do with the Mormons and polygamy, now it has got rid of the slavery question?" Mr. Colfax was carried away from the possible adjustment, which he might at a later date have effected with the leaders of the Mormon church, when he became as Vice-President the actual dictator of the Government on Utah affairs.

In sending out his book, " Across the Continent," dedicated to Mr. Colfax, Mr. Bowles strongly marks this change which had taken place in a few months, both in the minds of the Mormon leaders and in the policies and intentions of Mr. Colfax. In his supplementary papers he wrote: "Since our visit to Utah in June, the leaders among the Mormons have repudiated their professions of loyalty to the Government, denied any disposition to yield the issue of polygamy, and begun to preach anew, and more vigorously than ever, disrespect and defiance to the authority of the National Government.

They seem to be disappointed and irate that their personal attentions and assurances to Mr. Colfax and his friends did not win for them more tolerance of their peculiar institution, and something like espousal of their desire for admission as a State of the Union. New means are taken to organize and drill the militia of the Territory and to provide them with arms, under the auspices and authority of the Mormon Church; and an open conflict with the representatives of the Government is apparently braved, even threatened.

"Much of this demonstration is probably mere bravado; means to arouse the ignorant people, excite them against the Government, make them still more the fanatical followers of the Church leaders, and also to intimidate the public authorities, and induce them to continue the same let-alone and indulgent policy that has been the rule at Washington for so long. The Government always seems to have demonstrated just enough against the Mormons to irritate them and keep them compact and prepared to resist it, but never enough to make them really afraid, or to force them into any submissive steps. The bristling attitude of the Saints has ever had the apparent effect to qualify the Government purpose, and make it stop short in its proceeding to enforce the laws and National authority.

It is no wonder, therefore, that they repeat their frantic and fanatic appeals to their people, and their defiance to the Government, and grow more and more bold in them. They find that it works better than professions of loyalty and half-way offers of submission, one bad effect of which, for their own cause, is of course to demoralize their followers, and weaken their own authority over them.

"There is no evidence yet of any change in the policy of the executive authorities at Washington. While the new Federal Governor of the Territory, Mr. Durkee from Wisconsin, the Federal judges, and the superintendent of Indian affairs are both anti-Mormons and anti-polygamists, all or nearly all the other Federal officers in the Territory are both leading Mormons and practical polygamists—the postmasters, collectors of internal revenue, etc. The postmaster of Salt Lake City is one of Brigham Young's creatures, and editor of the Mormon daily paper there. The returns of internal revenue in the Territory are found to be, proportionately to similar populations and wealth, quite small; and there are reasons to believe that the taxes are not faithfully assessed and collected. General Conner, who has been returned to his old place, as military commander of the district of Utah alone, is assigned a force of only one thousand soldiers; though he asked for and expected to have five thousand. The lesser number remote from all possible reinforcement, is entirely inadequate to support the Governor and judges in any exercise of authority that they may dare to undertake, and that the Mormons may choose to resist. One thousand soldiers could very readily be wiped out—which is a favorite phrase of the Saints towards their enemies—by a sudden uprising of the fanatical followers of Brigham Young and his apostles.

"Excuse for such uprising is in much danger of being developed from the growing strength and impatience of the anti-Mormon elements in society at Salt Lake City, and the reckless, desperate character of some of those elements.

Miners from Idaho and Montana have come into that city to winter, to spend their profits, if successful, or to pick up a precarious living, if unlucky. Many discharged soldiers also remain there or in the neighboring districts. The growing travel and commerce across the continent floats in other persons, good, bad and indifferent as to habits and self-control; other accessions to the Gentile strength and agitation are constantly being made. The merchants of that class are increasing and becoming prosperous; those who have been silent and submissive under the Mormon hierarchy, dare now to demonstrate their real feelings, under the protection of sympathy and soldiers; the Daily Union Vedette continues to be published as organ of the soldiers and other 'Gentiles,' and is bold and unsparing and constant in its denunciations of the Mormon church and its influences; Rev. Norman McLeod, chaplain of the soldiers, and pastor of the Congregational Society in Salt Lake City, has returned from a summer's trip to Nevada and California, with funds for building a meeting-house, and increasing zeal against the Mormons; a Gentile theatre has been established; various social organizations, in the same interest, are increasing and growing influential over the young people; General Connor himself, his fellow officers and soldiers are all bitter in their hatred of the Mormons, and eager for the opportunities to subdue them to the governmental authority; Governor Durkee seems less disposed to be tolerant of the Mormon control and the Mormon disrespect to federal authority, than his predecessors generally have been; and the judges, goaded like all the rest of the Gentiles, by Mormon insults and Mormon defiance, and their own incapacity, under government neglect, to perform their duties, more than share the common feeling of antagonism to the Church leaders.

"Thus the two parties are growing more and more antagonistic, more and more into a spirit of conflict. Thus, too, while are rapidly aggregating and operating the means by which the Mormon problem is to be solved, even without the special help or interference of Government, are also coming into life the elements and the dangers of a more serious and personal collision, in which the Mormons, from their numerical superiority, would most probably be successful and, quite likely, wreak terrible vengeance on their enemies. Of course such a result would evoke full retribution on their own head; for then people and Government would arouse, and enforce speedy and complete subjugation.

"But these threatened and dreaded results ought to be and can be avoided. The Government has now the opportunity to guide and control the operation of natural causes to the overthrow of polygamy and the submission of the Mormon aristocracy, without the shedding of blood, without the loss of a valuable population and their industries. The steps, too, are, first, a sufficient military force in the Territory to keep the peace, to protect freedom of speech, of the press, and of religious proselytism; to forbid any personal outrages on the rights of the Mormons; and to prevent any revenges by them upon the Gentiles. And, next, the supplanting of all polygamists in federal offices by men not connected with that distinctive sin and offence of the church. These steps, wisely taken, firmly administered, would rapidly give the growing anti-polygamist elements such moral power as would insure a speedy and bloodless revolution. It may not be wise or necessary, at least at the present, in view of past indulgence, to undertake to enforce the federal law against polygamy; that may be held in abeyance until the effect of such proceedings as have been indicated are fully developed. In short, I would change the government policy from the ' do-nothing' to the 'make-haste-slowly' character; I would have its influence decidedly and continuously felt in the Territory, against the crime of polygamy.

"Neglecting to do this, there is danger of anarchy and deadly conflict springing up on that arena; there is also sure prospect that the people of the country at large will, in their impatience and disgust, force upon Congress such radical measures against the Mormons, as are, in regard to our past neglect and the present opportunity of peaceful revolution, to be almost as deeply deprecated. In either event, the responsibility will rest heavily and sharply upon the President and his Cabinet, who are permitting the affairs of the Territory to drift on in the present loose and dangerous way, either ignorant of, or indifferent to, the rapidly developing social conflict there." As regards the Utah militia Mr. Bowles, evidently, was laboring under a very prevalent mistake. It has always been represented by anti-Mormon writers, and rehearsed from time to time by the newspapers of the country, that the Utah militia was organized and kept up for the express purpose of rebellion against the United States, or, at least, to give the Mormon leaders the power to resist the Federal rule whenever it became obnoxious to then. In other words, the militia of the Territory was looked upon as the military arm of the Mormon Church, and the nucleus of this army was supposed to be a formidable band of " Danites,"

known also by another name—the "Avenging Angels" of the Church. Hence the annual muster and drill of the Utah militia, taking place so soon after the Colfax visit, signified to Mr. Bowles the arming and preparing for rebellion against the Federal authority: "an open conflict with the representatives of the Government is apparently braved, even threatened." It must be confessed that this view of the militia had been established by the action of the Utah war, when Brigham Young, as governor, put the Territory under martial law, ordered a United States army back, and made bold war speeches in the Tabernacle, and that the militia had gone out under its lieutenant-general to repel invasion. But the Utah militia had been organized for no such purpose. It has been shown, in this history, that the people of Utah had not been making any preparation to resist the expedition, nor had they expected any conflict with the Government, until the news burst upon them like a bombshell, while they were celebrating the tenth anniversary of their pioneer day, that an army was on the way to destroy them as a community. Then everywhere throughout the Territory the citizens arose spontaneously, not so much as a militia, but rather as a community to defend their church, their homes, their lives and their liberties, and to protect their wives and children; for it will be remembered that they expected nothing less than extermination from their Rocky Mountain refuges, if the Utah military expedition prevailed. But the Utah militia was organized with no contemplation of anything of this, much less with an intent of resistance to the Federal authority. It was organized in 1849, for the protection of the young colonies against Indian depredations and was kept up for the same purpose. It had, up to 1865, cost the settlers many valuable lives, and millions of dollars in time and substance, and there had been occasions when nearly all the able-bodied men in the settlements, both North and South were, half the year round, either under arms on guard at home, or away on Indian expeditions protecting distant settlements. Indeed, the often and continued Indian wars form no inconsiderable portion of Utah's history, and Salt Lake City, being the headquarters, was always conspicuous in the military action and display, especially during the annual muster and review of the troops "over Jordan," when President D. H. Wells figured as lieutenant-general, and apostles and bishops as major-generals, brigadier-generals and colonels yet this fact by no means constituted the militia the army of the Church. Just such an occasion had come in the year 1865. It was the year of the Black Hawk war.

CHAPTER XLI.

HISTORY OF THE UTAH MILITIA FOR THE YEARS 1865, 1866, AND 1887. THE GOVERNOR CALLS UPON CAMP DOUGLAS FOR AID AGAINST THE INDIANS BUT IS REFUSED. THE GOVERNMENT ORDERS THE UTAH MILITIA FOR THAT SERVICE. SECRETARY RAWLINS SUBMITS THE REPORT TO CONGRESS. THE GOVERNMENTS DEBT TO OUR CITIZENS OF OVER A MILLION DOLLARS FOR MILITARY SERVICES UNPAID.

The following State document, which is, in itself, quite a chapter of the Indian history of our Territory, gives a very different rendering of the military activity in the fall of 1865, of which Mr. Bowles wrote to the public: "New means are taken to organize and drill the militia of the Territory, and to provide them with arms, under the auspices and authority of the Mormon Church; and an open conflict with the representatives of the government is apparently braved, even threatened."

"War Department, March 25th, 1869.

"The Secretary of War has the honor to submit to the House of Representatives the accompanying communication from the adjutant-general of the Territory of Utah, inclosing a statement of the expenses incurred by the Territory in the suppression of Indian hostilities during the years 1865, 1866 and 1867.

"Jno. A. Rawlins, Secretary of War.

"Adjutant General's Office, Utah Territory,

"Salt Lake City, Feb. 9th, 1869.

"I have the honor herewith to forward to you the accounts of expenses incurred by the Territory of Utah, in the suppression of Indian hostilities in said Territory during the years 1865, 1866 and 1867.

"The seat of this war has been chiefly in Sanpete, Sevier and Piute Counties, and it may be necessary to give a brief description of that part of the Territory to enable you to more readily understand the situation of those inhabitants, and the necessity that existed for a strong military force constantly in the field during the season of hostilities.

"San Pete Valley is one hundred and twenty miles south of this city, and extends southward some sixty miles, and is from five to fifteen miles wide, surrounded by lofty and rugged mountains, from which streams of water flow down into the valley at intervals of from six to ten miles. On these streams and near the base of the mountains, the settlements and towns are mostly located. There are in this valley, which was first settled in 1849, nine large and, until the war, flourishing settlements, viz: Fountain Green, Moroni, Coalville, Fairview, Mount Pleasant, Springtown, Fort Ephraim, Manti, and Fort Gunnison, each with a population of from five hundred to two thousand inhabitants. The San Pete River runs through the valley from north to south, and empties into the Sevier river below Fort Gunnison. Near this point Sevier County joins San Pete and extends directly south some sixty miles up the Sevier Valley, In Sevier County there was, when the war commenced, four thriving settlements, viz: Salina, Glenwood, Richfield and Alma, with a population of about fifteen hundred. Piute County lies directly south of Sevier. In these, as in San Pete

County, the settlements are located on the streams near the base of the mountains, which are high and very rugged.

The war commenced on the tenth day of April, 1865, when a band of San Pete Utes, led by Black Hawk, killed Peter Ludwicksen near Manti, San Pete County, and on the following day, Barney Ward and Mr. Lambson, near Salina, Sevier County, and drove off a large herd of stock up the adjoining canyon. A company of cavalry was immediately mustered into service, gave them chase, and when about ten miles up the canyon received a deadly fire from the Indians from behind the rocks in an almost impregnable position. From the high and rugged mountains on both sides they could not be flanked. Two of our men were instantly killed and two wounded, and the company was obliged to fall back, until on the arrival of additional forces they again started in pursuit, and traveling one hundred miles over an extremely rugged country, overtook them near Fish Lake, gave them battle, killing and wounding several of the Indians, but the stock had been driven on toward the Elk mountains and could not be recovered. The war had now commenced, and all overtures of peace were peremptorily refused by the Indians. His Excellency J. D. Doty, then governor of the Territory, and Colonel O. H. Irish, then superintendent of Indian Affairs, were applied to for aid.

The superintendent requested the military authorities at Camp Douglas, in this city, to send a sufficient force to protect the settlers and to arrest the offending Indians. This was declined. See annual report of O. H. Irish, superintendent of Indian Affairs, Utah Territory, September 9th, 1865, to the Commissioner of Indian Affairs, Washington, D. C, published in the ' Report of the Secretary of the Interior,' 1865-66, page 314, of which the following is an extract: "' During the past year the Indians have been peaceful, with the exception of the difficulties with a band of outlaws in San Pete Valley, mentioned in my letter of the 28th of April last. At that time I requested the military authorities to send a sufficient force to protect the settlers and to arrest the offending Indians.

This was refused, and the settlers were left to take care of themselves. They organized a force of about eighty men and drove the Indians back to Grand River, killing about one-third of the number of those who were engaged in committing the depredations.

"O. H. Irish, Superintendent, etc.,

"May 26th.—The Indians killed John Given, wife and four children, near Thistle Valley, San Pete County, and Mr. Neilson, near North Bend, in the same county, and on the 29th, David M. Jones, near the same settlement, and drove off a large herd of horses and cattle. In consequence of these renewed outrages other companies of cavalry were mustered into service, and the stock in these counties, which had up to that time ranged in the valleys and sides of the mountains, were gathered up and herded in the vicinity of the settlements by the inhabitants.

"Notwithstanding every precaution and effort made by the militia and the settlers, in consequence of the rugged nature of the country and the situation of the settlements, it was impossible to prevent the enemy making an occasional raid on the settlements or some herd of stock, as they would come down from the mountains in force and return in an hour to an almost impregnable position in the canyon, or some previously unknown mountain pass.

"For the better protection of the settlements, all of the able-bodied men in those counties were mustered into service as home guards, and performed duty in this capacity, but no returns for this service are included in these accounts.

"The war continued, the Indians gaining accessions to their ranks, and having, during the summer, massacred between thirty and forty men, women and children. The last raid in 1865, was on Fort Ephraim, San Pete County, in the month of October, when five men and two women were killed, and two men wounded, and two hundred head of stock taken. Many battles were fought during the summer and some forty of Black Hawk's warriors killed.

"On the approach of winter the Indians withdrew to the Colorado River, living on the plunder of the past summer, their successes having furnished them with horses to mount all who would join their ranks, and plenty of beef to feed them—strong inducements to Indians.

"Nothing reliable was heard of the enemy for some time, but it was rumored that they were daily increasing in numbers and making preparations for another campaign so soon as the melting snow in the mountains would permit.

"Early in the month of February, 1866, their intentions were defined by making a raid on a small settlement in Kane County, Southern Utah, killing Dr. Whitmore and a young man by the name of McIntyre, and driving off a large flock of sheep, some horses and cattle; and in a few days making another raid on Berryville, in the same county, killing two men and one woman, and taking some horses and cattle; and as the snow disappeared from the mountains north, so they continued to advance on the settlements in force, having been joined by a number of the Navajos and a band of Elk Mountain Utes. The war, which at its commencement, looked small, began to assume alarming proportions, and, as the settlers had to rely on the militia of the Territory, Lieutenant-General Daniel H. Wells ordered all the able-bodied men that could be spared from San Pete, Sevier and Piute Counties to be immediately mustered into service as cavalry and infantry, and organized for defense. Before the organization was completely effected, another raid was made upon Marysvale, Piute County, April 2nd; two men were killed and a band of horses captured. Their next raid was on Salina, Sevier County, April 20th. Here two men were killed, and two hundred head of cattle and horses taken. See letters of Colonel F. H. Head, Superintendent of Indian Affairs, Utah Territory, to the Commissioners of Indian Affairs, Washington, D. C, published in 'Indian Affairs, 1866,' on pages 128, 130, of which the following is extracted:

"'Utah Superintendence,
"' Great Salt Lake City, April 30, 1866

"'Sir: Black Hawk, a somewhat prominent chief of the Ute Indians, has been engaged for more than a year past in active hostilities against the settlements in the southern portion of this Territory. His Land consisted at first of but forty-four men, who were mostly outlaws and desperate characters from his own and other tribes. During the summer and autumn of 1865 he made several successful forays upon the weak and unprotected settlements in San Pete and Sevier Counties, killing in all thirty-two whites, and drove away to the mountains upward of two thousand cattle and horses.

"' Forty of his warriors were killed by the settlers in repelling his different attacks. His success in stealing, however, enabled him to feed abundantly and mount all Indians who joined him, and the prestige acquired by his raids was such that his numbers were constantly on the increase, despite his occasional losses of men. He spent the winter near where the Grand and Green Rivers unite to form the Colorado. On the 20th instant he again commenced his depredations by making an attack upon Salina, Sevier County. He succeeded in driving to the mountains about two hundred cattle, killing two men who were guarding them, and compelling the abandonment of the settlement.

"'His band, from what I consider entirely reliable information, now numbers about one hundred warriors, one-half of whom are Navajos from New Mexico.

"'In view of these circumstances, and for the purpose of preventing accessions to the ranks of the hostile Indians, I have, after consultation with Governor Durkee, desired Colonel Potter, commanding the United States troops in this district, to send two or three companies of soldiers to that portion of the Territory to protect the settlements and repel further attacks. Colonel Potter has telegraphed to General Dodge for instructions in reference to my application. I should be much pleased to have an expression of your views as to the policy to be pursued in this matter.

"' Very respectfully, your most obedient servant,

"'F. H. Head, Superintendent.

"Hon. D. N. Cooley,

"'Commissioner of Indian Affairs, Washington, D. C,

"And under date of 21st June, in a similar communication, he states (see page 130 of said published report): "' I advised you in my communication of the 30th April that I had applied to the military authorities to send two or three companies of troops to protect the settlers in those portions of the Territory most exposed to Indian raids, and that 'Colonel Potter, commanding at this point, had telegraphed for instructions. A copy of the response to such communication is herewith enclosed.

"' The morning of my departure (from Uintah) I was informed by Tabby, the head chief, that when he received notice of my arrival in the valley, himself and all his warriors were on their way to join the hostile Indians in the southern portion of the Territory, in their war upon the settlements. He also informed me that Black Hawk, having secured a number of recruits among the Elk Mountain Utes to swell his force to three hundred warriors, was then setting out from the Elk Mountain country to attack the weaker settlements in San Pete County.

"' On reaching this city on my return from Uintah, I communicated the facts in my possession relative to Black Hawk, to Governor Durkee. General Wells, one of the principal militia officers, after consulting with the Governor, has raised two or three companies of militia, and proceeded to the threatened locality to protect the settlers from the expected attack.

" F. H. Head, Superintendent:

"'Fort Leavenworth, Kansas, May 2nd, 1866.

"'General Pops telegraphs that the superintendent of Indian affairs will have to depend for the present on the militia to compel the Indians to behave at Salina.

"' By command of Major-General Dodge.

"'Samuel C. Mackey,

"'Acting Assistant Adjutant-General,

"' Col. Carroll H. Potter,
"'Commanding District of Utah.'

"Accordingly, steps were immediately taken to place all the settlements south and east of Salt Lake City in a better state of defense, and troops were mustered into service from Salt Lake and other counties, and dispatched to the scenes of hostilities. The weaker settlements in Summit, Wasatch, San Pete, Sevier, Piute, Beaver, Iron, Kane, and Washington, were abandoned and removed to the stronger.

Substantial forts were built, and all the stock in the above-named counties was gathered up and guarded. Overtures of peace were made by the settlers whenever opportunity offered but were defiantly refused by the Indians; and on the 11th day of June, Lieutenant-General D. H. Wells started from Salt Lake City, and on the 14th arrived at Fort Gunnison, San Pete County, and took command in person, remaining in San Pete, Sevier and Piute Counties three months. Notwithstanding every precaution, and the energy and faithfulness of the militia troops in service, such was the extent and mountainous character of the country, that the enemy, lying secreted, would occasionally succeed in making a dash on some weak point and capturing a herd of stock. Thus it continued through the summer, while all that part of the Territory for three hundred miles in extent was paralyzed, but more particularly was it the case in San Pete, Sevier and Piute Counties. No improvements were made. The saw mills in the canyons were silent; and in many cases were burnt up or otherwise destroyed by the Indians.

Very little grain was raised in consequence of the number of men in the service in those counties During the summer about twenty persons were massacred, and a very large amount of stock was taken, and many flourishing settlements were broken up and abandoned. Several skirmishes occurred through the summer, in which between thirty and forty of the Indians were killed and wounded.

"The Indians again drawing off for winter quarters, on the first day of November the last of the militia troops were mustered out.

"Peace again reigned for a short time. The mountains and passes were again blockaded with snow, and the inhabitants had a short interval to prepare for winter.

"Nothing of importance was heard from the Indians until early in January, 1867, when they commenced the war for another year by making a raid on Pine Valley, Washington County, the extreme southern part of the Territory, capturing a band of horses. Captain Andrews, with a company of cavalry, followed them, recovered most of the horses and killed seven Indians. All was quiet again till March, when another raid was made on Richfield, Sevier County.

Here they killed one man, one woman, and a girl fourteen years of age. The killing of the females was accompanied with great atrocity. Reliable information was received that they were still determined on war, and troops were again mustered into service in San Pete, Sevier and Piute Counties, also one company of cavalry and one of infantry in Salt Lake and Utah Counties. With the aid of these two companies, in addition to the forces raised in these three counties, further depredations were prevented until the 2nd of June, when Major Vance and Sergeant Houtz were waylaid and killed at Twelve Mile Creek, San Pete County; and on the 12th, they made a raid on Beaver, Beaver County capturing a large herd of stock. This county is west of Piute County.

"August 14th, they made a raid on Springtown, San Pete County, killing two men, wounding another, and capturing a band of horses. Colonel R. N. Allred, with a company of cavalry chased and gave them battle, recovering some of the horses.

"September 18th, another raid was made on Beaver, Beaver County, and two hundred head of horses and cattle were taken.

"This was the last raid of the season, as, through the activity of the militia troops, the depredations were less frequent and not so extensive as previously.

"Great praise is accorded to the superintendent of Indian affairs, Colonel F. H. Head, for his untiring exertions with the Indians to promote peace. He finally succeeded in obtaining an interview with Black Hawk and obtained his promise that he would refrain from further depredations on the whites, and that he would use his influence to have the war entirely stopped. He expressed a fear, however, that some of the outlaws would continue depredations, which has been the case, as several raids have been made since this interview, but it is generally believed that Black Hawk has kept his promise.

"In the spring of 1868, these renegades attacked a company of whites while camped on the Sevier River, killed two men and wounded one. During the summer they made several raids on stock in San Pete Valley; and in November attacked a party of emigrants in southern Utah and took a large band of horses and mules. Some active service was performed during the summer and autumn of 1868, but as the returns have not been received at this office, they are not included in the accompanying accounts, which amount in the aggregate, for the three years, 1865, 1866, and 1867, as per recapitulation sheet herewith forwarded, to the sum of one million one hundred and twenty-one thousand and thirty-seven dollars and thirty-eight cents ($1,121,037.38).' "In conclusion, I beg leave to respectfully refer you to a memorial of the Legislature of this Territory, approved by his Excellency Charles Durkee, Governor, of which the following is a copy:

"'*MEMORIAL TO CONGRESS PRAYING FOR AN APPROPRIATION TO DEFRAY THE EXPENSES OF THE LATE INDIAN WAR IN UTAH TERRITORY.*

"'To the Honorable the Senate and House of Representatives of the United States in Congress assembled.

"'Gentlemen:—Your memorialists, the Governor and Legislative Assembly of the Territory of Utah, would most respectfully represent to your Honorable Body that, for the last three years, we have had a vexatious Indian war on our hands, the seat of which has been in Sevier, Piute, and San Pete Counties, extending more or less to the counties of Wasatch, Utah, Millard, Beaver, Iron, Washington and Kane, rendering a strong military force constantly necessary in the field. Colonel Irish, former Superintendent of Indian affairs, called on General Connor to protect the settlements of this Territory from Indian depredations; the General replied that if those depredations were committed upon any settlements remote from the mail line he could not do it. Colonel Head, present Superintendent of Indian affairs, called on Colonel Potter to protect the settlements of this Territory where Indian hostilities existed. Colonel Potter sent east for instructions in the case and received answer from General Sherman that we must rely on the militia of the Territory. During this war Sevier and Piute Counties were abandoned by six extensive and flourishing settlements, it being considered impracticable to defend them there. Their removal was effected at the loss of nearly all they had, their stock and teams being mostly stolen and driven away by the Indians, and they were removed by the citizens of San Pete County. Likewise four settlements on the borders of San Pete County were broken up and removed at much expense and loss. Also fifteen settlements in Iron, Kane and Washington Counties, besides two or three small settlements in Wasatch County. In this war we have furnished our own soldiers, arms, ammunition, transportation, cavalry horses, and supplies, for the years 1865, 1866, and 1867.

We have borne a heavy burden, and we ask for compensation and aid, as most of our citizens at and near the seat of this war have become greatly reduced and impoverished thereby, and likewise the other settlements that have had to remove are more or less so. We therefore ask your Honorable Body to appropriate $1,500,00, to compensate the citizens for their service, transportation and supplies in suppressing Indian hostilities in the Territory of Utah during the years before named, or so much thereof as will cover the expenses, as per vouchers and testimonies now in the adjutant-general's office, which will accompany this memorial, or follow it at an early day, and your memorialists, as in duty bound, will ever pray.

"All of which is respectfully submitted.
"Your obedient servant,
"H. B. Clawson, Adjutant-General, Utah Territory.
"Hon. John M. Schofield,
"Secretary of War, Washington City, D. C."

To this State document may be supplemented, from the Adjutant-General's office, instructions and special orders issued by Lieutenant-General Wells to his commanding officers, covering the very time, of which it was charged, that the said General Wells was organizing, mustering and drilling his forces for overt acts against the Federal administration in Utah.

"Headquarters Nauvoo Legion,
"Adjt.-Gen'l's Office, Great Salt Lake City, May 23, 1866.
"Major General Robt. T. Burton:
"Dear Brother: It is considered best for you to have out a patrol guard to watch and protect herds, and to observe the movements and indications of the Indians, speaking and treating them kindly, and endeavoring to influence those with whom they shall meet to be peaceable and friendly, and at the same time let them see that we are on the alert, and do not intend to let them have our stock without asking for it.

"It is believed that a few men in each settlement in your district can perform this service and extend their patrols and observations up into the canyons, where people are working at the mills and getting out wood and timber; and to all such most likely places for Indians to secrete themselves and steal forth to make depredations upon the people and their property. Men and not boys should be entrusted to take charge of herds and should go armed and prepared to defend themselves.

"It may be thought there is no danger of hostile Indians making any demonstration in your neighborhood; but the surest way to avoid it is to be prepared to meet it, and not give them a chance.

"Men should be posted in the night time where they can be concealed and see without being seen, and thus be able to give timely information, or afford timely relief, or assistance in the protection of life and property, and not do like some, make themselves a target for an Indian to shoot at, and stand and be killed when they ought to be shooting.

"Be vigilant in carrying the same into effect, and make full returns to this office of all services rendered, &c.

"Respectfully yours,
"D. H. Wells."

SPECIAL ORDERS NO. 1.

"Adjutant-General's Office, G. S. L. City, April 15th, 1867.

"1st. Brigadier General Warren S. Snow is hereby temporarily relieved from the duties of his command over San Pete and Piute Military District and Brigadier-General W. B. Pace, of the Utah Military District, assigned to that duty.

"2nd. General Pace will be provided with a full company of cavalry from Great Salt Lake and Utah Military Districts, fully armed and equipped, supplied and provisioned from their respective districts, except flour, meat, and forage, which will be furnished from San Pete.

"3rd. Gen. Pace will repair to the scene of his duties with the troops aforesaid as soon as practicable, and locating his command at or near Gunnison, will detail working parties either to go to the canyons, labor on fords, guard stock, or parties traveling into the canyons, or elsewhere, and to aid and assist the people exposed to the inroads and depredations of the Indians, in defending themselves against hostile demonstrations of the foe. He will also lose no time in organizing the forces herein placed under his command as will, in the most efficient manner, render such aid and assistance as is or may become necessary and proper to secure and protect those settlements from depredations from the Indians.

"4th. Gen. Pace is hereby directed to see that a strict and correct account is kept, and prompt returns made to this office of all expenses incurred, and service performed, as also any and all movements or dispositions made of all the forces placed under his command, and in all things exercise that just discretion and efficiency which should characterize an energetic and yet prudent and careful commander.

"D. H. Wells,
" Lieut. General, Commanding Nauvoo Legion.

" SPECIAL ORDERS NO. 2.

"Adjutant-General's Office, "G. S. L. City, April 15th, 1867.

"1st. Major-General Robert T. Burton, of the Great Salt Lake Military District will raise three platoons of cavalry from his command for the San Pete expedition, and have them properly officered and organized, and in readiness to march on Monday next, the 22nd instant, with arms, ammunition, accoutrements, and supplies for six months, except flour, meat and forage, which will be provided elsewhere.

"2nd. Men must be selected, and not boys allowed to go as substitutes, and must be furnished with suitable transportation, and tools for working parties, which will be detailed from the command to assist in the construction of forts, etc., as well as to assist in defending the people against Indian depredations.

"3rd. The troops thus organized and provided will rendezvous at Provo, Utah Military District, and report to Brigadier-General Wm. B. Pace, who is assigned to take the command of the San Pete and Piute Military Districts, and they will act under his direction.

"4th. The horses must be provided with ropes for tying up and hobbles, and a few pack saddles should also be furnished in case of wanting to make a sudden excursion after Indians.

"5th. General Burton is at liberty to assign a captain or an adjutant as he and General Pace shall agree upon, as it would be proper for one or the other to go from his command with this detachment.

Daniel H. Wells,
Lieutenant General Commanding Nauvoo Legion.

TO GOVERNOR DURKEE.

Adjutant-General's Office, Great Salt Lake City, Dec. 31st, 1867.
" To His Excellency Charles Durkee, Governor of Utah Territory.

Dear Sir: I take pleasure in forwarding to your Excellency the accompanying abstract return of the Nauvoo Legion, the militia of our Territory; made out from the latest reports that have been received from each district and showing the aggregate number of the militia so far enrolled, with their individual arms, ammunition and equipments. They number twelve thousand and twenty-four (12,024), including cavalry, artillery and infantry, would doubtless be largely increased by a full enrollment of all persons liable to military duty, unusually seen in attendance at our general musters.

"The apparent difficulty of obtaining fire arms among the infantry arises chiefly from the annual emigrations of many poor persons, who are destitute of weapons on their arrival.

"As your Excellency is aware, our settlers have now had a three years' war with Utah Indians, during which a very large amount of stock has been driven off from our settlements, and seventy of our citizens killed and wounded by them.

It has also involved a great loss of their property in breaking up the settlements throughout Sevier, Piute, Kane and parts of San Pete and other counties. During this time various detachments of troops have been sent from the more densely settled districts to the settlements more immediately in the scene of actual Indian hostilities, to assist in repressing the Indians, defending the settlers, and guarding against their sudden attacks.

"A small portion of the outlay for these expenditures has been paid out of the Territorial funds, but it is believed that an appropriation should be made by the General Government to reimburse the Territory, and defray all expenses, accounts of which are in preparation accordingly against the General Government.

"Without reliable information of their intentions, it is hoped and believed that the Indians are now more peaceably inclined, and trust that the ensuing spring and summer may not open up as they have the last three years with an Indian war upon our hands.

"With much respect,

"H. B. Clawson,
"Adjutant-General Nauvoo Legion, the Militia of Utah Territory."

ACCOUNTS SENT TO HON. W. H. HOOPER, M. C.
"Adjutant General's Office,
"Salt Lake City, Feb 10, 1869.
"Hon. W. H. Hooper, M. C, Washington City, D. C.

"Dear Sir: By to-day's express I forward to your address the accounts of expenses incurred by the Territory of Utah in the suppression of Indian hostilities in said Territory during the years 1865-6-7, amounting to the sum of one million, one hundred and twenty-one thousand and thirty-seven dollars and thirty-eight cents ($1,121,037.38); also a communication from myself to the Hon. John M. Schofield, Secretary of War, to accompany said accounts. By reference to that communication you will perceive that a large amount of service was rendered by the male inhabitants of the localities of the war, as home guards, for which no charge is made; nothing but active service being included in those accounts, it having been our constant effort to keep the expenses as light as possible, and it is believed here that an equal amount of service by almost any other people would have been quadrupled in cost. These accounts will now be in your hands, and it is believed that the government, at an early day, through the wisdom of your efforts, will fully reimburse to the Territory of Utah the amounts of those expenses.

"Very truly yours,
"H. B. Calwson,
"Adjutant-General, Utah Territory.

The report of the adjutant-general of the Utah militia, to the Secretary of War, was accompanied by the following voucher:

"Executive Office, Utah Territory, Salt Lake City, January 9, 1869.
"I, Charles Durkee, Governor of Utah Territory, do hereby certify that the military service rendered by the militia of this Territory, comprised in the foregoing accounts, was absolutely necessary, and was therefore sanctioned and authorized by me at the times specified, and that the accounts are just.
"Charles Durkee, Governor."

This is the same governor—of whom Mr. Bowles wrote, "Governor Durkee seems less disposed to be tolerant of Mormon control and the Mormon disrespect to federal authority than his predecessors generally have been,"—who certifies to the General Government that he had "sanctioned and authorized" the service of the Utah militia as "absolutely necessary," and that "the accounts are just."

Hut this debt of one million, one hundred and twenty-one thousand and thirty-seven dollars and thirty-eight cents, owed by the Government to the citizens of Utah, to this day remains unpaid.

CHAPTER XLII.

WADE'S BILL. CONTEMPLATED RECONSTRUCTION OF THE MILITIA. ABSOLUTE POWER IN CIVIL AND MILITARY AFFAIRS TO BE GIVEN THE GOVERNOR. THE MORMON CHURCH TO BE DISQUALIFIED FROM OFFICIATING IN MARRIAGE CEREMONIES. ACKNOWLEDGEMENT OF PLURAL MARRIAGE SUFFICIENT PROOF OF "UNLAWFUL COHABITATION." AIMS ON THE CHURCH PROPERTY AND TREASURY. THE TRUSTEE-IN-TRUST TO BE UNDER THE GOVERNOR'S THUMB.

Notwithstanding the Utah Militia was employed in the service of the Government in the years 1865, 1866, and 1867, protecting the country against the Indians; notwithstanding, as it turned out, this service was performed at their own cost, the impression had been established in the public mind that it was a standing army of rebellion, and that it ought to be broken up by the strong military arm of the Government, should Congress find itself inadequate to the task.

Indeed, from the year 1866 to the year 1870, there was fast working up in the United States a movement against the Mormon power, very much as it had been before the Utah War, when the two great political parties laid Utah upon the altar to appease a common hate of Mormondom, and then worked up the "war of rebellion " between themselves.

The first exposition of the resolution to put down "Mormon Utah" and supplant it with a "Gentile Utah," presented to Congress during the work of re-constructing the South, was the bill of Senator Ben. Wade. In the Senate of the United States, June 30, 1866, Senator Wade asked, and by unanimous consent obtained leave to bring in his bill, which was read twice, referred to the Committee on Territories, and ordered printed; and on the 12th of July, 1866, the bill was reported by Mr. Wade with amendments. Although this bill did not pass, nearly all its aims have since become operative in subsequent bills; in the Government direction of Utah affairs; in the disbanding of the militia; in the jurisdiction and decisions of the courts; in the Utah Commission; in a half-supplanted Legislature and the controlling power of the Governor, both in civil and military affairs. Indeed the salient points of the Wade bill may be reviewed as very like the face of the history of Utah from that date to the present. First take,

"Sec. 10. And be it enacted, that there shall be in the militia of said Territory no officer of higher rank or grade than that of major-general, and all officers, civil and military, shall be selected, appointed and commissioned by the Governor; and every person who shall act or attempt to act as an officer, either civil or military, without being first commissioned by the Governor, and qualified by taking the proper oath, shall be guilty of misdemeanor, and upon conviction thereof, shall be subject to a fine not exceeding one thousand dollars and imprisoned in the Penitentiary not exceeding one year, or both such fine and imprisonment at the discretion of the court.

"Sec. 11. And be it further enacted, That the militia of said Territory shall be organized and disciplined in such manner and at such times as the Governor of said Territory shall direct. And all the officers thereof shall be appointed and commissioned by the Governor. As commander-in-chief the Governor shall make rules and regulations for the enrolling and mustering of the militia, and he shall yearly, between the first and last days of October, report to the Secretary of War the number of men enrolled and their condition, the state of discipline, and the number and description of arms belonging to each company, division, or organized body. Aliens shall not be enrolled and mustered into the militia."

"Sec. 22. And be it further enacted, That all commissions and appointments, both civil and military, heretofore made or issued, or which may be made or issued before the 1st day of January, eighteen hundred and sixty-seven, shall cease and determine on that day, and shall have no effect or validity thereafter."

In this bill there is no intelligent aim at the purpose and existence of the Utah militia, nor any knowledge shown of its circumstantial history: all that is seen is the design of the bill itself. The first aim regarding it was to take the militia altogether out of the hands of the Territorial Legislature, and to confer powers extraordinary upon the Governor, not only as commander-in-chief, but as the originator, sustainer and dictator: "the militia of said Territory shall be organized and disciplined in such manner and at such times as the Governor of said Territory shall direct," etc. The second aim was to abolish the office of lieutenant-general. He disposed of—his office having no longer an existence, all the officers before under him would soon also pass away, their "appointments and commissions" expiring before January, 1867. Thereafter all the officers were not only to be "commissioned," but also selected and "appointed" by the Governor, and indeed the entire militia re-organized by him as the originating source, under this contemplated act of Congress. Clearly the militia of the Territory would have been practically abolished or set aside, as it afterwards was by the proclamation of Governor Shaffer, or it would have been transformed to an anti-Mormon force, to act as a posse commitatus for the Governor in the execution of the designs of the bill. Even had such a design been proper for the utter suppression of the Mormon power in America, still there would have been no relation between it and the purpose of the existence of the Utah militia. The following, from the many documents of a similar nature in the adjutant-general's office, will strikingly illustrate this and be a very favorable contrast to the bills and aims in question:

REPORT OF THE BOARD OF OFFICERS.

"The militia of the Territory of Utah (under the governor as commander-in-chief) shall be commanded by a lieut.-general, and formed into an independent military body called the Nauvoo Legion, and shall be organized into platoons, companies, battalions, regiments, brigades, divisions and departments as hereinafter provided for."

The necessity for such a military body will be seen from the following documents.

In general orders No. 2, under date of January 21st, 1854, we find the following—

"Rule 4. They will preserve a good organization of their entire force, and fill up the minute companies for prompt and energetic action in accordance with general orders No. 1, of 28th Nov., 1853; and act on the defensive whenever it becomes necessary for the protection of their respective districts.

"Rule 5. It is wise in time of peace to prepare for war, although peace can as yet scarcely be said to exist.

"No time should be lost in preparing and completing the forts and defenses in the various districts; as we think it is well understood that our settlements must be based on a permanent system of defense.

"In enlarging the forts or locating new ones for the accommodation of the increasing population, great care and judgment should be exercised in selecting such places as are beyond the reach of covert, (and unless included) beyond the rifle range of ridges, benches and mountains—and so as to command water for the use of the forts, and as much of the surrounding country as possible.

"Rule 6. The safety and future success of the settlements depend much upon guarding against surprise, or being deceived by pretended friendship, at the same time exercising friendly relations with all, clothing and feeding them for their labor. It is humane and politic to feed the strangers when they first come, keeping a good look out for them, and if they remain too long giving them work, encouraging them by giving them fair wages for what they do, and making them as comfortable as possible according to the circumstances of the post, when they evince a disposition to comply with reasonable requirements.

[Signed] Brigham Young,
Daniel H. Wells,
Lieut.-General Commanding Nauvoo Legion.'"

We further review the bill:

"Sec. 2. And be it further enacted, That the marshal or other officer, in selecting grand or petit jurymen, shall select them from the body of the people of the district. And in the trial of any case in which the United States shall be a party, the United States shall have the same right to challenge jurors that the other party has.

"Sec. 3. That it shall be the duty of the United States marshal, in person or by his deputies, to attend all the courts held by the United States justices or judges in said Territory, and to serve and execute all process and orders issued or directed by said courts or by the judges thereof.

"Sec. 5. And be it further enacted, That the probate judge shall be appointed by the Governor" etc.

"Sec. 6. And be it further enacted, That the judges of the Supreme Court of said Territory may make rules and regulations as to the mode and manner of taking appeals from one court to another in said Territory, so that the just rights of the parties may be secured and preserved."

"Sec. 12. And be it further enacted, That marriages in said Territory may be solemnized only by any justices of the Supreme Court, justices of the peace duly elected and qualified in their proper townships or precinct, or by any priest or minister of the gospel (not Mormon), regularly ordained and settled or established in said Territory, between parties competent to enter into the marriage contract. And the person solemnizing such marriage shall sign and deliver to the husband and wife a certificate thereof, wherein shall be set forth the names, the ages and the places of the parties, and the place and date of such solemnization, together with the names of witnesses, not less than two, present at such solemnization, which certificate may be recorded in the office of the proper register of the county. * * * And such certificates or a certified copy of the record shall be evidence in any court of the facts therein set forth as above required."

"Sec. 13. And be it further enacted, That if any officer herein authorized to solemnize marriage shall, knowingly and willfully, solemnize a marriage to which either of the parties are disqualified to enter into the marriage contract he shall be guilty of a misdemeanor, and upon conviction before a court having competent jurisdiction, he shall be sentenced to pay a fine of not less than one hundred dollars, and stand committed until the fine shall be paid.

Sec. 14 proposed to annul all the land grants and water privileges to the first settlers made by the Legislature up to that date. About one-sixth of the bill was devoted to that part. Had it passed it would have despoiled and ruined hundreds of families who made these Rocky Mountain colonies successful.

"Sec. 15. And be it further enacted, That all that part of Section two, of the act or ordinance entitled 'An ordinance incorporating the Church of Jesus Christ of Latter-day Saints, which declares that the real and personal property of said church shall be free from taxation; and all that part of Section three of said ordinance, which declares that the said church has the original right to solemnize marriages compatible with the revelations of Jesus Christ; and also, all that part of said section which declares that said church does and shall possess and enjoy continually the power and authority in and of itself to originate, make, pass and establish rules, regulations, ordinances, laws, customs, and criterions for the good order, safety, government, conveniences, comfort and control of said church, and for the punishment or forgiveness of all offences relative to fellowship, according to church covenant— that the pursuit of bliss and the enjoyment of life, in every capacity of public associations and domestic happiness, temporal expansion or spiritual increase upon earth may not legally be questioned—be, and the same is hereby disapproved and annulled.

Sec. 17. "Marriage, so far as its validity in law is concerned in said Territory is hereby declared a civil contract, to which the consent of parties, capable in law of contracting, is essential."

"Sec. 18. That it shall not be lawful for said church or its officers or members to grant divorces or solemnize marriages."

Sections 19 and 20 compelled the Trustee-in-Trust of the Mormon Church to make a full report on oath every year, between the first and last days of November, to the Governor of the Territory, of all church properties, moneys in bank, notes, deposits with the church, etc. The Trustee failing to comply, the Governor, within the expiration of three days after the time was authorized to file a complaint before one of the U. S. justices, requiring a warrant for the marshal to arrest said Trustee, who "shall, on a day set by said justice," be tried, and if found guilty, be liable to a fine of not more than $2,000 and imprisonment in the Penitentiary of not more than two years, or fine not less than five hundred dollars and not less than six months in the Penitentiary. All church property and revenues above $20,000 were to be taxed.

"Sec. 25. And be it further enacted, That in prosecutions for the crime of polygamy, proof of cohabitation by the accused as husband or wife, or the acknowledgments of the party accused of the existence of marital relation shall be sufficient to sustain the prosecution."

Evidently the design of Senator Wade's bill was to dismantle both "church and state," and to take from the people all their inherent powers, placing them in the hands of Congress and Federal officers appointed specifically for the purpose of suppressing the people of Utah as a Mormon community—styled at that time the " Mormon hierarchy," and a year or two later still more acceptably dubbed by Chief Justice McKean "the Mormon polygamic theocracy." Hence the grand enabling sections of the bill were, either to altogether abolish the Utah militia, or to transform it to an anti-Mormon force, to act as the Governor's posse commitalus, under the directions of the Secretary of War, to whom he was periodically to report.

A few months later Senator Cragin's bill superseded Wade's bill. It was, however, substantially the same, with trifling addenda and a few idiosyncrasies of its own; of the latter the following is an extract: "No man, a resident of said Territory, shall marry his mother, his grandmother, daughter, step-mother, grandfather's wife, son's wife, grandson's wife, wife's mother, wife's grandmother, wife's daughter, wife's granddaughter, nor his sister, his half-sister, his brother's daughter, sister's daughter, or mother's sister.

No woman shall marry her father, grandfather, son, grandson, step-father, grandmother's husband, daughter's husband, granddaughter's husband, husband's father, husband's son, husband's grandson, nor her brother, half-brother, brother's son, sister's son, father's brother or mother's brother."

If he or she did either of this, the penalty was to be imprisonment, at hard labor, in the penitentiary, for not more than fifteen years nor less than six months.

But this special legislation against Mormon Utah was suspended by the great controversy which arose between Congress and President Andrew Johnson.

Moreover, President Johnson was opposed to the special legislation contemplated; Delegate Hooper was consulted in the choice of officers not objectionable to the people; and in 186$ the delegate succeeded in obtaining the passage of several bills of most vital interest not only to Salt Lake City but the entire Territory.

CHAPTER XLIII.

OPENING OF THE FIRST COMMERCIAL PERIOD. REMINISCENCES OF THE EARLIEST MERCHANTS. CAMP FLOYD. THE SECOND COMMERCIAL PERIOD. UTAH OBTAINS AN HISTORICAL IMPORTANCE IN THE COMMERCIAL WORLD. ORGANIZATION OF Z. C. M. I.

It is time that we take up the commercial vein of the history of our city and Territory, having reached a period when the commercial thread became closely woven in the general and political history of our most peculiar commonwealth.

The history of Utah commerce is very unique. In some respects there is not a State or Territory in America whose commercial history will compare with that of our Territory. Its character has been as peculiar as its commonwealth, and that has given to it a typing quite uncommon in its genius; yet the typing is in accord with the co-operative policies which the age has devised in solving the problem between capital and labor. There is also much stirring romance in its history. Its story and incidents are almost as romantic as the commerce of Arabia, whose mammoth caravans, in their journeys across the deserts, have given subject and narrative to the most gorgeous romances in the whole range of literature.

The journeys of the trains of these merchants of the West over the Rocky Mountains and the vast arid plains between Salt Lake City and the Eastern States, and their arduous tasks and adventurous experiences will fitly compare with the history of the merchants in the East in olden times when civilization herself was fostered by commerce; and, moreover, in the early days of Utah, it took as much commercial courage, perseverance and ability to establish the commerce of this Territory as it did that of any nation known in history. On the very face of the record, we may discern that the men who did this work were no ordinary men. They were capable of making their mark in any land; and if Utah, in the early days, afforded them great opportunities, it was their boundless energies and commercial ambitions that first created those opportunities and made a people comparatively affluent who had been buried in isolation and in the depths of poverty.

In the year 1849, which was two years after the entrance of the Pioneers, the first regular stock of goods for the Utah market was brought in by Livingston & Kinkead. Their stock was valued at about $20,000. They opened in John Pack's adobe house in the Seventeenth Ward. It is now pulled down. It stood on the northeast corner of the lot now occupied by the new residence of the late John Pack and near where is now built the Seventeenth Ward Schoolhouse. In that day, it was the most convenient house in the city that these merchants could obtain and also one of the largest.

The following year, 1850, Holliday & Warner appeared, who constituted the second firm in the commercial history of our Territory. William H. Hooper came to Salt Lake City in charge of their business. They opened in a little adobe building which had been erected for a school house on President Young's block, east of the Eagle Gate. This little school house was esteemed a big store in those days. Holliday & Warner next removed to the building now occupied as the Museum.

The merchant's quarter soon began to define itself better than we see it in the primitive examples referred to, and Main Street grew into importance. The unerring scent of commerce tracked the direction which business was about to take, notwithstanding Main Street was dubbed Whiskey Street and often rebuked in the Tabernacle presumably for its many demerits; but such men as Jennings and Hooper, J. R. Walker, Godbe and Lawrence—who have been temperate all their lives,—redeemed it from the odium and made Main Street the quarter of princely merchants.

Main Street first began to define itself from the extreme upper quarter. John & Enoch Reese were the third firm in historical date established in Salt Lake City, and they built the second store on Main Street, upon the ground now occupied by Wells, Fargo & Co. J. M. Horner & Co., was the fourth firm, and they did business in the building occupied by the Deseret News Co. This firm continued in business but a short time and was succeeded by that of Hooper & Williams. Livingston, Kinkead & Co., changed to Livingston & Bell. Their commercial mart was the Old Constitution Buildings, which was the first merchant store erected in Utah. It was undoubtedly in the "Old Constitution" that the commercial focus of Main Street was best defined in the earliest days; and when Mr. Bell became postmaster the street also put on some official dignity. Business, however, gravitated down street. In this quarter, Gilbert & Gerrish, before the Utah war, became noted as one of the principal Gentile firms; and Gilbert occupied his stand after the settlement of the difficulty with the United States and the evacuation of the troops. It was also at this quarter of Main Street where William Nixon flourished and where the majority of the young commercial men of Salt Lake City of that epoch, including the Walker Brothers, were educated under him.

William Nixon was an Englishman and a Mormon. His commercial career was first marked in Saint Louis. To this day the "boys" educated under him speak of William Nixon as the "father of Utah merchants;" it was the name that he delighted in while he lived. He was proud of the distinction. In some respects he seemed to be an uncommon man—like William Jennings, a natural merchant who did business sagaciously by instinct and found the methods and directions of trade by commercial intuition. The Walker Brothers were his chief pupils, and they speak of William Nixon much in this vein.

On the arrival of the Walker family in St. Louis, Father Walker became acquainted with William Nixon, to whom he sold goods purchased by him at auction. Nixon, at that time, was a regular merchant doing business on Broadway, in St. Louis. The elder Walker secured his son, David F. Walker—Mr. " Fred." as he is more familiarly known—a clerkship under the St. Louis merchant. At that date young Walker was but thirteen years of age. John Clark, who was one of the managers of departments in Z. C. M. I. from its commencement, was with Nixon before the Walker Brothers; so also was another of our prominent citizens and capitalists, Mr. Dan. Clift. These young men emigrated to Utah; Mr. "Fred" Walker went to fill their vacant place. Soon afterward, William Nixon himself emigrated, and Father Walker having then recently died, the four sons with the mother resolved to emigrate to Utah that same season,—the Walker Brothers, it will be remembered, being originally Mormon boys. As soon as they arrived in Salt Lake City, which was in September, 1852, Mr. "Fred" again went to clerk for Nixon and soon afterwards Joseph R. Walker also went into the same employ. Henry W. Lawrence, John Chislett, George Bourne, James Needham, David Candland and John Hyde were also commercially educated under Mr. Nixon; Thomas Armstrong was his book-keeper. William Nixon soon became recognized in our commercial history as a very successful merchant doing a large business. It was he who built the second store down street. Gilbert & Gerrish, who had been doing business at the Old Museum followed with a new stock of goods; and John Kimball, with his brother-in-law Henry W. Lawrence, as his clerk, opened next door to Nixon. This removal threw the main business into that quarter of the street; and it was not until Jennings' Eagle Emporium was reared, with Kimball & Lawrence on the opposite corner, and Godbe's Exchange Buildings were erected on the east side of the street, that business returned towards the original location, which at length has been crowned with the erection of the magnificent buildings of Z. C. M. I. Other Mormon merchants also rose, some of whom have since left Utah. There was the firm of Staines & Needham, John M. Brown, Gilbert Clements, Chislett & Clark; and, after the period of the Utah war, Ransohoff, Kahn, and other Jew merchants began to pour into the city.

Here something should be noted of Thomas Williams, Hooper's first partner. The merchant Williams was a Mormon young man of much promise in Nauvoo before the exodus. He was with the people in their exodus and was a member of the famous Mormon Battalion. He was one of the company of J. M. Horner & Co., which was afterwards changed to Hooper & Williams, and he built the third store on Main Street, on the site now occupied by the Deseret National Bank.

The firm of Hooper & Williams, existed until the spring of 1857, when Williams sold his interest to W. H. Hooper, and emigrated, with his family, to Weston, Missouri, where he engaged in the hotel business. Subsequently, in 1858, he returned to Utah, and in 1860 he, together with his brother-in-law, Pimena Jackman, was killed by Indians while en route to Southern California, to which point they were proceeding for a train of merchandise. Thomas Williams was the man who first took William S. Godbe by the hand and gave him a commercial training. It is said that he was a man of excellent business qualities.

It was the merchants of Utah who first brought the Mormon community fairly into socialistic importance. And this affirmation is true of them, both in their results at home and the influence which they exercised abroad for the good of the people and the glory of Utah. Moreover, in the general sense of the public weal, this affirmation is as true of the Walker Brothers and Godbe and Lawrence as it is of Jennings and Hooper, or Eldredge and Clawson. The very construction of society and the necessities and aims of commerce convert the enterprises and life work of this class of men into the public good. Over quarter of a century, for instance, the Walker Brothers and Godbe and Lawrence have been identified with the material prosperity and destiny of this Territory. The welfare of the country is their own good as a class;—the glory of the commonwealth glorifies their houses and augments their own fortunes. Of all men, the life-work and enterprise of the class who establish commerce, build railroads, develop the native mineral resources of the country, and construct the financial power of the State, must perforce tend to the public prosperity as well as conserving and preserving society. And if this is the case with those influential men of commerce and great enterprises who have gone outside the pale of the Church, yet are still identified with the community in all their essential interests, how much more, specially speaking, is it the case with those men who have remained inside the pale of the Church and built up her commercial and financial power? The Church owes to her apostles of commerce and finance more than many would like to confess; and yet in this point of their extraordinary service to the

Church is at once the significance and potency of Zion's Co-operative Mercantile Institution.

This will be strikingly illustrated in the circumstantial history of Z. C. M. I, A cursory view has been given of the destitute condition of the Mormon people during the first period of the settlement of these Valleys. As late as 1856, there was a famine in Utah, and the community was barely preserved by the leaders wisely rationing the whole and dividing among the people their own substance. But it was neither the economy and wisdom of the leaders, nor the plentiful harvests that followed, that redeemed Utah from the depths of her poverty, and the anomalous isolation of a people reared in lands of civilization and plenty. She was redeemed from her social destitution by a train of providential circumstances on the one hand, and the extraordinary activities of her merchants on the other. As we have seen, the providence came in a United States army; the temporary existence of Camp Floyd; the departure of the troops, leaving their substance to the community; the needs of the Overland Mail line; the construction of the telegraph lines; and then again the arrival of another U. S. army under Colonel Connor, and the establishment of Camp Douglass with several thousand soldiers to disburse their money in Salt Lake City alter their pay-days, besides the constant supplies which the camp needed from our country, and often labor from our citizens. It was then, under these changed and propitious circumstances, that our Utah merchants put forth their might, and built up a commercial system for our Territory as strange and wonderful in its growth and history as that of any State that has risen in America. As early as 1864, and right in the time of the great civil war of the nation, when the cities of the South were under devastation, Hooper and Eldredge purchased in New York a bill of goods at prime Eastern cost of over one hundred and fifty thousand dollars, the freight of which added to it another eighty thousand. A little later in the same year, William Jennings purchased of Major Barrows a train of goods in Salt Lake City worth a quarter of a million, including the freight. In 1865, this merchant purchased in New York at one time a stock of goods amounting to half a million, Eastern cost, the freight upon which was $250,000. During these same years Godbe and Mitchell went East and purchased for the people on "commission goods to the amount of several hundred thousand dollars; and Kimball & Lawrence were at that period also in their most flourishing condition. And all this commercial activity instanced above was on the Mormon side, exclusive of the mammoth merchandise business carried on by the Walker Brothers, besides that of lesser merchants not ranked among the Mormon commercial houses. During this period also, William Jennings built his Eagle Emporium; Godbe his Exchange Buildings; Woodmansee Brothers their stone store now occupied by Osborne & Co.; and Walker Brothers the new store where they still do business, but which, like the Eagle Emporium, has been since enlarged.

Here we pause in the historic record before the era of Z. C. M. I. began, not touching as yet the boundaries of the great commercial period in which has risen the Deseret National Bank, and the commercial palace reared by Z. C. M. I., which wilt compare favorably with almost any mercantile building in America.' Consider then the primitive condition of the community in their isolation and destitution and behold what wonders these apostles of commerce wrought in so short a time. It was their work, be it repeated, that first brought Utah into social importance, carving out a material prosperity for the Mormons. This affirmation is not made to underrate the

Apostles of the Church, who had done a still more wonderful part in their missionary operations, their emigrations, peopling these Valleys of the Rocky Mountains and founding the cities and settlements of as rare a State as ever sprang up in the history of the world,—and these commercial and financial apostles, whom the Church herself has brought forth have built a temporal superstructure upon the foundation which their prophets and elders laid.

Utah in her early days was utterly destitute of cash; all her internal trade being conducted by barter and the due-bill system. Yet as early as 1864, paradoxical as it may seem, her merchants were dispersing for her millions of gold and greenbacks. Some of them, as we have seen, could purchase in New York from a hundred thousand to half a million dollars' worth of goods at a time. The great wholesale houses of New York, Chicago and St. Louis scarcely ever met any such customers in all America as their Utah patrons, either in commercial integrity or weight. These achievements were only possible by these Utah merchants creating the millions before they disbursed them. True, no small amount of money was brought in by the emigrants from the old countries, but this was soon exhausted by their need of States goods and the purchase of homes; thus simply exchanging the money into hands eager to send it out of the country for States goods. In fine, the bulk of the money was created at home by our merchants in their commerce, turning the produce of the country into cash. For example, one of Wm. Jennings' contracts with the Overland Mail line was to supply it with 75,000 bushels of grain; another contract to be filled to General Connor for 6,000 sacks of flour at a time when flour brought five dollars in gold per hundred weight. On their part the Walkers and others shipped immense quantities of flour, fruit, etc., to the mining Territories. Thus, it will be seen that these merchants did not take money out of the people but created it for them; besides supplying the home market with gigantic stocks of States goods. It must be confessed that Utah commerce, before the opening of our mines, gave all the money to a few hands. And this was one of the immediate causes that brought forth Zion's Co-operative Mercantile Institution; as the leaders of the' Church conceived it to be their duty, at length, to construct for the community a broader and more equitable system of commercial existence; so that all could participate, to the extent of their means, in the profits realized and the reduction in price of the co-operative system. That this was the genuine aim of the Institution its history will show, notwithstanding some blunders may have been made in the execution of the design.

As a necessary result of these operations, our merchants not only redeemed the community from social destitution and converted a rural town into a commercial city; but they brought Utah into an importance abroad and greatly reformed the Eastern mind concerning the "strange people" who inhabit these distant Valleys. As all know, in the earlier days the Mormon community was esteemed by the good folks in the Eastern States as a monstrous society which had grown up in America. The exaggerated stories told of the Mormons by the ex-Federal officers, together with the existence of the institution of polygamy, had given them an unenviable notoriety; while their exoduses, the Utah war, and other unique incidents of their history, attached to them a peculiar distinction as a troublesome little nation of modern Israelites which had hidden itself in the solitudes of the Rocky Mountains. But our Utah merchants made the community more comprehensible. The people abroad could not understand the theology and peculiar institutions of this Mormon Israel; but they could appreciate the importance of the Utah trade; and when at length the grand commercial organization of the Z. C. M. I. was formed, the financial potency of the community was greatly enhanced. The business men of New York, Chicago, Boston and St. Louis have become deeply concerned in preserving the Mormons, and in the general prosperity of Utah. The mission of Mormonism has been an enigma in the age, but the purchase in New York of millions of dollars' worth of goods by the Mormon merchants was a record easily read by the commercial men of that city, years ago; and the subsequent history of Z. C. M. I. has financially established the community in all the great business centers of America. Our Utah merchants have now long been esteemed as sound-headed, enterprising, honorable men; and this is equally true of those who have gone out of the Church, as of those who remained inside and became the pillars of Zion's Co-operative Mercantile Institution.

The foregoing sketches of our commerce and commercial men have prepared us to comprehend the vital importance of the Church preserving within herself this vast monetary and mercantile power. Herein was nascent the wisdom of the cooperative idea, and in it resides the original justification of President Young's energetic efforts to so preserve the financial power by the construction of some order of mercantile communism applicable to the Church. The President was at the onset abundantly reproached for his co-operative movement or—as some worded it—compulsory mercantile combination; and several of those who had been his staunchest adherents up to that period left his side in consequence. The impartial historian, however, cannot but justify Brigham Young as the head and guide of Mormon society. The truth is that in 1868-9 the Mormon Church was brought face to face with implacable necessities which seemed about to weaken her; and these necessities were of a commercial and financial character. She had to subdue or be subdued,—a point on which the dominant will of a man like Brigham Young could decide in a moment. The issue of those times was— should she hold her temporal power or loose it?—Should the vast money agencies which had so grown up among her own people, in the country which she had settled, at length overwhelm her; or should she, by combinations of her own, place those agencies at her back and preserve her supreme potency? Brigham Young answered those vital questions in the organization of Z. C. M. I.

At the time referred to, these financial and mercantile issues were, after President Young, chiefly held in the hands of three men, namely; William Jennings, William H. Hooper and Horace S. Eldredge. The subject, then, at this stage, grows so suggestive of the existence of Z. C. M. I. as the necessary commercial handmaid of the Church that we must dwell awhile on a circumstantial exposition.

Early in our commercial history, there grew up a conflict between the merchants and the Church. To become a merchant was to antagonize the Church and her policies; so that it was almost illegitimate for Mormon men of enterprising character to enter into mercantile pursuits; and it was not until Jennings, Hooper and Eldredge redeemed Utah from this conflict by resigning to the Church their own basis that Utah commerce developed into proper forms and became inspired with the true genius of mercantile enterprise. To-day there is no such commercial war as existed in 1868 and out of which Z. C. M. I. was evolved; and yet when Mr. T. B. H. Stenhouse wrote his Rocky Mountain Saints the salient part of the commercial record of his book was all concerning this " irrepressible conflict" between the merchants and the priesthood. The firm of the Walker Brothers is described as the head and front of this conflict on the merchant side, as Brigham Young was on the side of the

Mormon Commonwealth. But the Church was too powerful to be subdued; and the merchants were desirous at one moment to give up the fight. Says Mr. Stenhouse: "With such a feeling of uneasiness, nearly all the non-Mormon merchants joined in a letter to Brigham Young, offering, if the Church would purchase their goods at twenty-five per cent, less than their valuation, they would leave the Territory. Brigham answered them cavalierly that he had not asked them to come into the Territory, did not ask them to leave it, and that they might stay as long as they pleased.

"It was clear that Brigham felt himself master of the situation; and the merchants had to 'bide their time' and await the coming change that was anticipated from the completion of the Pacific Railroad. As the great iron way approached the mountains, and every day gave evidence of its being finished at a much earlier period than was at first anticipated, the hope of what it would accomplish nerved the discontented to struggle with the passing day."

Here is at once described the Gentile and apostate view of the situation of those times, and confined as it is to the salient point, no lengthy special argument in favor of President Young's policies could more clearly justify his mercantile cooperative movement. It was the moment of life or death to the temporal power of the Church! When it be also considered that the organization of Z. C. M. I. not only preserved this power in the hands of the community, but that it redeemed the Territory from this irritating commercial conflict, it is evident that the scheme was both potent and wise. The historian has nothing to do with the argument of the conflict at issue in any of its forms, but simply with the fact of its existence and the necessities of the Mormon community at that time. The point that stands boldly out in the period under review is, that the organization of Z. C. M. I. at that crisis saved the temporal supremacy of the Mormon commonwealth.

But the co-operative idea and genius originated not with the merchants. Cooperation, indeed, is the true offspring of the Church. It was not conceived in the spirit of the world but in the spirit of the gospel; and it was begotten early in the Mormon dispensation, though it was not successfully applied to the community until 1869.

Joseph Smith, the founder of the Church of Latter-day Saints, was the Prophet of a co-operative system designed to be applied not only to this Church but ultimately to all society. It was the means by which a universal social redemption was to be brought about, and in this result was the beginning of a Millennium for the race. Without social redemption, no millennial reign was possible; so taught the Prophet Joseph and such apostles as Parley P. Pratt, Orson Pratt and John Taylor fifty years ago. These men were the teachers of a co-operative system, based on gospel principles, to the disciples of the last generation, whose children scarcely dream that their fathers were inspired by such a philosophy and spirit or that they believed that in the success and spread of a true communistic gospel over the whole earth the reign of righteousness was to be brought in as the consummation of the 'Latter-day mission. But such was original Mormonism; and it was Joseph Smith who was the Prophet of this communistic gospel in which was to be evolved the best methods of a co-operative commonwealth inspired by the spirit of the broadest social benevolence. This system was styled the "Order of Enoch," and it signified simply and truly a society based upon a perfect co-operative order, practically worked in all its affairs by co-operative principles and inspired by the spirit of a universal Christ-like benevolence. It was, in fine, the order of the Kingdom of Heaven to be established upon the earth in the last days.

Its peculiar style—the "Order of Enoch"—signified to the Mormon understanding that such a perfect communistic system existed in the earliest patriarchal age among Enoch and his people. Thus socially considered, we may form a pretty lucid and comprehensive idea of what Enoch's walking with God in the early age of the world signified; and from the revelations given by the Prophet Joseph historically of Enoch and his people, it appears that their supreme social boast was that there were "no poor in Zion." Such a Zion was to be established in the last days; and in the consummation of a social system which would truly and most perfectly realize Zion, according to the conception of the Prophet Joseph, was the grand socialistic aim of the Mormon mission. Co-operation is as much a cardinal and essential doctrine of the Mormon Church as baptism for the remission of sins; and every Mormon Elder who understands the philosophy of his own system could affirm that without co-operation society cannot be saved. Furthermore, it has been the ambition of the Mormon leaders to evolve their own social system. Hence their wonderful "gatherings"—the emigration of a hundred and fifty thousand converts from Europe; their founding of hundreds of cities and settlements under a temporal Priesthood of Bishops, and hence also their patriarchal and polygamic institutions. We are not, however, in this chapter, about to treat of the strange religious and social system of the Mormons; but to speak of the efforts of Brigham Young in 1868-9 and '70 to transform this people into a grand co-operative community and afterwards to perfect them as the " United Order of Enoch."

The co-operative exposition, then, shows us that early in his day, Joseph Smith attempted to found a communistic church,—not after the order of the French Communists and sceptics, nor even after that of the more reverent Robert Owen; but such a communistic church or social and religious brotherhood as the great English socialist believed Jesus and his apostles attempted to establish on the earth as the pattern of things in the heavens. Apostasy and persecutions, however, prevented the Mormon Prophet from consummating this grand "design of the Heavens" to found, through him, a socialistic-religious brotherhood on the earth ushering in the earth's Millennium. But the Mormon apostles and the elders generally believe that all this would be ultimately consummated in their mission. At home and abroad this splendid ideal—which Robert Owen, in his latter moments especially, would have reveled in as a vision of New Jerusalem— often formed the subject of the most inspired sermons of the elders. Thus it continued as an ideal in the Mormon faith for nearly a quarter of a century after the death of the Mormon Prophet, before Brigham Young vigorously attempted to carry the plan into execution.

The reasons of this delay were—first, the extraordinary and unfavorable circumstances of the Mormon people during that period. There was the exodus from Nauvoo and then the peopling of these numerous valleys with the tens of thousands of destitute emigrants from Europe. They had also to convert the desert into a fruitful field. The law of their condition might have been well expressed in Lincoln's homely injunction—" Root, hog, or die." This period, therefore, was not the one to establish the order of Zion—for such the "Order of Enoch" is—nor to open effectively a probationary and preparatory period with some prudent cooperative plan upon which the moneyed men of the country as well as the people could unite.

According to these views of the true genius of the Mormon commonwealth and the proper socialistic aims of the Church, a Zion's Co-operative plan is most legitimate. Upon it, Mormon society must sooner or later be completely and perfectly constructed or the Church will fail to embody her own social philosophy.

This communistic gospel of the Mormons thirty years ago attracted the attention of the great socialistic apostles of England and won their admiration. It did so with George Jacob Holyoak and his class; and the famous and learned socialist, Brontier O'Brian, in one of the most powerful and discriminating editorials ever written upon the Mormons and their commonwealth, said in Reynolds' Newspaper that the Mormons had "created a soul under the rib of death!" It was a matter of supreme astonishment to these great apostles of socialism to find a Christian Church in this age working abreast of themselves in social reforms; and they boldly and justly proclaimed that the Mormons were the only people in Christendom who were building upon the true social base-work as exemplified in the early Christian Church. And what made the Mormon movement, in its socialistic aspects, so singular and interesting to these men was the fact that the Mormons were working out a new social order harmonious with the co-operative and communistic plans of a Robert Owen, yet with God in their system and a mighty faith in their people inspiring them to a great social reconstruction. They frankly confessed that in this respect the Mormon apostles had the advantage of all other reformers of the social system.

* * * * *

The Mormons as a community were about to test the strength of their temporal bulwark. They were also, for the first time in their history, to meet an adequate trial of the communistic genius of their Church, at once in its potency in the sense of a community's aggregated force and in the adhesive and the preserving qualities of that genius in the sense of a communistic power of resistance.

But we must return to the historical narrative of the period, that we may review the salient points of the situation during the years 1868-69-70. Early in 1868, the merchants were startled by the announcement " that it was advisable that the people of Utah Territory should become their own merchants;" and that an organization should be created for them expressly for importing and distributing merchandise on a comprehensive plan. When it was asked of President Young, "What do you think the merchants will do in this matter; will they fall in with this cooperative idea?" he answered, "I do not know, but if they do not we shall leave them out in the cold, the same as the Gentiles, and their goods shall rot upon their shelves."

This surely was implacable; but, as already observed, Brigham Young and the Mormons as a peculiar community had in 1868 come face to face with implacable necessities. They had, in fact, to cease to be a communistic power in the world and from that moment exist as a mere religious sect or preserve their temporal cohesiveness. The Mormons from the first have existed as a society, not as a sect. They have combined the two elements of organization—the social and the religious. They are now a new society-power in the world and an entirety in themselves. They are indeed the only religious community in Christendom of modern birth. They existed as such in Ohio; in Missouri, in Illinois, and finally in Utah; and to preserve themselves as a community they made an exodus to the isolation of the Rocky Mountains. They intend forever to preserve themselves as a community; that was the plain and simple meaning of Brigham Young's answer concerning the merchants in

1868. It was not an exodus which was then needed to so preserve them, but a Zion's Co-operative Mercantile Institution.

The subsequent history abundantly shows as much; many times since, as we shall find by tracing the lines of the Mormon financial influences abroad, Z. C. M. I. has moved the commercial world everywhere to the preservation of that peculiar community of which it has become the temporal bulwark. There was, therefore, at once the extraordinary sagacity of a great society organizer as well as genuine Mormon fidelity in President Young's answer. If the merchants do not fall in with Zion's Co-operative movement to preserve herself intact "we will leave them out in the cold, the same as the Gentiles." President John Taylor or George Q. Cannon would have answered precisely the same. Indeed, this was the united decision of the Apostles upon the co-operative necessities of the times, and it was a co-operation among the mercantile and financial class of the community that was so essentially required in 1868-69-70. To appreciate the radical necessity of such a combination of the Mormon moneyed classes at that time will be to sociologically understand the birth and subsequent history of Z. C. M. I. and the immense service which three or four of the chief commercial and moneyed men of the Territory did to the community in resigning their own base-work to a Zion's Institution, thus setting the example to the lesser mercantile powers throughout the Territory.

The co-operative plan having been sufficiently evolved in the mind of President Young and his apostolic compeers, the President called a meeting of the merchants in the City Hall, October, 1868. It was there and then determined to adopt a general co-operative plan throughout the Territory to preserve the commerce and money resources of the people within themselves, and thus also to preserve the social unity. As yet, however, the methods of co-operation were not perfected nor the idea of a Z. C. M. I. completely evolved. It was necessary for the merchants themselves to work out the idea into practical shape, it being their special movement, though inspired by the Church from the very impulse of her own genius. To be true to the integrity of history, it must be confessed that of themselves the merchants never would have re-constructed themselves upon a co-operative plan. The inspiration of the moment was from the Church, while its success was in such men as Jennings and Hooper and Eldredge and Clawson; but especially was the commercial basework of Mr. Jennings, with his Eagle Emporium, required for the foundation of an Institution colossal enough to represent a community. Brigham Young was wise enough to know the necessary parts of the combination.

The initial movement of co-operation having been made, meeting followed meeting; a committee was appointed to frame a constitution and by-laws, and, without seeing the end from the beginning, their part of the programme was carried out, and an institution formed on paper; subscriptions were solicited, and cash fell into the coffers of the Treasurer pro tem. This was during the winter months of 1868. With the turn of the year a committee was appointed to commence operations. They waited upon the President for advice, who, in his quiet but decided way, said: "Go to work and do it." After a little conversation, the question was again suggested: "What shall we do?" With the same sententious brevity, the reply came, "Go to work and do it." "But how?" the questioners continued; "we haven't enough money; we haven't the goods; we have no building; we haven't sufficient credit." "Go to work and do it, and I will show you how," was the President's finality to those who came to seek counsel.

To some minds these sententious answers of Brigham Young will be merely illustrations of a despotic resolve to force into existence a mercantile co-operation by the power which he held over the Latter-day Saints in all the world. That universal dominance of the head of the Church is admitted; and in 1868, before the opening of the Utah mines, and the existence of a mixed population, there was no commercial escape from the necessities of a combination. But while the imperativeness of President Young's resolve may be frankly confessed, his sagacity was as strongly illustrated as the absoluteness of his purpose. Indeed, these famous replies of Brigham, which were current in the public conversations of Salt Lake City at the' time, may be considered, with their significance brought out, as fine tributes to the commercial power and capacity of three or four men, easily named, who could "go to work and do it" better than he could advise them. The co-operative genius evolved in the gatherings of the people into a community in Ohio, Missouri, Illinois and Utah, had already manifested itself. To fail in Mormon cooperation was, therefore, something that Brigham Young could not understand.

To sum up, then, the people possessed the genius of co-operation, and Brigham Young possessed the will; while around him there was a small circle of men who, for commercial energy and honor, instincts for great enterprises, and financial capacity generally, would be esteemed as pre-eminent in any commercial state in the world.

Thus considered, Brigham Young's famous words, "Go to work and do it," have an extraordinary commercial weight. They signified, in the strongest possible brevity of expression, first, perhaps, faith in himself; next, faith in the people; and, lastly, confidence in the organic capacity and financial power of a few men whom he had clearly defined in his mind. Those who have repeated with any other meaning these words of Brigham Young—words which are as types of the period—have but poorly appreciated the historical import of his mighty injunction.

Review the commercial and financial combination as defined in Brigham Young's mind at that moment. There was, perhaps, first, the Hon. William H. Hooper. He had served the people faithfully in Congress ever since the " Utah War," and the President esteemed him as the keystone of the commercial arch.

As a far-seeing, watchful politician, also William H. Hooper could perfectly comprehend at once the political and commercial complications of the times and foresee that, as the people's Delegate, he would soon have to grapple in Congress with the same essential problem that Brigham Young had to grapple with at home.

This was, to preserve the community intact and sufficiently resistive toward all antagonistic forces; and scarcely a year had passed ere the Hon. William H. Hooper fully realized this in his defense of the Mormons against the Cullom Bill. He, therefore, in the crisis of 1869-70—the date now reached—could well appreciate Brigham Young's words, "Go to work and do it!"

There was, probably, next in the President's mind, Horace S. Eldredge. He had been with the people in their troubles in Missouri and Illinois, had conducted t their emigrations and was one of the commercial founders of the Mormon commonwealth in Utah. Therefore Horace S. Eldredge was a proper foundation stone of Z. C. M. I.

The third—and in some respects the most important man defined in the President's mind—was William Jennings. In 1869, he could have carried a million dollars to either side in means and credit. He had the goods at that moment in Salt Lake City; he had built his Eagle Emporium, which was quite worthy of Zion's Co-operative Mercantile Institution to open business in, and he had abundance of commercial credit either East or West to sustain the president in his great design. After these three first named, came John Sharp, Feramorz Little, Henry W. Lawrence and William S. Godbe; besides H. B. Clawson, who was Brigham Young's son-in-law and late business manager, and at this time in partnership with Horace S. Eldredge. Undoubtedly, President Young was depending upon all these above named.

The combinations thus reviewed, reconsider the conversations of the occasion when that committee waited on President Young, for the record is given with historical exactness: "Go to work and do it."

"But how?"

"I will show you—" substantially implying: "you have plenty of money; you have buildings; you have abundance of goods; you have sufficient credit."

The President was right; and the merchants realized that there was no getting around his solid views.

To the everlasting honor of William Jennings be it said, he did not betray the President and the people in their co-operative movement. Mr. Stenhouse treats his act as a shrewd piece of business policy: but the true historian can only consider it as an act commensurate with the needs of those times. William Jennings resigned his business basis to Z. C. M. I., sold his stock to it for over $200,000, and rented his Eagle Emporium for three years to the institution at an annual rental of $8,000. Eldredge & Clawson also sold their stock and resigned their business basis to Z. C. M. I., and other leading firms followed the example.

The organization of Z. C. M. I., was at length effected in the winter of 1868-69. It consisted of a president, vice-president, secretary, treasurer and seven directors. Brigham Young was very properly chosen president; J. M. Bernhisel, vice-president; Wm. Clayton, Secretary and D. O. Calder, treasurer; George A. Smith, William Jennings, G. Q. Cannon, William H. Hooper, H. S. Eldredge, H. W. Lawrence, and H. B. Clawson, directors; H. B. Clawson, superintendent.

Several changes, however, were soon made in the Board and officers of the Institution. Thomas G. Webber succeeded William Clayton as the secretary, Thomas Williams was elected at the same time treasurer. Henry W. Lawrence retired from the Institution and sold his interest in it to Horace S. Eldredge.

The policy which had been wisely and considerately pursued in purchasing the stock of existing firms, or receiving them as investments at just rates, shielded from embarassment those who would otherwise have inevitably suffered from the inauguration and prestige of the Z. C. M. I.

Simultaneously with the framing of the parent institution, local organizations were formed in all the settlements of the Territory; each feeling itself in duty bound to sustain the one central depot and to make their purchases from it. The people, with great unanimity, became shareholders in their respective local co-operatives, and also in the parent institution; so that they might enjoy the profits of their own investment and purchases. Thus, almost in a day, was effected a great re-construction of the commercial relations and methods of an entire community which fitted the purposes of the times and preserved the temporal unity of the Mormon people as well as erecting for them a mighty financial bulwark.

CHAPTER XLIV.

POLITICAL SIGNIFICANCE TO UTAH OF THE ELECTION OF GRANT AND COLFAX. THE "FATHERS OF THE CHURCH " SPEAK TO THE NATION ON THE SUBJECT OF ABOLISHING POLYGAMY. COLFAX'S DISAPPOINTMENT AND IRE. A DELEGATION OF CHICAGO MERCHANTS VISIT SALT LAKE ON THE COMPLETION OF THE U. P. R. R; ALSO DISTINGUISHED STATESMEN. BRIGHAM YOUNGS FAMOUS CONVERSATION WITH SENATOR TRUMBULL. COUNCIL OF THE CHICAGO MERCHANTS, STATESMEN AND UTAH GENTILES HELD AT THE HOUSE OF J. R. WALKER. TRUMBULL RELATES THE CONVERSATION WITH BRIGHAM. A GENERAL WAR TALK. THE SECOND VISIT OF COLFAX TO SALT LAKE CITY.

We return to the general history. The election of U. S. Grant to the presidency of the United States, and of Schuyler Colfax to the vice-presidency, signified to Utah, a persistent policy on the part of the Government to grapple with Utah affairs. Originally, as we have seen, in the letters of Mr. Bowles, from Salt Lake City, the programme was intended to be comparatively mild and tolerant toward the Mormon people, though firm and decisive, and the base of operations a solid ground for the Mormon people to reconstruct themselves upon, under the direction of the Government.

It is most probable that Mr. Colfax had forecast a settlement of the difficult Mormon problem through the coalition of himself and Brigham Young, the one representing the government and will of United States, and the other the Mormon Church as a party to a compromise. This seems to have been the meaning of those passages referring to Mr. Colfax's " suggestion " "that he had hoped the prophets of the church would have a new revelation on the subject, which should put a stop to the practice ;" adding "that as the people of Missouri and Maryland, without waiting for the action of the general Government against slavery, themselves believing it to be wrong and an impediment to their prosperity, had taken measures to abolish it, so he hoped that the people of the Mormon Church would move for the abandonment of polygamy, and thus all objection to the admission of Utah as a Slate be taken away: but that until it was, no such admission was possible, and that the Government could not continue to look indifferently upon the enlargement of so offensive a practice. And not only what Mr. Young said, but his whole manner left with us the impression that, if public opinion and the Government united vigorously, but at the same time discreetly, to press the question, there would be found some way to acquiesce in the demand and change the practice of the present fathers of the Church."

Speaker Colfax—politician though he was—may well be pardoned for entertaining for a while the pretty plan, suggested in the above, for the solution of the Mormon problem. On his part, with the presidency of the United States in his prospect, or at least the vice-presidency, and with the powerful Republican party, then in its giant strength, at his back, he could doubtless have kept his part of the compact had it been made. Utah would have become a State—a Republican State, held in vassalage by the very Mormon vote itself to the partly which had created it; polygamy would have been abolished by a new revelation, which of course to Mr.

Colfax simply meant the will and say-so of Brigham Young, and the Mormon Church would soon have become defunct in every sense of its past existence. The accomplishment of this project would have been a great triumph in Mr. Colfax's life, scarcely less than would have been his election to the Presidential Chair. As President of the United States he would have been but one among many; as solver of the Mormon problem he would have stood alone in American history. Already since the Mormons left " the borders of civilization " in 1846, up to the date of the first Colfax visit, five Presidents of the United States had held the Mormon community in their hands. Mr. Polk had designed to occupy California for the nation, by the Mormon community, two years before the discovery of gold threw the nation on to the Pacific Coast as from a tidal wave; Mr. Filmore had, in the popular mind, clothed the Mormon Church in the habiliments of a Territory and endowed Brigham Young with gubernatorial power and prestige; Mr. Pierce, much to the disgust of both political friends, and foes who would gladly have seen Utah dismantled, re-appointed Brigham Young; Mr. Buchanan had the Utah war forced upon, him, first by the action of his predecessors, and finally by the will and pleasure of both political parties; Mr. Lincoln had sent word "if Brigham Young and the Mormons will let me alone I will let them alone;" but in the consummation of the whole to Mr. Colfax was to be given the triumph of dismantling the Mormon Church, by a new revelation from herself, and the transformation of an Israelitish commonwealth into a Gentile or apostate State. The plan was well conceived from a politician's point of view, and in a worldly sense there was much statesmanship in it. But Brigham Young and the Apostles understood it, much better than Mr. Colfax and his friends— both as touching the policy of the compromise, the new revelation and the consequences that would overtake their church. It is an old Mormon adage, which we quote, not apply—" When God and the Devil strike hands, the kingdom of God is no more."

The "fathers of the Church" hastened to correct the mistakes of Mr. Colfax and his friends relative to their being any possibility of a compromise on their part and rebuked them for giving out to the world that a new revelation might soon be expected through them, abandoning polygamy. Mr. Bowles in his supplementary papers calls attention to this apostolic utterance. He wrote: "My readers may be interested to know the reply of the Mormons to my letters on the subject of polygamy. The Deseret News, the official organ of the church, had such a reply in August, 1865, from which I quote: "As a people we view every revelation from the Lord as sacred. Polygamy was none of our seeking. It came to us from Heaven, and we recognized in it, and still do, the voice of Him whose right it is not only to teach us but ta dictate and teach all men, for in his hand is the breath of the nostrils, the life and existence of the proudest, most exalted, most learned or puissant of the children of men. It is extremely difficult, nay utterly impossible, for those who have not been blessed with the gift of the Holy Ghost, to enter into our feelings, thoughts and faith in these matters. They talk of revelation given, and of receiving counter revelation to forbid what has been commanded, as if man was the sole author, originator and designer of them. Granted that they do not believe the revelations we have received come from God; granted they do not believe in God at all—if they so desire—do they wish to brand a whole people with the foul stigma of hypocrisy, who, from their leaders to the last converts that have made the dreary journey to these mountain wilds for their faith, have proved their honesty of purpose and deep sincerity of faith by the most sublime sacrifices? Either that is the issue of their reasoning, or they imagine that we serve the most accommodating Deity ever dreamed of in the wildest vagaries of the most savage polytheist.

Either they imagine we believe man concocts and devises the revelations which we receive, or that we serve a God who will oblige us at any time by giving revelations to suit our changing fancies, or the dictation of men who have declared the canon of revelation full, sealed up the heavens as brass, and utterly repudiated the affairs of the Almighty in the affairs of men; by the first of these suppositions we would be gross hypocrites; by the other gross idiots.

"Know gentlemen of the press, and all whom it may concern, that though a repugnance to this doctrine may be expressed by one in a thousand of the people whom you call 'Mormons,' he is not one, nor recognized as such by that community of which he may be called a member. If one revelation is untrue, all are untrue; if one was revealed by God, all have their origin in the same Divine source."

This now is the true utterance of the Church, whether it pleases or displeases the State. This is the voice of Brigham Young and his fellow apostles as " prophets, seers, and revelators," and not as a party indulging over "strawberries " and the dinner table, in "the freest and frankest" conversation "ever known" between the Church and the State over the subject of the sacred oracles and the fitness of their speech to the times and conformity to the wishes and suggestions of the State. No church, with a priesthood and the oracles, could faithfully answer differently to the answer which this one gave through the Deseret News. The Catholic Church in its last four hundred years of controversy with the State, to say nothing of the early days of the church under the Roman emperors, is proof that no such church can compromise with the State, or renounce anything that constitutes its type.

When once the mistake came home to Mr. Colfax, through the apostolic rebuke of the Deseret News, he, perhaps, also clearly saw, and too keenly felt, the humility of the State, occupying a false position in the presence of the Church.

He had been self-deceived,—undoubtedly he thought imposed upon by Brigham Young—but really led away by the plausibility of his plan to solve the polygamic difficulty, by inducing the "fathers of the Church" to compromise with the government for a State, with amnesty for all the past, and recognition of existing family relations up to a certain date.

It is fairly due to Mr. Colfax to believe that his policy of settlement was conceived in the spirit of generosity and consideration, towards the Mormon people at least, and that the glowing speeches, made very much as a tribute to them, by himself and companions, were thoroughly genuine, but it is also certain that Mr. Colfax was, with the sequel, both disappointed and chagrined. From that time, there was no man in America more indisposed to compromise with the Mormon Church than he—not even the Apostle John Taylor, with whom Mr. Colfax discussed the Utah-Mormon question after he became Vice-President. It was in this stern spirit of uncompromise that Mr. Colfax made his second visit to Salt Lake City in October, 1869.

In the beginning of July, 1869, a delegation of Chicago merchants, seeking the trade of the West, with several distinguished American statesmen, arrived in Salt Lake City. It was by far the most important body of representative men of the Nation and its commerce that had visited the West; and their advent to our city, at that juncture, had a potent influence in the affairs of our Territory, not only in its commerce, but in the subsequent congressional legislation. The party consisted of the following persons—statesmen, bankers, merchants, etc.

Hon. L. Trumbull, U. S. Senator for Illinois; General R. J. Ogelsby, ex-governor of Illinois; Hon. N. B. Judd, M. C; Hon. J. V. Arnold; Hon. W. 8. Hinkley; Rev. Clinton Locke, D. D.; J. Medill, editor of the Chicago Tribune; J. M. Richards, president of the Chicago Board of Trade; Messrs. J. L Hancock, O. S. Hough, J. V. Farwell, J. H. Bowen, F. D. Gray, W. T. Allen, A. Cowles ,G. M. Kimbark, E. W. Blatchford, G. S. Bowen, C. G. Hammond, O. Lunt, T. Dent, C. G. Wicker, B. F. Haddock, S. Wait, E. V. Robbins, J. A. Ellison, C. Tobey, J. R. Nichols, E. F. Hollister, E. G. Keith, C. Gossage. J. Stockton, D. W. Whittle, Mr. Mead, O. L. Grant, (brother of President E. G. Squires, and others.

Headed by Col. James H. Bowen, to whom great credit was due for the efficient manner in which everything connected with the excursion had been managed; the Delegation called on President Young, at n o'clock A. M., July 10th, 1869.

Col. Bowen, surrounded by the members of the party, delivered the following address: "President Brigham Young: We call upon you this morning as members of a representative commercial party from the city of Chicago, who are en route upon a visit to San Francisco, the purpose of which is to facilitate commercial relations with localities made tributary by the completion of the Union and Central Pacific railroads.

"Esteeming the Territory of Utah one of the important localities, we have come to its capital to greet you and those engaged in commercial transactions in your midst, and to invite co-operation in our efforts.

"We also come to congratulate you upon the auspicious and speedy completion of the great national highway, that binds together the distant extremes of our country, that relieves the people of their long and profound isolation and places them and their products within a few days of steam locomotion of the great markets of the Union, thereby increasing the value of their labor and reducing the cost of their goods, and adding immensely to their wealth and their comforts, and placing them within easy reach of all the social as well as material enjoyments of life.

"In passing swiftly through the far-famed Echo and Weber canyons, we were deeply awed and grandly impressed with the majesty of the scenery and filled with wonder at the herculean task accomplished in the building of the railway through and over such seemingly insurmountable obstacles of nature in so incredibly short a space of time. A considerable share of the credit and honor of this achievement properly belongs to you and your people, who rendered hearty, efficient and timely aid to the company charged with the completion of this gigantic national highway, and we hope you will live long to enjoy the fruits of these beneficial labors. You will have further cause of congratulation when the branch road is completed which shall connect the capital of Utah with the main line, which work we are glad to learn is rapidly progressing towards completion.

"We have examined and scrutinized your wonderful development and the utilization of the barren nature which surrounded you in your early occupation of the valley. It demonstrates what can be reached by skillful industry and well-directed energy and is worthy of high commendation.

"Allow me the pleasure of introducing to you the members of our party, collectively and individually." President Young replied: " Col. J. H. Bowen, chairman of the representative commercial party of the city of Chicago, and gentlemen: I will briefly say in behalf of my friends here, and on my own part, gentlemen, you are each and all welcome; we are pleased to see you; we sincerely hope you are well and enjoying yourselves and that your excursion to the West will be productive of much benefit to all concerned.

"We congratulate you on the energy displayed by the commercial men of Chicago in advancing the business interests of the West, and we accept this as an index of more abundant success in the future. We are with you, heart and hand, in all that promotes the public good.

"We thank you for your congratulation and duly appreciate the high estimate which you hold of our labors. It is true we are the pioneers of this Western civilization, and that we have to some extent assisted in the development of the resources of the great West. It is true that we have built over 300 miles of the great Pacific Railroad, an enterprise for which, by the way, we memorialized Congress in 1852; but this of the past. Our labors are before the world, they speak for themselves. Our aim is to press onward, diligently to perform the part allotted to us in the great drama of life, and, having ever in view the glory of God and our country, the rights of man, and social independence, strive for the maintenance of those glorious principles which compose our Federal Constitution." Col. Bowen then introduced the gentlemen of the party, and a general and very agreeable conversation of upwards of an hour ensued.

This call upon ex-Governor Young, as the founder of Salt Lake City, and the pomp and formality of the interview, gave a very proper initial to the business and purposes of the delegation; but their council on Utah affairs was held at the residence of Mr. J. R. Walker. There the delegation met representative Gentiles of the city, Federal officials, military men, and non-Mormon merchants, among whom were the Walker Brothers, Colonel Kahn, John Chislett, General P. Edward Connor, Major Charles H. Hempstead, Judges Hawley and Strickland, O. J. Hollister, R. H. Robertson, Major Overton, and Captain Thomas H. Bates.

Designedly marked was the absence of Chief Justice Wilson, and Secretary Mann, whose fair standing with the Mormon people rendered them altogether unfitted for this very pronounced non-Mormon assembly. The meeting was a sort or informal national council, held on the spot, over Utah affairs, and it meant the determination of capacious special legislation, such as was quickly thereafter developed in the Cullom Bill. General Connor and Major Hempstead were there to give to the distinguished visitors emphatic views of the Mormon leaders, consonant with the early relations between the City and Camp Douglas, when its guns were planted on the city and its provost guard paraded our streets; the Federal officers were there to ask for special legislation, the removal of Chief Justice Wilson and Secretary Mann, and the appointment of such men as were soon afterwards sent by President Grant, in the persons of Governor Shaffer and Judge McKean, all aiming to make the Federal power absolute in the control of the affairs of the Territory; and the non-Mormon merchants were there to represent to the Chicago merchants the commercial crisis of that period, in which, to use the phrase of the time, they were "left out in the cold," by the establishing of Zion's Co-operative Mercantile Institution.

The two large rooms of Mr. Walker's residence were filled. Over forty persons were present. The munificent host had abundantly suppled his distinguished guests with champagne. Colfax and his friends, on their first visit to our city, fell upon strawberry beds, and discussed social problems with Brigham and the apostles over the dinner table, where the blessing was surely asked and "peace" and the "good Spirit" invoked. But this meeting was belligerent. Champagne was better suited to its purposes than either strawberries or blessings. The spirit of war was invoked rather than the " good spirit of peace." There was, they say, that day " the fullest and freest expression that had ever occurred in Utah," all of course with a strong, decided anti-Mormon animus and aim. "Everybody gave vent;" "war talk ran around;" Senator Trumbull related to the company that famous conversation between him and President Young, in which the latter had said to the effect that, if the Federal officers didn't behave themselves, he would have them ridden out of the city; and from this meeting the report of that conversation between Senator Trumbull and President Young ran throughout the United States; and gave to Vice-President Colfax the advantage to push General Grant almost to the verge of actual war against Mormon Utah. Such was the bearing of that counsel held at the house of Mr. J. R. Walker, over Utah affairs, in July, 1869.

The telegrams from San Francisco brought news that on the return of the Vice-President from the "Golden State" he would tarry for several days in Salt Lake City.

At a meeting of the City Council, held at the City Hall, October 1st, 1869, Aldermen Clinton, Richards and Pyper, committee, presented the following preamble and resolution, which were unanimously adopted:

"Whereas, His Excellency Schuyler Colfax, Vice-President of the United States, and party, are about to visit our city on their way returning from California to the East, and being desirous to contribute to their pleasure by extending to them a cordial welcome;

"Therefore, be it resolved by the City Council of Salt Lake City, that the hospitalities of said city be tendered to the Vice-President and party, during their stay, as a feeble but hearty demonstration of our sympathies with a great Nation, who have by their suffrages, conferred upon him such eminence in their political existence, and that appropriate committees be appointed to carry this resolution into effect."

In pursuance of the foregoing, Alderman S. W. Richards and Councilor Theodore McKean were appointed a committee on behalf of the Council to meet said party, with suitable coaches at Uintah Station and accompany them to the city.

Mayor D. H. Wells, Hon. W. H. Hooper, Alderman J. Clinton and Marshal J. D. T. McAllister were appointed a committee of reception, on arriving at the Townsend House, in this city, where ample arrangements would be made for entertainment during their stay.

On the 3rd of October, the delegation from the City Council met the Colfax party at Uintah Station, from which point the party was escorted to the city, where they arrived in the afternoon, and were received by the reception committee, headed by Mayor Wells and Hon. W. H. Hooper, who was at that time our Delegate to Congress. The hospitalities of the city was tendered to "the distinguished visitors," who, however, declined on the ground that the party was traveling in a strictly private capacity; and having spent a brief, but seemingly cordial interview with the representatives of the city, the Vice-President excused himself and party on account of fatigue, etc., of the journey.

It was understood, however, by this time, that the vice-President entertained a deep and abiding resentment towards the Mormon leaders, and an utter indisposition for further intercourse with the " fathers," either of the Church or the city. Mr. Stenhouse, in his book, thus notes the cause of the offense: "Mr. Colfax politely refused to accept the proffered courtesies of the city.

Brigham was reported to have uttered abusive language in the Tabernacle towards the Government and Congress, and to have charged the President and vice-President with being drunkards and gamblers. O.ie of the aldermen who waited upon Mr. Colfax to tender him the hospitalities of the city, could only say that ' he did not hear Brigham say so.' The weakness of the denial confirmed the information obtained from so many sources that the Prophet had really said so, and Mr. Colfax followed his own programme during his stay."

CHAPTER XLV.

THE VICE-PRESIDENT ARRANGING FOR WAR ON THE SAINTS. HE IS LET INTO THE SECRET OF THE PROJECTED GODBEITE SCHISM AND ENCOURAGES IT. HIS QUESTION-" WILL BRIGHAM YOUNG FIGHT?" OUTBURST OF THE SCHISM. THE NEW YORK HERALD SENDS ON A SPECIAL AGENT WITH INSTRUCTIONS TO SUPPORT THE SECEDERS.

There can be no doubt that Vice-President Colfax came up to Utah this time with a war programme very nearly perfected in his mind. His deep chagrin at the indignity which he believed Brigham Young had put upon the Government and himself, had made him the uncompromising enemy of the apostolic head of Mormondom, and the institutions and rule that seemed to derive life from his potent administration and his supreme will. Colfax, in fact, had resolved on the entire overthrow of Brigham Young and the domination of the Mormon hierarchy over Utah. He had unquestionably represented to President Grant that Mormondom was nothing less than a standing Rebeldom, which, ever and anon, hurled defiance or insult in the face of the general Government, and that Brigham Young had been at the head and front of it for a quarter of a century. To be convinced, with a man like Grant, was to resolve to conquer "Polygamic Theocracy" by a Federal rule in Utah as iron-heeled as that placed upon any of the rebel States of the South. The method generally approved by the country at that time was to work up the action by the most summary Congressional legislation, and to consummate it by military force. Hence, at that moment, the entire country looked upon another Mormon war as imminent, for an internal revolution had not been dreamt of then by the Government or thought possible by any outside observer. It was under such an aspect of affairs that the Colfax party made its second visit to Utah; and his coming practically meant a warning to the Mormon people, or a proclamation of the war intentions of the Government, just as they chose.

The arrival of the Vice-President found the Jew and Gentile merchants in consternation over co-operation. The Federal officers were in despair of ever being able to grapple with the problem, without military invasion of the situation, and the whole Gentile population saw themselves about to be more than ever "left out in the cold." Even the Walker Brothers were almost inclined to end their long controversy with the Church and leave Utah to her fate. But Colfax sought to rekindle the smouldering fire of a radical Gentile antagonism and pledged to the opposition the support of the Government to all intents and purposes.

Just at this crisis, it was deemed prudent, by certain of the confidants, to entrust the Vice-President with the secret that a number of influential Elders who were capable of controlling the commercial issue of the times, and able to affect Mormondom by the local press, were actually on the eve of revolution. This was better, even, than Mr. Colfax could have hoped to arrange by his visit and official encouragement; but, at first, he seemed more desirous to see these Mormon Protestants enlist in a crusade inaugurated by the Government, than that they should occupy the situation by a reform movement. A " Utah Expedition," sent by General Grant, would be thorough in its work and speedy in its cure. On the other hand a Protestant reform movement would be conservative, peaceful and necessarily slow in its issues.

The Vice-President put himself in communication with the heretics. Mr. Stenhouse was honored with a long drive and a confidential chat with him, before his departure from the city of the Saints.

"Will Brigham Young fight?" enquired Mr. Colfax, bringing the question home to the issue that he most desired.

"For God's sake, Mr. Colfax!" exclaimed Stenhouse, "keep the United States off. If the Government interferes and sends troops, you will spoil the opportunity, and drive the thousands back into the arms of Brigham Young, who are ready to rebel against the ' one-man power.' Leave the Mormon elders alone to solve their own problems. We can do it; the Government cannot. If you give us another Mormon war, we shall heal up the breach, go back in full fellowship with the church and stand by the brethren. What else could we do? Our families, friends and life-companions are all with the Mormon people. Mr. Colfax, take my word for it, the Mormons will fight the United States, if driven to it in defense of their faith, as conscientious religionists always have fought. The Mormons are naturally a loyal people. They only need to be broken off from the influence of Brigham Young. Depend upon it, Mr. Colfax, the Government had better let us alone with this business, simply giving its protection to the ' New Movement men.'"

These were substantially the pleadings of Mr. Stenhouse to the significant question of Vice-President Colfax—"Will Brigham Young fight?"

Mr. S. related to me the conversation between himself and the Vice-President on the same day of this fortunate ride and timely discussion of the Utah question. Stenhouse's replies will show the tenor of the Vice-President's own remarks, without my presuming to reproduce him from memory. His capital words, however—"Will Brigham Young fight?" were driven like a nail into the minds of the elders who were just about to commence their schism.

Nor was the conversation between Mr. Stenhouse and the Vice-President upon the Mormon question and the crisis of the hour, unsupported by similar views and utterances, to members of the Government and to Federal officials, by the men who were undertaking to revolutionize Utah and her institutions. They believed that they could affect Mormondom to its center for good, or at least bring over a large class of influential elders into a Protestant movement with a very respectable following.

In briefly reviewing the events of those times Mr. Stenhouse himself has said: "The Vice-President and his friends were made acquainted with the forthcoming opposition from members of the Church, and took much interest in the ' Movement,' believing as they did that the one-man power and the infallibility of the priesthood had seen their day."

As the " New Movement" was fostered by the United States Government and became the nucleus of the "Liberal Party" of Utah, it is historically proper to give it a circumstantial narrative. In coupling the " New Movement " with the visit of Vice-President Colfax to our City, Mr. Stenhouse says: "Another and unlooked-for phase of Mormon experience was soon to demand public attention. Two elders were trying to establish a literary paper—The Utah Magazine—the proprietors were W. S. Godbe and E. L. T. Harrison; the latter was the editor. Elder Harrison had essayed once before, with his friend Edward W. Tullidge, to make literature a profession among the Saints, and had established the Peep O' Day; but they met with insurmountable difficulties, and the paper stopped. The Magazine, with even Mr. Godbe's willing hand and ready purse to support it, realized that the effort to establish a purely literary paper in Utah was premature. The career of the Magazine was fast hastening to a close, and by way of rest and recreation, the editor accompanied the merchant to New York. * * * "Away from Utah, and traveling over the Plains, the old rumbling stage coach afforded the two friends, as every traveler in those days experienced, an excellent opportunity for reflection. On their way, they compared notes respecting the situation of things at home and spoke frankly together of their doubts and difficulties with the faith. They discovered, clearly enough that they were—in the language of the orthodox—'on the road to apostasy,' yet in their feelings they did not want to leave Mormonism or Utah. A struggle began in their minds.

"One proposition followed another, and scheme after scheme was the subject of discussion, but not one of those schemes or propositions, when examined, seemed desirable; they were in tenable mental anguish. Arrived in New York and comfortable in their hotel, in the evening they concluded to pray for guidance.

They wanted light, either to have their doubts removed and their faith in Mormonism confirmed, or yet again to have the light of their own intellects increased that they might be able to follow unwaveringly their convictions. In this state of mind the two elders assert that they had an extraordinary spiritualistic experience.

"They returned to Utah, and to a very small circle of friends confided what has here been only very briefly related, and their story was listened to. Elder Eli B. Kelsey, a Mormon of twenty-seven years standing, and who was also a president of Seventies, was the intimate friend of Mr. Godbe, and Edward W. Tullidge another 'Seventy,' was the bosom friend of Mr. Harrison. Elder Henry W. Lawrence, a wealthy merchant, a bishop's counsellor, and a gentleman of the highest integrity, was early informed in confidence of this "New Movement," and gave to his friend, Mr. Godbe, valuable material support. The Magazine, that had before this been hastening to an end, took a new lease of life, and became a brilliant, well-conducted paper."

During the absence of the merchant Godbe and Elder Harrison, in the fall of 1868, the co-operative institution had been projected; and it is quite a curious fact, seeing it afterwards antagonized the policies of President Young, that the Utah Magazine, which had been left in the charge of Tullidge, had for several weeks vigorously and enthusiastically sustained the co-operative movement; this, however, was fairly paralled by the other fact that Henry W. Lawrence was one of the first pillars of Z. C. M. I.

The organization was effected in the beginning of 1869, with a president, vice-president, and five directors. Brigham Young, president, Delegate Hooper, vice-president, George A. Smith, George Q. Cannon, Horace Eldredge, Wm. Jennings and Henry W. Lawrence, directors; Wm. Clayton, secretary; H. B. Clawson, superintendent. * At the very time when this organization was formed, the ""New Movement" had already been resolved upon; so that though Henry W. Lawrence put 530,000 into the Z. C. M. I. and became one of its directors, he was, to so express the historical complexity, a " New Movement" leader. The force of circumstances in those times, compelled the members of the " New Movement" to wait for the development of events which depended upon the action of President Young himself. There was nearly a total suspension. The very times hung on the man. He had been the " Man of Destiny " to Utah and was still.

During this period of suspension, there was abundance of opportunity for pause and reconsideration. There was a year's intellectual incubation before the "Movement" opened.

Having by their preliminary action provoked their excommunication from the Church, the Godbeite leaders, on Sunday, December 19, 1869, commenced public meetings in Salt Lake City, opening in the Thirteenth Ward Assembly Rooms, which was granted to them by President Young himself, on the application of Messrs. Godbe and Lawrence, through Bishop Woolley.

Immediately on the opening of the Movement, E. W. Tullidge wrote officially for his party to the New York Herald. The design was to impress upon the public mind the fact that an important Mormon schism had begun; that it would be vigorously prosecuted; that it would infuse Mormondom with new ideas, harmonious with the age, and that in time a peaceful revolution would be wrought out by the Mormons themselves, resulting in the very condition of things which the country desired to see in Utah. The New York Herald took similar views and urged them upon the American public by strong timely editorials on the Utah question. Nearly all the journals in the country followed in the wake, proclaiming "a great Mormon schism," and declaring the wisdom of "letting the Mormons alone to solve their own problem."

Of such importance did the events, which were at that crisis occurring in Salt Lake City seem to the American public, that, immediately on the receipt of Tullidge's letter, the New York Herald dispatched one of its chief special correspondents—Colonel Findley Anderson—formerly its principal correspondent in Europe. Colonel Anderson's brother was also the private and confidential secretary of young James Gordon Bennett. The reason of Bennett's sending so important a "special" to Salt Lake City was that the New York Herald might have on the spot one trusted to fully represent the leading journal of the country, while through its editorial columns it gave advice and impulse to the Government and the public touching Utah affairs in that crisis. Colonel Anderson was instructed to support the New Movement leaders, as well as to report their doings, and the influence of their action in Mormon society. The Harpers also, and George W. Curtis, indeed the whole staff of the Harpers, manifested an extraordinary interest in this "reformation in Utah," as the "Utah Schism" was styled in Harpers Weekly and Monthly; while the Springfield (Mass.) Republican petted the New Movement with a paternal spirit. Mr. Bowles' forecasting seemed to be at that moment fully realized. The New York Tribune was the only one of the great papers of the country that did not seem quite satisfied with the New Movement, and this was because the Tribune feared it lacked sufficient revolutionary force and determination to break up the "powerful Mormon hierarchy of Brigham Young." It was to Mr. Greeley and Whitelaw Reid merely another Mormon Church. The philosophers of the New York Tribune were not so far seeing and knowing as the Utah Gentiles, who were about to make this "other " Mormon Church the nucleus of an anti-Mormon political party.

On the part of the Government, from the onset, it gave countenance and favor to the Godbeite rebellion, and would have supported it by its military arm, had the opportunity occurred ; but this very movement against the parent Church, composed of apostate Mormon elders and leading Salt Lake merchants, prevented the interposition of the military arm, and greatly changed and modified the original intentions of the Government, as inspired by Vice-President Colfax, and determined by President Grant.

CHAPTER. XLVI.

FAMOUS DISCUSSION BETWEEN VICE-PRESIDENT COLFAX AND APOSTLE JOHN TAYLOR. SPEECH OF THE VICE-PRESIDENT AT SALT LAKE CITY. APOSTLE TAYLOR'S REPLY AND ANSWER TO THE COLFAX LETTER.

The review of Mormon affairs as made between Vice-President Colfax and Apostle John Taylor, afterward President of the Mormon Church, may properly be embodied as a representative chapter of this history; as the utterances of President Taylor very closely apply to the aspect of Utah's case at the present time, 1885. The review opens with Mr. Colfax's speech delivered on the portico of the Townsend House, Salt Lake City, October 5th, 1869: "Fellow Citizens:—I come hither in response to your call to thank the band from Camp Douglas for the serenade with which they have honored me, and to tender my obligations to the thousands before me, for having come from their homes and places of business ' to speed the parting guest.' "As I stand before you, to-night, my thoughts go back to the first view I ever had of Salt Lake City, four years ago last June. After traveling with my companions, Gov. Bross and Mr. Bowles, who are with me again, and Mr. Richardson, whose absence we have all regretted, over arid plains, and alkali valleys, and barren mountains, day after day, our stage coach emerged from a canyon one morning, and we looked down upon your city, covering miles in its area, with its gardens, green with fruit trees and shrubbery, and the Jordan, flashing in the sun beyond. And when, after stopping at Camp Douglas, which overlooks your city, to salute the flag of our country, and honor the officers and soldiers who keep watch and ward over it at this distant post, we drove down with your common council to the city, and saw its wide streets, and the streams which irrigate your gardens, rippling down all of them in their pebbly beds, I felt indeed that you had a right to regard it as a Palmyra in the desert. Returning now, with my family and friends, from a long journey on the Pacific coast, extending north to where the Columbia river tears its way through the mighty range which bars the way for all other rivers from the British to the Mexican line, we came to your city by the stage route from the railroad, through the fertile region that lines your lake shore, and find it as beautiful and attractive in its affluence of fruits and flowers as when we first visited it.

"I am gratified too, that our present visit occurred at the same time with your Territorial Fair, enabling us to witness your advance in the various branches of industry. I was specially interested in the hours I spent there, yesterday, with some of your leading citizens, in your cotton manufactures from the cotton you raise in Southern Utah, your woolen manufactures, the silk manufacture you have recently inaugurated, your leather and harness, the porcelain, which was new to me, your furniture, your paintings, and pictures, the fancy work of the ladies, and the fruits and vegetables which tell their own story of the fertility of your soil.

I rejoice over every indication of progress and self-reliance in all parts of the Union, and hope you may realize, by further development, how wise and beneficial such advancement is to communities like yours, remote from the more thickly settled portions of the Republic.

"I have enjoyed the opportunity, also, of visiting your Tabernacle, erected since I was here before, the largest building in which religious services are held on the continent, and of listening to your organ, constructed here, which, in its mammoth size, its volume of sound, and sweetness of tone, would compare favorably with any in the largest cities in the Union. Nor did I feel any the less interest on my present, than on my former visit, in listening to your leading men in their places of worship, as they expounded and defended their faith and practice, because that faith and practice differed so widely from my own. Believing in free speech, as all of us should, I listened attentively, respectfully, and courteously, to what failed to convince my mind, and you will doubtless hear me with equal patience, while I tell you frankly wherein we differ.

"But first let me say that I have no strictures to utter as to your creed on any really religious question. Our land is a land of civil and religious liberty, and the faith of every man is a matter between himself and God alone. You have as much right to worship the Creator through a president and twelve apostles of your church organization as I have through the ministers and elders and creed of mine.

And this right I would defend for you with as much zeal as the right of every other denomination throughout the land. But our country is governed by law, and no assumed revelation justifies anyone in trampling on the law. If it did, every wrong-doer would use that argument to protect himself in his obedience to it. The Constitution declares, in the most emphatic language, that that instrument and the laws made in conformity thereto, shall be the supreme law of the land.

Whether liked or disliked, they bind the forty million of people who are subject to that supreme law. If anyone condemns them as unconstitutional, the courts of the United States are open, before which they can test the question. But, till they are decided to be in conflict with the Constitution, they are binding upon you in Utah as they are on me in the District of Columbia, or on the citizens of Idaho and Montana. Let me refer now to the law of 1862, against which you especially complain, and which you denounce Congress for enacting. It is obeyed in the other Territories of the United States, or if disobeyed its violation is punished. It is not obeyed here, and though you often speak of the persecutions to which you were subject in the earlier years of your church, you cannot but acknowledge that the conduct of the government and the people of the United States towards you, in your later years, has been one of toleration, which you could not have realized in any other of the civilized nations of the world.

"I do not concede that the institution you have established here, and which is condemned by the law, is a question of religion. But to you who do claim it as such, I reply, that the law you denounce, only re-enacts the original prohibitions of your own Book of Mormon, on its 118th page, and your Book of Doctrine and Covenants, in its chapter on marriage; and these are the inspired records, as you claim them, on which your church was organized.

"The Book of Mormon, on the same page, speaks twice of the conduct of David and Solomon, as 'a grosser crime,' and those who follow their practice as 'waxing in iniquity.' The Book of Doctrine and Covenants is the discipline and creed of your church; and in its chapter on marriage, it declares, that as the Mormon church has been charged with the crimes of fornication and polygamy, it is avowed as the law of the church, that a man shall have but one wife, and a woman but one husband, till death shall part them.

"I know you claim that a subsequent revelation annulled all this; but I use these citations to show you that the Congressional law, which you denounce, only enacted what was the original and publicly proclaimed and printed creed on which your church was founded. And yet, while you assume that this later revelation gives you the right to turn your back on your old faith and disobey the law, you would not yourselves tolerate others in assuming rights for themselves under revelations they might claim to have received, or under religions they might profess. The Hindus claim, as part of their religion, the right to burn widows with the dead bodies of their husbands. If they were to attempt it here, as their religion, you would prevent it by force. If a new revelation were to be proclaimed here, that the strong men should have the right to take the wives of the weaker men, that the learned men should take the wives of the unlearned, that the rich men should take the wives of the poor, that those who were powerful and influential should have the right to command the labor and the services of the humbler, as their bond-slaves, you would spurn it, and would rely upon the law and the power of the United States to protect you.

"But you argue that it is a restraint on individual freedom; and that it concerns only yourselves. Yet you justify these restraints on individual freedom in everything else. Let me prove this to you. If a man came here and sought to establish a liquor saloon on Temple street without license, you would justify your common council, which is your municipal congress, in suppressing it by force, and punishing the offender besides. Another one comes here and says that he will pursue his legitimate avocation of bone boiling on a lot in the heart of your city.

You would expect your council to prevent it, and why? Because you believe it would be offensive to society and to the people around him. And still another says, that as an American citizen he will establish a powder mill on a lot he has purchased, next door to this hotel, where we have been so hospitably entertained.

You would demand that this should be prevented, because it was obnoxious to the best interests of the community. I might use other illustrations as to personal conduct which you would insist should be restrained, although it fettered personal freedom, and the wrong-doer might say only concerned himself. But I have adduced sufficient to justify Congress in an enactment they deemed wise for the whole people for whom they legislated. And I need not go further to adduce other arguments as to the elevation of woman; for my purpose has been in these remarks, to indicate the right of Congress to pass the law and to insist on obedience to it.

"One thing I must allude to, personal to myself. The papers have published a discourse delivered last April by your highest ecclesiastical authority, which stated that the President and Vice-President of the United States were both gamblers and drunkards. (Voices in the crowd, ' He did not say so.') I had not heard before that it was denied, but I am glad to hear the denial now. Whether denied or not, however, I did not intend to answer railing with railing, nor personal attack with invective. I only wished to state publicly in this city, where the charge is said to have been made, that it was utterly untrue as to President Grant, and as to myself, that I never gambled to the value of a farthing and have been a total abstinence man all the years of my manhood. However I may differ on political questions or others from any portion of my countrymen, no one has ever truthfully assailed my character. I have valued a good character far more than a political reputation or official honors, and wish to preserve it unspotted while life shall last.

"A few words more and I must conclude. When our party visited you four years ago, we all believed that, under wise counsels, your city might become the great city of the interior. But you must allow me to say that you do not seem to have improved these opportunities as you might have done. What you should do to develop the advantages your position gives you, seems obvious. You should encourage, and not discourage competition in trade. You should welcome, and not repel, investments from abroad. You should discourage every effort to drive capital from your midst. You should rejoice at the opening of every new store, or factory, or machine shop, by whomsoever conducted. You should seek to widen the area of country dependent on your city for supplies. You should realize that wealth will come to you only by development, by unfettered competition, by increased capital.

"Here I must close. I have spoken to you, face to face, frankly, truthfully, fearlessly. I have said nothing but for your own good. Let me counsel you once more to obedience to the law and thanking you for the patient hearing you have given me, and for the hospitalities our party have received, both from Mormon and Gentile citizens, I bid you all good night and good bye."

"American House, Boston, Mass.,
"October 20th, 1869.

" To the Editor of the Deseret Evening News:

"Dear Sir—I have read with a great deal of interest the speech of the Hon. Schuyler Colfax, delivered in Salt Lake City, October 5th, containing strictures on our institutions, as reported in the Springfield Republican, wherein there is an apparent frankness and sincerity manifested. It is pleasant, always, to listen to sentiments that are bold, unaffected and outspoken; and however my views may differ—as they most assuredly do—from those of the Hon. Vice-President of the United States, I cannot but admire the candor and courtesy manifested in the discussions of this subject; which, though to him perplexing and difficult, is to us an important part of our religious faith.

"I would not, however, here be misunderstood; I do not regard the speech of Mr. Colfax as something indifferent or meaningless. I consider that words proceeding from a gentleman occupying the honorable position of Mr. Colfax, have their due weight. His remarks, while they are courteous and polite, were evidently calmly weighed and cautiously uttered, and they carry with them a significance, which I, as a believer in Mormonism, am bound to notice; and I hope with that honesty and candor which characterize the remarks of this honorable gentleman.

"Mr. Colfax remarks: '" I have no strictures to offer as to your creeds on any really religious question. Our land is a land of civil and religious liberty, and the faith of every man is a matter between himself and God alone; you have as much right to worship the Creator, through a president and twelve apostles of your church organization, as I have through the ministers and elders and creed of mine; and this right I would defend for you with as much zeal as the right of any denomination throughout the land.' "This certainly is magnanimous and even-handed justice, and the sentiments do honor to their author; they are sentiments that ought to be engraven on the heart of every American citizen.

"He continues: '" But our country is governed by law and no assumed revelation justifies anyone in trampling on the law.' "At first sight this reasoning is very plausible, and I have no doubt that Mr. Colfax was just as sincere and patriotic in the utterance of the latter as the former sentences; but with all due deference permit me to examine these words and their import.

"That our country is governed by law we all admit; but when it is said that 'no assumed revelation justifies anyone in trampling on the law;' I should respectfully ask, what! not if it interferes with my religious faith, which you state 'is a matter between God and myself alone?' Allow me, sir, here to state that the assumed revelation referred to is one of the most vital parts of our religious faith; it emanated from God and cannot be legislated away; it is part of the 'Everlasting Covenant' which God has given to man. Our marriages are solemnized by proper authority; a woman is sealed unto a man for time and for eternity, by the power of which Jesus speaks, which 'sealed on earth and it is sealed in heaven.' With us it is ' Celestial Marriage; ' take this from us and you rob us of our hopes and associations in the resurrection of the just. This is not our religion? You do not see things as we do. Your marry for time only, 'until death does you part.' We have eternal covenants, eternal unions, eternal associations. I cannot, in an article like this, enter into details, which I should be pleased on a proper occasion to do. I make these remarks to show that it is considered, by us, a part of our religious faith, which I have no doubt did you understand it as we do, you would defend, as you state, 'with as much zeal as the right of every other denomination throughout the land.' Permit me here to say, however, that it was the revelation (I will not say assumed) that Joseph and Mary had, which made them look upon Jesus as the Messiah; which made them flee from the wrath of Herod, who was seeking the young child's life. This they did in contravention of law, which was his decree. Did they do wrong in protecting Jesus from the law? But Herod was a tyrant. That makes no difference; it was the law of the land, and I have yet to learn the difference between a tyrannical king and a tyrannical Congress. When we talk of executing law in either case, that means force, —force means an army, and an army means death. Now I am not sufficiently versed in metaphysics to discover the difference in its effects, between the asp of Cleopatra, the dagger of Brutus, the chalice of Lucretia Borgia, or the bullet or sabre of an American soldier.

"I have, sir, written the above in consequence of some remarks which follow: "' I do not concede that the institution you have established here, and which is condemned by the law, is a question of religion.' "Now, with all due deference, I do think that if Mr. Colfax had carefully examined our religious faith he would have arrived at other conclusions. In the absence of this I might ask, who constituted Mr. Colfax a judge of my religious faith? I think he has stated that ' the faith of every man is a matter between himself and God alone.' "Mr. Colfax has a perfect right to state and feel that he does not believe in the revelation on which my religious faith is based, nor in my faith at all; but has he the right to dictate my religious faith? I think not; he does not consider it religion, but it is nevertheless mine.

"If a revelation from God is not a religion, what is?

"His not believing it from God makes no difference; I know it is. The Jews did not believe in Jesus but Mr. Colfax and I do; their unbelief did not alter the revelation.

"Marriage has from time immemorial, among civilized nations, been considered a religious ordinance. It was so considered by the Jews. It is looked upon, by the Catholic clergy, as one of their sacraments. It is so treated by the Greek Church. The ministers of the Episcopal Church say, in their marriage formula, 'What God has joined together, let not man put asunder;' and in some of the Protestant churches their members are disfellowshipped for marrying what are termed unbelievers. So I am in hopes, one of these times, should occasion require it, to call upon our friend, Mr. Colfax, to redeem his pledge.

"' To defend for us our religious faith, with as much zeal as the right of every other denomination throughout the land.' "I again quote: 'But to you who do claim it as such, I reply that the law that you denounce only re-enacts the original prohibition of your own Book of Mormon, on its 118th page, and your Book of Doctrine and Covenants, in its chapter on marriage.' "In regard to the latter of these I would state that it was only considered a portion of the discipline of our Church, and was never looked upon as a revelation. It was published in the appendix to the Book of Doctrine and Covenants long before the revelation concerning Celestial Marriage was given. That, of course, superseded the former. The quotation from the Book of Mormon, given by Mr. Colfax, is only partly quoted. I cannot blame the gentleman for this: he has many engagements without examining our doctrines. I suppose this was handed to him. Had he read a little further he would have found it stated: "' For if I will, saith the Lord of Hosts, raise up seed unto me I will command my people; otherwise they shall hearken unto these things.' "In answer to this I say the Lord has commanded and we obey the command.

"I again quote: "And yet while you assume that this later revelation gives you the right to turn your back on your old faith and to disobey the law, you would not yourselves tolerate others in assuming rights for themselves under revelations they might claim to have received, or under religions they might profess.' "Mr. Colfax is misinformed here. All religions are tolerated by us, and all revelations or assumed revelations. We take the liberty of disbelieving some of them; but none are interfered with. And in relation to turning our back on our old religion we have never done it.

"Concerning our permitting the Hindus to burn their widows, it is difficult to say what we should do. The British government has tolerated both polygamy and the burning of Hindoo widows in India. If the Hindus were converted to our religion they would not burn their widows; they are not likely to come to Utah without. Whose rights have we interfered with? Whose property have we taken? Whose religious or political faith or rights have been curtailed by us? None. We have neither interfered with Missouri nor Illinois; with Kansas, Nebraska, Idaho, Nevada, Montana, California, nor any other State or Territory. I wish we could say the same of others, I hope we shall not be condemned for crimes we are expected to commit. It will be time enough to atone for them when done. We do acknowledge having lately started co-operative stores. Is this anything new in England, Germany, France or the United States? We think we have a right, as well as others, to buy and sell of and to whom we please.

We do not interrupt others in selling, if they can get customers. We have commenced to deal with our friends. We do acknowledge that we are rigid in the enforcement of law against theft, gambling, debauchery and other civilized vices. Is this a crime? If so, we plead guilty.

"But permit me here to return to the religious part of our investigations; for if our doctrines are religious, then it is confessed that Congress has no jurisdiction in this case and the argument is at an end. Mr. Webster defines religion as 'any system of faith and worship, as the religion of the Turks, of Hindus, of Christians.' I have never been able to look at religion in any other light. I do not think Mr. Colfax had carefully digested the subject when he said 'I do not concede that the institution you have established here, and which is condemned by law, is a question of religion.' "Are we to understand by this that Mr. Colfax is created an umpire to decide upon what is religion and what is not, upon what is true religion and what is false? If so, by whom and what authority is he created judge? I am sure he has not reflected upon the bearing of this hypothesis, or he would not have made such an utterance.

"According to this theory no persons ever were persecuted for their religion, there never was such a thing known. Could anybody suppose that that erudite, venerable, and profoundly learned body of men,—the great Sanhedrim of the Jews; or that those holy men, the chief priests, scribes and Pharisees, would persecute anybody for religion? Jesus was put to death,—not for his religion— but because he was a blasphemer: because he had a devil and cast out devils, through Beelzebub the prince of devils; because he, being a carpenter's son, and known among them as such, declared himself the Son of God. So they said, and they were the then judges, could anybody be more horrified than those Jews at such pretensions? His disciples were persecuted, proscribed and put to death, not for their religion, but because they 'were pestilent fellows and stirrers up of sedition,' and because they believed in an 'assumed revelation' concerning 'one Jesus, who was put to death, and who, they said, had risen again.' It was for false pretensions and a lack of religion that they were persecuted. Their religion was not like that of the Jews; ours, not like that of Mr. Colfax.

"Loyola did not invent and put into use the faggot, the flame, the sword, the thumbscrews, the rack and gibbet to persecute anybody, it was to purify the church of heretics, as others would purify Utah. His zeal was for the Holy Mother Church. The Nonconformists of England and Holland, the Huguenots of France and the Scottish Covenanters were not persecuted or put to death for their religion; it was for being schismatics, turbulent and unbelievers. Talk of religion, what horrid things have not been perpetrated in its name! All of the above claimed that they were persecuted for their religion. All of the persecutors, as Mr. Colfax said about us, did ' not concede that the institution they had established, which was condemned by the law, was religion;' or, in other terms, it was an imposture or false religion. What of the Quakers and Baptists of New England?

"You say we complain of persecution. Have we not cause to do it? Can we call our treatment by a milder term? Was it benevolence that robbed, pillaged and drove thousands of men, women and children from Missouri, was it Christian philanthropy that, after robbing, plundering, and ravaging a whole community, drove them from Illinois into the wilderness among savages?

"When we fled as outcasts and exiles from the United States we went to Mexican Territory. If not protected we should have been at least unmolested there.

Do you think, in your treaty with Mexico, it was a very merciful providence that placed us again under your paternal guardianship? Did you know that you called upon us in our exodus from Illinois for 500 men, which were furnished while fleeing from persecution, to help you to possess that country; for which your tender mercies were exhibited by letting loose an army upon us, and you spent about forty million of dollars to accomplish our ruin? Of course we did not suffer; "religious fanatics" cannot feel: like the eels the fish woman was skinning, "we have got used to it." Upon what pretext was this done? Upon the false fabrications of your own officers, and which your own Governor Cumming afterwards published as false. Thus the whole of this infamous proceeding war predicated upon falsehood, originating with your own officers and afterwards exposed by them. Did Government make any amends, or has it ever done it? Is it wrong to call this persecution? We have learned to our cost " that the king can do no wrong." Excuse me, sir, if I speak warmly. This people have labored under accumulated wrongs for upwards of thirty years past, still unacknowledged and unredressed. I have said nothing in the above but what I am prepared to prove. What is all this for? Polygamy? No—that is not even pretended.

Having said so much with regard to Mr. Colfax's speech, let me now address a few words to Congress and to the nation. I hope they will not object for I too am a teacher. And first let me inquire into the law itself, enacted in 1862. The revelation on polygamy was given in 1843, nineteen years before the passage of the Congressional act. We, as a people, believe that revelation is true and came from God. This is our religious belief; and right or wrong it is still our belief; whatever opinions others may entertain it makes no difference to our religious faith. The Constitution is to protect me in my religious faith, and other persons in theirs, as I understand it. It does not prescribe a faith for me, or anyone else, or authorize others to do it, not even Congress. It simply protects us all in our religious faiths. This is one of the Constitutional rights reserved by the people. Now who does not know that the law of 1862 in relation to polygamy was passed on purpose to interfere with our religious faith? This was as plainly and distinctly its object as the proclamation of Herod to kill the young children under two years old, was meant to destroy Jesus; or the law passed by Pharaoh in regard to the destruction of the Hebrew children, was meant to destroy the Israelites. If a law had been passed making it a penal offense for communities, or churches, to forbid marriage, who would not have understood that it referred to the Shaking Quakers, and to the priories, nunneries and priesthood of the Catholic Church? This law, in its inception, progress and passage, was intended to bring us into collision with the United States, that a pretext might be found for our ruin. These are acts that no honest man will controvert. It could not have been more plain, although more honest, if it had said the Mormons shall have no more wives than one. It was a direct attack upon our religious faith. It is the old story of the lamb drinking below the wolf and being accused by it of fouling the waters above. The big bully of a boy putting a chip on his shoulder and daring the little urchin to knock it off.

"But we are graciously told that we have our appeal. True, we have an appeal. So had the Hebrew mothers to Pharaoh; so had Daniel to Nebuchadnezzar; so had Jesus to Herod; so had Caesar to Brutus; so had those sufferers on the rack to Loyola; so had the Waldenses and Albigenses to the Pope; so had the Quakers and Baptists of New England to the Puritans. Why did they not do it? Please answer.

"Do statesmen and politicians realize what they are doing when they pass such laws? Do they know, as before stated, that resistance to law means force, that force means an army, and that an army means death? They may yet find something more pleasant to reflect upon than to have been the aiders and abettors of murder, to be stained with the blood of innocence, and they may try in vain to cleanse their hands of the accursed spot.

"It is not the first time that Presidents, Kings, Congresses and statesmen have tried to regulate the acts of Jehovah. Pharaoh's exterminating order about the Hebrew infants was one of acknowledged policy. They grew, they increased too fast. Perhaps the Egyptians had learned, as well as some of our Eastern reformers, the art of infanticide; they may have thought that one or two children was enough and so destroyed the balance. They could not submit to let nature take its vulgar course. But in their refined and polite murders, they found themselves dwindling and decaying, and the Hebrews increasing and multiplying; and no matter how shocking it might be to their refined senses, it stood before them as a political fact, and they were in danger of being overwhelmed by the superior fecundity of the Hebrews. Something must be done; what more natural than to serve the Hebrew children as they had served their own? and this, to us and the Christian world, shocking act of brutal murder, was to them simply what they may have done among themselves; perhaps more politely a la Madam Restelle, but not more effectually. The circumstances are not very dissimilar. When Jesus was plotted against by Herod and the infants put to death, who could complain? It was law: we must submit to law. The Lord Jehovah, or Jesus the Savior of the world, has no right to interfere with law. Jesus was crucified according to law. Who can complain? Daniel was thrown into a den of lions strictly according to law. The King would have saved him, if he could; but he could not resist law. The massacre of St. Bartholomew was in accordance with law. The guillotine of Robespierre of France, which cut heads off by the thousand, did it according to law. What right had the victims to complain? But these things were done in barbarous ages. Do not let us, then, who boast of our civilization, follow their example; let us be more just, more generous, more forbearing, more magnanimous. We are told that we are living in a more enlightened age. Our morals are more pure (?) our ideas more refined and enlarged, our institutions more liberal. 'Ours,' says Mr. Colfax, 'is a land of civil and religious liberty, and the faith of every man is a matter between himself and God alone," providing God don't shock our moral ideas by introducing something that we don't believe in. If He does let Him look out. We won't persecute, very far be that from us; but we will make our platform, pass Congressional laws and make you submit to them. We may, it is true, have to send out an army, and shed the blood of many; but what of that? It is so much more pleasant to be proscribed and killed according to the laws of the Great Republic, in the 'asylum for the oppressed,' than to perish ignobly by the decrees of kings, through their miserable minions, in the barbaric ages.

"My mind wanders back upwards of thirty years ago, when in the State of Missouri, Mr. McBride, an old gray-haired venerable veteran of the Revolution, with feeble frame and tottering steps, cried to a Missouri patriot: 'Spare my life, I am a Revolutionary soldier, I fought for liberty, would you murder me? What is my offense, I believe in God and revelation?' This frenzied disciple of a misplaced faith said, 'take that, you God d —— d Mormon,' and with the butt of his gun he dashed his brains out, and he lay quivering there,—his white locks clotted with his own brains and gore on that soil that he had heretofore shed his blood to redeem—a sacrifice at the shrine of liberty! Shades of Franklin, Jefferson and Washington, were you there! Did you gaze on this deed of blood? Did you see your companion in arms thus massacred? Did you know that thousands of American citizens were robbed, disfranchised, driven, pillaged and murdered, for these things seem to be forgotten by our statesmen. Were not these murderers punished? Was not justice done to the outraged? No. They were only Mormons, and when the Chief Magistrate was applied to, he replied 'Your cause is just, but I can do nothing for you.' Oh, blessed land of religious freedom!

What was this for. Polygamy? No. It was our religion then, it is our religion now. Monogamy or polygamy, it makes no difference. Let me here seriously ask: have we not had more than enough blood in this land? Does the insatiate moloch still cry for more victims?

"Let me here respectfully ask with all sincerity, is there not plenty of scope for the action of government at home? What of your gambling hells? What of your gold rings, your whisky rings, your railroad rings, manipulated through the lobby into your Congressional rings. What of that great moral curse of the land, that great institution of monogamy—Prostitution? What of its twin sister —Infanticide? I speak to you as a friend. Know ye not that these seething infamies are corrupting and destroying your people? and that like the plague they are permeating your whole social system? that from your gilded palaces to your most filthy purlieus, they are festering and stewing and rotting. What of the thirty thousand prostitutes of New York City and the proportionate numbers of other cities, towns and villages, and their multitudinous pimps and paramours, who are, of course, all, all, honorable men! Here is ample room for the Christian, the philanthropist, and the statesman. Would it not be well to cleanse your own Augean stables? What of the blasted hopes, the tortured and crushed feelings of the thousands of your wives whose whole lives are blighted through your intrigues and lasciviousness? What of the humiliation of your sons and daughters from whom you cannot hide your shame? What of the thousands of houseless and homeless children thrown ruthlessly, hopelessly and disgracefully upon the world as outcasts from society, whose fathers and mothers are alike ashamed of them and heartlessly throw them upon the public bounty, the living memorials of your infamy? What of your infanticide, with its murderous, horrid, unnatural, disgusting and damning consequences? Can you legislate for these monogamic crimes, or shall Madam Restell and her pupils continue their public murders and no redress? Shall your fair daughters, the princesses of America, ruthlessly go on in sacrificing their noble children on the altar of this Moloch—this demon? What are we drifting to? This 'bonehouse,' this "powder magazine' is not in Salt Lake City, a thousand miles from your frontiers; it is in your own cities and towns villages and homes. It carouses in your secret chambers and flaunts in the public highway; it meets you in every corner and besets you in every condition. Your infirmaries and hospitals are reeking with it; your sons and daughters, your wives and husbands are degraded by it. It extends from Louisiana to Minnesota, and from Maine to California. You can't hide yourselves from it; it meets you in your magazines and newspapers, and is disgustingly placarded on your walls,—a living, breathing, loathsome, festering, damning evil. It runs through your very blood, stares out your eyes and stamps its horrid mark on your features, as indelibly as the mark of Cain; it curses your posterity, it runs riot in the land, withering, blighting, corroding and corrupting the life blood of the nation.

"Ye American Statesmen, will you allow this demon to run riot in the land, and while you are speculating about a little political capital to be made out of Utah, allow your nation to be emasculated and destroyed? Is it not humiliating that these enormities should exist in your midst, and you, as statesmen, as legislators, as municipal and town authorities, as clergymen, reformers and philanthropists, acknowledge yourselves powerless to stop these damning crimes that are gnawing at the very vitals of the most magnificent nation on the earth? We can teach you a lesson on this matter, polygamists as we are. You acknowledge one wife and her children; what of your other associations unacknowledged? We acknowledge and maintain all of our wives and all of our children; we don't keep a few only, and turn the others out as outcasts, to be provided for by orphan asylums, or turned as vagabonds on the street to help increase the fearfully growing evil. Our actions are all honest, open and above board. We have no gambling hells, no drunkenness, no infanticide, no houses of assignation, no prostitutes.

Our wives are not afraid of intrigues and debauchery; nor are our wives and daughters corrupted by designing and unprincipled villains. We believe in the chastity and virtue of women and maintain them. There is not, to-day, in the wide world, a place where female honor, virtue and chastity, are so well protected as in Utah. Would you have us, I am sure you would not, on reflection, reverse the order of God, and exchange the sobriety, the chastity, the virtue and honor of our institutions, for yours, that are so debasing, dishonorable, corrupting, defaming and destructive? We have fled from these things, and with great trouble and care have purged ourselves from your evils, do not try to legislate them upon us nor seek to engulf us in your damning vices.

"You may say it is not against your purity that we contend; but against polygamy, which we consider a crying evil. Be it so. Why then, if your system is so much better, does it not bring forth better fruits! Polygamy, it would seem, is the parent of chastity, honor and virtue; Monogamy the author of vice, dishonor and corruption. But you would argue these evils are not our religion; we that are virtuous, are as much opposed to vice and corruption as you are.

Then why don't you control it? We can and do. You have your Christian associations, your Young Men's associations, your Magdalen and Temperance associations all of which are praiseworthy. Your cities and towns are full of churches, and you swarm with male and female lecturers, and ministers of all denominations.

You have your press, your National and State Legislatures, your police, your municipal and town authorities, your courts, your prisons, your armies, all under the direction of Christian monogamists. You are a nation of Christians. Why are these things not stopped? You possess the moral, the religious, the civil and military power but you don't accomplish it. Is it too much to say 'take the beam out of thine own eye and then shalt thou see clearly to remove the mote that is in thy brother's.' "Respectfully, etc.,

" John Taylor."

It is not necessary to give Mr. Colfax's reply to Apostle Taylor, as his points are all reviewed in the following rejoinder: "Mr. Colfax has replied to my article by another, published in the New York Independent, December 2nd, headed 'The Mormon Question.'

"I have always been taught to reverence men in authority. My religion has not lessened the force of that precept. I am sorry to be under the necessity of differing from the honorable gentleman who stands second in authority in the greatest and freest nation in the world. My motto has always been and now is: Honor to whom honor is due; yet, while I feel bound to pay homage to a man of his talent and position I cannot but realize that 'all men are now free and equal,' and that I live in a land where the press, thought and speech are free. If it had been a personal difference I should have had no controversy with Mr. Colfax, and the honorable gentleman, I am sure, will excuse me for standing up in the defense of what I know to be a traduced and injured people. I would not accuse the gentleman of misrepresentation. I cannot help knowing, however, that he is misinformed in relation to most of his historical details; and justice to an outraged community, as well as truth, requires that such statements should be met and the truth vindicated. I cannot but think that in refusing the proffered hospitality of our city which, of course, he had a perfect right to do, he threw himself among a class of men that were, perhaps, not very reliable in historical data.

"I am not surprised at his apparent prejudices; I can account for his antipathies, but cannot permit Mr. Colfax, even ignorantly, to traduce my friends without defense. He states that ' the demand of the people of Utah Territory for immediate admission into the Union, as a State, made at their recent conference meeting and to be presented by their delegate at the approaching session of Congress, compels the nation to meet face to face, a question which it has apparently endeavored to ignore.' "Is there anything remarkable in a Territory applying for admission into the Union? How have other States entered the Union since the admission of the first thirteen? Were they not all Territories in their turn, and generally applied to Congress for, and obtained admission? Why should Utah be an exception? She has from time to time, as a constitutional requisition, presented a petition with a constitution containing a republican form of government. Since her application California, Nevada, Kansas, Minnesota, Oregon and Nebraska have been admitted. And why should Congress, as Mr. Colfax says: 'endeavor to ignore Utah?' And why should it be so difficult a question to meet ' face to face?' Has it become so very difficult for Congress to do right? What is the matter? Some remarkable conversation was had between Brigham Young and Senator Trumbull. Now, as I did not happen to hear this conversation, I cannot say what it was. One thing, however, I do know, that I have seen hundreds of distinguished gentlemen call on President Young and they have been uniformly better treated than has been reciprocated. But something was said about United States officers. I am sorry to say that many United States officers have so deported themselves that they have not been much above par with us. They may indeed be satraps and require homage and obeisance; but we have yet to learn to bow the knee. Brigham Young does not generally speak even to a United States Senator with honeyed words and measured sentences; but as an ingenious and honest man. But we are told that ' the recent expulsion of prominent members of his Church for doubting his infallibility proves that he regards his power as equal to any emergency and has a will equal to his power.'

"I am sorry to have to say that Mr. Colfax is mistaken here. No person was ever dismissed from the Church of Jesus Christ of Latter-day Saints for disbelieving in the infallibility of President Young. I do not believe he is infallible, for one; and have so taught publicly. I am in the Church yet. Neither have I ever heard President Young make any such pretensions. Mr. Colfax is a good politician, but he makes sad blunders in polemics. He makes a magnificent Speaker and President of the Senate;

I am afraid, however, that as a preacher he would not be so successful. The honorable gentleman now proceeds to divide his subject and commences.

"'I. Their Fertilizing of the Desert.—For this they claim great credit, and I would not detract an iota from all they are legitimately entitled to.

It was a desert when they first emigrated thither. They have made large portions of it fruitful and productive, and their chief city is beautiful in location and attractive in its gardens and shrubbery. But the solution of it all is in one word— water. What seemed to the eye a desert became fruitful when irrigated, and the mountains, whose crests are clothed in perpetual snow, furnished, in the unfailing supplies of their ravines, the necessary fertilizer.'

'Water! *Mirabile dictu*!! Here I must help Mr. C. out. This wonderful little water nymph, after playing with the clouds on our mountain tops, frolicking with the snow and rain in our rugged gorges for generations, coquetting with the sun and dancing to the sheen of the moon, about the time the 'Mormons' came here took upon herself to perform a great miracle, and descending to the valley with a wave of her magic wand and the mysterious words, " hickory, diccory, dock,' cities and streets were laid out, crystal waters flowed in ten thousand rippling streams, fruit trees and shrubbery sprang up, gardens and orchards abounded, cottages and mansions were organized, fruits, flowers and grain in all their elysian glory appeared and the desert blossomed as the rose; and this little frolicking elf, so long confined to the mountains and water courses proved herself far more powerful than Cinderella or Aladdin. Oh! Jealousy, thou green-eyed monster! Can no station in life be protected from the shimmer of thy glamour!

Must our talented and honorable Vice-President be subjected to thy jaundiced touch? But to be serious, did water tunnel through our mountains, construct dams, canals and ditches, lay out our cities and towns, import and plant choice fruit-trees, shrubs and flowers, cultivate the land and cover it with the cattle on a thousand hills, erect churches, schoolhouses and factories, and transform a howling wilderness into a fruitful field and garden? If so, why does not the Green River the Snake River, Bear River, Colorado, the Platte and other rivers perform the same prodigies? Unfortunately for Mr. Colfax, it was Mormon polygamists who did it. The Erie, the Welland, the Pennsylvania and Suez canals are only water.

What if a stranger on gazing upon the statuary in Washington and our magnificent Capitol, and after rubbing his eyes were to exclaim, 'Eureka! It is only rock and mortar and wood.' This discoverer would announce that instead of the development of art, intelligence, industry and enterprise, its component parts were simply stone, mortar and wood. Mr. Colfax has discovered that our improvements are attributable to water. We next come to another division and quote their persecutions:

"'This is also one of their favorite themes. Constantly it is reiterated by their apostles and bishops, from week to week, and from year to year. It is discoursed about in their tabernacles and their ward and town churches. It is written about in their periodicals and papers. It is talked about with nearly every stranger that comes into their midst. They have been driven from place to place, they claim, solely on account of their religious belief. Their faith has subjected them to the wickedest persecution by unbelievers. They have been despoiled, they insist, of their property; maltreated in their persons, buffeted and cast out, because they would not renounce their professions and their revelations.' "This, sir, is all true; does it falsify a truth to repeat it? The Mormons make these statements and are always prepared to prove them. I referred to some of these things in my last; Mr. Colfax has not disproved them. He now states, 'I do not attempt to decide that the charges against them are well founded.' Why then are they made? Has it become so desirable to put down the Mormons that unfounded charges must be preferred against them?

"' Their church was first established at Manchester, New York, in 1830, and their first removal was in 1831, to Kirtland, Ohio, which they declared was revealed to them as the site of their New Jerusalem.' (A mistake.) 'Thence their leaders went west to search a new location, which they found in Jackson County, Mo., and dedicated a site for another New Jerusalem there, and returned to Kirtland to remain for five years avowedly to make money;' (an error) 'a bank was established there by them; large quantities of bills of doubtful value issued, and growing out of charges of fraudulent dealing, Smith and Rigdon were tarred and feathered.' This is a gross perversion, Smith and Rigdon were tarred and feathered in March, 1832, in Hiram, Portage County; the bank was organized December 2nd, 1836, in Kirtland.

"Mr. C. continues: 'And unjustifiable as such outrages are this one was based on alleged fraud and not on religious belief.' Allow me to state that this persecution was based on religious belief and not on fraud, and that this statement is a perversion, for the bank was not opened until several years after the tiring and feathering referred to. But did the bank fail? Yes, in 1837, about five years after, in the great financial crisis; and so did most of the banks in the United States, in Canada, a great many in England, France and other parts of Europe. Is it so much more criminal for the Mormons to make a failure than others? Their bank was swallowed in the general financial maelstrom, and sometime after the failure of the bank the bills were principally redeemed.

"'They fled to Missouri, their followers joined them there, they were soon accused of plundering and burning habitations and with secret assassinations.' Was there no law in Missouri? The Missourians certainly did not lack either the will or the power to enforce it. Why were not these robbers, incendiaries, and assassins dealt with? Mr. C. continues: 'Nor do these charges against them rest on the testimony of those who had not been of their own faith; in October, 1838, T. B. Marsh, ex-president of the twelve apostles of their church, and Orson Hyde, one of the apostles, made affidavits before an officer in Ray County, Missouri, in which Marsh swore and Hyde corroborated it.

"'They have among them a company consisting of all that are true Mormons, called the Danites, who have taken an oath to support the heads of the church in all things, whether right or wrong. I have heard the Prophet say that he would yet tread down his enemies and walk over their dead bodies; that, if he was not let alone he would be a second Mohammed to this generation, and that he would make it one gore of blood from the Rocky Mountains to the Atlantic Ocean.' I am sorry to say that Thomas B. Marsh did make that affidavit, and that Orson Hyde stated that he knew part of it and believed the other; and it would be disingenuous in me to deny it; but it is not true that these things existed, for I was there and knew to the contrary; and so did the people of Missouri, and so did the Governor of Missouri. How do you account for their acts?

Only on the score of the weakness of our common humanity. We are living in troublous times, and all men's nerves are not proof against such shocks as we then had to endure. Mobs were surrounding us on every hand, burning our houses, murdering our people, destroying our crops, killing our cattle. About this time that horrible massacre at Haun's Mill took place, where men, women and children, were indiscriminately butchered, and their remains, for want of other sepulture, thrown into a well. Messages were coming in from all parts, of fire, devastation, blood and death. We threw up a few logs and fences for protection; this, I suppose, is what Mr. Colfax calls, 'fortifying their towns and defying the officers of law.' If wagons and fences and a few house logs are fortifications, we were fortified; and if the mob, whose hands were dripping with the blood of men, women and children, whom they had murdered in cold blood, were ' officers of the law' then we are guilty of the charge. I cannot defend the acts of Thomas B. Marsh or Orson Hyde, although the latter had been laboring under a severe fever, and was at the time only just recovering, no more than I could defend the acts of Peter when he cursed and swore and denied Jesus; nor the acts of Judas who betrayed Him; but, if Peter, after going out and 'weeping bitterly,' was restored, and was afterwards a chief apostle; so did Orson Hyde repent sincerely and weep bitterly, and was restored and has since been to Palestine, Germany and other nations. Thomas B. Marsh returned a poor broken down man and begged to live with us; he got up before assembled thousands and stated: 'If you wish to see the effect of apostacy, look at me.' He was a poor wreck of a man, a helpless driveling child, and he is since dead. A people are not to be judged by such acts as these. But the Governor of Missouri in his message says: "' These people had violated the laws of the land by open and armed resistance to them; they had instituted among themselves a government of their own, independent of, and in opposition to, the government of this State," (false); "they had, at an inclement season of the year, driven the inhabitants of an entire county from their homes, ravaging their crops and destroying their dwellings.' "Now, if the Governor had reversed this statement it would have been true; the falsity of it I stand prepared to prove anywhere. Mr. Governor it was your bull that gored our ox. We were robbed, pillaged and exiled, were you? Our men, women and children were murdered without redress; driven from their homes in an inclement season of the year, and died by hundreds, in the State of Illinois, in consequence of hardships and exposure.

"The legislature of Missouri, to cover their infamy, appropriated the munificent sum of £2,000 to help the suffering Mormons. Their agent took a few miserable traps, the sweepings of an old store; for the balance of the patrimony he sent into Davis County and killed our hogs, which we were then prevented from doing, and brought them to feed the poor Mormons as part of the legislative appropriation. This I saw. On this subject I could quote volumes. I will only say that when authenticated testimony was presented to Martin Van Buren, the President of the United States, he replied, 'Your cause is just; but I can do nothing for you.' "Mr. Colfax, in summing up, says, 'There is nothing in this as to their religion.' Read the following: "Tuesday, November 6th, 1838, General Clark made the following remarks to a number of men in Far West, Mo.: "' Gentlemen, you whose names are not attached to this list of names will now have the privilege of going to your fields and providing corn and wood for your families. Another article yet remains for you to comply with, that is, that you leave the State forthwith, and whatever may be your feelings concerning this, or whatever your innocence is nothing to me. The orders of the Governor to me were that you should be exterminated. I would advise you to scatter abroad and never again organize yourselves with bishops, presidents, etc., lest you excite the jealousies of the people.' "Is not this persecution for religion?

"Mr. Colfax next takes us to Nauvoo and says, 'In Nauvoo they remained until 1846; the disturbances which finally caused them to leave the city were not in consequence of their religious creed. Foster and Law, who had been Mormons, renounced the faith and established an anti-Mormon paper at Nauvoo called the Expositor. In May, 1844, the prophet and a party of his followers, on the publication of his first number, attacked the office, tore it down and destroyed the press.' "This is a mistake. The Expositor was an infamous sheet, containing vile and libelous attacks upon individuals, and the citizens generally, and would not have been allowed to exist in any other community a day. The people complained to the authorities about it; after mature deliberation the city council passed an ordinance ordering its removal as a nuisance, and it was removed. In a conversation with Governor Ford, on this subject, afterwards, when informed of the circumstances, he said to me, 'I cannot blame you for destroying it, but I wish it had been done by a mob.' I told him that we preferred a legal course, and that Blackstone described a libelous press as a nuisance and liable to be removed; that our city charter gave us the power to remove nuisances; and that if it was supposed we had contravened the law, we were amenable for our acts and refused not an investigation. Mr. Colfax's history says, 'The authorities thereupon called out the militia to enforce the law, and the Mormons armed themselves to resist it. The facts were that armed mobs were organized in the neighborhood of Carthage and Warsaw. The Governor came to Carthage and sent a deputation to Joseph Smith, requesting him to send another to him, with authentic documents in relation to the late difficulties. Dr. J. M. Bernhisel, our late delegate to Congress, and myself, were deputed as a committee to wait upon the Governor. His Excellency thought it best (although we had had a hearing before) for us to have a rehearing on the press question. We called his attention to the unsettled state of the country, and the general mob spirit that prevailed; and asked if we must bring a guard; that we felt fully competent to protect ourselves but were afraid it would create a collision. He said, 'We had better come entirely unarmed,' and pledged his faith and the faith of the State for our protection. We went unarmed to Carthage, trusting in the Governor's word. Owing to the unsettled state of affairs we entered into recognizances to appear at another time. A warrant was issued for the arrest of Joseph and Hyrum Smith, for treason. They were remanded to jail, and while there were murdered. Not ' by a party of mob,' as Mr. Colfax's history states, 'from Missouri,' but by men in Illinois, who, with blackened faces, perpetrated the hellish deed; they did not overpower the guard, as stated, the guard helped them in the performance of their fiendish act. I saw them for I was there at the time. I could a tile unfold that would implicate editors, officers, military and civil, ministers of the gospel, and other wolves in sheep's clothing.

"The following will show in part what our position was: "'A proclamation to the citizens of Hancock County :—Whereas, a mob of from one to two hundred men, under arms have gathered themselves together in the southwest part of Hancock County, and are at this time destroying the dwellings, and other buildings, stacks of grain and other property, of a portion of our citizens in the most inhuman manner, compelling the defenseless women and children to leave their sick beds and exposing them to the rays of the parching sun, there to lie and suffer without aid or assistance of a friendly hand, to minister to their wants, in their suffering condition. The rioters spare not the widow nor orphan, and while I am writing this proclamation, the smoke is arising to the clouds, and the flame is devouring four buildings which have just been set on fire by the rioters. Thousands of dollars worth of property has already been consumed, an entire settlement of about sixty or seventy families laid waste, the in habitants thereof are fired upon, narrowly escaping with their lives, and forced to die before the ravages of the mob. Therefore I command said rioters and other peace breakers to desist, forthwith, and I hereby call upon the law-abiding citizens, as a. posse commitatus of Hancock County, to give their united aid in suppressing the rioters and maintaining the supremacy of the law.

J. B. Backenstos,
Sheriff of Hancock Counly, Ills.'
"Mr. Backenstos was not a Mormon.

"We set out in search of an asylum, in some far-off wilderness, where we hoped we could enjoy religious liberty. Previous to our departure a committee composed of Stephen A. Douglass Gen. John J. Harding, both members of Congress, the Attorney General of Illinois, Major Warren and others, met in my house, in Nauvoo, in conference with the Twelve, to consult about our departure. They were then presented the picture of devastation that would follow our exodus, and felt ashamed to have to acknowledge that State and United States authorities had to ask a persecuted and outraged people to leave their property, homes and firesides for their oppressors to enjoy; not because we had not a good Constitution and liberal government, but because there was not virtue and power in the State and United States authorities to protect them in their rights. We made a treaty with them to leave; after this treaty, when the strong men and the majority of the people had left, and there was nothing but old and infirm men, buys, women and children to battle with, like ravenous wolves, impatient for their prey, they violated their treaty by making war upon them, and driving them houseless, homeless, and destitute across the Mississippi river.

"The archaeologist, the antiquarian, and the traveler need not then have gone to Herculaneum, to Pompeii, to Egypt or Yucatan, in search of ruins or deserted cities; they could have found a deserted temple, forsaken family altars, desolate hearth stones and homes, a deserted city much easier: the time, the nineteenth century; the place, the United States of America; the State, Illinois, and the city, Nauvoo.

"While fleeing, as fugitives, from the United States, and in Indian territory, a requisition was made by the Government for 500 men to assist in conquering Mexico, the very nation to whose Territory we were fleeing in our exile; we supplied the demand and though despoiled and expatriated, were the principal agents in planting the United States flag in Upper California.

"I again quote: "'In September, 1850, Congress organized Utah Territory, and President Fillmore appointed Brigham Young (who at Smith's death had become President of the Church) as Governor. The next year the Federal judges were compelled by Brigham Young's threats of violence to flee from the Territory, and the laws of the United States were openly defied. Col. Steptoe was commissioned Governor in place of Young, but after wintering with a battalion of soldiers at Salt

Lake, he resigned, not deeming it safe or prudent to accept.' "So far from this being the case, Col. Steptoe was on the best of terms with our community, and previous to his appointment as Governor, a number of our prominent Gentile citizens, judges, Col. Steptoe and some of his officers signed a petition to the President praying for the continuance of President Young in office.

He continues: 'In February, 1856, a mob of armed Mormons, instigated by sermons from the heads of the Church, broke into the United States court room and at the point of the bowie knife compelled Judge Drummond to adjourn his court sine die;" (this is a sheer fabrication, there never was such an occurrence in Utah) 'and very soon all the United States officers, except the Indian Agent, were compelled to flee from the Territory.' Now this same amiable and persecuted Judge Drummond brought with him a courtesan from Washington, whom he introduced as his wife, and had her with him on the bench. The following will show the mistake in regard to Col. Steptoe and others:

"' To His Excellency Franklin Pierce, President of the United States:

"' Your petitioners would respectfully represent that, Whereas, Governor Brigham Young possesses the entire confidence of the people of this Territory, without distinction of party or sect, and from personal acquaintance and social intercourse, we find him to be a firm supporter of the Constitution and laws of the United States, and a tried pillar of Republican institutions; and having repeatedly listened to his remarks, in private as well as in public assemblies, do know he is a warm friend and able supporter of Constitutional liberty, the rumors published in the States, to the contrary, notwithstanding; and having canvassed to our satisfaction, his doings as Governor and Superintendent of Indian affairs, and also the distribution of appropriations for public buildings for the Territory, we do most cordially and cheerfully represent that the same has been expended to the best interest of the nation; and whereas, his appointment would better subserve the Territorial interest than the appointment of any other man, "' We therefore take great pleasure in recommending him to your favorable consideration, and do earnestly request his appointment as Governor, and Superintendent of Indian affairs for this Territory.

"' Salt Lake City, Utah Territory, December 30th, 1854. J. F. Kinney, Chief Justice Supreme Court; Leonidas Shaver, Assistant Justice; E. J. Steptoe, Lt. Col. U. S. Army; John F. Reynolds, Bvt. Maj.; Rufus Ingales, Capt.; Sylvester Mowry, La Chett, L. Livingston, John C. Chandler, Robert O. Tyler, Benj. Allston, Lieutenants; Chas. A. Perry, Wm. G. Rankin, Horace R. Kirby, Medical Staff; U. S. A. Henry, C. Branch, C. C. Branham, C. J. Bipne, Lucian L. Bedell, Wm. Mac, J. M. Hochaday and other strangers.'

"There was really no more cause for an army then than there is now, and there is no more reason now, in reality, than there was then, and the bills of Messrs. Cragin and Cullom are only a series of the same infamies that we have before experienced, and are designed, as all unbiassed men know, to create a difficulty and collision, aided by the clamor of speculators and contractors, who have of course, a very disinterested desire to relieve their venerated uncle "by thrusting their patriotic hands into his pockets.

"I am sorry to be under the painful necessity of repudiating Mr. Colfax's history. It is said that ' corporations have no souls,' and nations are not proverbially conscientious about their nomenclature or records. Diplomacy generally finds language suited to its objects. When the British nation granted to the East India Company their stupendous monopoly, that company subjugated and brought really into serfdom about one hundred millions of human beings; and compelled many to raise poison (opium) instead of bread. History calls that 'trade and commerce.' After the Chinese had made a law making the introduction of opium contraband, in defiance of this law they sent cargoes of the tabooed article and illicitly introduced their poison. The Chinese, unwilling to be poisoned, confiscated and destroyed these contraband goods. History calls it a casus belli, and when the Chinese, unwilling to be coerced, resisted the British force, that nation slaughtered vast hordes of them, because they had the power; history calls it war. When they forced them to pay millions of dollars for the trouble they had in killing them, history calls it indemnification for the expenses of the war. When President Polk wanted to possess himself of the then Mexican Territory of Upper California, he sent General Taylor, with an army of occupation, into disputed Mexican territory, well knowing that an honorable nation would resent it as an insult, and that would be considered a casus belli and afford a pretext for making war upon the weak nation, and possessing ourselves of the coveted Territory; history calls it conquest and reprisals. It is true that we acted more honorably than Great Britain in awarding some compensation. President Buchanan, goaded by the Republicans, wished to show them that in regard to the Mormons he dared out-Herod Herod, by fitting up an army to make war upon the Mormons; but it was necessary to have a pretext. It would not have been popular to destroy a whole community in cold blood, so he sent out a few miserable minions and renegades for the purpose of provoking a collision. These men not only acted infamously here, but published false statements throughout the United States, and every kind of infamy—as is now being done by just such characters—was laid at the door of the Mormons. They said, among other things, that we had burned the U. S. records. These statements were afterwards denied by Governor Cumming. Mr. Buchanan had another object in view, and Mr. J. B. Floyd, Secretary of War, had also his axe to grind, and the whole combined "was considered a grand coup d'état. It is hardly necessary to inform Mr. Colfax that this army, under pretense of subjugating the Mormons, was intended to coerce the people of Kansas to his views, and that they were not detained, as stated by Mr. Colfax's history, which said: "the troops, necessarily moving slowly, were overtaken by the snows in November, and wintered at Bridger.' I need not inform Mr. Colfax that another part of this grand tableau originated in the desire of Secretary Floyd to scatter the U. S. forces and arms, preparatory to the Confederate rebellion. Such is history and such are facts.

"We were well informed as to the object of the coming of the army, we had men in all of the camps, and knew what was intended. There was a continual boast among the men and officers, even before they left the Missouri river, of what they would do with the Mormons. The houses were picked out that certain persons were to inhabit; farms, property and women were to be distributed.

'Beauty and booty,' were their watchword. We were to have another grand Norman conquest, and our houses, gardens, orchards, vineyards, fields, wives and daughters were to be the spoils. Instead of this Mr. Buchanan kept them too long about Kansas; the Lord put a hook in their jaws, and instead of reveling in sacked towns and cities and glutting their libidinous and riotous desires in ravishing, destroying and laying waste, they knawed dead mules' legs at Bridger, rendered palatable by the ice, frost and snow of a mountain winter, seasoned by the pestiferous exhalations of hecatomb of dead animals, the debris of a ruined army, at a cost to the nation of about forty millions. We had reason to say then 'the Lord reigns, let the earth be glad.' Oh, how wicked it was for President Young to resist an army like the above, prostituted by the guardians of a free and enlightened republic to the capacity of buccaneers and brigands!

"In the spring rumors prevailed of an intended advance of the army. Preferring compromise to conflict, we left Salt Lake City and the northern part of the Territory en masse and prepared ourselves, for what we then considered a coming conflict. After first preparing combustible materials and leaving a sufficient number of men in every settlement to destroy everything; had we been driven to it we should have made such a conflagration as never was witnessed in the U. S. Every house would have been burned and leveled to the ground, every barn, grain and hay stack, every meeting house, court house and store demolished; every fruit tree and shrub would have been cut down; every fence burned and the country would have been left a howling wilderness as we found it. We were determined that if we could not enjoy our homes in peace, that never again should our enemies revel in our possessions.

"I now come to Mr. Colfax's next heading, 'their polygamy:' "As this is simply a rehash of his former arguments, without answering mine, I beg to be excused inserting his very lengthy quotation, as this article is already long. In regard to our tolerations of all religions, Mr. C. entertains very singular ideas. We do invite men of almost all persuasions to preach to us in our tabernacles, but we are not so latitudinarian in our principles as to furnish meeting houses for all; we never considered this a part of the programme. Meeting houses are generally closed against us everywhere, and men are advised not to go and hear us; we open ours, and say to our congregation go and hear them, but we do not engage to furnish all. Neither is the following statement correct: 'About the same time he (Mr. Taylor) was writing it, Godbe and others were being expelled from the Church for disbelieving the infallibility of Brigham Young.' No person, as I before stated, was ever expelled from the Church for doubting the infallibility of President Young; it is but just to say that President Young, himself disclaims it. Mr. C. again repeats his argument in relation to the suttee, or burning of widows in India, and after giving a very elaborate and correct account of its suppression by English authority says:— "'Wherever English power recognized there this so-called religious rite is now sternly forbid demand prevented. England with united voice said stop!

and India obeyed.' "To present Mr. Colfax's argument fairly, it stands thus: The burning of Hindoo widows was considered a religious rite, by the Hindus. The British were horrified at the practice and suppressed it. The Mormons believe polygamy to be a religious rite. The American nation consider it a scandal and that they ought to put it down. Without entering into all the details, I think the above a fair statement of the question. He says ' the claim that religious faith commanded it was powerless, and it went down, as a relic of barbarism.' He says: 'History tells us what a civilized nation, akin to ours, actually did, where they had the power.' I wish to treat this argument with candor, although I do not look upon the British nation as a fit example for us; it was not so thought in the time of the Revolution. I hope we would not follow them in charging their cannon with Sepoys and shooting them off in this same India. I am glad, also, to find that our Administration views and acts upon the question of neutrality more honorably than our trans-Atlantic cousins. But to the point. The British suppressed the suttee in India, and therefore we must be equally moral and suppress polygamy in the United States. Hold! not so fast; let us state facts as they are and remove the dust. The British suppressed the suttee but tolerated eighty-three millions of polygamists in India. The suppression of the suttee and that of polygamy are two very different things. If the British are indeed to be our examplars, Congress had better wait until polygamy is suppressed in India. But it is absurd to compare the suttee to polygamy; one is murder and the destruction of life, the other is national economy and the increase and perpetuation of life. Suttee ranks truly with Infanticide, both of which are destructive of human life. Polygamy is salvation compared with either and tends even more than monogamy to increase and perpetuate the human race.

"I have now waded through Mr. Colfax's charges and have proven the falsity of his assertions and the tergiversation of his historical data. I will not say his but his adopted history; for it is but fair to say that he disclaims vouching for its accuracy.

"Permit me here again to assert my right as a public teacher, to address myself to Congress and the nation, and to call their attention to something that is more demoralizing, debasing, and destructive than polygamy. As an offset to my former remarks on these things, we are referred to our mortality of infants as "exceeding anything else known."

"Mr. Colfax is certainly in error here. In France, according to late statistical reports on *la mort d'enfants*, they were rated at from fifty to eighty per cent, of the whole under one year old. The following is from the Salt Lake City sexton's report for 1869:

"' Total interments during the year, 484; deducting persons brought from the country places for interment, and transients, 93; leaving the mortality of this city, 391.

Jos. E. Taylor, Sexton.

"'Having been often asked the question: Whether the death-rate was not considerably greater among polygamic families than monogamic, I will answer: Of the 292 children buried from Salt Lake City last year (1869), 64 were children of polygamists; while 228 were children of monogamists; and further, that out of this number, there was not even one case of infanticide.

Respectfully, Jos. E. Taylor.

"We had a sickly season last year among children; but when it is considered that we have twice as many children as any other place, in proportion to the number of inhabitants, the death-rate is very low, especially among polygamists.

"But supposing it was true, 'the argumentum ad hominum' which Mr. Colfax says he ' might use,' would scarcely be an argumentum ad judicum; for if all the children in Salt Lake City or Utah died, it would certainly not do away with that horrible crime, infanticide. Would Mr. Colfax say that because a great number of children in Utah, who were children of polygamists, died, that, therefore, infanticide in the United States is justifiable? and that the acts of Madame Restelle and her pupils were right and proper? I know he would not, his ideas are more pure, generous and exalted. Mr. Colfax says of us, 'I do not charge infant murder, of course." Now I do charge that infant murder prevails to an alarming extent in the United States. The following will show how near right I am. Extract from a book entitled, Serpents in a Dove's Nest, by Rev. John Todd, D. D. Boston. Lee and Shepherd.

"Under the head of 'Fashionable Murder," we read the following: "'By the advertisements of almost every paper, city and village in the land, offering medicines to be effectual 'from whatever causes' it is needed; by the shameless and notorious great establishments, fitted up and advertised as places where any woman may resort to effect the end desired, and which now number in the city of New York alone over four hundred, advertised and abundantly patronized, houses devoted to the work of abortionating; by the confession of hundreds of women made to physicians, who have been injured by the process; and by the almost constant and unblushing applications made to the profession from 'women in all classes of society, married and unmarried, rich and poor and otherwise, good, bad or indifferent,' to aid them in the thing—do we know of the frequency of this crime?' (p. 4 and 5.) 'I would not advise anyone to challenge further disclosures, else we can show that France, with all her atheism, that Paris, with all her license, is not as guilty, in this respect, as is staid New England at the present hour. Facts can be adduced that will make the ears tingle; but we don't want to divulge them; but we do want the womanhood of our day to understand that the thing can be no longer concealed; that commonness of fashion cannot do away with its awful guilt; it is deliberate and cold-blooded murder.' (p. 13, 14.) "These facts are corroborated by Dr. Story in a book, entitled, Why Not.

Lee and Shepherd, Boston. By the New York Medical Journal, September, 1866, by the Boston Commonwealth, Springfield, (Mass.) Worcester Palladium, Northampton Free Press, Salem Observer, and, as stated above, 'by the advertisements of almost every paper, city and village in the land.' I have statistics before me now, from a physician, stating the amount of prostitution, feticide and infanticide in Chicago; but bad as Chicago is represented to be, these statements are so enormous and revolting that I cannot believe them. Neither is the statement made by some of the papers, in regard to Mr. Colfax's association with the Richardson case, reliable. Men in his position have their enemies, and it is not credible that a gentleman holding such strong prejudice about, what he considers, the immorality of the Mormons, and whose moral ideas, in relation to virtue and chastity, are so pure, could lend himself as an accomplice to the very worst and most revolting phase of Free Loveism. And I would here solicit the aid of Mr. Colfax, with his superior intelligence, his brilliant talents and honorable position, to help stop the blighting, withering curse of prostitution, feticide and infanticide.

"I call upon philosophers and philanthropists to stop it; know ye not that the transgression of every law of nature brings its own punishment, and that as noble a race of men as ever existed on the earth are becoming emasculated and destroyed by it? I call upon physicians to stop it; you are the guardians of the people's health, and justice requires that you should use all your endeavors to stop the demoralization and destruction of our race. I call upon ministers of the gospel to stop it; know ye not the wail of murdered infants is ascending into the ears of the Lord of Sabaoth and that the whole nation is hastening to destruction whilst you are singing lullaby songs to murderers and murderesses? I call upon statesmen to stop it; know ye not that the statisticians inform us that our original stock is running out, and that in consequence of this crime we are being supplanted by foreigners, and that the enemies of the negro race are already exulting in the hope of their speedy extinction, by copying your vices. I call upon the fair daughters of America and their abettors their husbands and paramours to pause in their career of crime; you came of an honorable and pure stock, your fathers, mothers and grandmothers' hands were not stained with the blood of innocence; they could press their pillows in peace, without the fear of a visit from the shades of their wailing offspring. I call upon municipal and State authorities and especially upon Congress to stop this withering, cursing and damning blight.

I call upon all honorable men and women to use their influence to stop this growing evil. I conjure you by the love of God, by the ties of consanguinity, by a respect for our race and a love for our nation, by the moans of murdered infants and the fear of an avenging retribution, help stop this cursed evil!

"In the province of Gazaret, Hindustan, parents have been in the habit of destroying infant children as soon as born; and at the festival held at Gunga Sergoor, children were sacrificed to the Ganges from time immemorial; both of these the British nation suppressed. Shall we practice crimes in civilized and Christian America, that England will not allow heathens to perform, but put them down by the strong arm of the law? You indeed tell us that these things are " banned by you, banned by the law, banned by morality and public opinion;" your bans are but a mockery and a fraud, as are your New England temperance laws; your law reaches one in a thousand who is so unfortunate as to be publicly exposed. These crimes, of which I write, run riot in the land, a withering, cursing blight. The affected purity of the nation is a myth; like the whited walls and painted sepulchers, of which Jesus spake, "within there is nothing but rottenness and dead men's bones." Who, and what is banned by you? What power is there in your interdiction over the thirty thousand prostitutes and mistresses of New York and their amiable pimps and paramours? What of the thousands in the city of brotherly love, in Boston, in your large eastern, northern and southern cities? What of Washington? What of your four hundred murder establishments in New York and your New England operations in the same line? You are virtuous are you?

God deliver us from such virtue. It may be well to talk about your purity and bans to those who are ignorant; it is too bare-faced for the informed. I say, as I said before, why don't you stop this damning, cursed evil? I am reminded of the Shakesperian spouter who cried, 'I can call spirits from the vasty deep!' 'So can I,' said his hearer, 'but they won't come!' Now we do control these horrid vices and crimes, do you want to force them upon us? Such things are

"'A blot that will remain a blot in spite
Of all that grave apologists may write;
And, though a bishop try to cleanse the stain.
He rubs and scours the crimson spot in vain.'

"We have now a Territory out of debt; our cities, counties and towns are out of debt. We have no gambling, no drunkenness, no prostitution, feticide nor infanticide. We maintain our wives and children, and we have made the 'desert to blossom as the rose.' We are at peace with ourselves and with all the world. Whom have we injured? Why can we not be let alone?

"What are we offered by you in your proposed legislation? for it is well for us to count the cost. First—confiscation of property, our lands, houses, gardens, fields, vineyards, and orchards, legislated away by men who have no property, carpetbaggers, pettifoggers, adventurers, robbers, for you offer by your bills a premium for fraud and robbery. The first robs us of our property and leaves us the privilege, though despoiled, of retaining our honor, and of worshipping God according to the dictates of our own conscience. We have been robbed before; this we could stand again. Now for the second—the great privilege which you offer by obedience: Loss of honor and self-respect; a renunciation of God and our religion; the prostitution of our wives and children to a level with your civilization; to be cursed with your debauchery; to be forced to countenance infanticide in our midst, and have your professional artists advertise their dens of murder among us; to swarm, as you do, with pimps and harlots and their paramours; to have gambling, drunkenness, whoredom, and all the pestiferous effects of debauchery; to be involved in debt and crime, forced upon us; to despise ourselves, to be despised by our wives, children and friends, and to be despised and cursed of God, in time and in eternity. This you offer us and your religion to boot. It is true you tell us you will 'ban it' but your bans are a myth; you would open the flood gates of crime and debauchery, infanticide, drunkenness and gambling, and practically tie them up with a strand of a spider's web. You cannot stop these; if you would you have not the power. We have, and prefer purity, honor, and a clear conscience, and our motto today is, as it ever has been, and I hope ever will be 'the Kingdom of God or nothing.' "Respectfully, "John Taylor."

CHAPTER XLVII.

BIRTH OF THE UTAH LIBERAL PARTY. POLITICAL COALITION OF GENTILES AND MORMON SCHISMATICS. CONTEST AT THE MUNICIPAL ELECTION OF 1870. REPORT OF THE FIRST CENTRAL COMMITTEE OF THE LIBERAL PARTY.

In the beginning of the year 1870, in January and February, a political plan was devised to unite the Godbeites with the Gentiles. Both were few in number; even when united they were but an insignificant minority, compared with the party since known as the " People's" party. The coalition, however, was considered promising and prospectively formidable. On the one side, the schismatic Mormon elders and merchants were likely to have a large following throughout the Territory or, at least, it was expected that the schism would increase greatly and extend to every settlement, even though it should lack cohesion. Nothing seemed more probable than that there were thousands of men and women, who had grown up in the Mormon community, or been long connected with it, apart from any spiritualistic "New Movement" incubated at nightly seances at New York, who occupied similar positions, and entertained similar views regarding Mormonism, to those of Mr. Godbe and his compeers, and the Walker Brothers, Chislett and their class, who had left the Church years before. There were also many influential men who remained in the Mormon Church who said to Mr. Godbe and his friends, "You should have remained in the Church and fought out your issues. It was a great mistake to set up new a church."

And thus the " New Movement," or new " Church of Zion" was soon generally looked upon to be in and of itself a failure, while to the faithful Mormons, whose head of the Church was so prominent and sound, whose will so strong and organism matchless, this church of Zion, without a head, or even the power to organize a quorum of elders, was a thing of scorn. Henry W. Lawrence keenly felt this and forecasted failure in the object of the schism. The only resolution of any social potency was in a quick uniting of the Godbeites with the Gentiles, and the formation of a political party by such a coalition.

"The design was projected, and early in February, 1870, a political caucus was called, of the leading men concerned, to give birth to that party now known as the "Liberal" party. The meeting was held in the Masonic Hall. Eli B. Kelsey was chosen chairman, whereupon the leaders made their preliminary speeches, formulated methods for the city election close at hand, with Henry W. Lawrence at the head of their ticket for Mayor of Salt Lake City. The Gentiles, with political sagacity, kept in the background, merely playing the parts as advisers, helpers and voters. Of course the object of this maneuver was to make their coalition party a political entering-wedge 'into' the Mormon Church, by calling out the Mormon friends of the men on the ticket. The preliminary work having been done,' the meeting adjourned to be held next at Walker Brother's old store, where the " New Movement " held its service and public meetings; Eli B. Kelsey was continued as chairman, and a committee was appointed to make a public call for the ratification of the Liberal ticket.

Accordingly the city was duly, placarded, informing the public of the meeting and its object; and the invitation given was" Come one, come all!" It was an unfortunate wording; for it was addressed to the "people" of Salt Lake City to "come one, come all" to nominate their municipal officers for the forthcoming election. The Mormons were "the people"—"The People's party"—a name, indeed, which came into political significance from that very election.

The People's party resolved to accept the invitation and give the Liberals a surprise. It was a party coup d'état, perhaps, not quite fair, yet without that fell design which the Liberal party has marked in the first chapter of its own history.

It was in fact, merely a political move of party managers to show the people how futile an opposition party was, and how easily overwhelmed.

But it is necessary to the completeness of the historical data of our city, as due to the Utah Liberal party, which has since repeatedly contested the elections for Delegate to Congress to give its first chapter as presented by its own central committee at the time.

The Deseret News of February 10, 1870, thus called attention to " the Mass Meeting:"

"By a placard which is posted up in several places in the city, signed ' many voters,' we see that it is the intention to hold a public Mass Meeting this, Thursday, Evening, at half past six o'clock, in the building known as Walker Brothers' original store, on East Temple Street. The object of the meeting, set forth by the placard, is ' for the nomination of a People's Free and Independent Ticket for Mayor, Aldermen, Councilors, etc., to be voted for on Monday, the 14th instant.' "The placard is headed in large letters, 'Come One, Come All.' A full meeting is desired, and as the object is one of general interest to all classes of our citizens, we hope there will be a crowded attendance. We want to see a good ticket nominated for city officers and the occasion is one in which every citizen should be interested."

On Saturday, February 12, 1870, the following appeared in the 7th number of the Mormon Tribune, published by Godbe & Harrison:

"A CARD BY THE COMMITTEE.

"The Mass Meeting, called by many voters, in Walker Brothers' original store, Thursday evening, February 10, was overwhelmed by a characteristic maneuvering on the part of the Church authorities. The Deseret Evening News promptly announced the meeting and gave a significant hint for a grand coup d'état. And we are well informed that A. Milton Musser went to the different wards of the city and instructed the bishops and teachers to have the people of their wards turn out en masse, and defeat the object for which the meeting was called.

The principal of the Deseret University, also instructed his pupils to be on hand. A large crowd took possession of the street in front of the building long before the hour appointed for the meeting. The pressing demand for admittance, rendered it necessary to open the doors a six o'clock, whereupon the crowd rushed in with screams and yells, jumping over and breaking the seats in the most reckless manner. At the head of the crowd marched J. D. T. McAllister, acting bishop of the Eighth Ward and Territorial marshal, and Bishop J. C. Little. Mr. Eli B. Kelsey stated that this was an adjourned meeting of which he was the regular chairman; but as they took possession by force they were welcome to do so.

Without a moment's delay, Bishop J. C. Little was nominated for chairman of the meeting, Mr. E. L. Sloan was elected secretary, and Mr. Grimshaw reporter.

Bishop Little called for nominations, when the whole orthodox ticket was nominated one by one by acclamation; the more sober and thoughtful portion of the audience ignoring the whole proceedings, considering that a gross outrage had been perpetrated by the Church officials. We sincerely regret the unmistakable animus betrayed in the whole affair; and we feel more than ever the need of a change.

"We call upon every free American citizen to rally to the polls on Monday next, and vote the Independent ticket, thereby manifesting their disapproval of proceedings rarely equaled—certainly never outdone in the Kansas elections."

"Independent Ticket: Mayor—Henry W. Lawrence; aldermen—First Municipal Ward, Samuel Xahn; Second Municipal Ward, J. R. Walker; Third Municipal Ward, Orson Pratt, Jr.; Fourth Municipal Ward, E. D. Woolley; Fifth Municipal Ward, James Gordon. Councilors—Nat Stein, Anthony Godbe, John Cunnington, John Lowe, Marsena Cannon, Fred T. Perris, Dr. W. F. Anderson, Wm. Sloan, Peter Rensheimer; city recorder, Wm. P. Appleby; city treasurer, B. G. Raybould; city marshal, Ed. Butterfield.

"By order of the
"Central Committee."

The following correspondence passed between the Liberal central committee and the mayor:

"Salt Lake City, Feb. 12, 1870.
" Daniel H. Wells, mayor Salt Lake City.
"Dear Sir :—You are doubtless aware there is an Independent ticket nominated by many voters of this city to be submitted to the people for their suffrage, at the municipal election on Monday, the 14th instant. We, therefore, respectfully ask, on behalf of those wishing to sustain said ticket, that one judge of election and one clerk be appointed from the Independent party, by you or the city council, to act in these positions at said election; and would respectfully ask that John M. Worley, and William P. Appleby be appointed for those positions, which is according to the usages of the country.

"This committee is desirous that none but legal votes shall be cast at the coming election, and to this end ask of you the assurance that the usual challenges and ballot box shall be protected by you and the police force of this city. Will you please return an answer by bearer?

"By order of the committee,
"J. M. Orr, Chairman."

"Mayor's Office, Salt Lake City, Feb. 13th, 1870.
"J. M. Orr, Esq., Chair. Cen. Com.
"Sir :—Your note dated 12th inst. asking for a change to be made in the board of judges and clerks of election is just received, and I hasten to answer.

"Col. Jesse C. Little, Seymour B. Young and John Needham, Esqs., have been chosen judges, and F. A. Mitchell and R. V. Morris, Esqs., clerks of said election.

" These gentlemen were selected and appointed to act as said judges and clerks by the city council on Tuesday, 1st inst., and, I am sanguine, command the confidence of the entire people, and will doubtless act justly and wisely in the performance of the duties thus devolved upon them.

"Rest assured that every protection will be afforded for voters to vote their respective tickets without partiality or hindrance.

"If, as is sometimes the case, during the day, the polls should be crowded, I would recommend the voters to be patient, for all will have the opportunity afforded to them to vote during the day. And it is designed to enforce the strictest order.

Respectfully,

D. H. Wells, Mayor."

The municipal election on the Monday, February 14th, was quite peaceful, showing on either side but little of the animus which the commencement seemed to promise. The Deseret News merely noted the result of the election, with an item relative to the counting of votes. The Liberal party were the speakers to the public on the occasion, as will be seen from the report of the first central committee of the Liberal party.

"To the editors of the Mormon Tribune: "The undersigned, a committee representing the Independent voters of Salt Lake City and County, desire to state to the public the circumstances connected with the organization of the first Independent political party in this Territory, as also the facts of the recent election.

"On Wednesday, February 9th, a meeting was held at the Masonic Hall, of those opposed to the existing state of our city government. An organization was effected, a central committee was appointed to serve for one year, and a ticket for city officers, composed of old and respected citizens without regard to creed or religious belief, nominated-by acclamation. A mass meeting was also appointed for the following night to be held at Walkers' original store, for the ratification of the nominations, and an exchange of views on the questions before the people. Long previous to the hour appointed, the street in front of, and the building itself, were taken possession of by a crowd of men, determined to defeat the purposes of the meeting. We have already stated in the Tribune the result of their endeavors, the same number of your journal, however, contained the original, regularly nominated Independent ticket, as submitted to the people on Monday last. During the election many irregularities, to say the least, were reported to us (by a sub-committee of challengers appointed by us) which we were and are powerless to remedy. They state that— "Many voted who were not citizens of the United States.

"Many who were not citizens of Salt Lake City.

"Many who were not of lawful age; and the ballot boxes when filled were set aside and not properly sealed or guarded.

"It is needless to recapitulate the numerous obstacles thrown in the way of those desirous of voting the Independent ticket, or the annoyances to which our challengers were subjected. Suffice it to say that without these, and the existing law of the Territory compelling the numbering and identifying of each vote, a system practically robbing every citizen of his freedom of ballot, the result would have been far different. The means used by our opponents to prevent a fair election and an impartial count prove their fears on this point.

"The result of the election, as announced by the judges—no member of our committee being allowed to be present at the counting of the votes—shows an average of about three hundred votes for the Independent ticket, and we regard our commencement in the great work of vindicating the rights of free speech, free thought and a free press in this Territory a promising one. To sum up the reward of five days' work: After twenty years of self-constituted city government, to which we have paid thousands in taxation, without an exhibit of receipts or expenses, and for that time not daring to express a sentiment in opposition to those held by the dominant party, we have in the election of Monday last demonstrated to the country the existence of American institutions in this Territory, and believe that the seed sown on that day will bear such fruits that before many months the State of Utah, freed from all relics of past tyranny and oppression, will be found marching with the great sisterhood of States, keeping step with the progress of the Union.

"In concluding we would return thanks to those of our fellow citizens who have by their confidence placed us in our responsible and prominent positions before the public. The responsibility we realize,—the publicity was unsought.

The duties of our positions we will discharge, as long as honored by their confidence, in the fear of God and love of humanity, unshaken loyalty to our country and with 'charity for all' who differ from us and 'malice towards none.'

"Respectfully,
"J. M. Orr,
"J. R. Walker,
"Joseph Salisbury,
"T. D. Brown,
"James Brooks,
"Samuel Kahn,
"R. H. Robertson,
"Central Committee."

The People's ticket of that year was: Mayor—Daniel H. Wells; aldermen—First Municipal Ward, Isaac Groo; Second, Samuel W. Richards; Third, A. H. Raleigh; Fourth, Jeter Clinton; Fifth, A. C Pyper. Councilors—Robert T. Burton, Theodore McKean, Thos. Jenkins, Heber P. Kimball, Henry Grow, John Clark, Thos. McLellan, John R. Winder, Lewis S. Hills; Recorder—Robert Campbell; treasurer—Paul A. Schettler; marshal—John D. T. McAllister.

CHAPTER XLVIII.

PASSAGE OF THE WOMAN'S SUFFRAGE BILL. GRAND MASS MEETING OF THE "SISTERS" PROTESTING AGAINST THE CULLOM BILL, THEN BEFORE CONGRESS. EXTRAORDINARY RESOLUTIONS AND HEROIC SPEECHES OF THE WOMEN OF MORMONDOM.

The year 1870 was also signalized by the passage of the female suffrage bill, which event was destined to make Mormon Utah politically distinguished among all the advocates of woman's suffrage throughout the world.

The Phrenological Journal for November, 1870, in its biographical article on "William H. Hooper, the Utah Delegate and female suffrage advocate," says: "Utah is a land of marvels. She gives us, first, polygamy, which seems to be an outrage against ' woman's rights,' and then offers the nation a 'female suffrage bill,' at this time in full force within her own borders. Was there ever a greater anomaly known in the history of society? The women of Utah hold' political power to-day. They are the first in the nation to whom the functions of the state have been extended, and it is just as consistent to look for a female member of Congress from Utah as a member of Congress sent to Washington by the women's vote. Let the women be once recognized as powers in the state as well as in society and in the church, and their political rights can be extended to any length, according to the temper of the public mind, of which the female element forms so large a part.

"There is in our innovative age much discussion on the abstract justice, and also on the practical propriety of extending political power to the women of America; and the women of England have made the same demand in the political motions of our old Saxon fatherland. This may be caused by one of the great impulses of the times, for we are certainly living in an age of impulses. It is also an age of marvels; not merely in steam and electricity, but in our social states and philosophies of society. Indeed, until modern times, the phrase 'social science' was not known; but these new problems and marvels of society have led statesmen and philosophers to recognize a positive 'social science,' and the term sociology to-day is just as legitimate as the term geology. And it is very singular that those advanced minds who are beginning to reduce government and the social development to systems of positive philosophy, bring in the function of political power for woman. Of course your political gamblers and legislative charlatans are against the innovations which female suffrage bills would work out in the age; but such philosophical lawgivers of society and government as John Stuart Mill, and also statesmen like Cobden and Bright of England, are contemplating the extension of political power to the women as one of the grand methods for the world's future good.

"Our present object is not, however, to contend for the benefits to accrue to society through the agencies of woman brought to bear upon the State, as they have been in the Church and in the general spheres of life, but to note the extraordinary circumstances of political power having been first granted to and exercised by the women of Utah. We see that female suffrage is both accepted and strongly maintained as one of the great social problems of the future, not only to advance the world, but to assert the dignity and cause of womanhood; that it is thus accepted and maintained by the boldest female reformers of America and the great masters of social science in England. That is one side of the case, and in that view we find no subject for astonishment, for the men and women whose very names represent mind in the reform movements of the times will be certain to be found in the vanguard of civilization; but*that the women of Utah, who have been considered representatives of womanhood in its degradation, should suddenly be found on the same platform with John Stuart Mill and his sisterhood, is truly a matter for astonishment. And moreover, when we look upon the Mormon "kingdom of God," as the Saints denominate it, as the first nationality in the world which has granted to woman political power and created her the chief part of the State as well as the Church, one cannot but confess that the Mormons in this have stolen a march upon their betters.

"Three years ago a friend of the Mormons informed us that the Delegate of Utah was in New York, just from Washington, bound for Utah before Brigham Young the extraordinary design of giving to the women of Mormondom political power. And the circumstance was the more marked from the singular facts that the legislative minds, aided by the American press, were proposing just at that time a scheme for Congress to force female suffrage upon Utah, to give to the women of that Territory the power to break up the institution of polygamy and emancipate themselves from their supposed serfdom and the degradation of womanhood. This done, the conclusion, of course, was that Mormonism and the Mormons would become converted and transformed into respectable monogamic problems, easy of solution by our multitude of Christian and other civilizing agencies."

The incident referred to in the Phrenological Journal relative to William H. Hooper as the female suffrage delegate from Utah, may be supplemented with the narrative itself. Mr. Julian, of Indiana, offered a bill to the House in 1867 in substance, "A Bill to solve the Polygamic Problem." Upon its presentation and announcement, Delegate Hooper immediately called upon Mr. Julian, saying, "That bill has a high-sounding title. What are its provisions?" He replied, simply a bill of one section, providing for the enfranchisement of the women of Utah. "Mr. Julian," said the Delegate, "I am in favor of that bill." He inquired, "Do you speak for your own leading men?" Mr. Hooper replied, "I do not; but I know of no reason why they should not also approve of it."

When Mr. Hooper returned to Utah, he held a conversation with President Brigham Young upon this subject. "Brother Hooper," inquired the President, "are you in favor of female suffrage?" "I know of no reason why I should not be," he answered. No more was said; but from that time the subject seemed to develop itself in the mind of the President and soon afterwards it was taken up by the Legislative body and passed by an unanimous vote.

The following is a copy of the bill:

"An Act, giving women the elective franchise in the Territory of Utah.

"Sec. 1.—Be it enacted by the Governor and the Legislative Assembly of the Territory of Utah: That every woman of the age of twenty-one years, who has resided in this Territory six months next preceding any general or special election, born or naturalized in the United States, or who is the wife, or widow, or the daughter of a naturalized citizen of the United States, shall be entitled to vote at any election in this Territory.

"Sec. 2.—All laws, or parts of laws, conflicting with this act are hereby repealed.

"Approved February 12, 1870."

It has been charged by the anti-Mormons, that woman suffrage in Utah was only designed to further enslave the Mormon women; that they took no part in its passage and have had no soul in its exercise. Nearly the reverse of this is the case as the records will show. Here follow the minutes of a general meeting of the great Female Relief Society, held in Salt Lake City, February 19, 1870—just seven days after the passage of their bill:

"Minutes.—Most of the wards of the city were represented. Miss E. R. Snow was elected president, and Mrs. L. D. Alder secretary.

"Meeting opened with singing; prayer by Mrs. Harriet Cook Young.

"Miss Eliza R. Snow arose and said, to encourage the sisters in good works, she would read an account of our indignation meeting, as it appeared in the Sacramento Union; which account she thought a fair one. She also stated that an expression of gratitude was due acting-Governor Mann, for signing the document granting woman suffrage in Utah, for we could not have had the right without his sanction and said that Wyoming had passed a bill of this kind over its governor's head, but we could not have done this.

"The following names were unanimously selected to be a committee for said purpose: Eliza R. Snow, Bathsheba W. Smith, Sarah M. Kimball, M. T. Smoot, H. C. Young, Z. D. Young, Phoebe Woodruff, M. I. Home, M. N. Hyde, Eliza Cannon, Rachel Grant, Amanda Smith.

"Mrs. Sarah M. Kimball said she had waited patiently a long time, and now that we were granted the right of suffrage, she would openly declare herself a woman's rights woman, and called upon those who would do so to back her up, whereupon many manifested their approval. She said her experience in life had been different from that of many. She had moved in-all grades of society; had been both rich and poor; had always seen much good and intelligence in woman.

The interests of man and woman cannot be separated; for the man is not without the woman nor the woman without the man in the Lord. She spoke of the foolish custom which deprived the mother of having control over her sons at a certain age; said she saw the foreshadowing of a brighter day in this respect in the future. She said she had entertained ideas that appeared wild, which she thought would yet be considered woman's rights; spoke of the remarks made by Brother Rockwood, lately, that women would have as much prejudice to overcome, in occupying certain positions as men would in granting them and concluded by declaring that woman was the helpmate of man in every department of life.

"Mrs. Phoebe Woodruff said she was pleased with the reform and was heart and hand with her sisters. She was thankful for the privilege that had been granted to women but thought we must act in wisdom and not go too fast. She had looked for this day for years. God has opened the way for us. We have borne in patience, but the yoke on woman is partly removed. Now that God has moved upon our brethren to grant us the right of female suffrage, let us lay it by, and wait till the time comes to use it, and not run headlong and abuse the privilege. Great and blessed things are ahead. All is right and will come out right, and woman will receive her reward in blessing and honor. May God grant us strength to do right in his sight.

"Mrs. Bathsheba W. Smith said she felt pleased to be engaged in the great work before them and was heart and hand with her sisters. She never felt better in her life, yet never felt more her own weakness, in view of the greater responsibilities which now rested upon them, nor ever felt so much the necessity of wisdom and light; but she was determined to do her best. She believed that woman was coming up in the world. She encouraged her sisters with the faith that there was nothing required of them in the duties of life that they could not perform.

"Mrs. Prescinda Kimball said: I feel comforted and blessed this day. I am glad to be numbered in moving forward this reform; feel to exercise double diligence and try to accomplish what is required at our hands. We must all put our shoulder to the wheel and go ahead. I am glad to see our daughters elevated with man, and the time, come when our votes will assist our leaders, and redeem ourselves. Let us be humble, and triumph will be ours. The day is approaching when woman shall be redeemed from the curse placed upon Eve, and I have often thought that our daughters who are in polygamy will be the first redeemed. Then let us keep the commandants and attain to a fulness, and always bear in mind that our children born in the priesthood will be saviors on Mount Zion.

"Mrs. Zina D. Young said she was glad to look upon such an assemblage of bright and happy faces and was gratified to be numbered with the spirits who had taken tabernacles in this dispensation, and to know that we are associated with kings and priests of God; thought we do not realize our privileges. Be meek and humble and do not move one step aside but gain power over ourselves. Angels will visit the earth, but are we, as handmaids of the Lord, prepared to meet them? We live in the day that has been looked down to with great anxiety since the morn of creation.

"Mrs. M. T. Smoot said: 'We are engaged in a great work, and the principles that we have embraced are life and salvation unto us. Many principles are advanced on which we are slow to act. There are many more to be advanced.

Woman's rights have been spoken of. I have never had any desire for more rights than I have. I have considered politics aside from the sphere of woman; but, as things progress, I feel it is right that we should vote though the path may be fraught with difficulty.' "Mrs. Wilmarth East said she would bear testimony to what had been said.

She had found by experience that ' obedience is better than sacrifice.' I desire to be on the safe side and sustain those above us; but I cannot agree with Sister Smoot in regard to woman's rights. I have never felt that woman had her privileges. I always wanted a voice in the politics of the nation, as well as to rear a family. I was much impressed when I read the poem composed by Mrs. Emily Woodmansee—' Who Cares to Win a Woman's Thought.' There is a bright day coming; but we need more wisdom and humility than ever before. My sisters, I am glad to be associated with you—those who have borne the heat and burden of the day and ask God to pour blessings on your head.

"Eliza R. Snow; in closing, observed, that there was a business item she wished to lay before the meeting, and suggested that Sister Bathsheba W. Smith be appointed on a mission to preach retrenchment all through the South, and woman's rights if she wished.

"The suggestion was acted upon, and the meeting adjourned with singing 'Redeemer of Israel,' and benediction by Mrs. M. N. Hyde."

The municipal election in Salt Lake City, which occurred but two days after the approval of the bill in question, presented, as we have seen, the first political issue in our city, from any organized opposition party; but the new voting element placed in the hands of the People's party by the passage of this bill was not brought largely into requisition. Only a few of the "sisters " claimed the honor of voting on the occasion. The first of these was Miss Seraph Young, a niece of President Young.

But probably the most remarkable woman's rights demonstration of the age, was that of the women of Utah, in their great mass meetings, held throughout the Territory, in all its principal cities and settlements, in January of 1870 relative to the Cullom bill.

On the 13th of January, 1870, "notwithstanding the inclemency of the weather, the old tabernacle," says the Deseret News, "was densely packed with ladies of all ages, and, as that building will comfortably seat five thousand persons, there could not have been fewer than between five and six thousand present on the occasion."

It was announced in the programme that there were to be none present but ladies. Several reporters of the press, however, obtained admittance, among whom was Colonel Finley Anderson, special correspondent of the New York Herald.

The meeting was opened with a very impressive prayer from Mrs. Zina D. Young; and then, on motion of Miss Eliza R. Snow, Mrs. Sarah M. Kimball was elected president. Mrs. Lydia Alder was chosen secretary, and Mrs. M. T. Smoot, Mrs. M. N. Hyde, Isabella Horn, Mary Leaver, Priscilla Staines and Rachel Grant, were appointed a committee to draft resolutions. This was done with executive dispatch; for many present had for years been leaders of women's organizations. The president arose and addressed a few pithy remarks to the vast assemblage. She said: "We are to speak in relation to the government and institutions under which we live. She would ask, have we transgressed any law of the United States?

[Loud 'no' from the audience.] Then why are we here to-day? We have been driven from place to place, and wherefore? Simply for believing and practicing the counsels of God, as contained in the gospel of heaven. The object of this meeting is to consider the justice of a bill now before the Congress of the United States. We are not here to advocate woman's rights, but man's rights. The bill in question would not only deprive our fathers, husbands and brothers of enjoying the privileges bequeathed to citizens of the United States, but it would deprive us, as women, of the privilege of selecting our husbands; and against this we unqualifiedly protest."

During the absence of the committee on resolutions speeches were delivered and then the committee on resolutions reported the following: "Resolved, That we, the ladies of Salt Lake City, in mass-meeting assembled, do manifest our indignation, and protest against the bill before Congress, known as ' the Cullom bill,' also the one known as ' the Cragin bill,' and all similar bills, expressions and manifestoes.

"Resolved, That we consider the above named bills foul blots on our national escutcheon—absurd documents—atrocious insults to the honorable executive of the United States Government, and malicious attempts to subvert the rights of civil and religious liberty.

"Resolved, That we do hold sacred the constitution bequeathed us by our forefathers, and ignore, with laudable womanly jealousy, every act of those men to whom the responsibilities of government have been entrusted, which is calculated to destroy its efficiency.

"Resolved, That we unitedly exercise every moral power and every right which we inherit as the daughters of American citizens, to prevent the passage of such bills, knowing that they would inevitably cast a stigma on our republican government by jeopardizing the liberty and lives of its most loyal and peaceful citizens.

"Resolved, That, in our candid opinion, the presentation of the aforesaid bills indicates a manifest degeneracy of the great men of our nation; and their adoption would presage a speedy downfall and ultimate extinction of the glorious pedestal of freedom, protection, and equal rights, established by our noble ancestors.

"Resolved, That we acknowledge the institutions of the Church of Jesus Christ of Latter-day Saints as the only reliable safeguard of female virtue and innocence; and the only sure protection against the fearful sin of prostitution, and its attendant evils, now prevalent abroad, and as such, we are and shall be united with our brethren in sustaining them against each and every encroachment.

"Resolved, That we consider the originators of the aforesaid bills disloyal to the constitution, and unworthy of any position of trust in any office which involves the interests of our nation.

"Resolved, That, in case the bills in question should pass both Houses of Congress, and become a law, by which we shall be disfranchised as a Territory, we, the ladies of Salt Lake City, shall exert all our power and influence to aid in the support of our own State government."

These resolutions were greeted with loud cheers from nearly six thousand women and carried unanimously.

CHAPTER XLIX.

BRIEF REVIEW OF UTAH IN CONGRESS, FROM ITS ORGANIZATION TO THE PASSAGE OF THE CULLOM BILL. GREAT SPEECH OF DELEGATE HOOPER IN CONGRESS AGAINST THE BILL, IN WHICH HE REVIEWS THE COLONIZING WORK OF THE MORMONS IN THE WEST, AND JUSTIFIES HIS POLYGAMOUS CONSTITUENTS.

In the exhibition of these wonderful mass meetings of fifty thousand organized Mormon women held throughout the Territory, to preserve their sacred institutions, the reader has a marked example typical of the Mormon people; but we must now give a more regular review of the Congressional subject relative to Utah.

Utah can scarcely be said to have possessed any political or congressional history until the period of the Utah war. Previously her condition and career had been almost entirely primitive and patriarchal. The Hon. John M. Bernhisel, delegate from Utah through this period, had served his constituents faithfully; but no feature of that service stands out so prominent as to require special mention. The general history, up to this time, may therefore be considered as including the congressional.

The "Mormon war," of course, had somewhat interrupted the relations between Utah and the nation. In the eyes of the American public, Utah had been in rebellion; although, as we have seen, the controversy had been amicably settled, and the Mormons had been pardoned of all their political offences.

It was under this aspect of affairs that William H. Hooper was elected delegate to Congress, from Utah, in August, 1859. His position was a delicate one, his task arduous, and the case he had to handle certainly a very peculiar and complex case, looking at it from whatever point of view. Notwithstanding his constituents held that they were in the right in the late controversy which had nearly come to bloodshed, and notwithstanding their affirmation that they had stood upon their constitutional ground, and had merely resisted, by a practical but a justifiable protest, an unconstitutional invasion of the rights of American citizens, delegate Hooper well knew that the general public took another view of the case. But the great advantage which Hooper possessed, and which enabled him to master the situation, was in his thorough appreciation of the views and shapings of both sides. Therefore, while the delegate was prepared to stand by his people, in the defense of all their constitutional rights, and to ward off any new difficulty, he was equally ready to "see eye to eye" with members of Congress. This was the exact reason why Brigham Young sent him; indeed, one of Brigham's greatest gifts is manifested in his choice of the fittest instruments for the work and the times.

Fortunately, also, when Hooper went to Congress as delegate in 1859, the members were disposed to humor the Mormon view of the Utah expedition and troubles, and he in turn humored them most politicly.

As we have seen, the public, and especially journalists and Congressmen, were only too willing to treat the Utah war as Buchanan's affair, and wipe the hands of the nation clean of it. With this feeling came the good-natured inclination to let the Mormons have all they asked for, if they only asked in reason. And Congress had a Utah delegate of a most sagacious, practical turn of mind, who understood his points too well to ask for more than was certain to be granted, contenting himself, in the rest, in working up a good feeling towards his constituents.

Delegate Hooper settled everything he touched. There were two sessions of the Utah Legislature unrecognized and unpaid; Governor Young's accounts against the U. S. Treasury were unsettled; and the expenses of the Indian war of 1850, were still due to the Territory. All this the energetic and influential delegate brought to a settlement. Besides this financial triumph, a bill which passed the House, for the suppression of polygamy, never became a law, and the thirty-sixth Congress ended, leaving Utah affairs comparatively tranquil.

Notwithstanding that in the thirty-sixth Congress, Utah had met a very fair adjustment, and that it was indeed the only one in which Utah, up to this date, had risen to anything like political importance in the nation, the Hon. John M. Bernhisel was returned to the thirty-seventh Congress. This may have been intended as a recognition of the past service of that gentleman, before his final retirement from public life, but it is evident that he was not so well fitted for the post as Delegate Hooper. Dr. Bernhisel was originally rather a professional than a political character,—something of a Mormon elder in Congress, representing a religious people; whereas, Hooper was a successful merchant, and full of political sagacities. It is true the latter might not have been able to have prevented the passage of the anti-polygamic bill of 1862, but he certainly would have rallied a host of political friends against it. Without wasting his strength to show the "unconstitutionality" of the bill, he would have adopted the more practical line of argument that the bill must, from its very nature, remain inoperative for years, thus giving, tacitly, a license for the continuation of polygamy. This has been abundantly recognized by members of Congress since. The bill of 1862 has been considered by them to be as great a nuisance as polygamy itself. Surely Hooper would have foreshadowed the difficulties of special legislation, in such a delicate matter as the marriage question of an entire community. Moreover, in 1862, the whole responsibility of the abolition of thousands of plural marriages rested entirely with Congress, there having been no primary agitation of the matter by the people of Utah themselves. But the thirty-seventh Congress, in its innocence, passed that bill, committing almost as great a blunder as did Buchanan in the case of the Utah war.

The Hon. John M. Bernhisel returned to his constituents, and the Hon. John F. Kinney was elected to succeed him. For a number of years, Judge Kinney had been Chief Justice of Utah, but he had been just removed by Lincoln, it is said, for too faithfully serving the Mormons. Be that as the reader may please to consider, the Mormons were grateful, and resolved that the Chief Justice should not go from them in disgrace. They accordingly elected him to represent them in the thirty-eighth Congress; and so the Chief Justice, instead of returning to his friends in the East, under a cloud, went to Washington in triumph, to take his seat in the Congress of the United States.

Judge Kinney was a brilliant man, and he soon won golden opinions from both constituents and strangers, by his eloquent efforts in Congress. But he was not essentially identified with the destiny of Utah, although a constant friend of the people, and it became evident that the congressional career of a Gentile, representing a purely Mormon constituency, must tend more to his political advancement than to their potency. He might have built a pinnacle on their political destiny; they could build nothing on his political fame. They had the example of Judge Douglas before them—" the Mormon-made Senator"—who in his career nearly reached the Presidency of the United States, yet who recommended to Congress the expediency of cutting the " loathsome ulcer out "—the "ulcer" being the people who, in his rise to fame, had done so much to uplift him. In justice, however, it should be said that Judge Kinney served his constituents well and faithfully.

With the return of Hon. W. H. Hooper to the thirty-ninth Congress, the prestige of home delegates was restored. His influence was greater than ever, both at home and in Washington. The very change for a time from Mormon to Gentile had enhanced that influence and illustrated the eminent consistency of a man who was politically in harmony with Congress, yet in destiny one with the Mormon people, representing them as their delegate. We are ever impressed with that law which is described as the "eternal fitness of things; " so Congress could better understand and respect William H. Hooper maintaining the integrity of the Mormon commonwealth and reconciling it with the rights of the American citizen, than it could the representation of Utah in those days, by a Gentile delegate. Hooper had by far the greatest influence in Congress; his earnestness in controversy was respected by his congressional colleagues, even when they were resolutely bent on an anti-Mormon policy; and the very fact that he was a well-known monogamist only rendered his defense of the religious rights of his polygamic constituents more truly American in spirit.

During the thirty-ninth and fortieth Congresses, to the commencement of Grant's administration, 1869, nothing very formidable was proposed or carried out against the founders of Utah. Bills were introduced by Mr. Ashley, then chairman of the Territorial Committee, and others, looking to the disintegration of the Territory; but only a passive recognition was given those measures by Congress. Gentile delegations also went to Washington from Utah urging legislation against the Mormons; but Congress was busy with the great question of "reconstruction," and the impeachment of President Johnson, and thus Utah, a minor question, was overlooked.

The passive action of Congress towards Utah, coupled with the wholesome legislation of the Johnson period, among which was the establishment of the present land system, the enlargement of the postal service, and a partial recognition of local self-government, warranted the hope that a brighter day was dawning for the Territory, inasmuch as the delegate was consulted in the choice of Federal officers who were not objectionable to the people.

But, with the commencement of Grant's administration, a new warfare was opened, and early in the first session under his Presidency, the Cullom bill was introduced in the House. Its monstrosity was such that scarcely a section did not propose measures in violation of the most sacred provisions of the Constitution. It is understood that this bill was framed in Utah. It was like a resume of the Cragin bill; and Senator Cragin at once adopted it as his protege. He could well afford this, for it was a more perfected anti-Mormon measure than his own, bristling with formidable points of special legislation against " Polygamic Theocracy," wherever touched. General Cullom fathered the bill in the House; Senator Cragin introduced it in the Senate. The Cullom bill was published and reviewed by nearly all the journals in the country. From the standpoint of newspaper criticism, it was very difficult to tell exactly what was its moral character.

There was, however, a pretty general confession that it was an infamous bill; yet, with a strange consistency, it was quite as candidly confessed that it was not nearly bad enough to satisfy the popular desire.

Sargent, Axtell and Fitch spoke against the bill. The Hon. Thomas Fitch's speech was one of the most powerful efforts of oratory that Congress has had the privilege of listening to in these latter days. Not, however, from the bill itself did Mr. Fitch conjure the effectiveness of his speech, but over the prospect of the blood and the millions of money which it must cost the nation to enforce its provisions. Fitch's speech created so much sensation in the House that General Cullom himself proposed the temporary recommittal of the bill.

The Cullom bill not only stirred the entire nation to a desire for special legislation against the Mormons, but also Mormondom to its very center.

The crowning moment came. Delegate Hooper was on the floor of the House with his plea for religious liberty, which we quote from the Congressional Record. He said: "Mr. Speaker.—I wish to make a few remarks concerning the extraordinary bill now under consideration. While so doing, I crave the attention of the House, for I am here, not alone as one of the people sought to be cruelly oppressed; not only as the delegate representing Utah; but as an American citizen, to utter my solemn protest against the passage of a bill that aims to violate our dearest rights and is fraught with evil to the Republic itself.

"I do not propose to occupy the time of the House by dwelling at length upon the vast contributions of the people of Utah to the wealth of the nation.

There is no member in the House who does not recollect in his schoolboy days the vast region of the Rocky Mountains characterized in the geographies as the Great American Desert.' 'There' said those veracious text books, 'was a vast region wherein no man could live. There were springs and streams, upon the banks of which could be seen the bleaching bones of animals and of men, poisoned from drinking of the deadly waters.' Around the borders of the vast desert, and in its few habitable parts, roamed the painted savages, only less cruel and remorseless than the desert itself.

"In the midst of this inhospitable waste to-day dwell an agricultural, pastoral, and self-sustaining people, numbering 120,000 souls. Everywhere, can be seen the fruits of energetic and persistent industry. The surrounding mining Territories of Colorado, Idaho, Montana, Arizona and Nevada, in their infancy, were fed and fostered from the surplus stores of the Mormon people. The development of the resources of these mining Territories was alone rendered possible by the existence at their doors of an agricultural people, who supplied them with the chief necessities of life at a price scarcely above that demanded in the old and populous States. The early immigrants to California paused on their weary journey in the redeemed wastes of Utah, to recruit their strength, and that of their animals, and California is to day richer by thousands of lives and millions of treasure, for the existence of this half-way house to El Dorado.

"To the people of Utah, therefore, is to be attributed no inconsiderable part in the production of the vast mineral wealth which has poured into the coffers of the nation from our mining States and Territories.

"This, however, is but a tithe of our contributions to the nation's wealth. By actual experiment we have demonstrated the practicability of redeeming these desert wastes. When the Pacific slope and its boundless resources shall have been developed; when beyond the Rocky Mountains 40.000,000 of people shall do homage to our flag, the millions of dwellers in Arizona, Nevada, Idaho, Colorado and Montana, enriched by the products of their redeemed and fertilized deserts, shall point to the valley of Great Salt Lake as their exemplar, and accord to the sturdy toilers of that land due honor, in that they inaugurated the system and demonstrated its possible results. These results are the offering of Utah to the nation.

"When Robert Fulton's first steamboat moved from New York to Albany, so far as concerned the value of the vessel, he had made scarce a perceptible addition to our merchant marine; but the principle, the practicability of which he then demonstrated, was priceless, and enriched the nation more than if she had received the gift of the vessel, built from and loaded with solid gold.

"I will not, Mr. Speaker, trespass upon the time of the House by more than thus briefly adverting to the claims of Utah to the gratitude and fostering care of the American people.

"For the first time in the history of the United States, by the introduction of the bill under consideration, a well-defined and positive effort is made to turn the great law-making power of the nation into a moral channel and to legislate for the consciences of the people.

"Here, for the first time, is a proposition to punish a citizen for his religious belief and unbelief. We have before us a statute book designating crime. To restrain criminal acts, and to punish the offender, has heretofore been the province of the law, and in it we have the support of the accused himself. No man comes to the bar for trial with the plea that the charge upon which he is arraigned constitutes no offence, His plea is * Not guilty.' He cannot pass beyond and behind the established conclusions of humanity. But this bill reaches beyond that code into the questionable world of morals—the debatable land of religious beliefs; and, first creating the offense, seeks with malignant fury of partisan prejudice and sectarian hate to measure out the punishment.

"The bill before us declares that that system which Moses taught, that God allowed, and from which Christ, our Savior, sprung, is a crime, and that any man believing in it and practicing it—I beg pardon, the bill, as I shall presently show, asserts that belief alone is sufficient—that any so offending shall not be tried, but shall be convicted, his children declared bastards, his wives turned out to starve, and his property be confiscated, in fact, for the benefit of the moral reformers, who, as I believe, are the real instigators in this matter.

"The honorable member from Illinois, the father of this bill, informs us that this is a crime abhorred by men, denounced by God, and prohibited and punished by every State in the Union. I have a profound respect for the motives of the honorable member. I believe he is inspired by a sincere hostility to that which he so earnestly denounces. No earthly inducement could make him practice polygamy. Seduction, in the eyes of thousands, is an indiscretion, where all the punishment falls upon the innocent and unoffending. The criminal taint attaches when the seducer attempts to marry his victim. This is horrid. This is not to be endured by man or God, and laws must be promulgated to prevent and punish.

"While I have this profound regard for the morals and motives of the honorable member, I must say that I do not respect, to the same extent, his legal abilities. Polygamy is not denounced by every State and Territory, and the gentleman will search in vain for the statute or criminal code of either defining its existence and punishment. The gentleman confounds a religious belief with a criminal act. He is thinking of bigamy when he denounces polygamy, and in the confusion that follows, blindly strikes out against an unknown enemy. Will he permit me to call his attention to the distinction? Bigamy means the wrong done a woman by imposing upon her the forms of matrimony while another wife lives, rendering such second marriage null and void. The reputation and happiness of a too confiding woman is thus forever blasted by the fraudulent acts of her supposed husband, and he is deservedly punished for his crime. Polygamy, on the contrary, is the act of marrying more than one woman, under a belief that a man has a right, lawfully and religiously, so to do, and with the knowledge and consent of both his wives.

"I suppose, Mr. Speaker, that in proclaiming the old Jeffersonian doctrine that that Government is best which governs least, I would not have even a minority upon the floor. But when I say that in a system of self-government such as ours, that looks to the purest democracy, and seeks to be a government of the people, for the people, and by the people, we have no room for the guardian, nor, above all, for the master, I can claim the united support of both parties. To have such a government; to retain such in its purest strength, we must leave all questions of morals and religion that lie outside the recognized code of crime to the conscience of the citizen. In an attempt to do otherwise than this, the world's abiding places have been washed with human blood, and its fields made rich with human bones.

No government has been found strong enough to stand unshaken above the throes of religious fanaticism when driven to the wall by religious persecution. Ours, sir, would disappear like the " baseless fabric of a vision" before the first blast of such a convulsion. Does the gentleman believe, for example, that in aiming this cruel blow at a handful of earnest followers of the Lord in Utah, he is doing a more justifiable act than would be, in the eyes of a majority of our citizens, a bill to abolish Catholicism, because of its alleged immorality; or a law to annihilate the Jews for that they are Jews, and therefore obnoxious? Let that evil door once be opened; set sect against sect; let the Bible and the school books give place to the sword and the bayonet, and we will find the humanity of to-day the humanity of the dark ages, and our beautiful government a mournful dream of the past.

"This is not only philosophically true, but, sir, it is historically a fact. In making the appeal, I stand upon the very foundation-stone of our constitutional Government. That they might worship God in accordance with the dictates of conscience, the fathers fled from their homes in Europe to the wilds in America.

For this they bore the fatigues or perished in the wilds of a savage-haunted continent; for this they poured out their blood in wars, until every stone in the huge edifice that shelters us as a nation is cemented by the blood of a martyr. Upon this, however, I need not spend my time or yours; a mere statement of the proposition is a conclusive argument from which the people, in their honest instincts, will permit no appeal. In our Constitution, still perfect and fresh as ever, we have a clause that cannot be changed and leave a vestige of a free government.

In the original instrument we find this language: "No religious tests shall ever be required as a qualification to any office or public trust under the United States."

But this was not considered sufficiently comprehensive for a free people, and subsequently we find it declared, "Congress shall make no law respecting an establishment of religion or prohibiting the free exercise thereof."

"Upon the very threshold of my argument, however, I am met by the advocates of this extraordinary bill with the assumption that polygamy is not entitled to be considered as a portion of our religious faith; that under the Constitution we are to be protected and respected in the enjoyment of our religious faith, but that we are not entitled to consider as a portion thereof the views held by us as a people in reference to the marriage relation. One eminent disputant, as an argument, supposes a case where a religious sect might claim to believe in the rightfulness of murder, and to be protected in the enjoyment of that right. This is not in any sense a parallel case. Murder by all law, human and divine, is a crime; polygamy is not. In a subsequent portion of my remarks, I will show, that not only the authority of the Old Testament writers, but by numerous leading writers of the Christian church, the doctrine of polygamy is justified and approved.

The only ground upon which any argument can be maintained that our views of the marriage relation are not to be considered as a portion of our religious faith, is that marriage is a purely civil contract, and therefore outside the province of religious doctrine. No sect of Christians can, however, be found who will carry their beliefs to this extent. The Catholic Church, the most ancient of Christian churches, and among the most powerful in numbers of the religious denominations of our country, upon this point is in accord with the Mormon church. Marriage, according to the faith of the Catholic church, is one of its sacraments; is not in any sense a civil contract, but a religious ordinance, and the validity of a divorce granted by a civil court is denied. And not in any Christian church is the marriage contract placed on a par with other civil contracts—with a swap of horses or a partnership in trade. It is a civil contract, in that a court of equity, for certain specified causes, may dissolve it; but not otherwise. Upon the marriage contract is invoked the most solemn sanctions of our Christians; the appointed ministers and servants of God, by their presence and aid, give solemnity and efficiency to the ceremonial, and upon the alliance is invoked the Divine guidance and blessing. To most intents and purposes, with every Christian denomination, the marriage ceremony is regarded as a religious ordinance. Upon this point, therefore, and a vital point in the discussion of the question before us, the Catholic church in fact, and the other religious denominations in theory and usual practice, are with the Mormons in their position, that the supervision and control of the marital relation is an integral and essential portion of their religious faith and practice, in the enjoyment of which they are protected by the Constitution.

"The Mormon people are a Christian denomination. They believe fully in the Old and New Testaments in the divinity of Christ's mission, and the upbuilding and triumph of his church. They do not believe, however, that light and guidance from above, ceased with the crucifixion on Calvary. On the other hand, they find that in all ages, whenever a necessity therefor existed, God has raised up prophets to speak to the people, and to manifest to them his will and requirements. And they believe that Joseph Smith was such a prophet; that the time had arrived when there was a necessity for further revelation, and through Joseph Smith it was given to the world.

"Upon this point of continuous revelation, which is really one of the turning points of the controversy, we are in accord with many of the most eminent divines of the Christian church, and with the most earnest and vigorous thinkers of our own day.

"Upon the departure of the Pilgrim Fathers from Holland to America, the Rev. John Robinson, their beloved pastor, preached a farewell sermon, which showed a spirit of mildness and tolerance truly wonderful in that age, and which many who claim to be ministers of God would do well to imitate in this: '"Brethren, we are quickly to part from one another, and whether I may ever live to see your faces on earth any more, the God of heaven only knows; but whether the Lord hath appointed that or not, I charge you before God and his blessed angels, that you follow me no further than you have seen me follow the Lord Jesus Christ. If God reveal anything to you by any other instrument of His, be as ready to receive it as you were to receive any truth from my ministry; for I am fully persuaded, I am very confident, that the Lord has more truth yet to break forth out of His holy word.

"' For my part I cannot sufficiently bewail the condition of the reformed churches, who are come to a period in religion, and will go at present no further than the instruments of their information. The Lutherans cannot be drawn beyond what Luther saw. Whatever part of His will our good God has revealed to Calvin, they will rather die than embrace it; and the Calvinists, you see, stick fast where they were left by that great man of God, who yet saw not all things.

"' This is a misery much to be lamented, for though they were burning and shining lights in their time, yet they penetrated not into the whole counsel of God; but were they now living, would be as ready to embrace further light as that which they first received. I beseech you to remember that it is an article of your covenant, that you shall be ready to receive whatever truths shall be made known to you from the written word of God.'"

"And says Ralph Waldo Emerson, in one of his golden utterances 'I look for the hour when that supreme beauty which ravished the souls of those Hebrews and through their lips spoke oracles to all time, shall speak in the West also.

The Hebrew and the Greek Scriptures contain immortal sentences that have been the bread of life to millions. But they have no epical entirety; are fragmentary; are not shown in their order to the intellect. I look for the new Teacher that shall follow so far these shining laws that he shall see some full circle; shall see their rounding, complete grace; shall see the world to the mirror of the soul.' "Conceding, therefore, that new revelation may be at all times expected in the future of our race, as they have been at all times vouchsafed in the past, and the whole controversy ends. A man has arisen named Joseph Smith, he claims to be a prophet of God, and a numerous community see fit to admit the justice of such claim. It is a religious sect; it has to-day vindicated its right to live by works and sacrifices which are the admiration even of its enemies. It brings forward certain new doctrines; of church government; of baptism even for their dead; of the marriage relation. Upon what point is it more probable that light from above would be given to our race, than upon the marriage relation? The social problem is the question of the age. The minds of many of the foremost men and women of our days are given to the study of the proper position and relations of the sexes. The wisest differ—differ honestly and unavoidably. Endless is the dispute and clamor of those honestly striving to do away with the social evil; to ameliorate the anomalous condition of the wronged and suffering women of to-day. And while this is so; while thousands of the good and pure of all creeds and parties are invoking the Divine guidance in their efforts for the good of our fallen humanity, is it strange that the Divine guidance thus earnestly besought should come—that the prayer of the righteous be answered? The Mormon people believe that God has thus spoken; that through Joseph Smith he has indicated that true solution of the social questions of our day; and while they persecute or question no man for differing honestly with them, as to the Divine authority of such revelations, they firmly insist that in their following of what they believe to be the will of God, they are entitled to the same immunity from persecution at the hands of the Government, and the same liberty of thought and speech, wisely secured to other religious beliefs by the Constitution.

"Upon the point whether polygamy can properly be considered as a part of our religious faith and practice, I beg leave humbly further to submit, sir, that the decision rests solely on the conscience and belief of the man and woman who proclaim it to be a religious belief. As I have said, it is not numbered among the crimes of that code recognized by all nations having any form of government under which criminals are restrained or punished, and to make it such, a new code must be framed. My people proclaim polygamy as a part of their religious belief. If they are honest in this, however much this may be in error, they stand on their rights under the Constitution, and to arrest that error you must appeal to reason, and not to force. I am here, not to argue or demonstrate the truthfulness of their faith; 1 am not called upon to convince this honorable House that it is either true or false; but if I can convince you that this belief is honorably and sincerely entertained, my object is accomplished.

"It is common to teach, and thousands believe that the leaders of the sect of Latter-day Saints, popularly known as Mormons, are hypocrites, while their followers are either ignorant, deluded men and women, or people held to their organization by the vilest impulses of lust. To refute these slanders, I can only do as the earlier Christians did, point to their sufferings and sacrifices, and I may add, the unanimous testimony of all, that aside from what they consider the objectionable practice of polygamy, my constituents are sober, moral, just, and industrious in the eyes of all impartial witnesses. In this community, removed by long reaches of wastes from the moral influences of civilization, we have a quiet, orderly and Christian community. Our towns are without gambling hells, drinking saloons, or brothels, while from end to end of our Territory the innocent can walk unharmed at all hours. Nor is this due to an organized police, but to the kind natures and Christian impulses of a good people. In support of my argument of their entire sincerity, I with confidence appeal to their history.

"The Mormon Church was established at Fayette, New York, in the year 1830. In 1831, the headquarters of the people was removed to Kirtland, Ohio, and considerable numbers of missionaries were sent out to preach the new religion various parts of the Northern States. Many converts were made and removed Kirtland, but they were subject to various petty annoyances and persecutions r the surrounding people. Land not being abundant or easily acquired for the rapidly increasing numbers, the new converts were advised to locate in Jackson County,

Missouri, where land was abundant and cheap—where, in fact, but few settlers had preceded our people. The Mormons soon became a prosperous and wealthy community; the same habits of industry and thrift which they have ever maintained being even then vigorously inculcated by their leaders. Many hundred thousand acres of Government land were purchased, fine farms and thriving settlements were established, and the first printing press in western Missouri put in operation. But the wealth acquired by the people was desired by our neighbors; the lawless border-men, who afterwards made the frontiers of Kansas their battlefield, attacked, plundered, and murdered our settlers, and finally drove them from their delightful homes, which they appropriated to themselves. The title to much of the land in Jackson and other counties is to-day in Mormons, who were then driven from their homes. During the trouble incident to the expulsion of the Mormons, hundreds of men, women, and children were murdered, or died from diseases caused by exposure to the inclemencies of the weather. The wretched refugees afterwards located in Clay, Caldwell, and Davis counties, Missouri, where there were almost no settlers, and where, within a few years their industries had again built up thriving settlements and accumulated large herds of stock. The outrages of Jackson County were then repeated, the Mormons driven from their homes, which were seized by the marauders and thousands of women and children driven forth homeless, and the prey for the border-ruffians whose cupidity had been excited by the wealth of the industrious exiles. Hundreds perished from cold, exposure and starvation. But their leaders, sustained by an undying faith, again called together their scattered and impoverished followers and removing to Illinois, founded the city of Nauvoo.

"For several years they were comparatively undisturbed; they built up one of the most thriving and beautiful cities of the State. Far as the eye could reach from the eminence of their temple, the well-tilled farms and gardens, the comfortable farm-houses, the mills and factories, and well-filled schools, attested the industry, the thrift, and the wealth of the once persecuted people. But again their wealth created envy in the lawless border-men of the new State. Without what even their enemies claim was justifiable cause, and in a manner which Governor Ford characterized as a permanent disgrace to the people of the State, they were attacked, pillaged, and driven across the river; their houses burned; their women and children driven forth unsheltered in the inclement season of the year; their leaders brutally murdered.

"The annals of religious persecution, so fruitful of cruel abuse, can give nothing more pitiable and heart-rending than the scenes which followed this last expulsion. Aged men and women, the sick and feeble, children of tender years, and the wounded, were driven into the flats of the river, yet in sight of their once happy houses, to perish from exposure and starvation. While over our broad land the church bells of Christian communities were ringing out peace and good-will to men; while to the churches thronged thousands to hear preached the gospel of charity and forgiveness; these poor, heart-sick followers of the same Redeemer, were driven in violence from their houses to perish like wild beasts in the swamps and wilderness. The gentlemen charged us with hypocrisy and depraved lust for motives, with such a record as this to mock their charge! The world has many hypocrites, and is well filled with wicked men, but they keep about them the recompense of sin, and have other histories than this I give you, and which history no man can deny.

"Word went out to the world that Mormonism had finally been annihilated. But again the scattered hosts were gathered together, and set out on a pilgrimage, that since that of the children of Israel has been without parallel in the history of the human race. They had no stores, they were beggared in the world's goods yet with earnest religious enthusiasm they toiled on through unknown deserts, over unexplored mountain ranges, and crossed plains haunted by savages, only less cruel than the white Christian who had driven them forth in search of that promised land, where at last they could worship God in accordance with the dictates of their own consciences, and find unbroken that covenant of the Constitution which guards this sacred right. Ragged, foot-sore, starving, wretched, they wandered on. Delicately nurtured women and their children dug roots, or subsisted on the bark of trees or the hides of animals. From Nauvoo to Salt Lake, the valley of their promised land—1,500 miles—there is to-day scarce a mile along that dreary and terrible road, where does not repose the body of some weary one, whom famine, or sickness, or the merciless savage, caused to perish by the way.

"It was while on this pilgrimage that an order came from the Government for five hundred men to serve as soldiers in the Mexican war. The order was promptly obeyed. These devoted men, who had received only cruel persecution from the people they were called upon to protect on the field of battle, dedicated their poor, helpless wives to God, and themselves to their country. Leaving their families to struggle on as best they could, these brave, patriotic men followed our flag into New Mexico and California, and were at last disbanded at San Diego, with high praise from their officers, but with scanty means to return to those they loved, and whom they had left to suffer, and perhaps to perish on the way.

"Thus, Mr. Speaker, three times did this persecuted people, before their location in Utah, build up for themselves pleasant and prosperous homes, and by their industry surrounded themselves with all the comforts and appliances of wealth; and three times were they, by an unprincipled and outrageous mob, driven from their possessions, and reduced to abjectest poverty. And bear it in mind, that in every instance the leader of these organized mobs offered to all who would abandon and deny their faith, toleration and the possession of their homes and wealth. But they refused the tempting snare. They rejoiced that they were, thought worthy to suffer for the Master, and, rather than to deny their faith, they welcomed privation; they sacrificed all that earth could offer; they died the saintly martyr's death.

"Mr. Speaker, is this shining record that of a community of hypocrites? What other Christian denomination of our country can show higher evidences of earnestness, of devoted self-sacrifice for the preservation of their religious faith?

"In further presentation of my argument, Mr. Speaker, that the doctrine of polygamy is an essential feature in our religious faith, and that in our adherence thereto we are advocating no new or unsupported theory of marriage, I crave the indulgence of the House while I cite some few from the numerous writers of weight and authority in the Christian Church, who have illustrated or supported the doctrine.

"Now, sir, far be it from me to undertake to teach this learned House, and above all, the Hon. Chairman of the Committee on Territories great theological truths. If there be any subject with which this honorable body is especially conversant, it is theology. I have heard more Scripture quoted here, and more morality taught, than in any other place it was ever my fortune to serve. With great diffidence then, I venture to suggest to the supporters of this bill, that while polygamy had its origin in holy writ, taught as I have said before by the greatest of all law-makers, and not only tolerated, but explicitly commanded by the Almighty, as I shall presently show, monogamy, or the system of marriage now recognized by so many Christian nations, originated among the Pagans of ancient Greece and Rome.

"I know, sir, that the report accompanying the bill fetches vast stores of theological information to bear; informs us that polygamy is contrary to the Divine economy and refers to the marriage of the first human couple, and cites the further testimony of the Bible, and that of the history of the world. Setting aside the last named as slightly too voluminous for critical examination in the present discussion, we will take up, as briefly as possible, the Divine authorities, and the commentaries and discussions thereon by eminent Christian writers and see how far my people have been misled by clinging to them. As for the illustrious example quoted of our first parents, all that can be said of their marriage, is that it was exhaustive. Adam married all the women in the world, and if we find teaching by the example, we must go among his descendants, where examples can be found among the favored people of God, whose laws were of Divine origin, and whose conduct received sanction or punishment at His hands.

"At the period of the Reformation in Germany, during the early part of the 16th century, those great reformers, Luther, Melancthon, Zwingle, and Bucer, held a solemn consultation at Wittenburg, on the question, "Whether it is contrary to the Divine law for a man to have two wives at once?" and decided unanimously that it was not; and upon the authority of the decision, Philip, Landgrave of Hesse, actually married a second wife, his first being still alive. This fact is recorded in D'Aubigne's History of the Reformation, and by other authors of that period.

"Dr. Hugo Grotius, a celebrated Dutch jurist and statesman and most eminent law-writer of the seventeenth century, states 'the Jew's laws allow a plurality of wives to one man.' "Hon. John Selden, a distinguished English author and statesman, a member of Parliament for 1624, and who represented the University of Oxford in the Long Parliament of 1640, in his work entitled, ' Uxor Hebraica,' the Hebrew Wife, says that ' polygamy was allowed, not only among the Hebrews, but in most other nations throughout the world; and that monogamy is a modern and a European custom, almost unknown to the ancient world.' "Dr. Samuel Puffendorf, professor of law in the University of Heidelberg, in Germany, and afterwards of Lund, in Sweden, who wrote during the latter part of the 17th century, in his great work on the law of nature and nations, says that " the Mosaic law, was so far from forbidding this custom (polygamy) that it seems in several places to suppose it;' and in another place he says, in reference to the rightfulness thereof, ' the polygamy of the fathers, under the old covenant, is an argument which ingenious men must confess to be unanswerable.' "Rev. Gilbert Burnet, Bishop of Salisbury, the particular friend of William III., who was eminent among both historians and theologians, wrote a tract upon this subject, near the beginning of the 18th century. The tract was written on the question, 'Is a plurality of wives in any case lawful under the gospel?'"

The Hon. Delegate cited passages from the tracts and learned arguments from the pens of eminent Christian divines allowing polygamy to disciples whose faith and conscience had been educated by the Hebrew Scriptures to the adoption of plural marriage. And Mr. Hooper's argument was sonorous with a purer constitutional tone from the fact that he himself, like these divines, was in his own life a strict monogamist: it was purely the Hon. Delegate's Constitutional plea for the religious liberty of a conscientious people whom he represented before the Assembly of the Nation. The close of his argument on polygamy and the peroration of this remarkable speech shall be preserved in their historical entirety;— "Rev. David A. Allen, D. D., a Congregationalist, and a missionary of the American Board of Commissioners for Foreign Missions, after a professional residence of twenty-five years in Hindustan, published a work in 1856, entitled 'India, Ancient and Modern,' in which he says, pp. 551-3: "'Polygamy is practiced in India among the Hindus, the Mohammedans, the Zoroastricans, and the Jews. It is allowed and recognized by the institutes of Menu, by the Koran, by the Zendavesta, and, the Jews believe, by their scriptures, the Old Testament. It is recognized by all the courts in India, native and English. The laws of the British Parliament recognize polygamy among all these classes, when the marriage connection has been formed according to the principles of their religion and to their established forms and usages. The marriage of a Hindoo or a Mohammedan with his second or third wife is just as valid and as legally binding on all parties as his marriage with his first wife; just as valid as the marriage of any Christian in the Church of England. * * * * This man cannot divorce any of his wives if he would, and it would be great injustice and cruelty to them and their children if he should. * * * * His having become a Christian and embraced a purer faith will not release him from those obligations in view of the English Government and courts, or of the native population. Should he put them away, or all but one, they will still be legally his wives, and cannot be married to another man. And further, they have done nothing to deserve such unkindness, cruelty, and disgrace at his hands.

* * * So far from receiving polygamy as morally wrong, they not unfrequently take a second or third wife with much reluctance, and from a painful sense of duty to perpetuate their name, their family and their inheritance.' "In an appendix to this work, Dr. Allen informs the world that the subject of polygamy had been brought before the Calcutta Missionary Conference, a body composed of the missionaries of the various missionary societies of Great Britain and America, and including Baptists, Congregationalists, Episcopalians, Methodists, Presbyterians, and others, in consequence of the application of Christian converts, who, having several wives each, to whom they had been legally married, now desired admittance into the Christian Churches. After frequent consultation and much consideration, the conference, says Dr. Allen, came unanimously to the following conclusion: "'If a convert, before becoming a Christian, has married more wives than one, in accordance with the practice of the Jewish and primitive Christian churches, he shall be permitted to keep them all, but such a person is not eligible to any office in the church.' "These facts, as Dr. Allen asserts them, have a direct and important bearing upon this bill and the accompanying report. They prove that one of its main charges, that polygamy is abhorrent to every Christian nation, is false, for the British Empire is a Christian nation, and Hindustan is an integral part of that empire, as much so as its American provinces are, or as Ireland is. Hindustan is a civilized country, with schools and colleges, and factories and railroads, and telegraphs and newspapers. Yet the great mass of the people, comprising more than eighty millions, are polygamists, and as such they are recognized and protected by the laws of the British Parliament,

and the courts of the Queen's Bench; and the English and American missionaries of the gospel who reside there, and have resided there many years, and who know the practical working of polygamy, have assembled together in solemn conference and unanimously pronounced it to be right, and in accordance with the practice of the primitive Christian churches; and the French, the Spanish, the Dutch; the Portuguese, and other Christian nations are known to pursue a similar policy, and to allow the different peoples under their governments, the free and unmolested enjoyment of their own religions and their own marriage system, whether they are monogamous or polygamous.

"I trust, Mr. Speaker, that I have not wearied your patience by this citation of learned authorities upon the antiquity and universality of the polygamic doc trines. My object in this part of my argument is not to prove that polygamy is right or wrong, but simply to illustrate that a doctrine, the practice of which has repeatedly been commanded by the Almighty; which was the rule of life with the Jews at the time they were the chosen people of God, and were, in all things, governed by His dictation; which has among its supporters many of the most eminent writers of the Christian church of all ages, and which is now sanctioned by law and usage in many of the Christianized provinces of the British Empire, is not wrong in itself. It is a doctrine, the practice of which, from the precedents cited, is clearly not inconsistent with the highest purity of character, and the most exemplary Christian life. My opponents may argue that it is unsuited to the civilization of the age or is the offspring of a religious delusion; but if so, its remedy is to be sought through persuasion, and not by the exercise of force; it is the field for the missionary and not for the jurist or soldier. It is a noble and a Christian work to purify and enlighten a benighted soul; to lift up those who are fallen and ready to perish; but from all the pulpits of the land comes up the cry that the fields are white for the harvest, while the laborers are few. So soon, however, as the Luthers, the Melancthons, the Whitfields of to-day, have wiped out the immorality, licentiousness and crime of older communities, and have made their average morality equal to that of the city of Salt Lake, let them transfer their field of labor to the wilds of Utah, and may God forever prosper the right.

"I trust, Mr. Speaker, that men abler and more learned in law than I, will discuss the legal monstrosities of this bill, fraught with evil, as it is, not only to the citizen of Utah, but to the nation at large; but must be pardoned for calling special attention to the seventh section, which gives to a single officer, the United States marshal, with the clerk of the court, the absolute right of selecting a jury; and, further, to the tenth section, which provides that persons entertaining an objectionable religious theory—not those who have been guilty of the practice of polygamy, but who have simply a belief in the abstract theory of plural marriage—shall be disqualified as jurors.

"To see what a fearful blow this is at the very foundation of our liberties; what a disastrous precedent for future tyranny, let us recall for a moment the history of the trial by jury; something with which all are as familiar as with the decalogue, but which, like the ten commandments, may occasionally be recalled with profit. Jury trial was first known as a *trill per pais*; by the country; and the theory was, that when a crime has been committed, the whole community came together and sat in judgment upon the offender. This process becoming cumbersome as the population increased, twelve men were drawn by lot from the country, thus securing, as was supposed, a representation of the average public sentiment of the whole country, and which was further secured by requiring the finding of the jury to be unanimous.

'A fair trial by jury, by our Anglo-Saxon ancestors, was regarded as so precious, that in Magna Charta it is more than once insisted on as the principal bulwark of English liberty.

"Blackstone says of it: 'It is the glory of the English law. It is the most transcendent privilege which any subject can enjoy or wish for, that he cannot be affected either in his property, his liberty, or his person, but by the unanimous consent of twelve of his neighbors and equals; a provision which has, under Providence, secured the just liberties of this nation for along succession of ages.'

"Our own people have been no whit behind the English in their high appreciation of the trial by jury. In the original Federal Constitution, it was provided simply that the ' trial of all crimes, except in cases of impeachment, shall be by jury.' The framers of the Constitution considered that the meaning of 'trial by jury' was sufficiently settled by long established usage and legal precedent, and that by the provision just cited was sufficient. But such was not the view of the people. One of the most serious objections to the adoption of the Constitution by the States was its lack of clearness upon this most vital point, and Alexander Hamilton, in one of the ablest and most carefully considered numbers of The Federalist, endeavored to explain away this objection. The Constitution was adopted, but the nation was not satisfied; and one of the earliest amendments to that instrument further provided that 'no person shall be held to answer for a capital or otherwise infamous crime unless on presentment or indictment of a grand jury ' and that ' in all criminal prosecutions, the accused shall enjoy the right to a speedy and public trial by an impartial jury of the State and district wherein the crime shall have been committed, which district shall have been previously ascertained by law.' "Thus, Mr. Speaker, it will be observed with what scrupulous solicitude our ancestors watched over this great safeguard of the liberties of the people. Nothing was left to inference or established precedent, but to every citizen was guaranteed in this most solemn manner an impartial trial by a jury of his neighbors and his peers, residents of the district where the offence was charged.

"Now, sir, is there any member of this House who will claim or pretend that the provisions of this bill are not in violation of this most sacred feature in our bill of rights? The trial by jury by this bill is worse than abolished, for its form —a sickening farce—remains, while its spirit is utterly gone. A packed jury is worse than no jury at all. The merest tyro in law, knows that the essence of a trial by jury consists in the fact that the accused is tried by a jury drawn by lot from among his neighbors; a jury drawn without previous knowledge, choice or selection on the part of the Government; a jury which will be a fair epitome of the district where the offence is charged, and thus such a tribunal, as will agree to no verdict except such as, substantially, the whole community would agree to, if present and taking part in the trial. Any other system of trial by jury is a mockery and a farce. The standard of public morality varies greatly in a country so vast as ours, and the principle of a jury trial recognizes this fact, and wisely provides, in effect, that no person shall be punished who, when brought to the bar of public opinion in the community where the alleged offence is committed, is not adjudged to have been guilty of a crime. This most unconstitutional and wicked bill before us, defies all these well-established principles and strikes at the root of the dearest right of the citizen. I have an earnest and abiding faith in the bright future of my native land; but if our national career, as we may fondly hope, shall stretch out before us unending glories, it will be because of the prompt and decisive rebuke, by the representatives of the people here, of all such legislation as that sought in the bill before us.

"I have touched more fully, Mr. Speaker, upon the feature of the bill virtually abolishing jury trial, than upon any other, because of its more conspicuous disregard of constitutional right. But the whole bill, from first to last, is most damnable in its provisions, and most unworthy of consideration by the representatives of a free people. This is an age of great religious toleration. This bill recalls the fearful days of the Spanish inquisition, or the days when, in New England, Quakers were persecuted or banished, and witches burned at the stake. It is but a short time since the country hailed with satisfaction a treaty negotiated on the part of a Pagan nation through the efforts of a former member of this body, and whose recent death has filled our hearts with sadness, whereby the polygamous Chinese emigrants to our shores are protected in the enjoyment of their idolatrous faith, and may erect their temples, stocked with idols, and perform their, to us, heathenish worship in every part of our land unquestioned. And while the civilized nations of Europe have combined to sustain and perpetuate a heathen nation practicing polygamy in its lowest form and are hailing with acclamation the approach of its head, the American Congress is actually deliberating over a bill which contemplates the destruction of an industrious people, and the expulsion of the great organizer of border civilization. Can it be possible that the national Congress will even for a moment, seriously contemplate the persecution or annihilation of an integral portion of our citizens, whose industry and material development are the nation's pride, because of a slight difference in their religious faith? A difference, too, not upon the fundamental truths of our common Christianity but because of their conscientious adherence to what was once no impropriety even, but a virtue? This toleration in matters of religion, which is perhaps the most conspicuous feature of our civilization, arises not from any indifference to the sacred truths of Christianity, but from an abiding faith in their impregnability — a national conviction that truth is mighty and will prevail. We have adopted as our motto the sentiment of Paul; 'Try all things; prove all things, and hold fast to that which is good.' The ancient Jewish rabbi, in his serene confidence that God would remember his own, was typical of the spirit of our age: 'Refrain from these men and let them alone, for if this counsel or this work be of God, ye cannot overthrow it; but if it be of men, it will come to naught.' "I have the honor of representing here a constituency probably the most vigorously lied about of any people in the nation. I should insult the good sense of this House and of the American people did I stoop to a refutation of the countless falsehoods which have been circulated for years in reference to the people of Utah. These falsehoods have a common origin—a desire to plunder the treasury of the nation. They are the children of a horde of bankrupt speculators, anxious to grow rich through the sacrifice even of human life. During the administration of Mr. Buchanan, a Mormon war was inaugurated, in great measure through the statements of Judge W. W. Drummond, a man of infamous character and life, and who is cited as authority in the report accompanying this bill.

His statement, as there published, that the Mormons had destroyed all the records, papers, etc., of the supreme Federal court of the Territory, and grossly insulted the Federal officers for opposing such destruction, was, as I have been informed by unquestionable authority, one of, if not the principal cause of the so-called Mormon war. An army was sent to Utah; twenty or thirty millions of dollars were expended, before the Government bethought itself to inquire whether such statements were true; then inquiry was made, and it was learned that the whole statement was entirely false; that the records were perfect and unimpaired.

Whereupon the war ended, but not until colossal fortunes were accumulated by the hangers-on and contractors for the army, who had incited the whole affair.

These men, and numerous would-be imitators, long for the return of that golden age. Since the railroad was completed, many of the American people have looked for themselves. They see in Utah the most peaceful and persistently industrious people on the continent. They judge the tree by its fruits. They read that a community given up to lust does not build factories and fill up the land with thrifty farms. That a nation of thieves and murderers do not live without intoxicating liquors, and become famous for the products of their dairies, orchards, and gardens. A corrupt tree bringeth not forth the fruits of temperance, Christianity, industry and order.

"Mr. Speaker, those who have been so kind and indulgent as to follow me thus far will have observed that I have aimed, as best I might, to show—

"1. That under our Constitution we are entitled to be protected in the full and free enjoyment of our religious faith.

"2. That our views of the marriage relation are an essential portion of our religious faith.

"3. That in considering the cognizance of the marriage relation as within the province of church regulations, we are practically in accord with all other Christian denominations.

"4. That in our views of the marriage relation as a part of our religious belief, we are entitled to immunity from persecution under the Constitution if such views are sincerely held; that if such views are erroneous, their eradication must be by argument and not by force.

"5. That of our sincerity we have both by words, and works, and sufferings, given for nearly 40 years, abundant proof.

"6. That the bill, in practically abolishing trial by jury, as well as in many other respects, is unconstitutional, uncalled for, and in direct opposition to that toleration in religious belief which is characteristic of the nation and the age.

"It is not permitted, Mr. Speaker, that any one man should sit as the judge of another as regards his religious belief. This is a matter which rests solely between each individual and his God. The responsibility cannot be shifted or divided. It is a matter outside the domain of legislative action. The world is full of religious error and delusion, but its eradication is the work of the moralist and not of the legislator. Our Constitution throws over all sincere worshippers, at whatever shrine, its guarantee of absolute protection. The moment we assume to judge of the truthfulness or error of any creed, the constitutional guarantee is a mockery and a sham.

"Three times have my people been dispersed by mob violence, and each time they have arisen stronger from the conflict; and now the doctrine of violence is proposed in Congress. It may be the will of the Lord that, to unite and purify us, it is necessary for further violence and blood. If so, we humbly and reverently submit to the will of Him in whose hands are all the issues of human life. Heretofore we have suffered from the violence of the mob; now, the mob are to be clothed in the authority of an unconstitutional and oppressive law. If this course be decided upon, I can only say that the hand that smites us smites the most sacred guarantee of the Constitution, and the blind Samson, breaking the pillars, pulls down upon friend and foe alike the ruins of the State."

www.ingramcontent.com/pod-product-compliance
Lightning Source LLC
Chambersburg PA
CBHW050848160426
43194CB00011B/2072